CONTENTS

CONTENTS

WRISTWATCH ANNUAL

2024

THE CATALOG

of

PRODUCERS, PRICES, MODELS,

and

SPECIFICATIONS

BY PETER BRAUN

WITH MARTON RADKAI

ABBEVILLE PRESS PUBLISHERS

New York   London

A STRONG CHARACTER CAN BE IDENTIFIED BY THE WRIST.

Exemplify Character and Strength in a New York Minute
with the Wempe Iron Walker Carbon Chronograph 46.

WEMPE
IRON WALKER

Glashütte i/SA | Automatic Chronograph 46 | Carbon | Certified Chronometer | $8,025

Dear Reader,

If you are holding this book in your hand, no doubt you have a liking or even a passion for watches. As someone who shares that feeling, I have the duty to make the book worth your while in many ways. First, there is the choice of brands in the A-Z section. You might not always find all of your favorites, or the one model you really have, but there's a very wide selection to choose from. You might not encounter your favorite brand or model, but while browsing through the book, you may experience an epiphany and fall in love with a watch you never knew existed.

You can find many watches on the web, of course, but this is a paper book, and paper is patient, durable. You can take your time with it...time...one of the last commodities we can still have, as long as we can escape from the frenzy of ubiquitous and permanent connectivity. You won't be interrupted by ads for hearing aids, brutal video games, or cryptocurrencies that will make you rich instantly. The ads you find are carefully crafted to be informative and pleasant, so please check them out, because the advertisers are what keep us going.

Because this is in print and has lasting power, I am quite careful about the material I share with you. Watches are a physical product and holding them in your hand is a vital process in the appreciation of the watchmaking art. Most of these products have been seen and scrutinized by me or the intrepid Elizabeth Doerr, who writes about the independent watchmakers (page 10). A watch can seduce with many elements: like the dial, which can generate an emotion; like its shape and the material of the case, be it gold, steel, titanium, carbon, or some high-tech product. And then, there is the finishing on the dial, bridges, and plates, and the strap. Some people are entranced by complications, like a hypnotic central tourbillon (see HYT, for example), a moon phase, a fascinating way of displaying the date or a power reserve—find out in the following pages! Some watches kindle an old memory of vintage car gauges or a lost heirloom, others arouse your alter ego as a sports enthusiast, a jet pilot, a Navy Seal. Yet others simply touch us with the sheer artistry of the *métiers d'art*: miniature painting, jeweled images, marquetry mosaics, cloisonné enamel, or crafted meteorites.

It is an industry that seems infinite in its potential. As with music or any art, some form of immediate contact is vital, so touching watches is part of the passion. This is why I reserved some space at the end of this book (see page 334) for a non-exhaustive look at some of the annual trade fairs and festivals you may wish to attend while traveling. You can meet some of the people who work in the industry at these events. Just in case, I have included a few portraits starting on page 30, like Ming Thein, of the brand Ming; or Amande Berclaz, a young polymechanic who works a lathe; or Anny Weber, a determined Gen-Zer, who made her first, rather striking, watch under the tutelage of Paul Gerber.

Planning a yearly book like *Wristwatch Annual* generates a strange phenomenon: one topic seems to lead unconsciously to another. Ever since Vianney Halter told me (in 2008) that he would like to make a watch that did not tell time, I have been thinking of the relationship between time itself and watches. This led to reading the French philosopher Henri Bergson and delving into watches that seem to hide time more than reveal it (Beyond Time, page 18). Finally, while visiting the Hong Kong Watch and Clock Fair, I saw a concentration of the Chinese watchmaking world and became acquainted with the national fashion trend known as *guochao*. I also met up with Professor Hans-Georg Moeller in Macau, a specialist in Chinese philosophy and also the creator of the outstanding YouTube channel *Carefree Wandering*. He pointed out that Bergson and Daoism are very close. And

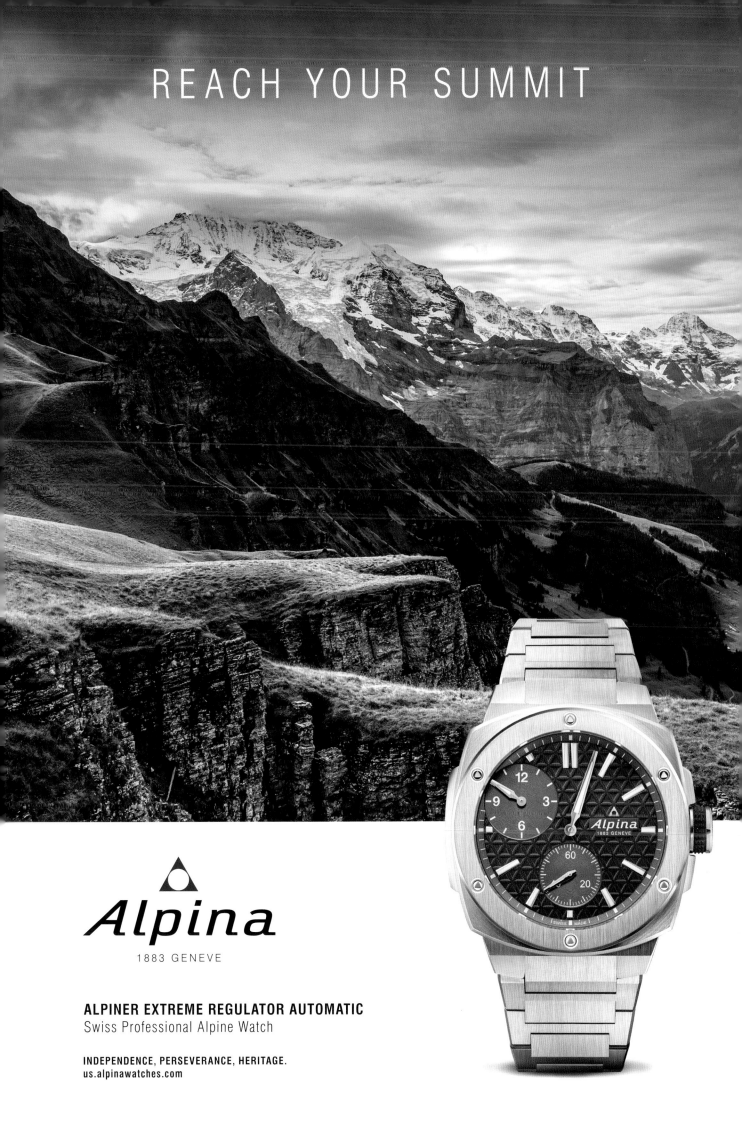

so the next chapter was decided: a carefree look at Chinese watchmaking and how some fundamental precepts of Daoism seem to influence the Chinese approach to creativity (see page 36).

As for new brands, there are many. First and foremost a number of Chinese brands, like the Shanghai Watch Company and CIGA Design. Sportive and dress watch brands have also found their way to the pages, like Lip and Norquain, Leica and Guinand, Edouard Koehn and Nove, the latter of which makes a very thin diver's watch. I cannot list them all, but I hope you enjoy the thrill of discovery as much as I did.

A word of thanks to close: Cindi Barton, Kourtnay King, Erin Morris, Stephanie Sarkany, and others helped review the text, managed the workflow in difficult times, laid out the chapters, and remained calm under pressure. Thanks, too, to Elizabeth Doerr for her annual contributions. And many thanks to the brands that advertise with *Wristwatch Annual* and who trust in the power of a real book filled with images and original copy. I would encourage you to visit them and check out their goods. Errors do occur, and if you run into one, please make gentle note of it so we can correct it. If you don't see your favorite watch or brand here, maybe next year! Have a great read and do take your time.

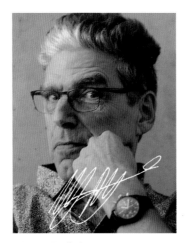

Marton Radkai

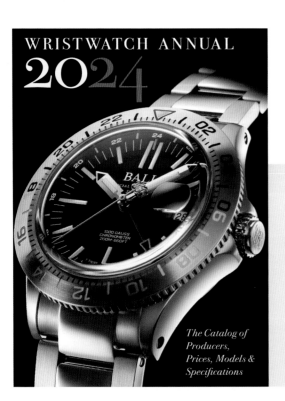

This year's Wristwatch Annual cover features Ball's **Engineer III Outlier** driven by the company's manufacture automatic caliber RRM7337-C with a quick-set GMT. It comes in a 40-millimeter, 904L stainless-steel case with a height of 13.8 millimeters and a screw-in crown. The COSC-certified caliber will run for 80 hours. The Amortiser patented anti-shock system delivers 5,000 G shock resistance and the mu-metal cage is anti-magnetic to 1,000 Gauss. Visibility is guaranteed by micro gas tubes on the inner GMT hour bezel, and SuperLumiNova on the 0-24 scale on the bidirectional outer bezel. The Engineer III Outlier is water-resistant to 20 atm and comes in a limited-edition of 1000 pieces.

LOUIS MOINET
1806

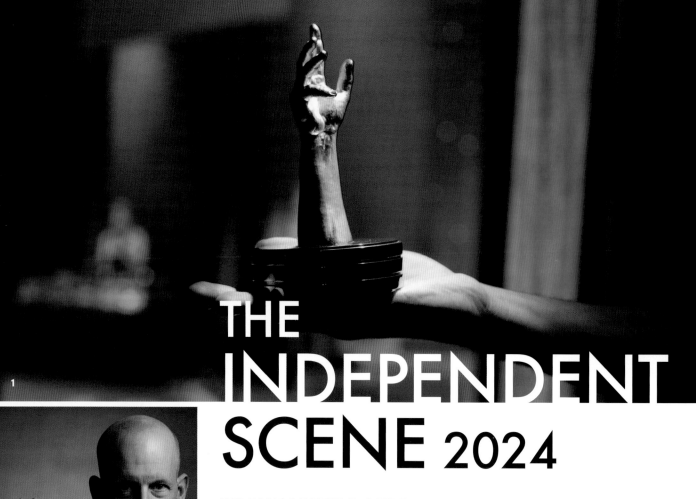

THE INDEPENDENT SCENE 2024

BY ELIZABETH DOERR

The world of independent watchmaking has been welcoming "new" faces and talents over the last few years and in pretty much every price class. In fact, our world of ticks and tocks is now graced with more independents than ever before.

The proliferation of independent watchmakers and brands is probably down to the success and reputation of the AHCI (Académie Horlogère des Créateurs Indépendents/ Horological Academy of Independent Creators)—and perhaps, at least in part, because so many members get lots of extra attention through awards like those given at the Grand Prix d'Horlogerie de Genève—but also the unaffiliated independent creatives that successfully came after the AHCI, like MB&F and De Bethune.

NOT SO NEW, BUT AS YET UNKNOWN

Formerly at the mechanical heart of Ulysse Nardin's technical oeuvres in the post-Schnyder/Oechslin era, **Stéphane von Gunten** decided to strike out on his own and introduced the **Haute-Rive Honoris I** in 2023, which now holds the record for the longest power reserve for a wristwatch with a single spring barrel (40 days). The peripheral power-reserve indicator on the open

1. The coveted prize of the Grand Prix D'Horlogerie de Genève

2. and 3. Ancestor power: Stéphane von Gunten and his Haute-Rive Honoris I, honoring his ancestors with 1,000-hour reserve

MING

CELEBRATING FIVE YEARS OF THE ILLUMINATINGLY UNCONSTRAINED

WWW.MING.WATCH

back of the watch is in itself quite remarkable and highlights the importance of such. It also has a flying tourbillon and bezel winding. And it does all of this in an extremely elegant and wearable manner: the Honoris I clocks in at just 11.95 mm in height and 42.5 mm in diameter despite all the handmade mechanical goodness found within.

Artimo is a "supergroup" comprising highly technical and supremely talented former employees in various functions at various top-level companies, including Greubel Forsey, Audemars Piguet (including Audemars Piguet Renaud & Papi), F.P. Journe, Breguet, and even Philippe Dufour: Fabrice Deschanel, Claude Emmenegger; Stéphane Maturel, Didier Bretin, Emmanuel Jutier, and Manuel Thomas. This team's first watch, the **ART01**, is, quite literally, a revelation, because it was conceived to reveal the complex mechanics inside. It does so by placing a sapphire crystal with a hint of a bezel atop a titanium undercarriage that serves as a frame for the hand-finished titanium bridges. These, in turn, hold the skeletonized white-gold movement in place. The latter features a tourbillon with a double balance spring and an ergonomic function selector for time-setting and winding that makes use of a column wheel running two cams, one via vertical clutch.

THE REXHEPI CLAN

Rexhep Rexhepi has been on a massive roll for years, thanks in great part to the Chronomètre Contemporain series, which kicked off in 2018, sealing his then-growing and now supernova-like reputation and earning him a first award at the 2018 Grand Prix d'Horlogerie de Genève that year. In 2023, Rexhepi introduced another family member to the line: the **Chronomètre Antimagnétique**, a unique version of which was set to debut at (the unfortunately postponed) Only Watch 2023. The watch reflects his love of

precision timekeeping by using a Faraday cage to protect the perfectly hand-finished movement from the effects of magnetism in a tribute to both historical chronometers and modern life. The symmetrical movement of Rexhepi's own design and manufacture includes indirectly driven, zero-resetting central seconds controlled by an all-or-nothing system.

Xhevdet Rexhepi may not be the household name his brother is, but sooner or later his time will come. And once his **Minute Inerte** really catches on, that time could be very soon. Xhevdet left his brother's brand, Akrivia, in 2022 to get his own career rolling and realize his own ideas and identity, starting with this fabulous twist on the chronometer housed in a platinum case measuring only 38 x 8.5 mm. Its "complication" is an idiosyncratic second hand that goes about its usual business for 58 seconds before pausing for two seconds at the top, then continuing with the next minute.

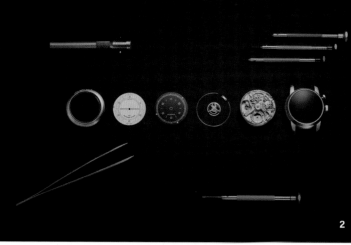

And speaking of Rexhep's successes, the young Geneva-based watchmaker has the honor of becoming the first watchmaker in Louis Vuitton's new series of collaborative timepieces with renowned independent watchmakers. This inaugural project is the **LVRR-01 Chronographe à Sonnerie**, a double-faced chronograph with a chiming complication powered by a completely new tourbillon movement developed from the ground up by Atelier Akrivia and its founder Rexhep Rexhepi in a redesigned Louis Vuitton Tambour case. The sapphire crystal dial of this miniature work of art gives us a good deal of information on the importance of this collaborative timepiece in the eyes of LV's director of watches, Jean Arnault: at a distance it seems to bear the conventional Akrivia logo, but up close the wording turns out to be a union of the two brand names, with "LV" subtly incorporated into "AKRIVIA." This represents the first time in history that Louis Vuitton has combined its logo with that of another brand.

The much-lauded newcomer **Simon Brette**, a former employee of MB&F, took home the Horological Revelation Prize with his revelatory **Chronomètre Artisans**, a watch practically masterminded by him (as he is not technically a watchmaker) as an engineer able to bring the right craftspeople together to make high art (shades of MB&F for sure!). What is perhaps the highest "wow factor" element about this watch right off the bat is the "dragon scale" engraving on the dial made by Yasmina Anti; but the zirconium case and unbelievably fine finishing of the clever movement seal the deal.

1. and 2. Mixing DNAs: Louis Vuitton meets Akrivia for the Chronographe à Sonnerie

3. Simon Brette spearheaded a group of twelve artisans for the Chronomètre Artisans

4. Gaël Petermann and Florian Bédat's second-born: a beautifully designed split-seconds chronograph

GRAND PRIX D'HORLOGERIE DE GENÈVE 2023 WINNERS

Gaël Petermann and Florian Bédat first met at the School of Watchmaking in Geneva in 2007. After that, they roomed together for some time in Dresden, Germany, where they continued to perfect their high watchmaking prowess at A. Lange & Söhne. They subsequently launched their eponymous brand **Petermann Bédat** in 2017 with the help of their workshop neighbor in Renens, Switzerland: Dominique Renaud. The first watch born of this intense alliance was the exquisitely finished Deadbeat Seconds 1967; it was so extraordinary that it won the Horological Revelation Prize at the Grand Prix d'Horlogerie de Genève in 2020. Continuing this excellent tradition, the duo's second watch, the **Chronographe Rattrapante**, won the Chronograph Prize at the 2023 GPHG.

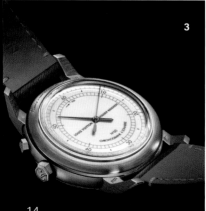

1. Behind the scenes of Simon Brette's Chronomètre Artisans

2. Special Jury Prize for Svend Andersen and Vincent Calabrese, founders of the AHCI

3. Traditional independent clockmaker's workbench (source: Marton Radkai)

4. Kari Voutilainen's winner for the Men's Complication Prize at the GPHG

AHCI NEWS

The heart of the independent scene is—and always has been in the modern era—the AHCI, a group of independent creators founded in 1985. The way of these individualistic watchmaker-inventors is indeed anachronistic, and though the products that emerge may not be everyone's cup of tea all of the time, they do attract the attention of collectors of rare taste who follow not only the horological escapades of these 30-odd men of varying age and nationality, but also the passion and personality that goes into each extremely limited timepiece.

At the 2023 Grand Prix d'Horlogerie de Genève, AHCI co-founders Svend Andersen and Vincent Calabrese were honored with the Special Jury Prize; this is the second time winning this award following 2010, when the whole group received this award. Additionally, Kari Voutilainen was awarded the Men's Complication Prize for his cushion-shaped World Timer. Not only is this watch almost fully hand-made, its Worldtime function has been designed for perfect convenience. All the user needs to do is press the crown inward to change both the reference city and the time zone.

Elizabeth Doerr is a freelance journalist specialized in watches and was senior editor of Wristwatch Annual *until the 2010 edition.*

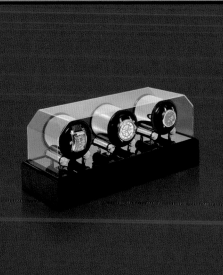

BEYOND TIME

BY MARTON RADKAI

1. The great astronomical clock in the Cathedral of Strasburg.

2. Blooming time: Lady Arpels Heures Florales.

When not focusing on the technical wizardry of watches, the marketing magicians of the industry will often talk loftily about the poetry, the art, the emotion in their products. These are vague terms often used almost casually, yet they do reveal a deeper aspect of watchmaking and watches, the romance with the unseizable, time itself.

At the 2022 edition of Watches and Wonders in Geneva, one of the timepieces presented that took many a breath away was the Heures Florales by Van Cleef & Arpels. This genuine work of art, a mix of gold, diamonds, sapphires, mother-of-pearl, and miniature painting, replicates a flower clock dreamed up by eighteenth-century Swedish taxonomist Carl Linnaeus, who had noticed that flowers seemed to have a schedule for opening and closing. Implementing this in a mechanical watch was quite a feat. And trying to read the time by counting the open flowers is not exactly user-friendly in our frenetic life. You could miss a train. There is a minute track, but it peaks out from an aperture in the middle case.

The philistine will rightfully ask: What's the use of this expensive object if it doesn't immediately tell time? Perhaps the creation of a beautiful piece, the mechanical hi-jinks coupled with the artistry, the value of so many crafts joining forces? And when all arguments have been exhausted, there is one left: the tribute paid to the most ephemeral and yet powerful of human dimensions, time itself, invisible and infinite but that tells us we are alive.

HOW MUCH TIME IS IT?

We often think of the watch merely as an instrument to give time in addition to performing other functions. The chronograph measures discrete time segments, the GMT

2

The legendary Military Chronograph revived.

CHRONOGRAPH 1 UTILITY – LIMITED EDITION

After more than 40 years, Porsche Design is bringing back an icon – with substantial
improvements: Military becomes Utility, stainless steel becomes titanium carbide.
While the design pays homage to the original, the use of the patented material titanium
carbide embodies progress and innovation in the art of horology.

www.porsche-design.com

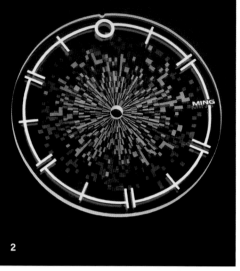

that the objects I make reference time," he told me in an interview. "The fact that this reference is available in these objects is anecdotal."

For Ming Thein, founder and CEO of the brand Ming (see Watch People, page 30), whose watches always radiate something mysterious, time is choice. "We don't need a watch to tell the time, our lives are regulated and organized in so many other ways," he wrote me. "The quantitative measure of time is easily found on our phones or computers. The last thing we need is another reminder of time pressure and the need to do things – ironically, watches both do this and liberate us from it, because it turns the act of measuring time into both choice and art."

PHYSICS AND METAPHYSICS

We can all agree with Ming, time is both liberator and taskmaster at the same time. Before real clocks existed, awareness of its passage was noted by observing natural cycles, like the seasons, sunrise and sunset, the moon, the stars, even the rumblings of a hungry stomach. Our connection to these movements still fills us with wonder, and it has inspired a slew of remarkably complex watches, most recently the Bovet Asterium, for example, or Louis Moinet's Cosmopolis with twelve different meteorites.

Yet, try as one may, defining time itself is like trying to nail pudding to a wall, much like its sibling, space. In his *Confessions,*

keeps us connected to home time while traveling, and so forth. Practically speaking, we would like to have the time now and know how much time we have left for a certain activity. It is time connected to an event in space.

Quite a few watches, however, seem designed, intentionally, or accidentally, to actually hide time delivery by esthetic distractions.

The seeds for this chapter, which has required a lot of research into non-horological material, was planted in 2008 at a three-way chat with Vianney Halter, Max Büsser (MB&F) and Felix Baumgartner (Urwerk). Right at the end, Halter, a kind of John Cage of watchmaking, casually announced he wanted to make a watch that didn't tell time. He came close with the Deep Space Resonance and Tourbillon, which draws all the attention to a massive triple tourbillon whirling around the center of the dial. If the minutes ring or the jumping hours were missing, no one would really notice. Other watches, like the Hautlence Labyrinth, presented at Baselworld in 2016 , go so far as to abandon the idea of time in favor of a game on the watch. Are these just marketing gimmicks?

The idea of scrambling a watch's basic time-giving function is not so far fetched when considering the essence of time itself. Halter is quite open about it. "It's by chance

1. Hautlence's Labyrinth, a non-watch.

2. The mysterious Ming time mosaic.

3. Louis Moinet's Cosmopolis focuses on twelve meteorites.

4. The case back of Bovet's Astérium reads the stars

5. and 6. *Space Odyssey* redux: Vianney Halter's Deep Space Resonance

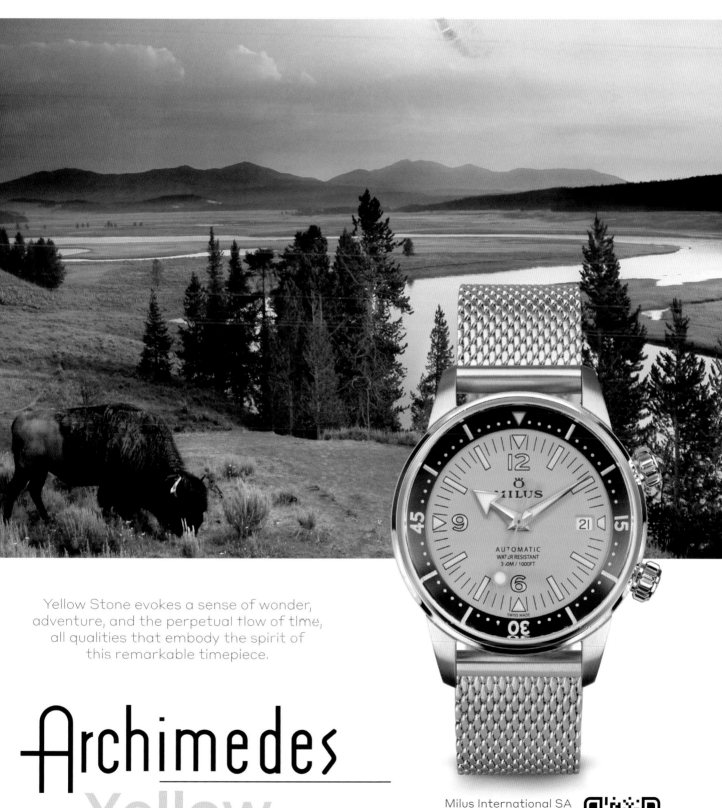

1. De Bethune pays homage to the cempasúchil, the "twenty flower" associated with the Day of he Dead

2. Father Time reminding us that time is always running out

3. El Cargador governs the year's events (Source: Yucatan Today)

philosopher and theologian St. Augustine of Hippo (354-430) wrote the famous and pithy statement: "What then is time? If no one asks me, I know. If I want to explain it to an inquirer, I do not know."

Well before the emergence of clocks and the like, many cultures the world round personified time to give it some form of three-dimensional presence. The ancient Greeks had what would become Father Time, Chronos, a key figure in the myth of creation, widely represented as an old man with a sickle, or portrayed with a child and an hour glass, symbolizing the two fixed events on our personal timelines, namely birth and death, the second being unavoidable and incomputable once the first has taken place. The Mayans, who were very concerned with time in natural cycles and had devised an extraordinarily complex set of calendars, had *El Cargador*, a figure carrying a heavy sack and representing the year with its good days, unlucky days, planting and harvesting days, and so on.

In the end, all cultures and religions have managed to quantify time, or put it in boxes, said the late mathematician and science historian, Gerald Withrow (1912-2000). In an essay entitled "Reflections on the History of the Concept of Time," he describes how Australian aborigines would place a rock in a tree fork to alert them to some scheduled event when the sun would strike it. As for the Chinese "different intervals of time were regarded as separate discrete units, so that time was in effect discontinuous. Just as space was decomposed into regions, so time was split up into eras, seasons and epochs." The primary purpose of developing clocks in the Middle Ages, he added, was not to "register the passage of time but rather from the monastic demand for accurate determination of the hours when the various religious offices and prayers should be said."

KNOWING TIME, FEELING TIME

If there is any thinker who managed to successfully explore the conundrum of time and give it real, experienceable meaning it was the French philosopher Henri Bergson (1856- 1941). In his doctoral thesis, later translated as *Time and Free Will: An Essay on the Immediate Data of Consciousness*, Bergson disentangles the notion of time and space, showing how the human mind tends to project time onto space, by seeing it as a mechanical sequence made up of multiple

BLAKJAK
TORNEK-RAYVILLE TYPE 7B

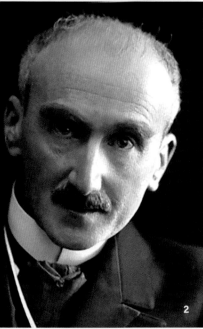

1. MB&F's HM11 Architect, time in the antechamber

2. Henri Bergson: separating time (duration) and space

3. Catharsis by Biver forgetting time

4. and 5. Time elicits an emotion: The wonders of the solar system with Van Cleef's Planetarium and Beauregard's exquisite turquoise Dahlia

segments—he illustrates this by observing a clock. This is the time we all share in some manner, or spatial, objective time. "Outside of myself, in space, there is only one unique position of the (clock) hands and the pendulum, because none of the past positions remain," he writes, "Inside me, a process of organization and mutual intermingling of the data of consciousness is taking place that makes up the true duration." By "data of consciousness," he is referring to all feelings and emotions, which he elevates to their rightful rank in contrast to our intelligence, which tends to distance us by needing to cut things up into little sequences of events.

Bergson's idea of time as duration is quite mind-blowing, to use a colloquial term, because he associates it to free will, the spontaneity of being in the now and evaluating each moment with what we feel. Elsewhere, he uses the term grace as a metaphor. "Gracefulness prefers curves to angular lines, because the curved line can change direction at any moment, but each new direction is hinted at in the one that preceded it." What he does, is resolve St. Augustine's dilemma by applying —humorously—Brandolini's system: Explaining or deconstructing time is not possible, your psychological or interior feeling however is just as good a tool.

"Our duration is irreversible," he wrote in his 1907 book *Creative Evolution*, "We cannot relive any part of it, because we would have to start by erasing the memory of everything that followed. We could, in a pinch, erase this memory from our intelligence, but not from our will." Those who seek to understand time have to conclude that it is a homogeneous dimension that exists as is, and human consciousness journeys through it, gathering experience and evolving. "The only time that exists for me is the present moment," Vianney Halter told me. "However,

I use this 'present time' to remember the past and project myself into the future." It's an echo of the opening lines of T. S. Eliot's poem "Burnt Norton":

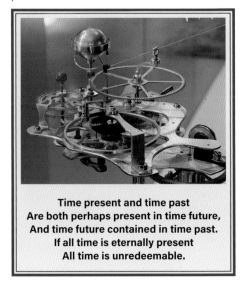

Time present and time past
Are both perhaps present in time future,
And time future contained in time past.
If all time is eternally present
All time is unredeemable.

HOMAGE TO TIME

In the very three-dimensional world of watchmaking, Ming Thein, Vianney Halter and others are therefore not alone in considering the measurement of time secondary to the artistry, or, poetry/emotion, if you will, of designing a watch. To put the hands of a watch on the back burner allows for more creativity, as myriad jewelry watches that are commonly sold to the female customer can testify to. From Chanel, Van Cleef and Arpels, or the Canadian stone-artist Alexandre Beauregard,

28
DB

DB28xs STARRY SEAS

38.7MM CASE
TITANIUM BALANCE WITH WHITE GOLD INSERTS
"DE BETHUNE" BALANCE-SPRING WITH FLAT TERMINAL CURVE
SILICON ESCAPE WHEEL
TRIPLE PARE-CHUTE SHOCK-ABSORBING SYSTEM

WWW.DEBETHUNE.COM

DE_BETHUNE

DE BETHUNE
L'ART HORLOGER AU XXIᵉ SIÈCLE

jeweled watches are not just symbols of wealth, they are genuinely a way of creating the emotional jolt that the marketing people sometimes refer to, an emotion that is intensely, intimately personal.

There are many subtle ways to balance time-telling with time giving. One clever solution, of course, is making minute repeaters. Sound has a special way of by-passing our intelligence and going straight to our intuition. Bergson even speaks of effect of hearing bells. The Catharsis, a single time-piece made by Jean-Claude Biver and his son, Pierre, for the Only Watch charity auction doesn't even have hands on the dial, only a sculptural poetic image of waves (sapphires) with a meteorite sun, an obsidian sky spangled with mother-of-pearl stars. Alongside the case is the telltale pusher to launch the carillon chimes. Polarizing, say some commentators, but perhaps unbeknownst to Biver, with his fifty brilliant years

plus in the industry, very much in the spirit of Bergson, as it will first be perceived by the wearer's consciousness.

H. Moser & Cie, the Schaffhausen-based brand that is in the MELB Group (it includes Hautlence) has a history of playing with the perception of time. One model, called Zzzz, was mounted in the rectangular Swiss Alp case and had a black dial with hands. It was meant as facetious take on the Apple Watch, which would power down when not in use (hence the zzzzs). By 2019, it had lost the hands to a minute repeater and the subsidiary seconds were replaced with a plain tourbillon just showing the passage of time. The last version has a Vantablack dial, a black case, and a subsidiary seconds dial that looks like the "waiting" animation we are all subjected to on our hand-held devices. Consensus suggests it's a watch, but its function is merely to symbolize time as an infinity.

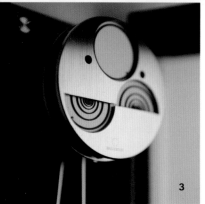

1. and 2. H. Moser & Cie and the Swiss Alps Watch: Giving more time by showing less

3. and 4. Independent Beat Haldimann: Just imagine what time it is with the H13 (top left) and H9 (bottom)

THE WORLD'S PREEMINENT TIMEPIECE EVENT

HKTDC
Hong Kong Watch & Clock Fair | E⁺PLUS

ufi
Approved
International
Event

3-7 SEP 2024
Hong Kong Convention and Exhibition Centre

27 AUG–14 SEP 2024
Click2Match (Online)

📱 HKTDC Marketplace
🌐 hkwatchfair.hktdc.com
📞 (852) 1830 668
✉ exhibitions@hktdc.org

See More !

In the same vein, Beat Haldimann's 2012 H9-Reduction should also be mentioned, because the hands are dissimulated behind a dark crystal, forcing the viewer to look closely. Was it a joke? On his website, there is a fictitious exchange, where a watch salesman explains that the customer has to imagine the time.

PLAY TIME

Between not telling time and being very 2+2=4 about it, there is another playful option that some brands have tried with success and that is stopping time or making it elastic. Franck Muller's perennial favorite, the Crazy Hours line, must be mentioned in this context, since the rearrangement of the hours on the dial will distract the viewer and interrupt thinking about the "now," as it were. A more subtle version of this idea is Itay Noy's ReOrder, with the hours emerging at various places on the dial as if haphazardly.

Franck Muller went even further, however with the Secret Hours. At rest, the hands are at 12 o'clock. To read time, you have to activate the pusher at 9 o'clock. Similarly, Hermès tapped the genius of Agenhor (Jean-Marc Wiederrecht) to create L'Heure Suspendu in the Arceau case. The idea is similar to the Franck Muller Secret Hours. Let us say you need a some time for yourself, maybe for a heart-to-heart conversation with a friend or a *rendez-vous doux*, but you'd like it to be open ended. Press the pusher at 2 o'clock and the minute and hour hands will take up a position straddling the 12, an "impossible" time. When your special time is up, press the button again, and the hands will pick up their journey in real time.

ELASTIC TIME

Finally, one watch that deserves mention in this context is the Key of Time made by Hublot about a decade ago. Thanks to very complicated mechanics, it allows the user to shorten or lengthen an hour by up to 20 minutes. "I may let my watch show me my own time, my own perception of time when I am at home or talking a walk," Jean-Claude Biver told me, "but since the rate can be modified according to my mood, according to my situation, in an unpleasant situation, I'm going to set my watch to 40 minutes per hour. At a conference, for example, I can get up and say: 'Gentlemen, my time is up.'" His slight smile suggests he may have tested that watch in real situations. The watch was

not a commercial success. "We would have had to sell it for 300,000 francs, and who's going to buy that for that money?" An excellent point, but as Ben Franklin did say, time is money. Of course, timelessness is priceless.

So, what exactly is time, and what is its relationship to watches, besides cutting time up into little pieces? German philosopher Hermann Broch, in his The Principle of Hope, boiled time down to "a clock without hands," which, as we've seen, has been done. And time is infinite until it becomes spatial. On a personal note, I feel it is like a deep invisible, inaudible vibration that accompanies human existence, like the inaudible vibration of a huge, imaginary organ pipe. We will only hear it sound when its frequency comes into contact with the vibrations of our own consciousness. This may sound a little esoteric, but it's worth remembering when you look at your plain three-hand watch, and it tells you have another half-hour till you meet a loved one, and time slows down in your mind.

1. Itay Noy makes the hours appear haphazradly

2. Hermès: stop time for your favorite moments

3. Hublot's Key of Time stretches or shortens hours

4. Franck Muller's Secret Hours stops time at will

5. Ancillary hours under the stinger: a creation by Jean-Mikaël Flaux

WATCH FACES

BY MARTON RADKAI

Watches are not really made by machines. They are conceived in the minds of passionate people and then executed by equally gifted people, who either have a clear vision of what they want and can then implement it, to use a rather coarse word, or who have the patience and manual skill to turn a blueprint or a rough sketch into a gem.

1

THE EYE OF TIME

The art of photography is being able to see what othes do not, capturing that as yet invisible "thing" and exposing it so common mortals can see it and have a sensation, feel an emotion. **Ming Thein** has the gift, and he transforms it into watches. His photographs often have a dreamy, expressionistic quality, where angles speak to each other, at times arguing, at times harmonizing. That same play between the ephemeral and the manifest, color striving to live in a monochrome world, appears in the watches of this young brand in full bloom.

Ming Thein was born in Malaysia but grew up in Australia and New Zealand. A troublemaker by his own account, a boy with a rapid mind, he raced through school and university and found himself in an adult world at the age of 16 (yes, that's right), and already imbued with a curiosity about watches. He took up photography as "something creative I could do when I had a bit of time," he says, "and a way for me to put my experience on watches without owning them."

Looking at watches and buying one, he found out, were two different things, especially since what he liked was often financially out of reach. "But there was a whole universe of interesting mechanics that one could learn about and sometimes see without having to buy any of it," he points out. "I think it was the mechanical part—I'm a creative person but I also have an affinity for machines and tangible objects. Watches are really a synthesis of all of these things at a very high level."

His photography led to design and consulting work, and, at some point in 2015, he took the step to actually making them: "We had the contacts to produce something, the experience as collectors to make something people like us might want to buy, and the

foolishness to believe we'd actually be able to make it work."

Eight years into the adventure, the name Ming is spoken in the highest terms. Ming taught himself CAD to facilitate the design work, while the actual construction is increasingly being done internally. His photographic eye is always at work, yet he is aware of the dialectic between the flattened out perspective of the 2D camera product and the finished watch. "The camera flattens out stereoscopic perspective," he wrote me, "watches must be designed with this taken into account. It's the reason we actively use reflection and layering, and I will never be able to representatively photograph our watches as they are intended to be viewed with a stereoscopic perspective."

Where does he get inspiration? Nothing specific, because creativity is a process for Ming: "I find it's much easier to be open and observant; the processing and translating happens in the subconscious and an idea forms."

2

1. Ming Thein, high-focus photographer, collector, designer, founder

2.Mysterious time, the Ming LW.01 Automatic

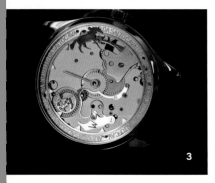

THE NEXT GENERATION

Many parents know that youthful passions, once inflamed, will stop at nothing. **Anny Weber**, born in 2002, was already fascinated by mechanics as a child. Once she finished high school, she went to Grenchen, Switzerland, to become a "rhabilleuse," a tough four-year study during which she learned how to take apart watches, replace or make parts from scratch, oil, and adjust—in short—everything. She also interned with Paul Gerber in Zurich. She was still a teenager at the time and already thinking of making a watch. "What fascinated me about the world of watchmaking back then was that a tiny speck of dust can stop the complex mechanism of an entire watch," she told me. "I also realized that the complexity of watches involves much more than just displaying the time."

She is 22 now and has already made two watches. One is a collaboration with Paul Gerber, her teacher, for the Waterford Festival of Time. The second is her "graduation watch," which is a tradition for all those who choose the watchmaking profession. The inspiration for the piece was her hobby, horseback riding. The watch, called "Da Salto Cavallo," which translates as "from the horse jump," has a little horse jumping from hour to hour on the edge of the dial. It looks fairly easy to the untrained eye, but it is in fact quite complicated. For one, the mechanism must gather power from the mainspring for thirty minutes to arm the horse, as it were, before releasing the tension for the jump. All this without shaking up the entire movement.

Anny Weber has now begun working with Paul Gerber and is still gathering the knowledge and experience: "For me, the mechanics in the watch are the key element, the different approaches, the craftsmanship and design behind it," she says. "I always find the history fascinating, because

watchmakers created amazing things at the time and with whatever resources available to them." It will be interesting to see where she goes.

BEFORE THE WATCH

In 2023, the Grand Prix d'Horlogerie de Genève awarded the Horological Revelation Prize to Simon Brette's Chronomètre Artisans. The plural "s" at the end is not an error. Twelve artisans worked on this champion and Brette pays tribute to them on his website. One is Matthieu Allègre, a young Frenchman who had a key role to play.

Before a watch is launched in 3D, it must be conceived. It gestates, or goes through many iterations, until it is ready to be born, built, and decorated. For this, you need a person who is visually imaginative and technically knowledgeable about elements like the case, lugs, rotors, bezels, and straps. That is **Mathieu Allègre's** work. Growing up, he developed a solid visual gift and a strong creative streak. When it came time to choose a profession, he found that industrial design suited him best. While studying at the Strate, a leading French school of design, he interned with a design company in Neuchâtel and became smitten with watches. "It's a demanding world," he told me in a written interview, "with a vast range of possibilities for expression in terms of volume creation, graphics, techniques, finishes, materials, and the historical diversity of the industry."

1. Paul Gerber and Anny Weber with their Waterford watch

2. and 3. Anny Weber and her study piece, Da Salto Cavallo

4. And 5. Matthieu Allègre, putting imagination onto paper

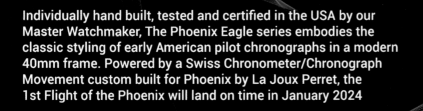

1

SANTA'S HELPER

"Les petites mains," the little hands, is an expression in the watchmaking industry to describe the thousands of women who sit day in, day out at workbenches filing, polishing, decorating, so that any watchmaker opening your watch for repair or servicing will be able to say: "Good work." There are parts you will not see, like the tiny feet holding the dial, which are cut from steel and lathed and machined to micro-millimeter diameter. These tiny, important parts are made by people like **Amande Berclaz**, who was born in Morges, Switzerland, spent her childhood in Israel, where her father ran a hotel, and then returned to her home country and ultimately became a polymechanic.

Amande's job is more than just machining, lathing, and drilling metal. She has to know how to service, fix, and occasionally build machines. It was not her first choice. "I wanted to become a marine biologist," she says, "but I had a passion for repairing motorcycles." She found a job at a company called BERMC in the Canton of Valais, which does everything from prototyping to manufacturing parts for a variety of industries, including automotive and watches. "I am currently working on product boxes and

Matthieu Allègre is young; his name means "joyful," with a hint of happy-go-lucky, and that seems to have imbued his demeanor. He seeks inspiration all over the place, but in the end, he says "you have to be able to identify the customer's expectations and be able to come up with proposals that are tailored to their needs. That's why I spend more time behind my screen than in a museum, even though it's a great place to think." In an industry where at times "crazy" is the way to be "disruptive," to wield an oft-used buzzword, his idea of an excellent watch is rather classical, or intelligently conceived: "The forms must be well proportioned, whether it be for the case, the movement, the strap or even the dial, including the typography. The overall look must be harmonious and coherent."

1. Matthieu Allègre, designer of Simon Brette's prizewinning Chronomètre Artisans

2. and 3. Amande Berclaz, from motorcycles to metal work, and modeling for fun

2

3

watch winders," she says, noting as well that the company does not disclose its clients. "The challenge in my job is finding ways to use time well and finding standard parts to make servicing easier."

Her favorite aspect of the job is the diversity. "If you are working on watch parts, you must be attentive to details," she notes. "When you're working on a piece weighing a ton, you need strength!" Amande is going places. As a polymechanic, she knows she can dream up something and make it real with her hands. And as a hobby, she does modeling. It's worth remembering the "little hands" when you glance at your watch.

STEADY HAND

Ismaël Nikles needs to know exactly what he is going to be doing before starting any project. He needs a blueprint approved by his customer, and then he needs a steady hand. His tools are a set of awls and files combined with enormous concentration. Imagine being sent a gold dial worth thousands of dollars with some enameling on it, and then having to engrave a regular pattern made of tiny indents onto the exposed metal, each dig needing to be exactly like the other. One slip, a few ounces of excessive pressure and the dial ends up in the recycling bin.

When brands speak of traditional crafts, they are referring to the work of people like Ismaël Nikles, whose atelier and home is in one of those large farmhouses that dot the Jura mountains, their façades pierced with windows to let in the light for the windowsill workbenches. It's here that some of the world's finest watches receive their final decoration. These men and women are usually very earthbound. They rarely boast about their work, but without it, what would watchmaking in Switzerland be? "We are Protestants," he says, "we are good craftspeople, but we just don't sell ourselves well."

Nikles studied microengineering, but his artist's soul drew him to a five-year course of study in La Chaux-de-Fonds to learn two of the many crafts (*métiers d'art* in French) that add to the beauty and value of a watch: engraving and chamfering. His clients are often luxury brands, who need him to decorate the dials, bridges, or mainplates, or carry out the fine work of chamfering the edges of a movement's bridges and plates. He also works for individual clients who bring him their watches for a special facelift. In one case, he even set his awls onto a rotor for the Detroit brand Shinola. And when not in his atelier, he's an avid cyclist.

1

1.–3. Ismaël Nikles, the traditional artisan engraver with his tools and his work

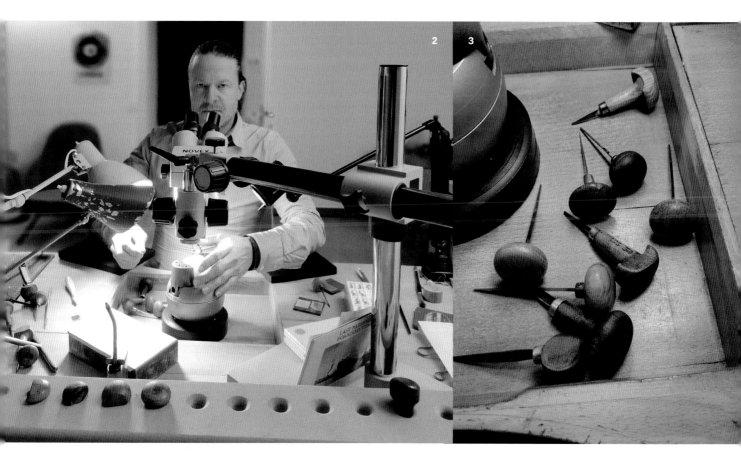

CAREFREE WATCHING

China is not only a very large country, but an economically powerful one notwithstanding the ups and downs. For the West, and specifically for Swiss watchmaking, the huge market that flourished rapidly since the 1980s has been very attractive but not always simple. As with Nietzsche's famous abyss, that market also looks into the West.

In November 2021, the audience of the Grand Prix d'Horlogerie de Genève (GPHG) was treated to something of a cultural surprise: the winner of the Challenge Prize for watches under 3,500 Swiss francs went to a Chinese company called CIGA Design for its Blue Planet. The dial of this 46-millimeter behemoth represents a view of our globe from the sky, with oceans in blue and a detailed, silvery, sculptural view of the land masses with mountains and valleys. A compass on the globe points to a static outer hour ring and a rotating inner minute ring.

CIGA Design (see page 116) had won several awards in Europe before, like Red Dot Awards for, among others, the minimalist Moon Phase Watch. The GPHG award, however, was a crowning achievement, perhaps even a watershed moment, since CIGA Design and other Chinese brands have been nominated, all of which have shown considerable originality in their designs. In 2023, there was Celadon's Century "Seven Wonders," with a cloisonné enamel dial (an ancient Chinese technique), a collaboration with AHCI master Lin Yong Hua. Fiyta's "Spacewalk" is a fun piece, with some very intricate engraving work.

1. Pride in Chinese motifs: a selection from Benjamin Chee's Celadon HH portfolio

2. CIGA Design's Blue Planet, a watch and a statement

3. Fiyta's mix of playful luxury and celebration of Chinese achievements

4. Celadon HH's Seven Wonders, a GPHG candidate

In 1999, master watchmaker Gerd-R. Lang had the original idea for the Kobold brand of watches and helped his 19-year-old protege, Michael Kobold, turn it into reality.

25 YEARS AGO, KOBOLD WATCHES WERE INVENTED

The Kobold brand quickly evolved from a Carnegie Mellon University class project to a serious enterprise. In 2000, explorer Sir Ranuph Fiennes became the brand's ambassador-in-chief. In 2003, actor James Gandolfini became the latest and most prominent Kobold ambassador. In 2002, the Kobold Soarway case was introduced after more than two years of research & development. The first watches with the innovative Soarway case were the Kobold Phantom and the Kobold Polar Surveyor Chronograph. In an industry teeming with recycled (or "re-imagined") case styles, the Soarway case continues to stand apart thanks its original design even today. In 2004, James Gandolfini's iconic design for a diver's watch was turned into reality with the release of the Kobold Seal. With James Gandolfini's help, Kobold then blazed the trail for the renaissance of American watchmaking. Kobold also set up the first high-end watch production in the Himalayas, survived a years-long effort to sabotage its operations, and along the way made thousands of customers very happy (and, as a result of the sabotage, a fistful very unhappy). No matter which way you turn it, Kobold is the little watch brand that has overcome every possible challenge and to this day continues developing uniquely designed and highly rugged watches. This incredible story of triumph over adversity is only possible thanks to the loyalty of Kobold collectors - the Koboldians.

A big thank-you to everyone who made the 25th anniversary of Kobold a success!

Kobold Phantom Safari Chronograph
41 mm diameter Soarway case
Automatic-winding

www.koboldwatch.com

1. Chinese motifs on a vase, the wages of Orientalism

2. Delivering the goods: China becomes the world's supplier of everything

3. Shanghai, where European nations settled during the "Century of Humiliation"

In spite of the frequent attempts by Chinese brands, though, breaking through the European armor seemed an impossible task. And one cannot help feel that this country, with its ancient culture and very different approach to life, is like a youngest, barely tolerated sibling trying to get into the older siblings' party.

The relationship between China and the West (a term of convenience) seems to be a constant blend of admiration and suspicion, curiosity and arrogance, avidity and, occasionally, fascination. We admire them for their inventions, like paper, gunpowder, and porcelain. When the latter appeared in seventeenth-century Europe—some brought over as ballast for ships—it launched the chinoiserie craze, an imitation Chinese decorative style marked by dragons, pagodas, and other "Chinese" objects and motifs. What stimulated Westerners, no doubt, was the sheer difference, sort of like the appreciation for the ancient spirituality of Daoism by the self-help and personal development industry.

The other side of that coin was the harsh reality of semi-colonialism and its collateral arrogance, as exemplified by the famous Macartney Embassy incident in 1793, and the "Century of Humiliation" beginning with the first Opium War. A curious note: most interaction with the Middle Kingdom always seems connected to trade or exploitation in one way or another.

THE AWAKENING GIANT

After centuries of feudalism, wars, revolution, and natural disasters, followed by Mao Zedong's own concoction of Marxist-Leninism and isolationism, China—its economy battered by poor planning and political constraints, but with a large population eager to improve their daily lives—developed a system of state capitalism that drove explosive growth within four decades. Today, its industries supply the planet with affordable goods, from EVs to electronics. And it has its own army of consumers eager to buy stuff and enjoy a more comfortable life.

For businesses in the West, including fashion houses and watch brands, the effusive market was a boon, and companies set about conquering it. "Right now, the Chinese need to learn about watches," was an often-heard trope when discussing how to approach these new consumers. Many big brands with name recognition led the charge, often with products made to entice the Chinese consumers of the new moneyed class. They bore traditional Chinese cultural symbols, notably the astrological signs or the Chinese calendar. With 2024 being the Year of the Dragon, the most powerful of the signs and one that combines benevolence, strength, and good luck, many luxurious timepieces have been made featuring that mythological creature.

The relationship, however, has often been lopsided and tinged with a somewhat patronizing attitude. Whenever China is discussed in terms of manufacturing, it is frequently in dismissive, even demeaning terms, as if the country was nothing more than a bottomless pit of cheap and garish stuff, counterfeits, bad copies, and generally low-quality products. "Sure you can buy a cheap tourbillon," a friend of mine told me with audible disdain, "but it will fall apart in a month." This prejudice, which in some cases may be justified, is also promoted by the steady stream of regular news that de-

CLAUDE MEYLAN

VALLÉE DE JOUX

Tortue de Joux

With its pure and timeless curves associated
with a proven mechanical, "Tortue de Joux"
introduces a new sculpture of time.

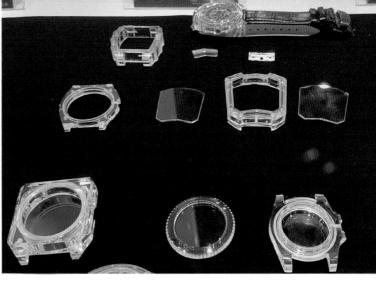

让设计师产生设计灵感的上海大厦建筑系现代主义风格的典型作品

1. and 2. Templates for your dream watch at the Hong Kong Watch and Clock Fair (left), sapphire crystals and cases at competitive prices "Made in China" (right)

3. The original Shanghai Watch factory

4. An industrial success: Mao and Chou En Lai thrilled with their Shanghais

5. The entry-level Shanghai, from novelty to nostalgia

picts China as a giant CNC machine park run by overworked, exhausted, underpaid drones exploited by covetous multinationals: a trade partner and enemy in the same breath, a recidivist violator of intellectual property. When I mentioned my journey to the Hong Kong Watch and Clock Fair (HKWCF), one watchmaker acquaintance looked at me and made a cross with his fingers, as if to ward off a vampire.

Chinese watchmakers are partially victims of their nation's success internationally. The country does indeed produce most of our consumer goods, and it is true that Chinese counterfeiters have proven to be very skillful, as one CEO of a major brand told me about seeing one such piece: "I couldn't tell the difference between the real and the fake." Is there a touch of envy? The fact is, they work hard, something no Swiss watchmaker could ever fault, and their business acumen and imagination is indeed impressive. One hall at the HKWCF I visited was filled by companies that make components like sapphire crystals and cases at very affordable prices. A slew of others did OEM/ODM work. In other words, anyone with an idea for a watch or a finished design can have a watch produced for ridiculously low sums: One quote I was given was $20

per watch as of 500 pieces. Some of these companies also make their own watches. While some Western brands also do OEM/ODM, many of these little companies, working mainly in Shenzhen, the "Silicon Valley of China," proved to be quite creative and could offer a wide range of attractive templates, like cases made of wood, or of recycled plastic mixed with ceramic, dials with real leaves, and so on.

Western watchmakers do demand highest quality and luxury, which has created a nimbus of invincibility in the struggle to maintain market share, but it is also a constraint. Quality labels, like "Swiss-made," which can only be applied to watches that are 60 percent made in Switzerland, serve as a tough rule that weighs on the margins for low-end brands, who will complain when cornered. Forgetting or ignoring that China has a strong native watchmaking industry, however, is perilous. The names CIGA Design, Fiyta, or Celadon mentioned above may be known to some, but they are just the tip of an iceberg in a sea of busy creativity and productivity, and they could easily become strong rivals or at least counterweights to the proud tradition in the West.

SEVEN-DAY CYCLE

 ITAY NOY   Independent Timepiece Maker | www.itay-noy.com | studio@itay-noy.com

1

THE RISING TIDE

Unbeknownst to many, perhaps, China has quite a long history of watchmaking with and without Western influence. In the nineteenth century, brands such as Vacheron Constantin and Bovet in particular had established themselves quite firmly in the country, so much so that the name Bovet became synonymous with any haute *horlogerie*. Local manufacturing could not maintain a high standard, and ultimately counterfeiting became a major problem. By the end of the century, however, the necessities for the average Chinese citizen boiled down to what was called the Three Great Things: a bicycle, a sewing machine, and a watch.

After the 1949 civil war that ushered in Mao Zedong and Communist rule, the watch of that trio earned a special ranking as a functional tool during the push to industrialize. "Factory and office workers who relied on timepieces to coordinate labor shifts and schedules used—and felt compelled to acquire—their own watches to counter management control over their time," wrote Karl Gerth, Professor of History at the University of California San Diego, in his book, *Unending Capitalism: How Consumerism Negated China's Communist Revolution*. In addition to the importance of timekeeping in factories, "railroad workers had to adhere to accurate schedules, especially when trains going in opposite directions shared the same tracks." The problem was that most available watches were for-

eign. So, the Party launched a program to build a domestic watch, and in 1955, a team in the city of Tianjin created the Five-Star brand, which ultimately became the Sea-Gull Watch Group. Meanwhile, a team of experienced watch repairers in Shanghai built a watch based on a Swiss movement but using Japanese and Soviet parts. The name of Shanghai stuck, and it became in some ways the standard. The brand continues to exist to this day (see page 276).

Watches are more than mere tools. Since not everyone could have one, their distribution was rationed, and thus they evolved into a status symbol, a troubling distinction in a nominally egalitarian society. They could be used as bribes, too. Gerth even mentions a movie in which the villain is identified because he is wearing six watches on one wrist, a rather fascinating precursor of the anti-corruption crackdown in 2012, when amateur sleuths started photographing the wrists of officials wearing western watches they could never afford on their regular salaries. On the positive side, watches also had a special symbolic value for the nation struggling to a certain extent with its legitimacy and international standing, as they "represented a small, everyday emblem of global competition that included the transformation, standardization, and internalization of time with the establishment of worldwide timekeeping," says Professor Gerth.

1. The name Bovet became synonymous with "watch" in nineteenth-century China

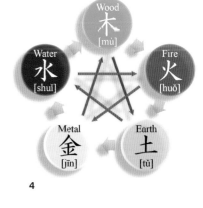

THE NEW WAVE

Thanks to the economic shake-up launched by Deng Xiaoping in the late 1970s, the country developed rapidly with investments in industry and a spirit of competition to rival any capitalist nation. Wealth fueled demand for consumer goods. In the world today, it is probably difficult to establish a clear distinction between daily necessities and luxuries. We don't wear uniforms, so fashionable clothing becomes part of daily life, and watches, be they smartwatches or fine mechanical objects from Europe, have become widely available as functional accessories.

The market for consumer goods in China is dynamic, yet it is still dominated at the higher end by Western companies. Some time around 2015, a cultural movement or trend known as *guochao* (national wave or trend), began, with a new focus on national and local culture and symbols. It was further boosted by a 2017 government plan to promote traditional craftsmanship. Some factors pushing *guochao* are economic and others social. Antonello Germano, a China market analyst with Daxue Consulting, sees it also as a reaction to the long-standing Eurocentrism in fashion: "Nowadays, Chinese consumers are aware of their influence on luxury sales, and they want to set trends and are urging brands to represent Chinese culture authentically, ditching the old orientalist view that shaped how Chinese style was shown in fashion." The word "authentic" is key.

Guochao expresses itself in many ways, notably the use of materials like jade and silk, or portraying certain traditional design and artistic elements of Chinese culture, like cranes, dragons, pandas, koi, and so forth. Colors, too, have significance, which explains some of the very lively fashions one might encounter in the street, in shows, or in shops. Red is a favorite, because it stands for good luck and vitality. Gold and yellow are connected to the mythical Yellow Emperor and signify prestige and prosperity. Purple is an expression of love and sometimes immortality. Colors in China, though, are also associated with the five elements, or *wuxing* 五行, a cornerstone of traditional Chinese medicine, with yellow standing for wood, red for fire, blue for earth, white for metal, and black for water. To the casual Western eye, this makes for a certain amount of gaudiness, not to say kitsch.

Not surprisingly, the rise of *guochao* is driven by a younger, Internet-savvy generation. Besides esthetics and a feeling of pride in their impressive cultural heritage, there is also a simple financial consideration. "Chinese brands are automatically associated with a higher value-for-money, more attentive customer care, and a greater variety of customized services," Antonello Germano told me. "Such functional elements are especially important to Gen Z."

This point was made during a presentation at the HKCWF by Jianmin Zhang, founder and CEO of CIGA Design, who stated that one of the goals of his brand was to make watches affordable for younger people. He also spoke of the brand's Blue Earth model and of the importance of preserving Earth's natural integrity. Interestingly, the brand Ideal Knight also has a watch named Blue Planet, and it's not just lip service to environmentalism. In the worldview of Daoism, that formidable body of thought in China going back over 2,500 years, it means much more. Nature taken

1. A celebration of Hong Kong's own movie formula, by Hedone

2. Chinese astrology, a perennial motif for consumers East and West

3. Pure purple and white, symbols of love, spiritual awareness and purity delivered by Micuch

4. The interaction of the elements in traditional Chinese medicine, also an esthetic clue

5. Guochau: shifting the spotlight onto Chinese culture

1

2

1. Hedone's Philosophe with yang (active) and yin (receptive) on the dial

2. CIGA Design's Oriental Jade, the Earth (square) meets Sky (square)

3. The hand-carved, slithering dragon by Genus

in the widest sense possible, or "heaven," is seen as a guide, a teacher, not only in the physical world, but also because it is always able to transform itself by adapting harmoniously with what we would call challenges (see page 47 for more). In the *Zhuangzi*, a seminal work in Daoism, one finds the sentence "Heaven and earth are born with me, and all things are one with me." Indeed, several CIGA Design models feature a round dial inside a square case with a skeletonized movement. The combination might be a hint at Bauhaus codes for one, but in China, Mr. Zhang pointed out, the circle represents the heavens and the square Earth. And the complex mechanism would then be all the things that happen between the two.

Another example of a Daoist concept appearing in a watch is less subtle at first glance. The Philosophe, by the brand Hedone (see page 163), makes use of the very famous *yin* and *yang* symbol that is casually used to represent wisdom and holisticness in the West. The dial design is a remarkable reminder of that "oneness before duality," where apparent opposites exist in a dynamic balance with each other. The escapement ticks away on the dial as the active (*yang*) principle, opposite the slow-moving, pensive clockface as the receptive/passive principle. As a note: The collection sells for around $500.

COMPETITION AND COOPERATION

As mentioned above, Western brands have been making a strenuous effort to create items geared towards the Chinese market, including watches. For this year, Bell & Ross created an eye-catching dragon that spreads over the entire watch, including the strap. After three years of hard work, the Swiss independent company Genus brought out a fascinating timepiece with an articulated gold dragon slithering across the dial counting out the minutes in ten-minute segments. It holds the traditional pearl in its jaws, a symbol of spiritual enlightenment. Priced at around $175,000, it is well beyond the wallet of most Chinese people young or old. On the other hand, the local brand, Lucky Harvey, has a very clever model costing $1,188 (88 is a very lucky number). Its dragon, hunched over the dial, lets a pearl out of its mouth every hour.

Another way of addressing the market is with collaborations. Atelier Wen, started by Robin Tallendier and Wilfried Buiron, who have extensive experience in China, boldly celebrates "made in China" rather than tryangg to hide it. Their first-born, the Porcelain Odyssey, looked back into history, a reminder of the old love for chinoiserie. The second model, Perception, is actually a collaboration

3

1

2

with one of the world's few hand-guilloché masters, Cheng Yu Cai, and features a meditative fish-scale pattern on the dial.

Clearly, Western brands cannot ignore the national feeling that is sweeping the country. "Even if some watchers consider it as mere nationalism," says Antonello Germano, "*guochao* is a much more complex cultural phenomenon that does not necessarily exclude foreign brands." Perhaps the diffuse precepts of *guochao* and its hint of populism and unseriousness are still anathema to luxury brands in the West. Yet, there is enormous potential in precisely that segment of the market. Generation Z is in the workplace in big, modern cities, and they are quick adopters, share everything online, and most importantly represent a globalized generation. And the Chinese watchmakers are seeking them out with dynamic, imaginative, fun, and bold products. One Swiss watchmaker was amazed at what he found at the HKWCF and warned: "We tend to rest on our laurels, and sure, Asia leaned on us for a while, but what I am seeing surpasses some of the things we do."

Understanding the market, what these consumers are looking for, demands careful study, or, better yet, an effort to understand and embrace the Chinese "feeling." For Wenzhuo Wu, Managing Editor of *Jing Daily*, some big fashion companies, like Loewe, have managed to strike the right nerve. For example, Loewe's campaign for their bags in monochrome ceramic colors attracted Chinese and global consumers. "Brands that take inspiration from local traditions need to do their research, show sincerity, and be transparent in crediting the culture," she wrote. "Otherwise, negative consumer sentiment can dilute the brand reputation that global companies have worked so hard to build."

The geopolitical encounter between the Western world and China is tense, even dangerously so. But as usual, this encounter is in fact full of rich exchanges and competition at the human level, especially with a new and globalized generation of consumers. The anthropologist Arjun Appadurai, in 1996, identified five "scapes" through which globalization expresses itself, including ideas. As such, watches and other goods can be seen as ambassadors, offering, in the words of Professor Hongmei Li from the University of Georgia in her article "Branding Chinese Products," "possibilities for creating communities of imagination and cultural identities outside the conventionally conceived stable national identity." For Jianmin Zhang, it seems it is natural to reach out across the artificial national divides on our blue planet. Commenting on the use of jade in a new model, he writes: "Ancient materials rejuvenated in novel forms. An ultimate balance is achieved between the ingenious forms of Western mechanical art and the sophisticated elements of traditional Chinese culture, between precision and elegance, and between metal and jade." The place to resolve these dualities and contradictions and achieve harmony is within ourselves.

3

4

1.–2. Two dragons: Lucky Harvey's (left) drops a pearl every hour, Bell & Rosses escapes from the watch

3.–4. Two interpretations of the Chinese calendar, by Blancpain (top) and XuShu Ma (bottom)

THE CREATIVE WAY

SILVER COBALT

1. **Laotzi, on his trip through the Han Valley on an ox**

2. **Human art meets perfect Nature**

3. **Happiewatch's earns its name by being frankly fun**

4. **The Cylindrex: An ingenious way of finding time**

The title of the previous chapter, "Carefree watching," arose after an encounter with Hans-Georg Moeller, professor at the University of Macau, an expert in Chinese philosophy, publisher of many books and keeper of the You Tube channel *Carefree Wandering*. I wanted to ask him about Chinese philosophy, the concept of time, and Henri Bergson, whose writing on the matter served as inspiration for the chapter "Beyond time." And something went click. . .

while a minute disc turns and "picks up" them up, like a commander ordering his troops. It was an enlightening moment, especially after visiting the Hong Kong Watch and Clock Fair, where many genuinely creative brands, like Angles Watches, exposed their creations. Angles explores the limits of wearability and produces some remarkable wrist devices, like the Cylindrex, which houses two automatic movements, or the massive Bastion, which shows the hours on four corners, like the towers of a fortress.

By the same token, I noticed some brands had brazenly copied some of the most noticeable Western brands, like Urwerk, MB&F, even Konstantin Chaykin. When politely pointing this out, I usually received an equally polite acquiescence. It was obviously another world, and I wondered about the spirit behind this approach, because the concepts of creativity

and aesthetics were not quite the same as in the West. So I began wandering.

Chinese cosmology is mainly governed by Daoism, which dominates Chinese and even much of Asian culture, even if it's not always consciously so, just as the Judeo-Christian cosmology governs Western culture, at times by willful antithesis. The term "Dao" translates as The Way, and its origins go back at least 2,500 years, to the wonderfully confusing and enlightening texts of Laozi (the *Tao Te Ching*) and *Zhuangzi* (the *Zhuangzi*). Much is in the form of poetry or parables full of stunning paradoxes that puzzle and delight scholars, philosophers, and anyone seeking knowledge to this day.

Taoism could almost be described as an anti-philosophy, in that it is strictly speaking—and oversimplifying for the sake of brevity—an expression of a process that imbues

1–2. **The path of creativity is in the gesture: imitation is respect**

3. **Angle Watch's Bastion, the watch as a fortress in time.**

4. **The art of calligraphy is repetition until perfecton is achieve.**

existence, be it of the individual, a society, Nature, or, indeed, the universe itself. As the *Tao Te Ching* describes it, everything between Heaven and Earth is imbued with the life force, *qi*, and "the space. . . is like a bellows, while empty, it is never exhausted, the more we activate them, the more it exhales." As living beings, we are encouraged to get inside those bellows and "wander" through life, carefree and at ease with whatever happens. This carefree wandering (逍遥遊), should be preceded with a heart-mind cleansing that frees us of spiritual, mental, and emotional clutter, like judgment, extreme goals, and so forth. You are permanently in the now, in a state of "action-in-in-action," or as it's known *wuwei* (無爲), which is the other fundamental precept.

"By loosening the bonds of our fixed preconceptions," says the *Internet Encyclopedia of Philosophy* in its entry on Zhuangzi, "we bring ourselves closer to an attunement to the potent and productive natural way (*dao*) of things." By the same token, this wandering, and especially the "inaction," should not be confused with laziness, as it is combined with a kind of inner peace. This stance or attitude is one that is particularly noticeable in martial arts, like Tai Chi, with its slow, flowing, repetitive gestures and its coopting

of the opponents action. And it is demonstrated in the story of the cook Ding in the *Zhuangzi*, who can cut up an ox perfectly. Because his practice taught him to cut it up without hitting the veins, muscles, or bones, he knows where the interstices are. So, he has had the same knife for nineteen years. His action is holistic, the gesture has been fully integrated.

In the West, our creative output is often done "by the sweat of one's brow," by brainstorming, by seeking uniqueness, exceptional quality for the sake of the outside world. It is goal oriented and produces wonderful results. In China, it is the gesture itself that counts. "Great painters often copied esteemed works by their predecessors as a way of fully inhabiting the minds of those earlier artists, a way of mastering their insights," writes David Hinton in *Art in America* on the ARTnews website. The creative is born inside, from a quality mentioned in the *Zhuangzi* as "virtue."

What does this have to do with the creative process and why is using others' work as a template seemingly acceptable? "Wandering facilitates creativity by engendering a plurality of new insights, experiences, and viewpoints," writes Charlene Tan in the *Journal of Creative Behavior*. "By seeing things

from different perspectives, such a person exercises open-minded flexibility and is liberated from one's presumptuous and in-grained ideas about the utility and value of things and people." In other words, the com-pulsion to make something beautiful is not that important.

In fact, as Belgian-Australian sinologist Pierre Ryckmans (1935-2014), who wrote as Simon Leys, pointed out in an essay on aes-thetics and ethics in China, a creative work reflects the virtue in the broadest sense of its author. "Even if the poet, the musician, the calligrapher, and the painter can thrill a few connoisseurs free of charge," he writes in the collection *Studio de l'inutilité*, "the pri-mary aim of his activity remains the culture and development of his interior life. Writing, painting, or playing the cithara is done to hone one's personality, to perfect oneself morally, by tuning one's individual human-ity to the rhythms of universal creation." This idea is illustrated by one of the most remarkable written interviews I have ever done. In response to a question about his concept of design, Jianmin Zhang, CEO and founder of CIGA Design, wrote:

Unfazed by the world's judgmental stare,
不在意频率不同的节奏

Unruffled by rhythms that differ, unaware.
你的时间痕迹只属于你自己

The marks you leave, a testament true,
你的时间只需你懂

Your time, your journey, is solely for you.

Once the "gesture" has been mastered, and the personal and commercial pressure of having to please has been discarded, the imagination of the designer can wander freely. The goal of creating beauty can, in-deed, become a constraint. In an article for *Psyche Magazine*, Julianne Chung, assistant professor of philosophy at York University in Toronto wrote: "If we focus on the task of achieving something original, we'll explore only the range of possibilities deemed suf-ficiently likely to yield that result, leaving out a lot that could have contributed to achiev-ing something original." This explains why one finds "copies" of some of the great mas-ters of Western horology. It is an aspiration to emulate them, a sign of deep respect, coupled with unfettered creativity that grows with the Way.

1. Zhuangzi (c.369-c.286 BC), carefree creator of instructive and often absurdly amusing parables

2. and 3. XuShu Ma phonograph-inspired watch, Happiewatch's boldly playful adoption of a well-known design.

ACCUTRON

Accutron c/o Citizen Watch America
Empire State Building
350 Fifth Avenue, 29th Floor
New York, NY 10118

Website:
https://www.accutronwatch.com/

Founded:
1960 (relaunched in 2020)

Distribution:
Accutron
customercare@accutronwatch.com
866-419-84-63

Most important collections/price range:
Spaceview 2020, Spaceview Evolution and
Accutron DNA / $3,500 to $5,000; Astronaut /
$3,500; Legacy / $1,290 to $1,600

Well before quartz regulars blew up the watch market, engineers were tinkering with the idea of building an electric watch. There is some debate as two who succeeded first, but it was probably the Elgin 725, a collaboration with the French company Lip, that was the first. It had a traditional mechanical movement with a button cell battery-run mechanism. It failed to thrill the market, however. But it did get another company, Bulova Watch Company, interested in the technology. Over the next few years, with the aid of a Swiss engineer named Max Hetzel, the company came up with a clever system using a tiny 360 Hertz tuning fork and a transistor. The Accutron, a combination of the terms accurate and electronic, was unveiled in 1960 as the world's first fully electronic watch. It was an instant success and even attracted NASA among others.

In 2020, Accutron was relaunched as a separate brand with its iconic Spaceview design. The company's design and engineering team based in Tokyo reworked the engine and the design to create a brand-new proprietary electrostatic energy movement. It is run by twin turbines that rotate very fast between two electrodes using the wearer's movements. The energy, stored in an accumulator, powers two motors. One drives the sweep-second hand, and a step motor powers the hour and minute hands. Both motors are synchronized through integrated circuits to provide accuracy to +/- 5 seconds a month.

Accutron decided to steer close to the original when it comes to design. Fans will easily recognize the cherished dial-less model with its green accents. As for the Spaceview, it was in its time a landmark achievement, with its case stripped down to expose the unique tuning fork movement. Accutron also features automatic timepieces inspired from the brand's most iconic historical timepieces.

DNA Casino
Reference number: 28A205
Movement: Accutron caliber NS30; quartz resonator with dual stepper motor and electrostatic drive system for the hands; ø 36 mm, height 6.48 mm; 28 jewels
Functions: hours, minutes, sweep seconds
Case: stainless steel, ø 45.1 mm, height 15.6 mm; sapphire crystal; water-resistant to 5 atm
Band: rubber, double folding clasp
Price: $3,500; limited edition of 100 pieces

DNA Casino
Reference number: 28A206
Movement: Accutron caliber NS30; quartz resonator with dual stepper motor and electrostatic drive system for the hands; ø 36 mm, height 6.48 mm; 28 jewels
Functions: hours, minutes, sweep seconds
Case: stainless steel, ø 45.1 mm, height 15.6 mm; sapphire crystal; water-resistant to 5 atm
Band: rubber, double folding clasp
Price: $3,500; limited edition of 100 pieces

DNA Casino
Reference number: 28A207
Movement: Accutron caliber NS30; quartz resonator with dual stepper motor and electrostatic drive system for the hands; ø 36 mm, height 6.48 mm; 28 jewels
Functions: hours, minutes, sweep seconds
Case: stainless steel, ø 45.1 mm, height 15.6 mm; sapphire crystal; water-resistant to 5 atm
Band: rubber, double folding clasp
Price: $3,500; limited edition of 100 pieces

DNA Casino

Reference number: 28A208
Movement: Accutron caliber NS30; quartz resonator with dual stepper motor and electrostatic drive system for the hands; ø 36 mm, height 6.48 mm; 28 jewels
Functions: hours, minutes, sweep seconds
Case: stainless steel, ø 45.1 mm, height 15.6 mm; sapphire crystal; water-resistant to 5 atm
Band: rubber, double folding clasp
Price: $3,500; limited edition of 100 pieces

Spaceview Evolution

Reference number: 26A209
Movement: Accutron caliber NS30; quartz resonator with dual stepper motor and electrostatic drive system for the hands; ø 36 mm, height 6.48 mm; 28 jewels
Functions: hours, minutes, sweep seconds
Case: stainless steel, ø 43.5 mm, height 15.9 mm; sapphire crystal; water-resistant to 5 atm
Band: reptile skin, double folding clasp
Price: $3,950

Spaceview Evolution

Reference number: 26A210
Movement: Accutron caliber NS30; quartz resonator with dual stepper motor and electrostatic drive system for the hands; ø 36 mm, height 6.48 mm; 28 jewels
Functions: hours, minutes, sweep seconds
Case: stainless steel, ø 43.5 mm, height 15.9 mm; sapphire crystal; water-resistant to 5 atm
Band: reptile skin, double folding clasp
Price: $3,950

Astronaut

Reference number: 2SW8A002
Movement: automatic, Sellita Caliber SW330, ø 26.20 mm, height 4.10 mm; 25 jewels; 28,800 vph; 56-hour power reserve
Functions: hours, minutes, sweep seconds; second time zone with GMT hand
Case: stainless steel, ø 41 mm, height 13.85 mm; sapphire crystal; partial transparent case back; water-resistant to 10 atm
Band: stainless steel, double folding clasp
Remarks: the Astronaut "T" design first launched in 1968 features a distinctive day/night bezel.
Price: $3,500; limited to 300 numbered pieces

Legacy x Le Kool

Reference number: 2SW6A002LK
Movement: automatic, Sellita Caliber SW200-1, ø 25.60 mm, height 4.6 mm; 26 jewels; 28,800 vph; 42-hour power reserve
Functions: hours, minutes, sweep seconds
Case: stainless steel, ø 34 mm, height 12.6 mm; Football Cross Hatch case design; sapphire crystal; partially transparent case back; water-resistant to 3 atm
Band: metallic leather, pin buckle
Remarks: "565" known as the Football Cross Hatch watch in 1966
Price: $1,550
Variations: comes with two extra black and gold metallic leather straps

Legacy x Le Kool

Reference number: 2SW7A004LK
Movement: automatic, Sellita Caliber SW200-1, ø 25.60 mm, height 4.6 mm; 26 jewels; 28,800 vph; 42-hour power reserve
Functions: hours, minutes, sweep seconds
Case: gold-tone stainless steel, ø 34 mm, height 12.6 mm; crown placement at 4 o'clock; sapphire crystal; partial transparent case back; water-resistant to 3 atm
Band: metallic leather, pin buckle
Remarks: historical "412" case design, the original case design for Accutron's iconic Spaceview
Price: $1,600
Variations: comes with two extra black and bronze metallic leather straps

Lange Uhren GmbH
Ferdinand-A.-Lange-Platz 1
D-01768 Glashütte
Germany

Tel.:
+49-35053-44-0

E-mail:
info@lange-soehne.com

Website:
www.alange-soehne.com

Founded:
1990

Number of employees:
750 employees, almost half of whom are watchmakers

U.S. distributor:
A. Lange & Söhne
645 Fifth Avenue
New York, NY 10022
800-408-8147

Most important collections/price range:
Lange 1 / $40,300 to $359,400; Saxonia / $19,700 to $287,800; 1815 / $27,300 to $253,500; Richard Lange / $36,800 to $247,800; Zeitwerk / $89,200 to $141,300; Odysseus / $34,900 to $56,500

ACCUTRON

...ermans tend to ...o died in January ...own of Glashütte. ...firm was originally ...d Adolph had origi-...on. And shortly after ...d again. ..., which are at the heart ...de of German silver (an ...r the hand-engraved bal-...calibers number sixty-nine ...se. They are decorated and ...positions. Patented innova-...set" for the second hand, and ...notably one for the Lange 31, ...rs. Materials for the cases have ...ellow and "honey" gold, stainless

tions incl...
the three differen...
whose mainspring provid...
grown as well and now include p...
steel, and titanium.

Lange's products, which are designed with great care, always surprise. The entry-level family is the classic, visually balanced, three-hand Saxonia, while the Lange 1, introduced in 1994, is considered the collection flagship. In 2019, the company created a stir among watch fans when the Odysseus, with a custom automatic movement and weekday and date display, staked a claim in the sports watch club. A wealth of novelties appeared in 2020, notably several inside "honey gold" cases, including a Zeitwerk with a minute repeater. And the Odysseus's stainless-steel model has now been joined by a titanium version, as well as a white gold model with an integrated leather or rubber strap, taking daily sports routine to the high end, as it were.

Odysseus

Reference number: 363.117
Movement: automatic, Lange Caliber L155.1 Datomatic; ø 32.9 mm, height 6.2 mm; 31 jewels; 28,800 vph; hand-engraved balance cock, 1 screw-mounted gold chaton, swan-neck fine adjustment; parts finished and assembled by hand; 50-hour power reserve
Functions: hours, minutes, subsidiary seconds; large date, weekday
Case: titanium, ø 40.5 mm, height 11.1 mm; sapphire crystal; transparent case back; water-resistant to 12 atm
Band: titanium, folding clasp
Price: $56,500; limited to 250 pieces (boutique edition)
Variations: In stainless steel ($34,900)

Odysseus

Reference number: 363.038
Movement: automatic, Lange Caliber L155.1 Datomatic; ø 32.9 mm, height 6.2 mm; 31 jewels; 28,800 vph; hand-engraved balance cock, 1 screw-mounted gold chaton, swan-neck fine adjustment; parts finished and assembled by hand; 50-hour power reserve
Functions: hours, minutes, subsidiary seconds; large date, weekday
Case: white gold, ø 40.5 mm, height 11.1 mm; sapphire crystal; transparent case back; water-resistant to 12 atm
Band: calf leather, buckle
Price: $47,400
Variations: with rubber strap ($47,400)

Lange 1

Reference: 191.039
Movement: hand-wound, Lange Caliber L121.3; ø 30.6 mm, height 5.7 mm; 47 jewels; 21,600 vph; 8 screw-mounted gold chatons, swan-neck fine adjustment, hand-engraved balance cock, parts finished and assembled by hand; 72-hour power reserve
Functions: hours, minutes, subsidiary seconds; power reserve indicator; large date
Case: white gold, ø 38.5 mm, height 9.8 mm; sapphire crystal; transparent case back; water-resistant to 3 atm
Band: reptile skin, buckle
Price: $40,300
Variations: in pink gold ($40,300); platinum ($53,000)

Grand Lange 1

Reference number: 137.033
Movement: hand-wound, Lange Caliber L095.1;
ø 34.1 mm, height 4.7 mm; 42 jewels; 21,600 vph;
7 screw-mounted gold chatons, swan-neck fine
adjustment, hand-engraved balance cock, parts finished
and assembled by hand; 72-hour power reserve
Functions: hours, minutes, subsidiary seconds; power
reserve indicator; large date
Case: pink gold, ø 41 mm, height 8.2 mm; sapphire
crystal; transparent case back, water-resistant to 3 atm
Band: reptile skin, buckle
Price: $48,100
Variations: in white gold ($48,100)

Little Lange 1 Moon Phase

Reference number: 182.086
Movement: hand-wound, Lange Caliber L121.2;
ø 30.6 mm, height 6 mm; 44 jewels; 21,600 vph;
8 screw-mounted gold chatons, swan-neck fine
adjustment, hand-engraved balance cock, parts finished
and assembled by hand; 72-hour power reserve
Functions: hours, minutes, subsidiary seconds; power
reserve indication, large date, moon phase
Case: white gold, ø 36.8 mm, height 9.5 mm; sapphire
crystal; transparent case back; water-resistant to 3 atm
Band: reptile skin, buckle
Remarks: dial covered in dark blue aventurine
Price: $49,400
Variations: with diamond bezel ($62,300)

Lange 1 Time Zone

Reference number: 136.029
Movement: hand-wound, Lange Caliber 141.1;
ø 34.1 mm, height 6.7 mm; 38 jewels; 21,600 vph;
3 screw-mounted gold chatons; parts finished and
assembled by hand; 38-hour power reserve
Functions: hours, minutes, subsidiary seconds;
additional 12-hour display (second time zone)
day/night indication (double), power reserve indicator,
daylight savings indication; large date
Case: white gold, ø 41.9 mm, height 10.9 mm; sapphire
crystal; transparent case back, water-resistant to 3 atm
Band: reptile skin, buckle
Price: $57,800
Variation: in pink gold ($57,800)

Lange 1 Perpetual Calendar

Reference number: 345.033
Movement: automatic, Lange Caliber L021.3;
ø 35.8 mm, height 8.8 mm; 63 jewels; 21,600 vph;
off-center balance, 5 screw-mounted gold chatons,
hand-engraved balance cock, gold rotor with platinum
oscillating mass; 50-hour power reserve
Functions: hours, minutes, subsidiary seconds; day/
night indication; perpetual calendar with large date,
weekday, month, moon phase, leap year
Case: pink gold, ø 41.9 mm, height 12.1 mm; sapphire
crystal; transparent case back; water-resistant to 3 atm
Band: reptile skin, buckle
Price: $113,400
Variations: white gold with pink gold dial ($116,000),
limited to 150 pieces

Saxonia Thin

Reference number: 205.086
Movement: hand-wound, Lange Caliber L093.1;
ø 28 mm, height 2.9 mm; 21 jewels; 21,600 vph; screw
balance, swan-neck fine adjustment, hand-engraved
balance cock, 3 gold chatons; 72-hour power reserve
Functions: hours, minutes
Case: white gold, ø 39 mm, height 6.2 mm; sapphire
crystal; transparent case back
Band: reptile skin, buckle
Remarks: copper-blue aventurine dial
Price: $26,400
Variations: in pink or white gold in a 37-millimeter
case with silver-colored dial ($21,200)

Saxonia Outsize Date

Reference number: 381.032
Movement: automatic; Lange Caliber L086.8;
ø 30.4 mm, height 5.2 mm; 40 jewels; 21,600 vph; hand-
engraved balance cock, screw balance, swan-neck fine
adjustment; 72-hour power reserve
Functions: hours, minutes, subsidiary seconds; large
date
Case: pink gold, ø 38.5 mm, height 9.6 mm; sapphire
crystal; transparent case back; water-resistant to 3 atm
Band: reptile skin, buckle
Price: $30,800
Variations: white gold ($30,800); with black dial

Saxonia Moon Phase

Reference number: 384.026
Movement: automatic, Lange Caliber L086.5;
ø 30.4 mm, height 5.2 mm; 40 jewels; 21,600 vph; hand-engraved balance cock, screw balance, swan-neck fine adjustment; 72-hour power reserve
Functions: hours, minutes, subsidiary seconds; large date, moon phase
Case: white gold, ø 40 mm, height 9.8 mm; sapphire crystal; transparent case back; water-resistant to 3 atm
Band: reptile skin
Price: $34,900
Variations: in pink gold ($34,900)

Datograph Up/Down

Reference number: 405.035
Movement: hand-wound, Lange Caliber L951.7;
ø 30.6 mm, height 8.1 mm; 46 jewels; 18,000 vph;
4 screw-mounted gold chatons, swan-neck fine adjustment, hand-engraved balance cock;
60-hour power reserve
Functions: hours, minutes, subsidiary seconds; power reserve indicator; flyback chronograph with precisely jumping minute counter; large date
Case: platinum, ø 41 mm, height 13.4 mm; sapphire crystal; transparent case back; water-resistant to 3 atm
Band: reptile skin, buckle
Price: $110,300
Variations: in pink gold ($94,400)

Datograph Perpetual

Reference number: 410.038
Movement: hand-wound, Lange Caliber L952.1;
ø 32 mm, height 8 mm; 45 jewels; 18,000 vph; off-center balance; in-house balance spring, column wheel control of the chronograph functions; 4 screw-mounted gold chatons, 36-hour power reserve
Functions: hours, minutes, subsidiary seconds; day/night indicator; flyback chronograph with precisely jumping minute counter; perpetual calendar with large date, weekday, months moon phase, leap year
Case: white gold, ø 41 mm, height 13.5 mm; sapphire crystal; transparent case back; water-resistant to 3 atm
Band: reptile skin, buckle
Price: $158,900

Zeitwerk Date

Reference number: 148.038
Movement: hand-wound, Lange Caliber L043.8;
ø 37 mm, height 8.9 mm; 70 jewels; 18,000 vph;
2 screw-mounted gold chatons, constant force mechanism (remontoir), hand-engraved balance cock;
72-hour power reserve
Functions: hours and minutes (digital, jumping), subsidiary seconds; power reserve indicator; date
Case: white gold, ø 44.2 mm, height 12.3 mm; sapphire crystal; transparent case back; water-resistant to 3 atm
Band: reptile skin, buckle
Price: $115,000

Zeitwerk Striking Time

Reference number: 145.032
Movement: hand-wound, Lange Caliber L043.2;
ø 36 mm, height 10 mm; 78 jewels; 18,000 vph; 2 screw-mounted gold chatons, constant force mechanism (remontoir), hand-engraved balance cock, acoustic signal at the top of the hour and every quarter hour;
36-hour power reserve
Functions: hours and minutes (digital, jumping), subsidiary seconds; power reserve indicator
Case: pink gold, ø 44.2 mm, height 13.1 mm; sapphire crystal; transparent case back; water-resistant to 3 atm
Band: reptile skin, folding clasp
Price: $141,300
Variations: in white gold ($141,300)

1815 Up/Down

Reference number: 234.032
Movement: hand-wound, Lange Caliber L051.2;
ø 30.6 mm, height 4.6 mm; 29 jewels; 21,600 vph;
7 screw-mounted gold chatons, three-quarter plate, screw balance, hand-engraved balance cock, parts finished and assembled by hand; 55-hour power reserve
Functions: hours, minutes, subsidiary seconds; power reserve indicator
Case: pink gold, ø 39 mm, height 8.7 mm; sapphire crystal; transparent case back; water-resistant to 3 atm
Band: reptile skin, buckle
Price: $31,800
Variations: white gold ($31,800)

1815 Annual Calendar

Reference number: 238.032
Movement: hand-wound, Lange Caliber L051.3;
ø 30.6 mm, height 5.7 mm; 26 jewels; 21,600 vph;
3 screw-mounted gold chatons, hand-engraved
balance cock, parts finished and assembled by hand;
72-hour power reserve
Functions: hours, minutes, subsidiary seconds; annual
calendar with date, weekday, month, moon phase
Case: pink gold, ø 40 mm, height 10.1 mm; sapphire
crystal; transparent case back; water-resistant to 3 atm
Band: reptile skin, buckle
Price: $48,000
Variations: white gold ($48,000)

1815 Chronograph

Reference number: 414.028
Movement: hand-wound, Lange Caliber L951.5;
ø 30.6 mm, height 6.1 mm; 34 jewels; 21,600 vph;
4 screw-mounted gold chatons, hand-engraved
balance cock, parts finished and assembled by hand;
60-hour power reserve
Functions: hours, minutes, subsidiary seconds;
flyback chronograph
Case: white gold, ø 39.5 mm, height 11 mm; sapphire
crystal; transparent case back; water-resistant to 3 atm
Band: reptile skin, buckle
Price: $67,800
Variations: in pink gold ($67,800), white gold
"boutique exclusive"

1815 Rattrapante Perpetual Calendar

Reference number: 421.025
Movement: hand-wound, Lange Caliber L101.1;
ø 32.6 mm, height 9.1 mm; 43 jewels; 21,600 vph;
4 screw-mounted gold chatons; hand-engraved
balance cock, parts finished and assembled by hand;
42-hour power reserve
Functions: hours, minutes, subsidiary seconds;
power reserve indicator; split-seconds chronograph;
perpetual calendar with date, weekday, months moon
phase, leap year
Case: platinum, ø 41.9 mm, height 14.7 mm; sapphire
crystal; transparent case back; water-resistant to 3 atm
Band: reptile skin, folding clasp
Price: $253,500

Richard Lange

Reference number: 232.032
Movement: hand-wound, Lange Caliber L041.2;
ø 30.6 mm, height 6 mm; 26 jewels; 21,600 vph; hand-
engraved balance cock, 2 screw-mounted gold
chatons, parts finished and assembled by hand;
in-house manufactured balance spring with a patented
anchoring clip; 38-hour power reserve
Functions: hours, minutes, sweep seconds
Case: white gold, ø 40.5 mm, height 10.5 mm; sapphire
crystal; transparent case back; water-resistant to 3 atm
Band: reptile skin, buckle
Price: $36,800
Variations: In pink gold (boutique edition, $36,800)

Richard Lange Minute Repeater

Reference number: 606.079
Movement: hand-wound, Lange Caliber L122.1;
ø 30 mm, height 5.4 mm; 40 jewels; 21,600 vph;
4 screw-mounted gold chatons, hand-engraved
balance cock, parts finished and assembled by hand;
72-hour power reserve
Functions: hours, minutes, subsidiary seconds;
minute repeater
Case: platinum, ø 39 mm, height 9.7 mm; sapphire
crystal; transparent case back; water-resistant to 2 atm
Band: reptile skin, folding clasp
Remarks: limited to 50 pieces (boutique edition)
Price: on request

Richard Lange Jumping Seconds

Reference number: 252.029
Movement: hand-wound, Lange Caliber L094.1;
ø 33.6 mm, height 6 mm; 50 jewels; 21,600 vph;
zero-reset mechanism, constant force escapement
(remontoir); 42-hour power reserve
Functions: off-center hours and minutes, large
seconds (jumping); winding reminder
Case: white gold, ø 39.9 mm, height 10.6 mm; sapphire
crystal; transparent case back; water-resistant to 3 atm
Band: reptile skin, buckle
Price: $88,600
Variations: pink gold with silver-colored dial, limited
to 100 pieces ($88,300); platinum ($84,200)

Caliber L155.1 Datomatic

Automatic; swan-neck fine adjustment; second stop mechanism, platinum oscillating mass; single spring barrel; 50-hour power reserve
Functions: hours, minutes, subsidiary seconds; date, weekday
Diameter: 32.9 mm
Height: 6.2 mm
Jewels: 31, including a screw-mounted gold chaton
Balance: glucydur with regulating screws
Frequency: 28,800 vph
Balance spring: made in-house
Remarks: components hand-finished and -assembled; 312 parts

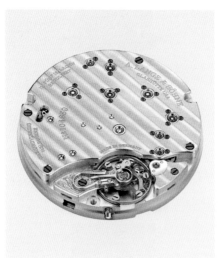

Caliber L121.1

Hand-wound; stop-seconds mechanism, 8 screw-mounted gold chatons, swan-neck fine adjustment; double spring barrel; 72-hour power reserve
Functions: hours, minutes, subsidiary seconds; power reserve indicator; large date
Diameter: 30.6 mm
Height: 5.7 mm
Jewels: 43
Balance: glucydur with eccentric adjustment cams
Frequency: 21,600 vph
Balance spring: made in-house
Shock protection: Kif
Remarks: plates and bridges of untreated German silver, decorated and assembled mostly by hand, hand-engraved balance cock

Caliber L141.1

Hand-wound; stop-seconds mechanism, 3 screw-mounted gold chatons, swan-neck fine adjustment; single spring barrel; 38-hour power reserve
Functions: hours, minutes, subsidiary seconds; 2nd time zone, 2 day/night indicators, power reserve indicator, daylight saving time
Diameter: 34.1 mm
Height: 6.7 mm
Jewels: 38
Balance: glucydur with eccentric adjustment cams
Frequency: 21,600 vph
Hairspring: made in-house Kif
Remarks: German silver plates and bridges, hand-finished and assembled, hand-engraved balance cock

Caliber L021.3

Automatic; unidirectional gold rotor with a platinum oscillating mass; single spring barrel, 50-hour power reserve
Functions: hours, minutes, subsidiary seconds; day/night indicator; perpetual calendar with large date, weekday, month, moon phase, leap year
Diameter: 35.8 mm
Height: 8.8 mm
Jewels: 63, including 5 screw-mounted gold chatons
Balance: glucydur with eccentric regulating cams 21,600 vph
Balance spring: in-house manufacture
Remarks: assembled and decorated by hand, hand-engraved balance cock; 621 components

Caliber L086.5

Automatic; single spring barrel; 72-hour power reserve
Functions: hours, minutes, subsidiary seconds; large date, moon phase
Diameter: 30.4 mm
Height: 5.2 mm
Jewels: 40
Balance: glucydur
Frequency: 21,600 vph;
Balance spring: made in-house
Remarks: German silver plates, hand-engraved balance cock; 325 parts

Caliber L951.6

Hand-wound; stop-seconds mechanism, jumping minute counter; single spring barrel; 60-hour power reserve
Functions: hours, minutes, subsidiary seconds; power reserve indicator; flyback chronograph; large date
Diameter: 30.6 mm **Height:** 7.9 mm **Jewels:** 46
Balance: glucydur with weighted screws
Frequency: 18,000 vph
Hairspring: made in-house
Shock protection: Incabloc
Remarks: three-quarter plate of untreated German silver, hand-assembled and decorated according to highest quality standards, hand-engraved balance cock; 451 parts

Caliber L952.1

Hand-wound; single spring barrel; 36-hour power reserve

Functions: subsidiary seconds; day/night indicator; flyback chronograph with exactly jumping minute counter, perpetual calendar with large date, weekday, months moon phase, leap year

Diameter: 32 mm

Height: 0 mm

Jewels: 45, including 4 screw-mounted gold chatons

Balance: glucydur with eccentric regulating cams

Frequency: 18,000 vph

Balance spring: in-house manufacture

Remarks: parts finished and assembled by hand, hand-engraved balance cock; 556 parts

Caliber L132.1

Hand-wound; column-wheel control of chronograph functions; single spring barrel; 55-hour power reserve

Functions: hours, minutes, subsidiary seconds; power reserve indicator; flyback chronograph, with triple flyback for comparative time measurements up to 12 hours, precisely jumping chrono and flyback minute counter, continuous chrono and split-second hour counter

Diameter: 30.6 mm **Height:** 9.4 mm

Jewels: 46, including 5 screw-mounted gold chatons, glucydur with eccentric adjustment cams

Frequency: 21,600 vph

Balance spring: made in-house

Remarks: German-silver plates and bridges, hand-engraved balance cock; 567 parts

Caliber L043.8

Hand-wound; jumping minute, constant force mechanism (remontoir), patented barrel spring mechanism, stop-seconds mechanism; single spring barrel; 72-hour power reserve

Functions: hours, minutes (digital, jumping), subsidiary seconds; power reserve indicator, acoustic signal every 10 minutes and on the hour (with switch-off mechanism); date

Diameter: 37 mm **Height:** 8.9 mm **Jewels:** 70

Balance: glucydur with eccentric adjustment cams

Frequency: 18,000 vph

Balance spring: made in-house with hairspring clamp

Shock protection: Incabloc

Remarks: three-quarter plate of German silver; 516 parts

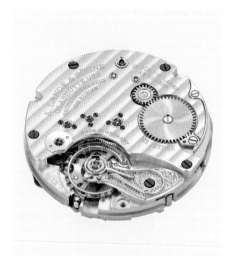

Caliber L051.3

Hand-wound; swan-neck fine adjustment, stop-seconds, German silver mainplate and bridges; single spring barrel, 72-hour power reserve

Functions: hours, minutes, subsidiary seconds; annual calendar with date, weekday, months, moon phase

Diameter: 30.6 mm

Height: 5.7 mm

Jewels: 26, including 3 screw-mounted gold chatons

Balance: glucydur with weighted screws

Frequency: 21,600 vph

Balance spring: in-house manufacture

Remarks: parts finished and assembled by hand, hand-engraved balance cock; 345 parts

Caliber L101.1

Hand-wound; stop-second system; single spring barrel, 42-hour power reserve

Functions: hours, minutes, subsidiary seconds; power reserve indicator; split-seconds chronograph; perpetual calendar with date, weekday, months moon phase, leap year

Diameter: 32.6 mm

Height: 9.1 mm

Jewels: 43, including 4 screw-mounted gold chatons

Balance: glucydur with weighted screws

Frequency: 21,600 vph

Balance spring: in-house manufacture

Shock protection: Kif

Remarks: parts finished and assembled by hand, hand-engraved balance cock; 528 parts

Caliber L122.1

Hand-wound; stop-second system; single spring barrel, 72-hour power reserve

Functions: hours, minutes, subsidiary seconds; minute repeater

Diameter: 30 mm

Height: 5.4 mm

Jewels: 40, including 4 screw-mounted gold chatons

Balance: glucydur with weighted screws

Frequency: 21,600 vph

Balance spring: in-house manufacture

Shock protection: Kif

Remarks: parts finished and assembled by hand, hand-engraved balance cock; 414 parts

ALEXANDER SHOROKHOFF

The ultimate goal for the watch connoisseur may be realizing one's own ideas for time-pieces. In the first stages of his life, Alexander Shorokhoff, born in Moscow in 1960, was an engineer and then an architect with his own construction company. This turned out to be an excellent platform to begin expanding into the field of fine timepieces. In 1992, shortly after the break-up of the Soviet Union, Shorokhoff founded a distribution company in Germany to market Russia's own Poljot watches. This gave him the insight and practice needed to launch phase two of his plan: establishing his own manufacturing facilities for an independent watch brand under his own name.

At Shorokhoff Watches, three main creative lines are bundled under the general concept "Art on the Wrist": Heritage, Avantgarde, and Vintage. The three lines share a design with a distinctly artistic orientation. They all focus on technical quality, sophisticated hand-engraving, and the cultural backdrop. "We consider watches not only as timekeepers, but also as works of art," says Alexander Shorokhoff. It's a statement that is clearly expressed by the product. The brand is at home in the world of international and Russian art and culture (models named Dostoevsky, Leo Tolstoy, and Peter Tchaikovsky, for example). Each dial is designed down to the smallest detail. The engraving and finishing of the movements are unique as well. These timepieces are bold, innovative, and visually striking, which explains numerous and illustrious design awards.

The movements are mostly Swiss-made, with some Russian movements thrown in. They are taken apart in Alzenau, reworked, decorated, and then reassembled with great care, which is why the brand has stamped each watch with "Handmade in Germany." Some of the modules used in these timepieces were developed by the company itself. Before a watch leaves the *manufacture*, it is subjected to strict quality control. The timepiece's functionality must be given the cleanest bill of health before it can be sent out to jewelers around the world.

Alexander Shorokhoff Uhrenmanufaktur
Hanauer Strasse 25
63755 Alzenau
Germany

Tel.:
+49-6023-919-93

E-mail:
info@alexander-shorokhoff.de

Website:
www.alexander-shorokhoff.de

Founded:
2003

Number of employees:
17

Annual production:
approx. 1,500-2,000 watches

Distributor:
About Time Luxury Group
210 Bellevue Avenue
Newport, RI 02840
401-846-0598

Most important collections/price range:
Heritage / starting at approx. $4,500;
Avantgarde / starting at approx. $1,500;
Vintage / starting at approx. $800

Avantgarde "Swan Lake AVG"

Reference number: AS.PT-SL3
Movement: hand-wound, Caliber 2612.AS (based on Poljot 2612/ AS1475); ø 26 mm, height 5.8 mm; 18 jewels; 18,000 vph; hand-engraved and finished; 38-hour power reserve
Functions: hours, minutes, sweep seconds; alarm
Case: stainless steel, ø 40 mm, height 11.5 mm; sapphire crystal; transparent case back; water-resistant to 3 atm
Band: reptile skin, pin buckle
Remarks: hinged double case
Price: $3,350; limited to 30 pieces

Avantgarde "Avantgarde 08"

Reference number: AS.AVG08
Movement: hand-wound, Caliber 2614.AS; ø 26 mm, height 4.3 mm; 17 jewels; 21,600 vph; hand-engraved and finished; 42-hour power reserve
Functions: hours, minutes, sweep seconds
Case: stainless steel, ø 43.5 mm, height 11.5 mm; sapphire crystal; transparent case back; water-resistant to 5 atm
Band: calfskin, pin buckle
Price: $1,500; limited to 50 pieces

Avantgarde "Shar"

Reference number: AS.SH05-5
Movement: automatic, Caliber 2671.AS (based on ETA 2671); ø 17.5 mm, height 4.8 mm; 25 jewels; 28,800 vph; hand-engraved oscillating mass; 42-hour power reserve
Functions: hours, minutes, sweep seconds; date
Case: stainless steel, spherical, with yellow-gold IP plating, ø 25 mm; sapphire crystal; water-resistant to 3 atm
Band: reptile skin, pin buckle
Remarks: malachite dial; hemispherical sapphire crystal; limited to 30 pieces
Price: $1,940

Avantgarde "Square & Round"

Reference number: AS.SR01-5
Movement: hand-wound, Caliber 3133.AS;
ø 31 mm, height 7.35 mm; 23 jewels; 21,600 vph;
hand-engraved and finished; 42-hour power reserve
Functions: hours, minutes, subsidiary seconds;
chronograph; date
Case: stainless steel, 45.5 x 45.5 mm, height 14.75 mm;
sapphire crystal; transparent case back;
water-resistant to 3 atm
Band: reptile skin, pin buckle
Price: $3,400; limited to 30 pieces

Avantgarde "Vintage 7 Matt"

Reference number: AS.V7-RS
Movement: automatic, Caliber 2616.2H.AS;
ø 26 mm, height 6.8 mm; 23 jewels; 18,000 vph;
hand-engraved and finished; 41-hour power reserve
Functions: hours, minutes, sweep seconds; date
Case: stainless steel, ø 39.5 mm, height 13.15 mm;
sapphire crystal; transparent case back;
water-resistant to 5 atm
Band: reptile skin, pin buckle
Price: $1,800; limited to 30 pieces

Avantgarde "CEO Skeleton"

Reference number: AS.31-CEO
Movement: hand-wound, Caliber 3105.AS
(based on Poljot 3105); ø 31 mm, height 5.38 mm;
17 jewels; 21,600 vph; skeletonized movement,
engraved and finished by hand; 42-hour power reserve
Functions: hours, minutes, subsidiary seconds
Case: stainless steel, ø 43.5 mm, height 13.2 mm;
sapphire crystal; transparent case back;
water-resistant to 5 atm
Band: reptile skin, pin buckle
Remarks: skeletonized dial
Price: $4,850; limited to 5 pieces

Avantgarde "Deep Ding 2"

Reference number: AS.DD15-RBR
Movement: automatic, Sellita Caliber SW200-1;
ø 25.6 mm, height 4.6 mm; 26 jewels; 28,800 vph;
hand-engraved rotor; 38-hour power reserve
Functions: hours, minutes, sweep seconds; date
Case: stainless steel with red-gold PVD,
ø 45 mm, height 13.75 mm; crown-activated inner
rotating scale ring with 0-60 scale; sapphire crystal;
water-resistant to 10 atm
Band: rubber, folding clasp
Remarks: comes with stainless-steel protective grille
for the case
Price: $2,500; limited to 37 pieces

Avantgarde "Neva Chrono"

Reference number: AS.CA05-NEV3
Movement: automatic, Caliber 2030.AS (based
on Dubois Dépraz 2030); ø 30 mm, height 7.5 mm;
49 jewels; 28,800 vph; 38-hour power reserve
Functions: hours, minutes, subsidiary seconds;
chronograph
Case: stainless steel, ø 43.5 mm, height 14.4 mm;
sapphire crystal; transparent case back;
water-resistant to 5 atm
Band: calfskin, pin buckle
Price: $3,200; limited to 100 pieces

Avantgarde "Crazy Balls"

Reference number: AS.CB01-2
Movement: automatic, Sellita Caliber SW200-1;
ø 25.6 mm, height 4.6 mm; 26 jewels; 28,800 vph; hand-
engraved and finished rotor; 38-hour power reserve
Functions: hours, minutes, sweep seconds; date
Case: stainless steel, ø 39 mm, height 10.6 mm;
sapphire crystal; transparent case back;
water-resistant to 5 atm
Band: ray skin, pin buckle
Price: $2,050; limited to 88 pieces

ALPINA

Alpina essentially grew out of a confederation of watchmakers known as the Alpina Union Horlogère, founded by Gottlieb Hauser. The group expanded quickly to reach beyond Swiss borders into Germany, where it opened a factory in Glashütte. For a while in the 1930s, it even merged with Gruen, one of the most important watch companies in the United States at the time.

After World War II, the Allied Forces decreed that the name Alpina could no longer be used in Germany, and so that brand was renamed "Dugena" for Deutsche Uhrmacher-Genossenschaft Alpina, or the German Watchmaker Cooperative Alpina.

Today, Geneva-based Alpina is no longer associated with that watchmaker cooperative of yore. Now a sister brand of Frederique Constant, it has a decidedly modern collection enhanced with a series of movements designed, built, and assembled in-house: the Tourbillon AL-980, the World Timer AL-718, the Automatic Regulator AL-950, the Small Date Automatic AL-710, and, more recently, the Flyback Chronograph Automatic AL-760, which features the patented Direct Flyback technology. Owners Peter and Aletta Stas sold it to Citizen Group in 2016.

Alpina has a history of pioneering advances in watchmaking. Its iconic Block Uhr of 1933 and the Alpina 4 of 1938, with an in-house automatic movement, set the pace for all sports watches, with a waterproof stainless-steel case and an amagnetic movement. In 2015, together with its sister company Frederique Constant, the company introduced its first Swiss-made Horological Smartwatch. In June 2020, it contributed the Alpiner X Alive to the trend toward health monitoring. And its contribution to World Oceans Day in 2022 was the Seastrong Diver 300 Automatic Calanda with a case made of 100 percent recycled stainless steel and a strap made of recycled plastic.

Two limited edition movements from its rich heritage were released for the brand's 140th birthday: an original manually-wound mechanical caliber 490 from 1938, carefully refurbished and decorated, and a replica of the legendary "Bumper" automatic caliber with pendulum oscillating weight.

Alpina Watch International SA
Route de la Galaise, 8
CH-1228 Plan-les-Ouates, Geneva
Switzerland

Tel.:
+41-0-22-860-87-40

E-mail:
info@alpina-watches.com

Website:
www.us.alpinawatches.com

Founded:
1883

Number of employees:
100

U.S. subsidiary:
Alpina Frederique Constant USA
350 5th Avenue, 29th Floor
New York, NY 10118
310-532-8463
customercare@alpinawatches.com

Most important collections/price range:
Alpiner Extreme / from approx. $1,695 to $2,595;
Seastrong / from approx $1,595 to $1,895;
Startimer Pilot / from approx. $695 to $2,995

Startimer Pilot Automatic
Reference number: AL-525G4TS26
Movement: automatic, Caliber AL-525 (based on Sellita SW200-1); ø 25.6 mm, height 4.6 mm; 26 jewels; 28,800 vph; 38-hour power reserve
Functions: hours, minutes, sweep seconds; date
Case: stainless steel, 41 mm, height 11.5 mm; sapphire crystal; transparent case back; screw-in crown; water-resistant to 10 atm
Band: textile, folding pin buckle
Price: $1,295
Variations: leather strap

Alpiner Extreme Chronograph Automatic
Reference number: AL-730SB4AE6B
Movement: automatic, Alpina Caliber AL-730; ø 30 mm, height 7.90 mm; 27 jewels; 28,800 vph; 62-hour power reserve
Functions: hours, minutes, subsidiary seconds; chronograph; date
Case: stainless steel, 41 x 42.5 mm, height 14.30 mm; sapphire crystal; transparent case back; screw-in crown; water-resistant to 10 atm
Band: stainless steel, folding clasp
Price: $2,595

Alpiner Extreme Regulator Automatic
Reference number: AL-650NDG4AE6B
Movement: automatic, Caliber AL-650 (base Sellita SW200-1); ø 25.6 mm, height 4.6 mm; 26 jewels; 28,800 vph; 38-hour power reserve
Functions: hours (off-center), minutes, subsidiary seconds
Case: stainless steel, 41 x 42.5 mm, height 12 mm; unidirectional bezel with 0-60 scale; sapphire crystal; water-resistant to 20 atm
Band: calf leather, buckle
Price: $2,595

Angelus
Manufacture La Joux-Perret SA
Boulevard des Eplatures 38
2300 La Chaux-de-Fonds
Switzerland

Tel:
+41-32-967-97-97

E-mail:
info@angelus-watches.com

Website:
www.angelus-watches.com

Founded:
1891; relaunched 2011

Number of employees:
about 100, including at the La Joux-Perret
manufacture

U.S. Distributor:
Angelus USA
510 West 6th Street, Suite 309
Los Angeles, CA 90014
213-622-1133
info@arnoldandsonusa.com

Most important collections/price range:
U23 / U30 / U41 / U50 / U51 / U53 / La Fabrique
$32,000; various tourbillons / $28,000 to $110,000

ANGELUS

The watch landscape in Switzerland has always been rich in small, vital brands. Many are no longer active, but their names still make for weepy eyes with connoisseurs and collectors. And every now and then, an older company is revived with varying degrees of success. It its day, Angelus, founded by Gustave and Albert Stolz in Le Locle in 1891, quickly forged a reputation for complicated watches, notably repeaters and chronographs. The brothers, Catholics, named the brand after the first word of a standard Catholic prayer and the midday church bells.

One of the brand's claims to fame was a two-handed chronograph, which became a hit in the thirties, culminating in a contract with the Hungarian air force in 1940. The company then built a chronograph with a date, and later one of the first digital dates. Meanwhile, it was creating excellent movements, one of which drove Panerai's Mare Nostrum in the fifties. Among its most iconic models was the waterproof repeater/alarm called the Tinkler, and, in the seventies, a five-minute repeater, which never really got off the ground due to the quartz crisis, which brought Angelus to its knees. . . .

In 2011, La Joux-Perret, a company known for movements and modules and which was already behind Arnold & Son, relaunched the brand. The breakout watch in 2015 designed by Sébastien Chaulmontet was the Tourbillon Lumière a modern, television-shaped behemoth recalling the travel clocks the company produced at one time. The company then moved to more recognizable, round watches, using in-house movements. The recent Chronodate is a revised version of a vintage Angelus. And the recent Gold & Carbon Flying Tourbillon has no real dial, so it can reveal its clever, minimalistic architecture.

A new collection called La Fabrique (the factory) was launched in collaboration with the Massena Lab design forge: a revived version of the Angelus Doctor's Watch from the 1960s.

Chronographe Médical x Massena LAB

Reference number: 0CHAS.A01A.V010S
Movement: hand-wound, Caliber A-5000; ø 29.40 mm, height 4.20 mm; 23 jewels; 21,600 vph; black DLC-coated, snailed, and beveled mainplate and bridges; 60-hour power reserve
Functions: hours, minutes, subsidiary seconds; 1-minute monopusher chronogaph; pulsometer; asthmometer
Case: titanium, ø 39 mm, height 9.2 mm; crown-adjustable unidirectional 60-minute timing bezel; double crown guards; sapphire crystal; transparent case back; water-resistant to 30 atm
Band: calfskin, pin buckle
Remarks: comes with an additional textile strap
Price: $19,900; limited to 99 pieces

Chronodate Titanium

Reference number: 0CDYF.B02A.M009T
Movement: automatic, Caliber A-500; ø 30 mm, height 7.9 mm; 26 jewels; 28,800 vph; finely finished movement with sandblasted or microbeaded parts, NAC-coated mainplate and bridges; tungsten and red gold rotor; 45-hour power reserve
Functions: hours, minutes, seconds; chronograph; power reserve indicator
Case: titanium monobloc, ø 42.5 mm, height 14.25 mm; sapphire crystal; carbon composite pushers and case back; water-resistant to 3 atm
Band: titanium, folding clasp
Price: $25,200
Variations: with white dial ($23,100); in red gold ($43,300); limited to 25 pieces per model; comes with black rubber strap ($23,100)

U53 Tourbillon Skeleton

Reference number: 0.TDDT.G01A.T008G
Movement: hand-wound, Caliber A- 300; ø 32.8 mm, height 4.3 mm; 23 jewels; 28,800 vph; flying 1-minute tourbillon; black DLC-coated, snailed, and beveled mainplate and bridges, skeletonized titanium bridges; 60-hour power reserve
Functions: hours, minutes, subsidiary seconds
Case: titanium, ø 46 mm, height 12.47 mm; crown-adjustable unidirectional 60-minute timing bezel; double crown guards; sapphire crystal; transparent case back; water-resistant to 30 atm
Band: rubber, buckle
Remarks: comes with an additional textile strap
Price: $42,800; limited to 25 pieces

ANONIMO

The brand Anonimo was launched in Florence, Italy. Watchmaking has a long history in Florence, going back to such innovators as Giovanni de Dondi (1318–1389), who built his first planetarium around 1368, and architect and goldsmith Lorenzo della Volpaia (1446–1512), who worked with calendars and astronomical instruments. And finally, there were the likes of the mathematician Galileo and the incomparable Leonardo da Vinci.

In more recent times, the Italian watch industry has been equipping submarine crews and frogmen with timepieces. The key technology comes from Switzerland, but the specialized know-how for making robust, water-resistant timepieces sprang from small enterprises with special competencies in building cases, notably of bronze. The founders of Anonimo understood this strength and decided to put it in the service of their "anonymous" brand—a name chosen to "hide" the fact that many small, discreet companies are involved in their superbly finished watches.

In 2013, armed with some fresh capital and a new management team, Anonimo came out with three watch families running on Swiss technology: the mechanical movements are a combination of Dubois Dépraz modules and tried-and-true Sellita movements. On the whole, though, the collections reflect exquisite conception and manufacturing, and the quality of the materials is unimpeachable: corrosion-resistant stainless steel, fine bronze, and titanium. The design is definitely vintage, a bit 1960s with a hint of a cushion case, but use of only three numerals—4, 8, and 12, which sketch an A on the dial—is quite modern. On the military models, the crown has been placed in a protected area between the two upper lugs. Thanks to a clever hinge system, that crown can be pressed onto the case for an impermeable fit or released for time setting. The Militare line is also home to a special-edition chronograph to celebrate Anonimo's status as official timer of the World Rally Championship, Italy section. Fans seeking a simpler dial have the Epurato line, including a number of different-colored dials, each with characteristic sunray effect. The Nautilo series was conceived for divers, chic and sportive and able to descend beyond 600 feet. The latest models look back to older Dino Zei Nautilos of the past, with hints of '60s-style cushion cases.

Anonimo SA
Chemin des Tourelles 4
CH-2400 Le Locle
Switzerland

Tel.:
+41-22-566-06-06

E-mail:
info@anonimo.com

Website:
anonimo.com

Founded:
1997; moved to Switzerland in 2013

U.S. distributor:
BeauGeste Luxury Brands
697 Third Avenue
New York, NY 10017
212-847-1371
www.beaugesteluxury.com

Most important collections/price range:
Epurato, Militare, Nautilo / $2,300 to $5,700

Militare Chrono DLC

Reference number: AM-1128.22.721.T74
Movement: automatic, Sellita Caliber SW300 with Dubois Dépraz 2035M module; ø 26.2 mm, height 6.5 mm; 49 jewels; 28,800 vph; 42-hour power reserve
Functions: hours, minutes, subsidiary seconds; chronograph
Case: stainless steel with black DLC, ø 43.5 mm, height 14.5 mm; sapphire crystal; transparent case back; water-resistant to 12 atm
Band: textile, buckle
Remarks: crown is pressed onto the case by upper lug for water-tight seal.
Price: $4,650

Nautilo 42mm Satin Blue

Reference number: AM-5009.09.103.M01
Movement: automatic, Sellita Caliber SW200-1; ø 25.6 mm, height 4.6 mm; 26 jewels; 28,800 vph; oscillating weight with côtes de Genève; 38-hour power reserve
Functions: hours, minutes, sweep seconds; date
Case: stainless steel, ø 42 mm, height 11.8 mm; unidirectional bezel with ceramic insert, with 0-60 scale; sapphire crystal; transparent case back; screw-in crown; water-resistant to 20 atm
Band: stainless steel, folding clasp with safety catch
Price: $2,980
Variations: with calfskin or rubber strap ($2,780)

Militare Chrono Bronze

Reference number: AM-1120.04.001.A01
Movement: automatic, Sellita Caliber SW300 with Dubois Dépraz 2035M module; ø 26.2 mm, height 6.5 mm; 49 jewels; 28,800 vph; 42-hour power reserve
Functions: hours, minutes, subsidiary seconds; chronograph
Case: bronze, ø 43.5 mm, height 14.5 mm; sapphire crystal; transparent case back; water-resistant to 12 atm
Band: calf leather, buckle
Remarks: crown is pressed onto the case by upper lug for water-tight seal
Price: $5,400

Armin Strom AG
Bözingenstrasse 46
CH-2502 Biel/Bienne
Switzerland

Tel.:
+41-32-343-3344

E-mail:
info@arminstrom.com

Website:
www.arminstrom.com

Founded:
2006 (first company 1967)

Number of employees:
22

Annual production:
approx. 1000 watches

U.S. representative:
Jean-Marc Bories
Head of North America
929-353-5395
Jean-marc@arminstrom.com

Most important collections/price range:
Masterpiece Collection, Resonance Collection,
Skeleton Collection, System 78 Collection / $9,900
to $100,000 plus

ARMIN STROM

For more than thirty years, Armin Strom's name was associated mainly with the art of skeletonizing. But this "grandmaster of skeletonizers" then decided to entrust his life's work to the next generation, which turned out to be the Swiss industrialist and art patron Willy Michel.

Michel had the wherewithal to expand the one-man show into a full-blown *manufacture* able to conceive, design, and produce its own mechanical movements. The endeavor attracted Claude Geisler, a very skilled designer, and Michel's own son, Serge, who became business manager. When this triumvirate joined forces, it was able to come up with a technically fascinating movement at the quaint little *manufacture* in the Biel suburb of Bözingen within a brief period.

The new movement went on to grow into a family of ten, which forms the backbone of a new collection, including a tourbillon with microrotor—no mean feat for a small firm. The ARF15 caliber of the Mirrored Force Resonance, for example, features two balance wheels placed close enough to influence each other (resonance) and give the movement greater stability.The two oscillating systems are coupled via a spiral spring with two counter-rotating coils, which was developed completely in-house. The company has innovated in many other directions, notably, in its System 78 line with a clever stop-work mechanism for an automatic movement, and development of a motor barrel, whereby the arbor drives the movement.

This essential portfolio has given the *manufacture* the industrial autonomy to implement its projects quickly and independently. Armin Strom has additionally created an online configurator (on its homepage) giving fans and collectors the opportunity to personalize their watches. All components can be selected individually and combined, from the dial, hands, and finishing to the straps. The finished product can be picked up at a local dealership or at the *manufacturer* in Biel/Bienne, including a tour of the place.

Orbit Manufacture Edition

Reference number: ST22-OR.90
Movement: automatic, Armin Strom Caliber ASS20; ø 35.52 mm, height 8.42 mm; 30 jewels; 25,200 vph; micro-rotor; spring barrel with Maltese cross stop-work for constant and limited force; finely finished movement; 72-hour power reserve
Functions: hours and minutes (off-center), subsidiary seconds; date
Case: stainless steel, ø 43.4 mm, height 12.6 mm; bezel in ceramic, with date scale; sapphire crystal; transparent case back; water-resistant to 5 atm
Band: stainless steel, double folding clasp
Price: $29,500

Tribute 1 Rose Gold

Reference number: RG21-TRI.70
Movement: hand-wound, Armin Strom Caliber AMW21; ø 33.5 mm, height 4.2 mm; 21 jewels; 25,200 vph; balance wheel with variable inertia, finely finished movement; 100-hour power reserve
Functions: hours, minutes, sweep seconds
Case: rose gold, ø 38 mm, height 9.38 mm; sapphire crystal; transparent case back; water-resistant to 5 atm
Band: reptile skin, double folding clasp
Price: $24,900; limited to 100 pieces

Mirrored Force Resonance Manufacture Edition Blue

Reference number: ST22-RF.05
Movement: hand-wound, Caliber ARF21; ø 37.2 mm, height 6.7 mm; 39 jewels; 25,200 vph; two independent regulating mechanisms connected by a resonance clutch spring that stabilize each other mutually; finely finished movement; 48-hour power reserve
Functions: hours and minutes (off-center), two subsidiary seconds
Case: stainless steel, ø 43 mm, height 11.55 mm; sapphire crystal; transparent case back; water-resistant to 3 atm
Band: Alcantara leather, double folding clasp
Price: $63,000; limited to 50 pieces

Mirrored Force Resonance Manufacture Edition Green

Reference number: ST22-RF.20
Movement: hand-wound, Caliber ARF21; ø 37.2 mm, height 6.7 mm; 39 jewels; 25,200 vph; two independent regulating mechanisms connected by a resonance clutch spring that stabilize each other mutually; finely finished movement; 48-hour power reserve
Functions: hours and minutes (off-center), two subsidiary seconds
Case: stainless steel, ø 43 mm, height 11.55 mm; sapphire crystal; transparent case back; water-resistant to 3 atm
Band: Alcantara leather, double folding clasp
Price: $63,000; limited to 50 pieces

Tribute 1 Blue

Reference number: ST21-TRI.05
Movement: hand-wound, Armin Strom Caliber AMW21; ø 33.5 mm, height 4.2 mm; 21 jewels; 25,200 vph; balance wheel with variable inertia, finely finished movement; 100-hour power reserve
Functions: hours, minutes, sweep seconds
Case: stainless steel, ø 38 mm, height 9.38 mm; sapphire crystal; transparent case back; water-resistant to 5 atm
Band: reptile skin, double folding clasp
Price: $14,900

Gravity Equal Force Ultimate Sapphire

Reference number: ST21-GEF.SA.VE.M.30
Movement: automatic, Armin Strom Caliber ASB19; ø 35.52 mm, height 11.67 mm; 28 jewels; 25,200 vph; micro-rotor; spring barrel with Maltese cross stop-work for constant and limited force; finely finished movement; 72-hour power reserve
Functions: hours and minutes (off-center), subsidiary seconds; power reserve indicator
Case: stainless steel, ø 41 mm, height 12.65 mm; sapphire crystal; transparent case back; water-resistant to 3 atm
Band: textile, double folding clasp
Price: $25,000

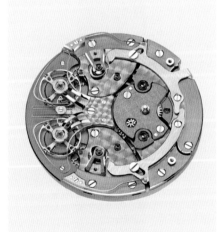

Caliber ASS20

Automatic; micro-rotor; spring barrel with Maltese cross stop-work for constant force; single barrel spring, 72-hour power reserve
Functions: hours and minutes (off-center), subsidiary seconds; date
Diameter: 35.52 mm
Height: 8,42 mm
Jewels: 30
Balance: screw balance with variable inertia
Frequency: 25,200 vph
Remarks: finely, hand-decorated movement; 273 parts

Caliber ARF21

Hand-wound; 2 separate regulating systems are connected by a resonance clutch spring and mutually stabilize each other; single barrel spring, 48-hour power reserve
Functions: hours and minutes (off-center), two independent, symmetrically mirrored subsidiary seconds
Diameter: 37.2 mm
Height: 6.7 mm
Jewels: 39
Balance: 2 balance wheels oscillating in opposite directions on a single hairspring
Frequency: 25,200 vph
Remarks: finely hand-decorated movement; 276 parts

Caliber AMW21

Hand-wound; single spring barrel; 100-hour power reserve
Functions: hours, minutes, sweep seconds
Diameter: 33.5 mm
Height: 4.2 mm
Jewels: 21
Balance: with variable inertia
Frequency: 25,200 vph
Hairspring: flat spring
Shock protection: Incabloc
Remarks: rose gold-plated bridges, finely finished movement; 135 parts

Arnold & Son
38, boulevard des Eplatures
CH-2300 La Chaux-de-Fonds
Switzerland

Tel.:
+41-32-967-9797

E-mail:
info@arnoldandson.com

Website:
www.arnoldandson.com

Founded:
1995

Number of employees:
approx. 30

U.S. distributor:
Arnold & Son USA
510 West 6th Street, Suite 309
Los Angeles, CA 90014
213-622-1133

Most important collections/price range:
Eight-Day / Globetrotter / Nebula / TB88, TBR, TE8
(Tourbillon), Time Pyramid, UTTE / from approx.
$10,000 to $325,000

ARNOLD & SON

John Arnold holds a special place among the British watchmakers of the eighteenth and nineteenth centuries because he was the first to organize the production of his chronometers along industrial lines. He developed his own standards and employed numerous watchmakers. During his lifetime, he is said to have manufactured around 5,000 marine chronometers, which he sold at reasonable prices to the Royal Navy and the West Indies merchant fleet. Arnold chronometers were packed in the trunks of some of the greatest explorers, from John Franklin and Ernest Shackleton to Captain Cook and Dr. Livingstone.

As Arnold & Son was once synonymous with precision timekeeping on the high seas, it stands to reason, then, that the modern brand should also focus its design policies on the interplay of time and geography as well as the basic functions of navigation. Independence from The British Masters Group has meant that the venerable English chronometer brand has been reorienting itself, setting its sights on classic, elegant watchmaking. With the expertise of watch manufacturer La Joux-Perret behind it (and the expertise housed in the building behind the complex on the main road between La Chaux-de-Fonds and Le Locle), the brand has been able to implement several new ideas.

Keeping it modern is, perhaps, the biggest challenge for any brand, and here Arnold shows remarkable skill. The Globetrotter has a bold split bridge over the dial, for example. Alternately, the brand chooses bold colors, like the "mintnight" for the new Perpetual Moon, which is a gradient green-to-blue. More subtle, perhaps, for the connoisseurs of Arnold & Son's watches: the movements have been reworked to fit into slightly smaller cases, which is entirely within the trend of the past few years. This has allowed the brand to revive some older models, like the DSTB and the Time Pyramid, and to improve some of the performance. The new caliber 6203 reappeared with a 55-hour power reserve.

Time Pyramid 42.5 Red Gold

Reference number: 1TPER.W01A.C153A
Movement: hand- wound, Arnold & Son Caliber 1615; ø 37.60 mm, height 4.4 mm; 27 jewels; 21,600 vph; skeletonized movement; finely finished movement, NAC-treated mainplate and bridges, gold-plated wheels, blued screws; double spring barrel; 90-hour power reserve
Functions: hours, minutes, subsidiary seconds; double power reserve indicator
Case: red gold, ø 42.5 mm, height 10.72 mm; sapphire crystal; transparent case back; water-resistant to 3 atm
Band: reptile skin, pin buckle
Remarks: pyramid-shaped movement inspired from table clocks by J. and R. Arnold
Price: $44,600; limited to 88 pieces
Variations: in platinum ($56,900, limited to 38 pieces)

DSTB Platinum

Reference number: 1ATCX.P01A.C200X
Movement: automatic, Arnold & Son Caliber 6203; ø 33 mm, height 5.54 mm; 32 jewels; 28,800 vph; true-beat escapement on the dial, finely finished movement, côtes de Genève on mainplate, blued screws; 55-hour power reserve
Functions: hours and minutes (off-center), subsidiary seconds (jumping)
Case: stainless steel, ø 42 mm, height 12.95 mm; sapphire crystal; transparent case back; water-resistant to 3 atm
Band: reptile skin, buckle
Remarks: white opal hour dial on salmon PVD main dial
Price: $56,500
Variations: in red gold ($44,200, limited to 38 pieces)

Perpetual Moon Mintnight

Reference number: 1GLMW.Z03A.C247A
Movement: hand-wound, Arnold & Son Caliber 1612; ø 29.4 mm, height 5.35 mm; 24 jewels; 21,600 vph; astronomically precise 122-year moon phase; finely finished mainplate, côtes de Genève, polished bridges, blued screws; 90-hour power reserve
Functions: hours, minutes; moon phase
Case: white gold set with 80 brilliant-cut diamonds, ø 38 mm, height 10.44 mm; sapphire crystal; transparent case back; water-resistant to 3 atm
Band: reptile skin, pin buckle set with 22 brilliant-cut diamonds **Remarks:** dial decorated with ruthenium crystal, tinted mother-of-pearl blue aventurine dial, blue lacquered moon disk, hand-engraved sculptural red gold moon and stars
Price: $67,000; limited to 18 pieces
Variations: series in various iterations

ARTYA

The business gurus like to use or create buzzwords for their processes like "agility," and "disruptive," and even "innovative," to describe more of the same with a few small changes. . . . In watchmaking, the approach often involves small engineering advances and a noisy campaign. Yvan Arpa, founder of ArtyA watches, does it differently.

This refreshingly candid personality who spent his *Wanderjahre* crossing Papua New Guinea on foot and practicing Thai boxing in its native land, lives, breathes, and garrulously posts his lived horology online, be it the diving trip to test his divers' watches, or some trek up a mountain.

After various trials and tribulations in the industry, Arpa founded ArtyA, where he could get his "monster" off the slab as it were, with a divine spark. "I had worked with water, rust, dust, and other elements, and then I really caught fire," says Arpa. Indeed, among his first creations were steel cases struck by artificial lightning from a Tesla generator.

Artya's watches hit nerves and drew a gamut of emotional responses. His dials shake up the owner and are often unique in the real sense of the word. No two ones are alike.

Thinking outside of the box is not enough for Arpa. He thinks out of the dial. He will personally go and test watches like the recent Depth Gauge, whose arched colored bands on the dial disappear as the watch reaches depths at which certain color frequencies fail. He continues to explore an artificial sapphire that changes color and which he uses not only to create mysterious watches but also bracelets. The recent Tiny Purity Tourbillon took a full 7 mm off its bigger sister (it's *la* montre in French) thanks to some serious reorganizing of the movement that included keeping the double barrel for the full 72-hour power reserve.

One of Arpa's not-so-secret weapons in the fight for market share is his artist wife, Dominique Arpa-Cirpka, who delivers dreamier dials that carefully mix textures and pigments or use real butterfly wings and collages of earth, shells, pigments, or fish scales. A simple tobacco leaf immediately carries one to a tropical island and the aroma of cigars, coffee, and rum.

Luxury Artpieces ArtyA SA
Route de Gy, 27
1252 Meinier
Switzerland

Tel.:
+41-22-752-4940

Website:
www.artya.com

Founded:
2010

Number of employees:
12

U.S. distributor:
BeauGeste Luxury Brands
www.beaugesteluxury.com

Most important collections/price range:
ArtyA Complications / $90,000 to $500,000;
Son of a Gun / $8,800 to $167,000;
Son of Art / $3,800 to $21,000;
Son of Earth / $4,300 to $183,000;
Son of Sound / $4,300 to $22,110;
Son of Gears / $6,550 to $16,550;
Race/ 7000 to 19,000

Tiny Purity Tourbillon NanoSaphir Chameleon

Movement: hand-wound, ArtyA exclusive tourbillon; ø 35 mm, height 10 mm; 28,800 vph; 17 jewels; 2 parallel-mounted spring barrels; 1-minute 18-millimeter flying tourbillon; fully skeletonized movement; 72-hour power reserve
Functions: hours, minutes, seconds on tourbillon cage
Case: extra-hard "NanoSapphire" case, crown, and lugs; 39 mm, height 13.4 mm; water-resistant to 3 atm
Remarks: case changes hues depending on the heat of the light
Band: leather, pin buckle
Price: $172,000; unique piece

Curvy Purity Tourbillon

Movement: hand-wound, ArtyA exclusive tourbillon; ø 35 mm, height 10 mm; 28,800 vph; 17 jewels; 2 parallel-mounted spring barrels; 1-minute, 18-millimeter flying tourbillon; fully skeletonized movement; hand-finished parts; 72-hour power reserve
Functions: hours, minutes, seconds on tourbillon cage
Case: sapphire crystal; 43 x 38.5 mm, height 12 mm; screwed-down transparent case back; water-resistant to 3 atm
Band: leather, pin buckle
Price: $145,000; limited to 13 pieces

Blue Star Sapphire

Movement: hand-wound, ArtyA exclusive skeleton Star movement with blue DLC treatment; ø 36.6 mm, height 4.5 mm; 18,000 vph; 17 jewels; fully skeletonized movement; 46-hour power reserve
Functions: hours, minutes
Case: extra hard sapphire case, crown and lugs; 46 mm, height 12.5 mm; transparent case back; water-resistant to 3 atm
Band: leather, pin buckle
Price: $29,000; unique piece

Son of Earth Dome Mars

Movement: automatic, exclusive ArtyOn COSC-certified chronometer movement; ø 25.6 mm, height 3.6 mm; 28,800 vph; 25 jewels; fully skeletonized movement; 42-hour power reserve
Functions: hours, minutes, sweep seconds
Case: stainless steel; ø 41 mm, height 14.8 mm; specially domed sapphire crystal; engraved case back; water-resistant to 3 atm
Band: reptile skin, buckle
Remarks: natural pigments used for coloring the dial
Price: $11,300; limited to 99 pieces
Variations: case with black DLC; various models with different dial colors

Blue Enamel Gold

Movement: exclusive ArtyOn COSC-certified chronometer movement; ø 25.6 mm, height 3.6 mm; 28,800 vph; 25 jewels 42-hour power reserve
Functions: hours, minutes, seconds; date
Case: stainless steel with DLC treatment, ø 44 mm, height 12 mm; engraved and screwed-down transparent case back; water-resistant to 3 atm
Band: leather, pin buckle
Price: $10,200; unique piece
Variations: multiple enamel colors

AquaSaphir

Movement: automatic, exclusive ArtyOn COSC-certified chronometer movement; ø 25.60 mm, height 3.60 mm; 25 jewels; 28,800 vph; rhodium-plated gold oscillator; COSC-certified chronometer; 42-hour power reserve
Functions: hours, minutes, sweep seconds; date
Case: sapphire crystal without any metal elements, ø 41 or 43 mm, height 12 mm; bezel in cyan NanoSapphire; transparent case back; water-resistant to 6 atm
Band: rubber, pin buckle
Remarks: gradated blue enamel dial; first sapphire diver's watch
Price: $44,900
Variations: white sapphire bezel ($33,900); dial made of a real Gibeon meteorite with visible Widmannstätten pattern

Burgundy Red Chrono Saphir

Movement: automatic, exclusive chronograph caliber; ø 30 mm, height 7.90 mm; 25 jewels; 28,800 vph; with côtes de Genève; 48-hour power reserve
Functions: hours, minutes, subsidiary seconds; chronograph; date
Case: sapphire crystal, ø 43 mm, height 14.5 mm; sapphire crystal crown; sapphire bezel transparent case back; water-resistant to 3 atm
Band: leather, pin buckle
Remarks: hand-applied enamel dial
Price: $44,500; unique piece

Depth Gauge Full Black

Movement: automatic, exclusive ArtyOn movement; ø 25.60 mm, height 3.60 mm; 25 jewels; 28,800 vph; with côtes de Genève; grey NAC coating on bridges; the rhodium-plated gold oscillator; COSC-certified chronometer; 42-hour power reserve
Functions: hours, minutes, sweep seconds
Case: stainless steel with black DLC, ø 44 mm, height 14 mm; unidirectional rotating bezel in steel with ceramic insert; transparent case back; water-resistant to 30 atm
Band: rubber, pin buckle
Remarks: depth gauge on dial with colored arches that disappear one by one the deeper the diver goes due to light wavelengths no longer reaching the dial.
Price: $8,800; limited to 99 pieces
Variations: in 41-millimeter, with full sapphire case

Diver Yellow Carbon

Movement: automatic, exclusive ArtyOn movement; ø 25.6 mm, height 3.6 mm; 28,800 vph; 25 jewels; COSC-certified chronometer; 42-hour power reserve
Functions: hours, minutes, sweep seconds; date
Case: carbon, ø 41 mm, height 12.45 mm; transparent case back; water-resistant to 30 atm
Band: rubber, pin buckle
Remarks: raw carbon dial
Price: $14,800
Variations: with bezels and straps in different colors

AUDEMARS PIGUET

Jules-Louis Audemars (b. 1851) and Edward-Auguste Piguet (b. 1853) knew they would follow in the footsteps of their fathers and grandfathers and become watchmakers. They were members of the same sports association, sang in the same choir, attended the same vocational school—and both became outstandingly talented watchmakers. The *manufacture*, founded over 140 years ago by these two, is still in family hands, and it has become one of the leading names in the industry.

In the history of watchmaking, only a handful of watches have really achieved cult status. One of them is the Royal Oak, which truly disrupted the idea that the quartz watch was the end-all in horology. Audemars Piguet contacted the designer Gérald Genta to create a watch for a new generation of customers, a sportive luxury timepiece with a modern look, which could be worn every day. The result was a luxurious watch of stainless steel. The octagonal bezel held down with boldly "industrial" hexagonal bolts onto a 39-millimeter case was provocatively big and was nicknamed "Jumbo." It ran on what was then the thinnest automatic movement, a slice 3.05 millimeters high. This iconic piece is still delivering.

The second key to the brand's enduring success was no doubt the acquisition of the atelier Renaud et Papi in 1992. APRP, as it is known, specializes in creating and executing complex complications, a skill it lets other brands share in as well.

The "Code 11.59," with its round bezel and case and octagonal barrel, has evolved since its launch in 2019. The Code 11.59 Universelle is the most complicated watch ever made by AP, with 40 functions, including 23 complications. A masterpiece of ergonomics and design, it took seven years to develop. The new Royal Oak Concept Split-Seconds Chronograph GMT takes its cue from the collection's signature high-tech features, taking the futuristic look and ergonomics of the Royal Oak Concept to a new level. The Code 11.59 by Audemars Piguet collection is, additionally, complemented by four new models—one in steel for the first time—that feature, among other things, a new dial design.

Manufacture d'Horlogerie
Audemars Piguet
Route de France 16
CH-1348 Le Brassus
Switzerland

Tel.:
+41-21-642-3900

E-mail:
info@audemarspiguet.com

Website:
www.audemarspiguet.com

Founded:
1875

Number of employees:
approx. 1,300

Annual production:
50,000 watches

U.S. distributor:
Audemars Piguet (North America) Inc.
Service Center of the Americas
3040 Gulf to Bay Boulevard
Clearwater, FL 33759

Most important collections/price range:
CODE 11.59 / from approx. $26,000; Millenary /
from approx. $28,400; Royal Oak /
from approx. $17,800; special concept watches
Note: Some prices given in Swiss francs (CHF)

Royal Oak "Jumbo" Extra-Thin

Reference number: 16202BA.00.1240BA.02
Movement: automatic, AP Caliber 7121; ø 29.6 mm, height 3.2 mm; 33 jewels; 28,800 vph; white-gold oscillating mass; 52-hour power reserve
Functions: hours, minutes, date
Case: yellow gold, ø 39 mm, height 8 mm; bezel fastened to case with 8 white-gold screws; sapphire crystal; transparent case back; water-resistant to 5 atm
Band: yellow gold, folding clasp
Price: $78,300

Royal Oak "Jumbo" Extra-Thin

Reference number: 16202BC.00.1240BC.02
Movement: automatic, AP Caliber 7121; ø 29.6 mm, height 3.2 mm; 33 jewels; 28,800 vph; white-gold oscillating mass; 52-hour power reserve
Functions: hours, minutes, date
Case: white gold, ø 39 mm, height 8 mm; bezel fastened to case with 8 white-gold screws; sapphire crystal; transparent case back; water-resistant to 5 atm
Band: white gold, folding clasp
Price: $78,300
Variations: in yellow gold ($78,300)

Royal Oak Automatic Self-Winding

Reference number: 15550BA.00.1356BA.01
Movement: automatic, AP Caliber 5900; ø 26.2 mm, height 3.9 mm; 29 jewels; 28,800 vph; finely finished movement; 60-hour power reserve
Functions: hours, minutes, sweep seconds; date
Case: yellow gold, ø 37 mm, height 9 mm; bezel fastened to case with 8 white-gold screws; sapphire crystal; transparent case back; water-resistant to 5 atm
Band: yellow gold, folding clasp
Price: $61,500

Royal Oak Offshore Self-Winding Chronograph

Reference number: 26238CE.00.1300CE.01
Movement: automatic, AP Caliber 4404; ø 32 mm, height 8 mm; 40 jewels; 28,800 vph; 70-hour power reserve
Functions: hours, minutes, subsidiary seconds; flyback chronograph; date
Case: ceramic, ø 42 mm, height 7.95 mm; bezel in ceramic, fastened to case with 8 white gold screws; sapphire crystal; transparent case back; ceramic crown and pushers, screw-in crown; water-resistant to 10 atm
Band: ceramic, folding clasp
Price: $84,400

Royal Oak Concept Split-Seconds Chronograph GMT Large Date

Reference number: 26650TI.00.D013CA.01
Movement: automatic, AP Caliber 4407; ø 32 mm, height 8.9 mm; 73 jewels; 28,800 vph; 72-hour power reserve
Functions: hours, minutes, subsidiary seconds; day/night indication; split-seconds chronograph; large date
Case: titanium, ø 43 mm, height 17.4 mm; bezel fastened to case with 8 white-gold screws; sapphire crystal; transparent case back; screw-in crown; water-resistant to 5 atm
Band: rubber, folding clasp
Price: CHF 170,000

Royal Oak Selfwinding Chronograph

Reference number: 26715ST.00.1356ST.01
Movement: automatic, AP Caliber 2385; ø 26.2 mm, height 5.5 mm; 37 jewels; 21,600 vph; movement entirely decorated by hand; 40-hour power reserve
Functions: hours, minutes, subsidiary seconds; chronograph; date
Case: stainless steel, ø 38 mm, height 11 mm; bezel fastened to case with 8 white-gold screws; sapphire crystal; screw-in crown and pushers; water-resistant to 5 atm
Band: stainless steel, folding clasp
Price: $36,200
Variations: various cases, straps, and dials

Royal Oak Perpetual Calendar Ultra-Thin

Reference number: 26586TI.00.1240TI.01
Movement: automatic, AP Caliber 5133; ø 32 mm, height 2.9 mm; 38 jewels; 19,800 vph; skeletonized gold rotor, finely finished movement; 40-hour power reserve
Functions: hours, minutes; day/night indication; perpetual calendar with date, weekday, month, moon phase, leap year
Case: titanium, ø 41 mm, height 6.2 mm; bezel fastened to case with 8 white-gold screws; sapphire crystal; transparent case back
Band: titanium, folding clasp
Price: $154,000; limited to 200 pieces

Royal Oak Offshore Chronograph

Reference number: 26420CE.00.A127CR.01
Movement: automatic, AP Caliber 4401; ø 32 mm, height 6.8 mm; 40 jewels; 28,800 vph; movement entirely decorated by hand; 70-hour power reserve
Functions: hours, minutes, subsidiary seconds; flyback chronograph; date
Case: ceramic with yellow-gold elements, ø 43 mm, height 14.4 mm; bezel fastened to case with 8 white-gold screws; sapphire crystal; water-resistant to 10 atm
Band: reptile skin, pin buckle
Remarks: comes with additional rubber strap
Price: $60,300

Royal Oak Offshore Flying Tourbillon Chronograph Automatic

Reference number: 26622CE.00.D062CA.01
Movement: automatic, AP Caliber 2967; ø 33.6 mm, height 8.4 mm; 40 jewels; 21,600 vph; flying tourbillon; 65-hour power reserve
Functions: hours, minutes; flyback chronograph
Case: ceramic, ø 43 mm, height 15.5 mm; bezel fastened to case with 8 white-gold screws; sapphire crystal; transparent case back; water-resistant to 10 atm
Band: rubber, folding clasp
Remarks: skeletonized dial
Price: CHF 285,000

CODE 11.59 Self-Winding Chronograph

Reference number: 26393QT.OO.A064KB.01
Movement: automatic, AP Caliber 4401;
ø 32 mm, height 6.8 mm; 40 jewels; 28,800 vph;
skeletonized gold rotor, finely finished movement;
70-hour power reserve
Functions: hours, minutes, subsidiary seconds;
flyback chronograph; date
Case: stainless steel, ø 41 mm, height 12.6 mm;
sapphire crystal; transparent case back;
water-resistant to 3 atm
Band: textile with rubber layer, pin buckle
Price: $37,400
Variations: various colors

CODE 11.59 Self-Winding Chronograph

Reference number: 26393ST.OO.A348KB.01
Movement: automatic, AP Caliber 4401;
ø 32 mm, height 6.8 mm; 40 jewels; 28,800 vph;
skeletonized gold rotor, finely finished movement;
70-hour power reserve
Functions: hours, minutes, subsidiary seconds;
flyback chronograph; date
Case: stainless steel, ø 41 mm, height 12.6 mm;
sapphire crystal; transparent case back;
water-resistant to 3 atm
Band: textile with rubber layer, pin buckle
Price: $35,000
Variations: various colors

CODE 11.59 Self-Winding

Reference number: 15210ST.OO.A056KB.01
Movement: automatic, AP Caliber 4302; ø 32 mm,
height 4.8 mm; 32 jewels; 28,800 vph; gold rotor,
finely finished movement; 70-hour power reserve
Functions: hours, minutes, sweep seconds; date
Case: white gold, ø 41 mm, height 10.7 mm; sapphire
crystal; transparent case back; water-resistant to 3 atm
Band: textile with rubber layer, pin buckle
Price: $25,300

Code 11.59 Minute Repeater Supersonnerie

Reference number: 26395NR.OO.D002KB.01
Movement: hand-wound, AP Caliber 2953;
ø 30 mm, height 6 mm; 32 jewels; 21,600 vph;
finely finished movement; 72-hour power reserve
Functions: hours, minutes, subsidiary seconds;
minute repeater
Case: ceramic, ø 41 mm, height 13.5 mm;
bezel, pink-gold lugs and case bottom; sapphire crystal
Band: textile with rubber layer, pin buckle
Remarks: sapphire crystal dial; special soundboard to
amplify the minute repeater
Price: CHF 325,000

Code 11.59 Flying Tourbillon

Reference number: 26396NR.OO.D002KB.01
Movement: automatic, AP Caliber 2950; ø 31.5 mm,
height 6.2 mm; 27 jewels; 21,600 vph; flying tourbillon;
skeletonized gold rotor; finely finished movement;
65-hour power reserve
Functions: hours, minutes
Case: ceramic, ø 41 mm, height 11.8 mm;
bezel, rose-gold case and lugs; sapphire crystal;
transparent case back; water-resistant to 3 atm
Band: textile with rubber layer, pin buckle
Price: $160,000

Code 11.59 Ultra-Complication "Universelle" (RD#4)

Reference number: 26398BC.OO.D002CR.02
Movement: automatic, AP Caliber 1000; ø 34.3 mm,
height 9.1 mm; 90 jewels; 21,600 vph; flying tourbillon;
60-hour power reserve
Functions: hours, minutes, sweep seconds; minute
repeater with large and small chimes; split-seconds
chronograph with flyback function; perpetual calendar
with large date, month, moon phase, leap year,
"supercrown" rapid setting
Case: white gold, ø 42 mm, height 15.6 mm;
sapphire crystal; transparent case back
Remarks: special soundboard to amplify the
minute repeater
Price: CHF 1,600,000

Caliber 7121

Automatic; skeletonized rotor, white-gold oscillating mass; single spring barrel, 55-hour power reserve
Functions: hours, minutes; date
Diameter: 29.6 mm
Height: 3.2 mm
Jewels: 33
Frequency: 28,800 vph
Remarks: finely finished movement; 268 parts

Caliber 5800

Automatic; skeletonized gold rotor; single spring barrel, 50-hour power reserve
Functions: hours, minutes, sweep seconds; date
Diameter: 23.3 mm
Height: 3.9 mm
Jewels: 28
Balance: with variable inertia
Frequency: 28,800 vph
Remarks: beveled and polished steel parts, plate with perlage, bridges with côtes de Genève; 189 parts

Caliber 2967

Automatic; flying tourbillon; skeletonized rotor; single spring barrel, 65-hour power reserve
Functions: hours, minutes; flyback chronograph
Diameter: 33.6 mm
Height: 8.4 mm
Jewels: 40
Frequency: 21,600 vph
Remarks: 526 parts

Caliber 7124

Automatic; fully skeletonized movement, skeletonized rotor, oscillating mass in rose gold; single spring barrel, 57-hour power reserve
Functions: hours, minutes
Diameter: 29.6 mm
Height: 2.7 mm
Jewels: 31
Frequency: 28,800 vph
Remarks: finely finished movement; 211 parts

Caliber 4401

Automatic; column-wheel control of chronograph functions; skeletonized gold rotor; single spring barrel, 70-hour power reserve
Functions: hours, minutes, subsidiary seconds; flyback chronograph; date
Diameter: 32 mm
Height: 6.8 mm
Jewels: 40
Balance: with variable inertia
Frequency: 28,800 vph
Remarks: beveled and polished steel parts, plate with perlage, bridges with côtes de Genève; 367 parts

Caliber 1000

Automatic; flying tourbillon; single spring barrel, 60-hour power reserve
Functions: hours, minutes, sweep seconds; minute repeater with large and small chimes; split-seconds chronograph with flyback function; perpetual calendar with large date, month, moon phase, leap year, "supercrown" rapid setting
Diameter: 34.3 mm
Height: 9.1 mm
Jewels: 90
Frequency: 21,600 vph
Remarks: special soundboard to amplify the minute repeater ("Supersonnerie"); over 1100 parts

AZIMUTH

Creativity can take on all forms and accept all forms as well. This appears to be the philosophy behind Azimuth, an independent watch brand that has sprouted an eclectic and surprising bouquet of watch designs. For the company, the path is by no means well-beaten: Azimuth always guarantees a raised eyebrow with avant-garde designs for luxury timepieces, with several iconic models like the Mr. Roboto, the Spaceship series, the automobile series and the TT and GT enjoying cult status.

Azimuth consistently explores the worlds of sci-fi with a few nods to pop culture, but it always does so boldly, sparing no expense to shape the watch cases themselves if need be. Dials featuring Astro Boy or the world's favorite cat Garfield mingle with iconic car-inspired pieces, like the Twin Turbo. And 2023 being the brand's twentieth anniversary, the followers of this unconventional company can expect some surprises. Mr. Roboto has been rebuilt using a block of sapphire crystal. The 3-dimensional eyes and mouth are visible from all angles, creating a perception of depth and intricacies. The complex CNC operation to cut the sapphire crystal makes this model by far the rarest Mr. Roboto ever created.

As for the Spaceship Predator, it appears in the form of the PVD Lava OverLand. It is in the Spaceship collection lineage, one of the company's most popular collections. It now comes in a titanium case and features enamel dial depicting a fierce flow of molten lava over land. Each dial is meticulously hand painted, meaning that no two dials are exactly alike.

Like all great artists, though, Azimuth is capable of doing "serious watches," and for that they purchased a venerable Swiss brand in 2013 called Montres Choisi.

Azimuth Watch Co. Sàrl
Rue des Draizes n° 5
CH-2000 Neuchâtel
Switzerland

Tel.:
+41-79-765-1466

E-mail:
gpi@azimuthwatch.com
chrislong@azimuthwatch.com

Website:
www.azimuthwatch.com

Founded:
2003

Number of employees:
6

U.S. distributor:
About Time Luxury Group
210 Bellevue Avenue
Newport RI 02840
401-952-4684

Most important collection/price range:
SP-1 / from $2,800

SP-1 Gran Turismo

Reference number: SP.SS.GT.N003
Movement: automatic, ETA Caliber 2671, ø 17.2 mm, height 4.80 mm; 25 jewels, 28,800 vph; 38-hour power reserve
Functions: hour, minutes, seconds
Case: stainless steel with black PVD, 50 mm x 45 mm, water-resistant to 3 atm
Band: calfskin strap, folding clasp
Price: $5,500; limited to 100 pieces
Variations: top case in stainless steel high-gloss polished, gold PVD treatment or camouflage design

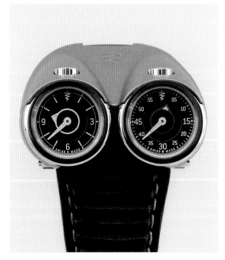

SP-1 Twin Turbo

Reference number: SP.SS.TT.N001
Movement: hand-wound, ETA Caliber 2512-1; ø 17.2 mm, height 2.85 mm; 17 jewels, 21,600 vph, 40-hour power reserve
Functions: hour, minutes; 2nd time zone
Case: stainless steel and aluminum, 51 mm x 50 mm; water-resistant to 3 atm
Band: calf strap, folding clasp
Remarks: 2 vintage movements, limited to 88 pieces
Price: $6,700
Variations: top hood in grey, anthracite or red (red limited to 50 pieces)

SP-1 Crazy Rider

Reference number: SP.SS.CR.N006
Movement: automatic, in-house modified Sellita Caliber SW 200-1; dimensions 47.7 mm x 4.35 mm; 26 jewels; 28,800 vph; 36-hour power reserve
Functions: 24-hour chain drive hour system, minutes
Case: stainless steel body, 55 mm x 36 mm; titanium bezel with black PVD; sapphire crystal, water-resistant to 3 atm
Band: calf leather, folding clasp
Price: $5,900
Variations: stainless-steel body with brown PVD

SP-1 Mr. Roboto R2

Reference number: SP.SS.ROT.N001
Movement: automatic, in-house modified ETA Caliber 2836-2; ø 32.5 mm, height 6.70 mm; 25 jewels 28,800 vph; sapphire rotor; 36-hour power reserve
Functions: regulator hours, retrograde minutes, 2nd time zone
Case: stainless steel, 47 mm x 55 mm; sapphire crystal, water-resistant to 3 atm
Band: calf leather, folding clasp
Price: $6,700
Variations: mid-case in titanium with blue PVD treatment

SP-1 Mr. Roboto Bronzo Artist Series

Reference number: SP.BR.MRB.L002
Movement: automatic, in-house modified ETA Caliber 2836-2; ø 32.50 mm, height 6.70 mm; 25 jewels; 28,800 vph; 36-hour power reserve
Functions: regulator hours, retrograde minutes, GMT
Case: bronze, 43 mm x 50 mm; sapphire crystal; water-resistant to 3 atm
Band: calf leather, bronze tang buckle
Remarks: individually hand-engraved bezel with a unique motif
Price: $10,400; unique piece

SP-1 Mr. Roboto Sapphire

Reference number: SP.SP.MRS.L003
Movement: automatic, in-house modified ETA Caliber 2836-2; ø 32.50 mm, height 6.70 mm; 25 jewels; 28,800 vph; power reserve 36 hours
Functions: regulator hours, retrograde minutes, GMT
Case: solid block CNC cut sapphire crystal, 43 mm x 50 mm; sapphire crystal; water-resistant to 3 atm
Band: rubber, folding clasp
Remarks: every piece has a unique Damascus dial pattern
Price: $23,000; limited to 20 pieces

SP-1 Spaceship Predator Lava OverLand

Reference number: SP.BR.PR.N002
Movement: hand-wound, ETA Caliber 6497-1; ø 36.6 mm, height 4.50 mm; 17 jewels; 18,800vph; micro-sandblasted finishing with blue screws; 40-hour power reserve
Functions: jumping hours, minutes
Case: bronze and stainless steel, ø 44 mm, domed sapphire crystal, water-resistant to 3atm
Band: rubber, bronze tang buckle
Remarks: limited to 100 pieces. Hand-painted dial
Price: $5,800

SP-1 Spaceship Predator PVD Lava OverLand

Reference number: SP.TI.PR.N003
Movement: hand-wound, ETA Caliber 6497-1; ø 36.6 mm, height 4.50 mm; 17 jewels; 18,800 vph; micro-sandblasted finishing with blue screws; 40-hour power reserve
Functions: jumping hours, minutes
Case: titanium with black PVD and stainless steel, diameter 44 mm; sapphire crystal, water-resistant to 3 atm
Band: rubber, folding clasp
Price: $5,800

Land Cruiser

Reference number: SP.SS.LC.L001
Movement: automatic, in-house modified Sellita Caliber SW 200-1, ø 34.4 mm, height 4.50 mm; 26 jewels; 28,800 vph; 36-hour power reserve
Functions: retrograde minutes, regulator hours
Case: stainless steel, 43 mm x 50 mm; sapphire crystal; water-resistant to 3 atm
Band: rubber, folding clasp
Remarks: comes with a special military ammo box
Price: $7,500; limited to 100 pieces

BALL WATCH CO.

Ball Watch Co. collections trace back to the company's origins and evoke the glorious age when trains puffing smoke and steam crisscrossed America. The General Railroads Timepiece Standards back then included such norms as regulation in at least five positions, precision to within thirty seconds per week, Breguet hairsprings, and so on. One of the chief players in developing the standards was Webster Clay Ball, a farm boy-turned-watchmaker from Fredericktown, Ohio. He decided to leave the homestead and apprentice as a watchmaker. He worked as a sales rep for Dueber watch cases and finally opened the Webb C. Ball Company in Cleveland. In 1891, he added the position of chief inspector of the Lake Shore Lines to his CV. His defining moment came when a hogshead's watch stopped for a few minutes, resulting in a lethal crash near Kipton, Ohio. Ball decided to establish quality benchmarks for watch manufacturing that included amag- netic technology. He also set up an inspection system for the timepieces. This standardized timekeeping tool gave rise to an expression in the American vernacular, to "be on the Ball." It also inspired the future Swiss Society of Chronometry (COSC), which governs the highest watch timing certification standards today.

Today, Ball Watch Co. still produces tool-like watches, including divers, although now the manufacturing is done in Switzerland. These rugged, durable watches aim to be "accurate in adverse conditions," so says the company tagline—and at a very good price. Since functionality is a top priority, Ball has developed several mechanisms like the patented SpringLOCK anti-shock system that prevents the balance spring from unfurling when jostled. Ball has also developed special oils for cold temperatures, and it is one of few brands to use tritium gas tubes to light up dials, hands, and markers. For those who need to read the time accurately in dark places—divers, pilots, commandos, hunters, etc.—this is essential.

BALL Watch Company SA
Rue du Châtelot 21
CH-2300 La Chaux-de-Fonds
Switzerland

Tel.:
0041-32-724-53-00

E-mail:
info@ballwatch.ch

Website:
www.ballwatch.com

Founded:
1891

U.S. distribution:
BALL Watch USA:
888-660-0691

Most important collections/price range:
Engineer, Fireman, Trainmaster / $1,300 to $6,500

Engineer Hydrocarbon EOD

Reference number: DM3200A-S1C-BK
Movement: automatic, Ball caliber RR1101-CSL; ø 25.6 mm, height 3.6 mm; 25 jewels; 28,800 vph; COSC-certified chronometer; SpringLOCK antishock system; SpringSEAL patented regulator anti-shock system; special movement oil to endure -45°C to 80°C / -49°F to 176°F; 42-hour power reserve
Functions: hours, minutes, sweep seconds; magnified date
Case: titanium, ø 42 mm, height 13.7 mm; stainless steel unidirectional bezel with micro gas tube inset; Mu-metal shield; sapphire crystal; special screwed-in crown protection cap; push-in crown; water-resistant to 30 atm; patented shock absorption ring
Band: titanium/stainless steel, folding clasp and extension link
Remarks: micro gas tube illumination; shock-resistant; anti-magnetic
Price: $3,349
Variations: ceramic bezel

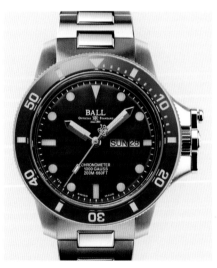

Engineer Hydrocarbon Original

Reference number: DM2218B-S2CJ-GR
Movement: automatic caliber Ball RR1102-CSL; ø 25.6 mm, height 5.05 mm; 25 or 26 jewels; 28,800 vph; COSC-certified chronometer; SpringLOCK antishock system; SpringSEAL patented regulator anti-shock system; 38-hour power reserve
Functions: hours, minutes, sweep seconds; day, date
Case: stainless steel, ø 43 mm, height 15.3 mm; sapphire unidirectional bezel with micro gas tubes; Mu-metal shield; sapphire crystal; crown protection system; water-resistant to 20 atm; Amortiser anti-shock system
Band: stainless steel, folding clasp and extension link
Remarks: micro gas tube illumination; shock-resistant; anti-magnetic
Price: $3,349
Variations: rubber strap; blue dial; black dial

Engineer Hydrocarbon DeepQUEST Ceramic

Reference number: DM3002A-S4CJ-BK
Movement: automatic, Ball Caliber RR1101-C; ø 25.6 mm, height 3.6 mm; 25 jewels; 28,800 vph; 42-hour power reserve
Functions: hours, minutes, sweep seconds; date; patented automatic helium release valve crown
Case: titanium, ø 42 mm, height 15.5 mm; ceramic unidirectional bezel; sapphire crystal; screwed-in crown; water-resistant to 100 atm
Band: titanium/stainless steel, folding clasp and extension link
Remarks: micro gas tube illumination; shock-resistant; anti-magnetic
Price: $3,999
Variations: rubber strap; green dial; black bezel

Engineer Hydrocarbon NEDU

Reference number: DC3226A-S3C-BE
Movement: automatic, Ball Caliber RR1402-C; ø 30 mm, height 7.9 mm; 25 jewels; 28,800 vph; COSC-certified chronometer; 48-hour power reserve
Functions: hours, minutes, subsidiary seconds; day, date; 12-hour chronograph operable underwater
Case: stainless steel, ø 42 mm, height 17.3 mm; patented helium system; ceramic unidirectional bezel; sapphire crystal; crown protection system; water-resistant to 60 atm
Band: titanium/stainless steel, folding clasp and extension link
Remarks: micro gas tube illumination; shock-resistant; anti-magnetic
Price: $4,849
Variations: black dial; rubber strap

Engineer Master II Diver Worldtime

Reference number: DG2232A-SC-GR
Movement: automatic, Ball Caliber RR1501-C; ø 31.4 mm, height 6.95 mm; 25 or 26 jewels; 28,800 vph; 38-hour power reserve; COSC-certified chronometer
Functions: hours, minutes, sweep seconds; day and date; world time indication; unidirectional diving bezel
Case: stainless steel, ø 42 mm, height 14.4 mm; sapphire crystal; transparent case back; screwed-in crown; water resistant to 30 atm
Band: stainless steel, folding clasp
Remarks: micro gas tube illumination; shock-resistant; anti-magnetic
Price: $3,399
Variations: black dial; rubber strap

Engineer Master II Diver Chronometer

Reference number: DM2280A-S1C-BKR
Movement: automatic, Ball Caliber; ø 25.6 mm, height 3.6 mm; 25 jewels; 28,800 vph; COSC-certified chronometer; 42-hour power reserve
Functions: hours, minutes, sweep seconds; date
Case: stainless steel, ø 42 mm, height 13.5 mm; inner bezel with micro gas tube illumination; Mu-metal shield; sapphire crystal; screwed-in crown; water-resistant to 30 atm
Band: stainless steel, folding clasp
Remarks: micro gas tube illumination; shock-resistant; anti-magnetic
Price: $2,599
Variations: blue dial; standard tubes colors; rubber strap

Engineer Master II Doolittle Raiders (40mm)

Reference number: NM3000C-S1-BK
Movement: automatic, Ball Caliber RR1103; ø 25.6 mm, height 4.6 mm; 25 or 26 jewels; 28,800 vph; 38-hour power reserve
Functions: hours, minutes, sweep seconds; date
Case: stainless steel, ø 40 mm, height 12.58 mm; Mu-metal shield; sapphire crystal; screwed-in crown; water-resistant to 10 atm
Band: stainless steel, folding clasp
Remarks: micro gas tube illumination; shock-resistant; anti-magnetic
Price: $1,949
Variations: blue dial; green dial; rainbow tubes colors

Engineer Master II Doolittle Raiders (46 mm)

Reference number: NM2638C-L1-GR
Movement: manual, Ball Caliber RR2102; ø 36.6 mm, height 4.5 mm; 17 jewels; 18,000 vph; 52-hour power reserve
Functions: hours, minutes, subsidiary seconds
Case: stainless steel, ø 46 mm, height 12.35 mm; sapphire crystal; push-in crown; water-resistant to 10 atm
Band: calf leather, folding clasp
Remarks: micro gas tube illumination; shock-resistant; anti-magnetic
Price: $2,399
Variations: blue dial; black dial; rainbow tubes colors

Engineer II Skindiver Heritage Manufacture Chronometer

Reference number: DD3208B-S2C-BKR
Movement: automatic, Ball Caliber RRM7309-C; ø 34.24 mm, height 5.16 mm; 25 jewels; 28,800 vph; COSC-certified chronometer; 80-hour power reserve
Functions: hours, minutes, sweep seconds; date
Case: stainless steel with TiC coating, ø 42 mm, height 15.2 mm; unidirectional sapphire bezel; sapphire crystal; transparent case back; screwed-in crown; water-resistant to 20 atm
Band: TiC coated stainless steel, folding clasp
Remarks: micro gas tube illumination; shock-resistant; anti-magnetic
Price: $3,449
Variations: blue dial; standard tubes colors; rubber strap

Engineer III Outlier

Reference number: DG9000B-S1C-BK
Movement: automatic, Ball Manufacture Caliber RRM7337-C; ø 26.2 mm, height 4.5 mm; 25 jewels; 28,800 vph; Amortiser anti-shock system; COSC-certified chronometer; 42-hour power reserve
Functions: hours, minutes, sweep seconds; magnified date; quick-set local 12-hour hand; three time zone indications
Case: stainless steel, ø 40 mm, height 13.8 mm; bidirectional steel bezel; Mu-metal shield; sapphire crystal; screwed-in crown; water-resistant to 20 atm
Band: stainless steel, folding clasp
Remarks: micro gas tube illumination; shock-resistant; anti-magnetic
Price: $3,449

Engineer III Marvelight Chronometer (36mm)

Reference number: NL9616C-S1C-PK
Movement: automatic, Ball caliber RR1101-C; ø 25.6 mm, height 3.6 mm; 25 jewels; 28,800 vph; COSC-certified chronometer; Amortiser anti-shock system; 42-hour power reserve
Functions: hours, minutes, sweep seconds; magnified date
Case: stainless steel, ø 36 mm, height 11.5 mm; Mu-metal shield; sapphire crystal; screw-in crown; water-resistant to 10 atm
Band: stainless steel, folding clasp
Remarks: micro gas tube illumination; shock-resistant; anti-magnetic
Price: $2,899
Variations: black dial; ice blue dial; green dial; rainbow tubes colors

Engineer III Marvelight Chronometer Day/Date

Reference number: NM9036C-S1C-IBE
Movement: automatic, Ball caliber RR1102-C; ø 25.6 mm, height 5.05 mm; 25 or 26 jewels; 28,800 vph; COSC-certified chronometer; Amortiser anti-shock system; 38-hour power reserve
Functions: hours, minutes, sweep seconds; day, magnified date
Case: stainless steel, ø 40 mm, height 13 mm; mu-metal shield; sapphire crystal; screwed-in crown; water-resistant to 10 atm
Band: stainless steel, folding buckle
Remarks: micro gas tube illumination; shock-resistant; anti-magnetic
Price: $2,599
Variations: black dial; blue dial; green dial; grey dial; rainbow tubes colors

Engineer III Legend II

Reference number: NM2126C-S5C-BE2
Movement: automatic, Ball Caliber RR1101-C; ø 25.6 mm, height 3.6 mm; 25 jewels; 28,800 vph; COSC-certified chronometer; 42-hour power reserve
Functions: hours, minutes, sweep seconds; magnified date
Case: stainless steel, ø 40 mm, height 11.5 mm; Mu-metal shield; sapphire crystal; screwed-in crown; water-resistant to 10 atm
Band: stainless steel, folding clasp
Remarks: micro gas tube illumination; shock-resistant; anti-magnetic
Price: $2,449
Variations: black dial; standard tubes colors

Engineer III Endurance 1917 GMT

Reference number: GM9100C-S2C-IBER
Movement: automatic, Ball Caliber RRM7337-C; ø 26.2 mm, height 4.5 mm; 25 jewels; 28,800 vph; 42-hour power reserve; COSC-certified chronometer; Amortiser anti-shock system; Special movement oil to endure -45°C / -49°F
Functions: hours, minutes, sweep second; magnified date; quick-set local 12-hour hand; second time zone indication
Case: stainless steel, ø 41 mm, height 13.15 mm; Mu-metal shield; sapphire crystal; screwed-in crown; water-resistant to 10 atm
Band: stainless steel, folding clasp
Remarks: micro gas tube illumination; shock-resistant; anti-magnetic
Price: $3,199
Variations: grey dial; blue dial; standard tubes colors

Engineer M Skindiver III Beyond

Reference number: DD3100A-S2C-BE
Movement: automatic, Ball Caliber manufacture RRM7309-C; ø 34.24 mm, height 5.16 mm; 25 jewels; 28,800 vph; COSC-certified chronometer; Amortiser anti-shock system; 80-hour power reserve
Functions: hours, minutes, sweep seconds; magnified date
Case: stainless steel, ø 41.5 mm, height 13.8 mm; sapphire unidirectional bezel; sapphire crystal; screwed-in crown; water-resistant to 30 atm
Band: stainless steel, folding clasp
Remarks: micro gas tube illumination; shock-resistant; anti-magnetic
Price: $3,699

Roadmaster Rescue Chronograph

Reference number: DC3030C-S1-WH
Movement: automatic, Ball Caliber RR1402; ø 30 mm, height 7.9 mm; 25 jewels; 28,800 vph; Amortiser anti-shock system; special movement oil to endure -45°C / -49°F; 48-hour power reserve
Functions: hours, minutes, subsidiary seconds; day, date; 12-hour chronograph; pulsometer
Case: titanium, ø 41 mm, height 14.8 mm; ceramic unidirectional bezel sapphire crystal; screwed-in crown; water-resistant to 10 atm
Band: titanium/stainless steel folding clasp
Remarks: micro gas tube illumination; shock-resistant; anti-magnetic
Price: $3,749
Variations: blue dial; ice blue dial

Roadmaster Marine GMT

Reference number: DG3000A-S4C-BK
Movement: automatic, Ball Caliber RR1203-C; ø 31.4 mm, height 5.75 mm; 25 or 26 jewels; 28,800 vph; COSC-certified chronometer; 38-hour power reserve
Functions: hours, minutes, sweep seconds; day and date
Case: titanium, ø 40 mm, height 14 mm; bidirectional bezel; sapphire crystal; screwed-in crown; transparent case back; water-resistant to 20 atm
Band: titanium/stainless steel folding buckle
Remarks: micro gas tube illumination; shock-resistant; anti-magnetic
Price: $3,249
Variations: blue dial

Roadmaster Pilot GMT

Reference number: DG3038A-S3C-BK
Movement: automatic, Ball Caliber RR1204-C; ø 31.4 mm, height 5.75 mm; 25 jewels; 28,800 vph; COSC-certified chronometer; 38-hour power reserve
Functions: hours, minutes, sweep seconds; magnified date; patented quick set mechanism for local 12-hour hand; three time zone indications
Case: titanium, ø 40 mm, height 14 mm; ceramic bidirectional bezel; sapphire crystal; transparent case back; screwed-in crown; water-resistant to 30 atm
Band: titanium/stainless steel folding clasp
Remarks: micro gas tube illumination; shock-resistant; anti-magnetic
Price: $3,249
Variations: blue dial; white dial

Trainmaster Eternity Ladies

Reference number: NL2080D-S2J-IBE
Movement: automatic, Ball Caliber RR1104; ø 17.2 mm, height 4.8 mm; 25 jewels; 28,800 vph; 38-hour power reserve
Functions: hours, minutes, sweep seconds; date
Case: stainless steel, ø 31 mm, height 10.35 mm; sapphire crystal; transparent case back; screwed-in crown; water-resistant to 3 atm
Band: stainless steel, folding clasp
Remarks: micro gas tube illumination; shock-resistant; anti-magnetic
Price: $2,649
Variations: black dial

Trainmaster Eternity

Reference number: NM2080D-S2J-IBE
Movement: automatic, Ball caliber RR1102; ø 25.6 mm, height 5.05 mm; 25 or 26 jewels; 28,800 vph; 38-hour power reserve
Functions: hours, minutes, sweep seconds; day and date
Case: stainless steel, ø 39.5 mm, height 11.8 mm; sapphire crystal; transparent case back; screw-in crown; water-resistant to 3 atm
Band: stainless steel, folding buckle
Remarks: micro gas tube illumination; shock-resistant; anti-magnetic
Price: $2,099
Variations: black dial; silver dial; crocodile leather

Fireman Victory

Reference number: NM2098C-S5J-SL
Movement: automatic, Ball Caliber RR1103; ø 25.6 mm, height 4.6 mm; 25 or 26 jewels; 28,800 vph; 38-hour power reserve
Functions: hours, minutes, sweep seconds; date
Case: stainless steel, ø 40 mm, height 11.3 mm; sapphire crystal; screw-in crowns; water-resistant to 10 atm
Band: stainless steel folding buckle
Remarks: micro gas tube illumination; shock-resistant; anti-magnetic
Price: $1,499
Variations: black dial; blue dial; calf leather

BAUME & MERCIER

Baume & Mercier, a company founded in 1830, has staked a claim on the market by its ability to keep a finger on the pulse of stylish, urban fashionistas who are looking for affordable yet remarkable timepieces. Since the early 2000s, it has created a number of noteworthy—and often copied—classics, like the Riviera and the Catwalk.

Joining the Richemont Group has boosted the brand's technical value. In 2018, after four years of development with ValFleurier, the group's movement manufacturer, and the RIMS research and innovation team, Baume & Mercier released its first in-house *manufacture* movement, the Baumatic Caliber BM12-1975A. In 2020, it added two new complications to the in-house caliber. Models using the caliber boast a five-day power reserve and accuracy of just –4/+6 seconds per day and amagnetism that is about twenty-five times higher than the current ISO norm.

The new BM14.1975 AC1/AC2 caliber is used in four of the Clifton models and drives a moon phase plus, in two models, a weekday and date display. To make way for the subsidiary dials and apertures, the crosshairs that "ordered" the dial of the simpler three-handers were removed.

The Hampton line was also extended with a series of watches whose rectangular shape recalls Art Deco predecessors. Most recently, the company rebooted the Riviera collection, which celebrated its fiftieth anniversary in 2023 and has been a perennial favorite for the whole half-century. The "new" Riviera comes in a 39-millimeter case and is equipped with the in-house Baumatic movement caliber, which was created exclusively for Baume & Mercier by the Richemont Group and presented in 2017. The high-performance movement boasts a power reserve of 120 hours with magnetic field protection. Best of all, it can be admired through a dial made of tinted sapphire glass that allows a view of the mechanics.

Baume & Mercier
Rue André de Garrini 4
CH-1217 Meyrin
Switzerland

Tel.:
+41-022-580-2948

Website:
www.baume-et-mercier.com

Founded:
1830

Annual production:
100,000 (estimated)

U.S. distributor:
Baume & Mercier
Richemont North America
New York, NY 10022
800-637-2437

Most important collections/price range:
Clifton (men) / $3,250 to $26,800;
Riviera (men and women) / $1,900 to $6,400 /
Classima (men and women) / $1,050 to $4,700;
Hampton (men and women) / $1,600 to $4,450

Riviera Azur
Reference number: M0A10716
Movement: automatic, Caliber Baumatic BM13.1975A; ø 28.2 mm, height 4.25 mm; 21 jewels; 28,800 vph; silicon anchor and escape wheel; balance wheel with variable inertia; skeletonized rotor; 120-hour power reserve
Functions: hours, minutes, sweep seconds; date
Case: stainless steel, ø 42 mm, height 11.97 mm; unidirectional bezel with aluminum ring with 0-60 scale, sapphire crystal; transparent case back, screw-in crown; water-resistant to 30 atm
Band: rubber, triple folding clasp
Remarks: transparent dial
Price: $4,150
Variations: with stainless steel bracelet and black dial ($4,500)

Riviera Perpetual Calendar
Reference number: M0A10742
Movement: automatic, Caliber Baumatic BM13.1975AC2 with Dubois Dépraz 55102 module; ø 28.2 mm, height 5.8 mm; 21 jewels; 28,800 vph; silicon anchor and escape wheel; balance wheel with variable inertia; skeletonized rotor; 120-hour power reserve
Functions: hours, minutes, sweep seconds; perpetual calendar with date, weekday, month, moon phase, leap year
Case: stainless steel, ø 40 mm, height 11.8 mm; bezel screwed to the case with 4 screws; sapphire crystal; transparent case back; water-resistant to 5 atm
Band: stainless steel, triple folding clasp
Price: $19,550, limited to 50 pieces

Riviera Baumatic
Reference number: M0A10720
Movement: automatic, Caliber Baumatic BM13.1975A; ø 28.2 mm, height 4.2 mm; 21 jewels; 28,800 vph; silicon anchor and escape wheel; balance wheel with variable inertia; skeletonized rotor; 120-hour power reserve
Functions: hours, minutes, sweep seconds; date
Case: stainless steel, ø 39 mm, height 10.31 mm; bezel in sand-blasted titanium, screwed to the case with 4 screws; sapphire crystal; transparent case back; water-resistant to 10 atm
Band: rubber, triple folding clasp
Remarks: transparent dial
Price: $4,150

Riviera GMT

Reference number: M0A10659
Movement: automatic, ETA Caliber 2893-2;
ø 25.6 mm, height 4.1 mm; 21 jewels; 28,800 vph;
42-hour power reserve
Functions: hours, minutes, sweep seconds; additional
24-hour display (2nd time zone); date
Case: stainless steel, ø 42 mm, height 10.96 mm; bezel
screwed to the case with 4 screws; sapphire crystal;
transparent case back; water-resistant to 10 atm
Band: rubber, triple folding clasp
Price: $3,100

Riviera

Reference number: M0A10730
Movement: automatic, Sellita Caliber SW200-1;
ø 25.2 mm, height 4.6 mm; 26 jewels; 28,800 vph;
38-hour power reserve
Functions: hours, minutes, sweep seconds; date
Case: stainless steel, ø 33 mm, height 9.6 mm;
bezel set with 4 diamonds; sapphire crystal;
transparent case back; water-resistant to 5 atm
Band: stainless steel, triple folding clasp
Price: $3,200

Clifton Baumatic COSC

Reference number: M0A10713
Movement: automatic, Caliber Baumatic BM13.1975A
COSC; ø 28.2 mm, height 4.2 mm; 21 jewels; 28,800 vph;
silicon anchor and escape wheel; balance wheel with
variable inertia; skeletonized rotor; 120-hour power
reserve; COSC-certified chronometer
Functions: hours, minutes, sweep seconds; date
Case: stainless steel, ø 40 mm, height 11,3 mm;
bezel with rose-gold PVD coating; sapphire crystal;
transparent case back; crown with rose-gold PVD;
water-resistant to 5 atm
Band: calfskin, triple folding clasp
Price: $4,200

Riviera Chronograph

Reference number: M0A10722
Movement: automatic, ETA Caliber 7750;
ø 30 mm, height 7.9 mm; 25 jewels; 28,800 vph;
42-hour power reserve
Functions: hours, minutes, subsidiary seconds;
chronograph; date and weekday
Case: stainless steel, ø 43 mm, height 14.1 mm; bezel
in sand-blasted titanium, screwed to the case with
4 screws; sapphire crystal; transparent case back;
water-resistant to 10 atm
Band: rubber, triple folding clasp
Price: $4,500

Riviera Azur

Reference number: M0A10717
Movement: automatic, Caliber Baumatic BM13.1975A;
ø 28.2 mm, height 4.25 mm; 21 jewels; 28,800 vph; silicon
anchor and escape wheel; balance wheel with variable
inertia; skeletonized rotor; 120-hour power reserve
Functions: hours, minutes, sweep seconds; date
Case: stainless steel, ø 42 mm, height 11.97 mm;
unidirectional bezel with aluminum ring, with
0-60 scale; sapphire crystal; transparent case back;
screw-in crown; water-resistant to 30 atm
Band: stainless steel, triple folding clasp
Remarks: transparent dial
Price: $4,350
Variations: with rubber strap and blue dial ($4,150)

Riviera Baumatic

Reference number: M0A10715
Movement: automatic, Caliber Baumatic BM13.1975A;
ø 28.2 mm, height 4.25 mm; 21 jewels; 28,800 vph; silicon
anchor and escape wheel; balance wheel with variable
inertia; skeletonized rotor; 120-hour power reserve
Functions: hours, minutes, sweep seconds; date
Case: stainless steel, ø 39 mm, height 10.21 mm;
bezel screwed to case with 4 screws; sapphire crystal;
transparent case back; water-resistant to 10 atm
Band: stainless steel, triple folding clasp
Remarks: transparent dial
Price: $3,750
Variations: various bands and dials

BELL & ROSS

If there is such a class as "military chic," Bell & Ross is undoubtedly one of the leaders. The Paris-headquartered brand develops, manufactures, assembles, and regulates its timepieces in a modern factory in La Chaux-de-Fonds in the Jura mountains of Switzerland. The early models had a certain stringency that one might associate with soldierly life, but in the past years, working with outside specialists, the company has ventured into even more complicated watches such as tourbillons and wristwatches with uncommon shapes. This kind of ambitious innovation has only been possible since perfume and fashion specialist Chanel—which also maintains a successful watch line in its own right—became a significant Bell & Ross shareholder and brought the watchmaker access to the production facilities where designer Bruno Belamich and team can create more complicated, more interesting designs for their aesthetically unusual "instrument" watches.

What sets Bell & Ross timepieces apart from those of other, more traditional professional luxury makers is their special, roguish look: a delicate balance between striking, martial, and poetic—think Lawrence of Arabia, the gallivanting warrior. And it is this beauty for the eye to behold that makes the company's wares popular with style-conscious "civilians" as well as with the pilots, divers, astronauts, sappers, and other hard-riding professionals drawn to Bell & Ross timepieces for their superior functionality. The plane-cockpit gauge look is especially strong in recent models, like the Radiocompass and the one paying tribute to France's air ace troop, Patrouille de France. The latest line, the BR 05, connects two geometric forms, the circular and the square. The result is a watch that gravitates more toward everyday usage, or what the brand calls "Urban Explorers," a modern version of the elemental being that slumbers in everyone.

Bell & Ross Ltd.
8 rue Copernic
F-75116 Paris
France

Tel.:
+33-1-73-73-93-00

E-mail:
sav@bellross.com

Website:
www.bellross.com

Founded:
1992

U.S. distributor:
Bell & Ross, Inc.
605 Lincoln Road, Suite 300
Miami Beach, FL 33139
888-307-7887
information@bellross.com
www.bellross.com

Most important collections/price range:
Instrument BR-X1, BR 01, BR 03, and BR 05 / approx. $3,100 to $450,000

BR 01 Cyber Skull bronze

Reference number: BR01-CSK-BR/SRB
Movement: hand-wound, Caliber BR-CAL.210; skull-shaped bridges, the jaw moves when winding the watch
Functions: hours, minutes
Case: bronze, 45 x 46.7 mm, height 13.7 mm; sapphire crystal; transparent case back; screw-in crown; water-resistant to 5 atm
Band: rubber, pin buckle
Price: $11,400; limited to 500 pieces

BR 03-93 GMT Blue

Reference number: BR0393-BLU-ST/SCA
Movement: automatic, Caliber BR-CAL.303 (based on ETA 2893-2); ø 25.6 mm, height 4.1 mm; 21 jewels; 28,800 vph; 42-hour power reserve
Functions: hours, minutes, sweep seconds; additional 24-hour display (2nd time zone); date
Case: stainless steel, 42 x 42 mm, height 12.3 mm; bidirectional bezel with aluminum insert, with 0-24 scale; sapphire crystal; screw-in crown; water-resistant to 10 atm
Band: calfskin, pin buckle
Price: $4,200

BR 03-92 Diver White bronze

Reference number: BR0392-D-WH-BR/SCA
Movement: automatic, Caliber BR-CAL.302 (based on ETA 2892-A2); ø 25.6 mm, height 3.6 mm; 21 jewels; 28,800 vph; 42-hour power reserve
Functions: hours, minutes, sweep seconds; date
Case: bronze, 42 x 42 mm, height 12.05 mm; unidirectional bezel with aluminum insert, with 0-60 scale; sapphire crystal; screw-in crown; water-resistant to 30 atm
Band: calfskin, pin buckle
Remarks: comes with extra rubber strap
Price: $4,700; limited to 999 pieces

BR-X5 Green Lum

Reference number: BR05A-GN-PG/SPG
Movement: automatic, Caliber BR-CAL.323 by Kenissi;
ø 33.8 mm, height 6.5 mm; 28 jewels; 28,800 vph;
70-hour power reserve
Functions: hours, minutes, sweep seconds; power
reserve indicator; date
Case: titanium with DLC and luminescent fiberglass
composite, 41 x 41 mm, height 12.8 mm; full-
luminescent bezel screwed to the monocoque case
with 4 screws; sapphire crystal; transparent case
back; screw-in crown and crown guard; water-
resistant to 10 atm
Band: rubber, folding clasp
Price: $13,300;limited to 500 pieces

BR 05 Green Gold

Reference number: BR05A-GN-PG/SCR
Movement: automatic, Caliber BR-CAL.322
(based on ETA 2892-A2); ø 25.6 mm, height 3.6 mm;
21 jewels; 28,800 vph; green galvanized movement
parts; 42-hour power reserve
Functions: hours, minutes, sweep seconds; date
Case: rose gold, 40 x 40 mm, height 10.33 mm;
bezel screwed to the monocoque case with 4 screws;
sapphire crystal; transparent case back;
screw-in crown; water-resistant to 10 atm
Band: reptile skin, folding clasp
Price: $22,600
Variations: with rose gold bracelet ($34,000)

BR 03-92 Patrouille de France 70th Anniversary

Reference number: BR0392-PAF7-CE/SCA
Movement: automatic, Caliber BR-CAL.302 (based on
ETA 2892-A2); ø 25.6 mm, height 3.6 mm; 21 jewels;
28,800 vph; 42-hour power reserve
Functions: hours, minutes, sweep seconds; date
Case: ceramic, 42 x 42 mm, height 10.4 mm; bezel
screwed to the monocoque case with 4 screws; sapphire
crystal; screw-in crown; water-resistant to 10 atm
Band: calfskin, pin buckle
Remarks: special edition for the 70th anniversary of
the founding of the "Patrouille de France" acrobatic
flying troop
Price: $6,500

BR 05 Skeleton Golden

Reference number: BR05A-CH-SKST/SRB
Movement: automatic, Caliber BR-CAL.322 (based on
ETA 2892-A2); ø 25.6 mm, height 3.6 mm; 21 jewels;
28,800 vph; green galvanized movement parts;
42-hour power reserve
Functions: hours, minutes, sweep seconds
Case: stainless steel, 40 x 40 mm, height 10.33 mm;
bezel screwed to the monocoque case with 4 screws;
sapphire crystal; transparent case back;
screw-in crown; water-resistant to 10 atm
Band: rubber, folding clasp
Remarks: skeletonized dial
Price: $6,600; limited to 500 pieces
Variations: with stainless steel bracelet ($7,100)

BR 03 Gyrocompass

Reference number: BR03A-CPS-CE/SRB
Movement: automatic, Caliber BR-CAL.302 (based on
ETA 2892-A2); ø 25.6 mm, height 3.6 mm; 21 jewels;
28,800 vph; 54-hour power reserve
Functions: hours, minutes, sweep seconds; date
Case: ceramic, 42 x 42 mm, height 10.4 mm; bezel
screwed to the monocoque case with 4 screws; sapphire
crystal; screw-in crown; water-resistant to 10 atm
Band: rubber with synthetic fabric, pin buckle with PVD
Price: $4,500; limited to 999 pieces

BR 03-92 Radiocompass

Reference number: BR0392-RCO-CE/SRB
Movement: automatic, Caliber BR-CAL.302 (based on
ETA 2892-A2); ø 25.6 mm, height 3.6 mm; 21 jewels;
28,800 vph; 54-hour power reserve
Functions: hours, minutes, sweep seconds; date
Case: ceramic, 42 x 42 mm, height 10.4 mm; bezel
screwed to the monocoque case with 4 screws; sapphire
crystal; screw-in crown; water-resistant to 10 atm
Band: rubber, pin buckle
Price: $4,100

BLANCPAIN

In its advertising, the Blancpain watch brand has always proudly declared that, since 1735, the company has never made quartz watches and never will. Indeed, Blancpain is Switzerland's oldest watchmaker, and by sticking to its ideals, the company was put out of business by the "quartz boom" of the 1970s.

The Blancpain brand we know today came into being in the mid-eighties, when Jean-Claude Biver and Jacques Piguet purchased the venerable name. The company was subsequently moved to the Frédéric Piguet watch factory in Le Brassus, where it quickly became largely responsible for the renaissance of the mechanical wristwatch. This success caught the attention of the Swatch Group—known at that time as SMH. In 1992, it swooped in and purchased both companies to add to its portfolio. Movement fabrication and watch production were melded to form the Blancpain Manufacture in mid-2010.

But being quartz-less does not mean being old-fashioned. Over the past several years, Blancpain president Marc A. Hayek has put a great deal of energy into developing the company's technical originality. In terms of complications, Blancpain watches have always been in a class of their own. The product families were all consolidated into four families: the Villeret; the legendary Fifty Fathoms diver's watches; Ladybird, a graceful series for women; and Metier's d'art, a collection of unique pieces that express the brand's artistic and watchmaking prowess.

The strong focus on diver's watches has also had an impact on the company's environmental efforts. Additionally, 2023 marks the seventieth anniversary of the Fifty Fathoms diver's watch, whose relaunch twenty years ago definitely gave the brand a boost. Three special models with 42-millimeter cases in stainless steel heralded the jubilee year, followed by the Fifty Fathoms Tech Gombessa, a remarkable novelty. This titanium watch, developed for rebreathing divers, has a three-hour hand with a correspondingly marked rotating bezel. Three hours is considered a possible dive time with new technology, in which the exhaled air is partially recycled and enriched with fresh oxygen.

Blancpain SA
Le Rocher 12
CH-1348 Le Brassus
Switzerland

Tel.:
+41-21-796-3636

Website:
www.blancpain.com

Founded:
1735

U.S. distributor:
Blancpain
The Swatch Group (U.S.), Inc.
1200 Harbor Boulevard
Weehawken, NJ 07086
201-271-4680

Most important collections/price range:
Villeret, Fifty Fathoms, Ladybird, Air Command,
Métiers d'Art / $9,800 to $420,000

Villeret Carrousel Répétition Minutes

Reference number: 00235-3631-55B
Movement: automatic, Blancpain Caliber 235; ø 32.8 mm, height 9.1 mm; 54 jewels; 21,600 vph; escapement with 1-minute flying carrousel
Functions: hours, minutes; minute repeater
Case: pink gold, ø 45 mm, height 15.35 mm; sapphire crystal; transparent case back
Band: reptile skin, folding clasp
Remarks: enamel dial
Price: $412,100

Villeret Tourbillon Carrousel

Reference number: 2322-3631-55B
Movement: hand-wound, Blancpain Caliber 2322; ø 35.3 mm, height 5.85 mm; 70 jewels; 21,600 vph; escapement with flying 1-minute tourbillon and 1-minute carousel with differential compensation; 3 spring barrels, 168-hour power reserve
Functions: hours minutes, power reserve indicator (on the movement side); date
Case: red gold, ø 44.6 mm, height 11.94 mm; sapphire crystal; transparent case back; water-resistant to 3 atm
Band: reptile skin, folding clasp
Remarks: enamel dial
Price: $319,000

Villeret Tourbillon Volant Une Minute 12 Jours

Reference number: 66240-3431-55B
Movement: automatic, Blancpain Caliber 242; ø 30.6 mm, height 6.1 mm; 43 jewels; 28,800 vph; 1-minute flying tourbillon; 288-hour power reserve
Functions: hours, minutes; power reserve display (on rear)
Case: platinum, ø 42 mm, height 11.65 mm; sapphire crystal; transparent case back; water-resistant to3 atm
Band: reptile skin, folding clasp
Remarks: enamel dial
Price: $155,400; limited to 188 pieces
Variations: in red gold ($133,100)

Villeret Carrousel Phases de Lune

Reference number: 6622L-3631-55B
Movement: automatic, Blancpain Caliber 225L; ø 31.9 mm, height 6.86 mm; 40 jewels; 28,800 vph; flying 1-minute carousel; 120-hour power reserve
Functions: hours, minutes; date, moon phase
Case: red gold, ø 42 mm, height 12.74 mm; sapphire crystal; transparent case back; water-resistant to 3 atm
Band: reptile skin, folding clasp
Remarks: enamel dial
Price: $135,300
Variations: in platinum (limited to 88 pieces, $168,000)

Villeret Tourbillon Volant Heure Sautante Minute Rétrograde

Reference number: 66260-3633-55B
Movement: hand-wound, Blancpain Caliber 260MR; ø 32 mm, height 5.85 mm; 39 jewels; 21,600 vph; one-minute flying tourbillon; 144-hour power reserve
Functions: hours (digital, jumping), minutes (retrograde)
Case: red gold, ø 42 mm, height 11 mm; sapphire crystal; transparent case back; water-resistant to 3 atm
Band: reptile skin, folding clasp
Remarks: enameled dial
Price: $155,400
Variations: red gold bracelet ($175,600); in platinum ($170,100, limited to 50 pieces)

Villeret Tourbillon Volant Une Minute 12 Jours

Reference number: 66240-3433-55B
Movement: automatic, Blancpain Caliber 242; ø 30.6 mm, height 6.1 mm; 43 jewels; 28,800 vph; flying one-minute tourbillon; 288-hour power reserve (12 days)
Functions: hours, minutes; power reserve indicator (on the rear)
Case: platinum, ø 42 mm, height 11.65 mm; sapphire crystal; transparent case back; water-resistant to 3 atm
Band: reptile skin, folding clasp
Remarks: hand-painted enamel dial with landscape motive
Price: on request; limited to 188 pieces

Villeret Perpetual Calendar

Reference number: 6656-3642-55B
Movement: automatic, Blancpain Caliber 5954; ø 32 mm, height 4.97 mm; 32 jewels; 28,800 vph; 72-hour power reserve
Functions: hours, minutes, sweep seconds; perpetual calendar with date, weekday, month, moon phase, leap year
Case: rose gold, ø 40 mm, height 11.1 mm; sapphire crystal; transparent case back; water-resistant to 3 atm
Band: reptile skin, folding clasp
Remarks: opaline dial
Price: $47,000
Variations: with rose-gold Milanese bracelet ($67,300)

Villeret Moonphase Complete Calendar GMT

Reference number: 6676-1127-55B
Movement: automatic, Blancpain Caliber 67A5; ø 27 mm, height 6 mm; 28 jewels; 28,800 vph; 2 spring barrels, 72-hour power reserve
Functions: hours, minutes; additional 24-hour display (second time zone); full calendar with date, weekday, month, moon phase
Case: stainless steel, ø 40 mm, height 11.8 mm; sapphire crystal; transparent case back; water-resistant to 3 atm
Band: reptile skin, folding clasp
Price: $16,800

Villeret Quantième Complet

Reference number: 6654-3640-55B
Movement: automatic, Blancpain Caliber 6654; ø 32 mm, height 5.5 mm; 28 jewels; 28,800 vph; 2 spring barrels, 72-hour power reserve
Functions: hours, minutes, sweep seconds; full calendar with date, weekday, month, moon phase
Case: rose gold, ø 40 mm, height 10.94 mm; sapphire crystal; transparent case back; water-resistant to 3 atm
Band: reptile skin, folding clasp
Price: $26,900
Variations: with rose gold Milanese bracelet ($48,200)

Villeret Ultra Thin

Reference number: 6223-3642-55B
Movement: automatic, Blancpain Caliber 1150;
ø 26.2 mm, height 3.25 mm; 28 jewels; 28,800 vph;
100-hour power reserve
Functions: hours, minutes, sweep seconds; date
Case: pink gold, ø 38 mm, height 8.35 mm; sapphire
crystal; transparent case back; water-resistant to 3 atm
Band: reptile skin, folding clasp
Price: $14,700
Variations: with rose-gold Milanese bracelet
($20,900); in stainless steel ($8,900)

Villeret Ultra Thin

Reference number: 6605-1127-55B
Movement: hand-wound, Blancpain Caliber 11A4B;
ø 27.4 mm, height 2.8 mm; 21 jewels; 21,600 vph;
100-hour power reserve
Functions: hours, minutes; power reserve indicator
(on the rear)
Case: stainless steel, ø 40 mm, height 7.39 mm;
sapphire crystal; transparent case back;
water-resistant to 3 atm
Band: reptile skin, folding clasp
Price: $10,700

Air Command

Reference number: AC02-12B40-63A
Movement: automatic, Blancpain Caliber F388B;
ø 31.8 mm, height 6.65 mm; 35 jewels; 28,800 vph;
50-hour power reserve
Functions: hours, minutes; flyback chronograph
Case: titanium, ø 42,5 mm, height 13.77 mm;
bidirectional bezel with ceramic insert, with
0-60 scale; sapphire crystal; transparent case back;
water-resistant to 3 atm
Band: calfskin, pin buckle
Price: $20,100
Variations: in rose gold ($32,300)

Fifty Fathoms Tourbillon 8 Jours

Reference number: 5025-12B40-052A
Movement: automatic, Blancpain Caliber 25C;
ø 26.2 mm, height 4.85 mm; 29 jewels; 28,800 vph;
flying tourbillon; 192-hour power reserve
Functions: hours, minutes, subsidiary seconds
(on the tourbillon cage)
Case: titanium, ø 45 mm, height 14.8 mm; unidirectional
bezel with sapphire crystal insert, with 0-60 scale;
sapphire crystal; transparent case back;
water-resistant to 30 atm
Band: textile, pin buckle
Price: $123,000
Variations: in rose gold ($139,100)

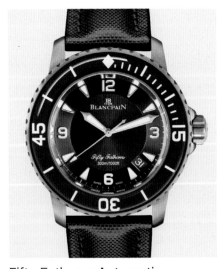

Fifty Fathoms Automatic

Reference number: 5015-12B40-052A
Movement: automatic, Blancpain Caliber 1315;
ø 30.6 mm, height 5.65 mm; 35 jewels; 28,800 vph;
silicon hairspring; 120-hour power reserve
Functions: hours, minutes, sweep seconds; date
Case: titanium, ø 45 mm, height 15.4 mm; unidirectional
bezel with sapphire crystal insert, with 0-60 scale;
sapphire crystal; transparent case back; water-
resistant to 30 atm
Band: textile, pin buckle
Price: $16,500
Variations: various bands and dials

Fifty Fathoms Automatic
Grande Date

Reference number: 5050-12B30-98B
Movement: automatic, Blancpain Caliber 6918B;
ø 32 mm, height 7.15 mm; 44 jewels; 28,800 vph; silicon
hairspring; 120-hour power reserve
Functions: hours, minutes, sweep seconds; large date
Case: titanium, ø 45 mm, height 16.27 mm;
unidirectional bezel with sapphire crystal insert, with
0-60 scale; sapphire crystal; transparent case back;
screw-in crown; water-resistant to 30 atm
Band: titanium, folding clasp
Price: $21,100

Fifty Fathoms Bathyscaphe Titanium

Reference number: 5000-1210-G52A
Movement: automatic, Blancpain Caliber 1315;
ø 30.6 mm, height 5.65 mm; 35 jewels; 28,800 vph;
silicon hairspring; 120-hour power reserve
Functions: hours, minutes, sweep seconds; date
Case: titanium, ø 43 mm, height 13.45 mm;
unidirectional bezel with ceramic insert, with
0-60 scale; sapphire crystal; transparent case back;
screw-in crown; water-resistant to 30 atm
Band: textile, pin buckle
Price: $12,200

Fifty Fathoms Bathyscaphe Sedna Gold

Reference number: 5000-36S40-052A
Movement: automatic, Blancpain Caliber 1315;
ø 30.6 mm, height 5.65 mm; 35 jewels; 28,800 vph;
silicon hairspring; 120-hour power reserve
Functions: hours, minutes, sweep seconds; date
Case: rose gold ("Sedna gold"), ø 43 mm, height
13.4 mm; unidirectional bezel with ceramic insert, with
0-60 scale; sapphire crystal; transparent case back;
screw-in crown; water-resistant to 30 atm
Band: textile, pin buckle
Remarks: special corrosion-resistant gold alloy
Price: $26,300

Fifty Fathoms Bathyscaphe Chronograph Flyback

Reference number: 5200-0153-B52A
Movement: automatic, Blancpain Caliber F385;
ø 31.8 mm, height 6.65 mm; 37 jewels; 36,000 vph;
silicon hairspring; 50-hour power reserve
Functions: hours, minutes, subsidiary seconds;
flyback chronograph; date
Case: ceramic, ø 43.6 mm, height 15.25 mm;
unidirectional bezel with ceramic insert, with
0-60 scale; sapphire crystal; transparent case back;
water-resistant to 30 atm
Band: textile, pin buckle
Price: $17,900

Villeret Women Quantième Phase de Lune

Reference number: 6126-2987-55B
Movement: automatic, Blancpain Caliber 913QL.P;
ø 23.7 mm, height 4.65 mm; 20 jewels; 28,800 vph;
40-hour power reserve
Functions: hours, minutes, sweep seconds;
date, moon phase
Case: rose gold, ø 33.2 mm, height 10.2 mm; bezel set
with diamond; sapphire crystal; transparent case back;
water-resistant to 3 atm
Band: reptile skin, folding clasp
Remarks: dial set with 8 diamonds
Price: $24,000

Villeret Women Date

Reference number: 6127-4628-55B
Movement: automatic, Blancpain Caliber 1151;
ø 27.4 mm, height 3.25 mm; 28 jewels; 28,800 vph;
100-hour power reserve
Functions: hours, minutes, sweep seconds; date
Case: stainless steel, ø 33.2 mm, height 9.15 mm;
bezel set with diamonds; sapphire crystal;
transparent case back; water-resistant to 3 atm
Band: reptile skin, folding clasp
Remarks: dial with eight diamond markers
Price: $11,700
Variations: various strap colors

Ladybird Complete Calendar Moon Phase

Reference number: 3663-2954-55B
Movement: automatic, Blancpain Caliber 6763;
ø 27 mm, height 4.9 mm; 30 jewels; 28,800 vph;
100-hour power reserve
Functions: hours, minutes, subsidiary seconds; full
calendar with date, weekday, month, moon phase
Case: red gold, ø 35 mm, height 10.57 mm; bezel set
with diamonds; sapphire crystal; transparent case
back; water-resistant to 3 atm
Band: reptile skin, folding clasp
Remarks: mother-of-pearl-dial set with 9 diamonds
Price: $30,300

BOVET

Bovet Fleurier S.A.
Le Château, CP20
CH-2112 Môtiers
Switzerland

Tel.:
+41-32-862-0808

E-mail:
info@bovet.com

Website:
www.bovet.com

Founded:
1822

Annual production:
around 1,000 timepieces

U.S. distributor:
Bovet LLC North America
305-974-4826

Most important collections/price range:
Amadeo Fleurier, Dimier, Pininfarina, Récital,
Virtuoso / $18,500 to $1,000,000

Note:
Model prices are given in Swiss francs

If any brand can claim real connections to China, it is Bovet, founded by Swiss business-man Edouard Bovet. Bovet emigrated to Canton, China, in 1818 and sold four watches of his own design there. On his return to Switzerland in 1822, he set up a company for ship-ping his Fleurier-made watches to China. The company name, pronounced "Bo Wei" in Mandarin, became a synonym for "watch" in Asia and at one point had offices in Canton. For more than eighty years, Bovet and his successors supplied the Chinese ruling class with valuable timepieces.

In 2001, the brand was bought by entrepreneur Pascal Raffy. He ensured the com-pany's industrial independence by acquiring several other companies as well, notably the high-end watchmaker Swiss Time Technology (STT) in Tramelan, which he renamed Dimier 1738. In addition to creating its own line of watches, this manufacture produces complex technical components such as tourbillons for Bovet watches. Assembly of Bovet creations takes place at the headquarters in the thirteenth-century Castle of Môtiers in Val-de-Travers not far from Fleurier.

Bovet is an equal opportunity manufacturer of fine watches for men and women. These high-end timekeepers do have several distinctive features. The first is intricate dial work, featuring not only complex architecture in the men's series, but also intricate guilloché patterns and very fine enameling techniques. Bovet has collaborated with car manufac-turers like Pininfarina and Rolls-Royce, for which it manufactured a bespoke dashboard clock that can be used as a table clock or wristwatch thanks to the Amadéo conversion system. This allows the wristbands to be easily attached or removed from the watch. Some models convert to table clocks, and the Amadeo Fleurier Miss Audrey series can even be worn as a necklace. In 2023, Bovet pushed the envelope even further, with such marvels as the Astérium, which shows the sky as seen from the earth and gives the sun time (equation complication), plus a complete calendar with astrological signs on the back. It is hardly any wonder, then, that this unique piece won the Calendar and As-tronomy Watch prize at the Grand Prix d'Horlogerie in Geneva.

Récital Asterium (front)
Reference number: R20N005/1/PU
Movement: hand-wound, Bovet Caliber 17DM02-SKY; ø 38 mm, height 12.45 mm; 18,000 vph; double-side flying tourbillon; fully skeletonized movement; 10-day power reserve
Functions (front): hours, minutes (retrograde at 3 o'clock), seconds; day/night display; calendar with day, date, month; double hemispheric moon phase; equation of time (at 9 o'clock); power reserve indicator (at 3 o'clock)
Remarks: the Asterium represents the sky seen from the earth; sidereal year shown, with 365 days, 6 hours, 9 minutes

Récital Asterium (back)
Functions (back): single hand traveling 365.25 days (thanks to the equation of time) for the calendar with date (on bezel and graduated track) and months; astrological signs, four seasons indication, solstices and equinoxes
Case: red gold, with white gold sections, reversed hand fitting, ø 46 mm, height 18.30 mm; sapphire crystal on both sides
Band: leather, pin buckle
Remarks: easy setting of annual calendar and all other functions with the crown; slant-top case
Price: CHF 495,000; unique piece

Virtuoso XI
Reference number: T10SQ002-SB1-GC24-C3
Movement: hand-wound, caliber 17BM03-GD, ø 38 mm, height 6.7 mm; 36 jewels; 18,000 vph, 1-minute flying tourbillon; 10-day power reserve
Functions: hours, minutes, seconds
Case: white gold, engraved and Bezel set with 60 baguette-cut diamonds, ø 44 mm; water-resistant to 3 atm;
Band: reptile skin, pin buckle
Remarks: slant-top case; all plates and bridges hand-engraved in Fleurisanne style on both sides, fully skeletonized movement
Price: CHF 375,000
Variations: comes without diamonds nor engraving on the case

Monsieur Bovet Teal Blue

Reference number: AI43043
Movement: hand-wound, Bovet Caliber 13BM09A1;
ø 29.1 mm, height 5.07 mm; 21,600 vph; 7-day power
reserve
Functions: hours, minutes, double coaxial seconds on
both sides of watch; power reserve indicator
Case: titanium, ø 43 mm, height 12.35 mm; sapphire
crystal; water-resistant to 3 atm
Band: rubber, pin buckle
Remarks: pin-wheel green guilloché; special
mechanism converts watch into a table clock, pendant,
or wristwatch
Price: CHF 60,000
Variations: white gold (CHF 68,200)

Miss Audrey Teal Blue Guilloché

Reference number: AS36062-SD12
Movement: automatic, Bovet Caliber 11BA15;
ø 25.60 mm, height 3.60 mm; 28,800 vph; 42-hour
power reserve
Functions: hours, minutes
Case: stainless steel, ø 36 mm, height 11 mm; crown
with sapphire cabochon; bezel and strap bolts set
with 103 round-cut diamonds; transparent case back;
water-resistant to 3 atm
Band: synthetic satin, pin buckle
Remarks: dial with dark turquoise guilloché; special
mechanism converts watch into a table clock, pendant,
or wristwatch
Price: CHF 26,000

Récital 23

Reference number: R230018-SD14
Movement: automatic, Bovet Caliber 11DA17-MP;
ø 30.52 mm x 34.80 mm, height 9.10 mm ; 28,800 vph;
62-hour power reserve
Functions: off-center hours and minutes, hemispheric
moon phase
Case: red gold, ø 43 mm, height 38.70 mm; case
set with 174 diamonds; crown and strap bolts with
sapphire cabochon, bezel set with 72 round-cut
diamonds; transparent case back; 10 brilliant-cut
diamond indexes; water-resistant to 3 atm
Band: reptile skin, pin buckle
Remarks: slant-top case
Price: CHF 120,000
Variations: case can be non-set (only bezel set with
diamonds, CHF 70,000)

Virtuoso VIII Chapter 2 Reimagined

Reference number: T10GD046
Movement: hand-wound, Bovet Caliber 17BM03-GD;
ø 38 mm, height 6.7 mm; 18,000 vph; 1-minute double-
faced flying tourbillon; decorated with blackened côtes
de Genève; 10-day power reserve
Functions: hours, minutes, seconds on tourbillon
cage; power reserve indicator; big date
Case: titanium, ø 44 mm, height 13.45 mm; transparent
case back; water-resistant to 3 atm
Band: reptile skin, buckle
Remarks: slant-top case
Price: CHF 221,500; limited to 8 pieces each
Variations: dials with green, blue, yellow and salmon
Super-LumiNova; red-gold case and guilloché dial (CHF
229,500)

Récital 21

Reference number: R210018
Movement: Caliber 13DM05-QPR, ø 36.30 mm, height
6.75 mm; 37 jewels; 21,600 vph; 5-day power reserve
Functions: hours, minutes, coaxial seconds; perpetual
calendar, day (on disk), date (retrograde) and month
and leap year in apertures; power reserve indicator
Case: titanium case, ø 44.40 mm, height 15.50 mm;
water-resistant to 3 atm
Band: rubber, pin buckle
Remarks: slant-top case
Price: CHF 90,000
Variations: different color dials; red-gold case
(95,000 CHF); limited to 60 pieces

Récital 27

Reference number: R270014
Movement: hand-wound, Caliber 13DM033FPL,
ø 36 mm, height 7.55 mm ; 37 jewels; 21,600 vph; 7-day
power reserve
Functions: hours, minutes; 3 time zone indicators,
2 with day/night indicators; moon phase; power
reserve indicator
Case: polished titanium ø 46.3, height 16.5; sapphire
crystal; 3 atm
Band: rubber, pin buckle
Remarks: slant-top case
Price: CHF 85,000
Variations: different color dials; red-gold case (CHF
90,000, limited to 60 pieces)

BREGUET

Abraham-Louis Breguet (1747–1823), who hailed from Switzerland, brought his craft to Paris in the *Sturm und Drang* atmosphere of the late eighteenth century. It was fertile ground for one of the most inventive watchmakers in the history of horology, and his products soon found favor with the highest levels of society.

Little has changed two centuries later. After a few years of drifting, in 1999 the brand carrying this illustrious name became the prize possession of the Swatch Group and came under the personal management of Nicolas G. Hayek, CEO. Hayek worked assiduously to restore the brand's roots, going as far as rebuilding the legendary Marie Antoinette pocket watch and contributing to the restoration of the Petit Trianon at Versailles.

Breguet is a full-fledged *manufacture*, and this has allowed it to forge ahead uncompromisingly with upscale watches and even jewelry. In modern facilities on the shores of Lake Joux, traditional craftsmanship still plays a significant role in the production of its fine watches, but at the same time, Breguet is one of the few brands to work with modern materials for its movements. After years focusing on the Reine de Naples, Tradition, Classique, and Marine collections, Breguet decided to spotlight pilot chronographs. In the post-war period, the company supplied the French Air Force with the standard pilot's chronograph in addition to on-board watches. Now, the model family has been supplemented by two new models in a historicized look, equipped with a brand new chronograph movement with automatic winding.

The two new watches are stylish interpretations of Breguet's Type XX line, which has indeed been delighting watch lovers for seventy years now: a "military" bicompax version, with, horizontally arranged small seconds and half-hour subdials, and a "civilian" tricompax version with three totalizers, including a 15-minute counter (a reminder of the days when you needed to track minutes for long-distance calls). A closer look at the model designations reveals that the "military" chronograph (reference 2057) is called "Type 20," written in Arabic numerals as in the original series from the fifties. The "civilian" version (reference 2067) is designated "Type XX," with Roman numerals.

Montres Breguet SA
CH-1344 L'Abbaye
Switzerland

Tel.:
+41-21-841-9090

Website:
www.breguet.com

Founded:
1775 (Swatch Group since 1999)

Number of Employees:
1,000

U.S. distributor:
Breguet
The Swatch Group (U.S.), Inc.
1200 Harbor Boulevard, 7th Floor
Weehawken, NJ 07086
201-271-1400

Most important collections:
Classique, Tradition, Héritage, Marine, Reine de Naples, Type XX, Type XXI, Type XXII

Tourbillon Extra-Plat 5367

Reference number: 5367PT 29 9WU
Movement: automatic, Breguet Caliber 581; ø 36 mm; 33 jewels; 28,800 vph; 1-minute tourbillon; silicon pallet fork and hairspring; 80-hour power reserve
Functions: hours, minutes, subsidiary seconds (on the tourbillon cage)
Case: platinum, ø 41 mm, height 7.45 mm; sapphire crystal; transparent case back; water-resistant to 3 atm
Band: reptile skin, triple folding clasp
Remarks: enamel dial
Price: $171,000
Variations: in rose gold ($155,600)

Classique Tourbillon Extra-Plat Squelette 5395

Reference number: 5395BR 1S 9WU
Movement: automatic, Breguet Caliber 581SQ; ø 36 mm; 33 jewels; 28,800 vph; 1-minute tourbillon; silicon escapement and hairspring; fully skeletonized movement; 80-hour power reserve
Functions: hours, minutes, subsidiary seconds (on the tourbillon cage)
Case: rose gold, ø 41 mm, height 7.7 mm; sapphire crystal; transparent case back; water-resistant to 3 atm
Band: reptile skin, folding clasp
Price: $237,500
Variations: in platinum $252,900

Classique 7147

Reference number: 7147BB 12 9WU
Movement: automatic, Breguet Caliber 502.3SD; ø 24.9 mm, height 2.4 mm; 35 jewels; 21,600 vph; silicon pallet fork and hairspring; 45-hour power reserve
Functions: hours, minutes, subsidiary seconds
Case: white gold, ø 40 mm, height 6.1 mm; sapphire crystal; transparent case back; water-resistant to 3 atm
Band: reptile skin, pin buckle
Remarks: hand-guilloché on dial
Price: $22,700
Variations: in rose gold $22,200

Classique Full Calendar

Reference number: 7337BB Y5 9VU
Movement: automatic, Breguet Caliber 502.3 QSE1;
ø 31 mm, height 3.8 mm; 35 jewels; 21,600 vph;
silicon hairspring, hand-guilloché on rose-gold
oscillating mass, numbered and signed movement
Functions: hours, minutes, subsidiary seconds; full
calendar with date, weekday, moon phase and age
Case: white gold, ø 39 mm, height 9.9 mm; sapphire
crystal; transparent case back; water-resistant to 3 atm
Band: reptile skin, folding clasp
Remarks: silver-plated hand-guilloché on gold dial
Price: $45,300
Variations: in rose gold $45,300

Classique 7137

Reference number: 7137BR 15 9VU
Movement: automatic, Breguet Caliber 502.3 DR1;
ø 27.1 mm, height 3.65 mm; 37 jewels; 21,600 vph;
silicon Breguet hairspring and escapement;
gold oscillating mass; 46-hour power reserve
Functions: hours, minutes; power-reserve indicator;
date, moon phase and age
Case: rose gold, ø 39 mm, height 8.65 mm; sapphire
crystal; transparent case back; water-resistant to 3 atm
Band: reptile skin, folding clasp
Remarks: hand-guilloche on gold dial
Price: $42,100
Variations: in white gold $42,100

Classique 5177

Reference number: 5177 BB 2Y 9V6
Movement: automatic, Breguet Caliber 777Q;
ø 27.1 mm; 26 jewels; 28,800 vph; silicon pallet lever,
escape wheel, and hairspring; 55-hour power reserve
Functions: hours, minutes, sweep seconds; date
Case: white gold, ø 38 mm, height 8.8 mm; sapphire
crystal; transparent case back; water-resistant to 3 atm
Band: reptile skin, pin buckle
Remarks: enamel dial
Price: $25,000

Classique Quantième Perpétuel

Reference number: 7327BB 11 9VU
Movement: automatic, Breguet Caliber 502.3.P;
ø 27.1 mm, height 4.5 mm; 35 jewels; 21,600 vph;
silicon Breguet hairspring and escapement;
gold oscillating mass; 45-hour power reserve
Functions: hours, minutes; perpetual calendar with
date, weekday, month (retrograde),
moon phase and leap year
Case: white gold, ø 39 mm, height 9.13 mm; sapphire
crystal; transparent case back; water-resistant to 3 atm
Band: reptile skin, folding clasp
Remarks: hand-guilloché on gold dial
Price: $80,200
Variations: in rose gold $80,200

Marine Équation Marchante

Reference number: 5887PT Y2 9WV
Movement: automatic, Breguet Caliber 581DPE;
ø 37.2 mm, 57 jewels; 28,800 vph; 1-minute tourbillon;
silicon anchor, anchor escape wheel and hairspring;
80-hour power reserve
Functions: hours, minutes, subsidiary seconds,
(on the tourbillon cage); "running" equation of time;
perpetual calendar with date (retrograde) weekday,
months, leap year
Case: platinum, ø 43.9 mm, height 11.75 mm; sapphire
crystal; transparent case back; water-resistant to 10 atm
Band: reptile skin, triple folding clasp
Price: $242,600
Variations: in rose gold $226,300

Marine Hora Mundi

Reference number: 5557BR YS 9WV
Movement: automatic, Breguet Caliber 77F1; 40 jewels;
28,800 vph; silicon anchor, anchor escape wheel, and
hairspring; 55-hour power reserve
Functions: hours, minutes, sweep seconds;
world-time display (two time zones, pusher-activated);
day/night indicator; date
Case: rose gold, ø 43.9 mm, height 13.8 mm; sapphire
crystal; transparent case back; water-resistant to 10 atm
Band: reptile skin, triple folding clasp
Remarks: hand-guilloché dial with continents made
of sapphire
Price: $72,700
Variations: with link bracelet $96,400 or rubber strap;
in white gold $72,700

Marine Date

Reference number: 5517TI Y1 5ZU
Movement: automatic, Breguet Caliber 777A;
ø 33.8 mm; 26 jewels; 28,800 vph; silicon pallet horns
and hairspring; 55-hour power reserve
Functions: hours, minutes, sweep seconds; date
Case: titanium, ø 40 mm, height 11.5 mm;
sapphire crystal; transparent case back
Band: rubber, folding clasp
Price: $18,300
Variations: with reptile skin or stainless-steel bracelet;
in rose gold ($30,100); in white gold ($30,100)

Marine Chronograph

Reference number: 5527BR G3 5WV
Movement: automatic, Breguet Caliber 582QA;
ø 32.7 mm; 28 jewels; 28,800 vph; silicon pallet lever
and hairspring; 48-hour power reserve
Functions: hours, minutes, subsidiary seconds;
chronograph; date
Case: rose gold, ø 42.3 mm, height 13.85 mm;
sapphire crystal; transparent case back;
screw-in crown; water-resistant to 10 atm
Band: rubber, folding clasp
Price: $35,700
Variations: with reptile skin ($35,700) or
link bracelet ($59,300); in white gold ($35,700);
in titanium ($22,700), titanium link ($25,400)

Marine Alarme Musicale

Reference number: 5547BB Y2 9ZU
Movement: automatic, Breguet Caliber 518F/1;
ø 27.1 mm; 36 jewels; 28,800 vph; silicon pallet fork and
hairspring; 45-hour power reserve
Functions: hours, minutes, sweep seconds;
additional 24-hour display (2nd time zone),
power reserve indicator for the chiming mechanism;
alarm (set to the minute); date
Case: white gold, ø 40 mm, height 13.05 mm; sapphire
crystal; transparent case back; water-resistant to 5 atm
Band: reptile skin, folding clasp
Price: $42,000
Variations: with rubber strap ($42,000) or
titanium link bracelet ($32,900); in titanium ($30,100);
in rose gold ($42,000)

Marine Dame 9518

Reference number: 9518BR 52 584 D000
Movement: automatic, Breguet Caliber 591A;
ø 25.6 mm; 25 jewels; 28,800 vph; silicon Breguet
hairspring and escapement, gold oscillating mass set
with 31 diamonds; 38-hour power reserve
Functions: hours, minutes, sweep seconds; date
Case: rose gold, ø 38.8 mm, height 9.89 mm; bezel with
50 diamonds; sapphire crystal; transparent case back;
water-resistant to 5 atm
Band: rubber, folding clasp
Remarks: hand-guilloché on mother-of-pearl-dial
Price: $36,700
Variations: with reptile skin strap; in white gold
($36,700); in stainless steel ($21,100)

Tradition Dame

Reference number: 7038BR 18 9V6 D00D
Movement: automatic, Breguet Caliber 505 SR;
ø 33 mm; 38 jewels; 21,600 vph; silicon Breguet
hairspring and pallet fork; 50-hour power reserve
Functions: hours and minutes (off-center),
subsidiary seconds (retrograde)
Case: rose gold, ø 37 mm, height 11.85 mm; bezel with
68 diamonds; sapphire crystal; transparent case back;
crown with ruby cabochon; water-resistant to 3 atm
Band: reptile skin, pin buckle set with 19 diamonds
Price: $40,200
Variations: in white gold $41,000

Tradition Quantième Rétrograde

Reference number: 7597BB GY 9WU
Movement: automatic, Breguet Caliber
505 Q; ø 33 mm; 38 jewels; 21,600 vph; silicon Breguet
hairspring and anchor pallets; 50-hour power reserve
Functions: hours and minutes (off-center);
date (retrograde)
Case: white gold, ø 40 mm, height 12.1 mm; sapphire
crystal; transparent case back; water-resistant to 3 atm
Band: reptile skin, folding clasp
Remarks: hand-guilloché on blued gold dial
Price: $40,800
Variations: in rose gold $39,900

Tradition Seconde Rétrograde

Reference number: 7097BR G1 9WU
Movement: automatic, Breguet Caliber 505 SR1;
ø 33 mm; 38 jewels; 21,600 vph; silicon Breguet
hairspring and anchor pallets; 50-hour power reserve
Functions: hours and minutes (off-center), subsidiary
seconds (retrograde)
Case: rose gold, ø 40 mm, height 11.8 mm; sapphire
crystal; transparent case back; water-resistant to 3 atm
Band: reptile skin, folding clasp
Remarks: hand-guilloché on silvered gold dial
Price: $34,400
Variations: in white gold $35,400

"Type 20"

Reference number: 2057ST 92 3WU
Movement: automatic, Breguet Caliber 7281;
ø 32.7 mm; 34 jewels; 28,800 vph; silicon Breguet
escapement and hairspring, gold oscillating mass;
60-hour power reserve
Functions: hours, minutes, subsidiary seconds;
flyback chronograph; date
Case: stainless steel, ø 42 mm, height 14.1 mm;
bidirectional bezel, with reference markings; sapphire
crystal; transparent case back; water-resistant to 10 atm
Band: calfskin, pin buckle
Remarks: comes with additional textile strap
Price: $18,000

"Type XX"

Reference number: 2067ST 92 3WU
Movement: automatic, Breguet Caliber 728; ø 32.7 mm;
38 jewels; 28,800 vph; silicon Breguet hairspring, gold
oscillating mass; 60-hour power reserve
Functions: hours, minutes, subsidiary seconds;
flyback chronograph; date
Case: stainless steel, ø 42 mm, height 14.1 mm;
bidirectional bezel, with 0-12 scale; sapphire crystal;
transparent case back; water-resistant to 10 atm
Band: calfskin, pin buckle
Remarks: comes with additional textile strap
Price: $18,000

Reine de Naples

Reference number: 8918BR 2C 364 DD0D
Movement: automatic, Breguet Caliber 537/3;
ø 19.7 mm; 26 jewels; 21,600 vph; silicon hairspring and
escapement; 45-hour power reserve
Functions: hours, minutes
Case: rose gold, 28.45 x 36.5 mm, height 10.05 mm;
bezel and flange set with 117 diamonds;
sapphire crystal; transparent case back; crown with
diamond cabochon; water-resistant to 3 atm
Band: calfskin, folding clasp with 26 diamonds
Remarks: enamel dial with drop-shaped diamond
Price: $38,300

Reine de Naples

Reference number: 8928BB 5W 944 DD0D 3L
Movement: automatic, Breguet Caliber 586/1;
ø 19.7 mm; 29 jewels; 21,600 vph; silicon hairspring and
pallet forks; 38-hour power reserve
Functions: hours, minutes
Case: white gold, 24.95 x 33 mm, height 10.05 mm;
bezel, flange, and lugs with 139 diamonds; sapphire
crystal; transparent case back; crown with diamond
cabochon; water-resistant to 3 atm
Band: reptile skin, folding clasp with 26 diamonds
Remarks: mother-of-pearl-dial
Price: $39,500

Reine de Naples

Reference number: 8999BB 8D 974 DD0D
Movement: automatic, Breguet Caliber 78CS;
45 jewels; 25,200 vph; balance wheel and escapement
on a 24-hour carousel; 57-hour power reserve
Functions: hours, minutes; additional 24-hour display
(2nd time zone), day/night indicator as animation on a
rotating titanium disc
Case: white gold, 34 x 42.05 mm, height 10.8 mm;
bezel, flange and lugs set with 184 diamonds;
sapphire crystal; transparent case back;
crown with diamond cabochon
Band: reptile skin, folding clasp
Remarks: hand-guilloché on gold dial set with
147 diamonds
Price: $237,500

BREITLING

When Léon Breitling opened his workshop in St. Imier in the Jura Mountains in 1884, he set a course focusing consistently on instrument watches with a distinctive design. High quality standards and the rise of aviation completed the picture.

Today, Breitling's relationship with air sports and commercial and military aviation is clear from its brand identity. The unveiling of its own, modern chronograph movement at Basel in 2009 was a major milestone in the company's history and also a return to its roots. The new design was to be "100 percent Breitling" and industrially produced in large numbers at a reasonable cost. Although Breitling's operations in Grenchen and in La Chaux-de-Fonds both boast state-of-the-art equipment, the contract for the new chronograph was awarded to a small team in Geneva. In 2006, the brand-new Caliber B01 made the COSC grade and has enjoyed great popularity ever since. For the team of designers, the innovative centering system on the reset mechanism that requires no manual adjustment was one of the great achievements.

Under CEO Georges Kern—of IWC fame—Breitling expanded beyond the pilot watch niche and tapped markets in the Far East. The new collections were streamlined and given more defined profiles, a recipe he brought in from his IWC days. The winged logo was replaced mostly with a coquettish "B."

The brand has also introduced a new hypoallergenic material called Breitlight and is boldly using bright colors, like bright red straps. But of course, the models of the past still have top billing. For its seventieth birthday, the Navitimer was equipped with the in-house Caliber B01, housed in a redesigned case. The water resistance remained the same, a modest 3 atmospheres (30 meters/100 feet). This is primarily due to the sealing of the rotating bezel— i.e., the slide rule—which the designers definitely did not want to dispense with.

In the past year, the collection was enlarged with new models for the Chronomat family, like the Chronomat GMT and the Super Chronomat 38. The Superocean, Top Time, and Premier collections have also been expanded.

Breitling
Léon Breitling-Strasse 2
2540 Grenchen
Switzerland

Tel.:
+41-32-654-5454

E-mail:
info.US@breitling.com

Website:
www.breitling.com

Founded:
1884

Annual production:
700,000 (estimated)

U.S. distributor:
Breitling U.S.A. Inc.
206 Danbury Road
Wilton, CT 06897
203-762-1180
www.breitling.com

Most important collections:
Navitimer, Avenger, Premier, Chronomat, Top Time, Superocean Heritage, Superocean, Professional, Classic Avi

Chronomat Automatic GMT 40

Reference number: A32398101A1A1
Movement: automatic, Breitling Caliber 32 (based on ETA 2893-2); ø 25.6 mm, height 4.1 mm; 21 jewels; 28,800 vph; 42-hour power reserve
Functions: hours, minutes, sweep seconds; additional 24-hour display (2nd time zone); date
Case: stainless steel, ø 40 mm, height 11.77 mm; unidirectional bezel with 0-60 scale; sapphire crystal; screw-in crown; water-resistant to 20 atm
Band: stainless steel, folding clasp
Price: $5,950

Chronomat Automatic GMT 40

Reference number: A32398101L1A1
Movement: automatic, Breitling Caliber 32 (based on ETA 2893-2); ø 25.6 mm, height 4.1 mm; 21 jewels; 28,800 vph; 42-hour power reserve
Functions: hours, minutes, sweep seconds; additional 24-hour display (2nd time zone); date
Case: stainless steel, ø 40 mm, height 11.77 mm; unidirectional bezel with 0-60 scale; sapphire crystal; screw-in crown; water-resistant to 20 atm
Band: stainless steel, folding clasp
Price: $5,950

Super Chronomat B01 44

Reference number: AB0136251B1S1
Movement: automatic, Breitling Caliber B01; ø 30 mm, height 7.2 mm; 47 jewels; 28,800 vph; column-wheel control of the chronograph functions; 70-hour power reserve; COSC-certified chronometer
Functions: hours, minutes, subsidiary seconds; chronograph; date
Case: stainless steel, ø 44 mm, height 14.4 mm; unidirectional bezel with 0-60 scale; sapphire crystal; transparent case back; screw-in crown; water-resistant to 20 atm
Band: rubber, folding clasp
Price: $9,450

Super Chronomat B01 42

Reference number: AB0134101C1A1
Movement: automatic, Breitling Caliber B01;
ø 30 mm, height 7.2 mm; 47 jewels; 28,800 vph;
column-wheel control of the chronograph functions;
70-hour power reserve; COSC-certified chronometer
Functions: hours, minutes, subsidiary seconds;
chronograph; date
Case: stainless steel, ø 42 mm, height 15.1 mm;
unidirectional bezel, with 0-60 scale; sapphire crystal;
transparent case back; screw-in crown;
water-resistant to 20 atm
Band: stainless steel, folding clasp
Price: $XXXXX
Variations: various cases, straps, and dials

Superocean Heritage B01 Chronograph 44

Reference number: AB0162121G1A1
Movement: automatic, Breitling Caliber B01;
ø 30 mm, height 7.2 mm; 47 jewels; 28,800 vph;
70-hour power reserve; COSC-certified chronometer
Functions: hours, minutes, subsidiary seconds;
chronograph; date
Case: stainless steel, ø 44 mm, height 15.5 mm;
unidirectional bezel with ceramic insert; sapphire
crystal; screw-in crown; water-resistant to 20 atm
Band: stainless steel Milanese bracelet, folding clasp
Price: $8,650
Variations: various bands and dials

Superocean Heritage B20 Automatic 46

Reference number: AB2020121L1S1
Movement: automatic, Breitling Caliber B20
(based on Tudor MT 5612); ø 31.8 mm, height 6.5 mm;
26 jewels; 28,800 vph; 70-hour power reserve;
COSC-certified chronometer
Functions: hours, minutes, sweep seconds; date
Case: stainless steel, ø 46 mm, height 14.9 mm;
unidirectional bezel with ceramic insert; sapphire
crystal; screw-in crown; water-resistant to 20 atm
Band: rubber, folding clasp
Price: $5,300
Variations: various cases, straps, and dials

Superocean Automatic 36

Reference number: A17377211C1A1
Movement: automatic, Breitling Caliber 17
(based on Sellita SW200-1); ø 25.6 mm, height 4.6 mm;
26 jewels; 28,800 vph; 38-hour power reserve;
COSC-certified chronometer
Functions: hours, minutes, sweep seconds
Case: stainless steel, ø 36 mm, height 12.21 mm;
unidirectional bezel with 0-60 scale; sapphire crystal;
water-resistant to 30 atm
Band: stainless steel, folding clasp
Price: $4,950
Variations: various cases, straps, and dials

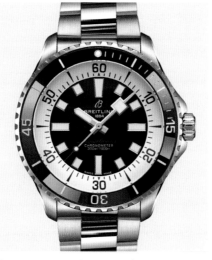

Superocean Automatic 44

Reference number: A17376211B1A1
Movement: automatic, Breitling Caliber 17
(based on Sellita SW200-1); ø 25.6 mm, height 4.6 mm;
26 jewels; 28,800 vph; 38-hour power reserve;
COSC-certified chronometer
Functions: hours, minutes, sweep seconds
Case: stainless steel, ø 44 mm, height 12.6 mm;
unidirectional bezel with 0-60 scale; sapphire crystal;
water-resistant to 30 atm
Band: stainless steel, folding clasp
Price: $5,250
Variations: various cases, straps, and dials

Superocean Automatic 44

Reference number: A17376211C1S1
Movement: automatic, Breitling Caliber 17
(based on Sellita SW200-1); ø 25.6 mm, height 4.6 mm;
26 jewels; 28,800 vph; 38-hour power reserve;
COSC-certified chronometer
Functions: hours, minutes, sweep seconds
Case: stainless steel, ø 44 mm, height 12.6 mm;
unidirectional bezel, with 0-60 scale; sapphire crystal;
water-resistant to 30 atm
Band: rubber, folding clasp
Price: $5,050
Variations: various cases, straps, and dials

Top Time B01 Ford Mustang

Reference number: AB01762A1L1X1
Movement: automatic, Breitling Caliber B01;
ø 30 mm, height 7.2 mm; 47 jewels; 28,800 vph;
70-hour power reserve
Functions: hours, minutes, subsidiary seconds;
chronograph
Case: stainless steel, ø 41 mm, height 13.3 mm;
sapphire crystal; transparent case back;
water-resistant to 10 atm
Band: calfskin, folding clasp
Price: $8,000

Top Time B01 Shelby Cobra

Reference number: AB01763A1C1X1
Movement: automatic, Breitling Caliber B01;
ø 30 mm, height 7.2 mm; 47 jewels; 28,800 vph;
70-hour power reserve
Functions: hours, minutes, subsidiary seconds;
chronograph
Case: stainless steel, ø 41 mm, height 13,3 mm;
sapphire crystal; transparent case back;
water-resistant to 10 atm
Band: calfskin, folding clasp
Price: $8,000

Premier B01 Chronograph 42

Reference number: AB0145221B1A1
Movement: automatic, Breitling Caliber B01;
ø 30 mm, height 7.2 mm; 47 jewels; 28,800 vph;
70-hour power reserve; COSC-certified chronometer
Functions: hours, minutes, subsidiary seconds;
chronograph; date
Case: stainless steel, ø 42 mm, height 13.6 mm;
sapphire crystal; transparent case back;
water-resistant to 10 atm
Band: stainless steel, folding clasp
Price: $9,500
Variations: with reptile skin strap ($9,100)

Premier B01 Chronograph 42

Reference number: AB0145171C1P1
Movement: automatic, Breitling Caliber B01;
ø 30 mm, height 7.2 mm; 47 jewels; 28,800 vph;
70-hour power reserve; COSC-certified chronometer
Functions: hours, minutes, subsidiary seconds;
chronograph; date
Case: stainless steel, ø 42 mm, height 13.6 mm;
sapphire crystal; transparent case back;
water-resistant to 10 atm
Band: reptile skin, folding clasp
Price: $9,100
Variations: with stainless steel bracelet ($9,500)

Navitimer B01 Chronograph 46

Reference number: AB0137211B1P1
Movement: automatic, Breitling Caliber B01;
ø 30 mm, height 7.2 mm; 47 jewels; 28,800 vph;
column-wheel control of the chronograph functions;
70-hour power reserve; COSC-certified chronometer
Functions: hours, minutes, subsidiary seconds;
chronograph; date
Case: stainless steel, ø 46 mm, height 13.9 mm;
bidirectional bezel, with integrated slide rule and
tachymeter scale; sapphire crystal; transparent case
back; water-resistant to 3 atm
Band: reptile skin, folding clasp
Price: $9,400
Variations: various cases, straps, and dials

Navitimer B01 Chronograph 43

Reference number: AB0138241C1P1
Movement: automatic, Breitling Caliber B01; ø 30 mm,
height 7.2 mm; 47 jewels; 28,800 vph; column-wheel
control of the chronograph functions; 70-hour power
reserve; COSC-certified chronometer
Functions: hours, minutes, subsidiary seconds;
chronograph; date
Case: stainless steel, ø 43 mm, height 13.6 mm;
bidirectional bezel, with integrated slide rule and
tachymeter scale; sapphire crystal; transparent case
back; water-resistant to 3 atm
Band: reptile skin, folding clasp
Price: $15,750
Variations: various cases, straps, and dials

Navitimer B01 Chronograph 43

Reference number: RB0138211B1R1
Movement: automatic, Breitling Caliber B01; ø 30 mm, height 7.2 mm; 47 jewels; 28,800 vph; column-wheel control of the chronograph functions; 70-hour power reserve; COSC-certified chronometer
Functions: hours, minutes, subsidiary seconds; chronograph; date
Case: red gold, ø 43 mm, height 13.6 mm; bidirectional bezel, with integrated slide rule and tachymeter scale; sapphire crystal; transparent case back; water-resistant to 3 atm
Band: red gold, folding clasp
Price: $38,700
Variations: various cases, straps, and dials

Chronomat 32

Reference number: R77310101A1R1
Movement: quartz, Breitling Caliber 77; COSC-certified chronometer
Functions: hours, minutes, sweep seconds; date
Case: red gold, ø 32 mm, height 8.54 mm; sapphire crystal; water-resistant to 10 atm
Band: red gold, folding clasp
Price: $21,500
Variations: various cases, straps, and dials

Super Chronomat Automatic 38

Reference number: U17356531L1U1
Movement: automatic, Breitling Caliber 17; ø 25.6 mm, height 4.6 mm; 25 jewels; 28,800 vph; 38-hour power reserve; COSC-certified chronometer
Functions: hours, minutes, sweep seconds; date
Case: stainless steel, ø 38 mm, height 11.88 mm; bezel in red gold, set with 32 diamonds; sapphire crystal; water-resistant to 10 atm
Band: stainless steel with red gold elements, folding clasp
Price: $14,250

Caliber B01

Automatic; column-wheel control of the chronograph functions; vertical clutch; single spring barrel, 70-hour power reserve; COSC-certified chronometer
Functions: hours, minutes, subsidiary seconds; chronograph; date
Diameter: 30 mm
Height: 7.2 mm
Jewels: 47
Balance: glucydur
Frequency: 28,800 vph
Remarks: 346 parts

Caliber B04

Automatic; column-wheel control of the chronograph functions; vertical clutch; single spring barrel, 70-hour power reserve; COSC-certified chronometer
Functions: hours, minutes, subsidiary seconds; additional 24-hour display (2nd time zone); chronograph; date
Diameter: 30 mm
Height: 7.4 mm
Jewels: 47
Balance: glucydur
Frequency: 28,800 vph

Caliber B05

Automatic; column-wheel control of chronograph functions; vertical clutch; time zone disk connected to hand mechanism by planetary transmission; single spring barrel; COSC-certified chronometer; 70-hour power reserve
Diameter: 30 mm
Height: 8.1 mm
Jewels: 56
Balance: glucydur
Frequency: 28,800 vph

BREMONT

Bremont watches have adventure in their DNA, as it were, but adventure with a bit of Anglo-Saxon understatement. They have been worn by a number of people who have exhibited their taste for derring-do, like polar explorer Ben Saunders or Levison Wood, who was the first person to walk the length of the Nile. And it's hardly any wonder, since the brand is the brainchild of brothers Nick and Giles English, themselves dyed-in-the-wool pilots and restorers of vintage airplanes. The brand name has a wild story as well: to avoid a storm, the brothers were forced to land their vintage biplane in a field in southern France. The farmer, a former World War II pilot, was more than happy to put them up for the night. His name: Antoine Bremont.

These British-made timepieces hit the market in 2007 and hit a nerve in those seeking a watch that tells the time and expresses some smoldering attraction to danger, perhaps. They use sturdy, COSC- or ISO-3159-certified automatic movements, extensively modified; hardened steel; a patented shock-absorbing system; and a rotor whose design recalls a flight of planes. The brand has steadily increased its production and programmatic scope. Bremont has sought its inspiration from such British icons as the Spitfire, Bletchley Park (where the German codes were broken during World War II), Jaguar sports cars, and even Boeing. Water sport is another area Bremont has explored, with models inspired by the legendary J-Class yachts, like the ladies' model AC I 32, and a special set devoted to the America's Cup.

In 2023, Bremont came out with an all-British, in-house made movement, the ENG300, tested mainly by Martin-Baker, a company that makes ejection seats for fighter jets, and that will belong to the H1 generation of watches. The concept model designed for the caliber is the MB Viper, a bright orange pilot's watch, with a round dial on a squarish bezel on top of an octagonal case, which is elegantly thin.

Bremont Watch Company
P.O. Box 4741
Henley-on-Thames
RG9 9BZ Oxfordshire
United Kingdom

Tel.:
+44-800-817-4281

E-mail:
info@bremont.com

Website:
www.bremont.com

Founded:
2002

Number of employees:
100+

Annual production:
several thousand watches

U.S. distributor:
Bremont Inc.
501 Madison Avenue, New York, NY 10022
855-273-6668
Michael.Pearson@bremont.com
Anthony.kozlowsky@bremont.com

Most important collections/price range:
ALT1, Armed Forces collection, Bremont Boeing, Bremont Jaguar, MB, SOLO, Supermarine, U-2, and limited editions / $3,600 to $42,500

S302 JET

Movement: automatic, Caliber BE-93-2AV (base Sellita SW330-1); ø 25.6 mm, height 4.1 mm; 25 jewels; 28,800 vph; ISO 3159-certified chronometer; 50-hour power reserve
Functions: hours, minutes, sweep seconds; additional 24-hour display (second time zone); date
Case: stainless steel with black DLC, ø 40 mm, height 13 mm; unidirectional ceramic bezel with 0-24 scale; sapphire crystal; transparent case back; screw-in crown; water resistant to 30 atm
Band: calfskin, pin buckle
Price: $4,250
Variations: with black rubber strap

S300 Kaimu

Movement: automatic, Caliber BE-92AV (base Sellita SW300); ø 25.6 mm, height 3.6 mm; 25 jewels; 28,800 vph; ISO.3159-certified chronometer; 38-hour power reserve
Functions: hours, minutes, sweep seconds; date
Case: stainless steel with PVD case middle, ø 40 mm, height 13 mm; unidirectional ceramic bezel with Super-LumiNova markers; screw-in crown; sapphire crystal; screw-down case back with decoration; water-resistant to 30 atm
Band: stainless steel; folding clasp
Price: $4,300
Variations: with reptile skin strap ($3,850)

MB Viper

Movement: automatic, Caliber ENG352; ø 30 mm, height 7.6 mm; 22 jewels; 25,200 vph; assembled in patented rubber anti-shock mount; custom-decorated tungsten rotor; gold-plated automatic bridge; H1 timing standard (like ISO 3159-certified) chronometer; free-sprung silicon escape wheel; 65-hour power reserve
Functions: hours, minutes, sweep seconds
Case: "Trip-Tick" stainless steel with black DLC and orange anodized aluminum; ø 43.5 mm, height 10.8 mm; unidirectional bezel with tachymeter scale; sapphire crystal; screw-in crown; water-resistant to 20 atm
Band: calf leather, folding clasp
Remarks: British-made movement with special endurance testing by ejection-seat maker Martin- Baker
Price: $5,995

B. R. M. Chronographes
(Bernard Richards Manufacture)
2 Impasse de L'Aubette
ZA des Aulnaies
F-95420 Magny-en-Vexin
France

Tel.:
+33-1-61-02-00-25

Fax:
+33-1-61-02-00-14

Website:
www.brm-chronographes.com

Founded:
2003

Number of employees:
20

Annual production:
approx. 2,000 pieces

U.S. distributor:
B.R.M Manufacture North America
25 Highland Park Village, Suite 100-777
Dallas, TX 75205
214-231-0144
usa@brm-manufacture.com

Price range:
$3,000 to $150,000

B. R. M. CHRONOGRAPHES

For Bernard Richards, the true sign of luxury lies in "technical skills and perfection in all stages of manufacture." The exterior of the product is of course crucial, but all of B.R.M.'s major operations for making a wristwatch—such as encasing, assembling, setting, and polishing—are performed by hand in his little garage-like factory located outside Paris in Magny-en-Vexin.

B.R.M. is devoted to the ultra-mechanical look combined with materials that derive from various industries, notably automotive. His inspiration at the start came from the 1940s, the age of axle grease, pinups, real pilots, and a can-do attitude. The design: three dimensions visible to the naked eye, big mechanical landscapes. The inside: custom-designed components, fitting perfectly into Richards's engineering ideal. Gradually, though, Richards has been modernizing.

B.R.M.'s unusual timepieces have mainly been based on the tried and trusted ETA movements. The new GMT, featuring a printed and UV-treated world on the dial, runs on one, for example. But Richards has set lofty goals for himself and his young venture, for he intends to set up a true *manufacture* in his French factory. His Birotor model is thus outfitted with the Precitime, a caliber conceived and manufactured on French soil. The movement features B.R.M.'s shock absorbers mounted on the conical springs of its so-called Isolastic system. Plates and bridges are crafted of ARCAP, rotors are made of Fortal HR—an aluminum alloy harder than some steels— and tantalum. The twin rotors, found at 12 and 6 o'clock, are mounted on double rows of ceramic bearings that require no lubrication.

Richards recently started a sailing-oriented collection, with the names of winds on the four compass points of a watch. And the Free Floating collection experiments with a trapezoidal case and an entirely "strung-up" movement inside. As for personalization, B. R. M. has a configurator that gives potential customers a free hand with colors and straps.

BM6-44-SA-N-CBL-AGR- ORCA BLANC

Movement: automatic, ETA Caliber 2824/2; ø 25.6 mm, height 4.60 mm; 25 jewels; 28,800 vph; full dial with hand painted hands and shock absorbers; 38-hour power reserve
Functions: hours, minutes, sweep seconds; date
Case: stainless steel with white lacquer, ø 44 mm, height 11 mm; stainless steel; crystal sapphire; transparent case back; screw-in crown; water-resistant to 10 atm
Band: Hypalon, pin buckle
Price: $5,050
Variations: 8 variations available with 44 mm case and 7 variations available with 34 mm case

V6-44-SA-N-SQ-5N

Movement: automatic, ETA Caliber 2824/2 modified in-house; ø 25.6 mm, height 4.60 mm; 25 jewels; 28,800 vph; skeletonized dial with hand painted automation bridge, hands and shock absorbers; 38-hour power reserve
Functions: hours, minutes, sweep seconds with stop-second device
Case: brushed stainless steel and black PVD, ø 44 mm, height 11; sapphire crystal; screw-in crown; antireflective on both sides; transparent case back; water-resistant to 10 atm
Band: leather, pin buckle
Price: $6,800
Variations: options with configurator

FF39-40-TG-LFN-BLM

Movement: automatic, B.R.M. Precitime in-house development (base ETA 2824/2); ø 25.6 mm, height 4.6 mm; 25 jewels; 28,800 vph; fully skeletonized movement; anodized Fortal (aluminum alloy) balance and rotor; Fortal casing ring mounted on shock absorbers; 38-hour power reserve
Functions: hours, minutes, stop sweep seconds
Case: grey titanium and polished black PVD stainless steel, trapezoidal form, 40 mm x 39 mm height 11.2 mm; bezel with black PVD; sapphire crystal; antireflective on both sides; sapphire crystal; transparent case back; water-resistant to 3 atm
Band: Alcantara, pin buckle
Remarks: the movement "floats" inside the case thanks to 5 silentblocs and two nitrile belts; carbon struts prevent lateral displacement
Price: $12,900
Variations: 36 variations available

BULGARI

Although Bulgari is one of the largest jewelry manufacturers in the world, watches have always played an important role for the brand. The purchase of Daniel Roth and Gérald Genta in the Vallée de Joux opened new prospectives for its timepieces, thanks to specialized production facilities and the watchmaking talent in the Vallée de Joux—especially where complicated timepieces are concerned. In March 2011, luxury goods giant Louis Vuitton Moët Hennessy (LVMH) secured all the Bulgari family shares in exchange for 16.5 million LVMH shares and a say in the group's future. The financial backing of the mega-group boosted the company's strategy to become fully independent.

Under the bold leadership of Guido Terrini, the watch division continued pushing the envelope with a series of increasingly thin and complicated automatics. After the tourbillon in 2014 came a minute repeater in 2016, which is 3.12 millimeters high and whose dial features slotted indices for better sound transmission. It was followed by the 5.15-millimeter-high Octo Finissimo Automatic run on the Caliber BVL 138. The Chronograph GMT (2019) was another record in streamlining. It is 6.9 millimeters high and runs on the BVL 318, featuring a hubless peripheral rotor and an hour hand that can be quickly and easily clicked through the time zones.

The sixth world record came in 2020 with the Octo Finissimo Tourbillon Chronograph Skeleton Automatic, which combines the essential complications of modern watchmaking in the thinnest possible case. And in November 2021, Bulgari picked up the coveted Aiguille d'Or of the Grand Prix d'Horlogerie de Genève for the Octo Finissimo Perpetual Calendar, which measures 5.8 millimeters. The Octo Finissimo Ultra held the record for thinnest mechanical watch, with a total height of 1.8 millimeters.

While working on another record, the product strategists in Neuchâtel are concentrating on the Octo Roma. With its octagonal case and distinctive round bezel, it doesn't fit into any common pattern; and yet the sporty watch, available in various sizes, has become the brand's top seller in just a few years.

Bulgari Horlogerie SA
Rue de Monruz 34
CH-2000 Neuchâtel
Switzerland

Tel.:
+41-32-722-7878

E-mail:
info@bulgari.com

Website:
www.bulgari.com

Founded:
1884 (Bulgari Horlogerie was founded in the early 1980s as Bulgari Time)

U.S. distributor:
Bulgari Corporation of America
555 Madison Avenue
New York, NY 10022
212-315-9700

Most important collections/price range:
Bulgari-Bulgari / from approx. $4,700 to $30,300; Diagono / from approx. $3,200; Octo Roma or Finissimo / from approx. $7,700 to $690,000 and above; Daniel Roth and Gérald Genta collections

Octo Roma Automatic

Reference number: 103739
Movement: automatic, Bulgari Caliber BVL 191; ø 25.6 mm; 26 jewels; 28,800 vph; 42-hour power reserve
Functions: hours, minutes, sweep seconds; date
Case: stainless steel, ø 41 mm, height 9.15 mm; sapphire crystal; water-resistant to 10 atm
Band: stainless steel, folding clasp
Price: $7,300

Octo Roma Automatic

Reference number: 103740
Movement: automatic, Bulgari Caliber BVL 191; ø 25.6 mm; 26 jewels; 28,800 vph; 42-hour power reserve
Functions: hours, minutes, sweep seconds; date
Case: stainless steel, ø 41 mm, height 9.15 mm; sapphire crystal; water-resistant to 10 atm
Band: stainless steel, folding clasp
Price: $7,300

Octo Roma Automatic

Reference number: 103741
Movement: automatic, Bulgari Caliber BVL 191; ø 25.6 mm; 26 jewels; 28,800 vph; 42-hour power reserve
Functions: hours, minutes, sweep seconds; date
Case: stainless steel, ø 41 mm, height 9.15 mm; sapphire crystal; water-resistant to 10 atm
Band: stainless steel, folding clasp
Price: $7,300

Octo Roma chronograph

Reference number: 103471
Movement: automatic, Bulgari Caliber BVL 399 (based on Bulgari BVL 191 with Dubois Dépraz module); 28,800 vph; 48-hour power reserve
Functions: hours, minutes, subsidiary seconds; chronograph; date
Case: stainless steel, ø 42 mm, height 12.4 mm; sapphire crystal; water-resistant to 10 atm
Band: stainless steel, folding clasp
Price: $9,150

Octo Roma Chronograph

Reference number: 103829
Movement: automatic, Bulgari Caliber BVL 399 (based on Bulgari BVL 191 with Dubois Dépraz module); 28,800 vph; 48-hour power reserve
Functions: hours, minutes, subsidiary seconds; chronograph; date
Case: stainless steel, ø 42 mm, height 12.4 mm; sapphire crystal; water-resistant to 10 atm
Band: stainless steel, folding clasp
Price: $9,150

Octo Roma Naturalia

Reference number: 103675
Movement: hand-wound, Bulgari Caliber BVL 206; ø 34 mm, height 5 mm; 21,600 vph; flying one-minute tourbillon; skeletonized movement, bridges with brown DLC; 64-hour power reserve
Functions: hours, minutes
Case: rose gold, ø 44 mm, height 11.35 mm; sapphire crystal; water-resistant to 5 atm
Band: reptile skin, folding clasp
Price: $149,000

Octo Roma Papillon Tourbillon

Reference number: 103748
Movement: hand-wound, Bulgari Caliber BVL 348; ø 35 mm, height 8.75 mm; 36 jewels; 21,600 vph; flying tourbillon; 60-hour power reserve
Functions: hours (digital, jumping), minutes ("butterfly" display)
Case: titanium with black DLC, ø 44 mm, height 11.9 mm; sapphire crystal; transparent case back; water-resistant to 5 atm
Band: reptile skin with rubber layer, folding clasp
Price: $119,000

Octo Roma Tourbillon Sapphire

Reference number: 103914
Movement: hand-wound, Bulgari Caliber BVL 206; ø 34 mm, height 5 mm; 21,600 vph; flying one-minute tourbillon; skeletonized movement, 11 bridges as hour markers, with green DLC; 64-hour power reserve
Functions: hours, minutes
Case: titanium with black DLC, sapphire case middle, ø 44 mm, height 11.65 mm; sapphire crystal; transparent case back; water-resistant to 5 atm
Band: reptile skin with rubber layer, folding clasp
Price: $78,000

Octo Finissimo S Chronograph GMT Titanium

Reference number: 103661
Movement: automatic, Bulgari Caliber BVL 318 Finissimo; ø 36 mm, height 3.3 mm; 37 jewels; 28,800 vph; hubless peripheral rotor with platinum oscillating mass; column-wheel control of the chronograph functions; finely finished with côtes de Genève; 55-hour power reserve **Functions:** hours, minutes, subsidiary seconds; additional 24-hour display (2nd time zone); chronograph
Case: titanium, ø 43 mm, height 6.9 mm; sapphire crystal; transparent case back; screw-in crown; water-resistant to 3 atm
Band: titanium, folding clasp
Remarks: ceramic-dial; currently the thinnest GMT chronograph movement with automatic winding
Price: $17,600

Octo Finissimo Minute Repeater

Reference number: 103015
Movement: hand-wound, Bulgari Caliber BVL 362;
ø 28.5 mm, height 3.12 mm; 21,600 vph;
42-hour power reserve
Functions: hours, minutes, subsidiary seconds;
minute repeater
Case: titanium, ø 40 mm, height 6.85 mm; sapphire
crystal; transparent case back; water-resistant to 3 atm
Band: titanium, double folding clasp
Price: on request; limited to 50 pieces

Octo Finissimo Perpetual Calendar

Reference number: 103788
Movement: automatic, Bulgari Caliber BVL 305;
ø 36 mm, height 2.75 mm; 30 jewels; 21,600 vph;
hubless peripheral rotor with platinum oscillating
mass; 60-hour power reserve
Functions: hours, minutes; perpetual calendar with
date (retrograde), weekday, month, leap year display
(retrograde)
Case: titanium, ø 40 mm, height 5.8 mm;
sapphire crystal; water-resistant to 3 atm
Band: titanium, folding clasp
Remarks: currently thinnest perpetual calendar
Price: $89,000
Variations: in platinum ($102,000)

Octo Finissimo Tourbillon Chronograph

Reference number: 103295
Movement: automatic, Bulgari Caliber BVL
388 Finissimo; height 3.5 mm; 21,600 vph; one-minute
tourbillon, single pusher for the chronograph functions,
hubless peripheral rotor with platinum oscillating
mass; 52-hour power reserve
Functions: hours, minutes, subsidiary seconds;
chronograph
Case: titanium, ø 43 mm, height 7.4 mm; sapphire
crystal; transparent case back; water-resistant to 3 atm
Band: titanium, folding clasp
Price: $170,000; limited to 50 pieces

Octo Finissimo Automatic

Reference number: 102713
Movement: automatic, Bulgari Caliber BVL
138 Finissimo; ø 36 mm, height 2.23 mm; 23 jewels;
21,600 vph; platinum micro-rotor; finely finished with
côtes de Genève; 60-hour power reserve
Functions: hours, minutes, subsidiary seconds
Case: titanium, ø 40 mm, height 6.9 mm; sapphire
crystal; transparent case back; screw-in crown;
water-resistant to 3 atm
Band: titanium, folding clasp
Price: $15,900

Octo Finissimo Chronograph GMT Titanium

Reference number: 103068
Movement: automatic, Bulgari Caliber BVL
318 Finissimo; ø 36 mm, height 3.3 mm; 37 jewels;
28,800 vph; hubless peripheral rotor with platinum
oscillating mass; column-wheel control of the
chronograph functions; finely finished with côtes de
Genève; 55-hour power reserve
Functions: hours, minutes, subsidiary seconds;
additional 24-hour display (2nd time zone); chronograph
Case: titanium, ø 42 mm, height 6.9 mm; sapphire
crystal; transparent case back; screw-in crown;
water-resistant to 3 atm
Band: titanium, folding clasp
Remarks: ceramic-dial; currently the thinnest GMT
chronograph movement with automatic winding
Price: $18,600

Octo Finissimo Tourbillon Automatic Carbon

Reference number: 103072
Movement: automatic, Bulgari Caliber BVL 288; ø 36 mm,
height 1.95 mm; 24 jewels; 21,600 vph; flying tourbillon;
hubless peripheral rotor; 52-hour power reserve
Functions: hours, minutes
Case: carbon, ø 42 mm, height 3.95 mm; sapphire
crystal; transparent case back; water-resistant to 3 atm
Band: carbon, double folding clasp
Remarks: currently the thinnest automatic watch
with a tourbillon
Price: $160,000

Bulgari Aluminum Chronograph

Reference number: 103383
Movement: automatic, ETA Caliber 2894;
ø 28.6 mm, height 6.1 mm; 37 jewels; 28,800 vph;
42-hour power reserve
Functions: hours, minutes, subsidiary seconds;
chronograph; date
Case: aluminum, ø 40 mm; titanium bezel with rubber
layer; sapphire crystal; water-resistant to 10 atm
Band: rubber, pin buckle
Price: $4,750

Bulgari Aluminum

Reference number: 103445
Movement: automatic, ETA Caliber 2892-A2;
ø 25.6 mm, height 3.6 mm; 21 jewels; 28,800 vph;
42-hour power reserve
Functions: hours, minutes, sweep seconds; date
Case: aluminum, ø 40 mm; titanium bezel with rubber
layer; sapphire crystal; water-resistant to 10 atm
Band: rubber, pin buckle
Price: $3,100

Bulgari Aluminum

Reference number: 103382
Movement: automatic, ETA Caliber 2892-A2;
ø 25.6 mm, height 3.6 mm; 21 jewels; 28,800 vph;
42-hour power reserve
Functions: hours, minutes, sweep seconds; date
Case: aluminum, ø 40 mm; titanium bezel with rubber
layer; sapphire crystal; water-resistant to 10 atm
Band: rubber, pin buckle
Price: $3,100
Variations: with black dial

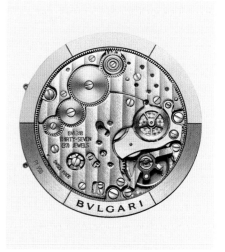

Caliber BVL 191

Automatic; central rotor with ceramic ball bearings;
single spring barrel, 42-hour power reserve
Functions: hours, minutes, sweep seconds; date
Diameter: 25.6 mm
Height: 3.8 mm
Jewels: 26
Balance: glucydur
Frequency: 28,800 vph
Hairspring: flat hairspring with fine adjustment
Shock protection: Incabloc
Remarks: perlage on mainplate and bridges,
polished steel parts and screw heads

Caliber BVL 138 "Finissimo"

Automatic; flying platinum micro-rotor; single spring
barrel, flying, 60-hour power reserve
Functions: hours, minutes, subsidiary seconds; date
Diameter: 36 mm
Height: 2.23 mm
Jewels: 23
Balance: glucydur
Frequency: 21,600 vph
Hairspring: flat hairspring with fine adjustment
Shock protection: Incabloc
Remarks: finely finished with côtes de Genève

Caliber BVL 318 "Finissimo"

Automatic; hubless peripheral rotor with platinum
oscillating mass; column-wheel control of the
chronograph functions; single flying spring barrel,
60-hour power reserve
Functions: hours, minutes, subsidiary seconds;
additional 24-hour display (2nd time zone); chronograph
Diameter: 36 mm
Height: 3.3 mm
Jewels: 37
Balance: glucydur
Frequency: 21,600 vph
Hairspring: flat hairspring with fine adjustment
Shock protection: Incabloc
Remarks: finely finished with côtes de Genève; currently
the thinnest automatic chronograph movement

CARL F. BUCHERER

While luxury watch brand Carl F. Bucherer is still rather young, the Lucerne-based Bucherer jewelry dynasty behind it draws its vast know-how from well over a century of experience in the conception and design of fine wristwatches, and over 130 years of experience in the sale of watches. Today, Carl F. Bucherer has worldwide presence. Though the retail side was bought up by Rolex in August 2023, it is one of the few independent Swiss watch *manufactures* that is still in the hands of the founding family. It is led these days by Jörg G. Bucherer, the grandson of the founder.

In 2005, Bucherer joined its Sainte-Croix-headquartered partner, Techniques Horlogères Appliquées SA (THA), to manufacture its own movement. THA was integrated into the Bucherer Group and the watch company renamed Carl F. Bucherer Technologies SA (CFBT).

The Swiss company also expanded its Lengnau location to create a competence center that can focus on manufacturing its own movements as well as in-house modern timepieces that combine unique design with the highest precision and outstanding functionality. Carl F. Bucherer is committed to technical innovation and found a strong niche in the field of peripheral technology (hubless gears with bearing and drive on the edge of the wheels). The company has proudly patented a peripheral winding mechanism as well as a "floating tourbillon" in a peripherally mounted cage. It even succeeded in building a peripherally controlled rate regulator for a minute repeater. With the introduction of the CFB Mastery Lab, a department created specifically for the innovative customization process of a watch, Carl F. Bucherer enables its customers to create unique timepieces.

Bucherer AG
Carl F. Bucherer
Langensandstrasse 27
CH-6002 Lucerne
Switzerland

Tel.:
+41-41-369-7070

E-mail:
info@carl-f-bucherer.com

Website:
www.carl-f-bucherer.com

Founded:
1919; repositioned under the name Carl F. Bucherer in 2001

Number of employees:
approx. 200

Annual production:
approx. 30,000 watches

U.S. distributor:
Carl F. Bucherer North America
1805 South Metro Parkway
Dayton, OH 45459
937-291-4366
info@cfbna.com;
www.carl-f-bucherer.com

Most important collections/price range:
Patravi, Manero, Heritage, Alacria, and Pathos / core price segment $5,000 to $30,000

Manero Tourbillon Double Peripheral Black

Reference number: 00.10920.16.33.01
Movement: automatic, Caliber CFB T3000; ø 36.5 mm, height 4.6 mm; 33 jewels; 21,600 vph; silicon escapement; flying tourbillon with invisible peripheral drive, hubless peripheral rotor with tungsten oscillating mass, hand-engraved bridges in white gold; 65-hour power reserve; COSC-certified chronometer
Functions: hours, minutes, subsidiary seconds (on the tourbillon cage)
Case: carbon with titanium inner case, ø 43.1 mm, height 12.3 mm; sapphire crystal; transparent case back; water-resistant to 3 atm
Band: rubber, folding clasp
Price: $63,400; limited to 30 pieces

Manero Peripheral Perpetual Calendar Black

Reference number: 00.10916.16.33.01
Movement: automatic, Caliber CFB A2055; ø 30.6 mm, height 5.73 mm; 33 jewels; 28,800 vph; hubless peripheral rotor with tungsten oscillating mass; 55-hour power reserve; COSC-certified chronometer
Functions: hours, minutes; perpetual calendar with date, weekday, month, double moon phase and leap year
Case: carbon with titanium inner case, ø 41.6 mm, height 12.49 mm; sapphire crystal; transparent case back; water-resistant to 3 atm
Band: rubber, folding clasp
Remarks: limited to 88 pieces
Price: $36,700

Manero Peripheral BigDate Black

Reference number: 00.10926.16.33.01
Movement: automatic, Caliber CFB A2011; ø 30.6 mm, height 6.3 mm; 33 jewels; 28,800 vph; hubless peripheral rotor with tungsten oscillating mass; 55-hour power reserve; COSC-certified chronometer
Functions: hours, minutes, subsidiary seconds; power-reserve indicator; large date and weekday
Case: carbon with titanium inner case, ø 41.6 mm, height 12.82 mm; sapphire crystal; transparent case back; water-resistant to 3 atm
Band: rubber, pin buckle with DLC
Remarks: limited to 188 pieces
Price: $22,900

Manero Flyback Black

Reference number: 00.10919.12.33.01
Movement: automatic, Caliber CFB 1970;
ø 30.4 mm, height 7.9 mm; 25 jewels; 28,800 vph;
42-hour power reserve
Functions: hours, minutes, subsidiary seconds;
flyback chronograph; date
Case: stainless steel with black DLC, ø 43 mm,
height 14.45 mm; sapphire crystal; transparent case
back; water-resistant to 3 atm
Band: rubber, folding clasp
Price: $8,100

Heritage BiCompax Annual Black

Reference number: 00.10803.12.32.01
Movement: automatic, Caliber CFB 1972;
ø 30 mm, height 7.3 mm; 47 jewels; 28,800 vph;
42-hour power reserve
Functions: hours, minutes, subsidiary seconds;
chronograph; annual calendar with large date, month
Case: stainless steel with black DLC, ø 41 mm, height
14.15 mm; sapphire crystal; transparent case back;
water-resistant to 3 atm
Band: rubber, folding clasp
Price: $8,800

Manero Tourbillon Double Peripheral Paradise

Reference number: 00.10928.03.39.11
Movement: automatic, Caliber CFB T3000;
ø 36.5 mm, height 4.6 mm; 33 jewels; 21,600 vph; silicon
escapement; flying tourbillon with invisible peripheral
drive, hubless peripheral rotor with tungsten oscillating
mass, hand-engraved bridges in white gold; 65-hour
power reserve; COSC-certified chronometer
Functions: hours, minutes, subsidiary seconds
(on the tourbillon cage)
Case: rose gold, ø 43.1 mm, height 11.57 mm; bezel set
with 40 tsavorites, sapphires, and rubies; sapphire
crystal; transparent case back; water-resistant to 3 atm
Band: rubber, folding clasp
Price: $158,000; limited to 18 pieces

Manero Peripheral

Reference number: 00.10924.08.13.01
Movement: automatic, Caliber CFB A2050; ø 30.6 mm,
height 5.3 mm; 33 jewels; 28,800 vph; hubless
peripheral rotor with tungsten oscillating mass;
55-hour power reserve; COSC-certified chronometer
Functions: hours, minutes, subsidiary seconds; date
Case: stainless steel, ø 40.6 mm, height 11.2 mm;
sapphire crystal; transparent case back;
water-resistant to 3 atm
Band: rubber, folding clasp
Price: $7,900
Variations: various colors

Patravi ScubaTec Verde

Reference number: 00.10632.23.93.01
Movement: automatic, Caliber CFB 1950.1;
ø 26.2 mm, height 4.6 mm; 25 jewels; 28,800 vph;
38-hour power reserve; COSC-certified chronometer
Functions: hours, minutes, sweep seconds; date
Case: stainless steel, ø 44.6 mm, height 13.45 mm;
unidirectional bezel with stainless steel with ceramic
insert, with 0-60 scale; sapphire crystal; screw-in
crown, helium valve; water-resistant to 50 atm
Band: rubber with recycled textile overlay, folding
clasp, with extension link
Price: $7,200

Manero Flyback chronograph

Reference number: 00.10927.08.13.22
Movement: automatic, Caliber CFB 1973;
ø 30.4 mm, height 7.9 mm; 29 jewels; 28,800 vph;
56-hour power reserve
Functions: hours, minutes, subsidiary seconds;
flyback chronograph; date
Case: stainless steel, ø 40 mm, height 14.45 mm;
sapphire crystal; transparent case back;
water-resistant to 3 atm
Band: stainless steel, folding clasp
Price: $7,700

CARL SUCHY & SÖHNE

Carl Suchy & Söhne
Prinz-Eugen-Strasse 48/Top 3
A-1010 Wien
Austria

Tel.:
+43-660-75-24-331

E-mail:
office@carlsuchy.com

Website:
www.carlsuchy.com

Founded:
1822/2017

Distribution:
Retail

Most important collection:
Waltz No1, Waltz No1 Skeleton, Belvedere

Reviving an old and venerable brand of anything can be a risky enterprise. Carl Suchy & Söhne, founded in 1822, was a clock and pocket-watch maker with a presence in Vienna and Prague and workshops in La Chaux-de-Fonds. The products were the ultimate in fashion at the time, made in the somewhat restrained, bourgeois Biedermeier style, which found favor well beyond Vienna's borders.

In 2016, a Viennese businessman with experience in "curating art" decided it was time for Vienna to have a watch brand again. The new Carl Suchy, however, would be an ode to this city, which was at the center of a huge empire.

The story begins with a modern timepiece reflecting the streamlined aesthetic concepts of architect Alfred Loos, whose main idea was encapsulated in a 1910 essay entitled "Ornament and Crime," in which he formulated his basic tenet: "Cultural evolution is equivalent to the removal of ornament from articles in daily use."

The Waltz N°1 was designed in a dialogue between CEO Robert Punkenhofer and a young graduate from the ECAL in Lausanne, Miloš Ristin, with the final product supervised by Swiss watchmaker Marc Jenni. A calm, thin model, it features a simple geometrical pattern with perpendicular guilloché on one half and a vertical guilloché on the other. At 6 o'clock, a small seconds disk turns, breaking up the pattern, but "clicking in place" twice each minute, sort of like a waltzing couple. The model was skeletonized for the second version, giving the dial face a peculiar look, as if the movement, a Vaucher 5401/180, was covered by a shutter.

In the meantime, the brand has come up with three distinct styles: Day, Night, and Danube, meaning white, black, and blue dials.

After devoting time and energy to a table clock, Carl Suchy & Söhne released a second collection, the Belvedere, a homage to the eponymous palace in Vienna, which appears as an engraving on the rotor. The watch—running on a Dubois Dépraz—is more the Waltz: the hands are richer like spires with a porthole attic window. They point to indices that are clearly inspired by the great arched entrance of Belvedere Palace.

Waltz N°1 Gold Dial

Reference number: W1.03.004
Movement: automatic, Vaucher Caliber VMF 5401; ø 30 mm, height 2.6 mm; 29 jewels; 21,600 vph; micro-rotor; finely finished movement with côtes de Genève; 42-hour power reserve
Functions: hours, minutes, subsidiary seconds (on a revolving disk)
Case: yellow gold, ø 41.5 mm, height 9.3 mm; sapphire crystal; transparent case back; crown with ceramic insert; water-resistant to 3 atm
Band: leather, buckle
Remarks: openings along the dial's guilloché lines; engraved serial number
Price: $23,400; limited to 5 pieces
Variations: with reptile skin strap

Belvedere Danube

Reference number: B.01.003
Movement: automatic, Caliber CSS201 (modified Dubois Dépraz DD90000); ø 32 mm, height 5.20 mm; 21 jewels; 28,800 vph; micro-rotor; finely finished movement; 42-hour power reserve
Functions: hours, minutes, sweep seconds; revolving date window
Case: stainless steel, ø 40.8 mm, height 12.2 mm; sapphire crystal; transparent case back; crown with black lacquer; water-resistant to 10 atm
Band: rubber, double folding clasp
Remarks: dial with horizontal and vertical guilloché pattern
Price: $8,200
Variations: with white (Day) or black (Night) dial

Waltz N°1 Black Dial

Reference number: W1.02.002
Movement: automatic, Vaucher Caliber VMF 5401/180; ø 30 mm, height 2.6 mm; 29 jewels; 21,600 vph; micro-rotor; 42-hour power reserve
Functions: hours, minutes, subsidiary seconds (on a revolving disk)
Case: stainless steel with black DLC, ø 41.5 mm, height 9.3 mm; sapphire crystal; transparent case back; crown with ceramic insert; water-resistant to 3 atm
Band: leather, double folding clasp
Remarks: dial with horizontal and vertical guilloché pattern with black PVD
Price: $13,000
Variations: blue or white dials

Cartier
1201 Genève
Switzerland

E-mail:
contact.na@cartier.com

Website:
https://www.cartier.com

Founded:
1847

Number of employees:
approx. 1,300 (watch manufacturing)

U.S. distributor:
Cartier North America
645 Fifth Avenue
New York, NY 10022
1-800-CARTIER
www.cartier.us

Most important collections:
Santos de Cartier, Panthère de Cartier, Baignoire,
Tank, Ballon Bleu de Cartier, Drive de Cartier,
Calibre de Cartier, Clé de Cartier, Ronde de Cartier,
Pasha de Cartier, Mystérieuse

CARTIER

Since the Richemont Group's founding, Cartier has played an important role in the lux-Cartier, founded as a maker of jewels in 1847, is today one of the main drivers of the Richemont Group, which it joined in 2012. It took a while for the company to find its footing and convince the market of its seriousness and potential in the watch industry. It was thanks to Carole Forestier-Kasapi—now at TAG Heuer—head of the watchmaking division that Cartier really made a splash and verticalized its production. It produced a host of outstanding calibers, beginning with the 1904 MC, a reference to the year in which Louis Cartier developed the first wristwatch made for men—a pilot's watch custom designed for his friend and early pioneer of aviation, Alberto Santos-Dumont. The automatic movement is powered by twin barrels and is available for chronographs or diver's watches. It is also now just one of a family of outstanding calibers that continue to push Cartier to the top rung of *haute horlogerie*.

In a period that values vintage, the Cartier brand has an advantage. More than a century of watchmaking has provided it with a steady stream of models to revive and modernize. The Pasha, Santos, Tank, Rotonde, Drive, and Calibre de Cartier are among the best-known and most successful watches in the world. And there is the series of "mystérieuse" watches, which in fine watchmaking stands for the invisible drive of an indicator or function.

Skeletonization has been on the menu recently, which is not surprising, since Cartier pushed the trend in 2009 already with the Santos. They released a new version of the Santos-Dumont with a newly developed movement that provides some animation on the dial: the micro-rotor of the automatic caliber 9629 MC bears a miniature of the Demoiselle (damselfly) airplanes designed by pilot Alberto Santos-Dumont, for whom Cartier once developed the watch.

Another skeletonized novelty appears in the Cartier Privé collection, which includes limited reissues of classics and the new Tank Normale. The highlight of these new versions is a model with skeletonized movement and 24-hour display. This turns reading habits upside down, as the hour hand circles the dial only once in 24 hours. The night hours are read in the lower, darker part of the dial, the day hours on the upper half, whose skeletonized bridges radiate like the sun's rays.

Tank Américaine

Reference number: WGTA0134
Movement: automatic, Cartier Caliber 1899 MC;
9 x 9 mm, height 3.63 mm; 24 jewels; 28,800 vph;
40-hour power reserve
Functions: hours, minutes
Case: rose gold, 24.4 x 44.4 mm, height 8.6 mm;
sapphire crystal; crown with sapphire cabochon;
water-resistant to 3 atm
Band: reptile skin, folding clasp
Price: $16,800
Variations: in stainless steel

Tank Louis Cartier

Reference number: WGTA0190
Movement: hand-wound, Cartier Caliber 1917 MC;
12.9 x 16.4 mm, height 2.9 mm; 19 jewels; 21,600 vph;
38-hour power reserve
Functions: hours, minutes
Case: yellow gold, 25.5 x 33.7 mm, height 6.6 mm;
mineral glass; crown with sapphire cabochon;
water-resistant to 3 atm
Band: reptile skin, pin buckle
Price: $13,000

Tank Louis Cartier

Reference number: WGTA0191
Movement: hand-wound, Cartier Caliber 1917 MC;
dimensions 12.9 x 16.4 mm, height 2.9 mm; 19 jewels;
21,600 vph; 38-hour power reserve
Functions: hours, minutes
Case: yellow gold, 25.5 x 33.7 mm, height 6.6 mm;
mineral glass; crown with sapphire cabochon;
water-resistant to 3 atm
Band: reptile skin, pin buckle
Price: $13,000

Cartier Privé Tank Normale

Reference number: WGHA0021
Movement: hand-wound, Cartier Caliber 9628 MC;
22.38 x 22.38 mm, height 3.9 mm; 23 jewels; 21,600 vph;
skeletonized movement with integrated decorative
elements and indices; 36-hour power reserve
Functions: 24-hour display, minutes
Case: yellow gold, 27.8 x 35.2 mm, height 8,15 mm;
sapphire crystal; transparent case back;
crown with sapphire cabochon
Band: reptile skin, pin buckle
Remarks: limited to 50 pieces
Price: $13,000

Cartier Privé Tank Normale

Reference number: WGTA0111
Movement: hand-wound, Cartier Caliber 070;
ø 15.29 mm, height 2.15 mm; 21 jewels; 25,200 vph;
38-hour power reserve
Functions: hours, minutes
Case: platinum, 27.7 x 32.6 mm, height 6.85 mm;
sapphire crystal; crown with ruby cabochon
Band: platinum, folding clasp
Remarks: limited to 100 pieces
Price: $13,000
Variations: in yellow gold

Tank Américaine

Reference number: WSTA0083
Movement: quartz
Functions: hours, minutes
Case: stainless steel, 19.4 x 35.4 mm, height 6.8 mm;
sapphire crystal; crown with spinel cabochon;
water-resistant to 3 atm
Band: reptile skin, pin buckle
Price: $3,950
Variations: in rose gold; in rose gold set with diamonds

Santos de Cartier

Reference number: WSSA0062
Movement: automatic, Cartier Caliber 1847 MC;
ø 25.6 mm, height 3.77 mm; 23 jewels; 28,800 vph;
40-hour power reserve
Functions: hours, minutes, sweep seconds; date
Case: stainless steel, 39.8 x 47.5 mm, height 9.38 mm;
sapphire crystal; crown with spinel cabochon;
water-resistant to 10 atm
Band: stainless steel, double folding clasp
Remarks: comes with additional reptile skin band with
QuickSwitch rapid changing system
Price: $7,750

Santos de Cartier

Reference number: WSSA0063
Movement: automatic, Cartier Caliber 1847 MC;
ø 25.6 mm, height 3.77 mm; 23 jewels; 28,800 vph;
40-hour power reserve
Functions: hours, minutes, sweep seconds
Case: stainless steel, 35.1 x 41.9 mm, height 8.83 mm;
sapphire crystal; crown with spinel cabochon;
water-resistant to 10 atm
Band: stainless steel, double folding clasp
Remarks: comes with additional reptile skin band with
QuickSwitch rapid changing system
Price: $7,050

Santos Dumont

Reference number: W2SA0028
Movement: quartz
Functions: hours, minutes
Case: stainless steel, 31.4 x 43.5 mm, height 7.3 mm;
bezel in yellow gold; sapphire crystal;
crown with spinel cabochon
Band: reptile skin, pin buckle
Price: $6,050

Santos Dumont

Reference number: WGSA0077
Movement: quartz
Functions: hours, minutes
Case: yellow gold, 32 x 41 mm, height 7.3 mm;
bezel in yellow gold; sapphire crystal;
crown with spinel cabochon
Band: reptile skin, pin buckle
Price: $13,000

Santos Dumont

Reference number: WGSA0082
Movement: hand-wound, Cartier Caliber 430 MC;
ø 20.55 mm, height 2.1 mm; 18 jewels; 21,600 vph;
38-hour power reserve
Functions: hours, minutes
Case: platinum, 33.9 x 46.6 mm, height 7.5 mm;
sapphire crystal; crown with ruby cabochon;
water-resistant to 3 atm
Band: reptile skin, pin buckle
Price: $11,200; limited to 200 pieces
Variations: in yellow gold; in rose gold ($16,800)

Santos Dumont

Reference number: WGSA0083
Movement: hand-wound, Cartier Caliber 430 MC;
ø 20,55 mm, height 2,1 mm; 18 jewels; 21,600 vph;
38-hour power reserve
Functions: hours, minutes
Case: rose gold, 33.9 x 46.6 mm, height 7.5 mm;
sapphire crystal; crown with jade cabochon;
water-resistant to 3 atm
Band: reptile skin, pin buckle
Price: $16,800; limited to 200 pieces
Variations: in yellow gold; in platinum ($11,200)

Santos Dumont Micro-Rotor

Reference number: WHSA0031
Movement: automatic, Cartier Caliber 9629 MC;
dimensions 23.2 x 23.2 mm, height 4.4 mm; 33 jewels;
25,200 vph; skeletonized movement with integrated
decorative elements, bridges with blue lacquer,
off-center micro-rotor; 44-hour power reserve
Functions: hours, minutes
Case: yellow gold with blue lacquer, 31.4 x 43.5 mm,
height 8 mm; sapphire crystal; transparent case back;
crown with sapphire cabochon; water-resistant to 3 atm
Band: reptile skin, pin buckle
Remarks: limited to 150 pieces
Price: $40,450

Santos Dumont Micro-Rotor

Reference number: WHSA0030
Movement: automatic, Cartier Caliber 9629 MC;
dimensions 23.2 x 23.2 mm, height 4.4 mm; 33 jewels;
25,200 vph; skeletonized movement with integrated
decorative elements, bridges with red lacquer,
off-center micro-rotor; 44-hour power reserve
Functions: hours, minutes
Case: rose gold, 31.4 x 43.5 mm, height 8 mm;
sapphire crystal; transparent case back; crown with
sapphire cabochon; water-resistant to 3 atm
Band: reptile skin, pin buckle
Price: $39,250

Santos Dumont Micro-Rotor

Reference number: WHSA0032
Movement: automatic, Cartier Caliber 9629 MC;
dimensions 23.2 x 23.2 mm, height 4.4 mm; 33 jewels;
25,200 vph; skeletonized movement with integrated
decorative elements, bridges with blue lacquer,
off-center micro-rotor; 44-hour power reserve
Functions: hours, minutes
Case: stainless steel, 31.4 x 43.5 mm, height 8 mm;
sapphire crystal; transparent case back; crown with
sapphire cabochon; water-resistant to 3 atm
Band: reptile skin, pin buckle
Price: $30,100

CHANEL

After putting the occasional jewelry watch onto the market earlier, family-owned Chanel opened its own horology division in 1987, a move that gave the brand instant access to the world of watchmaking art. While the brand's first collections were directed exclusively at its female clientele, it was actually with the rather simple and masculine J12 that Chanel finally achieved a breakthrough. That was in 1999, over twenty years ago. The designer was Jacques Helleu. The J12 collection showpiece, the Rétrograde Mystérieuse, was a stroke of genius—courtesy of the innovative think tank Renaud et Papi. Its sleek ceramic case and complex mechanics instantly propelled Chanel into the world of *haute horlogerie*.

It was designer Arnaud Chastaingt who reimagined the iconic J12. It still comes in brilliant ceramic. As part of a rejuvenation move, a new movement was added, built by Kenissi, a joint venture Chanel shares with Tudor and Breitling. It no longer has a silicon hairspring and has returned to the soft iron cage for protection from magnetic fields.

In the past few years, the brand turned its attention to a younger, dynamic crowd with models like the prize-winning "Vendôme" rectangular Boy·Friend with diamonds, a watch that would fit any wrist on the male-female spectrum.

In 2023, Chanel's communication spoke a lot of a so-called "Capsule Collection." Its thematic focus is called "Interstellar" and offers space for a slew of special wristwatch models from the J12, Première, Boy·Friend, and Code Coco collections. While most of the watches catch the eye with an overabundance of precious stones, the models of the J12 Interstellar subtly seduce with charming variations on the black-and-white theme that is virtually inherent in the sports watch, available in both white and black ceramic. Above all, the technically perfect implementation of the contrasting blocks arranged in blocks, stripes, or square pixels attracted a great deal of attention in the industry.

Chanel
135, avenue Charles de Gaulle
F-92521 Neuilly-sur-Seine Cedex
France

Tel.:
+33-1-41-92-08-33

Website:
www.chanel.com

Founded:
1914

Distribution:
retail and 200 Chanel boutiques worldwide

U.S. distributor:
Chanel Fine Jewelry and Watches
600 Madison Avenue, 19th Floor
New York, NY 10022
212-715-4741
www.chanel.com

Most important collections:
J12, Première, Boy.Friend, Monsieur de Chanel

J12 Diamond Tourbillon

Reference number: H7951
Movement: hand-wound, Chanel Caliber 5; ø 28.4 mm, height 6.25 mm; 29 jewels; 28,800 vph; flying tourbillon with diamond; 42-hour power reserve
Functions: hours and minutes (off-center)
Case: ceramic, ø 38 mm; bezel in white gold, with 34 baguette diamonds; sapphire crystal; transparent case back; crown with diamond; water-resistant to 5 atm
Band: ceramic, triple folding clasp (in white gold)
Remarks: skeletonized dial and hands set with 49 diamonds
Price: $194,040; limited to 55 pieces

J12 Cybernetic

Reference number: H7988
Movement: automatic, Chanel Caliber 12.1; ø 26 mm, height 4.99 mm; 26 jewels; 28,800 vph; winding rotor with tungsten oscillating mass; 70-hour power reserve; COSC-certified chronometer
Functions: hours, minutes, sweep seconds
Case: ceramic and stainless steel, ø 38 mm, height 12.6 mm; bezel in stainless steel with ceramic insert, with 0-60 scale; sapphire crystal; transparent case back; screw-in crown, in stainless steel, with ceramic cabochon; water-resistant to 5 atm
Band: ceramic, triple folding clasp (in stainless steel)
Price: $13,900; limited edition

Monsieur Tourbillon Meteorite

Reference number: H7956
Movement: hand-wound, Chanel Caliber 5.1; ø 28.4 mm, height 5.9 mm; 28 jewels; 28,800 vph; flying tourbillon; 72-hour power reserve
Functions: hours and minutes (off-center), subsidiary seconds (on the tourbillon cage)
Case: ceramic, ø 42 mm, height 10.85 mm; bezel in stainless steel; sapphire crystal; transparent case back; stainless-steel crown; water-resistant to 3 atm
Band: nylon with calfskin trim, triple folding clasp
Remarks: meteorite dial
Price: $128,000; limited to 55 pieces

Chopard & Cie. SA
8, rue de Veyrot
CH-1217 Meyrin (Geneva)
Switzerland

Tel.:
+41-22-719-3131

E-mail:
info@chopard.ch

Website:
www.chopard.ch

Founded:
1860

Distribution:
149 boutiques

U.S. distributor:
Chopard USA
75 Valencia Ave, Suite 1200
Coral Gables, FL 33134
1-800-CHOPARD
www.chopard.com/en-us

Most important collections/price range:
L.U.C / from $8,110; Happy Sport / from $4,420;
Imperiale / from $5,780; Classic Racing / from
$5,910; Alpine Eagle / from $9,810

CHOPARD

The Chopard *manufacture* was founded by Louis-Ulysse Chopard in 1860 in the tiny village of Sonvillier in the Jura mountains of Switzerland. In 1963, it was purchased by Karl Scheufele, a goldsmith from Pforzheim, Germany, and revived as a producer of fine watches and jewelry.

The past seventeen years have seen a breathtaking development, when Karl Scheufele's son, Karl-Friedrich, and his sister, Caroline, decided to create watches with in-house movements, thus restoring the old business launched by Louis-Ulysse back in the nineteenth century.

In 1996, out of nowhere, Chopard opened up its watchmaking *manufacture* in the sleepy town of Fleurier in the Val-de-Travers, which had not yet experienced the revival of the mechanical watch. Focus on vertical integration drove the opening of a second building, Fleurier Ebauches SA, a hub of caliber kits, including the L.U.C series. Chopard now has a line-up of eleven calibers, ranging from simple three-hander automatics to a tourbillon; a perpetual calendar; chronographs; an ultra-high-frequency chronometer; and a minute repeater, now with sapphire gongs that produce a very clear sound.

The sporty star of the collection is the Alpine Eagle and is unmistakably inspired by the Chopard classic of the 1980s, the St. Moritz. In keeping with the times, the new model has been modernized and upgraded in terms of its features and inner workings. In 2023, Chopard presented the 41 XPS, a new version with small seconds and a particularly thin movement; the L.U.C 96.40-L caliber measures just 3.3 millimeters. The Alpine Eagle collection uses the Chopard-exclusive "Lucent" steel alloy with a bright shimmer and the so-called Monte Rosa Pink dial, which was inspired by the eye of an eagle.

Mille Miglia Classic Chronograph

Reference number: 168619-3001
Movement: automatic, ETA Caliber A32.211;
ø 28.6 mm, height 6.1 mm; 37 jewels; 28,800 vph;
54-hour power reserve; COSC-certified chronometer
Functions: hours, minutes, subsidiary seconds;
chronograph; date
Case: stainless steel, ø 40.5 mm, height 12.9 mm;
sapphire crystal; transparent case back;
screw-in crown; water-resistant to 5 atm
Band: rubber, pin buckle
Price: $9,000

Mille Miglia Classic Chronograph

Reference number: 168619-3003
Movement: automatic, ETA Caliber A32.211;
ø 28.6 mm, height 6.1 mm; 37 jewels; 28,800 vph;
54-hour power reserve; COSC-certified chronometer
Functions: hours, minutes, subsidiary seconds;
chronograph; date
Case: stainless steel, ø 40.5 mm, height 12.9 mm;
sapphire crystal; transparent case back;
screw-in crown; water-resistant to 5 atm
Band: calfskin, pin buckle
Price: $9,210

Alpine Eagle Flying Tourbillon

Reference number: 298616-3001
Movement: automatic, L.U.C Caliber 96.24-L; ø 27.4 mm,
height 3.3 mm; 25 jewels; 25,200 vph; flying tourbillon,
2 spring barrels, micro-rotor; 65-hour power reserve;
Geneva Seal, COSC-certified chronometer
Functions: hours, minutes, subsidiary seconds
(on the tourbillon cage)
Case: stainless steel, ø 41 mm, height 8.03 mm;
bezel mounted to case with 8 screws; sapphire crystal;
transparent case back; water-resistant to 10 atm
Band: stainless steel, folding clasp
Price: on request

Alpine Eagle Large

Reference number: 298600-3002
Movement: automatic, Chopard Caliber 01.01-C;
ø 28.8 mm, height 4.95 mm; 31 jewels; 28,800 vph;
60-hour power reserve; COSC-certified chronometer
Functions: hours, minutes, sweep seconds; date
Case: stainless steel, ø 41 mm, height 9.7 mm; bezel
mounted to case with 8 screws; sapphire crystal;
transparent case back; water-resistant to 10 atm
Band: stainless steel, folding clasp
Price: $14,400
Variations: with rose-gold bezel ($22,600);
various dial colors

Alpine Eagle Large

Reference number: 298600-6001
Movement: automatic, Chopard Caliber 01.01-C;
ø 28.8 mm, height 4.95 mm; 31 jewels; 28,800 vph;
60-hour power reserve; COSC-certified chronometer
Functions: hours, minutes, sweep seconds; date
Case: stainless steel, ø 41 mm, height 9.7 mm; bezel
mounted to case with 8 screws; sapphire crystal;
transparent case back; crown in rose gold;
water-resistant to 10 atm
Band: stainless steel with rose gold elements,
folding clasp
Price: $22,600
Variations: various cases

Alpine Eagle 41 XPS

Reference number: 298623-3001
Movement: automatic, L.U.C Caliber 96.40-L;
ø 27.4 mm, height 3.3 mm; 29 jewels; 28,800 vph;
2 spring barrels, hairspring with Phillips end curve,
gold oscillating mass; 65-hour power reserve;
Geneva Seal, COSC-certified chronometer
Functions: hours, minutes, subsidiary seconds
Case: stainless steel, ø 41 mm, height 8.03 mm;
sapphire crystal; transparent case back;
screw-in crown; water-resistant to 10 atm
Band: stainless steel, folding clasp
Remarks: the shimmering "Lucent steel" is an alloy
using recycled steel
Price: $22,900

Alpine Eagle XL Chrono

Reference number: 298609-3001
Movement: automatic, Chopard Caliber 03.05-C;
ø 28.8 mm, height 7.6 mm; 45 jewels; 28,800 vph;
60-hour power reserve; COSC-certified chronometer
Functions: hours, minutes, subsidiary seconds;
flyback chronograph; date
Case: stainless steel, ø 44 mm, height 13.15 mm;
bezel mounted to case with 8 screws; sapphire crystal;
transparent case back; water-resistant to 10 atm
Band: stainless steel, folding clasp
Price: $21,000
Variations: various cases, bands, and dials

Alpine Eagle Frozen

Reference number: 295363-1006
Movement: automatic, Chopard Caliber 01.03-C;
ø 28.8 mm, height 4.95 mm; 27 jewels; 28,800 vph;
60-hour power reserve
Functions: hours, minutes
Case: white gold, ø 41 mm, height 9.7 mm;
bezel set with 36 rainbow sapphires; sapphire crystal;
transparent case back; screw-in crown;
water-resistant to 10 atm
Band: white gold, folding clasp
Remarks: dial set with 236 diamonds
Price: $86,700
Variations: in rose gold ($86,700)

L.U.C Full Strike Tourbillon

Reference number: 161987-5001
Movement: hand-wound, L.U.C Caliber 08.01-L;
ø 37.2 mm, height 7.97 mm; 63 jewels; 28,800 vph;
1-minute tourbillon; sapphire crystal gongs;
60-hour power reserve; Geneva Seal,
COSC-certified chronometer
Functions: hours, minutes, subsidiary seconds
(on the tourbillon cage); power-reserve indicator,
minute repeater
Case: rose gold, ø 42.5 mm, height 12.58 mm;
sapphire crystal; transparent case back
Band: reptile skin, folding clasp
Price: on request; limited to 20 pieces

L.U.C Flying T Twin

Reference number: 161978-5001
Movement: automatic, L.U.C Caliber 96.24-L; ø 27.4 mm, height 3.3 mm; 25 jewels; 25,200 vph; flying 1-minute tourbillon, 2 spring barrels; micro-rotor; 65-hour power reserve; Geneva Seal, COSC-certified chronometer
Functions: hours, minutes, subsidiary seconds (on the tourbillon cage)
Case: rose gold, ø 40 mm, height 7.2 mm; sapphire crystal; transparent case back; water-resistant to 3 atm
Band: reptile skin, pin buckle
Remarks: case manufactured of certified Fair mined gold; hand-guilloché on rose gold dial
Price: on request; limited to 50 pieces

L.U.C Full Strike Sapphire

Reference number: 168604-9001
Movement: hand-wound, L.U.C Caliber 08.01-L; ø 37.2 mm, height 7.97 mm; 63 jewels; 28,800 vph; 1-minute tourbillon; sapphire crystal gongs; 60-hour power reserve; Geneva Seal, COSC-certified chronometer
Functions: hours, minutes, subsidiary seconds; power-reserve indicator, minute repeater
Case: sapphire crystal, ø 42.5 mm, height 11.55 mm; sapphire crystal; transparent case back
Band: reptile skin, folding clasp
Remarks: skeletonized movement
Price: on request; limited to 5 pieces

L.U.C XPS 1860 Officer

Reference number: 161242-0001
Movement: automatic, L.U.C Caliber 96.01-L; ø 27.4 mm, height 3.3 mm; 29 jewels; 28,800 vph; 65-hour power reserve; Geneva Seal, COSC-certified chronometer
Functions: hours, minutes, subsidiary seconds; date
Case: yellow gold, ø 40 mm, height 7.7 mm; sapphire crystal; transparent case back; water-resistant to 3 atm
Band: reptile skin, pin buckle
Remarks: hinged case back
Price: $35,500

L.U.C Perpetual Chrono

Reference number: 168611-3001
Movement: hand-wound, L.U.C Caliber 03.10-L; ø 33 mm, height 8.32 mm; 42 jewels; 28,800 vph; German-silver mainplate and balance cock; 60-hour power reserve; Geneva Seal, COSC-certified chronometer
Functions: hours, minutes, sweep seconds; day/night indication; flyback chronograph; perpetual calendar with large date, weekday, month, moon phase, leap year
Case: titanium, ø 45 mm, height 15.06 mm; sapphire crystal; transparent case back; water-resistant to 3 atm
Band: calfskin, folding clasp
Price: $81,600; limited to 20 pieces

L.U.C Time Traveler One

Reference number: 168574-3008
Movement: automatic, L.U.C Caliber 01.05-L; ø 35.3 mm, height 6.52 mm; 39 jewels; 28,800 vph; 60-hour power reserve; COSC-certified chronometer
Functions: hours, minutes, sweep seconds; world time display (2nd time zone); date
Case: titanium (ceramicized), ø 42 mm, height 12.09 mm; crown-activated inner bezel with reference cities; sapphire crystal; transparent case back; water-resistant to 5 atm
Band: textile, pin buckle
Price: $17,000; limited to 250 pieces

L.U.C Strike One

Reference number: 161949-5001
Movement: automatic, L.U.C Caliber 96.32-L; ø 33 mm, height 5.6 mm; 33 jewels; 28,800 vph; 2 spring barrels, hairspring with Phillips end curve, sapphire crystal gongs, rose gold micro-rotor; 65-hour power reserve; Geneva Seal, COSC-certified chronometer
Functions: hours, minutes, subsidiary seconds, hour chiming
Case: rose gold, ø 40 mm, height 9.86 mm; sapphire crystal; transparent case back
Band: reptile skin, pin buckle
Price: $66,600; limited to 25 pieces

Caliber L.U.C 96.24-L

Automatic; flying tourbillon; gold micro-rotor; double spring barrel, 65-hour power reserve; Geneva Seal, COSC-certified chronometer
Functions: hours, minutes
Diameter: 27.4 mm
Height: 3.3 mm
Jewels: 25
Balance: glucydur
Frequency: 25,200 vph
Hairspring: flat hairspring, Nivarox 1
Remarks: 190 parts

Caliber L.U.C 96.32-L

Automatic; sapphire crystal gongs; rose-gold micro-rotor; double spring barrel, 65-hour power reserve; Geneva Seal, COSC-certified chronometer
Functions: hours, minutes, subsidiary seconds, hour chiming
Diameter: 33 mm
Height: 5.6 mm
Jewels: 33
Frequency: 28,800 vph
Hairspring: hairspring with Phillips end curve
Remarks: 275 parts

Caliber L.U.C 01.01-C

Automatic; single spring barrel, 60-hour power reserve; COSC-certified chronometer
Functions: hours, minutes, sweep seconds; date
Diameter: 28.8 mm
Height: 4.95 mm
Jewels: 31
Balance: glucydur
Frequency: 28,800 vph
Hairspring: flat hairspring, Nivarox 1
Remarks: 207 parts

Caliber L.U.C 03.05-C

Automatic; column-wheel control of chronograph functions, vertical clutch; single spring barrel, 60-hour power reserve; COSC-certified chronometer
Functions: hours, minutes, subsidiary seconds; flyback chronograph; date
Diameter: 28.8 mm
Height: 7.6 mm
Jewels: 45
Balance: glucydur
Frequency: 28,800 vph
Hairspring: flat hairspring
Remarks: slotted movement bridges; skeletonized rose-gold winding rotor

Caliber L.U.C 03.10-L

Hand-wound; single spring barrel, 60-hour power reserve; Geneva Seal, COSC-certified chronometer
Functions: hours, minutes, sweep seconds; day/night indication; flyback chronograph; perpetual calendar with large date, weekday, month, moon phase, leap year
Diameter: 33 mm
Height: 8.32 mm
Jewels: 42
Balance: Variner with four weighted screws
Frequency: 28,800 vph
Hairspring: flat hairspring
Remarks: German silver mainplate and balance cock

Caliber L.U.C 08.01-L

Hand-wound; sapphire crystal gongs for the repeater mechanism; single spring barrel, 60-hour power reserve; Geneva Seal, COSC-certified chronometer
Functions: hours, minutes, subsidiary seconds; power-reserve indicator, minute repeater
Diameter: 37.2 mm
Height: 7.97 mm
Jewels: 63
Frequency: 28,800 vph
Hairspring: hairspring with Phillips end curve
Remarks: German silver mainplate and balance cock; 533 parts

Christophe Claret SA
Route du Soleil d'Or 2
CH-2400 Le Locle
Switzerland

Tel.:
+41-32-933-0000

E-mail:
info@christopheclaret.com

Website:
www.christopheclaret.com

Founded:
manufacture 1989, brand 2009

Number of employees:
70

Distribution:
Contact the *manufacture* directly.

Most important collections:
Traditional complications (Maestro/Mecca/
Allegro/Aventicum/Maestoso/Kantharos/Soprano/
Concertino), Extreme line (X-TREM-1), gaming
watches (Poker/Baccara/Blackjack), and ladies'
complications line (Margot, Layla, Marguerite)
Prices are given in Swiss francs at near parity.

CHRISTOPHE CLARET

Individuals like Christophe Claret eat, drink, and breathe watchmaking and have developed careers based on pushing the envelope to the very edge of what's possible. By the age of twenty-three, the Lyon-born Claret was in Basel, where he was spotted by the late Rolf Schnyder of Ulysse Nardin and commissioned to make a minute repeater with jacquemarts. In 1989, he opened his *manufacture*, a nineteenth-century mansion extended with a state-of-the-art machining area. Indeed, Claret embraces wholeheartedly the potential in modern tools to create the precise pieces needed to give physical expression to exceedingly complex ideas.

Over the years, Claret created complications and movements for many major brands, like Ulysse Nardin and Harry Winston. Twenty years after establishing his business, Claret finally launched his own complex watches: models like the DualTow, turbocharged as the X-TREM-1, are perennial favorites of Claret. It has hours and minutes on two tracks, a minute repeater, and a complete view of the great ballet of cams and levers inside. Then came the Adagio, again a minute repeater, with a clear dial that has room for a second time zone and large date. In 2011, Claret wowed the watch world with a humorous, on-the-wrist gambling machine, telling time and allowing the wearer to play blackjack, craps, or roulette.

The list goes on and on. In the recent Al-Ula, Claret returned to his Aventicum's mechanism to highlight a hologram in the center of the watch; in this case, the center highlights the archeological site of Mada'in Salih in Al-Ula, Saudi Arabia. Even when exhibiting pure engineering art, as with the Maestro, though, Christophe Claret always manages to slip in a special complication, like the "memo," which lets the wearer set a small reminder of some upcoming date, for example. As for the Legend series, it reappears as Monaco: a tourbillon with a minute repeater pealing with Westminster chimes to celebrate a famous wedding in classy Monaco, that of Grace Kelly and Prince Rainier III.

Monaco

Reference number: MTR.NBC98.937
Movement: hand-wound, Christophe Claret Caliber NBC98; ø 37 mm, height 9.03 mm; 36 jewels; 21,600 vph; striking mechanism (gong) with 4 melodies and 4 jaquemart automatons; 1-minute tourbillon with the princely family emblem; 60-hour power reserve
Functions: hours, minutes; minute, quarter and hourly repeater with Westminster chimes (on demand)
Case: titanium, 47 mm, height 15 mm; sapphire crystal; transparent case back; water-resistant to 3 atm
Remarks: hand-painted dial by André Martinez featuring a Monaco Grand Prix in the 60s
Band: reptile skin, folding clasp
Price: CHF 650,000; unique piece
Variation: gold case (CHF 680,000)

Maestro Indian

Reference number: MTR.DMC16.330-337
Movement: hand-wound, Christophe Claret Caliber DMC16; ø 36.25 mm, height 10.50 mm; 33 jewels; 21,600 vph; skeletonized and step-shaped "Charles X" bridges; inverted movement construction with balance on the dial; 2 serial spring barrels;168-hour power reserve
Functions: hours, minutes, manually activated memo display (pusher switches sapphire at 4 o'clock to a ruby or diamond; two stones of same color means the owner has something coming up); large date (double digit) on a cone
Case: titanium, ø 42 mm, height 16.06 mm; sapphire crystal; transparent case back; water-resistant to 3 atm
Band: reptile skin, folding clasp
Price: CHF 72,000; limited to 7 pieces

Al-Ula

Reference number: MTR.AVE15.600-617
Movement: automatic, Christophe Claret Caliber AVE 15; ø 26.2 mm, height 3.37 mm; 28 jewels; 28,800 vph; invisible sapphire crystal rotor with five weights; 72 hours power reserve
Functions: hours (with anticorodal anodized aluminum pointers for lighter weight), minutes
Case: titanium, ø 44 mm, height 18.5 mm; sapphire crystal; transparent case back
Band: reptile skin, folding clasp
Remarks: mirascope optics that make a sculptural, hologram projection of a miniature of the famous archeological site of Mada'in Saleh micro-engraved in the middle of the dial
Price: CHF 69,000; limited to 17 pieces
Variations: in rose gold (CHF 77,000), limited to 17 pieces

CHRONOSWISS

Chronoswiss celebrated its fortieth anniversary in 2023, but the festivities were dampened by the death of the brand's founder, Gerd-Rüdiger Lang. He loved to joke about having "the only Swiss watch factory in Germany," as the brand used Swiss technology with concepts and designs "made in Germany," in Karlsfeld, near Munich, to be precise.

Lang also created regulator watches in the 1980s, a pioneering idea that found many fans of new ways to tell the time. Whether in a rectangular or round case, with a tourbillon or without, the off-center dial became the absolute identity of Chronoswiss watches and remains so to this day.

Chronoswiss has always been a little on the edge of the industry in terms of style and technical developments. It created the enduring *manufacture* caliber C.122—based on an old Enicar automatic movement with a patented rattrapante mechanism—and its Chronoscope chronograph has earned a solid reputation for technical prowess. The Pacific and Sirius models, additions to the classic collection, point the company in a new stylistic direction designed to help win new buyers and the attention of the international market.

In March 2012, a Swiss couple, Oliver and Eva Ebstein, purchased Chronoswiss and moved the company headquarters to Lucerne, Switzerland. They decided to remain faithful to the brand's codes. In-house calibers beat inside, and the design became edgier, with daring skeletonizing feats and bold colors. The new tagline, "Modern Mechanical," suggests the brand's direction.

The fortieth anniversary was still celebrated, with another redesign of the Delphis, with jumping hour and retrograde minute. The dial of the Delphis Oracle is in "curved-hand guilloché" with grand-feu enamel lines curving mellifluously under the hands of the minute and small seconds. The movement that powers this timepiece was developed by La Joux-Perret exclusively.

Chronoswiss AG
Löwenstrasse 16b
CH-6004 Lucerne
Switzerland

Tel.:
+41-41-552-21-80

E-mail:
luzern@chronoswiss.com

Website:
www.chronoswiss.com

Founded:
1983

Number of employees:
approx. 20

Annual production:
About 3,000 wristwatches

U.S. distributor:
Chronoswiss US Service Office
Shami Fine Watchmaking
372 Fairfield Rd
Fairfield, NJ 07004
973-785-0004

Most important collections/price range:
Approx. 30 models including, Space Timer, Flying Regulator, Open Gear ReSec, Lunar Chronograph, Opus Chronograph, SkelTec, Sirius Artist, (no current collection) approx. $5,800 to $47,000

Delphis Oracle
Reference number: CH-1421.1E-BLBK
Movement: automatic, Chronoswiss Caliber C.6004; ø 36.5 mm; 37 jewels; 28,800 vph; finely finished movement; 55-hour power reserve
Functions: hours (off-center, jumping), minutes (retrograde), subsidiary seconds
Case: red gold, ø 42 mm, height 14.5 mm; sapphire crystal; transparent case back; water-resistant to 10 atm
Band: rubber, folding clasp
Remarks: special edition for the 40th anniversary of the Delphis, with a vaulted dial with hand-made guilloché
Price: $39,800

Space Timer Jupiter Gold
Reference number: CH-9341.2-CUBK
Movement: automatic, Chronoswiss Caliber C.308; ø 32.8 mm; 33 jewels; 28,800 vph; hands mechanism (transmission wheel) visible on the dial side; finely finished movement; 42-hour power reserve
Functions: hours (off-center), minutes, sweep seconds; date
Case: red gold, ø 44 mm, height 15.2 mm; sapphire crystal; transparent case back; water-resistant to 10 atm
Band: reptile skin, folding clasp
Price: $28,600; limited to 50 pieces

Open Gear ReSec Aurora
Reference number: CH-6923-TUBK2
Movement: automatic, Chronoswiss Caliber C.301; ø 36.5 mm; 33 jewels; 28,800 vph; hands mechanism (transmission wheel) visible on the dial side; finely finished movement; 42-hour power reserve
Functions: hours (off-center), minutes, subsidiary seconds (retrograde)
Case: stainless steel, ø 44 mm, height 13.35 mm; sapphire crystal; transparent case back; water-resistant to 10 atm
Band: textile, folding clasp
Price: $11,600; limited to 50 pieces

Open Gear ReSec Endorphin

Reference number: CH-6928-PUBK1
Movement: automatic, Chronoswiss Caliber C.301; ø 36.5 mm; 33 jewels; 28,800 vph; hands mechanism (transmission wheel) visible on the dial side; finely finished movement; 42-hour power reserve
Functions: hours (off-center), minutes, subsidiary seconds (retrograde)
Case: stainless steel with violet CVD, ø 44 mm, height 13.35 mm; sapphire crystal; transparent case back; water-resistant to 10 atm
Band: reptile skin, folding clasp
Price: $12,900; limited to 50 pieces
Variations: with textile strap

Open Gear ReSec Blue on Black

Reference number: CH-6925M-EBBK
Movement: automatic, Chronoswiss Caliber C.301; ø 36.5 mm; 33 jewels; 28,800 vph; hands mechanism (transmission wheel) visible on the dial side; finely finished movement; 42-hour power reserve
Functions: hours (off-center), minutes, subsidiary seconds (retrograde)
Case: stainless steel with black DLC, ø 44 mm, height 13.35 mm; sapphire crystal; transparent case back; water-resistant to 10 atm
Band: textile, folding clasp
Price: $12,500; limited to 50 pieces

Open Gear Paraiba

Reference number: CH-8753.1-TUBK4
Movement: automatic, Chronoswiss Caliber C.299; ø 35.2 mm, height 6.11 mm; 31 jewels; 28,800 vph; hands mechanism (transmission wheel) visible on the dial side; finely finished movement; 42-hour power reserve
Functions: hours (off-center), minutes, subsidiary seconds
Case: stainless steel, ø 41 mm, height 13.85 mm; sapphire crystal; transparent case back; water-resistant to 10 atm
Band: textile, folding clasp
Remarks: hand-guilloché on dial
Price: $11,600; limited to 50 pieces

Open Gear Purple Panther

Reference number: CH-8755.1-PUBK
Movement: automatic, Chronoswiss Caliber C.299; ø 35.2 mm; height 6.11 mm; 31 jewels; 28,800 vph; hands mechanism (transmission wheel) visible on the dial side; finely finished movement; 42-hour power reserve
Functions: hours (off-center), minutes, subsidiary seconds
Case: stainless steel with black DLC, ø 41 mm, height 12.7 mm; sapphire crystal; transparent case back; water-resistant to 10 atm
Band: textile, folding clasp
Remarks: hand-guilloché on dial
Price: $11,600; limited to 50 pieces

Opus chronograph

Reference number: CH-7543.1S-SI
Movement: automatic, Chronoswiss Caliber C.741 S (Basis ETA 7750); ø 30 mm, height 7.9 mm; 25 jewels; 28,800 vph; entirely skeletonized movement with decorative, skeletonized rotor; 46-hour power reserve
Functions: hours, minutes, subsidiary seconds; chronograph; date
Case: stainless steel, ø 41 mm, height 14.8 mm; sapphire crystal; transparent case back; water-resistant to 10 atm
Band: reptile skin, folding clasp
Price: $13,600

Lunar chronograph

Reference number: CH-7543L-BL
Movement: automatic, Chronoswiss Caliber C.755 (Basis ETA 7750); ø 30 mm, height 7.9 mm; 25 jewels; 28,800 vph; côtes de Genève, perlage on movement, skeletonized rotor; finely finished movement; 46-hour power reserve
Functions: hours, minutes, subsidiary seconds; chronograph; date, moon phase
Case: stainless steel, ø 41 mm, height 14.8 mm; sapphire crystal; transparent case back; water-resistant to 3 atm
Band: reptile skin, folding clasp
Price: $10,300

CIGA DESIGN

Jianmin Zhang hails from China's northwestern province of Qinghai and is considered one of the country's top industrial designers. He built a reputation for creating guidance systems for large architectural projects, like the Shanghai Expo and the Beijing Olympics. It may sound like it's a long way from designing watches, but showing the way in physical space is not that far from showing the way in time.

In 2016, he founded CIGA Design (apparently from a Chinese word meaning amazing) with a mission to make high-quality, aesthetically eye-catching watches at an affordable price for the young generation. China's very efficient and low-cost production opportunities made this possible: all he needed was good design. And so, CIGA began manufacturing a range of watches, from sleek Bauhaus-inspired one-handers to edgily futuristic and minimalist pieces, like the J Series Zen, to more complex pieces with skeletonized or open-worked dials.

Jianmin Zhang is keenly aware of the new "national trend" (guochao), with consumers seeking Chinese-themed products, though not necessarily made in China. A number of models won awards in Europe, but in 2021, the Blue Planet clinched the Challenge Prize at the Grand Prix d'Horlogerie in Geneva. The watch features a detailed view of Earth from the sky, with engraved silver land masses. The time-telling mechanism is complex, with a static hour ring and a rotating minute ring that coordinate with the little compass on the globe that acts as a single hand. The watch is a general statement for ecology, but there are many Chinese references as well, like the compass, a Chinese invention. The other is the symbiotic duality of Earth and Sky so firmly anchored in Chinese culture and Daoism. This idea appears in other watches, where the combination of geometrical shapes, such as the square and the circle, could be considered a reference to the Bauhaus or the Chinese symbols for Earth and Sky.

At any rate, CIGA Design always mixes technical highlights with their design. The Magician comes with three different cases, and the Gorilla, a symbol of resilience and inner wisdom, features a clever suspension mechanism to protect the in-house skeleton movement, which is held in place by an X-shaped structure.

CIGA Design
43F, Block A, Tanglang Squre Office Bldg
Liuxian Blvd, Nanshan District
Shenzhen, Guangdong 518000
China

Tel.:
+86-755-827-951-80

E-mail:
waterman@cigadesign.com

Website:
www.cigadesign.com

Founded:
2016

Number of employees:
109

U.S. Distribution:
Online sales
www.cigadesign.com

Most important collections:
Blue Planet, Magician, Edge, Zen, Denmark Rose

Ice Age

Movement: automatic, unique CIGA Design movement; 30 jewels; 28,800 vph; 40-hour power reserve
Functions: hours, minutes
Case: ceramic, silver plating; ø 43 mm, height 15.5 mm; sapphire crystal; water-resistant to 3 atm
Band: ceramic; folding clasp
Remarks: comes with additional silicone strap
Price: $1,499
Variations: as Blue Planet, Blue Planet gilding version

Gorilla

Movement: automatic, CD-01; 28,800 vph; fully skeletonized movement based on an X structure; special suspension to protect the movement from shocks; 40-hour power reserve
Functions: hours, minutes
Case: stainless steel, with luminous effect at night, 44 mm x 46 mm, height 11.8 mm; sapphire crystal; water-resistant to 3 atm
Band: silicone, folding clasp
Remarks: comes with additional Nylon strap
Price: $379
Variations: case construction allows for various color combinations: in black/purple ($379), in silver/red ($379), in titanium/blue ($479), in titanium/gold ($569)

Edge

Movement: automatic, Seagull ST25; ø 30.4, height 7.4 mm, 25 jewels; 21,600 vph; 40-hour power reserve
Functions: hours, minutes, sweep seconds
Case: stainless steel, 48 mm x 40.8 mm, height 12.3 mm; sapphire glass, skeleton design, water-resistant to 3 atm
Band: silicone, folding clasp
Remarks: comes with additional calfskin band
Price: $279
Variations: in steel blue ($279), in steel red ($279), in titanium black ($399), in titanium orange ($399)

Claude Meylan
Route de l'Hôtel de Ville 2
CH-1344 L'Abbaye
Switzerland

Tel.:
+41-21-841-14-57

E-mail:
info@claudemeylan.ch

Website:
www.claudemeylan.ch

Founded:
originally mid-18th century; revived in mid-20th century and purchased in 2011

Number of employees:
7

Annual production:
approx. 2,500 pieces

Most important collections/price range:
Tortue, Lac, Lionne, Abbaye / $4,500 to $6,850;
Légendes series / up to $33,000

CLAUDE MEYLAN

In the quest for recognition, many companies, especially the smaller ones, look for a niche in which they can excel. The Swiss brand Claude Meylan, located in L'Abbaye near Joux Lake in the heart of watch country, specializes in skeletonization, which is the art of removing as much material as possible from bridges, plates, the dial, even the hands. The exercise is not just for fun. First, it transforms a watch, making it transparent and allowing a view of the mechanical innards. Second, it allows for imaginative designs using what's left of the material, notably the bridges. These can be either abstract or representative.

Skeletonization has become popular in recent years, but it's not as simple as it might sound. As the various metal components are hollowed out and properly finished with chamfering and sanding, the tensions within the material change. This can then have a deleterious effect on the functioning of the mechanism, since the bridges and plates are in fact used to hold and stabilize the movement.

In 1988, Claude Meylan founded his company. It was taken over soon after by another watchmaker, Henri Berney, who kept up the old tradition. In 2011, the next CEO, Philippe Belais, a man with long experience in the industry, took charge. He also heads Vaudaux, a maker of high-end boxes and cases in Geneva.

Claude Meylan's products, which show many different aspects of the art of skeletonization, live up to the brand's tagline: "Sculptors of time." The company has five main collections, all relating in some way to the region: Lac, for Joux Lake; l'Abbaye, the village where the company has its headquarters; Légendes, exploring local tales; Lionne, the tiny, 1,800-foot-long river with a big name (Lioness, because it sometimes becomes a raging torrent) that flows by the workshops; and, finally, Tortue, whose tonneau case is reminiscent of a turtle. Lately, the Lionne line has been evolving, with a smaller version to attract female watch fans, and the sur-mesure (bespoke) version that lets buyers have initials placed on the watch dial. The Tortue also has a version for smaller wrists. Remarkably, it was born in the mind of the company's communication officer, Pia de Chefdebien, who was asked to dream up her own mechanical watch. As someone with long experience with other independent brands with distinct looks, she conceived an almost totally transparent case, adding discreet ornamental motifs on the exposed mechanism of a modified ETA automatic.

Tortue Petite Fleur

Reference number: 6080-DIA
Movement: automatic, Caliber 7.75CM17; ø 26.5 mm, height 5 mm; 25 jewels; 28,800 vph; 38-hour power reserve; micro-rotor with 68 pavé diamonds
Functions: hours, minutes, seconds
Case: stainless steel, ø 31 x 31 mm, height 11 mm; sapphire crystal; transparent case back; water-resistant to 3 atm
Band: technical satin, buckle
Price: $7,700

Lionne Dentelles Lila

Reference number: 6043 L
Movement: hand-wound, Peseux 7001; ø 23 mm, height 2.50 mm; 17 jewels; 21,600 vph; skeletonized movement; 42-hour power reserve
Functions: hours, minutes
Case: stainless steel, ø 35 mm, height 11 mm; sapphire crystal; transparent case back; water-resistant to 3 atm
Band: leather, pin buckle
Remarks: lace
Price: $2,600
Variations: blue or brown dials

Lionne sur-mesure Initiales

Reference number: 6040-PI
Movement: hand-wound, Peseux 7040; ø 23.30 mm, height 3.10 mm; 17 jewels; 21,600 vph; skeletonized movement; 44-hour power reserve
Functions: hours, minutes
Case: yellow gold-plated stainless steel, ø 35 mm, height 11 mm; sapphire crystal; transparent case back; water-resistant to 3 atm
Band: leather, pin buckle
Remarks: personalization with initials on the dial
Price: $3,400

CORUM

Montres Corum Sàrl
Rue du Petit-Château 1
Case postale 374
CH-2301 La Chaux-de-Fonds
Switzerland

Tel.:
+41-32-967-0670

E-mail:
info@corum.ch

Website:
www.corum-watches.com

Founded:
1955

Number of employees:
50 worldwide

Annual production:
5,000 watches

U.S. distributor:
Montres Corum USA
CWJ BRANDS
1551 Sawgrass Corporate Parkway
Suite 109
Sunrise, FL 33323
954-279-1220
www.corum.ch

Most important collections/price range:
Admiral's Cup, Golden Bridge, Lab, Bubble, Coin,
Heritage, Romvlvs and Artisan / $4,400 to over
$1,000,000

Founded in 1955, Switzerland's youngest luxury watch brand, Corum, celebrated sixty years of unusual—and sometimes outlandish—case and dial designs in 2015. The brand has had quite a busy history but still by and large remains true to the collections launched by founders Gaston Ries and his nephew René Bannwart: the Admiral's Cup, Bridges, and Heritage. Among Corum's most iconic pieces is the legendary Golden Bridge baguette, or stick, movement, which has received a complete makeover in recent years with the use of modern materials and complicated mechanisms. It is built around the idea of concentrating all parts along a straight axis in the middle of a rectangular dial. The development of these extraordinary movements required great watchmaking craftsmanship.

The Bridges collection has always been an eye-catcher. It was originally the brainchild of the great watchmaker Vincent Calabrese, though these types of movements trace back further in time. Its introduction was a milestone in watchmaking history. And the Golden Bridge recently acquired a new highlight in the Golden Bridge Avant-Garde, with all components appearing to float in thin air, with six black indices framing the movement, themselves surrounded by a dangerous-looking black frame. It's very sleek and modern. But Corum also has more classical watches, like the sporty Admiral's Cup collection, which is divided into the staid Legend and the more athletic AC-One 45.

In 2013, the Chinese Citychamp Group became a shareholder and added much needed development cash and an extensive distribution network in Hong Kong and China. The Group has since also acquired the Rotary and Eterna brands, thus creating a strong manufacturing pool in Switzerland. Corum's vision is expressed in its logo: a key facing the sky, which symbolizes both the mysteries to be discovered as well as openness to the new. For a more popular experience of watch-wearing, the company revived the remarkable Bubble, which earned its moniker from the domed shape of the crystal, allowing room for all sorts of dial decoration.

Admiral 42 Automatic

Reference number: A395/04240
Movement: automatic, Caliber CO 395 (based on ETA 2895-2); ø 25.9 mm, height 4.35 mm; 27 jewels; 28,800 vph; 42-hour power reserve
Functions: hours, minutes, subsidiary seconds; date
Case: stainless steel, ø 42 mm, height 10.3 mm; sapphire crystal; transparent case back; water-resistant to 10 atm
Band: stainless steel, double folding clasp
Price: $4,700
Variations: in stainless steel /rose gold, limited to 50 pieces ($9,700); 38-mm diameter ($13,200 with diamond bezel)

Admiral 45 Chronograph

Reference number: A132/04254
Movement: automatic, Caliber CO 132; ø 25.6 mm, height 6.1 mm; 39 jewels; 28,800 vph; rotor with black PVD; 42-hour power reserve
Functions: hours, minutes, subsidiary seconds; chronograph; date
Case: titanium, ø 45 mm, height 14.4 mm; sapphire crystal; transparent case back; water-resistant to 30 atm
Band: titanium, double folding clasp
Price: $11,700; limited to 100 pieces
Variations: with rubber strap ($10,900); in a carbon-fiberglass and luminescent case with skeletonized movement ($41,500, limited to 25 pieces)

Golden Bridge Avant-Garde

Reference number: B313/04279
Movement: automatic, Caliber CO 313; 11.25 x 33.18 mm; 26 jewels; 28,800 vph; balance with variable inertia, baguette movement with gold bridges and plate, linear winding with a platinum sliding weight; 40-hour power reserve
Functions: hours, minutes
Case: titanium with black DLC and rose gold, 37.2 x 51.8 mm, height 13.7 mm; sapphire crystal; transparent case back; water-resistant to 3 atm
Band: reptile skin, double folding clasp
Remarks: baguette movement with linear sliding weight
Price: $48,100; limited to 150 pieces

CyS SA
Via Carlo Maderno 54
CH-6825
Switzerland

Tel.:
+41-21-552-18-82

E-mail:
contact@cuervoysobrinos.com

Website:
www.cuervoysobrinos.com

Founded:
1882

Annual production:
3,500 watches

Distributor:
Provenance Gems LLC
ines@provenancegems.com
800-305-3869

Most important collections/price range:
Historiador, Prominente, Torpedo, Robusto /
$2,000 to $20,000; higher for perpetual calendars
and tourbillon models

CUERVO Y SOBRINOS

Many brands have been going vintage to surf a wave of nostalgia in an age of techno-frigidity. Cuervo y Sobrinos, however, has vintage, nostalgia, romance, and a touch of derring-do as a genome set. The brand originated with Ramón Fernandos Cuervo, who emigrated from Spain to Cuba in 1862 and opened a jewelry business. Twenty years later, he recruited his sister's sons to help out with the booming business (that would be his nephews, the *sobrinos* of the brand name). Don Ràmon died in 1907, but the company continued to expand, adding wristwatches made in La Chaux-de-Fonds.

The advent of Communist rule on the island ended the streak of successes. But in 2002, an Italian watch enthusiast, Marzio Villa, resuscitated the brand. The tagline "Latin heritage, Swiss manufacture" says it all. These timepieces epitomize—or even romanticize—the island's heyday. The lines are at times elegant and sober, or blatantly vintage with fissured dial effect (the Historiador line), or radiate the ease of those who still have time on their hands, as it were. The color codes recall tobacco, coffee, the faded elegance of the age of steamships. A recent line recalls the rough and tumble life of one of America's iconic writers, Ernest Hemingway, who was an avid fisherman and big game hunter. The models are given a different logo of sorts on the case backs, namely an H with a cross bar representing a jumping marlin.

While some collections, like the Buceador, have some more modern models, the Espléndidos and Prominente collections are the ones that really epitomize the brand's DNA, with at times overly long, languorous, elegant, rectangular, thin cases and colors named "rhum," "salmon," or "tobacco."

Historiador Hemingway Icónico

Reference number: 3190.1ICB
Movement: automatic, CYS 8121 (Sellita 221-1 base);
ø 26 mm, height 5.05 mm, 26 jewels, 28,800 vph,
oscillating weight with côtes de Genève and logo;
38-hour power reserve
Functions: hours, minutes, sweep seconds;
sweep date with quick corrector
Case: stainless steel, ø 40 mm, height 11.75 mm;
sapphire crystal; screwed-down case back engraved
with Hemingway logo; water-resistant to 3 atm
Band: reptile skin, buckle
Price: $3,100; limited to 882 pieces
Variations: with cream dial

Historiador Hemingway GMT 'The Fisherman'

Reference number: 3192B.1B
Movement: automatic, CYS 5104 (Soprod
C125 base); ø 26.20 mm, height 4.10 mm, 25 jewels,
28,800 vph, oscillating weight with côtes de Genève
and Hemingway emblem; 38-hour power reserve
Functions: hours, minutes, sweep seconds;
12-hour display (2nd time zone); date
Case: stainless steel, ø 40 mm, height
11.75 mm; sapphire crystal; transparent case back with
Hemingway logo; water-resistant to 3 atm
Band: stainless steel, buckle
Price: $3,850

Historiador Cronógrafo 1946

Reference number: 3143.1S
Movement: automatic, CYS 8123 (ETA 2094 base);
ø 23.90 mm, height 5.50 mm, 33 jewels, 28,800 vph,
oscillating weight with côtes de Genève and logo;
42-hour power reserve
Functions: hours, minutes, subsidiary seconds;
chronograph with tachymeter scale
Case: stainless steel, ø 40 mm, height 12 mm; sapphire
crystal; transparent case back; water-resistant to 5 atm
Band: reptile skin, buckle
Price: $4,680; limited to 100 pieces

Historiador Asturias

Reference number: 3101.1ASB
Movement: automatic, CYS 5124 (La Joux-Perret G100);
ø 25.6 mm, height 4.45 mm, 24 jewels, 28,800 vph,
finished oscillating weight with engraving;
68-hour power reserve
Functions: hours, minutes, sweep seconds; date
Case: stainless steel, ø 40 mm, height 9.9 mm;
sapphire crystal; screw-down transparent case back;
water-resistant to 5 atm
Band: leather, folding clasp
Price: $2,520
Variations: with red, green, or grey dial

Historiador Asturias Pequenos Segundos

Reference number: 3102.1ASV
Movement: automatic, CYS 5124 (La Joux-Perret
G100 base); ø 25.6 mm, height 4.45 mm, 24 jewels,
28,800 vph, finished oscillating weight with engraving;
68-hour power reserve
Functions: hours, minutes, subsidiary seconds; date
Case: stainless steel, ø 40 mm, height 9.9 mm;
sapphire crystal; screw-down transparent case back;
water-resistant to 5 atm
Band: leather, folding clasp
Price: $2,750
Variations: with blue, salmon, or silver dial

Vuelo Emilio Carranza Bicompax

Reference number: 3202.1CN.BI
Movement: automatic, CYS 5160 (Selitta SW 295 base
G100); ø 25.6 mm, height 5.6 mm, 31 jewels, 28,800 vph,
finished oscillating weight with applied logo;
38-hour power reserve
Functions: hours, minutes, subsidiary seconds; date
Case: stainless steel, ø 44 mm, height 11.6 mm;
sapphire crystal; screw-down case back;
water-resistant to 3 atm
Band: leather, folding clasp
Remarks: engraving on back homage to pioneering
Mexican pilot Emilio Carranza (1905-1928)
Price: $4,120

Espléndidos Vitola

Reference number: 2451.1CC
Movement: automatic, Caliber CYS 5103
(base Soprod M100); ø 25.6 mm, height 3.6 mm;
25 jewels; 28,800 vph; oscillating weight with CyS logo;
42-hour power reserve
Functions: hours, minutes, sweep seconds; date
Case: stainless steel, ø 47 x 35 mm, height 10 mm;
sapphire crystal; transparent case back;
water-resistant to 5 atm
Band: reptile skin, folding clasp
Price: $3,050
Variations: various dial colors

Prominente Icónico

Reference number: 1012.1AM
Movement: automatic, Caliber CYS 5103
(base Soprod M100); ø 25.6 mm, height 3.6 mm;
25 jewels; 28,800 vph; oscillating weight with CyS
logo; 42-hour power reserve
Functions: hours, minutes, sweep seconds; date
Case: stainless steel, ø 52 x 33.75 mm, height 10 mm;
sapphire crystal; transparent case back;
water-resistant to 5 atm
Band: reptile skin, folding clasp
Price: $4,200

Prominente Icónico Doble Tiempo

Reference number: 1112.1NM
Movement: automatic, Caliber CYS 5024 (base ETA
2671 modified in-house); ø 17.2 mm, height 4.8 mm;
25 jewels; 28,800 vph; 44-hour power reserve;
rotor with fan decoration and CyS engraving
Functions: hours, minutes; additional 24-hour display
Case: stainless steel, 52 mm x 30.5 mm, height 9.5 mm;
sapphire crystal; double transparent case backs
affixed with 6 screws; water-resistant to 3 atm
Band: reptile skin, folding clasp
Remarks: black guilloché dial
Price: $5,050
Variations: silver, tobacco, salmon guilloché dials

Czapek & Cie.
18 Rue de la Corraterie
CH-1204 Geneva
Switzerland

Tel.:
+41-22-557-41-41

E-mail:
info@czapek.com

Website:
www.czapek.com

Founded:
2012

U.S. distributor:
Horology Works
11 Flagg Road
West Hartford, CT 06117
860-986-9676
info@horologyworks.com

Most important collections/price range:
Antarctique, Quai des Bergues men's and ladies'
watches, Place Vendôme, Faubourg de Cracovie /
$12,000 $226,000

CZAPEK & CIE.

Born in Bohemia (Czech Republic today) in 1811, watchmaker Frantiszek Czapek fought in the failed Polish insurrection of 1832 against Russia and then fled to Geneva. In 1839, he joined another Pole, Antoine de Patek, in a business venture. When the contract expired in 1845, Patek decided on a partnership with Jean Philippe, inventor of the keyless watch. Czapek went on to become purveyor of watches to Emperor Napoleon III and author of a book on watches. Then he vanished without a trace sometime in the late 1860s.

His "resurrection" is due to entrepreneur, art specialist, and occasional watch collector Harry Guhl, who registered the name and set up a management team that included Xavier de Roquemaurel and Sébastien Follonier. They chose Czapek's model No. 3430 as a model upon which to build up a new brand. It is an intriguing piece with elongated Roman numerals, elegant fleur-de-lis hands, and two oddly placed subdials at 7:30 and 4:30, one for small seconds, the other featuring a clever double hand for the seven-day power reserve and days of the week.

The team's claim to fame is collaborating with friends of the brand to create new models, which are always implemented by outstanding Swiss suppliers like Donzé for the grand-feu dials with the secret signature, and Aurélien Bouchet for the fine fleur-de-lis hands.

Over the years, Czapek has gradually diversified, producing classically stylish watches, like the Place Vendôme and the Faubourg de Cracovie. Recently, the company has even moved into some serious complications, with a split-seconds chronograph coupled with some impressive skeletonizing to show off, legitimately, the mechanism on the dial side. The Antarctique Dark Sector, with its mysterious dial, illustrates perfectly why watchmakers started to make transparent case backs. Czapek's name is old, but the brand is showing some very modern, technical strivings.

Antarctique Titanium Dark Sector

Movement: automatic, Czapek Caliber SXH5; ø 30 mm, height 4.2 mm; 28 jewels; 28,800 vph; micro-rotor of recycled platinum, balance wheel with gold regulating eccentric screws; finely finished movement; 60-hour power reserve
Functions: hours, minutes, sweep seconds
Case: titanium, ø 40.5 mm, height 10.6 mm; sapphire crystal; transparent case back; water-resistant to 12 atm
Band: titanium, folding clasp
Price: $36,000; limited to 100 pieces per year
Variations: with leather or rubber strap; in 38.5 mm diameter

Antarctique Révélation

Movement: automatic, Czapek Caliber SXH7; ø 30 mm, height 4.2 mm; 25 jewels; 28,800 vph; micro-rotor of recycled platinum; skeletonized movement; 60-hour power reserve
Functions: hours, minutes, subsidiary seconds
Case: stainless steel, ø 40.5 mm, height 10.6 mm; sapphire crystal; transparent case back; water-resistant to 12 atm
Band: stainless steel, folding clasp
Remarks: limited to 100 pieces per year
Price: $44,600

Antarctique Sashiko Azure

Movement: automatic, Czapek Caliber SXH5; ø 30 mm, height 4.2 mm; 28 jewels; 28,800 vph; micro-rotor of recycled platinum, balance wheel with gold regulating eccentric screws; finely finished movement; 60-hour power reserve
Functions: hours, minutes, sweep seconds
Case: stainless steel, ø 38.5 mm, height 10.6 mm; sapphire crystal; transparent case back; water-resistant to 12 atm
Band: stainless steel, folding clasp
Remarks: dial decorated in traditional sashiko stitching style; comes with pink dial
Price: $28,200

DAMASKO

When it comes to sheer toughness, Damasko has built up quite a track record ever since its founding in 1994, in Germany. But it's not visible at first glance. These unadorned watches with clean, sharp lines are almost archetypical watches. They are robust, indestructible even, and will not need much servicing.

The company's claim to fame lies in its choice of materials, such as polycrystalline silicon hairsprings and components made of a special ice-hardened steel. This special patent involves adding nitrogen and carbon to the molten stainless steel and then cooling it quickly. The resulting material, which has been used in machines like the space shuttle, is extremely hard and does not corrode easily, so these are watches that will keep their look for a long time.

In fact, the research done by this small brand, located near Regensburg in southern Germany, has generated over one hundred patents for the brand, as well as registered samples and designs. The "German" look means well-groomed dials and an immediate view of the time, thanks to contrasting hues.

These watches boast outstanding technical quality, which combines with a very clear stylistic concept. The collection ranges from very classical-functional pilot watches to a line of timeless sportive chronographs, and some very elegant watches for daily use. The latest models in the Damasko watch collection are the DC76/2 and DC86/2 chronographs with manufacture movement C51 and the DK36 as a three-hand watch with manufacture caliber A26-3. An innovative feature is the chronograph with a sweep minute totalizer.

Many of the models run on ETA movements, but Damasko also assembles its own caliber, the A35, which allows for a manufacturing depth of ninety percent. Parts made in the small factory include plates, bridges, pinions, balance, spring barrel, and rotors. Despite this, Damasko watches manage to stay in the affordable range.

Damasko GmbH
Unterheising 17c
93092 Barbing
Germany

Tel.:
+49-9401-80481

E-mail:
sales@damasko-watches.com

Website:
www.damasko-watches.com

Founded:
1994

Number of employees:
30

Distribution:
U.S. Sales
Island Watch
273 Walt Whitman Road, Suite 217
11746 Huntington Station, NY
631-470-0762
sales@longislandwatch.com

Price range:
$1,000 to $4,000

DC 76/2

Movement: automatic, Damasko Caliber C51-6; ø 30.4 mm, height 7.9 mm; 27 jewels; 28,800 vph; sweep seconds and minutes; shock-resistant and antimagnetic according to the German industrial norm (DIN); 50-hour power reserve
Functions: hours, minutes, subsidiary seconds; additional 24-hour display; chronograph; date Case: stainless steel (genuine instrument steel), ø 41 mm, height 14.6 mm; sapphire crystal; screw-in crown; water-resistant to 10 atm
Band: calfskin, pin buckle
Price: $3,474
Variations: with rubber strap ($3,474)

DC 86/2 Orange Black

Movement: automatic, Damasko Caliber C51-6; ø 30.4 mm, height 7.9 mm; 27 jewels; 28,800 vph; sweep seconds and minutes; shock-resistant and antimagnetic according to the German industrial norm (DIN); 50-hour power reserve
Functions: hours, minutes, subsidiary seconds; additional 24-hour display; chronograph; date
Case: ice-hardened stainless steel, ø 42 mm, height 14.4 mm; bidirectional bezel, with 0-12 scale; sapphire crystal; screw-in crown; water-resistant to 10 atm
Band: calfskin, pin buckle
Price: $3,688
Variations: with leather-rubber strap ($3,688)

DS 30 Blue

Movement: automatic, ETA Caliber 2824-2; ø 25.6 mm, height 4.6 mm; 25 jewels; 28,800 vph; antimagnetic according to the German industrial norm (DIN); 38-hour power reserve
Functions: hours, minutes, sweep seconds; date
Case: stainless steel (submarine steel), ø 39 mm, height 9.95 mm; sapphire crystal; screw-in crown; water-resistant to 20 atm
Band: calfskin, pin buckle
Price: $1,077
Variations: various colors for the hands

DK 36

Movement: automatic, Damasko Caliber A26-3;
ø 25.6 mm, height 5.05 mm; 20 jewels; 28,800 vph;
antimagnetic according to the German industrial norm
(DIN); 42-hour power reserve
Functions: hours, minutes, sweep seconds; date and
weekday
Case: ice-hardened stainless steel, ø 40 mm, height
12.3 mm; sapphire crystal; screw-in crown; water-
resistant to 10 atm
Band: calfskin, pin buckle
Price: $1,736
Variations: with leather-rubber strap ($1,750)

DK 36 Black

Movement: automatic, Damasko Caliber A26-3;
ø 25.6 mm, height 5.05 mm; 20 jewels; 28,800 vph;
shock-resistant and antimagnetic according to the
German industrial norm (DIN); 42-hour power reserve
Functions: hours, minutes, sweep seconds;
date and weekday
Case: ice-hardened stainless steel, with Damest
coating, ø 40 mm, height 12.3 mm; sapphire crystal;
screw-in crown; water-resistant to 10 atm
Band: calfskin, pin buckle
Price: $1,826
Variations: with leather-rubber strap ($1,839)

DK 32

Movement: automatic, Damasko Caliber A26-2;
ø 25.6 mm, height 4.6 mm; 20 jewels; 28,800 vph;
shock-resistant and antimagnetic according to the
German industrial norm (DIN); 42-hour power reserve
Functions: hours, minutes, sweep seconds; date
Case: stainless steel (submarine steel), ø 39 mm,
height 9.95 mm; sapphire crystal; screw-in crown;
water-resistant to 20 atm
Band: calfskin, pin buckle
Price: $1,618
Variations: with leather rubber strap ($1,502)

DSub 50

Movement: automatic, Damasko Caliber A26-2;
ø 25.6 mm, height 4.6 mm; 20 jewels; 28,800 vph;
shock-resistant and antimagnetic according to the
German industrial norm (DIN); 42-hour power reserve
Functions: hours, minutes, sweep seconds; date
Case: stainless steel (submarine steel) with Damest
coating, ø 43 mm, height 12.6 mm; unidirectional bezel
with 0-60 scale; sapphire crystal; screw-in crown;
water-resistant to 30 atm
Band: rubber, folding clasp
Price: $2,263

DC 72

Movement: automatic, Damasko Caliber C51-2;
ø 30.4 mm, height 7.9 mm; 27 jewels; 28,800 vph;
sweep seconds and minutes; shock-resistant and
antimagnetic according to the German industrial norm
(DIN); 50-hour power reserve
Functions: hours, minutes; chronograph; date
Case: ice-hardened stainless steel (genuine
instrument steel), ø 41 mm, height 14.6 mm; sapphire
crystal; screw-in crown; water-resistant to 10 atm
Band: calfskin, pin buckle
Price: $2,761

DC 80

Movement: automatic, Damasko Caliber C51-1;
ø 30.4 mm, height 7.9 mm; 27 jewels; 28,800 vph;
sweep seconds and minutes; shock-resistant and
antimagnetic according to the German industrial norm
(DIN); 50-hour power reserve
Functions: hours, minutes; chronograph
Case: ice-hardened stainless steel, ø 42 mm, height
13.9 mm; bidirectional bezel, with 0-60 scale; sapphire
crystal; screw-in crown; water-resistant to 10 atm
Band: calfskin, pin buckle
Price: $2,868
Variations: with leather-rubber strap ($2,881)

DAVOSA

One of the more important brands occupying the lower segment of the market is Davosa, which manufactures a wide range of watches with all the complications one might want but in an affordable segment: pilot watches, quality divers (with helium valve), dress watches, and ladies' watches. The brand has even come out with an apnea training watch that can be removed from its case and stood upright. These timepieces use solid Swiss movements (Sellita and ETA), which are occasionally modified to fit the watches' specific designs. Among these dressy-in-a-sporty-sort-of-way timepieces, one finds a limited-edition automatic chronograph with a moon phase, at under $2,400.

To create a broad portfolio requires experience, and that is something Davosa has in spades. The company was founded in 1891, when farmer Abel Frédéric Hasler from Tramelan, in Switzerland's Jura mountains, spent the winter months making silver pocket watch cases. The following generation of Haslers took up the flame. However, playing the role of unassuming private-label watchmakers, they remained in the background and let their customers in Europe and the United States run away with the show. It wasn't until after World War II that brothers Paul and David Hasler dared produce their own timepieces.

The long experience with watchmaking and watches culminated in 1987 with the brothers developing their own line of watches under the brand name Davosa. The Haslers then signed a partnership with the German distributor Bohle. In Germany, mechanical watches were experiencing a new boom, so the brand was able to evolve quickly. In 2000, Corinna Bohle took over as manager of strategic development. Davosa now reaches well beyond Switzerland's borders and has become an integral part of the world of mechanical watches. It has streamlined its offering, which is now divided into three families: diving, performance, and pilot.

DAVOSA Swiss
Bohle GmbH
Bunsenstrasse 1a
32052 Herford
Germany

Tel.:
+49 (0)5221 9942400

E-mail:
info@davosa.com

Website:
www.davosa.com

Founded:
1881

U.S. distributor:
Davosa U.S.A,
S Biscayne Blvd 200
FL 33131, Miami, USA
877-DAVOSA1
info@davosa-usa.com
www.davosa-usa.com

Most important collections/price range:
Apnea Diver, Argonautic, Classic, Gentleman, Military, Newton, Pilot, Ternos, Titanium / $600 to $2,400

Argonautic BG Automatic

Reference number: 161.528.70
Movement: automatic, Davosa Caliber DAV3021 (based on Sellita SW200-1); ø 25.6 mm, height 4.6 mm; 26 jewels; 28,800 vph; 38-hour power reserve
Functions: hours, minutes, sweep seconds; date
Case: stainless steel, ø 43 mm, height 13.5 mm; unidirectional bezel with ceramic insert, with 0-60 scale; sapphire crystal; screw-in crown, helium valve; water-resistant to 30 atm
Band: stainless steel, folding clasp, with safety lock and extension link
Price: $899
Variations: various colors

Argonautic BGBS Automatic

Reference number: 161.528.10
Movement: automatic, Davosa Caliber DAV3021 (based on Sellita SW200-1); ø 25.6 mm, height 4.6 mm; 26 jewels; 28,800 vph; 38-hour power reserve
Functions: hours, minutes, sweep seconds; date
Case: stainless steel, ø 43 mm, height 13.5 mm; unidirectional bezel with ceramic insert, with 0-60 scale; sapphire crystal; screw-in crown, helium valve; water-resistant to 30 atm
Band: stainless steel, folding clasp, with safety lock and extension link
Price: $939

Argonautic Lumis Automatic

Reference number: 161.529.20
Movement: automatic, Davosa Caliber DAV3021 (based on Sellita SW200-1); ø 25.6 mm, height 4.6 mm; 26 jewels; 28,800 vph; 38-hour power reserve
Functions: hours, minutes, sweep seconds; date
Case: stainless steel, ø 43 mm, height 13.8 mm; unidirectional bezel with 0-60 scale; sapphire crystal; screw-in crown, helium valve; water-resistant to 30 atm
Band: stainless steel, folding clasp, with safety lock and extension link
Remarks: self-illuminating tritium gas on the dial
Price: $979
Variations: various colors

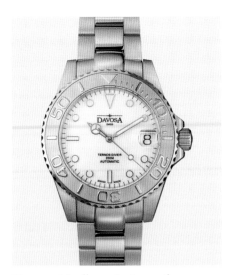

Ternos Medium Automatic

Reference number: 166.198.20
Movement: automatic, Davosa Caliber DAV3021
(based on Sellita SW200-1); ø 25.6 mm, height 4.6 mm;
26 jewels; 28,800 vph; 38-hour power reserve
Functions: hours, minutes, sweep seconds; date
Case: stainless steel with yellow-gold PVD, ø 36.5 mm,
height 11.8 mm; unidirectional bezel, with 0-60 scale;
sapphire crystal; screw-in crown; water-resistant to
20 atm
Band: stainless steel with yellow-gold PVD, folding
clasp with safety lock
Price: $948
Variations: various straps

Ternos Professional Megalume

Reference number: 161.583.10
Movement: automatic, Davosa Caliber DAV3021
(based on Sellita SW200-1); ø 25.6 mm, height 4.6 mm;
26 jewels; 28,800 vph; 38-hour power reserve
Functions: hours, minutes, sweep seconds; date
Case: stainless steel with black DLC coating, ø 42 mm,
height 15.5 mm; unidirectional bezel with ceramic
insert, with 0-60 scale; sapphire crystal;
screw-in crown; water-resistant to 50 atm
Band: rubber, folding clasp with safety lock
Remarks: dial entirely coated with SuperLumiNova C3,
limited to 500 pieces
Price: $1,159

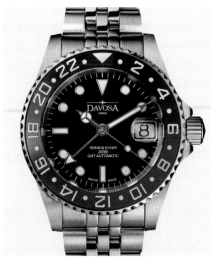

Ternos Ceramic GMT Automatic

Reference number: 161.590.07
Movement: automatic, Davosa Caliber DAV3032
(based on Sellita SW330-2); ø 25.6 mm, height 4.1 mm;
21 jewels; 28,800 vph; 50-hour power reserve
Functions: hours, minutes, sweep seconds;
additional 24-hour display (2nd time zone); date
Case: stainless steel, ø 40 mm, height 12.2 mm;
unidirectional bezel with ceramic insert,
with 0-24 scale; sapphire crystal; screw-in crown;
water-resistant to 20 atm
Band: stainless steel, folding clasp, with safety lock
Price: $1,459
Variations: various colors

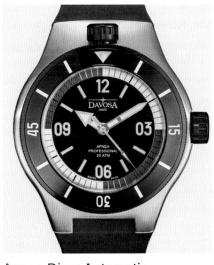

Apnea Diver Automatic

Reference number: 161.569.55
Movement: automatic, Davosa Caliber DAV3021
(based on Sellita SW200-1); ø 25.6 mm, height 4.6 mm;
26 jewels; 28,800 vph; 38-hour power reserve
Functions: hours, minutes, sweep seconds
Case: stainless steel, ø 46 mm, height 12.5 mm;
unidirectional bezel with 0-60 scale; crown-activated
scale ring with surfacing markings; sapphire crystal;
screw-in crown; water-resistant to 20 atm
Band: rubber, pin buckle
Remarks: crown unscrews to release a stand keeping
the watch upright for apnea exercises; comes with
additional red rubber strap
Price: $1,049

Newton Pilot Speedometer Automatic

Reference number: 161.587.25
Movement: automatic, Davosa Caliber DAV3023
(based on Sellita SW240-1); ø 29 mm, height 5.05 mm;
25 jewels; 28,800 vph; 38-hour power reserve
Functions: hours (in a window, digital, sliding),
minutes, sweep seconds (disk)
Case: stainless steel, ø 44 mm, height 12.8 mm;
sapphire crystal; transparent case back;
water-resistant to 5 atm
Band: calfskin, pin buckle
Price: $999
Variations: various colors

Newton Pilot

Reference number: 161.530.70
Movement: automatic, Davosa Caliber DAV3021
(based on Sellita SW200-1); ø 25.6 mm, height 4.6 mm;
26 jewels; 28,800 vph; 38-hour power reserve
Functions: hours, minutes, sweep seconds
Case: stainless steel, ø 40 mm, height 11.6 mm;
sapphire crystal; transparent case back;
water-resistant to 7 atm
Band: stainless steel, double folding clasp
Price: $1,099
Variations: various colors

DE BETHUNE

De Bethune was named after an eighteenth-century French navy captain from an old aristocratic family, the Chevalier De Béthune, who did extensive research into watch and clockmaking and whose name is associated with a particularly clever escapement. Similarly, Denis Flageollet had had many years of experience in the research, conception, and implementation of prestigious timepieces. So he and David Zanetta, a well-known consultant for a number of high-end watch brands, founded their own company in 2002 in what used to be the village pub and turned it into a stunning factory. The modern CNC machinery, combined with an outstanding team of watchmakers and research and development specialists allowed the company to rapidly produce prototypes and make small movement series with great dispatch. In order to become even more independent of suppliers, the little factory produced its own cases, dials, and hands.

De Bethune watches are aesthetically compelling, thanks to the use of simple color schemes, mirror-polished titanium, and discreet microlight engraving. The "delta" on many of the dials is natural decoration, explains Flageollet: "The triangle is essential to holding the gearwheel pivots, so why not turn them into a natural ogival arch?" This cool-modern visual is contrasted with certain classic elements that soften the brand's sharpness. These two aspects were brought together in a single two-sided watch released in early 2021, the Kind of Two.

Engineering innovations are also a De Bethune specialty. Among others, the company developed a hand-wound caliber with a power reserve of up to eight days, a self-regulating double barrel, a balance wheel in titanium and platinum that allows for an ideal inertia/mass ratio, a balance spring with a patented De Bethune end curve, and a triple "parachute" shock-absorbing system. It also boasts the lightest and one of the fastest silicon/titanium tourbillons on the market.

All this innovation requires investments, and in August 2021, the Watchbox trading platform became a majority owner of the small company. According to those in charge, however, no one intends to deviate master Denis Flageollet from his well-established tracks.

De Bethune SA
Chemin des Grangettes 19
CH-1454 L'Auberson
Switzerland

Tel.:
+41-22-310-22-71

E-mail:
geneva@debethune.com

Website:
www.debethune.ch

Founded:
2002

Number of employees:
40

Annual production:
200

U. S. Distribution:
Cellini Jewelers
212-888-0505
Govberg
877-798-7528

Most important collections:
Limited production of series, DB25, DB 28, DB 29

DB28 XS Starry Seas

Reference number: DB28XSTIS3
Movement: hand-wound, De Bethune Caliber DB2005; ø 30 mm; 27 jewels; 28,800 vph; self-regulating double spring barrel, titanium balance, silicon escape wheel, optimized for temperature fluctuations and air penetration; finely finished movement with "côtes de Bethune"; 6-day power reserve
Functions: hours, minutes
Case: polished titanium, ø 38.7 mm, height 7.4 mm; sapphire crystal; transparent case back; water-resistant to 3 atm
Band: reptile skin, pin buckle
Remarks: dial with random guilloché with white-gold stars
Price: $90,000

DBD Evergreen

Reference number: DBDRE
Movement: hand-wound, De Bethune Caliber DB2044; ø 30 mm; 29 jewels; 28,80000 vph; self-regulating double spring barrel, titanium balance, balance spring with De Bethune flat terminal, silicon escape wheel, optimized for temperature fluctuations and air penetration; 120-hour power reserve
Functions: digital and jumping hours and minutes; day, date, month
Case: polished titanium, ø 42.6 mm, height 9.4 mm; sapphire crystal; transparent case back; water-resistant to 3 atm **Band:** two-toned textile strap and reptile skin strap, pin buckle **Remarks:** côtes de Genève on the dial, côtes de Bethune on case back
Price: $242,000; limited to 20 pieces

DB Eight

Reference number: DB8RETIS1
Movement: hand-wound, De Bethune Caliber DB 3000; ø 30 mm; height 5.19 mm; 31 jewels; 28,800 vph; chromium-plated chronograph bridges, hand-chamfered parts; titanium balance wheel with white-gold inserts, silicon escape wheel, optimized for temperature fluctuations and air penetration; 60-hour power reserve
Functions: hours, minutes; monopusher chronograph with minute totalizer
Case: polished titanium, ø 42.4 mm, height 9.2 mm; sapphire crystal; transparent case back; water-resistant to 3 atm **Band:** reptile skin (extra-supple), pin buckle **Remarks:** radiating guilloché dial, clous de Paris on minute counter
Price: $85,000

Deep Blue Watches
1716 Coney Island Avenue
Suite 3r
Brooklyn, NY 11230

Tel.:
718-484-7717

Website:
www.deepbluewatches.com

E-mail:
info@deepbluewatches.com

Founded:
2007

Number of employees:
70

Annual output:
n/a

Distribution:
Retail and online

Most important collections/price range:
Master 1000, Diver 1000, Defender / $300 – 500;
Pro Sea Diver / $500-900; Daynight / $600-1,000;
Alpha, Marine, Ocean $700-1,500; Blue Water
$600-1,400

DEEP BLUE

As far as anyone can tell, the fish do not care what you are wearing on your wrist. For the diver, it has to be accurate, genuinely water-resistant, and readable in less-than-ideal conditions. Those are the basics—or should be— of any real diver's watch. The rest is in the eye of the beholder. And it seems that New York–based Deep Blue does not wander too far off home plate, as it were. The company was founded with the idea of providing divers with an array of tough watches that do the job and have the look and feel of a professional-quality diver's watch at a fraction of what you might expect to pay.

Little did they know in 2007 that Deep Blue watches would achieve cult status among divers. Deep Blue watches are accurate, robust, and ready for life in the open and underwater. There's no need to hide them in a safe, and getting banged up a little does them no harm—it's called patina, and it gives these timepieces the look and feel of a real tool watch... which is what they are.

The collection includes all sorts of models for every type of diving. The power is supplied by an array of ETA, Sellita, Miyota, and Seiko/Time calibers, and occasionally quartz movements. Some have special features like ceramic bezels; some are water-resistant to as much as 3,000 meters, like the Depthmaster, whose dimensions (ø 49 mm, height 19.5) and weight (300 g) will certainly contribute to the speed of the diver's descent. Lots of care has been given to lighting the dial, with generous application of Superluminova and the occasional use of autoluminescent tritium tubes, which may well attract some interesting fish.

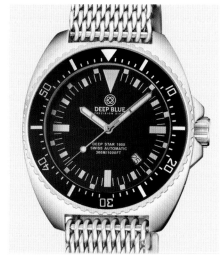

Deep Star 1000 Vintage Swiss Automatic

Reference number: DSTAREXPEDBLKWHITEBRC
Movement: automatic, Sellita Caliber SW-200-01; ø 25.6 mm, height 4.6 mm; 26 jewels; 28,800 vph; 38-hour power reserve
Functions: hours, minutes, sweep seconds; date
Case: stainless steel, ø 45 mm, height 15 mm; unidirectional ceramic bezel with 120 clicks; screw-down crown; helium release valve; transparent case back; sapphire crystal; water-resistant to 33 atm
Band: stainless steel mesh, folding clasp with extension; **Remarks:** tritium gas-filled tube illumination on hands and hour markers
Price: $799
Variations: silicon or rubber strap

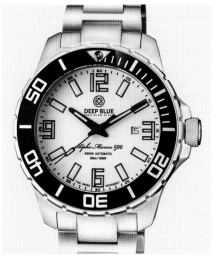

Daynight Alpha Marine 500 Tritium T-100 Swiss Automatic

Reference number: AM500TRITWHITBLUE
Movement: automatic, Sellita Caliber SW-200-1; ø 25.6 mm, height 4.6 mm; 26 jewels; 28,800 vph; 38-hour power reserve; **Functions:** hours, minutes, sweep seconds; date; **Case:** stainless steel, ø 45 mm, height 15 mm; unidirectional ceramic bezel with 0-60 scale and 120 clicks; screw-down crown and case back; transparent case back; helium release valve; sapphire crystal; water-resistant to 33 atm
Band: stainless steel, folding clasp with extension;
Remarks: tritium gas-filled tube illumination on hands and hour markers; full-lume blue dial; **Price:** $1,299
Variations: green lume dial; leather strap ($1,149)

Daynight Scuba 500 Tritium T-100 Swiss Automatic

Reference number: DNSCUBASW200BLACK
Movement: automatic, Sellita SW-200-1; ø 25.6 mm, height 4.6 mm; 26 jewels; 28,800 vph
Functions: hours, minutes, sweep seconds; 2nd time zone; date; **Case:** stainless steel, ø 45 mm, height 15 mm; unidirectional bezel with ceramic insert and 0-60 scale; transparent case back; sapphire crystal; water-resistant to 50 atm
Band: stainless steel, folding clasp with extension
Remarks: tritium gas–filled tube illumination on hands and hour markers
Price: $1,299
Variations: with rubber strap ($1,149)

DELMA

Industries all have their major players and their minor ones. The major brands attract the attention thanks, oftentimes, to lots of clamorous advertising plus name recognition. In the watch business, as in many others, there are smaller, less noisy brands that also produce quality watches.

Delma began as one of four brands produced by a company founded in 1924 by two brothers, Alfred and Adolf Gilomen. For several decades, they manufactured a number of different models, from classic pocket watches and dress watches to a fine chronograph marketed under the name Midland in 1946, which made a bit of a splash.

In 1966, after Gilomen's passing, the brand was sold to Ulrich Wütrich. He decided to use a single name, Delma, and focus production on diver's watches, without, however, losing the customers in search of a nice watch that could be used every day. In 1969, they came out with the Periscope, an automatic diver's able to go down to 50 atm (500 meters). It established a new style for the brand, one it has remained faithful to ever since. A few years later, Delma released the Shell Star, a professional diver's watch.

Today, the company is run by Wütrich's son, Fred Leibundgut and his son Andreas. The brand still produces casual watches, but its claim to fame is still its diver's. The Periscope and Shell Star, which were rereleased in 2021, have been revived with a modernized look and more pertinent technology. The Shell Star features a special table to help divers optimize their gas mixtures in dives up to 70 atm. Another line, the Blue Shark, was launched in 2011. It could survive a 3,000-meter (9,900-foot) plunge. To prove they could improve even on that, in 2019 Delma came out with the Blue Shark III, which can go to 4,000 meters. It has a 6.8-millimeter sapphire crystal, and a thick steel back, so you may not survive the plunge, but the watch will. And in 2023, the company bested that with the Blue Shark IV, adding 100 atm (1,000 meters/3,300 ft) to the diving depth.

Delma Watch Limited
Solothurnstrasse 47
2543 Lengnau
Switzerland

Tel.:
+41 32 654 22 11

E-mail:
info@delma.ch

Website:
www.delma.ch

Founded:
1924

Number of employees:
15

Annual production:
25,000 watches

U. S. Distribution:
Contact headquarters in Switzerland.

Most important collections/price range:
Aero, Racing, Diver, Dress, and Elegance collections / up to $4,000

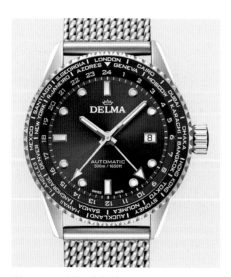

Cayman World Timer

Reference number: 41801.710.6.041
Movement: automatic, ETA 2893-2; ø 25.6 mm, height 4.1 mm; 21 jewels; 28,800 vph; decorated rotor; 42-hour power reserve
Functions: hours, minutes, seconds; 24-hour indicator (world timer with reference cities and places); date
Case: stainless steel, ø 42 mm, height 13.6 mm; sapphire crystal; bidirectional bezel; screw-in crown and see-through case back; water-resistant to 50 atm
Band: stainless steel Milanese mesh, folding clasp
Price: $2,750;
Variations: with leather strap ($2,625); various dials

Blue Shark IV

Reference number: 41701.760.6.154
Movement: automatic, Sellita SW-200-1; ø 25.6 mm, height 4.6 mm; 25 jewels; 28,800 vph; decorated rotor; 38-hour power reserve
Functions: hours, minutes, seconds; date
Case: stainless steel, ø 47 mm, height 18.5 mm; sapphire crystal; unidirectional bezel; helium valve; screw-in crown and case back; water-resistant to 500 atm
Band: stainless steel, folding clasp with safety lock
Price: $2,800; limited to 999 pieces
Variations: various dials ($2,950)

Quattro

Reference number: 41702.580.6.049
Movement: automatic, Valjoux 7750; ø 30 mm, height 7.9 mm; 29 jewels; 28,800 vph; custom rotor; 48-hour power reserve
Functions: hours, minutes, subsidiary seconds; chronograph; weekday, date
Case: stainless steel, ø 45 mm at bezel, height 14.7 mm; screw-down crown; sapphire crystal; transparent case back; water-resistant to 10 atm
Band: stainless steel, folding clasp
Price: $2,990
Variations: with blue or black dial

Santiago GMT Meridian Automatic

Reference number: 41702.756.6P014
Movement: automatic, Sellita SW-330-2; ø 25.6 mm, height 4.6 mm; 25 jewels; 28,800 vph; decorated rotor; 56-hour power reserve
Functions: hours, minutes, sweep seconds; 2nd time zone; date
Case: stainless steel, ø 43 mm, height 13.3 mm; sapphire crystal; unidirectional bezel with anodized aluminum with 0-24 scale; helium valve; screw-in crown; transparent case back (mineral glass); water-resistant to 50 atm
Band: stainless steel, folding clasp with safety lock
Price: $1,850; limited to 999 pieces
Variations: various dials ($2,950)

Commander Big Date

Reference number: 44601.720.6.038
Movement: automatic, ETA Caliber2892 (with Jaquet bi-date module) ; ø 25.6 mm (base caliber), height 3.6 mm; 26 jewels; 28,800 vph; custom rotor; 50-hour power reserve
Functions: hours, minutes, sweep seconds; date (with quick set)
Case: stainless steel black PVD, ø 45 mm, height 10.9 mm; sapphire crystal; screw-in crown; transparent case back (mineral glass); water-resistant to 5 atm
Band: leather, pin buckle
Price: $1,850; limited to 150 pieces

Cayman Field Automatic

Reference number: 41601.706.6.034
Movement: automatic, Sellita Caliber SW 200; ø 25.6 mm, height 4.6 mm; 26 jewels; 28,800 vph; custom rotor; 38-hour power reserve
Functions: hours, minutes, sweep seconds; date
Case: stainless steel, ø 42 mm, height 13.3 mm; unidirectional black anodized aluminum bezel; sapphire crystal; transparent case back (mineral glass); water-resistant to 50 atm
Band: canvas, pin buckle
Price: $1,226

Klondike Chronotec

Reference number: 41601.660.6.031
Movement: automatic, Valjoux 7750; ø 30 mm, height 7.9 mm; 29 jewels; 28,800 vph; custom rotor; 48-hour power reserve
Functions: hours, minutes, subsidiary seconds; chronograph; day, date; tachymeter
Case: stainless steel, ø 44 mm at bezel, height 14.8 mm; screw-down crown; sapphire crystal; transparent case back with mineral glass; water-resistant to 20 atm
Band: cordura rubber, pin buckle
Price: $3,575
Variations: white dial, different case colors; stainless steel bracelet (available in bicolor version) and folding clasp ($3,825)

Continental Pulsometer

Reference number: 41701.702.6.039
Movement: automatic, Sellita Caliber SW510; ø 30 mm, height 7.9 mm; 27 jewels; 28,800 vph; 48-hour power reserve
Functions: hours, minutes, subsidiary seconds; bicompax chronograph; date
Case: stainless steel, ø 42 mm at bezel, height 15.2 mm; screw-in crown; sapphire crystal; transparent case back with mineral glass; water-resistant to 10 atm
Band: calfskin, folding clasp
Remarks: dial with pulsometer, tachymeter, and telemeter for measuring heart rate, speed, and distance
Price: $2,800
Variations: with black, blue, green; yellow gold bezel and bicolor bracelet ($2,950)

Heritage Chronograph

Reference number: 41601.728.6.061
Movement: automatic, Sellita Caliber SW500; ø 30 mm, height 7.9 mm; 25 jewels; 28,800 vph; 62-hour power reserve
Functions: hours, minutes, subsidiary seconds; tricompax chronograph with tachymeter scale; day, date
Case: stainless steel, ø 42 mm at bezel, height 15.2 mm; screw-in crown; sapphire crystal; transparent case back with mineral glass; water-resistant to 10 atm
Band: calfskin, folding clasp
Price: $3,125

DETROIT WATCH COMPANY

Patrick Ayoub and Amy Ayoub launched Detroit Watch Company in 2013 with the first and only mechanical timepieces designed and assembled in Detroit, Michigan. Patrick, a car designer, and Amy, an interior designer, share a passion for original design and time-pieces and have worked hard to develop their brand, which draws inspiration from, and celebrates, the city of "Détroit."

Detroit means a lot of things to different people. Because the history of the people and places have shaped the city, Detroit's stories are also part of the Detroit Watch Company's collective story. The 1701, for instance, commemorates Antoine de la Mothe Cadillac, Knight of St. Louis, who, with his company of colonists, arrived at Détroit on July 24, 1701. On that day, under the patronage of Louis XIV and protected by the flag of France, the city, then called Fort Pontchartrain, was founded. These watches, while modern and chic, do recall the fairly clear-cut lines of an old church clock (*horloge*).

People phoning Detroit will understand why the company came out with a watch named 313. It's the area code of the city that brought not only cars, but also Motown (*motor + town*) music to the world. Needless to say, the dial looks like an old-fashioned phone dial. And where did Detroit's cars ride and race informally? On Woodward Avenue, the first mile of concrete highway in the USA, where carriages once rolled. It's the name for a collection of sporty chronographs. Finally, the city supplied the war effort against the Axis with many vital vehicles, including the B-24 Liberator bomber. No wonder the brand's line of watches includes an aviator collection.

The Detroit Watch Company timepieces are classically designed and hand-assembled in-house, and they may be purchased directly through the Detroit Watch Company web-site. The company also offers a wide range of straps and has a transparent and affordable servicing program.

Detroit Watch Company, LLC
P.O. Box 60
Birmingham, MI 48012

Tel:
248-321-5601

E-mail:
info@detroitwatchco.com

Founded:
2013

Number of employees:
3

Annual production:
400 watches

Distribution:
direct sales only

Most important collections/price range:
M1 Woodward classic, 1701 Pontchartrain GMT, 1701 Louis XIV; / $1,100 to $2,950

M1 Woodward Classic

Movement: automatic, Caliber Valjoux 7750; ø 30 mm, height 8.4 mm; 25 jewels; 28,800 vph; custom M1 rotor; 48-hour power reserve
Functions: hours, minutes, subsidiary seconds; chronograph; day, date
Case: stainless steel, ø 42 mm, height 14.5 mm; sapphire crystal; transparent case back, screw-down crown; water-resistant to 5 atm
Band: calf leather, folding clasp
Price: $2,275
Variations: various straps

M1 24hr Legends

Reference number: DWC M1W-EXH
Movement: automatic, Caliber Valjoux 7750; ø 30 mm, height 8.4 mm; 25 jewels; 28,800 vph; custom M1 rotor; 48-hour power reserve
Functions: hours, minutes, subsidiary seconds; chronograph; day, date
Case: stainless steel, ø 42 mm, height 14.5 mm; sapphire crystal; transparent case back, screw-down crown; water-resistant to 5 atm
Band: calf leather, folding clasp
Price: $2,275
Variations: race number 6, 98

M1 24hr Legends "Pink Pig"

Reference number: DWC-M1W-EXH
Movement: automatic, Caliber Valjoux 7750; ø 30 mm, height 8.4 mm; 25 jewels; 28,800 vph; custom M1 rotor; 48-hour power reserve
Functions: hours, minutes, subsidiary seconds; chronograph; day, date
Case: stainless steel, ø 42 mm, 14.5 mm; transparent case back; screw-down crown; water-resistant to 5 atm
Band: calf leather, folding clasp
Remarks: tribute to the pink car (Pink Bertha, aka, Pink Pig) driven by Willi Kaussen and Reinhold Jöst at Le Mans, 1971, which had the different parts of the animal written on the body
Price: $2,275
Variations: version with watch parts written on the dial

City Collection 313

Reference number: DWC-CITY-313
Movement: automatic, ETA Caliber 2824-2, ø 26.6 mm, height 4.6 mm; 26 jewels; 28,800 vph; 38-hour power reserve
Functions: hours, minutes, subsidiary seconds
Case: stainless steel, ø 42 mm, height 9.4 mm, sapphire crystal, transparent case back; water resistant to 5 atm
Band: calfskin, buckle
Price: $1,150
Variations: Also available in area codes: 202, 212, 305, 312, 415, 416, 504, 512, 713, 818, 310

Aviator Power Reserve

Reference number: DWC-A-PW
Movement: automatic (or manual winding), Sellita SW279-1; ø 25.6, height 5.6 mm, 26 jewels (manual winding: height 4.35 mm, 24 jewels); 28,800 vph; decorated movement with blued screws, perlage, côtes de Genève; 38-hour power reserve
Functions: hours, minutes, subsidiary seconds; power reserve indicator; date with quick corrector
Case: stainless steel, ø 42 mm, height 9.7 mm; sapphire crystal, transparent case back, screw-in crown; water-resistant to 5 atm
Band: calf leather, buckle
Price: $1,495
Variations: graphite dial, green dial

1701 Moonphase Chronograph

Reference number: PCT-Moon-Chrono
Movement: automatic, ETA Caliber 7751; ø 30 mm, height 7.9 mm; 25 jewels; 28,800 vph; 48-hour power reserve
Functions: hours, minutes, subsidiary seconds; chronograph; date, day, month; moon phase
Case: stainless steel, ø 42 mm, height 14.5 mm, sapphire crystal with anti-reflective coating, screw-down transparent case back with engraving; water resistant to 5 atm
Band: calfskin
Price: $2,750

Pontchartrain Watch Co. 1st Edition

Movement: automatic, Caliber ETA 2892-A2, ø 25.6 mm, height 3.6 mm; 28,800 vph; decorated movement with blued screws, perlage, côtes de Genève; 42-hour power reserve
Functions: hours, minutes, sweep seconds
Case: stainless steel, ø 42 mm, height 9.7 mm; sapphire crystal, transparent case back, screw-down crown; water-resistant to 5 atm
Band: calf leather, buckle
Price: $1,295
Variations: with stainless steel bracelet and folding clasp; black dial

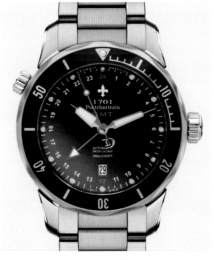

1701 Pontchartrain GMT- Great Lakes Edition

Reference number: DWC-1701GMTGLE-S1
Movement: automatic, ETA Caliber 2893-2, ø 26.6 mm, height 4.1 mm; 21 jewels; 28,800 vph; 42-hour power reserve
Functions: hours, minutes, sweep seconds; second time zone, date
Case: stainless steel, ø 42 mm, height 13 mm; sapphire crystal, unidirectional bezel, screw-down crown; helium valve; water resistant to 300 atm
Band: calfskin, buckle
Price: $1,495
Variations: 1701 Pontchartrain ($1,395)

1701 Pontchartrain Power Reserve

Reference number: DWC-1701-PW
Movement: automatic, Sellita SW279-1; ø 25.6, height 5.6 mm, 26 jewels; 28,800 vph; decorated movement with blued screws, perlage, côtes de Genève; 38-hour power reserve
Functions: hours, minutes, subsidiary seconds; power reserve indicator; date with quick corrector
Case: stainless steel, ø 42 mm, height 9.7; mm; sapphire crystal, transparent case back, screw-in crown; water-resistant to 5 atm
Band: calf leather, buckle
Price: $1,495

DLOKE

Founder and creator of DLoke watches, Donald R. Loke has a diverse and rich track record within the luxury watch industry. He's been a distributor, designer, service center manager (notably for the very complex Louis Moinet timepieces), and a restoration expert sought out by owners of some of the most complicated watches ever to be created. His training began at the Bowman Technical School where he earned both his Master Watchmaker and Clockmaker degrees, followed by training at the Centre De Perfectionnement Horloger (WOSTEP) in Neuchâtel, Switzerland, where he achieved perfect scores in both the technical and practical exams. A friend and fan of the late George Daniels, he's also a talented designer and engineer who decided to create his own complex dual-direct chronometer escapement. As if the mastery of the mystic arts of high watchmaking were not enough. As for the design, it is informed by a balanced and thoughtful approach and guided by adherence to traditional watchmaking canons. Loke has, after all, even designed watches for a well-known Swiss luxury brand.

DLoke currently has one watch in several iterations. But each model requires careful examination, as he applies many classical techniques to aesthetics. Rather than attack the senses with overwhelming displays of color and complication, radical shapes, or exotic materials, his method highlights how the devil really is in the details. Dials crafted in glowing white or deep blue Grand Feu enamel are the simple, but elegant backdrop hosting the composed set of sub dials, while asymmetrical hands merge with the applied markers to form a complete arrow as they cross one another. Even the case is an essay in less being more. While the dual crowns that oppose each other on the horizontal axis are quite visible, you'll have to look closely to note the presence of the integrated plungers that control the chronograph function.

Inside the Grade 5 titanium case beats a "quality one" grade customized Concepto 8100 chronometer/chronograph movement visible through the sapphire back. Each watch is hand-built to order by the master himself in very limited quantities.

DLoke
124 Bennets Farm Rd.
Ridgefield, CT 06877
USA

Tel:
203-570-8463

Email:
Lok.dr@gmail.com

Website:
www.drlokewatches.com

Founded:
2015

Number of employees:
3

Annual production:
75

Most important collection price:
Dress Chronograph / $8,950

Dress Chronograph
Reference number: DRL DC WB
Movement: automatic, Concepto 8100 Quality No. 1 Caliber; ø26 mm, height 7.9 mm; 25 jewels; 28,800 vph; rotor decorated with côtes de Genève; chronometer rated; 42-hour power reserve
Functions: hours, minutes; sweep chronograph, rotating inner bezel
Case: titanium; ø 43 mm, height 12.5 mm; sapphire crystal; transparent case back; water-resistant to 5 atm
Band: reptile skin, pin buckle
Price: $8,950

Dress Chronograph
Reference number: DRL DC WW
Movement: automatic, Concepto 8100 Quality No. 1 Caliber; ø26 mm, height 7.9 mm; 25 jewels; 28,800 vph; rotor decorated with côtes de Genève; chronometer rated; 42-hour power reserve
Functions: hours, minutes; sweep chronograph, rotating inner bezel
Case: titanium; ø 43 mm, height 12.5 mm; sapphire crystal; transparent case back; water-resistant to 5 atm
Band: reptile skin, pin buckle
Price: $8,950

Dress Chronograph
Reference number: DRL DC BW
Movement: automatic, Concepto 8100 Quality No. 1 Caliber; ø26 mm, height 7.9 mm; 25 jewels; 28,800 vph; rotor decorated with côtes de Genève; chronometer rated; 42-hour power reserve
Functions: hours, minutes; sweep chronograph, rotating inner bezel
Case: titanium; ø 43 mm, height 12.5 mm; sapphire crystal; transparent case back; water-resistant to 5 atm
Band: reptile skin, pin buckle
Price: $8,950

Montres DOXA SA
Rue de Zurich 23A
P.O. Box 6031
2500 Bienne 6
Switzerland

Tel.:
+41 32 344 42 72

E-mail:
contact@doxawatches.com

Website:
https://doxawatches.com

Founded:
1889

Number of employees:
40

Distribution:
DOXA USA
520 369 2872
usa@doxawatches.com

Most important collections/price range:
DOXA SUB dive watch collection / $950 to $4,900

DOXA

Watch aficionados who have visited the world-famous museum in Le Locle will know that the little castle in which it is housed once belonged to Georges Ducommun, the founder of Doxa. The *manufacture* was launched as a backyard operation in 1889 and originally produced pocket watches. Quality products and good salesmanship quickly put Doxa on the map, but the company's real game-changer came in 1967 with the uncompromising SUB 300, a heavy, bold diver's watch. It featured a unidirectional bezel with the official U.S. dive table engraved on it. The bright orange dial might seem quite ostentatious, but, in fact, it offers the best legibility under water. It also marked the beginning of a trend for colorful dials.

The popularity of Doxa watches was boosted early on by the commercialization of diving in the 1970s. Thriller writer Clive Cussler, chairman and founder of the National Underwater and Marine Agency (NUMA), even chose a Doxa as gear for his action hero Dirk Pitt.

The enduring vintage trend has shaped the recent development of the brand. Focus is on fewer lines with greater variations, with almost every model coming in different colors besides the striking orange: brilliant white, dreamy turquoise, bright yellow, and more.

Doxa has maintained its diving profile and, mostly, the cushion case and avoided too many fancy complications. The watches are usually three-handers with a date. The SUB 200 C-Graph is an automatic chronograph, however, and the SUB 300 Carbon Aqua Lung US Diver is, as the name says, made of a modern material. It's a revived and im-proved watch created in a collaboration with Aqua Lung, the company that essentially launched scuba diving with the creation of a demand regulator in 1943. In 2023, it re-ceived a companion, the ß (beta) Sharkhunter, a dark ceramic, elegant, diver's watch conceived for a night out or a day under water. The carbon case is light and robust and a good background for the no-decompression dive table—devised originally by the U.S. Navy— made up of an orange depth scale on the outer bezel and an inner scale for the dive timing.

SUB 300T Clive Cussler

Reference number: 840.80.031.15
Movement: automatic, ETA Caliber 2824-2; ø 25.6 mm, height 4.6 mm; 25 jewels; 28,800 vph; 42-hour power reserve
Functions: hours, minutes, sweep seconds; date
Case: stainless steel (distressed), ø 42.5 mm, height 14 mm; unidirectional bezel with 0-60 scale and decompression times; sapphire crystal; screw-in crown, automatic helium valve; water-resistant to 120 atm
Band: stainless steel, folding clasp, with extension link
Remarks: special edition paying tribute to novelist Clive Cussler, who had his hero, Dirk Pitt, wear a Doxa
Price: $2,690
Variations: with FKM-rubber strap ($2,650

SUB 300 Beta Sharkhunter

Reference number: 830.20.101ND.20
Movement: automatic, Sellita SW 200-1; ø 25.6 mm, height 4.6 mm; 26 jewels; 28,800 vph; COSC-certified chronometer 38-hour power reserve
Functions: hours, minutes, seconds; date
Case: ceramic with titanium inside case, ø 44.5, height 11.95 mm; unidirectional bezel with ceramic insert and screw-in crown in yellow gold; sapphire crystal; screw-down crown; water-resistant to 30 atm
Band: rubber, folding clasp with dive suit extension
Price: $6,950

DOXA Army

Reference number: 785.10.031.10
Movement: automatic, ETA Caliber 2824; ø 25.6 mm, height 4.6 mm; 25 jewels; 28,800 vph; 38-hour power reserve
Functions: hours, minutes, seconds; date
Case: stainless steel, ø 42.5 X 44.5 mm, height 11.95 mm; unidirectional rotating bezel in stainless steel with black ceramic inlay; sapphire crystal; screw-down crown; water-resistant to 30 atm
Band: stainless steel, folding clasp with wetsuit extension
Price: $2,090

EBERHARD & CO.

Chronographs weren't always the main focus of the Eberhard & Co. brand. In 1887, Georges-Emile Eberhard rented a workshop in La Chaux-de-Fonds to produce a small series of pocket watches, but it was the unstoppable advancement of the automotive industry that gave the young company its inevitable direction. By the 1920s, Eberhard was producing timekeepers for the first auto races. In Italy, Eberhard & Co. functioned well into the 1930s as the official timekeeper for all important events relating to motor sports. And the Italian air force later commissioned some split-second chronographs from the company, one of which went for 56,000 euros at auction.

Eberhard & Co. is still doing well, thanks to the late Massimo Monti. In the 1990s, he associated the brand with legendary racer Tazio Nuvolari. The company dedicated a chronograph collection to Nuvolari and sponsored the annual Gran Premio Nuvolari vintage car rally in his hometown of Mantua.

With the launch of its four-counter chronograph, this most Italian of Swiss watchmakers underscored its expertise and ambitions where short time/sports time measurement is concerned. Indeed, Eberhard & Co.'s Chrono 4 chronograph, featuring four little counters all in a row, has brought new life to the chronograph in general. CEO Mario Peserico has continued to develop it, putting out versions with new colors and slightly altered looks.

The brand is pure vintage, so it will come as no surprise that it regularly reissues and updates some of its older, popular models and its Caliber EB 140, a beautifully simple, 28,800-vph movement that can be admired through the case back of its 1887 Hand-Wound model. The latest model to be revived for a contemporary audience is the Scientigraf, which was first issued in 1961. Besides being shielded from magnetism, its modernized cathedral hands come in an orange or "radium" Super-LumiNova.

Eberhard & Co.
73, Ave. Léopold-Robert
CH-2300 La Chaux-de-Fonds
Switzerland

Tel.:
+41-32-342-5141

E-mail:
info@eberhard1887.com

Website:
www.eberhard1887.com

Founded:
1887

Distribution:
Contact main office for information
Astor Time Ltd
Riva Paradiso 12
6900 Lugano Paradiso
Switzerland
+41-91-993-2601
info@eberhard1887.com

-Most important collections:
Chrono 4; 8 Jours; Tazio Nuvolari; Extra-fort; Gilda; Scafograf

1887 Remontage Manuel
Reference number: 21028.01 CT
Movement: hand-wound, Eberhard Caliber EB 140; ø 31.6 mm; 18 jewels; 28,800 vph; finely finished movement; 40-hour power reserve
Functions: hours, minutes, sweep seconds; date
Case: stainless steel, ø 41.8 mm, height 9.6 mm; sapphire crystal; transparent case back; water-resistant to 3 atm
Band: textile, pin buckle
Price: $4,230

Chrono 4 "21-42"
Reference number: 31073.05 CN CU
Movement: automatic, Eberhard Caliber EB 250-12 1/2 (base ETA 2894-2); ø 33 mm, height 7.5 mm; 53 jewels; 28,800 vph; 4 totalizers in a row; 42-hour power reserve
Functions: hours, minutes, subsidiary seconds; additional 12-hour display; chronograph; date
Case: stainless steel, ø 42 mm, height 13.3 mm; sapphire crystal; screw-in crown; water-resistant to 5 atm
Band: rubber, buckle
Remarks: the "21-42" collection stands for the launch year (2021) of the anniversary edition (20 years Chrono 4), and the case diameter of 42 mm
Price: $7,100

Chrono 4 "21-42"
Reference number: 31073.12 CP
Movement: automatic, Eberhard Caliber EB 250-12 1/2 (base ETA 2894-2); ø 33 mm, height 7.5 mm; 53 jewels; 28,800 vph; 4 totalizers in a row; 42-hour power reserve
Functions: hours, minutes, subsidiary seconds; additional 12-hour display; chronograph; date
Case: stainless steel, ø 42 mm, height 13.3 mm; sapphire crystal; screw-in crown; water-resistant to 5 atm
Band: reptile skin, buckle
Remarks: the "21-42" collection stands for the launch year (2021) of the anniversary edition (20 years Chrono 4), and the case diameter of 42 mm
Price: $6,490

Tazio Nuvolari

Reference number: 31075.02 CPT
Movement: automatic, ETA Caliber 7750; ø 30 mm, height 7.9 mm; 25 jewels; 28,800 vph; 42-hour power reserve
Functions: hours, minutes; chronograph
Case: stainless steel, ø 41 mm, height 13.2 mm; sapphire crystal; screw-in crown; water-resistant to 5 atm
Band: calfskin, pin buckle
Price: $4,200

Scafograf 300 MCMLIX

Reference number: 41034V.09 CP
Movement: automatic, Sellita Caliber SW200-1; ø 25.6 mm, height 4.6 mm; 26 jewels; 28,800 vph; 38-hour power reserve
Functions: hours, minutes, sweep seconds; date
Case: stainless steel, ø 43 mm, height 12.6 mm; unidirectional bezel with ceramic insert, with 0-60 scale; sapphire crystal; screw-in crown, helium valve; water-resistant to 30 atm
Band: calfskin, pin buckle
Remarks: the diver's watch is based on a 1959 model
Price: $3,420

Scafograf 300 MCMLIX

Reference number: 41034V.10 CP
Movement: automatic, Sellita Caliber SW200-1; ø 25.6 mm, height 4.6 mm; 26 jewels; 28,800 vph; 38-hour power reserve
Functions: hours, minutes, sweep seconds; date
Case: stainless steel, ø 43 mm, height 12.6 mm; unidirectional bezel with ceramic insert, with 0-60 scale; sapphire crystal; screw-in crown, helium valve; water-resistant to 30 atm
Band: calfskin, pin buckle
Remarks: the diver's watch is based on a 1959 model
Price: $3,420

Scientigraf Chrono

Reference number: 31077CA2C
Movement: automatic, ETA 2894-2; ø 41 mm, height 13.55 mm; 37 jewels; 28,800 vph; antimagnetic with soft iron core; 42-hour power reserve
Functions: hours, minutes, subsidiary seconds; chronograph (30-minute totalizer at 9 o'clock)
Case: stainless steel, ø 41 mm, height 13.55 mm; sapphire crystal; screw-in crown; water-resistant to 10 atm
Band: stainless steel, folding clasp
Price: $5,230

Extra-fort Grande Taille "Roue à Colonnes"

Reference number: 31956.9 CP
Movement: automatic, La Joux-Perret Caliber 8000; ø 30.4 mm, height 7.5 mm; 27 jewels; 28,800 vph; column-wheel control of the chronograph functions; 55-hour power reserve
Functions: hours, minutes, subsidiary seconds; chronograph; date
Case: stainless steel, ø 41 mm, height 13.9 mm; sapphire crystal; screw-in crown; water-resistant to 5 atm
Band: reptile skin, pin buckle
Price: $5,240
Variations: with folding clasp

8 Jours Grande Taille

Reference number: 21027.7 CP
Movement: hand-wound, Eberhard Caliber EB 896.1 (based on ETA 7001); ø 34 mm, height 5 mm; 25 jewels; 21,600 vph; 2 spring barrels, 192-hour power reserve
Functions: hours, minutes, subsidiary seconds; power-reserve indicator
Case: stainless steel, ø 41 mm, height 10.85 mm; sapphire crystal; transparent case back; water-resistant to 3 atm
Band: reptile skin, pin buckle
Price: $5,440
Variations: with white dial

EDOUARD KOEHN

Edouard Koehn Master Watchmaker Sárl
Rue des 22-Cantons 36
2300 La Chaux-de-Fonds
Switzerland

Tel.:
+41 (0)79 137 60 29

Website:
www.edouardkoehn.com
www.edouardkoehnUS.com

Founded:
2018

US Distribution:
TWI2 Inc.
76 Division Ave
Summit, NJ 07901
724-263-2286
info@totallyworthit.com

Annual production:
approx. 300 pieces

Most important collections/price range:
World Heritage / $9,950; Tempus I/ $7,950;
Tempus II / $9,950; Tempus III / $8,950

Well before Germany became a Federal Republic, it was already a large collection of states, some small, others large, run by a potpourri of noblemen and -women and high clergymen. One particularly wealthy state was the Grand Duchy of Saxe-Weimar-Eisenach, today in the German state of Thuringia. As with all courts, it gave out royal warrants to suppliers of outstanding goods and services. Among these warrants was one for the clockmaker Karl Köhn. In 1859, his son, Edouard Koehn—he later Gallicized his name—set off to Geneva to learn watchmaking with the top school. In 1861, he joined the very successful firm of Patek Philippe, and was soon promoting that brand as far away as the USA. He also made partner.

Koehn was an outstanding salesman and above all a fine watchmaker, notably of quite thin pocket watches. He also has a patent to his name for an improvement on a Breguet retrograde system. In 1891, he purchased the company of the Swedish watchmaker Henri-Robert Ekegren and started producing highly complicated pocket watches on his own.

The company went dormant in the 1930s, not an unusual event. But it was revived recently and has come out with two rather bold collections. One is the Tempus, which has two versions. The Tempus I is a tricompax chronograph with a sportive, angular look and feel. It comes in a skeletonized version or with an elegant clous-de-Paris dial for a slightly tamer look. The Tempus II is a bicompax chrono activated with a single pusher, in itself a special complication. Both models feature a brushed ceramic bezel, a material that at least hints at hi-tech.

As for the World Heritage, it is the watch for travelers, with a central 24-hour, 24-city function surrounded by a pretty wave guilloché. Travelers will appreciate the alarm function, always handy when taking power naps.

These watches all use modified Concept calibers and are made and assembled in La Chaux-de-Fonds, one of Switzerland's horological hubs.

World Heritage Ice Blue

Reference number: EK-WTA05IBASBK
Movement: automatic, Caliber EK-MVTWTA01 (modified Concepto base); ø 30.40 mm, height 7.60 mm; 31 jewels; 28,800 vph; double barrel for time and alarm mechanism; 48-hour power reserve
Functions: hours, minutes, sweep seconds, 24-hour display (world time, with 24 reference cities); day/night indicator; alarm (around 12 seconds)
Case: titanium, ø 42 mm, height 14.5 mm; sapphire; transparent case back; water-resistant to 50 meters
Band: reptile skin, folding clasp
Remarks: wave-pattern guilloché on the dial
Price: $9,950
Variations: comes with different color dials

Tempus I Red, White, and Blue

Reference number: EK-CHR04SRBE-SR-RD
Movement: automatic, Caliber EK-CHR-MVT01 (modified Concepto base); ø 30.40 mm, height 8.40 mm; 27 jewels; 28,800 vph; semi skeleton; 48-hour power reserve
Functions: hours, minutes, subsidiary seconds; chronograph
Case: stainless steel with black DLC, ø 43 mm, height 15 mm; ceramic bezel; sapphire crystal; transparent case back; water-resistant to 10 atm
Band: rubber, pin buckle
Remarks: skeleton dial
Price: $7,950
Variation: with black skeleton dial

Tempus II Open-Heart Gradient Blue

Reference: EK-CHR06MPRBE
Movement: automatic, Caliber EK-CHRMP-MVT01 (modified Concepto base); ø 30.40 mm, height 8.40 mm; 29 jewels; 28,800 vph; inverted escapement construction; 48-hour power reserve
Functions: hours, minutes, subsidiary seconds; monopusher chronograph
Case: stainless steel with black DLC, ø 43 mm, height 15 mm; ceramic bezel; sapphire crystal; transparent case back; water-resistant to 10 atm
Band: rubber, pin buckle
Remarks: skeleton dial
Price: $9,950
Variation: with silver, gold, or green dial

Fabergé
1 Cathedral Piazza
London SW1E 6BP
United Kingdom

Tel:
+44-20-7518-7297

E-mail:
information@faberge.com

Website:
www.faberge.com

Founded:
1842, current watch department relaunched 2013

Annual production:
approx. 350 watches

U.S. distributor:
Contact: sales@faberge.com

Most important collections:
Flirt; Summer in Provence; Compliquée;
Visionnaire (DTZ and Chronograph); Altruist;
Dalliance

FABERGÉ

Peter Carl Fabergé (1846–1920), son of a Saint Petersburg jeweler of French Protestant stock and supplier to the Romanovs, is a legend. In 1885, he was commissioned by Czar Alexander III to produce a special Easter egg for the czarina. It earned him the good graces of the Romanovs, but when the Bolsheviks took over in 1918, he had to leave the country. His sons maintained the jewelry business, setting up shop in Paris.

After being sold several times during the twentieth century, the name Fabergé finally ended up in the hands of Pallinghurst, a holding company with investments in mining, which include the famous Gemfields, a specialist in colored stones.

In 2013, Fabergé decided to launch a new portfolio of watches. Utilizing colored stones and platinum was a foregone conclusion. Victor Mayer, a former licensee, took on the enamel guilloché dials of the Fabergé Flirt core collection, which received a Vaucher movement. For the men's watch, Renaud et Papi produced a subtly modern flying tourbillon with a geometrically openworked dial. But the pièce de résistance, the Lady Compliquée, was assigned to Jean-Marc Wiederrecht of Agenhor, who created a movement driving a retrograde peacock's tail (Peacock) or a wave of frost (Winter) to display the minutes, while the hours circle the dial in the opposite direction. It won a prize at the prestigious Grand Prix d'Horlogerie de Genève.

Sourcing quality paid up for Fabergé new and genuinely innovative watches, which are still in the portfolio, like the iteration of the Visionnaire DTZ, which features an almost invisible rotor oscillating just on the edge of the dial and a second time zone under a magnifying glass in the middle. The Visionnaire Chronograph has the three chrono hands stacked atop each other in the middle of the dial and required an entirely new module from Agenhor. Meanwhile, the brand has not neglected chicness and a younger crowd. The Lady Libertine appeared with fascinating gem layouts, and the Flirts deliver mostly bright colors for the wrist, with or without diamonds. The Altruist collection also offers elegant pieces, including a series of hand-painted dials to support conservation efforts in sub-Saharan Africa.

Flirt

Movement: automatic, Vaucher Caliber 3000;
ø 23.3 mm, height 3.9 mm; 28 jewels; 28,800 vph;
white gold rotor; 50-hour power reserve
Functions: hours, minutes
Case: rose gold, ø 36 mm, height 5 mm; transparent case back; sapphire crystal; water resistant to 3 atm
Band: reptile skin, pin buckle
Remarks: black lacquered case middle ring with two-tiered black dial
Price: $14,000
Variations: various dial colors, set with diamonds

Compliquée Peacock Black Sapphire

Movement: hand-wound, Caliber AGH6901 exclusive for Fabergé; ø 32.7 mm, height 3.58 mm; 38 jewels; 21,600 vph; 50-hour power reserve
Functions: hours (on disk at crown), minutes (retrograde)
Case: platinum, 38 mm, height 12.90 mm; 54 diamonds on bezel; transparent back; sapphire crystal; water-resistant to 3 atm
Band: reptile skin, platinum pin buckle
Remarks: after the 1908 Fabergé Peacock Egg; dial set with diamonds, tourmalines, and tsavorites, engraved peacock on the dial with wings
Price: $108,500
Variations: Peacock Ruby, Peacock Diamond and Ruby, Peacock Emerald, and more

Altruist Wilderness Cape Buffalo

Reference number: 2821/1
Movement: automatic, Vaucher Caliber 3000;
ø 23.3 mm, height 3.9 mm; 28 jewels; 28,800 vph;
white gold rotor; 50-hour power reserve
Functions: hours, minutes
Case: rose gold, ø 41 mm, height 5 mm; rose-gold crown with finger grip case back set with 5 responsibly sourced emeralds; sapphire crystal; water resistant to 3 atm
Band: Alcantara, pin buckle
Remarks: miniature painting of Cape buffalo by André Martinez; part of a sub-Saharan wildlife series created to support conservation projects; comes with hand-painted watercolor of the dial image
Price: $45,000; limited to 5 pieces
Variations: various wildlife images on the dial

FERDINAND BERTHOUD

Chronométrie Ferdinand Berthoud SA
20, rue des Moulins
CH-2114 Fleurier
Switzerland

E-Mail:
contact@ferdinandberthoud.ch

Website:
www.ferdinandberthoud.ch

Founded:
2013

U.S. distributor:
Cellini Jewelers
430 Park Avenue at 56th Street
New York, NY 10022
212-888-0505
www.cellinijewelers.com

Collections / price range:
Exclusively built chronometers: $150,000 to
$260,000

The old saying "nomen est omen" could be the slogan for many brands in the watch industry, whose strategy and style is all in the name they choose. Karl-Friedrich Scheufele, himself vice president of a brand named after a Swiss watchmaker, Louis-Ulyssse Chopard, stumbled upon another historical personality when he founded his manufactory in the Jura in 1996. Berthoud (1727-1807) was one of the most important watchmakers of his era, a contemporary of Abraham-Louis Breguet and Thomas Mudge, a master watchmaker at the French court and supplier to the Royal Navy. He was also the author of numerous books and writings on the theory of watchmaking. Finally, he was not French, but Swiss, born in Val-de-Travers near Fleurier.

Reviving that eighteenth-century DNA seemed worthwhile. In 2015, the first Berthoud watch of the modern era was presented in Paris, a chronometer, of course. The movement of the FB 1 was equipped with a constant force mechanism using a traditional chain and fusee. It also features an unusual power reserve display (53 hours) and a rather large tourbillon under a filigree one-armed cock.

The FB 1R model presented in 2016 had a special regulator dial with a discreet time display, and the FB 1L iteration that followed a little later shows the moon phase and moon age in an unconventional manner. In 2020, Ferdinand Berthoud launched a completely new collection with the FB 2RE, which is conspicuously inspired by Berthoud's marine chronometer No. 6 and has a sophisticated mechanism chain and fusee constant force escapement (*remontoir d'égalité*) and a jumping seconds.

The FB 3 chronometer was unveiled in 2022. Powered by a mechanical movement with a cylindrical balance-spring, it is the only timepiece of its kind to be awarded a COSC chronometer certificate. The elegance of its 42 mm case, inspired by nineteenth-century pocket watches, reveals the movement and provides a stage for the regulating organ.

Only a few dozen of these exquisite timepieces are produced each year. They are all developed, manufactured, decorated, adjusted and tested by hand in the workshops of Chronométrie Ferdinand Berthoud in Fleurier (Switzerland).

Chronomètre FB 3

Reference number: FB 3SPC.1
Movement: hand-wound, Ferdinand Berthoud Caliber FB-SPC; ø 34 mm, height 6.84 mm; 47 jewels; 21,600 vph; balance wheel with variable inertia with 4 regulating screws and 8 weighted screws, German silver mainplate and bridges; 72-hour power reserve; COSC-certified chronometer
Functions: hours, minutes, subsidiary seconds; power-reserve indicator
Case: white gold, ø 42.3 mm, height 9.43 mm; sapphire crystal; transparent case back; water-resistant to 3 atm
Band: reptile skin, pin buckle
Price: on request

Chronomètre FB 3

Reference number: FB 3SPC.2
Movement: hand-wound, Ferdinand Berthoud Caliber FB-SPC; ø 34 mm, height 6.84 mm; 47 jewels; 21,600 vph; balance wheel with variable inertia with 4 regulating screws and 8 weighted screws, German silver mainplate and bridges; 72-hour power reserve; COSC-certified chronometer
Functions: hours, minutes, subsidiary seconds; power-reserve indicator
Case: rose gold, ø 42.3 mm, height 9.43 mm; sapphire crystal; transparent case back; water-resistant to 3 atm
Band: reptile skin, pin buckle
Price: on request

Chronomètre FB 2T

Reference number: FB 2T.1
Movement: hand-wound, Caliber FB-T.FC-2; ø 35.5 mm, height 7.96 mm; 45 jewels; 21,600 vph; one-minute tourbillon, constant force via chain and fusée, balance wheel with variable inertia, hairspring with Phillips end curve, flying spring barrel; German silver bridges; 53-hour power reserve; COSC-certified chronometer
Functions: hours and minutes (off-center), sweep seconds; power-reserve indicator
Case: white gold, with lateral windows, ø 44 mm, height 14.3 mm; sapphire crystal; transparent case back; water-resistant to 3 atm
Band: reptile skin, folding clasp
Price: on request; limited to 38 movements in various iterations

Montres Journe SA
17 rue de l'Arquebuse
CH 1204 Geneva
Switzerland

Tel.:
+41-22-322-09-09

E-mail:
info@fpjourne.com

Website:
www.fpjourne.com

Founded:
1999

Number of employees:
135

Annual production:
850–900 watches

U.S. distributor:
Montres Journe America
Epic Hotel
270 Biscayne Boulevard Way
Miami, FL 33131
305-572-9802
america@fpjourne.com

Most important collections:
Souveraine, Octa, lineSport, Elégante
(Prices are in Swiss francs. Use daily exchange
rate for calculations.)

F.P.JOURNE

Born in Marseilles in 1957, François-Paul Journe might have become something else had he concentrated in school. He was kicked out and went to Paris, where he completed watchmaking school before going to work for his watchmaking uncle. And he has never looked back. By the age of twenty he had made his first tourbillon and soon was producing watches for connoisseurs.

He then moved to Switzerland, where he started out with handmade creations for a limited clientele and developed the most creative and complicated timekeepers for other brands before taking the plunge and founding his own in the heart of Geneva. The timepieces he basically single-handedly and certainly single-mindedly—hence his tagline *invenit et fecit*—conceives and produces are of such extreme complexity that it is no wonder they leave his workshop in relatively small quantities. Journe has won numerous top awards, some several times over. He particularly values the Prix de la Fondation de la Vocation Bleustein-Blanchet, since it came from his peers.

The family of Journe watches is divided into four collections: the automatic Octa collection, with classic complications based on a very powerful caliber, the 1300.3, which offers 120 hours of power; the lineSport, focusing on contemporary sportive aesthetics; and the Elégante collection, an electromechanical watch providing 8 to 18 years of autonomy, depending on whether it is in daily use or in sleeping mode; and the Souveraine. The fourth features a minute repeater, a constant force tourbillon with dead-beat seconds, and a unique Chronomètre à Résonance with two escapements beating in resonance and providing chronometer precise timekeeping, especially in its most recent version, where it is equipped with a remontoir system to even out the mainspring's torque. The FFC of 2023, driven by the 1300.1 Caliber, is an oddity in the F.P.Journe world, as it was conceived by Francis Ford Coppola for the Only Watch charity auction. The jumping hours are shown by the fingers of a single metallic hand, a replica of one of the first prosthetic hands made by the sixteenth-century French medical genius, Ambroise Paré.

Chronomètre à Résonance

Movement: hand-wound, F.P.Journe Caliber 1520 in 18K rose gold; ø 34.6 mm, height 6.9 mm; 62 jewels; 21,600 vph; 2 independent balances mutually influence and stabilize each other via resonance; rose-gold plate and bridges; 42-hour power reserve
Functions: hours, minutes, subsidiary seconds, left dial 24 hours, right dial 12 hours; power reserve indicator
Case: platinum, ø 40 or 42 mm, height 10.8 mm; sapphire crystal; transparent case back; water-resistant to 3 atm
Band: reptile skin, platinum pin buckle
Remarks: 2 constant force mechanisms, one single barrel, one differential, 2 secondary gear trains
Price: CHF 136,000
Variations: 6N gold (CHF 133,000)

FFC

Movement: automatic F.P.Journe Caliber 1300.3 in rose gold; ø 34.20 mm, height 8.10 mm; 63 jewels; 21,600 vph; titanium bridges with Titalyt coating; 120-hour power reserve chronometry-certified; rose-gold rotor
Functions: hours (animated fingers, instantly jumping), rotating minutes dial
Case: platinum, ø 40 or 42 mm, height 10.7 mm; sapphire crystal; transparent case back; water-resistant to 3 atm
Band: reptile skin, pin buckle
Remarks: concept by Francis Ford Coppola; special finger code for reading time: 1 - 4 o'clock: index to pinkie then thumb (5); 6 - 9 o'clock: thumb to 4th finger; 10, no fingers; 11 pinkie alone, 12 pinkie and thumb
Price: CHF 820,000

LineSport Chronomètre Rattrapante

Movement: hand-wound, F.P.Journe Caliber 1518 in aluminum alloy; ø 33.6 mm, height 6.80 mm; 29 jewels; 21,600 vph; aluminum alloy plate and bridges; 80-hour power reserve without chronograph
Functions: hours, minutes, seconds; monopusher split-seconds chronograph; large date
Case: titanium, ø 44 mm, height 12.1 mm; tachymetric bezel with ceramic inlay; sapphire crystal; transparent case back; water-resistant to 3 atm
Band: titanium bracelet and folding clasp
Remarks: aluminum alloy dial with engraved sapphire counters
Price: CHF 116,600
Variations: 6N gold (CHF 86,000), platinum (CHF 68,100); both with Caliber 1518 in rose gold

FRANCK MULLER

Francesco "Franck" Muller has been considered one of the great creative minds in the industry ever since he designed and built his first tourbillon watch back in 1986. In fact, he never ceased amazing his colleagues and competition ever since, with his astounding timepieces that combined complications in a new and imaginative manner.

But a while ago the "master of complications" stepped away from the daily business of the brand, leaving space for the person who had paved young Muller's way to fame, Vartan Sirmakes. It was Sirmakes, previously a specialist in watch cases, who had contributed to the development of the double-domed, tonneau-shaped Cintrée Curvex case, with its elegant, 1920s retro look. He also presided over numerous complications, like the Crazy Hours, which shake up the notion of time itself. Franck Muller also created the Gigatourbillons, which are 20 millimeters across and are now appearing in various other collections.

Even a brand that prides itself on a traditional look must make some concessions to modern aesthetics. The more recent Vanguards and pieces like the Skafander reveal an edginess that generates attractive tensions in that traditional Art-Deco tonneau-shaped case that is so typical of the brand. Lately, Franck Muller has turned its attention to vivacious colors and playful dials, which in the somewhat stringent days of a pandemic seem to suggest entertaining lights at the end of the tunnel. And in a brand known for its tonneau shape, a square or round watch will look "disruptive," to use a marketing buzzword.

This remarkable company is vertically integrated, meaning when you purchase a watch, it has been entirely conceived and built "in-house," from the strap to the caliber. In fact, Franck Muller seems to operate almost independently of other watchmakers. In 1997, Muller and Sirmakes founded the Franck Muller Group Watchland, which holds the majority interest in several other companies, ten of which are watch brands, like Backes & Strauss, Martin Braun, or Pierre Kunz.

Groupe Franck Muller Watchland SA
22, route de Malagny
CH-1294 Genthod
Switzerland

Tel.:
+41-22-959-88-88

E-mail:
contact@franckmuller.ch

Website:
www.franckmuller.com

Founded:
1991

Number of employees:
approx. 500 (estimated)

U.S. distributor:
Franck Muller USA, Inc.
207 W. 25th Street, 8th Floor
New York, NY 10001
212-463-8898
www.franckmuller-usa.com

Most important collections:
Giga Tourbillon, Aeternitas, Revolution, Evolution 3-1, Vanguard, Cintrée Curvex

Curvex CX Giga Tourbillon

Reference number: CX 38L T G PR SQT 5N 5N
Movement: hand-wound, FM 2111-T; 43.0 mm x 32.9 mm, height 9.35 mm; 25 jewels; 28,800 vph; 20-mm tourbillon driven by four barrel springs, finely finished movement; partially skeletonized dial; 96-hour power reserve
Functions: hours, minutes, sweep seconds; power reserve indicator
Case: rose gold, 56.1 mm x 40 mm, height 11.7 mm; sapphire crystal; transparent case back; water-resistant to 3 atm
Band: reptile skin, buckle
Price: $27,800
Variations: with carbon or stainless-steel case

Vanguard Damas Racing

Reference number: V 45 SC SQ TRC GD AMAC. NR
Movement: automatic, FM Caliber 2800-SQ01; ø 26.60, height 3.75 mm; 21 jewels; 28,800 vph; finely finished movement, côtes de Genève on bridges, perlage on mainplate; non-magnetic Damascus steel; 42-hour power reserve
Functions: hours, minutes, sweep seconds; chronograph; large date
Case: Damascus steel, 53.7 mm x 44 mm, height 12.7 mm; sapphire crystal; transparent case back; water-resistant to 3 atm
Band: reptile skin with textile overlay, folding clasp
Remarks: numerals of Damascus steel, applied by hand
Price: $24,200
Variations: in black scheme

Curvex Flash Grand Central Tourbillon

Reference number: CX 40 T CTR FLASH AC ACBR
Movement: automatic, FM Caliber FM 2536-SC, ø 25.6 mm, height 3.2 mm; 25 jewels; 28,800 vph; central 20-mm tourbillon, finely finished movement; 42-hour power reserve
Functions: hours, minutes, sweep seconds
Case: carbon, 58.6 mm x 40 mm, height 10.5 mm; sapphire crystal; transparent case back; water-resistant to 3 atm
Remarks: indices made of composite polymer
Band: Nylon on leather, pin buckle
Price: $123,000
Variations: orange, yellow, blue, or green scheme

Curvex CX Piano

Reference number: CX 33 SC AT FO PIANO ACNR
Movement: automatic, FM Caliber 2536-SC; ø 25.6 mm, height 3.2 mm; 25 jewels; 28,800 vph; 42-hour power reserve
Functions: hours, minutes, sweep seconds
Case: black stainless steel, 48.4 x 33.5 mm, height 9.1 mm; inner bezel under sapphire crystal; transparent case back; water-resistant to 3 atm
Band: black satin, pin buckle
Remarks: dial coated in 20 layers of lacquer
Price: $9,970
Variations: stainless steel ($9,400), rose or yellow gold ($18,100), gold with diamonds ()

Vanguard Crazy Hour Lady

Reference number: V 32 CH COL DRM D (RG) -5N
Movement: automatic, FM Caliber 2038-CH; 36.20 mm x 24.80 mm, height 5.40 mm; 23 jewels; 28,800 vph; finely finished movement; 40-hour power reserve
Functions: jumping "crazy" hours, minutes, sweep seconds
Case: rose gold, 39 mm x 29 mm, height 7.2 mm; sapphire crystal; transparent case back; water-resistant to 3 atm
Band: reptile skin, pin buckle
Price: $36,400

Vanguard Krypton Racing

Reference number: V 45 SC DT KRYPTON CARBONE NR (VE) CARB
Movement: automatic, FM Caliber 2536-SCDT; ø 25.60 mm, height 3.60 mm; 25 jewels; 28,800 vph; finely finished movement, perlage on mainplate, gold and rhodium plating on components; 42-hour power reserve
Functions: hours, minutes, sweep seconds; date
Case: carbon with green inserts, 53.7 mm x 44 mm, height 12.7 mm; sapphire crystal; transparent case back; water-resistant to 3 atm
Band: reptile skin, pin buckle
Price: $15,300

Master Square

Reference number: 6000 H SC DT COL DRM R
Movement: automatic, M Caliber 2536-SCDT; ø 25.60 mm, height 3.60 mm; 25 jewels; 28,800 vph; finely finished movement, perlage on mainplate, gold and rhodium plating on components; 42-hour power reserve
Functions: hours, minutes, sweep seconds
Case: rose gold, 36.4 mm x 36.4 mm, height 10.2 mm; sapphire crystal; transparent case back; water-resistant to 3 atm
Band: reptile skin, pin buckle
Price: $23,500
Variations: comes in many variations, with and without diamonds.

Round R43 Small Second

Reference number: R 43 S6 AT FO AC AC AC
Movement: automatic, FM Caliber 708; ø 28.90 mm, height 3.85 mm; 26 jewels; 21,600 vph; finely finished movement with côtes de Genève and perlage; dial with guilloché; 38-hour power reserve
Functions: hours, minutes, subsidiary seconds
Case: stainless steel, 43 mm, height 7.7 mm; sapphire crystal; transparent case back; water-resistant to 3 atm
Remarks: case set with 178 diamonds
Band: reptile skin, pin buckle
Price: $10,000
Variations: rose gold ($26,100), rose-gold bezel ($13,800)

Vanguard Crazy Hours Hom Nguyen

Reference number: V 41 CH HN COL DRM LTD (BC)
Movement: automatic, Franck Muller Caliber MVD FM 2800; ø 26.20 mm, height 5.60 mm; 19 jewels; 28,800 vph; finely finished movement with côtes de Genève and perlage on bridges and mainplate; bidirectional rotor; 42-hour power reserve
Functions: hours, minutes, sweep seconds
Case: rose gold, 49.95 mm x 41 mm, height 12.7 mm; sapphire crystal; transparent case back; water-resistant to 3 atm
Remarks: dial designed by French artist of Vietnamese origin Hom Nguyen
Band: reptile skin, pin buckle
Price: $17,500
Variations: comes with black dial, or black and white scheme

FREDERIQUE CONSTANT

Frederique Constant SA
Chemin du Champ des Filles 32
CH-1228 Plan-les-Ouates (Geneva)
Switzerland

Tel.:
+41-22-860-0440

E-mail:
info@frederique-constant.com

Website:
www.us.frederiqueconstant.com

Founded:
1988

Number of employees:
150

U.S. distributor:
Alpina Frederique Constant USA
350 5th Avenue, 29th Floor
New York, NY 10118
646-438-8124
customercare@usa.frederiqueconstant.com

Most important collections/price range:
Manufacture collection / from approx. $3,195 to $44,995; Highlife collection / from approx $2,295 to $48,995; Classics Collection / from approx $1,095 to $2,850

Peter and Aletta Stas, the Dutch couple who founded Frederique Constant, have always sought to make high-end watches for consumers without deep pockets. So high-end, in fact, that in 2004 they went public with their first movement produced entirely in-house and equipped with silicon components.

The brand was founded in the 1988 and named for Aletta's great-grandmother Frederique Schreiner and Peter's great-grandfather Constant Stas. The couple parlayed affordable watches with very classic—i.e., not boat-rocking—design into a modern factory in Geneva's industrial Plan-les-Ouates.

In 2016, Frederique Constant and sister brand Alpina were sold to the Japanese brand Citizen. The factory in Geneva was expanded in 2019 to almost double its original size. This permitted a production projection of 250,000 watches per year by 2025. In 2021, Frederique Constant achieved a mechanical breakthrough, with a compact silicon escapement rather than a normal escapement with balance. The oscillator vibrates at a frequency of 288,000 vibrations per hour. The Slimline Monolithic Manufacture ticks ten times faster than most mechanical watches and appears to achieve far better chronometric results as well. The new escapement—a genuine horological innovation—can be viewed through an opening at 6 o'clock.

Frederique Constant celebrated its 35th anniversary in 2023, and the company has its eye on the future. In addition to its main collections, by which it aims to bring high-quality, affordable watchmaking to the market, the company has at the same time gradually expanded its product range to include more exclusive pieces for discerning collectors. The tourbillon is undoubtedly one of the most popular high complications, and now Frederique Constant has one at a reasonable price.

Highlife Tourbillon Perpetual Calendar Manufacture
Reference number: FC-975BL4NH6B
Movement: automatic, Caliber FC-975 in-house caliber; ø 30 mm, height 6.7 mm; 33 jewels; 28,800 vph; perpetual calendar; one-minute tourbillon ;38-hour power reserve
Functions: hours, minutes; perpetual calendar with date, weekday, month, leap year
Case: stainless steel, ø 41 mm, height 12.65 mm, sapphire crystal, transparent case back, water-resistant up to 10 atm
Band: stainless-steel bracelet, folding clasp
Price: $28,995; limited to 88 pieces
Variations: comes with additional navy-blue rubber strap

Highlife Chronograph Automatic
Reference number: FC-391SB4NH6B
Movement: automatic, Caliber FC-391 (based on La Joux Perret L110); ø 30.4 mm, height 7.6 mm; 26 jewels; 28,800 vph; 60-hour power reserve
Functions: hours, minutes, subsidiary seconds; chronograph; date
Case: stainless steel, ø 41 mm, height 14.22 mm; sapphire crystal; transparent case back; water-resistant to 10 atm
Band: stainless steel, folding clasp
Price: $3,895
Variations: comes with additional black rubber strap

Highlife Automatic COSC
Reference number: FC-303G3NH6B
Movement: automatic, Caliber FC-303 (based on Sellita SW200); ø 25.6 mm, height 4.6 mm; 26 jewels; 28,800 vph; COSC-certified chronometer; 38-hour power reserve
Functions: hours, minutes, seconds; date
Case: stainless steel, ø 39 mm, height 10.34 mm; sapphire crystal; transparent case back; water-resistant to 10 atm
Band: stainless-steel, folding clasp
Price: $2,295
Variations: comes with additional green rubber strap

Classic Tourbillon Manufacture Meteorite

Reference number: FC-980MT3HPT
Movement: automatic, Caliber FC-980 in-house caliber; ø 30 mm; 33 jewels; 28,800 vph; one-minute tourbillon; silicon escape wheel and anchor; finely finished movement; 38-hour power reserve
Functions: hours, minutes, subsidiary seconds (on the tourbillon cage)
Case: platinum, ø 39 mm, height 10.99 mm; sapphire crystal; transparent case back; water-resistant to 3 atm
Band: reptile skin, folding clasp
Price: $44,995; limited to 35 pieces

Classic Tourbillon Manufacture

Reference number: FC-980G3H9
Movement: automatic, Caliber FC-980-4; ø 30 mm; 33 jewels; 28,800 vph; one-minute tourbillon; silicon escape wheel; finely finished movement; 38-hour power reserve
Functions: hours, minutes, subsidiary seconds (on the tourbillon cage)
Case: rose gold, ø 39 mm, height 10.99 mm; sapphire crystal; transparent case back; water-resistant to 3 atm
Band: reptile skin, folding clasp
Price: $27,995; limited to 150 pieces

Classic Tourbillon Manufacture

Reference number: FC-980S3H6
Movement: automatic, Caliber FC-980 in-house caliber; ø 30 mm; 33 jewels; 28,800 vph; one-minute tourbillon; silicon escape wheel and anchor; finely finished movement; 38-hour power reserve
Functions: hours, minutes, subsidiary seconds (on the tourbillon cage)
Case: stainless steel, ø 39 mm, height 10.99 mm; sapphire crystal; transparent case back; water-resistant to 3 atm
Band: reptile skin, folding clasp
Remarks: limited to 350 pieces
Price: $15,695

Classic Power Reserve Big Date Manufacture

Reference number: FC-735MT3HPT
Movement: automatic, Caliber FC-735 in-house caliber; 32 jewels; 28,800 vph; 50-hour power reserve
Functions: hours, minutes, seconds, power reserve indicator; big date; moon phase
Case: platinum, ø 40 mm, height 12.19 mm; sapphire crystal; transparent case back; water-resistant to 3 atm
Band: reptile skin, folding clasp
Price: $27,995; limited to 35 pieces

Classic Power Reserve Big Date Manufacture

Reference number: FC-735G3H9
Movement: automatic, Caliber FC-735 in-house caliber; 32 jewels; 28,800 vph; 50-hour power reserve
Functions: hours, minutes, seconds, power reserve indicator; big date; moon phase
Case: rose gold, ø 40 mm, height 12.19 mm; sapphire crystal; transparent case back; water-resistant to 3 atm
Band: reptile skin, folding clasp
Price: $19,995; limited to 350 pieces

Classic Power Reserve Big Date Manufacture

Reference number: FC-735S3H6
Movement: automatic, Caliber FC-735 in-house caliber; 32 jewels; 28,800 vph; 50-hour power reserve
Functions: hours, minutes, seconds, power reserve indicator; big date; moon phase
Case: stainless steel, ø 40 mm, height 12.19 mm; sapphire crystal; transparent case back; water-resistant to 3 atm
Band: Reptile skin, folding clasp
Price: $4,995

Classics Vintage Rally Healey Automatic COSC

Reference number: FC-301HGRS5B6
Movement: automatic, Caliber FC-301 (based on Sellita SW200); certified by the COSC; ø 25.6 mm, 26 jewels; 28,800 vph; 38-hour power reserve
Functions: hours, minutes, seconds
Case: stainless steel, ø 40 mm, height 10.3 mm; sapphire crystal; water-resistant to 5 atm
Band: calfskin, pin buckle
Remarks: comes in a collector's gift set, complete with miniature replica of the NOJ393.
Price: $1,995; limited to 1,888 pieces

Classics Heart Beat Moonphase Date

Reference number: FC-335MCGRW4P26
Movement: automatic, Caliber FC-335 (based on Sellita SW200-1); ø 25.6 mm; 26 jewels; 28,800 vph; plate openworked over the escapement; 38-hour power reserve
Functions: hours, minutes, sweep seconds; date, moon phase
Case: stainless steel, ø 40 mm, height 10 mm; sapphire crystal; transparent case back; water-resistant to 6 atm
Band: calfskin, pin buckle
Price: $1,995

Classics Premiere

Reference number: FC-301DGR3B6
Movement: automatic, Caliber FC-301 (based on LJP g100) ø 25.6 mm, height 4.45 mm; 26 jewels; 28,800 vph; tungsten oscillating mass; 68-hour power reserve
Functions: hours, minutes, seconds
Case: stainless steel, ø 38.5 mm, height 10.67 mm; sapphire crystal; transparent case back; water-resistant to 3 atm
Band: calfskin, pin buckle
Price: $1,895; limited to 500 pieces

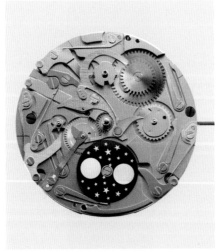

Caliber FC-980-4

Automatic; one-minute tourbillon; silicon escape wheel; single spring barrel, 38-hour power reserve
Functions: hours, minutes, subsidiary seconds
Diameter: 30 mm
Height: 5.7 mm
Jewels: 33
Balance: silicon
Frequency: 28,800 vph
Hairspring: flat hairspring
Shock protection: Incabloc
Remarks: perlage on mainplate, côtes de Genève on bridges, gold-plated rotor; 188 parts

Caliber FC-775

Automatic, single spring barrel, 38-hour power reserve
Functions: hours, minutes, perpetual calendar with date, weekday, month, moon phase and leap year
Diameter: 30.5 mm
Height: 6.67 mm
Jewels: 26
Frequency: 28,800 vph
Hairspring: flat hairspring with fine adjustment
Shock Protection: Incabloc II
Remarks: perlage on mainplate, côtes de Genève on bridges, gold-plated rotor; 191 parts

Caliber FC-718

Automatic; single spring barrel, 42-hour power reserve
Functions: hours, minutes, sweep seconds; 2nd time zone (world time display); date
Diameter: 30 mm
Height: 6.2 mm
Jewels: 26
Frequency: 28,800 vph
Hairspring: flat hairspring with fine adjustment
Shock protection: Incabloc
Remarks: crown-controlled functions; perlage on mainplate, côtes de Genève on bridges

Garrick Watchmakers
Unit 2, Fletcher Way, Norwich, Norfolk
NR3 3ST
England

Tel.:
+44 (0)1603-327272

E-mail:
info@garrick.co.uk

Website:
www.garrick.co.uk

Founded:
2013

Employees:
9

Annual production:
70 watches maximum

U. S. Distribution:
direct sales

Most important collections/price range:
Regulator and S series / £2,500 to £30,000
Prices only in pounds sterling

GARRICK

Britain has contributed enormously to the development of watchmaking, so it's hardly astonishing to find that the country is home to a growing number of brands vying on the international markets. Garrick Watchmakers is one of them. It was founded in 2013 in Devon by David Brailsford together with Simon Michlmayr, one of the top English watchmakers. The aim of these two men was to revive the old tradition of English watchmaking and to achieve the greatest possible vertical integration in the construction of their watches.

Wherever possible, Garrick either manufactures in its own workshop in Norwich, Norfolk or purchases from English suppliers. The company goes so far as to make its own hands, which is rare in the industry, since hands are very time-consuming to manufacture. The elaborately designed dials, too, are also entirely made in-house. Even cases are produced in England.

In the beginning Garrick had to delve deep into the history of English watchmaking and precision mechanics to regain the necessary knowledge to realize his vision. While the first models were still based on a Unitas caliber, the Portsmouth was presented in 2016, the first of what are now six of the company's own *manufacture* calibers. The same year saw the appearance of the Regulator, which uses its 42-millimeter case for three subdials and an opening on the free-sprung balance designed and built by the company. It was reinterpreted slightly for 2023. The so-called Trinity balance is made of a nonmagnetic alloy, Sircumet. To adjust the rate, the balance wheel is equipped with rim screws. The hairspring's position can be changed as well. In addition to genuine enamel dials, Garrick specializes in guilloché and finely engraved dials.

Garrick Watchmakers build no more than seventy watches every year. Thanks to its vertical manufacturing and the fact that each Garrick is made to order, customers are free to get some parts customized and create unique pieces. When ordering, make sure you check lead-time, though, because these are handmade pieces.

S6

Movement: hand-wound, Garrick Caliber BF03 (modified ETA 6498); ø 36.6 mm, height 4.5 mm; 19 jewels; 18,000 vph; skeletonized balance cock with swan neck regulator, hand-matted, rhodium-plated, beveled parts; engraved barrel and crown wheel cover, hand-polished chatons; 53-hour power reserve
Functions: hours, minutes, subsidiary seconds
Case: stainless steel, ø 42 mm, height 11 mm; sapphire crystal; transparent case back; water-resistant to 10 atm
Band: reptile skin, pin buckle
Remarks: engine turned or frosted dial with applied ink-filled chapter ring
Price: £6,245
Variations: engine turned dials

S2

Movement: hand-wound, Garrick Caliber UT-G06; 21 jewels; 21,600 vph; heat-blued cheater ring; gold or silver frosted finish; screw-mounted, hand-polished chatons; 45 -hour power reserve
Functions: hours, minutes, sweep dead-beat seconds
Case: stainless steel, ø 42 mm, height 10 mm; sapphire crystal; transparent case back; water-resistant to 10 atm
Band: reptile skin or calfskin; pin buckle
Price: £19,995
Variations: gold case; calfskin, buffalo, or ostrich strap; with heat-blued chapter ring and hands; options for personalization

Regulator MK II

Movement: hand-wound, Garrick Caliber UT-G02; 19 jewels; 18,000 vph; free-sprung; 48-hour power reserve
Functions: hours, minutes, sweep seconds
Case: stainless steel, ø 42 mm, height 14 mm; sapphire crystal; water-resistant to 3 atm
Band: calfskin, buckle
Remarks: finely structured metal dial, applied chapter rings
Price: £9,995
Variations: with engine turned dial (£10,995)

GIRARD-PERREGAUX

This venerable watch *manufacture* headquartered in La Chaux-de-Fonds is one of those with a very long history. It all began in 1791, though the genuinely successful part of the story is concentrated in the second half of the nineteenth century, 1867 to be precise, when Girard-Perregaux contributed a piece of watchmaking history with the aesthetically and technically sophisticated "Tourbillon with three golden bridges." Girard-Perregaux maintained its position at the forefront of Swiss watchmaking in the twentieth century with one of the first wrist-worn men's watches, as well as several pioneering achievements in mechanical watchmaking.

Italian entrepreneur Luigi ("Gino") Macaluso helped the brand achieve new greatness after 1992. In the wake of the renaissance of the mechanical watch, Girard-Perregaux managed to establish itself as a luxury manufacturer around the turn of the millennium. Following Macaluso's death in 2010, the company was purchased by the international Kering Group until it was taken over by its own management team led by CEO Patrick Pruniaux in the spring of 2022.

The tourbillon—in increasingly modern guises—remains the brand's focus, but along with the vintage trend and, no doubt, some nostalgia for the rational, elegant watches of older days, Girard-Perregaux decided to modernize the Laureato, a collection that was first introduced in 1975. It is considered one of the icons of the 1970s thanks to its sporty, striking aesthetics, octagonal bezel over a round base circle, and metal bracelet seamlessly integrated into the case. The recently rebuilt and modernized *manufacture* in La Chaux-de-Fonds quickly produced several remarkable creations based on the distinctive sports watch.

Girard-Perregaux has also released a number of special edition Laureato models to pay tribute to the brand's long-term partnership with the British sports car manufacturer Aston Martin and the Formula 1 team, such as the Green Ceramic, whose dial displays the pattern of the AM logo of the mid-1920s.

Girard-Perregaux
1, Place Girardet
CH-2300 La Chaux-de-Fonds
Switzerland

Tel.:
+41-32-911-3333

Website:
www.girard-perregaux.com

Founded:
1791

U.S. distributor:
Girard-Perregaux
Tradema of America, Inc.
7900 Glades Road, Suite 200
Boca Raton, FL 33434
833-GPWATCH
www.girard-perregaux.com

Most important collections/price range:
Laureato / Vintage 1945 / approx. $7,500 to $625,000; ww.tc / $12,300 to $23,800; GP 1966 / $7,500 to $291,000

Laureato 42mm Automatic
Reference number: 81010-11-431-11A
Movement: automatic, GP Caliber 01800-0013; ø 30 mm, height 3.97 mm; 28 jewels; 28,800 vph; 54-hour power reserve
Functions: hours, minutes, sweep seconds; date
Case: stainless steel, ø 42 mm, height 10.68 mm; sapphire crystal; transparent case back; water-resistant to 10 atm
Band: stainless steel, double folding clasp
Price: $14,300

Laureato 42mm Automatic
Reference number: 81010-11-3153-1CM
Movement: automatic, GP Caliber 01800-0013; ø 30 mm, height 3.97 mm; 28 jewels; 28,800 vph; 54-hour power reserve
Functions: hours, minutes, sweep seconds; date
Case: stainless steel, ø 42 mm, height 10.68 mm; sapphire crystal; transparent case back; water-resistant to 10 atm
Band: stainless steel, double folding clasp
Price: $14,300

Laureato 42mm Skeleton
Reference number: 81015-11-001-11A
Movement: automatic, GP Caliber 01800-0006; ø 30 mm, height 4.16 mm; 25 jewels; 28,800 vph; balance wheel with variable inertia, rotor in rose gold, fully skeletonized movement; 54-hour power reserve
Functions: hours, minutes, subsidiary seconds
Case: stainless steel, ø 42 mm, height 10.68 mm; sapphire crystal; transparent case back; water-resistant to 10 atm
Band: stainless steel, triple folding clasp
Remarks: skeletonized dial
Price: $43,600

Laureato 42mm Green Ceramic Aston Martin Edition

Reference number: 81010-32-3081-1CX
Movement: automatic, GP Caliber 01800-0013; ø 30 mm, height 3.97 mm; 28 jewels; 28,800 vph; 54-hour power reserve
Functions: hours, minutes, sweep seconds; date
Case: ceramic, ø 42 mm, height 11.08 mm; sapphire crystal; transparent case back; water-resistant to 10 atm
Band: ceramic, double folding clasp
Remarks: special edition for the sponsoring partner, Aston Martin
Price: $25,800; limited to 388 pieces

Laureato 38mm Green Ceramic Aston Martin Edition

Reference number: 81005-32-3080-1CX
Movement: automatic, GP Caliber 03300-0130; ø 25.6 mm, height 3.36 mm; 27 jewels; 28,800 vph; 46-hour power reserve
Functions: hours, minutes, sweep seconds; date
Case: ceramic, ø 38 mm, height 10.27 mm; sapphire crystal; transparent case back; water-resistant to 10 atm
Band: ceramic, double folding clasp
Remarks: special edition for the sponsoring partner, Aston Martin
Price: $25,000; limited to 188 pieces

Laureato Chronograph 42mm

Reference number: 81020-11-131-11A
Movement: automatic, GP Caliber 03300-0137/0138/0141; ø 25.95 mm, height 6.5 mm; 63 jewels; 28,800 vph; 46-hour power reserve
Functions: hours, minutes, subsidiary seconds; chronograph; date
Case: stainless steel, ø 42 mm, height 12.01 mm; sapphire crystal; water-resistant to 10 atm
Band: stainless steel, double folding clasp
Price: $18,600

Laureato Absolute Light & Shade

Reference number: 81071-43-2022-1CX
Movement: automatic, GP Caliber 01800-0006; ø 30 mm, height 4.16 mm; 25 jewels; 28,800 vph; balance wheel with variable inertia, rhodium-plated rose-gold rotor, fully skeletonized movement; 54-hour power reserve
Functions: hours, minutes, subsidiary seconds
Case: sapphire crystal, ø 44 mm, height 11.56 mm; bezel mounted on case with 8 titanium screws; sapphire crystal; transparent case back; water-resistant to 3 atm
Band: rubber, titanium folding clasp
Price: $99,600

Free Bridge

Reference number: 82000-11-631-FA6A
Movement: automatic, GP Caliber 01800-1170; ø 36.2 mm, height 5.94 mm; 23 jewels; 28,800 vph; 54-hour power reserve
Functions: hours, minutes
Case: stainless steel, ø 44 mm, height 12.2 mm; sapphire crystal; transparent case back; water-resistant to 3 atm
Band: calfskin, triple folding clasp
Price: $21,600

Neo Bridges

Reference number: 84000-21-001-BB6A
Movement: automatic, GP Caliber 08400-0001; ø 32 mm, height 5.45 mm; 29 jewels; 21,600 vph; symmetrical skeletonized construction; NAC-coated mainplate, PVD-coated bridges; micro-rotor; 54-hour power reserve
Functions: hours, minutes
Case: titanium, ø 45 mm, height 12.18 mm; sapphire crystal; transparent case back; water-resistant to 3 atm
Band: reptile skin, triple folding clasp
Price: $31,100

GLASHÜTTE ORIGINAL

Glashütter Uhrenbetrieb GmbH
Altenberger Strasse 1
D-01768 Glashütte
Germany

Tel.:
+49-350-53-46-0

E-mail:
info@glashuette-original.com

Website:
www.glashuette-original.com

Founded:
1951 foundation as VEB Glashütter Uhrenbetriebe
1990 privatization and registration as Glashütter Uhrenbetrieb GmbH;

Annual production:
N/A

U.S. distributor:
Glashütte Original
The Swatch Group (U.S.), Inc.
1200 Harbor Boulevard
Weehawken, NJ 07087
201-271-1400

Most important collections/price range:
Senator, Pano, Spezialist, Vintage, Ladies /
$4,900 to $152,300

Is there a little nostalgia creeping into the designers at Glashütte Original? Or is it just understated ecstasy for older looks? The retro touches that started appearing again a few years ago with the Sixties Square Tourbillon are still in vogue as the company delves into its own past for inspiration, such as the use of a special silver treatment on dials.

Glashütte Original *manufacture* roots go back to the mid-nineteenth century, though the name itself came later. The company, which had a sterling reputation for precision watches, became subsumed in the VEB Glashütter Uhrenbetriebe, a group of Glashütte watchmakers and suppliers who were collectivized as part of the former East German system. After reunification, the company took up its old moniker of Glashütte Original, and in 1995, the *manufacture* released an entirely new collection. Later, it purchased Union Glashütte. In 2000, the Swiss Swatch Group acquired the whole company and invested in expanding the production space at Glashütte Original headquarters. The company decided to separate out Union Glashütte, whose models are not distributed in the USA, by the way.

Manufacturing depth has reached 95 percent. All movements are designed by a team of experienced in-house engineers, while the components they comprise, such as plates, screws, pinions, wheels, levers, spring barrels, balance wheels, and tourbillon cages, are manufactured in the upgraded production areas. These parts are lavishly finished by hand before assembly by a group of talented watchmakers. Even dials are in-house. Among the highlights of its catalogue are the Senator Chronometer, which boasts second and minute hands that automatically jump to zero when the crown is pulled, allowing for extremely accurate time setting; and the Spezialist, a diver's watch that is modeled on a design from 1969, which was developed especially for frogmen and sports divers and is not only precise but particularly resistant to shocks. Its SeaQ line comes in a wide range of iterations.

Alfred Helwig Tourbillon 1920 – Limited Edition

Reference number: 1-54-01-01-01-01
Movement: hand-wound, Glashütte Original Caliber 54-01; ø 30.2 mm, height 6 mm; 20 jewels; 21,600 vph; flying tourbillon; Glashütte three-quarter plate with ribbing, screw balance with 10 weighted screws and 8 regulating screws, 2 diamond capstones; blued screws, finely finished movement; 100-hour power reserve
Functions: hours, minutes, subsidiary seconds
Case: rose gold, ø 40 mm, height 11.6 mm; sapphire crystal; transparent case back; water-resistant to 3 atm
Band: reptile skin, pin buckle
Remarks: gold dial
Price: $121,800; limited to 25 pieces

PanoLunarTourbillon

Reference number: 1-93-02-05-05-05
Movement: automatic, Glashütte Original Caliber 93-02; ø 32.2 mm, height 7.65 mm; 48 jewels; 21,600 vph; flying tourbillon, screw balance with 10 weighted and 8 regulating screws, 2 diamond capstones, blued screws, hand-engraved plate, skeletonized rotor with gold oscillating mass, finely finished movement; 48-hour power reserve
Functions: hours and minutes (off-center), subsidiary seconds (on the tourbillon cage); panorama date, moon phase
Case: red gold, ø 40 mm, height 13.1 mm; sapphire crystal; transparent case back; water-resistant to 5 atm
Band: reptile skin, folding clasp
Price: $132,000

PanoInverse – Limited Edition

Reference number: 1-66-12-01-03-62
Movement: hand-wound, Glashütte Original Caliber 66-12; ø 38.3 mm, height 5.95 mm; 31 jewels; 28,800 vph; Glashütte three-quarter plate, screw balance with 18 weighted screws, duplex swan-neck fine adjustment; inverted movement, blued screws, finely finished movement; 41-hour power reserve
Functions: hours and minutes (off-center), subsidiary seconds; power-reserve indicator
Case: platinum, ø 42 mm, height 12 mm; sapphire crystal; transparent case back; water-resistant to 5 atm
Band: reptile skin, double folding clasp
Remarks: micro-engraved "skyscraper" motif on both sides
Price: $46,700; limited to 50 pieces

PanoMaticCalendar

Reference number: 1-92-09-02-05-62
Movement: automatic, Glashütte Original Caliber 92-09; ø 32.6 mm, height 7 mm; 47 jewels; 28,800 vph; screw balance with 18 weighted screws, duplex swan-neck fine regulator, hand-engraved balance cock, Glashütte three-quarter plate with ribbing, blued screws; 100-hour power reserve
Functions: hours and minutes (off-center), subsidiary seconds; annual calendar with panorama date, month (retrograde), moon phase
Case: red gold, ø 42 mm, height 12.4 mm; sapphire crystal; transparent case back; water-resistant to 5 atm
Band: reptile skin, double folding clasp
Price: $29,700
Variations: in platinum (limited to 150 pieces, $39,100)

PanoMaticLunar

Reference number: 1-90-02-23-35-61
Movement: automatic, Glashütte Original Caliber 90-02; ø 32.6 mm, height 7 mm; 47 jewels; 28,800 vph; screw balance with 18 weighted screws, duplex swan-neck fine regulator, hand-engraved balance cock, Glashütte three-quarter plate with ribbing, blued screws, skeletonized rotor with gold oscillating mass, finely finished movement; 42-hour power reserve
Functions: hours and minutes (off-center), subsidiary seconds; panorama date, moon phase
Case: red gold, ø 40 mm, height 12.7 mm; sapphire crystal; transparent case back; water-resistant to 5 atm
Band: reptile skin, folding clasp
Price: $21,800
Variations: in stainless steel ($10,700)

Senator Cosmopolite

Reference number: 1-89-02-05-02-64
Movement: automatic, Glashütte Original Caliber 89-02; ø 39.2 mm, height 8 mm; 63 jewels; 28,800 vph; Glashütte three-quarter plate, screw balance with 4 regulating screws, swan-neck spring to regulate rate, hand-engraved balance cock; 72-hour power reserve
Functions: hours, minutes, subsidiary seconds; additional 12-hour display (2nd time zone), world time for 35 time zones, day/night indication for home and destination; power-reserve indicator; panorama date
Case: stainless steel, ø 44 mm, height 14 mm; sapphire crystal; transparent case back; water-resistant to 5 atm
Band: textile, folding clasp
Price: $21,900
Variations: with reptile skin strap; in red gold ($31,000)

Senator Chronometer

Reference number: 1-58-01-02-05-30
Movement: hand-wound, Glashütte Original Caliber 58-01; ø 35 mm, height 6.47 mm; 58 jewels; 28,800 vph; Glashütte three-quarter plate with stripe finish, screw balance with 18 weighted screws, swan-neck fine adjustment; hand-engraved balance cock, finely finished movement; 45 hours power reserve; DIN-certified chronometer
Functions: hours, minutes, subsidiary seconds; day/night indicator, power reserve indicator; panorama date
Case: red gold, ø 42 mm, height 12.47 mm; sapphire crystal; transparent case back; water-resistant to 5 atm
Band: reptile skin, folding clasp
Price: $26,240
Variations: in white gold ($32,500)

Senator Excellence Perpetual Calendar

Reference number: 1-36-02-02-05-61
Movement: automatic, Glashütte Original Caliber 36-02; ø 32.2 mm, height 7.35 mm; 49 jewels; 28,800 vph; silicon hairspring, screw balance with 4 regulating screws, swan-neck fine regulator, Glashütte three-quarter plate with ribbing, blued screws, skeletonized rotor with gold oscillating mass; 100-hour power reserve
Functions: hours, minutes, sweep seconds; perpetual calendar with panorama date, weekday, month, moon phase, leap year
Case: red gold, ø 42 mm, height 12.8 mm; sapphire crystal; transparent case back; water-resistant to 5 atm
Band: reptile skin, folding clasp
Price: $33,300
Variations: in stainless steel ($16,240)

Senator Chronograph Panorama Date

Reference number: 1-37-01-05-02-36
Movement: automatic, Glashütte Original Caliber 37-01; ø 34.8 mm, height 7.65 mm; 53 jewels; 28,800 vph; screw balance with 4 regulating screws, swan-neck spring to regulate rate; ribbing on mainplate, blued screws; 70-hour power reserve
Functions: hours, minutes, subsidiary seconds; power-reserve indicator; flyback chronograph; panorama date
Case: stainless steel, ø 42 mm, height 14.6 mm; sapphire crystal; transparent case back; water-resistant to 10 atm
Band: textile, folding clasp
Price: $13,700
Variations: with calfskin strap; with stainless steel bracelet ($14,900)

SeaQ

Reference number: 1-39-11-10-90-34
Movement: automatic, Glashütte Original Caliber 39-11; ø 26 mm, height 4.3 mm; 25 jewels; 28,800 vph; swan-neck fine regulator, Glashütte three-quarter plate with ribbing, skeletonized rotor with heavy metal oscillating mass, finely finished movement; 40-hour power reserve
Functions: hours, minutes, sweep seconds; date
Case: stainless steel, ø 39.5 mm, height 12.15 mm; unidirectional bezel in yellow gold with ceramic insert, with 0-60 scale; sapphire crystal; screw-in crown, in yellow gold; water-resistant to 20 atm
Band: textile, folding clasp
Price: $12,500

SeaQ

Reference number: 1-39-11-06-80-33
Movement: automatic, Glashütte Original Caliber 39-11; ø 26 mm, height 4.3 mm; 25 jewels; 28,800 vph; swan-neck fine regulator, Glashütte three-quarter plate with stripe, skeletonized rotor with heavy metal oscillating mass, finely finished movement; 40-hour power reserve
Functions: hours, minutes, sweep seconds; date
Case: stainless steel, ø 39.5 mm, height 12.15 mm; unidirectional bezel with ceramic insert, with 0-60 scale; sapphire crystal; screw-in crown; water-resistant to 20 atm
Band: rubber, folding clasp
Price: $9,000
Variations: with synthetic strap ($9,000); with stainless steel bracelet ($9,900)

SeaQ Chronograph

Reference number: 1-37-23-02-81-36
Movement: automatic, Glashütte Original Caliber 37-23; ø 31.6 mm, height 8 mm; 65 jewels; 28,800 vph; Screw balance with 4 regulating screws, swan-neck spring to regulate rate; ribbing on mainplate, blued screws, skeletonized rotor with gold oscillating mass, finely finished movement; 70-hour power reserve
Functions: hours, minutes, subsidiary seconds; flyback chronograph; panorama date
Case: stainless steel, ø 43.2 mm, height 16.95 mm; unidirectional bezel with ceramic insert, with 0-60 scale; sapphire crystal; transparent case back; screw-in crown; water-resistant to 30 atm
Band: textile, pin buckle
Price: $13,900

SeaQ Panorama Date

Reference number: 1-36-13-03-90-34
Movement: automatic, Glashütte Original Caliber 36-13; ø 32.2 mm, height 6.7 mm; 39 jewels; 28,800 vph; silicon hairspring, screw balance with 4 regulating screws, swan-neck spring to regulate rate, Glashütte three-quarter plate with ribbing; 100-hour power reserve
Functions: hours, minutes, sweep seconds; panorama date
Case: red gold, ø 43.2 mm, height 15.65 mm; unidirectional bezel with ceramic insert, with 0-60 scale; sapphire crystal; transparent case back; screw-in crown; water-resistant to 30 atm
Band: textile, folding clasp
Price: $24,900

SeaQ Panorama Date

Reference number: 1-36-13-04-91-34
Movement: automatic, Glashütte Original Caliber 36-13; ø 32.2 mm, height 6.7 mm; 39 jewels; 28,800 vph; silicon hairspring, screw balance with 4 regulating screws, swan-neck spring to regulate rate, Glashütte three-quarter plate with ribbing; 100-hour power reserve
Functions: hours, minutes, sweep seconds; panorama date
Case: stainless steel, ø 43.2 mm, height 15.65 mm; unidirectional bezel in red gold with ceramic insert, with 0-60 scale; sapphire crystal; transparent case back; screw-in red-gold crown; water-resistant to 30 atm
Band: textile, folding clasp
Price: $11,200
Variations: with rubber strap/pin buckle ($11,500)

SeaQ Panorama Date

Reference number: 1-36-13-07-83-33
Movement: automatic, Glashütte Original Caliber 36-13; ø 32.2 mm, height 6.7 mm; 39 jewels; 28,800 vph; silicon hairspring, screw balance with 4 regulating screws, swan-neck spring to regulate rate, Glashütte three-quarter plate with ribbing; 100-hour power reserve
Functions: hours, minutes, sweep seconds; panorama date
Case: stainless steel, ø 43.2 mm, height 15.65 mm; unidirectional bezel with ceramic insert, with 0-60 scale; sapphire crystal; transparent case back; screw-in crown; water-resistant to 30 atm
Band: rubber, folding clasp
Price: $11,500
Variations: with stainless steel bracelet ($12,400)

Seventies Chronograph Panorama Date

Reference number: 1-37-02-09-02-63
Movement: automatic, Glashütte Original Caliber 37-02; ø 31.6 mm, height 8 mm; 65 jewels; 28,800 vph; screw balance with 4 regulating screws; swan-neck spring to regulate rate; ribbing on mainplate, blued screws, skeletonized rotor with gold oscillating mass, finely finished movement; 70-hour power reserve
Functions: hours, minutes, subsidiary seconds; power-reserve indicator; flyback chronograph; panorama date
Case: stainless steel, 40 x 40 mm, height 14.1 mm; sapphire crystal; transparent case back; screw-in crown; water-resistant to 10 atm
Band: rubber, folding clasp
Price: $13,400

Sixties Subsidiary Seconds

Reference number: 1-39-60-01-01-04
Movement: automatic, Glashütte Original Caliber 39-60; ø 26.2 mm, height 5.9 mm; 30 jewels; 28,800 vph; swan-neck fine regulator, Glashütte three-quarter plate with ribbing, skeletonized rotor with gold oscillating mass, finely finished movement; 40-hour power reserve
Functions: hours, minutes, subsidiary seconds
Case: rose gold, ø 42 mm, height 12.4 mm; sapphire crystal; transparent case back; water-resistant to 3 atm
Band: reptile skin, pin buckle
Price: $16,000

Sixties Panorama Date

Reference number: 2-39-47-06-02-04
Movement: automatic, Glashütte Original Caliber 39-47; ø 30.95 mm, height 5.9 mm; 39 jewels; 28,800 vph; swan-neck fine regulator, Glashütte three-quarter plate with ribbing, skeletonized rotor with gold oscillating mass, finely finished movement; 40-hour power reserve
Functions: hours, minutes, sweep seconds; panorama date
Case: stainless steel, ø 42 mm, height 12.4 mm; sapphire crystal; transparent case back; water-resistant to 3 atm
Band: reptile skin, pin buckle
Price: $8,000
Variations: with silver or black dial ($8,000); in rose gold ($12,800)

SeaQ

Reference number: 1-39-11-09-82-70
Movement: automatic, Glashütte Original Caliber 39-11; ø 26 mm, height 4.3 mm; 25 jewels; 28,800 vph; swan-neck fine regulator, Glashütte three-quarter plate with ribbing, skeletonized rotor with heavy metal oscillating mass, finely finished movement; 40-hour power reserve
Functions: hours, minutes, sweep seconds; date
Case: stainless steel, ø 39.5 mm, height 12.15 mm; unidirectional bezel set with 47 diamonds and one sapphire; sapphire crystal; screw-in crown; water-resistant to 20 atm
Band: stainless steel, folding clasp
Price: $17,300
Variations: with textile strap ($16,100)

PanoMaticLunar

Reference number: 1-90-02-46-32-61
Movement: automatic, Glashütte Original Caliber 90-02; ø 32.6 mm, height 7 mm; 47 jewels; 28,800 vph; screw balance with 18 weighted screws, duplex swan-neck fine regulator, hand-engraved balance cock, Glashütte three-quarter plate with ribbing, blued screws, skeletonized rotor with gold oscillating mass, finely finished movement; 42-hour power reserve
Functions: hours and minutes (off-center), subsidiary seconds; panorama date, moon phase
Case: stainless steel, ø 40 mm, height 12.7 mm; sapphire crystal; transparent case back; water-resistant to 5 atm
Band: reptile skin, folding clasp
Price: $10,700
Variations: with pin buckle ($10,200); various dial colors in red gold ($21,800)

Lady Serenade

Reference number: 1-39-22-09-16-04
Movement: automatic, Glashütte Original Caliber 39-22; ø 26 mm, height 4,3 mm; 25 jewels; 28,800 vph; swan-neck fine regulator, Glashütte three-quarter plate with ribbing; finely finished movement; 40-hour power reserve
Functions: hours, minutes, sweep seconds; date
Case: stainless steel, ø 36 mm, height 10.2 mm; bezel in rose gold, set with 52 brilliant cut diamonds; sapphire crystal; transparent case back; crown in rose gold with a diamond; water-resistant to 5 atm
Band: reptile skin, folding clasp
Remarks: mother-of-pearl-dial
Price: $14,100
Variations: various cases, straps, and dials

Caliber 36

Automatic; seconds-stop mechanism; single spring barrel, 100-hour power reserve
Functions: hours, minutes, sweep seconds
Diameter: 32.2 mm
Height: 4.45 mm
Jewels: 27
Balance: screw balance with 4 regulating screws
Frequency: 28,800 vph
Hairspring: silicon
Shock protection: Incabloc
Remarks: very fine movement finishing, three-quarter plate with Glashütte ribbing, skeletonized rotor, with gold oscillating mass;
Related caliber: 36-02 (perpetual calendar), 36-03 (panorama date), 36-04 (panorama date and moon phase)

Caliber 37

Automatic; single spring barrel, 70-hour power reserve
Functions: hours, minutes, subsidiary seconds; power-reserve indicator; flyback chronograph; panorama date
Diameter: 31.6 mm
Height: 8 mm
Jewels: 65
Balance: screw balance with 4 regulating screws
Frequency: 28,800 vph
Hairspring: flat hairspring, swan-neck fine regulator for rate
Remarks: finely finished movement, chamfered edges, polished steel parts, blued screws, mainplate with Glashütte ribbing, skeletonized rotor with 21-ct gold oscillating mass

Caliber 39

Automatic; seconds-stop mechanism; single spring barrel, 40-hour power reserve
Functions: hours, minutes, sweep seconds (base caliber)
Diameter: 26.2 mm
Height: 4.3 mm
Jewels: 25
Balance: glucydur
Frequency: 28,800 vph
Hairspring: flat hairspring, swan-neck fine regulator
Shock protection: Incabloc
Related caliber: 39-55 (GMT, 40 jewels), 38-52 (automatic, 25 jewels), 39-50 (perpetual calendar, 48 jewels), 38-41/39-42 (panorama date, 44 jewels), 39-31 (chronograph, 51 jewels), 39-21/39-22 (date, 25 jewels)

Caliber 54-01

Hand-wound; flying tourbillon; 2 diamond capstones; single spring barrel, 100-hour power reserve
Functions: hours, minutes, subsidiary seconds
Diameter: 30.2 mm
Height: 6 mm
Jewels: 20
Balance: screw balance with 10 weighted screws and 8 regulating screws
Frequency: 21,600 vph
Hairspring: flat hairspring
Remarks: very fine movement finishing, chamfered edges, polished steel parts, screw-mounted gold chatons, blued screws, three-quarter plate with Glashütte ribbing, hand-engraved balance cock

Caliber 66-12

Hand-wound; seconds-stop mechanism; single spring barrel, 41-hour power reserve
Functions: hours and minutes (off-center), subsidiary seconds; power reserve indicator
Diameter: 38.3 mm
Height: 5.95 mm
Jewels: 31
Balance: screw balance with 18 weighted screws
Frequency: 28,800 vph
Hairspring: flat hairspring, double swan-neck regulator to fine-tune rate and beat
shock protection: Incabloc
Remarks: laser-processed structural parts (mainplate with skyscraper motif) with black rhodium plating

Caliber 61

Hand-wound; single spring barrel, 42-hour power reserve
Functions: hours and minutes (off-center), subsidiary seconds; flyback chronograph; panorama date
Diameter: 32.2 mm
Height: 7.2 mm
Jewels: 41
Balance: screw balance with 18 weighted screws
Frequency: 28,800 vph
Hairspring: flat hairspring, swan-neck fine regulator
Remarks: very fine movement finishing, chamfered edges, polished steel parts, screw-mounted gold chatons, blued screws, bridges, and balance cock with Glashütte ribbing, hand-engraved balance cock

Caliber 65

Hand-wound; single spring barrel, 42-hour power reserve

Functions: hours, minutes (off-center), subsidiary seconds; power reserve indicator; panorama date
Diameter: 32.2 mm
Height: 6.1 mm
Jewels: 48
Balance: screw balance with 18 weighted screws
Frequency: 28,800 vph
Hairspring: flat hairspring, duplex swan-neck fine adjustment for rate
Shock protection: Incabloc
Remarks: finely finished movement, three-quarter plate with Glashütte stripe finish, hand-engraved balance bridge

Caliber 89-02

Automatic; single spring barrel, 72-hour power reserve

Functions: hours, minutes, subsidiary seconds; 2nd time zone, world time with 37 time zones, day/night indicator, power reserve indicator; panorama date
Diameter: 39.2 mm
Height: 8 mm
Jewels: 63
Balance: screw balance with 4 gold regulating screws
Frequency: 28,800 vph
Hairspring: flat hairspring, duplex swan-neck fine adjustment for rate symmetry
Shock protection: Incabloc
Remarks: winding gears with double sun brushing, three-quarter plate with Glashütte stripe finish, hand-engraved balance bridge

Caliber 90

Automatic; single spring barrel, 42-hour power reserve

Functions: hours, minutes (off-center), subsidiary seconds; panorama date, moon phase
Diameter: 32.6 mm
Height: 5.4 mm
Jewels: 28
Balance: screw balance with 18 weighted screws
Frequency: 28,800 vph
Hairspring: flat hairspring, duplex swan-neck fine adjustment for rate symmetry
Shock protection: Incabloc
Remarks: eccentric, skeletonized, 21-ct gold oscillating mass, hand-engraved balance bridge

Caliber 91-02

Automatic; inverted movement with rate regulator on dial side; single spring barrel, 42-hour power reserve

Functions: hours, minutes (off-center), subsidiary seconds; panorama date
Diameter: 38.2 mm
Height: 7.1 mm
Jewels: 49
Balance: screw balance with 18 weighted screws
Frequency: 28,800 vph
Hairspring: flat hairspring, duplex swan-neck fine adjustment for rate symmetry
Shock protection: Incabloc
Remarks: finely finished movement, three-quarter plate with Glashütte stripe finish

Caliber 93-02

Automatic; flying tourbillon, single spring barrel, 48-hour power reserve

Functions: hours, minutes (off-center), subsidiary seconds (on tourbillon cage); panorama date, moon phase
Diameter: 32.2 mm
Height: 7.65 mm
Jewels: 48, plus 2 diamond capstones
Balance: screw balance with 18 weighted screws in rotating frame
Frequency: 21,600 vph
Hairspring: flat hairspring
Remarks: finely finished movement, off-center skeletonized rotor, with gold oscillating mass

Caliber 92-09

Automatic; double spring barrel, 100-hour power reserve

Functions: hours and minutes (off-center), subsidiary seconds; annual calendar with panorama date, month (retrograde), moon phase
Diameter: 34.8 mm
Height: 7.65 mm
Jewels: 53
Balance: screw balance with 4 regulating screws
Frequency: 28,800 vph
Hairspring: flat hairspring
Remarks: very fine movement finishing, chamfered edges, polished steel parts, mainplate with Glashütte ribbing, blued screws, off-center skeletonized rotor, with 21-ct-gold oscillating mass

GRAHAM

In the mid-1990s, unusual creations gave an old English name in watchmaking a brand-new life. In the eighteenth century, George Graham perfected the cylinder escapement and the dead-beat escapement with a temperature compensated pendulum, and he built an orrery, a mechanical model of the solar system. Graham certainly earned the right to be considered one of the big wheels in watchmaking history.

Despite his merits in the development of precision timekeeping, it was the mechanism he invented to measure short times on clocks (a kind of chronograph) that became the trademark of his wristwatch company. It consisted of a second set of hands that could be engaged to or disengaged from the constant flow of energy of the movement. Not surprisingly, the current Graham collection includes quite a few fascinating chronograph variations.

In 2000, the company released the Chronofighter, with its striking thumb-controlled lever mechanism—a modern twist on a function designed for World War II British fighter pilots, who couldn't activate the crown button of their flight chronographs with their thick gloves on. The company has also started a special series to "give back," as it were. Made of a special carbon, this U.S. Navy SEAL Chronofighter also features a special camo look designed to help hide soldiers from satellite cameras. A part of the sales of these watches will go to the nonprofit Navy SEAL Foundation. And as was to be expected, the carbon Chronofighters, which are much lighter than the stainless steel versions, are now available as a separate line. Staying in the "watch as survival tool" mode, Graham has also come up with a Chronofighter whose dial includes a gram ingot of gold (around $65 at time of writing). The buyer gets a little hammer to break the sapphire crystal in an emergency.

The Fortress line has also been designed in the same military look but without the prominent lever on the side. Instead, the chronograph functions are selected by a single pusher that is on the left-hand side of the watch, housed in a large onion-shaped crown.

Graham
Boulevard des Eplatures 38
CH-2300 La Chaux-de-Fonds
Switzerland

Tel.:
+41-32-910-9888

E-mail:
info@graham1695.com

Website:
www.graham1695.com

Founded:
1995

Number of employees:
approx. 30

Annual production:
5,000–7,000 watches

U.S. distributor:
Graham Watchmakers
169 East Flagler Street, Suite 932
Miami, FL 33131
305-890-6409
m.leemon@graham1695.com

Most important collections:
Geo.Graham, Chronofighter, Silverstone, Swordfish

Chronofighter Superlight Carbon Skeleton Orange

Reference number: 2CCCK.O01A
Movement: automatic, Graham Caliber G1790 (base ETA 7750); ø 30.4 mm, height 8.5 mm; 29 jewels; 28,800 vph; skeletonized movement, black coating on mainplate and bridges, finely finished movement; 48-hour power reserve
Functions: hours, minutes, subsidiary seconds; chronograph
Case: carbon fiber, ø 47 mm, height 15.2 mm; sapphire crystal; transparent case back; crown and pushers with finger lever on the left side; water-resistant to 10 atm
Band: rubber, buckle
Remarks: skeletonized dial
Price: $15,950

Fortress Green Limited

Reference number: 2FOAS.G05A
Movement: automatic, Graham Caliber G1750 (based on ETA A08.L01); ø 37.2 mm, height 8 mm; 25 jewels; 28,800 vph; single pusher for chronograph functions; 48-hour power reserve
Functions: hours, minutes, subsidiary seconds; chronograph; date
Case: stainless steel, ø 47 mm, height 16.9 mm; sapphire crystal; transparent case back; water-resistant to 10 atm
Band: calfskin, pin buckle
Price: $7,950; limited to 100 pieces

Chronofighter Vintage Grey Emergency Gold

Reference number: 2CVAS.A03A
Movement: automatic, Graham Caliber G1747; ø 30 mm, height 8 mm; 25 jewels; 28,800 vph; 48-hour power reserve
Functions: hours, minutes, subsidiary seconds; chronograph; date
Case: stainless steel, ø 44 mm, height 12 mm; sapphire crystal; transparent case back; crown with finger lever on the left side; water-resistant to 10 atm
Band: calfskin, pin buckle
Remarks: 1 gram of fine gold integrated into the dial; comes with hammer to break the sapphire crystal
Price: $8,950; limited to 25 pieces

Seiko Holdings
Ginza, Chuo, Tokyo
Japan

Website:
www.grand-seiko.com

Founded:
1960

Number of employees:
90,000 (for the entire holding)

U.S. distributor:
Grand Seiko Corporation of America
1111 MacArthur Boulevard
Mahwah, NJ 07430
201-529-5730
info@grand-seiko.us.com
www.grand-seiko.us.com

Most important collections/price range:
Elegance, Sport, Heritage / approx. $5,000 to
$59,000

GRAND SEIKO

In 2017, Shinji Hattori, president of the Seiko Watch Company, announced that the Grand Seiko line had become a separate *manufacture* brand with a very clear identity. For the brand's fiftieth anniversary in 2010, the Grand Seiko collection was given a host of new models and started being sold in the European market.

What makes the Grand Seiko collection special is the "Spring Drive" technology invented by a Seiko engineer. It took twenty-eight years to perfect. It's mostly mechanical but with a small, crucial electronic regulating element to tame the energy from the mainspring. The caliber has been continuously improved over time, notably with the use of a special alloy called SPRON, used for the mainspring and the hairspring.

Recent models based on that platform include the Spring Drive Chronograph with the automatic caliber 9R86 with ratchet wheel control and vertical chronograph clutch. The caliber 9S86 Hi-Beat vibrates at 36,000 vph.

It's no surprise, then, that classic watch fans have welcomed the Grand Seikos into their midst. The look is just retro enough to hint at the company's original watches of the 1960s, and the innovations are vigorous enough to keep the brand in the public eye. In 2022 the high-end skeletonized constant-force tourbillon named "Kodo," which means "heartbeat" in Japanese, drew a lot of welcome attention. Indeed, its carefully tuned escapement sounds like a beating heart.

In 2023, the Evolution 9 line was extended with the Tentagraph, a contraction of "ten beats per second, three days power reserve, chronograph." It is a high-frequency chrono with a 72-hour power reserve driven by a manufacture caliber 9SC5 based on the modern Hi-Beat caliber 9SA5. The chronograph version also has a date display, double pulse escapement, automatic winding, and a double barrel. To top it off, the chronograph functions are driven by a column wheel and a vertical clutch. These technical details ensure a longer durability of the movement and smooth starting and stopping of the stopwatch hand. The balance's frequency of 36,000 vph also makes it possible to measure or display tenths of a second.

Evolution 9 "Tentagraph"
Reference number: SLGC001
Movement: automatic, Grand Seiko Caliber 9SC5; 60 jewels; 36,000 vph; column-wheel control of chronograph functions; two-barrel springs, 72-hour power reserve
Functions: hours, minutes, subsidiary seconds; chronograph; date
Case: titanium, ø 43.2 mm, height 15.3 mm; sapphire crystal; transparent case back; screw-in crown; water-resistant to 10 atm
Band: titanium, folding clasp, with safety
Price: $13,700

Evolution 9 Hi-Beat 36,000 "White Birch"
Reference number: SLGH005
Movement: automatic, Grand Seiko Caliber 9SA5; ø 31.6 mm, height 5.18 mm; 47 jewels; 36,000 vph; antimagnetic to 4,800 A/m; 80-hour power reserve
Functions: hours, minutes, sweep seconds; date
Case: stainless steel, ø 40 mm, height 11.7 mm; sapphire crystal; transparent case back; screw-in crown; water-resistant to 10 atm
Band: stainless steel, folding clasp
Price: $9,100

Evolution 9 Spring Drive 5 Days "Ushio"
Reference number: SLGA015
Movement: automatic, Grand Seiko Caliber 9RA5; ø 31.6 mm, height 5.18 mm; 47 jewels; electromagnetic tri-synchro regulator escapement with sliding wheel; antimagnetic to 4,800 A/m; 120-hour power reserve
Functions: hours, minutes, sweep seconds; power-reserve indicator; date
Case: titanium, ø 43.8 mm, height 13.8 mm; unidirectional bezel with 0-60 scale; sapphire crystal; screw-in crown; water-resistant to 20 atm
Band: titanium, folding clasp, with extension link
Remarks: dial texture inspired by the seas around Japan (*ushio* = tide)
Price: $11,600

Evolution 9 Spring Drive 5 Days "Ushio"

Reference number: SLGA023
Movement: automatic, Grand Seiko Caliber 9RA5;
ø 31.6 mm, height 5.18 mm; 47 jewels; electromagnetic
tri-synchro regulator escapement with sliding wheel;
antimagnetic to 4,800 A/m; 120-hour power reserve
Functions: hours, minutes, sweep seconds;
power-reserve indicator; date
Case: stainless steel, ø 43.8 mm, height 13.8 mm;
unidirectional bezel with 0-60 scale; sapphire crystal;
screw-in crown; water-resistant to 20 atm
Band: stainless steel, folding clasp, with Extension link
Remarks: dial texture inspired by the seas around
Japan (*ushio* = tide)
Price: $11,600

Heritage Automatic Hi-Beat 36.000 GMT

Reference number: SBGJ267
Movement: automatic, Grand Seiko Caliber 9S86;
ø 28.4 mm, height 6.6 mm; 37 jewels; 36,000 vph;
antimagnetic to 4,800 A/m; 55-hour power reserve
Functions: hours, minutes, sweep seconds;
additional 24-hour display (2nd time zone); date
Case: stainless steel, ø 40 mm, height 14 mm;
sapphire crystal; transparent case back;
screw-in crown; water-resistant to 10 atm
Band: stainless steel, folding clasp
Price: $7,200

Heritage Automatic Hi-Beat 36.000 GMT

Reference number: SBGJ263
Movement: automatic, Grand Seiko Caliber 9S86;
ø 28.4 mm, height 6.6 mm; 37 jewels; 36,000 vph;
antimagnetic to 4,800 A/m; 55-hour power reserve
Functions: hours, minutes, sweep seconds;
additional 24-hour display (2nd time zone); date
Case: stainless steel, ø 40 mm, height 14 mm;
sapphire crystal; transparent case back;
screw-in crown; water-resistant to 10 atm
Band: stainless steel, folding clasp
Price: $7,200

Elegance Hi-Beat GMT Sekki "Yukigesho"

Reference number: SBGJ271
Movement: automatic, Grand Seiko Caliber 9S86;
ø 28.4 mm; 37 jewels; 36,000 vph; antimagnetic to
4,800 A/m; 55-hour power reserve
Functions: hours, minutes, sweep seconds;
additional 24-hour display (2nd time zone); date
Case: stainless steel, ø 39.5 mm, height 14 mm;
sapphire crystal; transparent case back;
water-resistant to 3 atm
Band: stainless steel, folding clasp
Remarks: dial inspired by snow-covered scenery
(*yukigesho* in Japanese)
Price: $7,100

Sport Spring Drive "Tokyo Lion"

Reference number: SBGA481
Movement: automatic, Grand Seiko Caliber 9R65;
ø 30 mm, height 5.1 mm; 30 jewels; electromagnetic
tri-synchro regulator escapement with sliding wheel;
antimagnetic to 4,800 A/m; 72-hour power reserve
Functions: hours, minutes, sweep seconds;
power-reserve indicator; date
Case: titanium, ø 44.5 mm, height 14.3 mm; bezel with
ceramic insert; sapphire crystal; transparent case
back; screw-in crown; water-resistant to 20 atm
Band: titanium, folding clasp
Price: $10,400

Sport Spring Drive GMT "Hotaka Peaks"

Reference number: SBGE295
Movement: automatic, Grand Seiko Caliber 9R66;
ø 30 mm, height 5.1 mm; 30 jewels; 36,000 vph;
electromagnetic tri-synchro regulator escapement
with sliding wheel; antimagnetic to 4,800 A/m;
72-hour power reserve
Functions: hours, minutes, sweep seconds;
additional 24-hour display (2nd time zone),
power-reserve indicator; date
Case: stainless steel, ø 44 mm, height 14.7 mm;
bidirectional bezel with 0-24 scale; sapphire crystal;
screw-in crown; water-resistant to 20 atm
Band: stainless steel, folding clasp
Price: $6,200

Guinand GmbH
Hausener Weg 61
D-60489 Frankfurt am Main
Germany

Tel:
+49-69-780-099

E-Mail:
vertrieb@guinand-uhren.de

Website:
www.guinand-uhren.de

Founded:
1865

Number of employees:
6

Annual production:
Around 1000 watches

Distribution:
Direct sales online or in the showroom

Most important collections/price range:
Pilot watches, chronographs, divers and dress
watches / starting around $1,500

GUINAND

Guinand is one of those watch brands that does not make too much brouhaha in the business, but rather maintains its base of faithful clients who know an affordable, readable, reliable watch when they see one. It was founded in 1865, in Les Brenets, Switzerland, just north of the watch hub, Le Locle. Early on, the company focused on chronographs and managed to survive for quite a while. Thanks to solid manufacturing capacity and a focus on, among other things, pilot watches, the company drew the attention of Helmut Sinn, who was just starting his own company in Frankfurt and needed a partner with expertise in chronographs. In the 1990s, Helmut Sinn bought Guinand, but in 2015, the company became independent again.

Today, Guinand continues to manufacture high-quality mechanical wristwatches in smallish batches but always using the quality components and applying the same excellent craftsmanship.

All Guinand watches are conceived, developed, designed, and manufactured in-house. And thanks to a focus on development, the timepieces are always at the cutting edge of technology. Any special functions requiring modification of the movements are usually designed in-house. A current example is the chronograph caliber GUI-02 with day/night indication using a central 24-hour hand. For the pilot's chronographs, Guinand has developed a case that meets the highest standards with a triple-sealed crown and FKM-R sealing system as well as a specially hardened rotating bezel mounted on ball-bearings.

Guinand attaches particular importance to craftsmanship in the manufacture of its watches. Each watch is assembled by a single watchmaker and then goes through quality control and a final test lasting several days, after which a final inspection certificate is issued. This process is done for every watch produced. The watches are only sold in the company's own showrooms and via the manufacturer's own online store. This direct sales model enables personal contact with the customer.

Pilot Chrono FR

Reference number: 40.50.X.03.Tricompax.FR
Movement: automatic, Sellita Caliber SW510A;
ø 30 mm, height 7.9 mm; 27 jewels; 28,800 vph; finely decorated movement; 60-hour power reserve
Functions: hours, minutes, subsidiary seconds; chronograph; date
Case: stainless steel, ø 40.7 mm, height 15.2 mm; black bidirectional bezel with hard coating and 0-60 scale; sapphire crystal; transparent case back; screw-in crown; water-resistant to 20 atm
Band: stainless steel, folding clasp
Price: $2,100
Variations: with calfskin strap ($1,960)

Flieger Chrono Greyline

Reference number: 40.50.X.03.Tricompax.Greyline
Movement: automatic, Caliber GUI-02 (based on Sellita SW510A); ø 30 mm, height 8.15 mm; 27 jewels; 28,800 vph; decorated movement; 60-hour power reserve
Functions: hours, minutes, subsidiary seconds; additional 24-hour display (2nd time zone); chronograph; date
Case: stainless steel, ø 40.7 mm, height 15.2 mm; black bidirectional bezel with hard coating and 0-24 scale; sapphire crystal; transparent case back; screw-in crown; water-resistant to 20 atm
Band: calfskin, pin buckle
Price: $2,200
Variations: with stainless steel bracelet ($2,360)

G44 Deepwave

Reference number: G44.T.S.01
Movement: automatic, Sellita Caliber SW200;
ø 25.6 mm, height 4.60 mm; 26 jewels; 28,800 vph; finely decorated movement; 40-hour power reserve
Functions: hours, minutes, sweep seconds; date
Case: stainless steel, ø 40.75 mm, height 12.2 mm; unidirectional bezel with 0-60 scale with hard-coated insert; sapphire crystal; screw-in crown; water-resistant to 30 atm
Band: stainless steel, folding clasp easy length adjustment
Remarks: black dial with hour bars made entirely of luminescent ceramic
Price: $1,595
Variations: with textile strap ($1,370)

HABRING²

The name Habring² stands for Maria Kristina Habring and her husband, Richard. This very gifted, fun, and creative couple have been manufacturing fine mechanical works of art in a small workshop in Austria's Völkermarkt. "You get two for one," Richard jokes with the ease of someone whose name, when uttered, triggers sage nodding. Before setting off on his own, he had a very distinguished career at IWC developing a split-seconds chronograph.

The couple's first watch labeled with their own name came out in 2004: a simple three-handed watch based on a refined and unostentatiously decorated ETA pocket watch movement, the Unitas 6498-1. The exceptional quality visible in every detail made Habring² an instant success among connoisseurs.

Since then, they have worked on a wide range of products, notably their movements, like the Caliber A09, which is available in both a manual and a bidirectionally wound automatic version, or the versatile A11, which appears in numerous models with a few iterations. All the little details that differentiate this caliber are either especially commissioned or are made in-house. Its sporty version drives a pilot's watch.

Also more or less in-house are the components of Habring²'s Seconde Foudroyante, with the foudroyante mechanism fed by a separate spring barrel. For the twentieth anniversary of the IWC double chronograph, Habring² built a limited, improved edition. The movement, based on the ETA 7750 "Valjoux," was conceived in 1991-1992 with an additional module between the chronograph and automatic winder.

Suffice to say, the four-member team's technical sophistication is remarkable. They do not shy away from modern materials like silicon, or technologies, or ion etching. But they also keep their feet on the ground, using classic materials like steel. And whatever they can't do in-house, they will purchase to ensure quality, like the perpetual calendar module that goes into the brand's flagship model, the Perpetual Doppel.

Habring² Uhrentechnik OG
Hauptplatz 16
A-9100 Völkermarkt
Austria

Tel.:
+43-4232-51-300

E-mail:
info@habring.com

Website:
www.habring2.com

Founded:
1997

Number of employees:
4

Annual production:
250 watches

U.S. retailers:
Martin Pulli (USA-East)
215-508-4610
www.martinpulli.com
Brandon Skinner (USA-West)
760-765-5657
www.horologybythesea.com

Most important collections/price range:
Felix / from $5,800; Erwin / from $7,200;
Doppel Felix / from $9,800; COS Felix /
from $8,900

Felix Sport

Reference number: Felix
Movement: hand-wound, Habring Caliber A11B;
ø 30 mm, height 4.2 mm; 18 jewels; 28,800 vph;
Triovis-fine regulator, finely finished movement;
48-hour power reserve
Functions: hours, minutes, subsidiary seconds
Case: stainless steel, ø 38.5 mm, height 7 mm;
sapphire crystal; transparent case back;
water-resistant to 3 atm
Band: calfskin, pin buckle
Price: $5,500

Erwin Tuxedo

Reference number: Erwin
Movement: hand-wound, Habring Caliber A11MS;
ø 30 mm, height 5.7 mm; 21 jewels; 28,800 vph;
antimagnetic escapement with Carl Haas hairspring,
finely finished movement; 48-hour power reserve
Functions: hours, minutes, sweep seconds (jumping)
Case: stainless steel, ø 38.5 mm, height 9 mm;
sapphire crystal; transparent case back;
water-resistant to 3 atm
Band: stainless steel, folding clasp
Price: $6,800
Variations: various dials

Foudroyante Felix

Reference number: Foudroyante Felix
Movement: hand-wound, Habring Caliber A11MF;
ø 30 mm, height 6.6 mm; 23 jewels; 28,800 vph;
antimagnetic escapement with Carl Haas hairspring
45-hour power reserve
Functions: hours, minutes, sweep seconds (jumping);
"foudroyant" indication of 1/8th of a second
("seconde foudroyante")
Case: stainless steel, ø 38.5 mm, height 11 mm;
sapphire crystal; transparent case back;
water-resistant to 3 atm
Band: calfskin, pin buckle
Price: $7,900
Variations: various dials

Chrono-Felix

Reference number: Chrono-Felix
Movement: hand-wound, Habring Caliber A11C-H1;
ø 30 mm, height 6.5 mm; 25 jewels; 28,800 vph;
tangential screw fine regulator, antimagnetic
escapement with Carl Haas hairspring; monopusher
for chronograph functions; 48-hour power reserve
Functions: hours, minutes, subsidiary seconds;
chronograph
Case: stainless steel, ø 38.5 mm, height 11 mm;
sapphire crystal; transparent case back;
water-resistant to 5 atm
Band: calfskin, pin buckle
Price: $7,900
Variations: various dials

Chrono-Felix Top Second

Reference number: Chrono-Felix Top Second
Movement: hand-wound, Habring Caliber A11FC;
ø 30 mm, height 7 mm; 25 jewels; 28,800 vph;
tangential screw fine regulator, antimagnetic
escapement with Carl Haas hairspring; monopusher
for chronograph functions; 48-hour power reserve
Functions: hours, minutes, rate display
(blinking seconds dot); chronograph
Case: stainless steel, ø 38.5 mm, height 11 mm;
sapphire crystal; transparent case back;
water-resistant to 3 atm
Band: textile, pin buckle
Price: $8,975

Doppel 38

Reference number: Doppel38
Movement: hand-wound, Habring Caliber A11R-H1;
ø 30 mm, height 7 mm; 27 jewels; 28,800 vph;
tangential screw fine regulator, antimagnetic
escapement with Carl Haas hairspring; monopusher
for chronograph functions; 48-hour power reserve
Functions: hours, minutes, subsidiary seconds;
split-seconds chronograph
Case: stainless steel, ø 38.5 mm, height 11.5 mm;
sapphire crystal; transparent case back;
water-resistant to 3 atm
Band: calfskin, pin buckle
Price: $10,300
Variations: various dials

Doppel 38

Reference number: Doppel38
Movement: hand-wound, Habring Caliber A11R-H1;
ø 30 mm, height 7 mm; 27 jewels; 28,800 vph;
tangential screw fine regulator, antimagnetic
escapement with Carl Haas hairspring; monopusher
for chronograph functions; 48-hour power reserve
Functions: hours, minutes, subsidiary seconds;
split-seconds chronograph
Case: stainless steel, ø 38.5 mm, height 11.5 mm;
sapphire crystal; transparent case back;
water-resistant to 3 atm
Band: calfskin, pin buckle
Price: $10,300
Variations: various dials

Chrono-Felix Perpetual

Reference number: Chrono-Felix Perpetual
Movement: hand-wound, Habring Caliber A11CP;
ø 30 mm, height 7.3 mm; 25 jewels; 28,800 vph;
tangential screw fine regulator, antimagnetic
escapement with Carl Haas hairspring; monopusher
for chronograph functions; 48-hour power reserve
Functions: hours, minutes; chronograph;
perpetual calendar with date, weekday, month,
moon phase, leap year
Case: stainless steel, ø 38.5 mm, height 12 mm;
sapphire crystal; transparent case back;
water-resistant to 3 atm
Band: calfskin, pin buckle
Price: $26,500

Chrono-Felix Perpetual

Reference number: Chrono-Felix Perpetual
Movement: hand-wound, Habring Caliber A11CP;
ø 30 mm, height 7.3 mm; 25 jewels; 28,800 vph;
tangential screw fine regulator, antimagnetic
escapement with Carl Haas hairspring; monopusher
for chronograph functions; 48-hour power reserve
Functions: hours, minutes; chronograph; perpetual
calendar with date, weekday, month, moon phase,
leap year
Case: stainless steel, ø 38.5 mm, height 12 mm;
sapphire crystal; transparent case back;
water-resistant to 3 atm
Band: calfskin, pin buckle
Price: $26,500

HAGER

Keeping it simple is the best way to get things going. Hager, owned and operated by American service veteran Pierre "Pete" Brown, is simply named after Hagerstown where the company was started in 2009. The business model was equally streamlined: create high-quality and affordable automatic watches accessible to those who have never experienced the joy of owning a mechanical watch. The look: rugged and refined, for individuals with a sense of adventure in their bones.

It began with sports watches, classic divers. They were designed by Brown and his small team in Hagerstown. All the cues are there for the watch connoisseur, the brushed and polished cases with beveled edges, two-tiered stadium dial, with brass markers and hands outlined in black and coated with Super-LumiNova. The domed sapphire crystal, 120-click ceramic bezel and 24 click GMT ceramic bezels are also enhanced with Super-LumiNova. The cases are rated at 20 atm, meaning they are good for more than just washing the dishes. Inside them beats one of a variety of automatic winding Swiss and Japanese mechanical movements that are both encased and regulated in the USA. Lately, Hager has started making its own movements by using trusty ETA calibers as a basis.

Since its modest beginnings, Hager has expanded its line of watches and styles without, however, abandoning the sportive touch. For the elegant, yet casual dresser needing an everyday time-telling tool, there is the Pheon (an arrowhead), with a sandwich dial, or the square Interceptor. Brown has even produced a pocket watch with a tourbillon for under $3,000. Affordable luxury, one might say. "We aren't just selling watches," he says, "we are selling the experience of owning a luxury timepiece." The fact that a Hager was chosen by the CIA to celebrate the Company's 75th anniversary says a lot.

Hager Watches
36 South Potomac Street
Suite 204
Hagerstown, MD 21740
USA

Tel.:
240-232-2172

E-mail:
info@hagerwatches.com

Website:
www.hagerwatches.com

Founded:
2009

Number of employees:
2

Annual production:
1,000–1,500 watches

Most important collections/price range:
Commando, GMT Aquamariner, U2, Interceptor, Pheon / $550 to $3,000

Hager Glacier Blue Fumé

Reference Number: 21006
Movement: automatic, Caliber MD7082 (base ETA 2895 clone stamped and assembled USA); ø 25.6 mm, height 4.35 mm, 27 jewels; 28,800 vph; 42-hour power reserve
Functions: hours, minutes, subsidiary seconds
Case: stainless steel with rose gold PVD, ø 40 mm, height 9.3 mm; screw-in crown; sapphire crystal; transparent case back; water-resistant to 5 atm.
Band: leather, buckle
Price: $895
Variations: multiple color convex sunburst patterned dials

Hager CIA 75th Anniversary Limited Edition

Reference Number: 2023LE
Movement: automatic, Caliber MD7081 (base ETA 2824 clone stamped and assembled in the USA); ø 26 mm, height 4.6 mm, 25 jewels; 28,800 vph; 40-hour power reserve
Functions: hours, minutes, sweep seconds; date; 2nd time zone
Case: stainless steel, ø 42 mm x 49.5 mm, height 13 mm; screw-in crown; sapphire crystal; custom imprinted CIA 75th Anniversary case back; water resistant to 30 atm
Band: stainless steel with 2-button clasp and 2-button slidelock extension system
Price: $1,500

Hager P02 Skeleton Pocket Watch

Reference Number: P02
Movement: hand-wound automatic, Caliber MDI-40, ø 33 mm, height 5.7 mm, 20 jewels; 28,800 vph; 1-minute flying tourbillon; 65-hour power reserve
Functions: hours, minutes
Case: stainless steel skeletonized structure, ø 42 mm x 42 mm; height 12.87 mm; sapphire crystal; transparent case back; water resistant to 3 atm.
Band: with brown leather fob
Price: $2,800

Hanhart 1882 GmbH
Hauptstrasse 33
D-78148 Gütenbach
Germany

Tel.:
+49-7723-93-44-0

Fax:
+49-7723-93-44-40

E-mail:
info@hanhart.com

Website:
www.hanhart.com

Founded:
1882 in Diessenhofen, Switzerland;
in Germany since 1902

Number of employees:
22

Annual production:
approx. 1,000 chronographs and 30,000
stopwatches

U.S. distributor:
WatchBuys
888-333-4895
www.watchbuys.com

Most important collections/price range:
Mechanical stopwatches / from approx. $600;
Pioneer / from approx. $1,070; Primus / from
approx. $2,300

HANHART

The reputation of this rather special company really goes back to the twenties and thirties. At the time, the brand manufactured affordable and robust stopwatches, pocket watches, and chronograph wristwatches. These core timepieces were what the fans of instrument watches wanted, and so they were thrilled as the company slowly abandoned its quartz dabbling of the eighties and reset its sights on the brand's rich and honorable tradition. A new collection was in the wings, raising expectations of great things to come. Support by the shareholding Gaydoul Group provided the financial backbone to get things moving.

Hanhart managed to rebuild a name for itself with a foot in Switzerland and the other in Gütenbach in southern Germany, but it began to drift after the 2009 recession. Following bankruptcy, the company reorganized under the name Hanhart 1822 GmbH and moved everything to its German hometown. It has also returned to its stylistic roots: the characteristic red start/stop pusher graces the new collections, even on the bi-compax chronos of the Racemasters, which come with a smooth bezel. Pilots' chronographs have never lost any of their charm, either, and Hanhart was already making them in the 1930s, notably the Caliber 41 and the Tachy Tele, with asymmetrical pushers and the typical red pusher. These timepieces have to survive extreme conditions, like shocks and severe temperature fluctuations. Hanhart's long tradition and expertise with flyers' chronographs struck a chord with the Austrian Army. It ordered a special edition of the Primus series decorated with the coat-of-arms of the Austrian Airforce on the dial and certified by the military.

Pioneer 417 ES 1954

Reference number: H701.210-7010
Movement: hand-wound, Sellita Caliber SW510 M; ø 30 mm, height 7.9 mm; 23 jewels; 28,800 vph; 58-hour power reserve
Functions: hours, minutes, subsidiary seconds; chronograph
Case: stainless steel, ø 39 mm, height 13.3; bidirectional bezel, with reference markings; sapphire crystal; water-resistant to 10 atm
Band: calfskin, pin buckle
Remarks: antimagnetic to 16,000 A/m
Price: $2,340

Primus Desert Pilot

Reference number: 740.250-372
Movement: automatic, Sellita Caliber SW510 (modified); ø 30 mm, height 7.9 mm; 27 jewels; 28,800 vph; 48-hour power reserve
Functions: hours, minutes, subsidiary seconds; chronograph; date
Case: stainless steel, ø 44 mm, height 16 mm; sapphire crystal; transparent case back; screw-in crown; water-resistant to 10 atm
Band: textile with calfskin overlay, folding clasp
Remarks: movable lugs
Price: $3,140

Pioneer Mk I Reverse Panda

Reference number: 714.211-7010
Movement: automatic, ETA Caliber 7753 (modified); ø 30 mm, height 7.9 mm; 27 jewels; 28,800 vph; monopusher control of chronograph functions; 42-hour power reserve
Functions: hours, minutes, subsidiary seconds; chronograph
Case: stainless steel, ø 40 mm, height 15 mm; bidirectional bezel, with reference markings; sapphire crystal; water-resistant to 10 atm
Band: calfskin, pin buckle
Price: $2,470
Variations: with stainless steel bracelet

HAUTLENCE

Time can be read in so many ways. Back in 2004, after spending years in the Swiss watch industry, Guillaume Tetu and Renaud de Retz decided that their idea for tracking it was new and unique. They were not watchmakers, but they knew whom to bring on board for the genesis of Hautlence, an anagram of Neuchâtel, the town where their small company made its debut. And soon, the first HL model was produced: a large, rectangular timepiece with the ratios of a television set and a lively and visible mechanical life, with a connecting rod between a retrograde minute and an hour chain, and other mechanical oddities.

Being unique in terms of design and mechanical hijinks, however, is not a recipe for immediate success, as many high-tech brands know. The road to finding that ideal balance between engineering and design and public perception is often rocky.

Fast forward to the 2020s. Hautlence is now a (founding) member of MELB Holding, headed by two men steeped in the watch business, Georges-Henri Meylan (formerly of Audemars Piguet) and former Breguet CFO Bill Muirhead. The industrial look with the "television" proportions has become the only Hautlence shape, though it has been given a more distinctive shape, with rounded edges. The use of blue rubber straps has also given the company a clear profile. More importantly, the intricate mechanisms have evolved and become more subtle, though no less complicated.

This all led to the Sphere, with jumping hours on a sphere and retrograde minutes. At the 2023 Grand Prix d'Horlogerie in Genva, the first series captured the Innovation Prize.

Two other collections, the Linear Series 1 and the Vagabonde, allow the company to experiment with other complications, like tourbillons, or with designs that can really fit on the space afforded by the "television set." In 2023, the company collaborated with Black Badger, makers of a kind of luminescent ceramic named Badgerite.

Hautlence
Rundbuckstrasse 10
CH - 8212 Neuhausen am Rheinfall
Switzerland

Tel.:
+41-32-924-00-60

E-Mail:
info@hautlence.com

Website:
www.hautlence.com

Founded:
2004

Number of employees:
10

Annual production:
150-200 watches

U.S. distributor:
Westime
8569 Westime Sunset Boulevard
West Hollywood, CA 90069
310-289-0808
info@westime.com
www.westime.com

Most important collections:
Concepts d'Exception, Vagabonde Series 4,
Linear Series 1

HL Sphere 01

Reference number: BA80-ST00
Movement: hand-wound, HTL A-80; ø 32.00 mm, height 5.5 mm; 37 jewels; 21,600 vph; components decorated and finished by hand; 72-hour power reserve
Functions: spherical jumping hours, retrograde minutes
Case: satin-finished and polished steel, 50.80 mm × 43 mm, height 10.9 mm (11.90 mm with sapphire crystal), polished white gold crown; transparent case back; water-resistant to 10 atm
Band: reptile skin, folding clasp
Remarks: spherical hour, with braked retrograde minute system; intermediate sapphire dial with minute numerals in Globolight; winner of GPHG Innovation Prize
Price: $74,800; limited to 28 pieces

Vagabonde Tourbillon Series 3

Reference number: AD30-ST00
Movement: automatic, in-house D30 caliber; 39.4 x 32.6 mm, height 7.7 mm; 39 jewels; 21,600 vph; double hairspring tourbillon with pawl bidirectional winding system; decorated and finished by hand; 72-hour power reserve
Functions: "wandering" hours and minutes
Case: satin-finished and polished steel with blue PVD; 43 mm x 50.8 mm x 11.9 mm; crown with rubber ring; 3D beveled sapphire crystal; water-resistant to 10 atm
Band: rubber, pin buckle with blue PVD
Remarks: cooperation with design studio Black Badger: two-level dial with etched pattern on copper-niobium superconductor base dial and intermediate sapphire dial with engraved minute track
Price: $71,500; limited to 28 pieces

Linear Series 2

Reference number: AD50-ST01
Movement: automatic, in-house D50 caliber; 37.4 x 33.0 mm, height 8.2 mm; 21,600 vph; 39 jewels; movement decorated and finished by hand; 1-minute flying tourbillon; 72-hour power reserve
Functions: retrograde linear jumping hours,
Case: satin-finished and polished steel with black PVD; 43 mm x 50.80 mm x 11.90 mm; crown with rubber ring; bezel with black PVD3D beveled sapphire crystal; water-resistant to 10 atm
Band: rubber, steel clasp
Remarks: complex dial construction, rhodium-plated base dial, intermediate sapphire dial with engraved minute track
Price: $71,020; limited to 28 pieces

Hedone Company
Flat A-6, 9th Floor,
Block A, Mai Hing Industrial Building,
16-18 Hing Yip Street,
Kwun Tong, Kowloon,
Hong Kong

Tel.:
+852-234-184-36

Email:
info@hedone-watch.com

Web:
www.hedone-watch.com

Number of employees:
8

Distribution:
Online sales and through the company website

Most important collections/prices range
Philosophe, Sculpteur, Architect, La Rose / $485
to $1,200

HEDONE WATCH

In the many and often endless deliberations by professional and amateur thinkers, the branch of philosophy known as hedonism often gets a bad name. This is partly due to the fact that it seems to fly in the face of a capitalist work ethic that demands suffering. Yet, there is something to say about taking pleasure in life itself. After all, what would be the point of living otherwise?

The question is: Does the name Hedone mean anything special in Chinese? No, says Jacky Wong, it's a reference to hedonism, having a positive attitude, and doing things with good humor and fun.

By the same token, one of the brand's most noticeable—or iconic—models is the Philosophe, which borrows the famous yin-yang symbol from Daoism for the design of the dial. On the one side is the yin principle, the receptive, passive principle, life in the third dimension, perhaps. The oscillating balance, which appears on the dial as well is the active principle, the yang, the spiritual. The day/night indicator is also a reminder of this duality.

Hedone founder and CEO Jacky Wong literally grew up with watches, spending summer vacations with his father at his watch factory. His dream was to follow in the paternal footsteps, so for the past twenty years, he has been involved in watches. "End users often buy into a brand, or follow a designer label, and the actual aesthetics and function of the timepieces often becomes the secondary concern," he said in an interview. "I want to correct that, and bring back affordable, beautiful watches that are truly a joy to own.

Armed with a team that can rework and assemble movements and watches in-house, Wong has explored several aesthetic avenues. The Architecte line features a sober dial with a clever day and month date appearing on two parallel slits on the dial. The Sculpteur collection is a classic skeleton watch, a kind of complication the brand has extended to the ladies' La Rose collection, which features a bridge shaped like a rose. Finally, Wong has a line of hand-painted dials celebrating the Hong Kong movie scene, which has made a number of cult movies already.

Philosophe

Reference number: H1001.0001
Movement: automatic, HM8202 Caliber; ø 31.00 mm, height 5.75 mm; 20 jewels; 21,600 vph; rotor decorated with côtes de Genève; escapement on the dial; 36-hour power reserve
Functions: hours, minutes; day/night indicator
Case: stainless steel; ø 44 mm, height 12.5 mm; sapphire crystal; transparent case back; water-resistant to 3 atm
Band: calfskin, pin buckle
Price: $485
Variations: various color schemes

Architect

Movement: automatic, Miyota 8215 Caliber; ø 26.00 mm, height 5.67 mm; 21 jewels; 21,600 vph; rotor decorated with côtes de Genève; escapement on the dial; 42-hour power reserve
Functions: hours, minutes, sweep seconds; day/date on two arched apertures
Case: stainless steel; ø 44 mm, height 12.5 mm; sapphire crystal; transparent case back; water-resistant to 3 atm
Band: calfskin, pin buckle
Price: $530
Variations: various color schemes

Sculpteur

Reference number: H4102.0003
Movement: hand-wound, HM7130; ø 36.60 mm, height 4.23 mm, 17 jewels; 21,600 vph; skeletonized movement, with perlage on the mainplate; 40-hour power reserve
Functions: hours, minutes
Case: stainless steel, ø 42 mm, height 10.8 mm; sapphire glass, transparent case back, water-resistant to 5 atm
Band: calfskin, folding clasp
Price: $1,160
Variations: with blue PVD or gold PVD ($1,250)

HERMÈS

Thierry Hermès's timing was just right. When he founded his saddlery in Paris in 1837, France's middle class was up and coming and spending money on beautiful things and activities like horseback riding. Hermès became a household name and a symbol of good taste—not too flashy, not trendy, but quite useful. The advent of the automobile gave rise to luggage, bags, headgear, and soon Hermès, still in family hands today, diversified its range of products—foulards, fashion, porcelain, glass, perfume, and gold jewelry are active parts of its portfolio.

Watches were a natural addition, especially with the advent of the wristwatch in the years prior to World War I. Hermès even had a timepiece that could be worn on a belt. But some time passed before the company engaged in "real" watchmaking. In 1978, La Montre Hermès opened its watch manufactory in Biel.

Hermès went all in to acquire genuine expertise on watchmaking. "Our philosophy is all about the quality of time," says CEO Laurent Dordet. "It's about imagination; we want people to dream." The way there was through "poetic" complications that allowed the company to navigate between classy but plain watches and muscular tool timepieces bristling with complications. On the one hand there were the aesthetics: the lively leaning numerals of the Arceau series or the bridoon recalling the company's equine roots at 12 o'clock for holding the strap. The Cape Cod and Nantucket series recall some of the grand old days of Art Deco, with streamlined forms and orderly dials. As for in-house complications, they are produced in collaboration with external designers, notably Agenhor, one of the industry's top engineering firms. The Slim line includes a perpetual calendar with modern numerals that raise it above the standard retro watch. The clever "Temps Suspendu" lets the wearer stop time for a moment. There are also fascinating moon phase displays and charming countdowns that will add a little romantic pizzazz to the last hour before a rendezvous. For the Arceau Le Temps Voyageur (time as traveler), Hermès turned to Chronode in Le Locle for a special module that has the home time on a small dial traveling around the watch's face. And the H08 chronograph presented in 2023 goes hypermodern, with a carbon case and titanium crown.

La Montre Hermès SA
Erlenstrasse 31A
CH-2555 Brügg
Switzerland

Tel.:
+41-32-545-0400

E-mail:
info@hermes.com

Website:
www.hermes.com

Founded:
1978

Number of employees:
362

Annual production:
Around 90,000 (est.)

U.S. distributor:
Hermès of Paris, Inc.
55 East 59th Street
New York, NY 10022
800-441-4488
www.hermes.com

Most important collections/price range:
Arceau, Cape Cod, Clipper, Faubourg, Galop d'Hermès, Heure H, H08, Klikti, Kelly, Medor, Slim d'Hermès / $2,400 to $500,000

Arceau "Le Temps Voyageur"
Reference number: 057198WW00
Movement: automatic, Hermès Caliber H1837 (with "Le Temps Voyageur" module); ø 32.7 mm, height 4.4 mm; 35 jewels; 28,800 vph; 40-hour power reserve
Functions: hours and minutes (off-center, peripheral rotation); world time display (second time zone); date
Case: platinum, ø 41 mm; titanium bezel with black DLC; sapphire crystal; transparent case back; water-resistant to 3 atm
Band: reptile skin, double folding clasp
Remarks: the "continents" on the world map on the dial are fictitious and named after key terms from the world of Hermès
Price: $30,825 **Variations:** with calfskin strap; in stainless steel with 38-millimeter case ($24,725)

H08 Chronograph Monopoussoir
Reference number: 058938WW00
Movement: automatic, Hermès Caliber H1837 (with chronograph module); ø 30 mm, height 7 mm; 34 jewels; 28,800 vph; finely finished movement; 46-hour power reserve
Functions: hours, minutes, subsidiary seconds; chronograph; date
Case: carbon fiber with graphene coating, 41 x 41 mm; bezel in titan; sapphire crystal; transparent case back; titanium crown; water-resistant to 10 atm
Band: rubber, folding clasp
Price: $15,000

Arceau Petite Lune Storyteller
Reference number: 403044WW00
Movement: automatic, Hermès Caliber H1837 (base with "Petite Lune" module); ø 26 mm, height 5.3 mm; 21 jewels; 28,800 vph; finely finished movement; 42-hour power reserve Functions: hours, minutes; moon phase
Case: white gold, ø 38 mm; bezel set with 70 diamonds; sapphire crystal; transparent case back; crown with diamond cabochon; water-resistant to 3 atm
Band: reptile skin, pin buckle
Remarks: aventurine dial on mother-of-pearl base with 5 diamonds
Price: $47,350

Slim d'Hermès Squelette Lune

Reference number: 053606WW00
Movement: automatic, Hermès Caliber H1953;
29 jewels; 28,800 vph; skeletonized movement, micro-rotor, bridges with black PVD; 43-hour power reserve
Functions: hours, minutes; double moon phase
Case: titanium, ø 39.5 mm; bezel in platinum; sapphire crystal; transparent case back; white-gold crown; water-resistant to 3 atm
Band: reptile skin, pin buckle
Remarks: skeletonized dial
Price: $23,975

Slim d'Hermès Perpetual Calendar

Reference number: 053255WW00
Movement: automatic, Hermès Caliber H1950 with Agenhor module; ø 30 mm, height 4 mm; 32 jewels; 21,600 vph; micro-rotor; finely finished movement; 42-hour power reserve
Functions: hours, minutes; additional 12-hour display (2nd time zone), day/night indication; perpetual calendar with date, month, moon phase, leap year
Case: titanium, ø 39.5 mm, height 9.48 mm; platinum bezel; sapphire crystal; transparent case back; white-gold crown and pushers; water-resistant to 3 atm
Band: reptile skin, pin buckle
Price: $38,925
Variations: in titanium with rose-gold bezel ($38,925)

Slim d'Hermès "L'heure impatiente"

Reference number: 044960WW00
Movement: automatic, Hermès Caliber H1912 (base with "L'heure impatiente" module); ø 31.96 mm, height 5.9 mm; 36 jewels; 28,800 vph; mainplate and bridges with circular and Geneva ribbing; 50-hour power reserve
Functions: hours, minutes; "Heure impatiente" alarm function with 60-minute countdown
Case: rose gold, ø 40.5 mm, height 10.67 mm; sapphire crystal; transparent case back; water-resistant to 3 atm
Band: reptile skin, pin buckle
Price: $37,325

Kelly

Reference number: 056306WW00
Movement: quartz
Functions: hours, minutes
Case: stainless steel, with 24 diamonds, 20 x 20 mm; sapphire crystal; transparent case back; water-resistant to 3 atm
Band: stainless steel, folding clasp
Remarks: case as a detachable "padlock" on a stainless-steel bracelet
Price: $5,775
Variations: with stainless steel bracelet set with diamonds; without diamonds; in rose gold set with diamond

Nantucket

Reference number: 049592WW00
Movement: quartz
Functions: hours, minutes
Case: stainless steel, 17 x 23 mm, height 6 mm; sapphire crystal; water-resistant to 3 atm
Band: stainless steel, folding clasp
Price: $3,650
Variations: with diamonds ($9,025); in rose gold ($14,625); in rose gold set with diamonds ($20,250)

Arceau WOW

Reference number: 059572WW00
Movement: automatic, Hermès Caliber H1912;
ø 23.9 mm, height 3.7 mm; 24 jewels; 28,800 vph; finely finished movement; 50-hour power reserve
Functions: hours, minutes
Case: white gold, ø 38 mm; bezel with 82 diamonds; sapphire crystal; water-resistant to 3 atm
Band: calfskin, pin buckle
Remarks: mother-of-pearl-dial with hand-painted miniature; limited to 24 pieces
Price: $72,600

H. MOSER & CIE.

H. Moser & Cie has been making a name for itself in the industry as a serious watchmaker, though not averse to flashes of humor, like the Swiss Mad (sic) Watch made of Vacherin Mont d'Or cheese it presented in 2017 (the cheese for the case is mixed with a hardening resin). And there's the Swiss Alp watch, made to look like an Apple Watch, but with all the essential Moser codes: streamlined design, top-notch technical implementation.

The company was originally founded in Le Locle in 1825 by one Heinrich Moser (1805–1874), from Schaffhausen, at the tender age of twenty-one. Soon after, he moved to Saint Petersburg, Russia, where ambitious watchmakers were enjoying a good market. In 1828, H. Moser & Cie. was brought to life—a brand resuscitated in modern times by a group of investors and watch experts together with Moser's great-grandson, Roger Nicholas Balsiger.

With the support of a host of Swiss and German specialists, the company returned to quality fundamentals. Its claim to fame is movements that contain a separate, removable escapement module supporting the pallet lever, escape wheel, and balance. The latter is fitted with the Straumann spring, made by Precision Engineering, another one of the Moser Group companies.

This small company has considerable technical know-how, which is probably what attracted MELB Holding, owners of Hautlence, and now majority owners of H. Moser shares. Under a new CEO, the brand redefined its style: understatement, soft tones, and subtle technicity. The three core collections—Endeavour, Venturer, and Pioneer—feature "clean" dials in solid colors, including the blackest black, called Vantablack. The month hand on the Endeavour is a mere arrowhead in the center of the dial that points to the hours, which double as the months. The minimalism extends to watches that would otherwise clamor for more complexity. In 2020, the company launched the Streamliner collection with a chronograph that uses the Aghenor mechanism to drive sweep second and minute hands inside a very flowing case. The collection has grown by several models, including a perpetual calendar, and in 2023, a somewhat more streamlined model—it's in the name—with a salmon dial. In the meantime, MELB Holding has shares in Agenhor.

H. Moser & Cie.
Rundbuckstrasse 10
CH-8212 Neuhausen am Rheinfall
Switzerland

Tel.:
+41-52-674-0050

E-mail:
info@h-moser.com

Website:
www.h-moser.com

Founded:
1828

Number of employees:
80+

Annual production:
approx. 2,000 watches

U.S. distributor:
MELB AMERICAS
info@melb-americas.com
917-974-8245

Most important collections/price range:
Endeavour / approx. $17,500 to $352,000; Pioneer / approx. $14,200 to $86,900; Streamliner / approx. $21,900 to $175,000; Heritage / approx. $15,300 to $275,000; concept watches

Pioneer Centre Seconds Arctic Blue

Reference number: 3200-1217
Movement: automatic, Moser Caliber HMC 200; ø 32 mm, height 5.5 mm; 27 jewels; 21,600 vph; escapement with Straumann hairspring; 72-hour power reserve
Functions: hours, minutes, sweep seconds
Case: stainless steel, ø 42.8 mm, height 10.6 mm; sapphire crystal; transparent case back; screw-in crown; water-resistant to 12 atm
Band: rubber, pin buckle
Price: $14,200
Variations: various straps

Pioneer Tourbillon Arctic Blue

Reference number: 3804-1208
Movement: automatic, Moser Caliber HMC 804; ø 32 mm, height 5.5 mm; 21,600 vph; exchangeable escapement with Straumann double hairspring, flying one-minute tourbillon, skeletonized bridges with black PVD, oscillating mass in red gold; 72-hour power reserve
Functions: hours, minutes
Case: stainless steel, ø 42.8 mm, height 10.8 mm; sapphire crystal; transparent case back; screw-in crown; water-resistant to 12 atm
Band: rubber, folding clasp
Price: $54,900
Variations: various straps

Endeavour Perpetual Calendar Tantalum Blue Enamel

Reference number: 1800-2000
Movement: hand-wound, Moser Caliber HMC 800; ø 34 mm, height 6.3 mm; 32 jewels; 18,000 vph; exchangeable escapement with Straumann hairspring, "flash calendar" functions correctable forward and backward; twin spring barrels; fine finishing on movement; 168-hour power reserve
Functions: hours, minutes, subsidiary seconds; power reserve indicator; perpetual calendar with large date and small sweep month display; leap year display (movement side)
Case: tantalum, ø 42 mm, height 13.1 mm; sapphire crystal; transparent case back
Band: kudu leather, folding clasp
Remarks: stainless-steel case back, enamel dial
Price: $82,500

Streamliner Tourbillon Vantablack

Reference number: 6804-0400
Movement: automatic, Moser Caliber HMC 804; ø 32 mm, height 5.5 mm; 21,600 vph; exchangeable escapement with flying one-minute tourbillon, Straumann double hairspring, skeletonized bridges with black PVD, oscillating mass in red gold; 72-hour power reserve
Functions: hours, minutes
Case: red gold, ø 40 mm, height 12.1 mm; sapphire crystal; transparent case back; screw-in crown; water-resistant to 12 atm
Band: red gold, triple folding clasp
Remarks: Vantablack on the dial, a deep black that absorbs almost all light
Price: $120,000
Variations: various straps

Streamliner Centre Seconds Smoked Salmon

Reference number: 6200-1207
Movement: automatic, Moser Caliber HMC 200; ø 32 mm, height 5.5 mm; 27 jewels; 21,600 vph; escapement with Straumann hairspring; 72-hour power reserve
Functions: hours, minutes, sweep seconds
Case: stainless steel, ø 40 mm, height 12.1 mm; sapphire crystal; transparent case back; screw-in crown; water-resistant to 12 atm
Band: stainless steel, triple folding clasp
Price: $21,900

Endeavour Concept Minute Repeater Tourbillon Aqua Blue

Reference number: 1904-0400
Movement: hand-wound, Caliber HMC 904; ø 33 mm, height 9.62 mm; 35 jewels; 21,600 vph; exchangeable escapement with flying one-minute tourbillon, Straumann double hairspring, skeletonized tourbillon bridge, finely hand-finished movement; 90-hour power reserve
Functions: hours, minutes; minute repeater
Case: red gold, ø 40 mm, height 13.5 mm; sapphire crystal; transparent case back
Band: reptile skin, pin buckle
Remarks: gongs and chimes visible on the dial side; limited to 20 pieces
Price: $365,000
Variations: in titanium (limited to 20 pieces)

Caliber HMC 812

Hand-wound; exchangeable escapement with gold pallet lever and escape wheel; "flash calendar" functions correctable forward and backward; twin spring barrel, 168-hour power reserve
Functions: hours, minutes, sweep seconds; power reserve indicator; perpetual calendar with date, sweep month, leap year indicator on movement side
Diameter: 34 mm
Height: 6.3 mm
Jewels: 33
Balance: glucydur
Frequency: 18,000 vph
Hairspring: Straumann
Shock protection: Incabloc

Caliber HMC 902

Automatic; column-wheel control of chronograph functions; horizontal clutch with friction wheel to avoid intermeshing of gears and to minimize accidental jumps when chronograph is activated; inverted movement with tungsten winding rotor under the dial; double spring barrel; 54-hour power reserve
Functions: hours, minutes; flyback chronograph
Diameter: 34.4 mm
Height: 7.3 mm
Jewels: 55
Frequency: 21,600 vph
Remarks: developed with Agenhor, Geneva, for H. Moser & Cie.; 434 parts

Caliber HMC 200

Automatic; double spring barrel, 72-hour power reserve
Functions: hours, minutes, sweep seconds
Diameter: 32 mm
Height: 5.5 mm
Jewels: 27
Frequency: 21,600 vph
Hairspring: Straumann

HUBLOT

Ever since Hublot moved into a new, modern, spacious factory building in Nyon, near Geneva, the brand has evolved with stunning speed. The growth has been such that Hublot has even built a second factory, which is even bigger than the first. The ground-breaking ceremony took place on March 3, 2014, and the man holding the spade was then-Hublot chairman Jean-Claude Biver, who now also heads LVMH Group's Watch Division.

Hublot grew and continues to grow thanks to a combination of innovative watchmaking and vigorous communication. It was together with current CEO Ricardo Guadalupe that Biver developed the idea of fusing different and at times incompatible materials in a watch: carbon composite and gold, ceramic and steel, denim and diamonds. In 2011, the brand introduced the first scratchproof precious metal, an alloy of gold and ceramic named "Magic Gold." In 2014, Hublot came out with a watch whose dial is made of osmium, one of the world's rarest metals. Using a new patented process, Hublot has also implemented a unique concept of cutting wafer-thin bits of glass that are set in the open spaces of a skeletonized movement plate.

The "art of fusion" tagline drove the brand into all sorts of technical and scientific partnerships and created a buzz that is ongoing, apparently, regardless of the economic environment. Hublot's concept is based on the idea of "being the first, different and unique." To achieve that goal, it has associated its name with major sports events and brands, and has created technoid, martial, exuberant, eye-burning timepieces that holler rather than merely display the time.

The counterpoints to these are the models in the expanding Classic Fusion Original collection. They look like good old friends, with purist lines and reduced dimension. In fact, they come very close to the original Hublot from the 1980s.

Hublot SA
Chemin de la Vuarpillière 33
CH-1260 Nyon
Switzerland

Tel.:
+41-22-990-9000

E-mail:
info@hublot.ch

Website:
www.hublot.com

Founded:
1980

Number of employees:
over 800 worldwide

Annual production:
approx. 50,000 watches

U.S. Distributor:
Hublot of America, Inc.
2455 E Sunrise Blvd # 402,
Fort Lauderdale, FL 33304
954-568-9400

Most important collections/price range:
Big Bang / $11,000 to $1,053,000; Classic Fusion / $5,200 to $474,000; Manufacture Piece (MP) / $82,000 to $579,000

MP-13 Tourbillon Bi-Axis Retrograde

Reference number: 913.NX.1170.RX
Movement: hand-wound, Hublot Caliber 6200; 44 jewels; 21,600 vph; flying double-axis tourbillon with 30-second and 60-second rotation; 96-hour power reserve
Functions: hours (retrograde), minutes (retrograde)
Case: titanium, ø 44 mm, height 16.7 mm; sapphire crystal; transparent case back; water-resistant to 3 atm
Band: rubber, folding clasp
Price: $158,000; limited to 50 pieces

Big Bang Integrated Tourbillon Full Carbon

Reference number: 455.YS.0170.YS
Movement: automatic, Caliber HUB 6035; ø 34 mm, height 5.7 mm; 26 jewels; 21,600 vph; flying tourbillon; off-center micro-rotor; skeletonized movement; 72-hour power reserve
Functions: hours, minutes
Case: carbon fiber and Texalium, ø 43 mm; bezel fastened to case with 6 titanium screws; sapphire crystal; transparent case back; water-resistant to 3 atm
Band: carbon fiber, titanium folding clasp
Price: $127,000; limited to 50 pieces

Big Bang Integrated Tourbillon Full Blue Sapphire

Reference number: 455.JL.0120.JL
Movement: automatic, Caliber HUB 6035; ø 34 mm, height 5.7 mm; 26 jewels; 21,600 vph; flying tourbillon; off-center micro-rotor; skeletonized movement; 72-hour power reserve
Functions: hours, minutes
Case: sapphire crystal, ø 43 mm; bezel fastened to case with 6 titanium screws; sapphire crystal; transparent case back; water-resistant to 3 atm
Band: sapphire crystal, folding clasp in titanium
Price: $500,000; limited to 10 pieces

Big Bang Integrated Time Only King Gold

Reference number: 456.OX.0180.OX
Movement: automatic, Caliber HUB 1710 (based on Zenith Elite 670); ø 26.2 mm, height 3.7 mm; 27 jewels; 28,800 vph; 50-hour power reserve
Functions: hours, minutes, sweep seconds; date
Case: rose gold, ø 40 mm, height 9.25 mm; bezel fastened to case with 6 titanium screws; sapphire crystal; transparent case back; water-resistant to 10 atm
Band: rose gold, folding clasp
Remarks: sapphire crystal dial
Price: $49,400
Variations: various cases

Big Bang Integrated Time Only Black Magic

Reference number: 456.CX.0170.CX
Movement: automatic, Caliber HUB 1710 (based on Zenith Elite 670); ø 26.2 mm, height 3.7 mm; 27 jewels; 28,800 vph; 50-hour power reserve
Functions: hours, minutes, sweep seconds; date
Case: ceramic, ø 40 mm, height 9.25 mm; bezel fastened to case with 6 titanium screws; sapphire crystal; transparent case back; water-resistant to 10 atm
Band: ceramic, folding clasp
Remarks: sapphire crystal-dial
Price: $19,900
Variations: various cases

Classic Fusion Original Yellow Gold 42mm

Reference number: 542.VX.1230.RX.MDM
Movement: automatic, Hublot Caliber 1110 (based on Sellita SW300-1 a); ø 25.6 mm, height 3.6 mm; 25 jewels; 28,800 vph; 42-hour power reserve
Functions: hours, minutes, sweep seconds; date
Case: yellow gold, ø 42 mm, height 10 mm; bezel fastened to case with 6 titanium screws; sapphire crystal; water-resistant to 5 atm
Band: rubber, folding clasp
Price: $24,100

Classic Fusion Original Black Magic 42mm

Reference number: 565.VX.1230.RX.MDM
Movement: automatic, Hublot Caliber 1110 (based on Sellita SW300-1 a); ø 25.6 mm, height 3.6 mm; 25 jewels; 28,800 vph; 42-hour power reserve
Functions: hours, minutes, sweep seconds; date
Case: ceramic, ø 42 mm, height 10 mm; bezel fastened to case with 6 titanium screws; sapphire crystal; water-resistant to 5 atm
Band: rubber, folding clasp
Price: $10,000
Variations: various case sizes and types

Classic Fusion Original Titanium 38mm

Reference number: 565.NX.1270.RX.MDM
Movement: automatic, Hublot Caliber 1110 (based on Sellita SW300-1 a); ø 25.6 mm, height 3.6 mm; 25 jewels; 28,800 vph; 42-hour power reserve
Functions: hours, minutes, sweep seconds; date
Case: titanium, ø 38 mm, height 9.85 mm; bezel fastened to case with 6 titanium screws; sapphire crystal; water-resistant to 5 atm
Band: rubber, folding clasp
Price: $7,900
Variations: various case sizes and types

Classic Fusion Chronograph Orlinski Titanium

Reference number: 549.NI.1270.RX.ORL23
Movement: automatic, Caliber HUB 1153; ø 30 mm, height 6.9 mm; 59 jewels; 28,800 vph; 42-hour power reserve
Functions: hours, minutes, subsidiary seconds; chronograph; date
Case: titanium, ø 41 mm, height 12 mm; bezel fastened to case with 6 titanium screws; sapphire crystal; water-resistant to 5 atm
Band: rubber, folding clasp
Price: $14,600
Variations: with titanium bracelet ($18,200)

Square Bang Unico Sapphire

Reference number: 821.JX.0120.RT
Movement: automatic, Caliber HUB 1280 "Unico 2";
ø 30.4 mm, height 6.75 mm; 43 jewels; 28,800 vph;
mainplate and bridges with grey coating;
72-hour power reserve
Functions: hours, minutes, subsidiary seconds;
chronograph; date
Case: sapphire, 43 x 43 mm, height 14.5 mm; bezel
fastened to case with 6 titanium screws; sapphire
crystal; screw-in crown; water-resistant to 10 atm
Band: rubber, folding clasp
Price: $95,000
Variations: various cases

Square Bang Unico White Ceramic

Reference number: 821.HX.0170.RX
Movement: automatic, Caliber HUB 1280 "Unico 2";
ø 30.4 mm, height 6.75 mm; 43 jewels; 28,800 vph;
mainplate and bridges with grey coating;
72-hour power reserve
Functions: hours, minutes, subsidiary seconds;
chronograph; date
Case: ceramic, 43 x 43 mm, height 14.5 mm; bezel
fastened to case with 6 titanium screws; sapphire
crystal; screw-in crown; water-resistant to 10 atm
Band: rubber, folding clasp
Price: $26,200
Variations: various cases

Spirit of Big Bang King Gold White diamonds

Reference number: 682.OE.2080.RW.1204
Movement: automatic, Caliber HUB 1120 (based on
Sellita SW300-1); ø 25.6 mm, height 3.6 mm; 25 jewels;
28,800 vph; 40-hour power reserve
Functions: hours, minutes, sweep seconds; date
Case: rose gold, ø 32 mm, height 11.1 mm; bezel set with
44 diamonds, fastened to case with 6 titanium screws;
sapphire crystal; water-resistant to 10 atm
Band: rubber, folding clasp
Price: $27,300

Caliber HUB 1280

Automatic; column wheel control of chronograph
functions; silicon pallet lever and escapement,
removable escapement; double-pawl automatic winding
(Pellaton system), winding rotor with ceramic ball
bearing; single spring barrel, 72-hour power reserve
Functions: hours, minutes, subsidiary seconds;
flyback chronograph; date
Diameter: 30 mm
Height: 6.75 mm
Jewels: 43
Balance: glucydur
Frequency: 28,800 vph
Hairspring: flat hairspring with fine adjustment
Shock protection: Incabloc
Remarks: 354 parts

Caliber HUB 1201

Hand-wound; skeletonized movement; silicon anchor
and escape wheel; double spring barrel, 240-hour
power reserve
Functions: hours, minutes, subsidiary seconds;
power-reserve indicator; date
Diameter: 35.19 mm
Height: 6.8 mm
Jewels: 24
Balance: CuBe
Frequency: 21,600 vph
Hairspring: flat hairspring with fine regulator
Shock protection: Incabloc
Remarks: 223 parts

Caliber HUB 6035

Automatic; flying tourbillon; off-center mini-rotor,
skeletonized movement; single spring barrel,
72-hour power reserve
Functions: hours, minutes
Diameter: 34 mm
Height: 5.7 mm
Jewels: 26
Balance: glucydur
Frequency: 21,600 vph
Hairspring: flat hairspring with fine regulator
Shock protection: Incabloc
Remarks: 282 parts

HYT SA
Rue de Prébarreau 17
CH-2000 Neuchâtel
Switzerland

Tel.:
+41-32-323-2770

E-mail:
contact@hytwatches.com

Website:
www.hytwatches.com

Founded:
2012

Number of employees:
45 (including the sister company Preciflex)

Annual production:
approx. 350 wristwatches

U.S. retailers:
Contact main office in Neuchâtel for information
on U.S. retailers

Most important collections/price range:
Various models with a liquid time display /
$39,000-$390,000

HYT

The earliest timekeepers were water clocks, known as clepsydras. The ancient Greeks had already devised a system by which water was guided from one vessel into another through an orifice of a predetermined diameter. Time was read on a calibrated scale on the second vessel. The three founders of HYT loved this idea of displaying the passage of time with moving fluids, and so they set out to solve the many problems generated if one were to introduce a liquid into a watch.

They developed a closed system made up of a capillary tube that would serve as a time track. It had a special pump-tank at either end that could either receive or pump out liquid. The two tanks had their dedicated space at 6 o'clock. These were based on sensors used by NASA. The piston-driven bellows are made of ultrathin but robust material that bends easily and offers a stable surface. This allows very exact amounts of liquid to be pumped from one tank into the other.

HYT attracted a lot of attention with its unique way of showing time, but the investment costs were very high. In 2021, the company was acquired by Kairos Technology Switzerland (KTS), and an experienced CEO, Davide Cerrato, was hired to relaunch the brand. The new collections were developed by Eric Coudray and Paul Clementi, two top-notch watchmakers who work with TEC Group. The first models they produced were the Moon Runner and the Hastroid series, with a moon phase boldly placed in the center of the dial, or a power reserve indicator. The year 2023 saw the appearance of the Conical Tourbillon, which was nominated for a GPHG prize. The tourbillon turns in the middle under a large sapphire dome and carries three small spheres spinning like planets at different speeds. In one iteration, the spheres were replaced with sapphires.

Hastroid Blue Star

Reference number: H030306-A
Movement: hand-wound, HYT Caliber 501-CM; 41 jewels; 28,800 vph; module with two bellows and a capillary tube containing two immiscible fluids, the meeting between the two liquids is the hour pointer; 72-hour power reserve
Functions: hours (retrograde fluidic), minutes; subsidiary seconds; power reserve indication
Case: gradated blue-coated magnesium alloy and black-coated titanium, 52.30 x 48 mm, height 13.30 mm; sapphire crystal; crown in blue and black titanium DLC; water-resistant to 5 atm
Band: rubber, folding clasp
Price: $75,000 limited to 20 pieces

Conical Tourbillon

Reference number: H02759-A
Movement: hand-wound, HYT Caliber 501-CM; 41 jewels; 28,800 vph; module with two bellows and a capillary tube containing two immiscible fluids, the meeting between the two liquids is the hour pointer; conical tourbillon; 72-hour power reserve
Functions: hours (retrograde fluidic), minutes; subsidiary seconds; power reserve indication
Case: black-coated titanium and carbon, 52.30 x 48 mm, height 17.20 mm; titanium crown with black DLC; domed sapphire crystal; water-resistant to 5 atm
Band: rubber with microfiber, pin buckle
Remarks: chaotic animation around the dial of three spheres turning at different speeds
Price: $370,850 limited to 8 pieces

Moon Runner White Neon

Reference number: H02800-A
Movement: hand-wound, HYT Caliber 601-MO; 42 jewels; 28,800 vph; module with two bellows and a capillary tube containing two immiscible fluids; black-coated movement; 72-hour power reserve
Functions: hours (retrograde fluidic), minutes, subsidiary seconds; day, month, 3D central moon phase,
Case: carbon and titanium, 52.30 x 48 mm, height 21.80 mm; crown coated black and silver; sapphire crystal; black-coated titanium crown; water-resistant to 5 atm
Band: rubber, folding clasp
Remarks: high luminosity thanks to a combination of SuperLumiNova
Price: $125,000; limited to 10 pieces

ITAY NOY

Our relationship to precious objects is complex and ultimately reveals as much about ourselves as about the object. Furthermore, the relationship we build up with precious objects is special. Itay Noy's watches, each unique in its look and feel, seem made to foster this conversation and, in many ways, keep it going. Noy, who hails from and lives in Israel, produces watches that immediately fire up the imagination. They are each a talking piece for the public, a touchstone for the owner.

His journey began with the City Squares model, which shows time on the backdrop of a map of the owner's favorite or native city. In 2013, Noy showcased a square watch run on a Technotime automatic movement with a face-like dial that changes with the movement of the hands, a tongue-in-cheek reminder of our daily communication with our phones and the meaning of the frame.

Exploring this intimacy between the watch and the owner is an endless source of inspiration for Noy, a jeweler by trade who, with time, as it were, has begun reaching into the engineer's magic box. He has even worked on a bespoke movement with a Swiss firm. In 2016, he created the Chrono Gears, which essentially runs on a large, invisible circular gear that drives a.m. and p.m. indicators and more. A year later, Time Tone, another "dynamic dial," to use his term, gave the owner the choice of a colored hour disk that only he or she will know, while the minute hand does its work in the center of the dial. The Full Month shows the date or the moon appearing through a circle of digits carved into the dial. The 2019 object is a subtle reminder that hours are almost irrelevant, but every minute counts: ReOrder has the hours digitally flashing on a sandwich dial, haphazardly it would seem. And with the recent Time Quarters, Noy has managed once again to rearrange time on the dial, now into four independent quadrants.

ITAY NOY
19 Mazal Arieh
Old Jaffa
Israel

Tel.:
+972-352-473-80

E-mail:
studio@itay-noy.com

Website:
www.itay-noy.com

Founded:
2000

Number of employees:
4

Annual production:
150

U.S. Distribution:
Please contact Studio Itay Noy for information.
studio@itay-noy.com

Most important collections/price range:
Time Quarters, ReOrder, Full Month, Chrono Gears,
Part Time and Seven-Day Cycle / $2,400-$16,800

Shabbat

Reference number: SDC-SHABBAT
Movement: automatic, INS200; ø 29 mm, height 5.05 mm, 26 jewels 28,800 vph, 38-hour power reserve
Functions: hours, minutes, sweep seconds, quick-set date, and day window
Case: stainless steel ø 40 mm, height 8.4 mm; sapphire crystal, screw-down case back; water-resistant to 5 atm
Band: handmade leather band, folding clasp
Price: $4,900; limited edition & numbered 77 pieces

Seven-Day Cycle

Reference number: SDC.BL
Movement: automatic, INS200; ø 29 mm, height 5.05 mm, 26 jewels 28,800vph, 38-hour power reserve
Functions: hours, minutes, sweep seconds, quick-set date, and day window
Case: stainless steel; ø 40 mm, height 8.4 mm, sapphire crystal, screw-down case back, water-resistant to 5 atm
Band: hand-made leather band; double folding clasp
Price: $4,900; limited to 77 numbered pieces

Full Month

Reference number: FM-NUM.WT
Movements: automatic, Caliber IN.VMF5400; ø 30 mm, height 3 mm; 29 jewels; 21,600 vph; extra-thin micro-rotor, 48-hour power reserve
Functions: hours, minutes, sweep seconds; full date window
Case: stainless steel, 40 mm x 44 mm, height 7.44 mm; sapphire crystal; transparent case back, water-resistant to 5 atm
Band: hand-made leather band, double folding clasp
Price: $12,800; limited to 18 numbered pieces
Variations: black or brown leather band

Chrono Gears

Reference number: CG.BK
Movement: hand-wound IN.IP13; ø 36.6 mm, height 5.5 mm; 20 jewels; 21,600 vph; 42-hour power reserve
Functions: chronogear hand indicator for a.m./p.m., chronogear hand indicator for 8 time situations, central hours, minutes, seconds
Case: stainless steel, ø 44 mm, height 12 mm; sapphire crystal; transparent case back; water-resistant to 5 atm
Band: leather, double folding clasp
Price: $6,800; limited to 24 numbered pieces
Variations: blue or black

Time Quarters

Reference number: TT.4C
Movement: Hand-wound IN.AR; ø 36.6 mm, height 5.5 mm, 20 jewels 18,000 vph, 46-hour power reserve
Functions: dynamic dial with 4 time-display windows indicating, hours, minutes, and central seconds
Case: stainless steel, ø 44 mm, height 12 mm, sapphire crystal, transparent case back, water-resistant to 5 atm
Band: hand-made leather band, double folding clasp
Price: $6,800; limited edition & numbered 24 pieces
Variations: yellow, red, green or four-color time-displays

ReOrder

Reference number: RO.WT
Movement: hand-wound, Caliber IN.IP13; ø 36.6 mm, height 5.5 mm, 20 jewels, 21,600 vph, 42-hour power reserve
Functions: dynamic dial with 12 digit-shaped windows indicating the hours, minutes, and central seconds
Case: stainless steel, ø 44 mm, height 12 mm; sapphire crystal, transparent case back; water-resistant to 5 atm
Band: hand-made leather band, double folding clasp
Price: $6,800; limited to 24 numbered pieces
Variations: blue, white, and gold plated

Rally

Reference number: RALLY.BPVD
Movement: hand-wound skeleton 6498-1; ø 36.6 mm, height 4.5 mm, 17 jewels; 18,000 vph, 46-hour power reserve
Functions: hours, minutes, subsidiary seconds
Case: stainless steel with black PVD, ø 44 mm, height 12 mm; sapphire crystal dome, transparent case back; water-resistant to 5 atm
Band: hand-made leather band, double folding clasp
Price: $5,150; limited to 99 numbered pieces
Variations: stainless steel

Time Tone

Reference number: TT.BL
Movement: hand-wound, IN.IP13; ø 36.6mm, height 5.5 mm; 20 jewels, 21,600vph; 42-hour power reserve
Functions: dynamic dial with tone colour disc, minutes, and seconds
Case: stainless steel, ø 44 mm, height 12 mm; sapphire crystal, transparent case back; water-resistant to 5 atm
Band: hand-made leather band, double folding clasp
Price: $5,800; limited to 24 numbered pieces
Variations: blue or black

Identity Hebrew

Reference number: ID-HEB.BL
Movement: automatic, ETA Caliber 2824-2; ø 25.6 mm, height 4.6 mm; 25 jewels; 28,800 vph; 38-hour power reserve
Functions: hours, minutes, sweep seconds, quick-set date window
Case: stainless steel, ø 42.4 mm, height 10 mm; sapphire crystal; screw-down case back; water-resistant to 5 atm
Band: hand-made leather band, folding clasp
Price: $2,800; limited to 99 numbered pieces
Variations: black or brown leather band

IWC

International Watch Co.
Baumgartenstrasse 15
CH-8201 Schaffhausen
Switzerland

Tel.:
+41-52-635-6565

E-mail:
info@iwc.com

Website:
www.iwc.com

Founded:
1868

Number of employees:
approx. 750

U.S. distributor:
IWC North America
645 Fifth Avenue, 5th Floor
New York, NY 10022
800-432-9330

Most important collections/price range:
Da Vinci, Pilot's, Portuguese, Ingenieur, Aquatimer,
Pallweber / approx. $4,000 to $260,000

It was an American who laid the cornerstone for an industrial watch factory in Schaffhausen—now environmentally state-of-the-art facilities. In 1868, Florentine Ariosto Jones, a watchmaker and engineer from Boston, crossed the Atlantic to the then low-wage venue of Switzerland to open the International Watch Company Schaffhausen.

Jones was a talented designer as well, who had a significant influence on the development of watch movements. Soon, he gave IWC its own seal of approval, the *Ingenieursmarke* (Engineer's Brand), a standard it still maintains today. The company has never deviated from that course, in spite of many different owners. The portfolio includes the rugged and sportive Pilot and Big Pilot watches, the refined Da Vincis, elegant Portofinos, and complicated Portuguese.

IWC movements include the Jones caliber, named for the IWC founder, and the pocket watch caliber 89, introduced in 1946 as the creation of then-technical director Albert Pellaton. Four years later, Pellaton created the first IWC automatic movement. In 2020, IWC decided to equip all the Portuguese models with in-house calibers, including the automatic 52000 and 82000 caliber families, which use Pellaton or double-pawl winding mechanisms.

Pilot's watches nowadays play an important role in IWC's portfolio. The company has expanded the Top Gun line in the Pilot's Watches collection to include new models with ceramic cases. Already in 2019, the first models in sand-colored ceramic appeared.

As for the IWC Ingenieur, in Gérald Genta's revised version of 1976, it undoubtedly ranks as a living watch legend. The "Jumbo," so coveted by collectors today, was viewed rather suspiciously when it was presented almost fifty years ago and it sort of failed commercially, selling less than one thousand pieces. IWC's head of design, Christian Knoop adopted this model for the new generation of Ingenieurs. Because its dimensions were already quite close to today's wearing habits, Knoop limited himself to a little fine-tuning of the proportions and surfaces of the case and bezel. The smaller diameter required use of the automatic caliber 32111. And the Ingenieur Automatic 40 is somewhat thinner than its prototype. Concessions were made in terms of magnetic field protection: the wall thickness of the soft-iron dome was reduced, and the new Ingenieur is now only resistant to magnetic fields up to 40,000 A/m.

Ingenieur Automatic 40

Reference number: IW328902
Movement: automatic, IWC Caliber 32111; ø 28.2 mm, height 3.77 mm; 21 jewels; 28,800 vph; finely finished with côtes de Genève; 72-hour power reserve
Functions: hours, minutes, sweep seconds; date
Case: stainless steel, ø 40 mm, height 10.8 mm; bezel mounted to case with five visible screws; sapphire crystal; water-resistant to 10 atm
Band: stainless steel, folding clasp, with fine adjustment
Remarks: antimagnetic to 40,000 A/m using soft iron core
Price: $11,700
Variations: with blue-green dial; in titanium

Portofino Pointer Date

Reference number: IW359201
Movement: automatic, IWC Caliber 35160 (based on Sellita SW300-1 a); ø 25.6 mm, height 3.75 mm; 25 jewels; 28,800 vph; finely finished with côtes de Genève; 50-hour power reserve
Functions: hours, minutes, sweep seconds; date
Case: stainless steel, ø 39 mm, height 10.8 mm; sapphire crystal; water-resistant to 5 atm
Band: calfskin, folding clasp
Price: $5,500

Portofino Chronograph 39

Reference number: IW391502
Movement: automatic, IWC Caliber 69355; ø 30 mm, height 7 mm; 27 jewels; 28,800 vph; finely finished with côtes de Genève; 46-hour power reserve
Functions: hours, minutes, subsidiary seconds; chronograph
Case: stainless steel, ø 39 mm, height 13 mm; sapphire crystal; water-resistant to 5 atm
Band: calfskin, folding clasp
Price: $7,300
Variations: various bands and dials

Big Pilot's Watch IWC Racing Works

Reference number: IW501019
Movement: automatic, IWC Caliber 52110; ø 37.8 mm, height 7,45 mm; 31 jewels; 28,800 vph; 2 spring barrels; Pellaton winding system; antimagnetic soft iron core; 168-hour power reserve
Functions: hours, minutes, sweep seconds; power-reserve indicator; date
Case: titanium, ø 46.2 mm, height 15.4 mm; sapphire crystal; screw-in crown; water-resistant to 10 atm
Band: calfskin, folding clasp
Price: $15,300; limited to 500 pieces

Pilot's Watch Chronograph 41 Top Gun Oceana

Reference number: IW389404
Movement: automatic, IWC Caliber 69380; ø 30 mm, height 7.9 mm; 33 jewels; 28,800 vph; 46-hour power reserve
Functions: hours, minutes, subsidiary seconds; chronograph; date and weekday
Case: ceramic, ø 41.9 mm, height 15.5 mm; sapphire crystal; transparent case back; screw-in crown; water-resistant to 10 atm
Band: rubber with textile overlay, pin buckle
Price: $11,700

Pilot's Watch Chronograph 41 Top Gun

Reference number: IW389401
Movement: automatic, IWC Caliber 69380; ø 30 mm; height 7.9 mm; 33 jewels; 28,800 vph; 46-hour power reserve
Functions: hours, minutes, subsidiary seconds; chronograph; date and weekday
Case: ceramic, ø 41.9 mm, height 15.5 mm; sapphire crystal; transparent case back; screw-in crown; water-resistant to 10 atm
Band: rubber, pin buckle
Price: $8,750

Pilot's Watch Chronograph 41

Reference number: IW388109
Movement: automatic, IWC Caliber 69385; ø 30 mm, height 7.9 mm; 33 jewels; 28,800 vph; 46-hour power reserve
Functions: hours, minutes, subsidiary seconds; chronograph; date and weekday
Case: bronze, ø 41 mm, height 14.5 mm; sapphire crystal; transparent case back; screw-in crown; water-resistant to 10 atm
Band: textile, pin buckle
Price: $8,250

Pilot's Watch Chronograph 41 Mercedes-AMG Petronas F1-Team

Reference number: IW388108
Movement: automatic, IWC Caliber 69385; ø 30 mm, height 7.9 mm; 33 jewels; 28,800 vph; 46-hour power reserve
Functions: hours, minutes, subsidiary seconds; chronograph; date and weekday
Case: titanium, ø 41 mm, height 14.5 mm; sapphire crystal; transparent case back; screw-in crown; water-resistant to 10 atm
Band: rubber, pin buckle
Remarks: special edition celebrating the years-long cooperation with the Mercedes-AMG Petronas Formula One Team; comes with additional black calfskin strap
Price: $8,350

Pilot's Watch Chronograph 41

Reference number: IW388102
Movement: automatic, IWC Caliber 69385; ø 30 mm, height 7.9 mm; 33 jewels; 28,800 vph; 46-hour power reserve
Functions: hours, minutes, subsidiary seconds; chronograph; date and weekday
Case: stainless steel, ø 41 mm, height 14.5 mm; sapphire crystal; transparent case back; screw-in crown; water-resistant to 10 atm
Band: stainless steel, folding clasp
Price: $8,500
Variations: with calfskin strap ($7,600)

IWC

Big Pilot's Watch

Reference number: IW501015
Movement: automatic, IWC Caliber 52110; ø 37.8 mm,
height 7.45 mm; 31 jewels; 28,800 vph; 2 spring barrels;
Pellaton winding; antimagnetic soft iron core;
168-hour power reserve
Functions: hours, minutes, sweep seconds;
power-reserve indicator; date
Case: stainless steel, ø 46.2 mm, height 15.4 mm; sapphire
crystal; screw-in crown; water-resistant to 6 atm
Band: calfskin, folding clasp
Price: $13,200

Big Pilot's Watch Perpetual Calendar Top Gun Ceratanium

Reference number: IW503604
Movement: automatic, IWC Caliber 52615; ø 37.8 mm,
height 9 mm; 54 jewels; 28,800 vph; Pellaton winding;
168-hour power reserve
Functions: hours, minutes, subsidiary seconds;
power-reserve indicator; perpetual calendar with date,
weekday, month, moon phase, year display (four digits)
Case: special alloy based on ceramic and titanium
(Ceratanium), ø 46.2 mm, height 15.4 mm; sapphire
crystal; transparent case back; screw-in crown;
water-resistant to 6 atm
Band: special alloy using ceramic and titanium
(Ceratanium), folding clasp
Price: $56,700

Big Pilot's Watch 43 Top Gun

Reference number: IW329801
Movement: automatic, IWC Caliber 82100; ø 30 mm,
22 jewels; 28,800 vph; finely finished with côtes de
Genève; 60-hour power reserve
Functions: hours, minutes, sweep seconds
Case: ceramic, ø 43.8 mm, height 13.9 mm; sapphire
crystal; screw-in crown; water-resistant to 10 atm
Band: textile, folding clasp
Price: $10,500

Portuguese Automatic

Reference number: IW500701
Movement: automatic, IWC Caliber 52010; ø 37.8 mm,
height 7.5 mm; 31 jewels; 28,800 vph; Pellaton winding;
finely finished with côtes de Genève; 168-hour power
reserve
Functions: hours, minutes, subsidiary seconds; power-
reserve indicator; date
Case: red gold, ø 42.3 mm, height 14.1 mm; sapphire
crystal; transparent case back; water-resistant to
3 atm
Band: reptile skin, folding clasp
Price: $25,600

Portuguese Automatic 40

Reference number: IW358313
Movement: automatic, IWC Caliber 82200; ø 30 mm,
height 6.6 mm; 31 jewels; 28,800 vph; Pellaton winding;
finely finished movement with perlage and côtes de
Genève; 60-hour power reserve
Functions: hours, minutes, subsidiary seconds
Case: stainless steel, ø 40.4 mm, height 12.4 mm;
sapphire crystal; transparent case back;
water-resistant to 3 atm
Band: reptile skin, folding clasp
Price: $7,750
Variations: various cases, straps and dials

Portuguese Chronograph

Reference number: IW371611
Movement: automatic, IWC Caliber 69355; ø 30 mm,
height 6.95 mm; 27 jewels; 28,800 vph; column wheel
control; finely finished movement with perlage and
côtes de Genève; 46-hour power reserve
Functions: hours, minutes, subsidiary seconds;
chronograph
Case: red gold, ø 41 mm, height 13 mm; sapphire crystal;
transparent case back; water-resistant to 3 atm
Band: reptile skin, pin buckle
Price: $19,200

Caliber 82200

Automatic; double-pawl winding (Pellaton system); single spring barrel, 60-hour power reserve
Functions: hours, minutes, subsidiary seconds
Diameter: 30 mm
Height: 6.6 mm
Jewels: 31
Frequency: 28,800 vph
Hairspring: flat hairspring
Remarks: finely finished movement with perlage and côtes de Genève

Caliber 69355

Automatic; column-wheel control of chronograph functions; single spring barrel, 46-hour power reserve
Functions: hours, minutes, subsidiary seconds; chronograph
Diameter: 30 mm
Height: 7.9 mm
Jewels: 27
Balance: glucydur
Frequency: 28,800 vph
Hairspring: flat hairspring
Remarks: finely finished movement with perlage and côtes de Genève

Caliber 82650

Automatic; double-pawl winding (Pellaton system); single spring barrel, 60-hour power reserve
Functions: hours, minutes, sweep seconds; perpetual calendar with date, weekday, month, moon phase
Diameter: 30 mm
Height: 7.8 mm
Jewels: 46
Frequency: 28,800 vph
Hairspring: flat hairspring
Remarks: finely finished movement with perlage and côtes de Genève; 326 parts

Caliber 52615

Automatic; double-pawl winding (Pellaton system) with ceramic wheels; double spring barrel, 168-hour power reserve
Functions: hours, minutes, subsidiary seconds; power reserve indicator; perpetual calendar with month, weekday, date, double moon phase (for northern and southern hemispheres), 4-digit year display
Diameter: 37.8 mm
Height: 9 mm
Jewels: 54
Balance: with variable inertia
Frequency: 28,800 vph
Hairspring: Breguet
Shock protection: Incabloc

Caliber 89361

Automatic; double-pawl winding (Pellaton system), column-wheel control of chronograph functions; single spring barrel, 68-hour power reserve
Base caliber: 89000
Functions: hours, minutes, subsidiary seconds; flyback chronograph; date
Diameter: 30 mm
Height: 7.46 mm
Jewels: 38
Balance: glucydur with variable inertia
Frequency: 28,800 vph
Hairspring: flat hairspring
Shock protection: Incabloc
Remarks: concentric chronograph totalizer for minutes and hours

Caliber 98295 "Jones"

Hand-wound; single spring barrel, 46-hour power reserve
Base caliber: 98000
Functions: hours, minutes, subsidiary seconds
Diameter: 38.2 mm
Height: 5.3 mm
Jewels: 18
Balance: screw balance with fine adjustment cams
Frequency: 18,000 vph
Balance spring: Breguet
Shock protection: Incabloc
Remarks: exceptionally long regulator index; three-quarter plate of German silver, hand-engraved balance cock

JAEGER-LECOULTRE

The Jaeger-LeCoultre *manufacture* has had a long and tumultuous history. In 1833, Antoine LeCoultre opened his own workshop for the production of gearwheels. Having made his fortune, he then did what many other artisans did; in 1866, he had a large house built and brought together all the craftspeople needed to produce timepieces, from the watchmakers to the turners and polishers. He outfitted the workshop with the most modern machinery of the day, all powered by a steam engine. "La Grande Maison" was the first watch *manufacture* in the Vallée de Joux.

At the start of the twentieth century, the grandson of the company founder, Jacques-David LeCoultre, built slender, complicated watches for the Paris manufacturer Edmond Jaeger. The Frenchman was so impressed with these that, after a few years of fruitful cooperation, he engineered a merger of the two companies.

In the 1970s, the German VDO Group (later Mannesmann) took over the company and helped it weather the quartz crisis.

Thanks to its inclusion in the Richemont stable, Jaeger-LeCoultre continued to grow. A vast array of calibers (around 1,200), including minute repeaters, tourbillons, and other *grandes complications*, a lubricant-free movement, and more than 400 patents, tell their own story. Today, it is the largest employer in the Vallée de Joux—just as it was back in the 1860s. The most enduring collection produced by the brand is probably the Reverso, which can swivel around to show a second watch face on the back. The 2023 production shows that the Reverso collection still has life.

But Jaeger-LeCoultre also boasts other iconic collections, like the Master, the Polaris, and the Atmos. That's because the brand has always managed to unify technical wizardry with a very fine sense of aesthetics, which is expressed in many models illustrating the many métiers d'art from the watch world. The Master Grande Tradition Grande Complication, for example, displays sidereal time combined with a minute repeater that rings on sapphire crystal gongs soldered to the sapphire crystal itself for a more penetrating sound.

Manufacture Jaeger-LeCoultre
Rue de la Golisse, 8
CH-1347 Le Sentier
Switzerland

Tel.:
+41-21-852-0202

E-mail:
info@jaeger-lecoultre.com
client.relations.us@jaeger-lecoultre.com

Website:
www.jaeger-lecoultre.com

Founded:
1833

Number of employees:
Around 1,400

Annual production:
approx. 75,000 watches

U.S. distributor:
Jaeger-LeCoultre
645 Fifth Avenue
New York, NY 10022
1-877-552-1833
www.jaeger-lecoultre.com

Most important collections/price range:
Atmos / starting at $7,100; Duomètre / starting at $41,700; Master / starting at $7,250; Polaris / starting at $7,250; Rendez-Vous / starting at $7,850; Reverso / starting at $4,750

Reverso Hybris Artistica Calibre 179

Reference number: Q39424E1
Movement: hand-wound, JLC Caliber 179; 26.2 x 41 mm, height 6.85 mm; 52 jewels; 21,600 vph; spherical double-axis tourbillon with different rotational speeds (60 and 12.6 secs.), Gyrolab escapement with hemispheric hairspring; 40-hour power reserve
Functions: hours, minutes, subsidiary seconds (on the tourbillon cage); additional 24-hour display
Case: pink gold, 31 x 51.2 mm, height 13.63 mm; sapphire crystal; water-resistant to 3 atm
Band: reptile skin, double folding clasp
Remarks: case turns and swivels 180°; limited to 10 pieces
Price: $530,000

Reverso Tribute Duoface Tourbillon

Reference number: Q392242J
Movement: hand-wound, JLC Caliber 847; 17.2 x 22 mm, height 3.9 mm; 31 jewels; 21,600 vph; "two-sided" flying tourbillon with hidden operation; 38-hour power reserve
Functions: hours, minutes; additional time indication (2nd time zone on the rear), day/night indication
Case: pink gold, 27.4 x 45.5 mm, height 9.15 mm; sapphire crystal; water-resistant to 3 atm
Band: reptile skin, double folding clasp
Remarks: case turns and swivels 180°
Price: $138,000

Reverso Tribute Chronograph

Reference number: Q389257J
Movement: hand-wound, JLC Caliber 860; 17.2 x 22 mm, height 5.5 mm; 38 jewels; 28,800 vph; column-wheel control of the chronograph functions; 52-hour power reserve
Functions: hours, minutes; additional time indicator (2nd time zone) and chronograph on the rear
Case: pink gold, 29.9 x 49.4 mm, height 11.14 mm; sapphire crystal; water-resistant to 3 atm
Band: reptile skin, pin buckle
Remarks: case turns and swivels 180°; comes with an additional calfskin strap
Price: $38,300
Variations: in stainless steel ($25,000)

Reverso Tribute Chronograph

Reference number: Q389848J
Movement: hand-wound, JLC Caliber 860;
17.2 x 22 mm, height 5.5 mm; 38 jewels; 28,800 vph;
column-wheel control of the chronograph functions;
52-hour power reserve
Functions: hours, minutes; additional time indication
(2nd time zone) and chronograph on the rear
Case: stainless steel, 29.9 x 49.4 mm, height 11.14 mm;
sapphire crystal; water-resistant to 3 atm
Band: reptile skin, double folding clasp
Remarks: case turns and swivels 180°; comes with an
additional calfskin strap
Price: $25,000
Variations: in pink gold ($38,800)

Reverso Tribute Small Seconds

Reference number: Q7132521
Movement: hand-wound, JLC Caliber 822/2;
17.2 x 22 mm, height 2.94 mm; 19 jewels; 21,600 vph;
42-hour power reserve
Functions: hours, minutes, subsidiary seconds
Case: pink gold, 27.4 x 45.6 mm, height 7.56 mm;
sapphire crystal; water-resistant to 3 atm
Band: calfskin and textile, pin buckle
Remarks: case turns and swivels 180°; comes with an
additional calfskin strap
Price: $22,700
Variations: with black or red dial; in stainless steel
($10,600)

Reverso Tribute Small Seconds

Reference number: Q713257J
Movement: hand-wound, JLC Caliber 822/2;
17.2 x 22 mm, height 2.94 mm; 19 jewels; 21,600 vph;
42-hour power reserve
Functions: hours, minutes, subsidiary seconds
Case: pink gold, 27.4 x 45.6 mm, height 7.56 mm;
sapphire crystal; water-resistant to 3 atm
Band: calfskin, pin buckle
Remarks: case turns and swivels 180°; comes with an
additional calfskin or textile strap
Price: $22,700
Variations: with silver or red dial; in stainless steel
($10,600)

Reverso Tribute Small Seconds

Reference number: Q713256J
Movement: hand-wound, JLC Caliber 822/2;
17.2 x 22 mm, height 2.94 mm; 19 jewels; 21,600 vph;
42-hour power reserve
Functions: hours, minutes, subsidiary seconds
Case: pink gold, 27.4 x 45.6 mm, height 7.56 mm;
sapphire crystal; water-resistant to 3 atm
Band: calfskin and textile, pin buckle
Remarks: case swivels and turns 180°; comes with an
additional calfskin strap
Price: $22,700
Variations: with black or solver dial; in stainless steel
($10,600)

Reverso Tribute Small Seconds

Reference number: Q713842J
Movement: hand-wound, JLC Caliber 822/2;
17.2 x 22 mm, height 2.94 mm; 19 jewels; 21,600 vph;
42-hour power reserve
Functions: hours, minutes, subsidiary seconds
Case: stainless steel, 27.4 x 45.6 mm, height 8.5 mm;
sapphire crystal; water-resistant to 3 atm
Band: calfskin and textile, double folding clasp
Remarks: case turns and swivels 180°
Price: $10,600
Variations: in pink gold ($22,700)

Master Control Memovox Timer

Reference number: Q410257J
Movement: automatic, JLC Caliber 956AA;
ø 28 mm, height 7.47 mm; 24 jewels; 28,800 vph;
44-hour power reserve
Functions: hours, minutes, sweep seconds; alarm
(minute-increment setting); date
Case: pink gold, ø 40 mm, height 12.39 mm;
crown-activated alarm function on the dial center;
sapphire crystal; transparent case back;
water-resistant to 5 atm
Band: reptile skin, pin buckle
Price: $33,600

Master Control Calendar

Reference number: Q4148480
Movement: automatic, JLC Caliber 866AA;
ø 26 mm, height 6.15 mm; 34 jewels; 28,800 vph;
70-hour power reserve
Functions: hours, minutes, subsidiary seconds; full
calendar with date, weekday, month, moon phase
Case: stainless steel, ø 40 mm, height 10.95 mm;
sapphire crystal; transparent case back;
water-resistant to 5 atm
Band: calfskin, double folding clasp
Price: $14,600

Master Control Date

Reference number: Q4018480
Movement: automatic, JLC Caliber 899AC;
ø 26 mm, height 3.7 mm; 32 jewels; 28,800 vph;
70-hour power reserve
Functions: hours, minutes, sweep seconds; date
Case: stainless steel, ø 40 mm, height 8.78 mm;
sapphire crystal; transparent case back;
water-resistant to 5 atm
Band: calfskin, double folding clasp
Price: $9,550

Master Control Chronograph Calendar

Reference number: Q413812J
Movement: automatic, JLC Caliber 759; ø 25.6 mm;
37 jewels; 28,800 vph; silicon escapement, column-
wheel control of the chronograph functions, gold rotor;
65-hour power reserve Functions: hours, minutes,
subsidiary seconds; chronograph; full calendar with
date, weekday, month, moon phase
Case: stainless steel, ø 40 mm, height 12.05 mm;
sapphire crystal; transparent case back;
water-resistant to 5 atm
Band: stainless steel, double folding clasp
Price: $19,100

Master Control Calendar

Reference number: Q4148120
Movement: automatic, JLC Caliber 866AA;
ø 26 mm, height 6.15 mm; 34 jewels; 28,800 vph;
70-hour power reserve
Functions: hours, minutes, subsidiary seconds;
full calendar with date, weekday, month, moon phase
Case: stainless steel, ø 40 mm, height 10.95 mm;
sapphire crystal; transparent case back;
water-resistant to 5 atm
Band: stainless steel, double folding clasp
Price: $16,100

Master Ultra Thin Moon

Reference number: Q1368480
Movement: automatic, JLC Caliber 925AA;
ø 26 mm, height 4.9 mm; 30 jewels; 28,800 vph;
70-hour power reserve
Functions: hours, minutes, sweep seconds;
date, moon phase
Case: stainless steel, ø 39 mm, height 10.04 mm;
sapphire crystal; transparent case back;
water-resistant to 5 atm
Band: reptile skin, double folding clasp
Price: $11,900
Variations: in pink gold ($23,000)

Master Ultra Thin Moon

Reference number: Q1368471
Movement: automatic, JLC Caliber 925AA;
ø 26 mm, height 4.9 mm; 30 jewels; 28,800 vph;
70-hour power reserve
Functions: hours, minutes, sweep seconds; date,
moon phase
Case: stainless steel, ø 39 mm, height 10.04 mm;
sapphire crystal; transparent case back;
water-resistant to 5 atm
Band: reptile skin, double folding clasp
Price: $11,900
Variations: in pink gold ($23,000)

Master Ultra Thin Moon

Reference number: Q1368430
Movement: automatic, JLC Caliber 925/2;
ø 26 mm, height 4.9 mm; 30 jewels; 28,800 vph;
70-hour power reserve
Functions: hours, minutes, sweep seconds;
date, moon phase
Case: stainless steel, ø 39 mm, height 10.04 mm;
sapphire crystal; transparent case back;
water-resistant to 5 atm
Band: reptile skin, pin buckle
Price: $11,900
Variations: in pink gold ($23,000)

Master Ultra Thin Moon

Reference number: Q1362510
Movement: automatic, JLC Caliber 925AA;
ø 26 mm, height 4.9 mm; 30 jewels; 28,800 vph;
70-hour power reserve
Functions: hours, minutes, sweep seconds; date,
moon phase
Case: pink gold, ø 39 mm, height 10.04 mm; sapphire
crystal; transparent case back; water-resistant to 5 atm
Band: reptile skin, pin buckle
Price: $23,000
Variations: in stainless steel ($11,900)

Polaris Perpetual Calendar

Reference number: Q9082680
Movement: automatic, JLC Caliber 868AA;
ø 26 mm, height 4.72 mm; 54 jewels; 28,800 vph;
70-hour power reserve
Functions: hours, minutes, sweep seconds; perpetual
calendar with date, weekday, month, moon phase, year
display (four digits)
Case: pink gold, ø 42 mm, height 11.97 mm; sapphire
crystal; transparent case back; water-resistant to 10 atm
Band: rubber, pin buckle
Price: $52,500

Polaris Perpetual Calendar

Reference number: Q9088180
Movement: automatic, JLC Caliber 868AA;
sø 26 mm, height 4.72 mm; 54 jewels; 28,800 vph;
70-hour power reserve
Functions: hours, minutes, sweep seconds; perpetual
calendar with date, weekday, month, moon phase, year
display (four digits)
Case: stainless steel, ø 42 mm, height 11,97 mm;
sapphire crystal; transparent case back;
water-resistant to 10 atm
Band: stainless steel, folding clasp
Price: $36,100

Polaris Date Green

Reference number: Q906863J
Movement: automatic, JLC Caliber 899AB;
ø 26 mm, height 4.6 mm; 32 jewels; 28,800 vph;
70-hour power reserve
Functions: hours, minutes, sweep seconds; date
Case: stainless steel, ø 42 mm, height 13.1 mm;
crown-activated inner rotating scale ring with
0-60 scale; sapphire crystal; water-resistant to 20 atm
Band: rubber, double folding clasp
Price: $11,100

Polaris Date

Reference number: Q9068671
Movement: automatic, JLC Caliber 899A/1;
ø 26 mm, height 4.6 mm; 32 jewels; 28,800 vph;
70-hour power reserve
Functions: hours, minutes, sweep seconds; date
Case: stainless steel, ø 42 mm, height 13,1 mm;
crown-activated inner rotating scale ring with
0-60 scale; sapphire crystal; water-resistant to 20 atm
Band: rubber, double folding clasp
Price: $10,000

Caliber 860

Hand-wound; column wheel control of chronograph functions; single spring barrel, 52-hour power reserve
Functions: hours, minutes; additional 12-hour display (2nd time zone, on the rear); chronograph with retrograde minute counter (on the rear)
Dimensions: 17.2 x 22 mm
Height: 5.5 mm
Jewels: 38
Balance: glucydur
Frequency: 28,800 vph
Remarks: skeletonized movement; 300 parts

Caliber 956AA

Automatic; automatic winding for time and alarm mechanisms; single spring barrel, 44-hour power reserve
Functions: hours, minutes, sweep seconds; date; alarm
Diameter: 28 mm
Height: 7.47 mm
Jewels: 24
Balance: glucydur
Frequency: 28,800 vph
Hairspring: flat hairspring
Remarks: perlage on mainplate, bridges with côtes de Genève, element for sounding board; 271 parts

Caliber 899AC

Automatic; silicon escapement; gold rotor; single spring barrel, 70-hour power reserve
Functions: hours, minutes, sweep seconds; date
Diameter: 26 mm
Height: 3.7 mm
Jewels: 32
Frequency: 28,800 vph
Remarks: mainplate with perlage, bridges with côtes de Genève; 218 parts

Caliber 866AA

Automatic; silicon escapement; gold rotor; single spring barrel, 70-hour power reserve
Functions: hours, minutes, subsidiary seconds; full calendar with date, weekday, month, moon phase
Diameter: 26 mm
Height: 5.65 mm
Jewels: 34
Balance: glucydur
Frequency: 28,800 vph
Remarks: mainplate with perlage, bridges with côtes de Genève

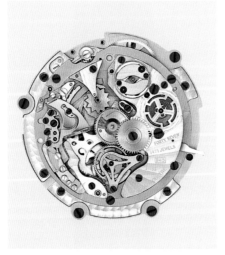

Caliber 945

Hand-wound; silicon anchor with integrated pallets, flying tourbillon rotates with dial in 56 minutes (sidereal time, star time); single spring barrel, 48-hour power reserve
Functions: hours, minutes, hours, quarter hour and minute repeater; perpetual calendar with, date, month, celestial map with zodiac signs
Diameter: 34.7 mm
Height: 12.62 mm
Jewels: 49
Balance: screw balance
Frequency: 28,800 vph
Hairspring: flat hairspring
Remarks: repetition with "trebuchet" hammers to strengthen the impulses; 527 parts

Caliber 925AA

Automatic; single spring barrel, 70-hour power reserve
Functions: hours, minutes, sweep seconds; date, moon phase
Diameter: 26 mm
Height: 4.9 mm
Jewels: 30
Frequency: 28,800 vph
Remarks: mainplate with perlage, bridges with côtes de Genève; 245 parts

Caliber 751

Automatic; column wheel control of chronograph functions; double spring barrel, 65-hour power reserve
Functions: hours, minutes, subsidiary seconds; chronograph
Diameter: 26.2 mm
Height: 5.7 mm
Jewels: 37
Balance: screw balance with 4 weights
Frequency: 28,800 vph
Hairspring: flat hairspring
Shock protection: Kif
Remarks: 262 parts

Caliber 822/2

Hand-wound; single spring barrel, 42-hour power reserve
Functions: hours, minutes, subsidiary seconds
Dimensions: 17.2 x 22 mm
Height: 2.94 mm
Jewels: 19
Balance: screw balance
Frequency: 21,600 vph
Hairspring: flat hairspring

Caliber 925/2

Automatic; single spring barrel, 70-hour power reserve
Functions: hours, minutes, sweep seconds; date, moon phase
Diameter: 26 mm
Height: 4.9 mm
Jewels: 30
Frequency: 28,800 vph
Remarks: 245 parts

Caliber 978F

Automatic; 1-minute tourbillon; gold rotor; single spring barrel, 45-hour power reserve
Functions: hours, minutes, subsidiary seconds (on the tourbillon cage); hand date (jumping from the 15th to the 16th of the month)
Diameter: 30 mm
Height: 7.2 mm
Jewels: 33
Balance: glucydur with weighted screws
Frequency: 28,800 vph
Hairspring: Breguet-Hairspring
Shock protection: Kif
Remarks: mainplate with perlage, bridges with côtes de Genève; 302 parts

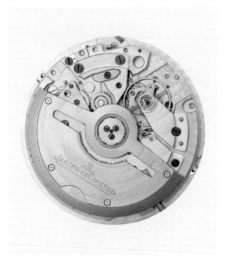

Caliber 868/A2

Automatic; single spring barrel, 70-hour power reserve
Functions: hours, minutes, sweep seconds; perpetual calendar with date, weekday, month, moon phase, 4-digit year display
Diameter: 26 mm
Height: 4.72 mm
Jewels: 46
Balance: glucydur
Frequency: 28,800 vph
Remarks: 332 parts

Caliber 868/1

Automatic; single spring barrel, 38-hour power reserve
Functions: hours, minutes, sweep seconds; perpetual calendar with date, weekday, month, moon phase, 4-digit year display
Diameter: 27.8 mm
Height: 4.72 mm
Jewels: 46
Balance: glucydur
Frequency: 28,800 vph
Remarks: 336 parts

JÖRG SCHAUER

Jörg Schauer's watches are first and foremost cool. The cases have been carefully worked, and the look is planned to draw the eye. After all, he is a perfectionist and leaves nothing to chance. He works on every single case himself, polishing and performing his own brand of magic for as long as it takes to display his personal touch. This time-consuming process is one that Schauer believes is absolutely necessary. "I do this because I place a great deal of value on the fact that my cases are absolutely perfect," he explains. "I can do it better than anyone, and I would never let anyone else do it for me."

Schauer, a goldsmith by training, has been making watches since 1990. He began by doing one-off pieces in precious metals for collectors and then opened his business and simultaneously moved to stainless steel. His style is to produce functional, angular cases with visibly screwed-down bezels and straightforward dials in plain black or white. Forget finding any watch close to current trends in his collection; Schauer only builds timepieces that he genuinely likes.

Purchasing a Schauer is not that easy. He has chosen a strategy of genuine quality over quantity and only produces about 50 watches annually. This includes special watches like the One-Hand Durowe, running on a modified Unitas made by the movement manufacturer Durowe, which Schauer acquired in 2002. It has been revived as the One-Hand 44. His production structure is a vital part of his success and includes prototyping, movement modification, finishing, case production, dial painting and printing—all done in Schauer's own workshop in Engelsbrand. Any support he needs from the outside he prefers to find among regional specialists.

Jörg Schauer
Durowe GmbH
Jörg Schauer
Pforzheimer Straße 41
75331 Engelsbrand
Germany

Tel.:
+49-(0)7235-975-87 45

E-mail:
info@durowe.com

Website:
www.durowe.com

Founded:
1990

Number of employees:
2

Annual production:
approx. 50 watches

Distribution:
direct sales; online shop; please contact the address in Germany

Chronograph Kulisse Edition 10 Jubiläum

Movement: automatic, ETA Caliber 7753; ø 30 mm, height 7.9 mm; 25 jewels; 28,800 vph; with decorative ribbing and blued screws; 48-hour power reserve
Functions: hours, minutes, subsidiary seconds; chronograph; date
Case: stainless steel, ø 42 mm, height 14.9 mm; bezel fixed with 12 screws; sapphire crystal; transparent case back; water-resistant to 5 atm
Band: reptile skin, folding clasp
Price: $4,500; limited to 130 pieces
Variations: with metal link bracelet ($4,800); with manual winding ($4,900)

One-Hand Jubiläum

Movement: automatic, ETA Caliber 2824-2; ø 25.6 mm, height 4.6 mm; 25 jewels; 28,800 vph; fine finishing, special engraved rotor; 38-hour power reserve
Functions: hours (each line stands for five minutes)
Case: stainless steel, ø 42 mm, height 10.2 mm; bezel fixed with 12 screws; sapphire crystal; transparent case back; water-resistant to 5 atm
Band: rubber, folding clasp
Price: $2,200; limited to 100 pieces
Variations: with metal link bracelet ($2,500)

Chronograph Kulisse Edition 15

Movement: automatic, ETA Caliber 7753; ø 30 mm, height 7.9 mm; 25 jewels; 28,800 vph; with decorative ribbing and blued screws, exclusive engraved "Schauer" rotor; 48-hour power reserve
Functions: hours, minutes, subsidiary seconds; chronograph; date
Case: stainless steel, ø 44 mm, height 15 mm; bezel fixed with 12 screws; sapphire crystal; transparent case back; water-resistant to 5 atm
Band: calfskin, folding clasp
Remarks: chronograph hands colors on request
Price: $4,700
Variations: with manual winding ($5,100); various bands; with carbon fiber dial

JS Watch Co. Reykjavik
Laugavegur 62
101 Reykjavik
Iceland

Tel.:
+354-551-05-00

E-mail:
info@jswatch.com

Website:
www.jswatch.com

Founded:
2003

Number of employees:
5

Annual production:
500 pieces

Distribution:
Retail and direct sales
info@jswatch.com
+354-551-41-00

Price range:
$1,978 to $14,147

JS WATCH CO.

When they weren't pillaging Europe and terrorizing populations from the British Isles to Russia, the Vikings were in fact a very hardworking and talented bunch. And when not roaming about, they tended their fields, herds, and houses, and, as a number of exhibitions in the past twenty years have shown, they made jewelry. Their work in this field was remarkable and fed their commercial supply chains, to use a modern term.

Iceland is where many descendants of the Norsemen live—a rugged and stark landscape, with over three hundred volcanoes and long winter nights. The ability to design and create fine jewelry lives on, and since 2003, the tiny country with a population of over 387,000 has been producing watches as well, thanks to four friends: designer Grimkell Sigurþórsson, watchmakers Sigurður Gilbertsson and Gilbert Guðjónsson, and Júlíus Heiðarsson.

Their first launch in 2005 of one hundred watches sold out within half a year, and so they persisted, using Swiss or German parts and movements (ETA, Sellita) but creating watches with some unique features paying tribute to their small but very intriguing country. The "execution top" movements provide solid chronometric performance and standard decoration, meaning lower prices but good quality. The timepieces are inspired and named after an event, place, or year in Iceland or Icelandic history. "We made the Sif N.A.R.T., which was named for the first helicopter of Iceland's Coast Guard rescue teams and the North Atlantic Rescue Timer," says Sigurþórsson, now the Director of Design and Marketing of the tiny company. In 2018, when Iceland qualified for the Football World Cup, JS Watch Co. was ready with a limited series.

The Gilbert collection pays tribute to the company's own watchmaker, Gilbert Guðjónsson, with sober, almost self-effacing timepieces. In the Vinland line, one finds a complicated chronograph collection sporting a tachymeter scale. To appeal to different tastes, there is a choice of dials, including one in red and black, a hint at the lava running under this mysterious country. The second Vinland, a special edition, has a rich guilloché dial and Norse engravings on the mainplate visible through the case back.

Vínland Chronograph

Reference number: VIN-CH-1
Movement: automatic, Sellita Caliber SW 510b, ø 30 mm, height 7.9 mm; 27 jewels; 28,800 vph; 62-hour power reserve
Function: hours, minutes, subsidiary seconds; chronograph
Case: stainless steel, ø 42 mm, height 14.2 mm; sapphire crystal; transparent case back; water-resistant to 10 atm
Band: reptile skin, buckle
Price: $6,990
Variations: white, black, or blue dial; roman or arabic numerals

Vínland Special Limited Edition

Reference number: VIN-SP-1
Movement: hand-wound, Caliber 6498, modified Unitas, ø 25.60 mm, height 3.60 mm; 17 jewels; 18,800 vph; partly blued swan-neck regulator; three-quarter plate with Norse engravings, blued screws; 46-hour power reserve
Functions: hours, minutes, subsidiary seconds
Case: stainless steel, ø 41 mm, height 10.9 mm; sapphire crystal transparent case back; water-resistant to 5 atm
Band: reptile skin, folding clasp
Price: $16,280
Variations: silver or gold, each limited to 25 pieces

Islandus Dakota 44 mm

Reference number: Dak-44-1
Movement: automatic, Soprod Caliber M100; ø 25.60 mm, height 3.60 mm; 25 jewels; 28,800 vph; 42-hour power reserve
Functions: central hours, minutes, sweep seconds; date
Case: stainless steel, ø 44 mm, height 11.5 mm; sapphire crystal; transparent case back; water-resistant to 5 atm
Band: calf leather, buckle
Price: $2,631
Variations: black or white dials; with Arabic numerals

JUNGHANS

The town of Glashütte in Saxony was already a watchmaking name to be reckoned with when Erhard Junghans (b. 1823) founded his factory in 1861 in Schramberg, a small town in the Black Forest . His son Arthur then developed it into a large-scale production site on the American industrial model. At the height of its success, the factory employed nearly three thousand men and women making nine thousand wall clocks and alarm clocks daily.

In the boom years after World War II, the company, with its logo featuring a star, produced mainly wristwatches. It went on to ring in modern times with its own solar and radio-controlled watches. Junghans was twice the official timekeeper at the Olympic Games.

In 2009, Dr. Hans-Jochem Steim, a successful entrepreneur and political figure from Schramberg, purchased the company, which had gone bankrupt. An infusion of cash allowed it to set up a new production and distribution schedule. Today, the brand boasts an extensive collection of high-quality wristwatches, ranging from genuine icons of design to major classics, all the way to sporty chronographs. In 2018, the company opened a watch- and clockmaking museum in the restored Terrassenbau, a century-old, terraced construction that allowed Junghans employees to work with strong natural lighting. In the same year, Junghans came out with a brand-new radio-controlled movement, the Caliber J101, designed to mix high-tech with a classic look. To satisfy a broad market, Junghans manufactures quartz and mechanical watches, all in a sober Bauhaus idiom. The latest products include the Meister S, a sporty, masculine watch, and a series of watches that combine the radio-controlled Caliber J101 with the latest in solar technology, all packaged in the traditional Junghans look. A brand-new time signal enables rapid synchronization with a smartphone thanks to a specially developed app.

In 2023, the company celebrated the 200th birthday of its founder with two limited edition models in 18-carat gold and two additional models in lemon yellow to match its sponsorship of the 54th FIS Nordic World Ski Championships, for which it has acted as "Official Timing Partner."

Uhrenfabrik Junghans
GmbH & Co. KG
Geisshaldenstrasse 49
D-78713 Schramberg
Germany

Tel.:
+49-742-218-0

E-mail:
info@junghans.de

Website:
www.junghans.de

Founded:
1861

Number of employees:
127

Annual production:
approx. 60,000 watches

U.S. distributor:
DKSH Luxury & Lifestyle North America Inc.
9-D Princess Road
Lawrenceville, NJ 08648
609-750-8800

Most important collections/price range:
Meister; Max Bill by Junghans; MEGA;
1972 Competition; Form / from approx. $395 to
$2,500; special pieces up to $17,000

1972 Competition FIS Edition Lemon

Reference number: 27/4305.00
Movement: automatic, Caliber J880.5 (based on Sellita SW510); ø 30 mm, height 7.9 mm; 25 jewels; 28,800 vph; rhodium-plated movement, blue screws, rotor with côtes de Genève; 48-hour power reserve
Functions: hours, minutes, subsidiary seconds; chronograph; date
Case: stainless steel, ø 45.5 mm, height 14.5 mm; sapphire crystal; screw-in crown; water-resistant to 10 atm
Band: calfskin, folding clasp
Remarks: homage to Junghans's history of sports time measurement
Price: $3,660; limited to 150 pieces

1972 Chronoscope Quartz Edition FIS Lemon

Reference number: 41/4369.00
Movement: quartz, Caliber J645.83
Functions: hours, minutes, subsidiary seconds; chronograph; date
Case: stainless steel, ø 43.3 mm, height 11.3 mm; unidirectional bezel with 0-60 scale; sapphire crystal; screw-in crown; water-resistant to 10 atm
Band: calfskin, pin buckle
Remarks: homage to Junghans's history of sports time measurement
Price: $970

1972 Competition

Reference number: 27/4203.00
Movement: automatic, Caliber J880.5 (based on Sellita SW510); ø 30 mm, height 7.9 mm; 25 jewels; 28,800 vph; rhodium-plated movement, blue screws, rotor with côtes de Genève; 48-hour power reserve
Functions: hours, minutes, subsidiary seconds; chronograph; date
Case: stainless steel, ø 45.5 mm, height 14.5 mm; sapphire crystal; screw-in crown; water-resistant to 10 atm
Band: calfskin, pin buckle
Remarks: homage to Junghans's history of sports time measurement
Price: $2,800; limited to 1972 pieces

Meister S Chronoscope

Reference number: 27/4228.44
Movement: automatic, Caliber J880.1 (based on Sellita SW500); ø 30 mm, height 7.9 mm; 25 jewels; 28,800 vph; rhodium-plated movement, blue screws, rotor with côtes de Genève; 48-hour power reserve
Functions: hours, minutes, subsidiary seconds; chronograph; date and weekday
Case: stainless steel, ø 45 mm, height 15.9 mm; sapphire crystal; screw-in crown; water-resistant to 20 atm
Band: stainless steel, double folding clasp
Price: $2,760
Variations: with rubber strap ($2,690)

Meister Chronoscope

Reference number: 27/4224.02
Movement: automatic, Caliber J880.1 (based on ETA 7750 or Sellita SW500); ø 30 mm, height 7.9 mm; 25 jewels; 28,800 vph; rhodium-plated movement, blue screws, rotor with côtes de Genève; 48-hour power reserve
Functions: hours, minutes, subsidiary seconds; chronograph; date and weekday
Case: stainless steel, ø 40.7 mm, height 13.9 mm; sapphire crystal; transparent case back; water-resistant to 5 atm
Band: ostrich leather, pin buckle
Price: $2,400

Meister Chronoscope

Reference number: 27/4222.02
Movement: automatic, Caliber J880.1 (based on ETA 7750 or Sellita SW500); ø 30 mm, height 7.9 mm; 25 jewels; 28,800 vph; rhodium-plated movement, blue screws, rotor with côtes de Genève; 48-hour power reserve
Functions: hours, minutes, subsidiary seconds; chronograph; date and weekday
Case: stainless steel, ø 40.7 mm, height 13.9 mm; sapphire crystal; transparent case back; water-resistant to 5 atm
Band: ostrich leather, pin buckle
Price: $2,400
Variations: various bands and dials

Meister Pilot Automatic Navy Blue

Reference number: 27/4397.00
Movement: automatic, Caliber J800.1.6 (based on Sellita SW261); ø 25.6 mm, height 4.6 mm; 26 jewels; 28,800 vph; rhodium-plated movement, rotor with côtes de Genève; 38-hour power reserve
Functions: hours, minutes, subsidiary seconds; date
Case: stainless steel with DLC, ø 43.3 mm, height 12.5 mm; bidirectional bezel, with 0-60 scale; sapphire crystal; water-resistant to 10 atm
Band: calfskin, pin buckle
Price: $2,260

Meister Pilot Chronoscope Navy Blue

Reference number: 27/3396.00
Movement: automatic, Caliber J880.4 (based on ETA 2824-2 with Dubois Dépraz module); ø 30 mm, height 7.6 mm; 49 jewels; 28,800 vph; rhodium-plated movement, rotor with côtes de Genève; 38-hour power reserve
Functions: hours, minutes, subsidiary seconds; chronograph
Case: stainless steel with DLC, ø 43.3 mm, height 14.4 mm; sapphire crystal; water-resistant to 10 atm
Band: calfskin, pin buckle
Price: $2,910; limited to 300 pieces

Meister Pilot Chronoscope Desert

Reference number: 27/3398.00
Movement: automatic, Caliber J880.4 (based on ETA 2824-2 with Dubois Dépraz module); ø 30 mm, height 7.6 mm; 49 jewels; 28,800 vph; rhodium-plated movement, rotor with côtes de Genève; 38-hour power reserve
Functions: hours, minutes, subsidiary seconds; chronograph
Case: stainless steel with DLC, ø 43.3 mm, height 14.4 mm; sapphire crystal; water-resistant to 10 atm
Band: calfskin, pin buckle
Price: $2,910
Variations: in stainless steel without DLC, with black or brown dial and strap ($2,790)

Meister Fein Automatic Edition Erhard

Reference number: 27/9301.00
Movement: automatic, Caliber J800.1 (based on Sellita SW200-1); ø 25.6 mm, height 4.6 mm; 26 jewels; 28,800 vph; rhodium-plated movement, blue screws, special two-armed rotor with engraved profile of Erhard Junghans; 38-hour power reserve
Functions: hours, minutes, sweep seconds; date
Case: yellow gold, ø 39.5 mm, height 11 mm; sapphire crystal; transparent case back; water-resistant to 3 atm
Band: calfskin, pin buckle
Price: $9,500; limited to 200 pieces

Meister Fein Automatic Edition Erhard

Reference number: 27/9300.00
Movement: automatic, Caliber J800.1 (based on Sellita SW200-1); ø 25.6 mm, height 4.6 mm; 26 jewels; 28,800 vph; rhodium-plated movement, blue screws, special two-armed rotor with engraved profile of Erhard Junghans; 38-hour power reserve
Functions: hours, minutes, sweep seconds; date
Case: white gold, ø 39.5 mm, height 11 mm; sapphire crystal; transparent case back; water-resistant to 3 atm
Band: calfskin, pin buckle
Price: $9,500; limited to 200 pieces

Meister Fein Automatic Signature

Reference number: 27/4355.00
Movement: automatic, Caliber J800.1 (based on Sellita SW200-1); ø 25.6 mm, height 4.6 mm; 26 jewels; 28,800 vph; rhodium-plated movement, blue screws, rotor with engraved plaque; 38-hour power reserve
Functions: hours, minutes, sweep seconds; date
Case: stainless steel, ø 39.5 mm, height 11 mm; sapphire crystal; transparent case back; water-resistant to 5 atm
Band: calfskin, pin buckle
Price: $1,910

Meister Fein Chronoscope MEGA Solar

Reference number: 59/7201.00
Movement: quartz, multi-frequency radio-controlled Caliber J110; time-zone recognition and setting to the second thanks to radio-controlled, app for time-setting; "perpetual" date (in quartz mode as well), solar cell charging
Functions: hours, minutes, subsidiary seconds; chronograph; perpetual calendar with date
Case: stainless steel with rose-gold PVD, ø 39.5 mm, height 9.5 mm; sapphire crystal; transparent case back; water-resistant to 5 atm
Band: calfskin, pin buckle
Price: $1,760
Variations: in stainless steel ($1,510)

Meister Fein Small Automatic

Reference number: 27/7232.00
Movement: automatic, Caliber J800.1 (based on Sellita SW200-1); ø 25.6 mm, height 4.6 mm; 26 jewels; 28,800 vph; rhodium-plated movement, blue screws, rotor with ribbing; 38-hour power reserve
Functions: hours, minutes, sweep seconds; date
Case: stainless steel with rose-gold PVD, ø 35 mm, height 10.1 mm; sapphire crystal; transparent case back; water-resistant to 5 atm
Band: calfskin, pin buckle
Price: $1,300

Max Bill Chronoscope Bauhaus

Reference number: 27/4303.02
Movement: automatic, Caliber J880.2 (based on Sellita SW500); ø 30 mm, height 7.9 mm; 25 jewels; 28,800 vph; 48-hour power reserve
Functions: hours, minutes; chronograph; date
Case: stainless steel, ø 40 mm, height 14.4 mm; sapphire crystal; water-resistant to 5 atm
Band: calfskin, pin buckle
Price: $2,500

Kleynod Ukrainian Watches
Kyrylivska Street 69
Kyiv, 04080 Ukraine

Tel.:
+38-067-223-1085

E-mail:
trade@kleynod.ua

Website:
www.kleynodwatches.com

Founded:
2002

Number of employees:
100

Annual production:
approx. 90,000 watches

U. S. Distributor:
V2Com Commerce LLC
775 Bloomfield Ave,
Suite 1B
Clifton, New Jersey 07012
973-272-8251
kleynodusa@gmail.com

Most important collections/price range
Mechanical and quartz: Antonov (quartz) / Classic
/ Embroidery / Kleynods of Independence /
Football Collection / Kleynod Forces; up to $785

KLEYNOD

Watches were a common gift in the former Soviet Union, so it may not come as a great surprise that millions of timepieces of all types were manufactured during that period. Today, many swamp the online auction markets, much appreciated for their rugged look, the very identifiable symbols (like the red star), and their robust construction. There were several big names, of course: Vostok, Sturmanskie, and Raketa, among others. Most are still with us these days as new post-Soviet brands in their own right and with distinctive looks.

Among the more recent enterprises is the Kyiv Ukranian Watch Factory, founded in 1997 in the Ukrainian capital. It was a manufacturer for the Russian brand Poljot, among others. Perhaps more notorious in Ukraine at least was the making of a watch for Ukrainian astronaut Leonid Kadeniuk, who was on the international STS-87 mission carried out by the space shuttle Columbia. In 2002, the company decided to create a distinct brand of its own. They chose the name Kleynod, which derives from the German *Kleinod*, or Polish *klejnot*, an old word for "gem."

The output is divided up into six main collections. For the sake of affordability, the movements used are mostly quartz, but a fair number of the watches do come equipped with Swiss-made Ronda movements. Still, they are all under the $1,000 mark. Perhaps more interesting though are the motifs on the dials that reflect a pride in the country's long history. The 3, 6, 9, and 12 that appear on the dial of the Kleynods of Independence collection may hardly be recognizable at first because they have been stylized to look like the *tryzub*, the distinctive Ukrainian trident, on a guilloché background, which originates back in the mists of the nation's history.

The numerals of the Classic model also mirror the style of the *tryzub*, though the dial is far simpler. As for the Embroidery collection, its geometrical decorative pattern suggests an ancient craft from certain regions of the country—other regions, notably in the east, lean towards floral patterns.

Classic Collection
Reference number: K 348-523
Movement: automatic, Caliber Ronda R-150; ø 25.6 mm, height 4.4 mm; 25 jewels; 28,800 vph; 40-hour power reserve
Functions: hours, minutes, sweep seconds; date
Case: stainless steel, 42 mm, height 10.6 mm; sapphire crystal; water-resistant to 5 atm
Band: leather, folding clasp
Remarks: guilloché in the center of the dial
Price: $570

Kleynods of Independence
Reference number: K 25-606
Movement: automatic, Caliber Ronda R-150; ø 25.6 mm, height 4.4 mm; 25 jewels; 28,800 vph; 40-hour power reserve
Functions: hours, minutes, sweep seconds; date
Case: stainless steel with gold plating (IPG), ø 44 mm, height 11.2 mm; sapphire crystal; water-resistant to 5 atm
Band: leather, folding clasp
Remarks: guilloché on the dial
Price: $715; limited to 2,500 pieces
Variations: comes in stainless steel, with white dial; also in tonneau version

Embroidery by Kleynod
Reference number: K 308-511 B
Movement: automatic, Caliber Ronda R-150; ø 25.6 mm, height 4.4 mm; 25 jewels; 28,800 vph; 40-hour power reserve
Functions: hours, minutes, sweep seconds; date
Case: stainless steel, ø 37 mm, height 10.4 mm; sapphire crystal; water-resistant to 5 atm
Band: natural leather with sateen on the top, buckle
Remarks: geometric pattern on the dial inspired by Ukrainian embroidery.
Price: $520

KOBOLD

Like many others in the field, Michael Kobold had already developed an interest in the watch industry in childhood. As a young man, he found a mentor in Chronoswiss founder Gerd-Rüdiger Lang, who encouraged him to start his own brand. This he did in 1998—at the age of nineteen while he was still a student at Carnegie Mellon University. Today, after twenty-five years, some, like the pandemic years, quite difficult, Kobold Watch Company stretches across three continents. Part is in Pittsburgh, where it manufactures cases and movement components; some components are also manufactured in Nepal, while the founder himself lives in his native Germany.

It is not surprising for a company whose motto is "Embrace Adventure." Explorers such as Sir Ranulph Fiennes, whom Guinness Book of World Records describes as "the world's greatest living explorer, have worn these tough mechanical instruments. The brand's centerpiece is the Soarway collection and the fabled Soarway case, which was originally created in 1999 by Sir Ranulph, master watchmaker; Chronoswiss founder Lang; and company founder Kobold, himself an avid mountain climber. Advice and funding came in part from the late James Gandolfini, better known to TV audiences as Tony Soprano.

Kobold's love of the Himalayas has driven his commitment to the people of Nepal. He produces leather accessories and straps there and uses the operation to offer women vocational training. In 2015, he launched the Soarway Foundation to help Nepal in the event of earthquakes. His love of that country is also behind the Fire Truck Expedition as a way to supply the mountain-clad country with key firefighting equipment.

Kobold has contributed to the renaissance of American watchmaking and originally set its sights even higher, namely on an in-house U.S.-made movement. Things have changed, though. "We make tough, rugged watches and so the case plays a more important role than the movement," says Kobold. "So for now, we're concentrating on making the toughest cases possible.

Kobold Time GmbH
Willibald-Alexis-Strasse 18
D-10965 Berlin
Germany

Tel.:
+49-151-105-500-10
1-877-SOARWAY

E-mail:
info@koboldwatch.com

Website:
www.koboldwatch.com

Founded:
1998

Number of employees:
8

Annual production:
maximum 2,500 watches

Distribution:
factory-direct, select retailers
1-877-SOARWAY

Most important collection/price range:
Soarway, Phantom, SMG / $2,650 to $48,000

Seal Ceramic James Gandolfini— Meteorite dial

Reference number: KD 842121C
Movement: automatic, ETA 2892-A2; ø 36 mm, height 3.6 mm; 21 jewels; 28,800 vph; 46-hour power reserve
Functions: hours, minutes, sweep seconds
Case: ceramic, ø 44 mm, height 17.0 mm; unidirectional rotating bezel with 60-minute divisions; Antireflective sapphire crystal; screwed-in crown; screwed-down case back; water-resistant to 100 atm
Band: rubber, signed buckle
Price: $8,500; limited to 51 pieces
Variations: varied dials, including Mount Everest summit rock, malachite, turquoise

SMG-2

Reference number: KD 5546142
Movement: automatic, Caliber ETA 2893-A2; ø 26.2 mm, height 4.1 mm; 21 jewels; 28,800 vph; 40-hour power reserve
Functions: hours, minutes, sweep seconds; 2nd time zone; date
Case: stainless steel, ø 43 mm, height 12.75 mm; unidirectional bezel with 0-60 scale; antireflective sapphire crystal; screwed-down case back; screwed-in crown; water-resistant to 20 atm
Band: rubber, buckle
Price: $6,450

Phantom SL Chronograph

Reference number: KD 7934552
Movement: automatic, ETA 7750; ø 25.6 mm, height 7.9 mm; 25 jewels; 28,800 vph; côtes de Genève, perlage, engraved and skeletonized gold-plated rotor; 38-hour power reserve
Functions: hours, minutes, subsidiary seconds; date, day; chronograph
Case: titanium, ø 40.5 mm, height 17 mm; bezel with tachymeter scale (blank bezel optional); screwed-in crown; sapphire crystal; screwed-down back; water-resistant to 20 atm
Band: reptile skin, buckle
Price: $3,450

Arctic Diver

Reference number: KD 9652155
Movement: automatic, ETA 2824; ø 25.6 mm, height
4.6 mm; 25 jewels; 28,800 vph; côtes de Genève,
perlage, engraved gold-plated rotor; soft iron core;
38-hour power reserve
Functions: hours, minutes, sweep seconds; date
(optional)
Case: DLC-coated titanium, ø 44.5 mm, height 15 mm;
unidirectional bezel with 60-minute divisions (blank
bezel optional); screwed-in crown; sapphire crystal;
screwed-down back; water-resistant to 50 atm
Band: rubber, buckle
Price: $5,650

Soarway Diver

Reference number: KD 1113145
Movement: automatic, ETA 2892; ø 25.6 mm, height
3.6 mm; 25 jewels; 28,800 vph; côtes de Genève,
perlage, engraved and skeletonized gold-plated rotor;
38-hour power reserve
Functions: hours, minutes, sweep seconds; date
(optional)
Case: DLC-coated stainless steel, ø 40.5 mm, height
10 mm; unidirectional bezel with 60-minute divisions,
screwed-in crown; antireflective sapphire crystal;
screwed-down back; water-resistant to 30 atm
Band: canvas, buckle
Price: $5,950

Phantom Safari Chronograph

Reference number: KD 7935455
Movement: automatic, ETA 7750; ø 25.6 mm, height
7.9 mm; 25 jewels; 28,800 vph; with côtes de Genève,
perlage, engraved and skeletonized gold-plated rotor;
38-hour power reserve
Functions: hours, minutes, subsidiary seconds; date,
day; chronograph
Case: titanium with DLC coating, ø 40.5 mm, height
17 mm; unidirectional bezel with 0-60 scale; screwed-
in crown; screw-locked push buttons; sapphire crystal;
screwed-down case back; water-resistant to 30 atm
Band: canvas, buckle
Price: $7,950

Seal

Reference number: KD 842121
Movement: automatic, ETA 2892-A2; ø 36 mm, height
3.6 mm; 21 jewels; 28,800 vph; 46-hour power reserve
Functions: hours, minutes, sweep seconds
Case: stainless steel, ø 44 mm, height 15 mm;
unidirectional rotating bezel with 0-60 scale; sapphire
crystal; screwed-down case back; screw
ed-in crown; water-resistant to 100 atm
Band: Calfskin, buckle
Price: $5,650

Polar Surveyor Chronograph

Reference number: KD 9266452
Movement: automatic, ETA 7750; ø 25.6 mm, height
7.9 mm; 25 jewels; 28,800 vph; côtes de Genève,
perlage, engraved and skeletonized gold-plated rotor;
38-hour power reserve
Functions: hours, minutes, subsidiary seconds; date,
day; chronograph; second time zone
Case: titanium, ø 40.5 mm, height 17 mm; unidirectional
bezel with 60-minute divisions; screwed-in crown;
screw-locked push buttons; sapphire crystal; screwed-
down back; water-resistant to 30 atm
Band: stainless steel, buckle
Price: $9,450

Himalaya Everest Edition

Reference number: KD 2143211
Movement: automatic, ETA 2892-A2; ø 36 mm, height
3.6 mm; 21 jewels; 28,800 vph; 46-hour power reserve
Functions: hours, minutes, sweep seconds
Case: stainless steel, ø 44 mm, height 14.0 mm;
sapphire crystal; screwed-down case back; water-
resistant to 10 atm
Band: calfskin, buckle
Remarks: dial made from Mount Everest summit rock
Price: $24,500

KUDOKE

Stefan Kudoke, a watchmaker from Frankfurt an der Oder, has made a name for himself as an extremely skilled and imaginative creator of timepieces. He apprenticed with two experienced watchmakers and graduated as the number one trainee in the state of Brandenburg. This earned him a stipend from a federal program promoting gifted individuals. He then moved on to one of the large *manufactures* in Glashütte, where he refined his skills in its workshop for complications and prototyping. At the age of twenty-two, with a master's diploma in his pocket, he decided to get an MBA and then devote himself to building his own company.

His guiding principle is individuality, and that is not possible to find in a serial product. So Kudoke began building unique pieces. By realizing the special wishes of customers, he manages to reflect each person's uniqueness in each watch. And he has produced some genuinely outstanding timepieces, like the ExCentro1 and 2 or more recently a watch with an octopus that seems to be climbing out of the case. Even his more minimalistic pieces, like the Kudoke 1 and 2 are deeply thought-out. They come in carefully chosen, yet toned-down colors like anthracite, that interact subtly with the shapes.

Kudoke has divided his output into two clear categories: HANDwerk, meaning crafts, and referring to straight watchmaking, and KUNSTwerk, which means artwork or art movement. The latter category gives him the opportunity to work his specialties, like artisanal engraving and goldsmithing. Under his hand, edges might be turned into graceful bodies, or a plate fragment might be turned into figures and garlands. His creativity has earned him a Grand Prix d'Horlogerie de Genève (GPHG) prize in the "Petite Aiguille" category in 2019. The small family-run company was one of the very few German brands to win this "Oscar" of the watch industry with its successful Kudoke 2 model.

Kudoke Uhren
Tannenweg 5
D-15236 Frankfurt (Oder)
Germany

Tel.:
+49-335-280-0409

E-mail:
info@kudoke.eu

Website:
www.kudoke.eu

Founded:
2007

Number of employees:
4

Annual production:
150 watches

Distribution:
Contact the brand directly for information

Price range:
between approx. $4,500 and $32,000

Kudoke 1 Red Gold
Reference number: K1_RG
Movement: hand-wound, Kudoke Caliber 1; ø 30 mm, height 4.3 mm; 18 jewels; 28,800 vph; hand-engraved and finished movement; blued hands; 46-hour power reserve
Functions: hours, minutes, subsidiary seconds
Case: rose gold, ø 39 mm, height 9.5 mm; sapphire crystal; transparent case back
Band: reptile skin, pin buckle
Price: $16,040

Kudoke 2 Yellow Gold
Reference number: K2_GG
Movement: hand-wound, Kudoke Caliber 1, 24-hour version; ø 30 mm, height 5.05 mm; 18 jewels; 28,800 vph; hand-engraved and finished movement; 46-hour power reserve
Functions: hours, minutes; additional 24-hour display
Case: stainless steel, ø 39 mm, height 10.7 mm; sapphire crystal; transparent case back
Remarks: sky disk hand-engraved and treated galvanically in three colors
Price: $13,760

Kudoke 3
Reference number: K3
Movement: hand-wound, Kudoke Caliber 1; ø 30 mm, height 4.3 mm; 18 jewels; 28,800 vph; hand-engraved and finished movement; 46-hour power reserve
Functions: hours (segment display), minutes
Case: stainless steel, ø 39 mm, height 10.3 mm; sapphire crystal; transparent case back
Band: reptile skin, pin buckle
Price: $9,910

LAURENT FERRIER

A rock rolling along a riverbed or being buffeted by coastal surf will, over time, achieve a kind of perfect shape, streamlined, flowing, smooth. It will usually become a comfortable touchstone for the human hand—a fine pebble, or *galet* in French. And that is the name given to the watches made by Laurent Ferrier in Geneva, Switzerland. The name refers to the special look and feel of the cases, which are just one hallmark of this very unusual, yet classical, watch brand.

Laurent Ferrier is a real person, the offspring of a watchmaking family from the Canton of Neuchâtel and a trained watchmaker. As a young man he had a passion for cars, too, and even raced seven times at the 24 Hours of Le Mans. In 2009, after thirty-five years of employment at Patek Philippe working on new movements, Ferrier decided he had been shaped enough by his industry. He gathered up his deep experience and founded his own enterprise. He was joined by his son, Christian Ferrier, a watchmaker in his own right, and fellow former race driver François Sérvanin.

In 2023, the Grand Sport Tourbillon Pursuit picked up the Tourbillon Prize at the Geneva "grand prix." Like other models in the collection, this one uses a natural escapement with a double hairspring, ensuring greater accuracy (a technical idea going back to Breguet). The tourbillon is once again concealed on the movement side, keeping the dial free of clutter.

The flagship Galet keeps evolving and being used to house different complications, like a second time zone. But Ferrier likes to return to roots, and the École Annual Calendar manages to put the calendar right on the dial along with time without the different functions running into each other. And the Square collection now has one of the most basic types of watch, a regulator, used by watchmakers since time immemorial to test their products' accuracy.

Laurent Ferrier
Route de Saint Julien 150
CH-1228 Plan-les-Ouates
Switzerland

Tel.:
+41-22-716-3388

E-mail:
info@laurentferrier.ch

Website:
www.laurentferrier.ch

Founded:
2010

Number of employees:
12

Annual production:
135

U.S. distributor:
Cellini Jewelers
430 Park Avenue
New York, NY 10022
212-888-0505
800.CELLINI
Contact@CelliniJewelers.com

Most important collections/price range:
Variations of the Galet / from $40,000 to $345,000

Grand Sport Tourbillon Pursuit

Reference number: LCF044.T1.RN1
Movement: hand-wound, Laurent Ferrier Caliber LF619.01; ø 31.60, height 5.57 mm; 21,600 vph; 23 jewels; Swiss lever escapement, tourbillon with double balance spring; finely decorated bridges and mainplate; semi-instantaneous calendar with correction forward or backward; 80-hour power reserve
Functions: hours, minutes, subsidiary seconds
Case: titanium, ø 44 mm, height 13.40 mm; domed and tinted sapphire crystal; transparent case back; ball-shaped crown; water-resistant to 10 atm
Band: titanium, folding clasp
Remarks: the tourbillon is on the back in traditional style
Price: $190,000

Sport Auto 40

Reference number: LCF040.T1.V1GCO
Movement: automatic, Laurent Ferrier Caliber LF270.01; ø 31.6 mm, height 4.85 mm; 28,800 vph; 31 jewels; platinum off-center micro-rotor; natural lever escapement with double escape wheel; finely decorated bridges and mainplate; 72-hour power reserve
Functions: hours, minutes, subsidiary seconds; date
Case: titanium, ø 41.5 mm, height 12.70 mm; satin-brushed bezel; ball-shaped crown; sapphire crystal, transparent screwed-down case back; water-resistant to 12 atm
Band: titanium, triple folding clasp
Remarks: white opaline dial
Price: $56,730; limited to 40 pieces

Classic Micro-Rotor Evergreen

Reference number: LCF004.R5.VR1
Movement: automatic, Laurent Ferrier Caliber FBN 229.01.01; ø 31.60 mm, height 4.35 mm; 21,600 vph; 35 jewels; silicon escapement, finely decorated bridges and mainplate; 72-hour power reserve
Functions: hours, minutes, subsidiary seconds
Case: red gold, ø 40 mm, height 11.10 mm; ball-shaped crown; sapphire crystal front, transparent case back; water-resistant to 3 atm
Band: calfskin with textile lining, pin buckle
Price: $68,380
Variations: dial also comes in the Square collection with stainless steel case (on request)

Ernst Leitz Werkstätten GmbH
Am Leitz-Park 4
D-35578 Wetzlar
Germany

Tel.:
+49 6441-899-330

E-mail:
pr@ernst-leitz-werkstaetten.com

Website:
www.ernst-leitz-werkstaetten.com

Founded:
2022

Number of employees:
7

U.S. Distribution
Retail, direct sales

Leica Store LA
424-777-0341
leicastore.la@leica-camera.com

Leica Store DC
202-787-5900
leicastore.dc@leica-camera.com

Most important collections/price range:
ZM 1 and ZM 2, Monochrom / $10,000 to $15,500

LEICA

Alongside fine watchmaking, the manufacture of photographic cameras has always been regarded as the supreme discipline of precision manufacturing. Leica Camera AG's decision to develop its own wristwatch collection was therefore a natural step. After all, the Leica M series still raises eyebrows of admiration amongst connoisseurs of fine cameras. They have always been compact, silent, extremely precise, and robust. The only thing that seems unusual is that Leica took 150 years to make this decision.

In 2023, following several starts and restarts, with models listed as L1 and L2 appearing briefly on the market, Leica finally launched the first two wristwatches designed and constructed from scratch. Discreetly hidden on the winding crown of the ZM 1 and ZM 2 "timepieces" is the trademark red dot upon which Leica-users would normally see the company's name. This brings us right to the heart of the matter.

Lehmann Präzision, located in Schramberg, in the Black Forest, was heavily involved in the project, having codeveloped the movement. The company is in fact not known for watches, but they do manufacture small components and assemble units. Professor Achim Heine, who has designed numerous Leica products over the years and thus has extensive background knowledge with regard to the company's design principles, was in charge of getting the right look.

Many features known from the cameras can therefore be found in the details on the watches, including the fine hands and indexes, the shape of the intricately crafted stainless-steel case, or the special fluting on the crowns (from the shutter button). The cambered sapphire crystal, of course, is reminiscent of Leica lenses. Among the technical charms are the stop-second pusher on the crown and a power reserve indicator made of two plates that turn onto each other like a camera's shutter.

For the past year, Leica has maintained a full-fledged watchmaker's atelier at the company's Wetzlar site, where the timepieces are prepared for shipment and any warranty claims are handled. Seven employees, including two watchmakers, represent the watch cosmos of the brand with the red dot in the Ernst Leitz workshops.

ZM 1

Movement: hand-wound, Leica Caliber ZM 1; ø 35.75 mm, height 6.35 mm; 26 jewels; 28,800 vph; automatic seconds zero reset; 60-hour power reserve
Functions: hours, minutes, subsidiary seconds; power-reserve indicator; date
Case: stainless steel, ø 41 mm, height 14.5 mm; sapphire crystal; transparent case back; patented crown with pusher that switches between winding and time-setting with a switch indicator; water-resistant to 5 atm
Band: calfskin, pin buckle
Price: $10,000

ZM 2

Movement: hand-wound, Leica Caliber ZM 2; ø 35.75 mm, height 8.4 mm; 26 jewels; 28,800 vph; automatic seconds zero reset; 60-hour power reserve
Functions: hours, minutes, subsidiary seconds; additional 12-hour display (2nd time zone), day/night indication, power reserve indicator (crown-activated scale ring on the flange); date
Case: stainless steel, ø 41 mm, height 14.5 mm; sapphire crystal; transparent case back; patented crown with pusher that switches between winding and time-setting with a switch indicator; water-resistant to 5 atm
Band: calfskin, pin buckle
Price: $14,000

ZM 1 Monochrom

Movement: hand-wound, Leica Caliber ZM 1; ø 35.75 mm, height 6.35 mm; 26 jewels; 28,800 vph; automatic seconds zero reset; 60-hour power reserve
Functions: hours, minutes, subsidiary seconds; power-reserve indicator; date
Case: stainless steel with black PVD, ø 41 mm, height 14.5 mm; sapphire crystal; transparent case back; patented crown with pusher that switches between winding and time-setting with a switch indicator; water-resistant to 5 atm
Band: calfskin, pin buckle
Price: $11,500
Variations: ZM 2 Monochrom ($15,500)

LIP

Like the Vallée de Joux, or Geneva, or La Chaux-de-Fonds, the town of Besançon, France, was at one time a major watchmaking hub. It even has an observatory, which was once upon a time needed to set watches.

In 1867, Emmanuel Lipmann founded a small watchmaking enterprise in this booming town and, together with his sons, quickly established himself as a specialist in stopwatches. They were an innovative family. In 1904, Ernest Lipmann had Pierre and Marie Curie, who had just discovered radium, prepare a special luminous material for dials. During the First World War, observation watches and chronographs equipped in this way were in great demand, but it was not until the 1930s that the brand began to take off with the first French mass-produced wristwatch caliber (T18).

In 1952, Fred Lipmann, who had been forced to change his name to Lip during the war under the Vichy Regime, released the first electromechanical wristwatch, and in the 1970s, Lip was quick to adopt quartz, becoming the first European quartz watch in series. There were problems, however, with Japanese and American competition, the oil crisis in 1973, and the drop in the dollar exchange rate. The company filed for bankruptcy. The unionized workers, however, resisted, and Lip became a household word in France. And they won. The workers' committee transferred the company to collective self-management and hired the designer Roger Tallon, who, with the legendary Mach 2000, contributed significantly to the unexpected and brief rise of the Lip brand. After renewed economic troubles, however, Lip was restructured into a cooperative in the 1980s and liquidated in 1990.

At the turn of the millennium, the brand was revitalized using Chinese technology, but it was not until 2014 that the brand returned to new production facilities at its former founding site in Besançon. Shortly afterwards, the first watches manufactured in France were shown, and since then, Lip has seen a steady rise in the favor of watch buyers. The interesting history of the brand, coupled with the distinctive aesthetics of the reinterpreted classics, and not least the very affordable prices of the product, even for well-equipped automatic watches, make Lip an insider tip for collectors and newcomers alike.

Montres Lip
Chemin des Maurapans
ZAC Valentin
F-25075 Besançon
France

Tel.:
+33 381 48 48 41

Email:
lip@smb-horlogerie.com

Website:
www.lip.fr

Founded:
1867/2014

Number of employees:
8

Distribution:
Retail, webshop

Price range:
$150 to $1,500

Grand Nautic Ski 41 mm
Reference number: 671521
Movement: automatic, Miyota Caliber 8215; ø 25.6 mm, height 5.67 mm; 21 jewels; 21,600 vph; 38-hour power reserve
Functions: hours, minutes, sweep seconds; date
Case: stainless steel, ø 41 mm, height 12 mm; crown-activated inner rotating scale ring with 0-60 scale; sapphire crystal; water-resistant to 20 atm
Band: polyurethane (Tropic), pin buckle
Price: $545

Big TV Titanium Skeleton
Reference number: 671656
Movement: automatic, Time Module NH72; ø 27.4 mm, height 5.32 mm; 24 jewels; 21,600 vph; skeletonized movement; 41-hour power reserve
Functions: hours, minutes, sweep seconds
Case: titanium, 35 x 35 mm, height 10 mm; sapphire crystal; water-resistant to 5 atm
Band: titanium, folding clasp
Price: $980

Mach 2000 Mini
Reference number: 671162
Movement: quartz
Functions: hours, minutes, sweep seconds
Case: stainless steel, 30 mm x 28 mm, height 5 mm; mineral glass; water-resistant to 3 atm
Band: calfskin, pin buckle
Remarks: design classic by Roger Tallon originally from the 1970s
Price: $196
Variations: various colors; with Milanese mesh bracelet ($207)

Longines Watch Co.
Rue des Longines 8
CH-2610 St-Imier
Switzerland

Tel.:
+41-32-942-5425

E-mail:
info@longines.com

Website:
www.longines.com

Founded:
1832

Number of employees:
worldwide approx. 2,000

U.S. distributor:
Longines
The Swatch Group (U.S.), Inc.
Longines Division
703 Waterford Way, Ste. 450
Miami, FL 33126
786-725-5393
www.longines.com

Most important collections/price range:
The Longines Master Collection, Longines
DolceVita, HydroConquest, Heritage Collection /
from approx. $1,000 to $10,000

LONGINES

The Longines winged hourglass logo is the world's oldest trademark, according to the World Intellectual Property Organization (WIPO). Since its founding in 1832, the brand has manufactured somewhere in the region of 35 million watches, making it one of the genuine heavyweights of the Swiss watch world. In 1983, Nicolas G. Hayek merged the two major Swiss watch manufacturing groups ASUAG and SIHH into what would later become the Swatch Group. Longines, the leading ASUAG brand, barely missed capturing the same position in the new concern; that honor went to Omega, the SIHH frontrunner. However, from a historical and technical point of view, this brand has what it takes to be at the helm of any group. Was it not Longines that equipped polar explorer Roald Amundsen and air pioneer Charles Lindbergh with their watches? It has also been the timekeeper at many Olympic Games and is a major sponsor at many other sports events, from riding to archery.

Longines now has an impressive portfolio of in-house calibers in stock, from simple manual winders to complicated chronographs. Thanks to this stock, it can supply Swatch Group with anything from cheap, thin quartz watches to heavy gold chronographs and calendars with quadruple retrograde displays. In addition to elegant ladies' watches and modern sports watches, remakes of great classics from the company's own history are a particular specialty of the house. There is, for example, the striking diver's watch whose rotating bezel is under sapphire crystal, including the Ultra-Chron with its high-speed oscillating movement, reissued exclusively for Longines with modern technology by the ETA movement factory. This year, lovers of the brand were able to enjoy a faithful replica of a pilot's watch from the 1930s, whose special feature is an internal marker time index that can be adjusted via the rotating bezel. The movement has been relocated inside the waterproof case.

Thanks to its many years of experience as a timekeeper at world championships and as a partner of international federations, Longines has also been able to forge close and lasting relationships with the world of sports, which are evidenced with great regularity in limited special editions.

Pilot Majetek

Reference number: L2.838.4.53.0
Movement: automatic, Longines Caliber L893.6 (based on ETA A31.501); ø 25.6 mm; 26 jewels; 25,200 vph; silicon hairspring, antimagnetic nickel-phosphorus escapement wheel and anchor (LIGA technology); 72-hour power reserve
Functions: hours, minutes, subsidiary seconds
Case: stainless steel, ø 42 mm, height 13.3; bidirectional bezel (under the crystal) with reference markings; sapphire crystal; screw-in crown; water-resistant to 10 atm
Band: calfskin, pin buckle
Remarks: modeled on a pilot's watch of the Czech air force ("Majetek")
Price: $3,750

Spirit Flyback

Reference number: L3.821.4.53.9
Movement: automatic, Longines Caliber L791.4 (based on ETA A08.261); ø 30 mm, height 7.9 mm; 28 jewels; 28,800 vph; silicon hairspring, column-wheel control of chronograph functions; 68-hour power reserve; COSC-certified chronometer
Functions: hours, minutes, subsidiary seconds; flyback chronograph
Case: stainless steel, ø 42 mm, height 17 mm; bidirectional bezel with ceramic insert, with 0-60 scale; sapphire crystal; transparent case back; screw-in crown; water-resistant to 10 atm
Band: textile, pin buckle
Price: $4,450

Spirit Zulu Time

Reference number: L3.802.5.53.2
Movement: automatic, Longines Caliber L844 (based on ETA A31.411); ø 25.6 mm, height 3.85 mm; 21 jewels; 25,200 vph; silicon hairspring, antimagnetic escapement (LIGA technology); 72-hour power reserve; COSC-certified chronometer
Functions: hours, minutes, sweep seconds (incremental setting of hour hand); additional 24-hour display (2nd time zone); date
Case: stainless steel, ø 42 mm, height 13.9 mm; bidirectional bezel in yellow gold with ceramic insert, with 0-24 scale; sapphire crystal; screw-in crown, in yellow gold; water-resistant to 10 atm
Band: calfskin, double folding clasp
Price: $4,200
Variations: various bands and dials

Ultra-Chron

Reference number: L2.836.4.52.6
Movement: automatic, Longines Caliber L836 (based on ETA C07.L11); ø 25.6 mm; 25 jewels; 36,000 vph; silicon hairspring, antimagnetic escapement (LIGA technology); Timelab-certified chronometer; 52-hour power reserve
Functions: hours, minutes, sweep seconds
Case: stainless steel, ø 43 mm, height 13.6 mm; bezel with sapphire crystal insert; sapphire crystal; water-resistant to 30 atm
Band: stainless steel, double folding clasp
Price: $3,600

HydroConquest GMT

Reference number: L3.790.4.06.2
Movement: automatic, Longines Caliber L844 (based on ETA A31.411); ø 25.6 mm, height 3.85 mm; 21 jewels; 25,200 vph; silicon hairspring, antimagnetic escapement (LIGA technology); 72-hour power reserve
Functions: hours, minutes, sweep seconds (incremental setting of hour hand); additional 24-hour display (2nd time zone); date
Case: stainless steel, ø 41 mm, height 12.9 mm; unidirectional bezel with ceramic insert, with 0-60 scale; sapphire crystal; screw-in crown; water-resistant to 30 atm
Band: textile, pin buckle
Price: $2,675

Conquest

Reference number: L3.830.4.72.6
Movement: automatic, Longines Caliber L888 (based on ETA A31.L01); ø 25.6 mm, height 3.85 mm; 21 jewels; 25,200 vph; silicon hairspring; 72-hour power reserve
Functions: hours, minutes, sweep seconds; date
Case: stainless steel, ø 40 mm, height 10.9 mm; sapphire crystal; transparent case back; water-resistant to 10 atm
Band: stainless steel, double folding clasp
Price: $1,975

Legend Diver Watch

Reference number: L3.774.4.90.2
Movement: automatic, Longines Caliber L888.5 (based on ETA A31.L11); ø 25.6 mm, height 3.85 mm; 21 jewels; 25,200 vph; silicon hairspring, antimagnetic escapement (LIGA technology); 72-hour power reserve
Functions: hours, minutes, sweep seconds
Case: stainless steel, ø 42 mm, height 12.7 mm; crown-activated inner rotating scale ring with 0-60 scale; sapphire crystal; screw-in crown; water-resistant to 30 atm
Band: textile, folding clasp
Price: $2,500

Dolce Vita

Reference number: L5.200.4.75.6
Movement: quartz
Functions: hours, minutes, subsidiary seconds
Case: stainless steel, 21.5 x 29 mm, height 6.75 mm; sapphire crystal; water-resistant to 3 atm
Band: stainless steel, folding clasp
Price: $1,850

Dolce Vita

Reference number: L5.512.7.71.0
Movement: quartz
Functions: hours, minutes, subsidiary seconds
Case: yellow gold, with 46 diamonds, 23 x 37 mm, height 7.2 mm; sapphire crystal; water-resistant to 3 atm
Band: reptile skin, pin buckle
Price: $8,950

Louis Erard SA
Ouest 2
CH-2340 Le Noirmont
Switzerland

Tel.:
+41-32-957-65-30

E-mail:
info@louiserard.com

Website:
www.louiserard.com

Founded:
1929

Number of employees:
15

Annual production:
not specified

Distribution/sales:
Exquisite Timepieces
4380 Gulfshore Blvd., N. Suite 800
Naples, Fl 34103
239-666-8163
exquisitetimepieces.com

Cellini Jewelers
430 Park Ave
New York, NY 10022
212-888-0505
cellinijewelers.com

Most important collections/price range:
Excellence, La Sportive, Heritage, / $1,000 to
$5,000

LOUIS ERARD

Once upon a time in the watchmaking workshops, there was a large clock that gave the minutes as the main time increment and the hours on a separate dial. This allowed the watchmakers to set and test the accuracy of the piece they were assembling. Over time, so-called regulator dials became popular with the public. It is said that train conductors preferred them because they needed accuracy to the minute.

Among the rare brands that have made regulator watches an important part of their output is Louis Erard. The company namesake (1893-1964), a watchmaker by trade, founded a watchmaking school in his native La Chaux-de-Fonds, and later a casing business for the thriving industry, and then a watchmaking company under his own name.

Erard's business acumen was as good as his technical skill. In the 1930s, he worked on the legendary Valjoux 72 chronograph movement, and in 1956, his company received the coveted right to manufacture movements. In fact, Louis Erard, the company, managed to weather the quartz crisis thanks to a careful modernization program in the 1970s launched by Erard's grandson.

In 1992, Louis Erard moved to Le Noirmont in the Jura Mountains. It had some trouble maintaining a profile, until Manuel Emch of Jaquet Droz and Romain Jérôme stepped in. The new directive was "make collecting affordable" mainly through daring collaborations with the likes of Label Noir, Alain Silberstein, Konstantin Chaykin, Massena Lab, and The Horophile. Collections are limited, and most watches are under $5,000 dollars.

The recipe seems to be working. It allows for creativity and bold products that still depend on solid watchmaking. Those who keep a close eye on the industry are always curious to see what the little company up in the Jura will be producing next.

Le Chronographe Monopoussoir Louis Erard x Massena LAB

Reference number: 85237NN57
Movement: automatic, Sellita W500MPC; ø 30 mm, height 7.90 mm; 25 jewels; 28,800 vph; carefully decorated with open-worked oscillating weight; 48-hour power reserve
Functions: hours, minutes; monopusher chronograph, minute totalizer
Case: stainless steel with black PVD, ø 43 mm, height 15.70 mm; sapphire crystal; transparent case back; water-resistant to 5 atm
Band: calfskin lining, buckle, quick strap change system
Collaboration: watch developed in association Massena Lab; special grained dial, blued hands
Price: $4,950; limited to 178 pieces
Variations: with silvery rhodium-plated dial

La Petite Seconde Metropolis Louis Erard x The Horophile

Reference number: 34248AA44-6
Movement: automatic, Sellita SW261-1; ø 25.60 mm, height 5.60 mm; 31 jewels; 28,800 vph; open-worked oscillating weight with Louis Erard logo, 38-hour power reserve
Functions: hours, minutes, subsidiary seconds
Case: stainless steel, ø 39 mm, height 12.82 mm; crown with fir-tree pattern; sapphire crystal; transparent case back; water-resistant to 5 atm
Band: calfskin, pin buckle, quick strap change system
Remarks: collaboration with The Horophile, real name Amr Sindi, a multifaceted figure focusing on design
Price: $2,900; limited to 178 pieces in all
Variations: slate dial or tobacco dial

Le Régulateur Louis Erard x Konstantin Chaykin Dusk to Dawn

Reference number: 85237AA89
Movement: automatic, Sellita SW266-1; ø 22 mm, height 5.60 mm; 31 jewels; 28,800 vph; open-worked oscillating weight with Louis Erard logo, 38-hour power reserve
Functions: hour disk, sweep minute, seconds disk
Case: stainless steel, ø 42 mm, height 12.25 mm; sapphire crystal; transparent case back; water-resistant to 5 atm
Band: toadskin with rabbit lining, pin buckle, quick strap change system
Remarks: eye (hour) and mouth (minutes) recall the evil goblin Likho of Slav mythology; available in a set of two watches as well
Price: $4,500; limited to 178 pieces
Variations: with green minute track; in 39-millimeter case

LOUIS MOINET

Les Ateliers Louis Moinet SA
Rue du Temple 1
CH-2072 Saint-Blaise
Switzerland

Tel.:
+41-32-753-6814

E-mail:
info@louismoinet.com

Website:
www.louismoinet.com

Founded:
2005

U.S. distributor:
Fitzhenry Consulting
1029 Peachtree Parkway, #346
Peachtree City, GA 30269
561-212-6812
Don@fitzhenry.com

Most important collections:
Memoris, Sideralis, Tempograph Chrome,
Spacewalker, Ultravox; numerous unique pieces

There's always something happening at Louis Moinet, but what really boosted the brand was a rather special historic discovery: in the race to be the first to invent something new, Louis Moinet (1768–1853), it seems, has emerged as the first maker of a chronograph. His *Compteur de tierces*, dating to 1816, was revealed to the public in 2013. This special chronograph counted one-sixtieth of a second with a frequency of 216,000 vph. It was built to make more accurate astronomical calculations.

The original Louis Moinet was a professor at the Academy of Fine Arts in Paris and president of the Société Chronométrique and was without a doubt one of the most inventive, multitalented men of his time. He worked with such eminent watchmakers as Breguet, Berthoud, Winnerl, Janvier, and Perrelet. Among his accomplishments is an extensive two-volume treatise on horology.

Following in such footsteps is hardly an easy task, but Jean-Marie Schaller and Micaela Bertolucci decided that their idiosyncratic creations were indeed imbued with the spirit of the great Frenchman. They work with a team of independent designers, watchmakers, movement specialists, and suppliers to produce the most unusual wristwatches filled with clever functions and surprising details. The Jules Verne chronographs have hinged levers, for example, and the second hand on the Tempograph changes direction every ten seconds.

Increasingly, this independent-minded brand is exploring the space-time continuum and the worlds of astronomy, space travel, science fiction, and even ancient spirituality. And they are winning Guinness World Records and all sorts of design prizes. The Mars Mission recalls the earliest snapshot of the planet and has a bit of Martian meteorite inside. The Astronef Techno features two satellite tourbillons revolving at different speeds around the dial over a microelectronic wafer. As for the Time to Race, the customer can pick a number and color pattern, and that watch will then be unique. The mission at Louis Moinet is to make watches that tell stories.

Astronef Techno

Reference number: LM-105.20.01
Movement: hand-wound, Louis Moinet Caliber LM105; ø 38.50 mm, height 13.60 mm; 56 jewels; 21,600 vph; 2 spring barrels, one for each of the the two satellite tourbillons rotating in opposite directions and at different rates, crossing paths 18 times per hour; each tourbillon has gold counterweights to ensure smooth rotation; 48-hour power reserve
Functions: hours, minutes
Case: titanium frame (ø 43.50 mm) with a sapphire crystal case, ø 41.60 mm, height 18.30 mm; transparent case back; water-resistant to 1 atm
Band: reptile skin, folding clasp
Remarks: dial cut from real microelectronic wafer; mechanism hidden in the base of the watch.
Price: $385,000; unique piece

Jules Verne Under the Sea

Reference number: LM-135.50.V5
Movement: hand-wound, Louis Moinet Caliber LM 35, ø 32 mm, height 5.70 mm; 26 jewels; 28,800 vph; 1-minute off-center flying tourbillon; two superimposed barrel springs arranged head to tail ("volte-face") to discharge energy simultaneously; 96-hour power reserve
Functions: hours, minutes
Case: red gold, ø 40.7 mm, height 15.12 mm; domed sapphire crystal; water-resistant to 3 atm
Band: reptile skin, folding clasp
Remarks: from a collection of 8 unique pieces each with a different slice of opal in the dial center; surrounded by hand-guilloché with special blue varnish
Price: $125,000

Mars Mission

Reference number: LM- 75.10B.MA-B
Movement: automatic, Louis Moinet Caliber LM45; ø 30.4 mm, height 6.6 mm; 22 jewels; 28,800 vph; côtes de Genève, circular-grained wheels, clous de Paris on rotor; 48-hour power reserve
Functions: hours, minutes, subsidiary seconds
Case: stainless steel, ø 43.2 mm, height 14.8 mm; transparent case back; water-resistant to 5 atm
Band: reptile skin, folding clasp
Remarks: a genuine meteorite fragment from Mars is in a frame at 3 o'clock; dial fashioned after the first ever photograph of Mars, taken by the Mariner 4 in 1965
Price: $22,500 ; limited to 100 pieces

Impulsion

Reference number: LM-114.40.20
Movement: hand-wound; Caliber LM114;
ø 32 mm, height 7.55 mm; 36 jewels; 28,800 vph; two
superimposed barrel springs arranged head to tail
("volte-face") to discharge energy simultaneously;
monopusher chronograph with column wheel control
as separate structure on the dial side; 1-minute off-
center tourbillon; 96-hour power reserve
Functions: hours, minutes, subsidiary seconds;
chronograph
Case: red gold , ø 42.50 mm, height 14.75 mm; sapphire
crystal, transparent case back; water-resistant to 3 atm
Band: reptile skin, folding clasp
Remarks: aventurine mainplate under open dial
Price: $149,900 ; limited to 28 pieces
Variations: with onyx mainplate, limited to 28 pieces

Time to Race

Reference number: LM-96.20.8R | LM-96.20.8B |
LM-96.20.8VF
Movement: automatic, Louis Moinet Caliber LM 96,
ø 30.40 mm, height 10.69 mm; 30 jewels; 28,800 vph;
column-wheel control; monopusher chronograph; screw
balance; oscillating mass with clous de Paris; mainplate with
côtes de Genève on movement side; 48-hour power reserve
Functions: hours, minutes, seconds, chronograph
Case: titanium, ø 40.7 mm, height 17.92 mm; sapphire crystal;
screw down transparent back; water-resistant to 5 atm
Band: rubber, folding clasp
Remarks: customers can choose their "lucky number"
and the one of several colors, so each piece is unique
and will never be made again
Price: $36,000

Japan Rocket

Reference number: LM-45.10.JP
Movement: automatic, Louis Moinet Caliber LM45;
ø 30.40 mm, height 6.60 mm; 22 jewels; 28,800 vph;
côtes de Genève, circular-grained wheels, clous de
Paris on rotor; 48-hour power reserve
Functions: hours, minutes, subsidiary seconds
Case: stainless steel, ø 43.20 mm, height 14.80 mm;
transparent case back; water-resistant to 5 atm
Band: reptile skin, folding clasp
Remarks: the dial contains a chip of lunar meteorite
and of the Gibeon meteorite, and a fragment of Japan's
H-IIB rocket fairing
Price: on request; limited to 20 pieces; available
exclusively in Japan

Tempograph Neo Onyx

Reference number: LM-125.10.50
Movement: automatic, Louis Moinet Caliber LM 85,
ø 30.40 mm, height 8.29 mm; 36 jewels; 28,800 vph;
screw balance with 18 screws; partially skeletonized
movement, oscillating mass with clous de Paris;
mainplate with côtes de Genève on movement side;
48-hour power reserve
Functions: hours, minutes, seconds (retrograde on
20-second scale with tricolored 1-minute totalizer on
subdial)
Case: stainless steel, ø 44 mm, height 14.75;
water-resistant to 5 atm
Band: reptile skin, folding clasp
Price: $29,900; limited to 28 pieces

Savanna Tiger

Reference number: LM-135.50.TI
Movement: hand-wound; Caliber LM35; ø 32 mm,
height 4.70 mm; 26 jewels; 28,800 vph; 1-minute off-
center tourbillon; two superimposed barrel springs
arranged head to tail ("volte-face") to discharge energy
simultaneously; 96-hour power reserve.
Functions: hours, minutes
Case: rose gold polished and satinated, ø 40.7 mm,
height 15.12 mm; domed sapphire crystal;
water-resistant to 3 atm
Band: reptile skin, folding clasp
Remarks: puzzle dial made of 81 pieces each
individually painted and arranged on four layers
Price: $159,000, unique piece

Cosmopolis

Reference number: LM-135.50.CO
Movement: hand-wound, Louis Moinet Caliber LM
35, ø 32 mm, height 5.70 mm; 26 jewels; 28,800 vph;
1-minute off-center flying tourbillon; two superimposed
barrel springs arranged head to tail ("volte-face") to
discharge energy simultaneously; 96-hour power
reserve
Functions: hours, minutes
Case: red gold, ø 40.7 mm, height 15.12 mm; domed
sapphire crystal; water-resistant to 3 atm
Band: reptile skin, folding clasp
Remarks: This timepiece features twelve different
meteorites and was awarded the title of "Most meteorite
inserts in a watch" by Guinness World Records
Price: on request; unique piece

MAURICE LACROIX

The roots of the brand Maurice Lacroix run deep, all the way to the late nineteenth century, in fact. The name Maurice Lacroix, however, was chosen in 1975 and carried the brand to respectable international success. In 2011, DKSH (Diethelm Keller & SiberHegner), a Swiss holding company that specializes in international market expansions, became the majority shareholder. This has ensured Maurice Lacroix a strong position in all major markets, with flagship stores and its own boutiques.

Nevertheless, the heart of the company remains the production facilities in the highlands of the Jura, in Saignelégier and Montfaucon, where the brand built La Manufacture des Franches-Montagnes SA (MFM) outfitted with state-of-the-art technology to produce very specific individual parts and movement components.

The watchmaker can thank the clever interpretations of "classic" pocket watch characteristics for its steep ascent in the 1990s. Since then, the *manufacture* has redesigned the complete collection, banning every lick of Breguet-like bliss from its watch designs. In the upper segment, *manufacture* models such as the chronograph and the retrograde variations on Unitas calibers set the tone. In the lower segment, modern "little" complications outfitted with module movements based on ETA and Sellita are the kings. The brand is mainly associated with the hypnotically turning square wheel, the "roue carrée."

The Aikon collection has been gaining in popularity ever since its introduction in 2016. It has a sort of back-to-the-roots quality: precise timekeeping, high readability, and exceptionally comfortable wear. And like all other Maurice Lacroix watches, the Aikon offers a lot of perceived value. The latest creation in the Aikon family is a collaboration with Tide Ocean SA, a company with the mission of recycling and upcycling plastic collected from the oceans: The AIKON #tide comes in a variety of bright colors. The design is genuinely cool. The new Pontos S Diver has been competing with the Aikon, however. The professionally equipped diver's watch made way for the revived sports watch line in 2016, but now it is coming back—a little less martial than before but more wearable and still a "real diver's watch" from the thick sapphire crystal to the screw-down crown.

Maurice Lacroix SA
Rüschlistrasse 6
CH-2502 Biel/Bienne
Switzerland

Tel.:
+41-44-209-1111

E-mail:
info@mauricelacroix.com

Website:
www.mauricelacroix.com

Founded:
1975

Number of employees:
about 250 worldwide

Annual production:
approx. 90,000 watches

U.S. distributor:
DKSH Premium Brand Distribution
31 NE 17th St
Miami, FL 33132
609-750-8800

Most important collections/price range:
Aikon / $890 to $2,900; Les Classiques / $950 to $4,300; Eliros / $690 to $1,390; Fiaba (ladies') / $980 to $2,900; Pontos / $1,750 to $7,900; Masterpiece manufacture models / $6,800 to $14,900

Masterpiece Gravity

Reference number: MP6118-SS001-115-1
Movement: automatic, Caliber ML 230; ø 37.2 mm, height 9.05 mm; 35 jewels; 18,000 vph; inverted movement with escapement on the dial; silicon anchor and escape wheel; 50-hour power reserve
Functions: hours and minutes (off-center), subsidiary seconds
Case: stainless steel, ø 43 mm, height 16 mm; sapphire crystal; transparent case back; water-resistant to 5 atm
Band: calfskin, folding clasp
Price: $10,900

Masterpiece Triple Retrograde

Reference number: MP6538-SS001-110-1
Movement: automatic, Sellita Caliber SW200-1 with Modul ML291; ø 25.6 mm; 47 jewels; 28,800 vph; 38-hour power reserve
Functions: hours, minutes, subsidiary seconds; additional 24-hour display (retrograde); date and weekday (retrograde)
Case: stainless steel, ø 43 mm, height 14 mm; sapphire crystal; transparent case back; water-resistant to 5 atm
Band: calfskin, folding clasp
Price: $6,050
Variations: various bands and dials

Aikon Master Grand Date

Reference number: AI6118-DLB0B-330-2
Movement: automatic, Caliber ML 331; ø 37.2 mm; 43 jewels; 18,000 vph; 50-hour power reserve
Functions: hours and minutes (off-center), subsidiary seconds; large date
Case: stainless steel with black DLC, ø 45 mm, height 15 mm; sapphire crystal; water-resistant to 10 atm
Band: rubber, double folding clasp
Price: $9,400
Variations: various cases, straps, and dials

Pontos S Diver

Reference number: PT6248-SS00L-330-J
Movement: automatic, Caliber ML 115 (based on
Sellita SW200-1); ø 25.6 mm, height 4.6 mm; 26 jewels;
28,800 vph; 38-hour power reserve
Functions: hours, minutes, sweep seconds; date
Case: stainless steel, ø 42 mm, height 12 mm; crown-
activated inner rotating scale ring with 0-60 scale;
sapphire crystal; screw-in crown; water resistant
to 30 atm
Band: rubber, pin buckle
Price: $2,050

Pontos S Chronograph

Reference number: PT6038-SSL24-130-2
Movement: automatic, Caliber ML 112 (based on
Sellita SW500); ø 30 mm, height 7.9 mm; 25 jewels;
28,800 vph; 48-hour power reserve
Functions: hours, minutes, subsidiary seconds;
chronograph; date and weekday
Case: stainless steel, ø 44 mm, height 15 mm;
sapphire crystal; water-resistant to 20 atm
Band: rubber with textile overlay, pin buckle
Price: $3,550

Pontos Chronograph

Reference number: PT6388-SS001-321-2
Movement: automatic, Caliber ML 112 (based on
Sellita SW500); ø 30 mm, height 7.9 mm; 25 jewels;
28,800 vph; 48-hour power reserve
Functions: hours, minutes, subsidiary seconds;
chronograph; date
Case: stainless steel, ø 43 mm, height 15 mm;
sapphire crystal; water-resistant to 10 atm
Band: calfskin, double folding clasp
Price: $3,200
Variations: various straps and dial colors

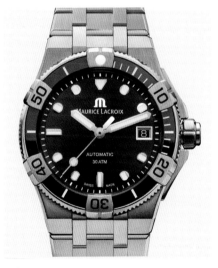

Aikon Automatic Chronograph Titanium

Reference number: AI6038-TT030-330-2
Movement: automatic, Caliber ML 112 (based on ETA
7750); ø 30 mm, height 7.9 mm; 25 jewels; 28,800 vph;
48-hour power reserve
Functions: hours, minutes, subsidiary seconds;
chronograph; date and weekday
Case: titanium, ø 44 mm, height 15 mm; sapphire
crystal; transparent case back; screw-in crown;
water-resistant to 20 atm
Band: titanium, double folding clasp
Price: $4,250

Aikon Automatic 42mm

Reference number: AI6008-SS00F-431-C
Movement: automatic, Caliber ML 115 (based on
Sellita SW200-1); ø 25.6 mm, height 4.6 mm; 26 jewels;
28,800 vph; 38-hour power reserve
Functions: hours, minutes, sweep seconds; date
Case: stainless steel, ø 42 mm, height 11 mm; sapphire
crystal; transparent case back; screw-in crown;
water-resistant to 20 atm
Band: stainless steel, double folding clasp
Price: $2,500
Variations: various dial colors

Aikon Venturer

Reference number: AI6057-SSL22-330-1
Movement: automatic, Caliber ML 115 (based on
Sellita SW200-1); ø 25.6 mm, height 4.6 mm; 26 jewels;
28,800 vph; 38-hour power reserve
Functions: hours, minutes, sweep seconds; date
Case: stainless steel, ø 38 mm, height 12 mm;
unidirectional bezel with ceramic insert, with
0-60 scale; sapphire crystal; screw-in crown;
water-resistant to 30 atm
Band: stainless steel, double folding clasp
Price: $2,400

Aikon Automatic Skeleton

Reference number: AI6007-SS002-030-1
Movement: automatic, Caliber ML 115 (based on
Sellita SW200-1); ø 25.6 mm, height 4.6 mm;
26 jewels; 28,800 vph; skeletonized movement;
38-hour power reserve
Functions: hours, minutes, sweep seconds
Case: stainless steel, ø 39 mm, height 11 mm; sapphire
crystal; transparent case back; screw-in crown;
water-resistant to 20 atm
Band: stainless steel, double folding clasp
Remarks: skeletonized dial
Price: $3,750

Aikon Automatic Date 35mm

Reference number: AI6006-SS00F-550-E
Movement: automatic, Caliber ML 115 (based on
Sellita SW200-1); ø 25.6 mm, height 4.6 mm; 26 jewels;
28,800 vph; 38-hour power reserve
Functions: hours, minutes, sweep seconds; date
Case: stainless steel, ø 35 mm; sapphire crystal;
transparent case back; water-resistant to 10 atm Band:
stainless steel, double folding clasp
Remarks: dial set with 8 diamonds
Price: $2,550
Variations: various dial colors

Aikon Quartz

Reference number: AI1108-SS002-630-1
Movement: quartz
Functions: hours, minutes, sweep seconds; date
Case: stainless steel, ø 40 mm, height 9 mm;
sapphire crystal; water-resistant to 10 atm
Band: stainless steel, double folding clasp
Price: $1,050

Aikon Quartz 35mm

Reference number: AI1106-SS002-150-1
Movement: quartz
Functions: hours, minutes, sweep seconds; date
Case: stainless steel, ø 35 mm, height 9 mm;
sapphire crystal; water-resistant to 10 atm
Band: stainless steel, double folding clasp
Remarks: dial with diamond indices (56 diamonds)
Price: $1,150

Aikon #tide Mahindra

Reference number: AI2008-04000-400-J
Movement: quartz
Functions: hours, minutes, sweep seconds; date
Case: plastic, ø 40 mm, height 11 mm; sapphire crystal;
water-resistant to 10 atm
Band: rubber, pin buckle
Remarks: case and clasp of upcycled ocean plastic;
special edition celebrating the cooperation with the
Mahindra Formel E Racing Team
Price: $900

Aikon #tide

Reference number: AI2008-AAAA1-3A0-0
Movement: quartz
Functions: hours, minutes, sweep seconds; date
Case: plastic, ø 40 mm, height 11 mm; sapphire crystal;
water-resistant to 10 atm
Band: rubber, pin buckle
Remarks: case and clasp of upcycled ocean plastic;
dial set with 44 synthetic diamonds
Price: $935

MB&F
Route de Drize, 2
CH-1227 Carouge
Switzerland

Tel.:
+41-22-786-3618

E-mail:
info@mbandf.com

Website:
www.mbandf.com

Founded:
2005

Number of employees:
40

Annual production:
approx. 350 watches

U.S. distributors:
Westime Los Angeles and Miami
310-470-1388 (Los Angeles)
786-347-5353 (Miami)
info@westime.com
Provident Jewelry, Florida
561-747-4449; nick@providentjewelry.com
Stephen Silver, Redwood City (California)
650-325-9500; www.shsilver.com
Cellini, New York
212-888-0505; contact@cellinijewelers.com
Watches of Switzerland Las Vegas
702-792-0183, www.watchesofswitzerland.com

Most important collections/price range:
Horological Machines / from $90,000; Legacy
Machines / from $64,000

MB&F

In the esoteric world of alternative time-tellers, there is one very durable prophet: Maximilian Büsser. After breaking away from brand constraints at Harry Winston, where he launched the Opus line, Büsser founded MB&F (that is, "and friends") with the mission of setting creators free. He acts as initiator and coordinator. His Horological Machines are developed and realized in cooperation with highly specialized watchmakers, inventors, and designers in an "idea collective" creating unheard-of mechanical timepieces of great inventiveness, complication, and exclusivity. The composition of this collective varies as much as each machine. Number 5 ("On the Road Again") is an homage to the 1970s, whereas HM10 is engineering imitating nature, as the watch turns into a bulldog, with bulging, conical "eyes" that tell the time and jaws that open and close to tell you the power reserve.

Contrasting sharply with the modern productions are the Legacy Machines, which re-interpret past mechanical feats. Some, like the incredibly complicated Sequential Evo, a collaboration with watch wizard Stephen McDonnell, feature two chronographs and a special switch, the "Twinverter" allowing for multiple time computations.

MB&F machines have won awards, several at the Grand Prix d'Horlogerie in different categories, even an Aiguille d'Or, an award that no one could begrudge Büsser, whose work and brand has tirelessly promoted the highest level of watchmaking. And though he is not himself a watchmaker, his spirit, his deep knowledge of engineering, and his sense of aesthetics are always present in each new watch. They are also vented freely in the M.A.D. Galleries the world round, where one finds "mechanical art objects" that are beautiful, intriguing, technically impeccable, and sometimes perfectly useless. They have their own muse and serve as worthy companions to the sci-fi-inspired table clocks that MB&F produces with L'épée 1938.

MB&F's connection to the automobile is deep-rooted: it began in 2012 with the HM5, followed by the HMX in 2015 and the HM8 in 2016, each featuring the instantly recognizable tachometer-style dial on the front of the case, echoing the bold futuristic design of the 1970s. A decade after the first automotive-inspired MB&F comes the higher-tech model: the HM8 Mark 2.

Legacy Machine Sequential EVO

Reference number: 09.ZR.OR
Movement: hand-wound, MB&F Caliber LM Sequential; ø 36.6 mm, height 12.6 mm; 59 jewels; 21,600 vph; dual spring barrel, inverted movement design with balance wheel hovering over the dial; dual chronograph mechanism with twin pushers to switch between modes; finely finished with côtes de Genève; 72-hour power reserve
Functions: hours and minutes (off-center); power reserve indicator; double chronograph with independent measurement
Case: zirconium; ø 44 mm, height 18.2 mm; sapphire crystal; transparent case back; water-resistant to 8 atm
Band: rubber, folding clasp
Price: $180,000
Variations: with black dial

Legacy Machine Perpetual

Reference number: 03.SL.S
Movement: hand-wound, MB&F Caliber LM3; ø 36.6 mm, height 12.6 mm; 41 jewels; 18,000 vph; double spring barrel, inverted movement design with balance wheel hovering over the dial; finely finished with côtes de Genève; 72-hour power reserve
Functions: hours and minutes (off-center); power reserve indicator; perpetual calendar with date, weekday, month, leap year (reverse counting)
Case: stainless steel, ø 44 mm, height 17.5 mm; sapphire crystal; transparent case back; water-resistant to 3 atm
Band: reptile skin, folding clasp
Price: $180,000
Variations: various limited-edition cases

HM8 Mark 2

Reference number: 82.TL.W
Movement: automatic, MB&F Caliber HM8; 30.5 x 36.1 mm, height 7.2 mm; 30 jewels; 28,800 vph; gold rotor; disk display reflected in a display window using prisms; 42-hour power reserve
Functions: hours (digital, jumping), minutes (digital)
Case: titanium with green carbon-Macrolon case cover, 41.5 x 47 mm, height 19 mm; sapphire crystal; transparent case back; water-resistant to 3 atm
Band: calfskin, pin buckle
Price: $78,000; limited to 33 pieces
Variations: with white case cover

MEISTERSINGER

MeisterSinger, headquartered in Münster, Germany, has made minimalism a hallmark of this brand, which was launched in 2001. Founder Manfred Brassler chose a look that, in many ways, returns to the very beginnings of watchmaking. Notably, watch hands have different functions. The seconds hand is essentially there to tell that the watch is working, and the hour hand is essentially a slower minute hand, so the two can be pressed into service for a single function, thereby making space on the dial for the eye to wander on their one-handed watches.

MeisterSinger customers are looking for that combination of technical and cultural tradition of early watchmaking with Swiss-made quality and a uniquely purified design, which has earned the brand three dozen awards to date.

Looking at these ultimately simplified dials does tempt one to classify the one-hand watch as an archetype. The single hand simply cannot be reduced any further, and the 144 minutes for 12 hours around the dial do have a normative function of sorts. In one model, the hour jumps very precisely in a window under 12 o'clock—hence its Italian name *Salthora*, or "jumping hour."

With the series novelty Singularis, MeisterSinger has released the second generation of watches with the in-house automatic caliber MSA01. The movement boasts two barrels and 120 hours of power reserve coupled with a unique design and finish. The brand has also been introducing more complications quietly, one watch at a time. There is the particularly large moon phase of the Stratoscope or the almost forgotten complication of the hour strike reserved for the Bell Hora. The Astroscope combines a day and date function with a look at heavenly bodies.

The Primatic features a power reserve display and comes in no less than four colors. The Perigraph has been revived with a modernized look. As for the Unimat, it is the brand's first amagnetic watch.

MeisterSinger GmbH & Co. KG
Hafenweg 46
D-48155 Münster
Germany

Tel.:
+49-251-133-4860

E-mail:
info@meistersinger.de

Website:
www.meistersinger.de

Founded:
2001

Number of employees:
13

Annual production:
approx. 10,000 watches

U.S. distributor:
Duber Time
1115 4th Street North, Unit #B
Saint Petersburg, FL 33701
727-202-3262
damir@dubertime.com

Price range:
from approx. $995 to $6,600

Bell Hora

Reference number: BHO918G
Movement: automatic, MeisterSinger Caliber MS-Bell (Basis Sellita SW200-1 with hour-striking module); ø 25.6 mm, height 6.9 mm; 26 jewels; 28,800 vph; 38-hour power reserve
Functions: hours (each line stands for 5 minutes), passing hour chime (can be turned off)
Case: stainless steel, ø 43 mm, height 13 mm; sapphire crystal; transparent case back
Band: calfskin, folding clasp
Price: $4,699
Variations: various dial colors

Pangaea

Reference number: PM9901G
Movement: automatic, Sellita Caliber SW300-1; ø 25.6 mm, height 3.6 mm; 25 jewels; 28,800 vph; 42-hour power reserve
Functions: hours (each line stands for 5 minutes)
Case: stainless steel, ø 40 mm, height 9.8 mm; sapphire crystal; transparent case back
Band: calfskin, pin buckle
Price: $2,499
Variations: with blue or ivory dial

Primatic

Reference number: PR918
Movement: automatic, Sellita Caliber SW270; ø 25.6 mm, height 5.6 mm; 26 jewels; 28,800 vph; 38-hour power reserve
Functions: hours (each line stands for 5 minutes); power-reserve indicator; date
Case: stainless steel, ø 41.5 mm, height 13 mm; sapphire crystal; transparent case back
Band: stainless steel, folding clasp
Price: $2,699
Variations: various dial colors

N° 01

Reference number: AM3303
Movement: hand-wound, Sellita Caliber SW210;
ø 25.6 mm, height 3.4 mm; 19 jewels; 28,800 vph;
42-hour power reserve
Functions: hours (each line stands for 5 minutes)
Case: stainless steel, ø 43 mm, height 11.5 mm;
sapphire crystal; water-resistant to 5 atm
Band: calfskin, pin buckle
Price: $1,849
Variations: with white or blue dial

Perigraph

Reference number: AM1001G
Movement: automatic, Sellita Caliber SW200-1;
ø 25.6 mm, height 4.6 mm; 26 jewels; 28,800 vph;
38-hour power reserve
Functions: hours (each line stands for 5 minutes);
date (rotating disk display)
Case: stainless steel, ø 43 mm, height 11,5 mm;
sapphire crystal; transparent case back;
water-resistant to 5 atm
Band: calfskin, pin buckle
Price: $2,499
Variations: with blue or ivory dial

Neo Azure

Reference number: NE914
Movement: automatic, Sellita Caliber SW200-1;
ø 25.6 mm, height 4.6 mm; 26 jewels; 28,800 vph;
38-hour power reserve
Functions: hours (each line stands for 5 minutes); date
Case: stainless steel, ø 36 mm, height 9.7 mm;
Plexiglas; water-resistant to 3 atm
Band: calfskin, pin buckle
Price: $1,449
Variations: various dial colors

Lunascope

Reference number: LS908G
Movement: automatic, MeisterSinger Caliber MS-Luna
(based on Sellita SW220-1); ø 25.6 mm, height 5.8 mm;
26 jewels; 28,800 vph; 38-hour power reserve
Functions: hours (each line stands for 5 minutes);
date, moon phase
Case: stainless steel, ø 41 mm, height 12 mm; sapphire
crystal; transparent case back; water-resistant to 5 atm
Band: calfskin, folding clasp
Price: $4,649
Variations: with horse leather ($4,699); with stainless
steel Milanese bracelet ($4,830)

Astroscope

Reference number: S-AS902Y
Movement: automatic, Sellita Caliber SW220-1;
ø 25.6 mm, height 5.1 mm; 26 jewels; 28,800 vph;
38-hour power reserve
Functions: hours (each line stands for 5 minutes); date
and weekday
Case: stainless steel, ø 40 mm, height 10.5 mm;
sapphire crystal; transparent case back; water-
resistant to 5 atm
Band: calfskin, buckle
Remarks: weekdays are represented by the moon,
Mars, Mercury, Jupiter, Venus, Saturn and the sun. The
indication is a white dot that seems to jump around
erratically across the dial
Price: $2,649

Unomat

Reference number: ED-UN915
Movement: automatic, Sellita Caliber SW400-
1; ø 31 mm, height 4.67 mm; 26 jewels; 28,800 vph;
antimagnetic; 38-hour power reserve
Functions: hours (each line stands for 5 minutes); date
Case: stainless steel, ø 43 mm, height 13.2 mm; sapphire
crystal; screw-in crown; water-resistant to 30 atm
Band: silicone, pin buckle
Price: $2,649
Variations: with blue or green dial

MIDO

Mido SA
Chemin des Tourelles 17
CH-2400 Le Locle
Switzerland

Tel.:
+41-32-933-35-11

Website:
www.mido.ch

Founded:
1918

Number of employees:
50 (estimated)

Annual production:
over 100,000

U.S. distributor:
Mido, division of The Swatch Group (U.S.) Inc.
703 Waterford Way, Suite 450
Miami, FL 33126
www.midowatches.com

Most important collections/price ranges:
Baroncelli / $460 to $1,450; Commander /
$710 to $2,000; Multifort / $620 to $2,230;
Ocean Star / $890 to $1,900

Among the legacies of World War I was the popularization of the wristwatch, which had freed up soldiers' and aviators' hands to fight and steer, respectively, and permitted artillery officers to coordinate barrages. And, not surprisingly, this led to a kind of reindustrialization of the watch industry. Among the earliest companies to appear on the scene was Mido, which was founded on November 11, 1918—Armistice Day—by Georges Schaeren in Solothurn, Switzerland. The name means "I measure" in Spanish.

At first, the brand produced colorful and imaginative watches that were well suited to the Roaring Twenties. But in the 1930s Mido began making more serious, robust, sportive timepieces better suited for everyday use. For the watch fan of today, water resistance and self-winding are normal. Mido, however, was already offering this functionality in the 1930s with the introduction of the Multifort. This Swiss manufacturer also developed a number of very practical novelties like the Radiotime model (1939) and the Multicenter-chrono (1941), which today have become genuine collectors' items.

In 1971 the Schaeren family sold the company to the General Watch Co. Ltd., a holding company belonging to ASUAG, which, in turn became the SMH and, ultimately, Swatch Group. Mido continues to produce mostly mechanical watches with about one-quarter of its production devoted to quartz movements. In 1998, Mido decided to revive some of its older watchmaking values. The Multifort, Commander, Battalion, and Baroncelli collections are each in their own way expressions of that mission. Nothing "in your face," just affordable timepieces with the basic hallmarks of a good Swiss watch, like côtes de Genève on the rotors and, in some cases, even COSC certification. An exception may be the Ocean Star Decompression Worldtimer, which revives some of the "crazy seventies" loudness on the dial. By the same token, it features practical scales for decompression times and a second time zone, all at a fairly modest price.

Ocean Star Decompression Worldtimer

Reference number: M0268291704100
Movement: automatic, Mido Caliber 80.661 (based on ETA C07.661); ø 25.6 mm, height 5.22 mm; 25 jewels; 21,600 vph; with côtes de Genève; 80-hour power reserve
Functions: hours, minutes, sweep seconds (incremental setting of hour hand); additional 24-hour display (2nd time zone); date
Case: stainless steel, ø 40.5 mm, height 13.43 mm; bidirectional bezel with aluminum insert, with reference cities; sapphire crystal; screw-in crown; water-resistant to 20 atm
Band: rubber, pin buckle
Remarks: comes with additional stainless steel Milanese mesh bracelet
Price: $1,310

Ocean Star Decompression Worldtimer

Reference number: M0268291705100
Movement: automatic, Mido Caliber 80.661 (based on ETA C07.661); ø 25.6 mm, height 5.22 mm; 25 jewels; 21,600 vph; with côtes de Genève; 80-hour power reserve
Functions: hours, minutes, sweep seconds (incremental setting of hour hand); additional 24-hour display (2nd time zone); date
Case: stainless steel, ø 40.5 mm, height 13.43 mm; bidirectional bezel with aluminum insert, with reference cities; sapphire crystal; screw-in crown; water-resistant to 20 atm
Band: stainless steel Milanaise, folding clasp
Remarks: comes with additional rubber strap
Price: $1,310

Multifort M Chronometer

Reference number: M0384311109700
Movement: automatic, Mido Caliber 80.821 COSC (based on ETA C07.821); ø 25.6 mm, height 5.22 mm; 25 jewels; 21,600 vph; silicon hairspring; 80-hour power reserve; COSC-certified chronometer
Functions: hours, minutes, sweep seconds; date and weekday
Case: stainless steel, ø 42 mm, height 11.99 mm; sapphire crystal; transparent case back; water-resistant to 10 atm
Band: stainless steel, folding clasp
Price: $1,350

Ocean Star 200C

Reference number: M0424301704100
Movement: automatic, Mido Caliber 80.621 (based on
ETA C07.621); ø 25.6 mm, height 5.22 mm; 25 jewels;
21,600 vph; with côtes de Genève; 80-hour power reserve
Functions: hours, minutes, sweep seconds;
date and weekday
Case: stainless steel, ø 42.5 mm, height 12.25 mm;
unidirectional bezel with ceramic insert, with
0-60 scale; sapphire crystal; screw-in crown;
water-resistant to 20 atm
Band: rubber, folding clasp, with extension link
Price: $1,140

Ocean Star GMT Special Edition

Reference number: M0266291104100
Movement: automatic, Mido Caliber 80.661 (based on
ETA C07.661); ø 25.6 mm, height 5.22 mm; 25 jewels;
21,600 vph; with côtes de Genève; 80-hour power
reserve
Functions: hours, minutes, sweep seconds
(incremental setting of hour hand); additional 24-hour
display (2nd time zone); date
Case: stainless steel, ø 44 mm, height 13.43 mm;
unidirectional bezel with ceramic insert, with
0-60 scale; sapphire crystal; screw-in crown;
water-resistant to 20 atm
Band: stainless steel, folding clasp
Remarks: comes with additional textile strap
Price: $1,460

Ocean Star 600 Chronometer Black DLC Special Edition

Reference number: M0266083305100
Movement: automatic, Mido Caliber 80.821 COSC Si
(based on ETA C07.821); ø 25.6 mm, height 5.22 mm;
25 jewels; 21,600 vph; silicon hairspring; 80-hour
power reserve; COSC-certified chronometer
Functions: hours, minutes, sweep seconds; date
Case: stainless steel with black DLC, ø 43.5 mm, height
14.05 mm; unidirectional bezel with ceramic insert,
with 0-60 scale; sapphire crystal; screw-in crown;
helium valve; water-resistant to 60 atm
Band: stainless steel with black DLC, folding clasp,
with extension link
Remarks: comes with extra rubber strap; certified
according to European diving equipment standard
Price: $1,930

Commander Big Date

Reference number: M0216261109100
Movement: automatic, Mido Caliber 80.651
(based on ETA C07.651); ø 29.4 mm, height 5.77 mm;
25 jewels; 21,600 vph; Rotor with côtes de Genève;
80-hour power reserve
Functions: hours, minutes, sweep seconds; large date
Case: stainless steel, ø 42 mm, height 11.97 mm;
sapphire crystal; transparent case back;
water-resistant to 5 atm
Band: stainless steel, double folding clasp
Price: $990

Multifort Skeleton Vertigo

Reference number: M0384363705100
Movement: automatic, Mido Caliber 80.631 (based on
ETA C07.631); ø 25.6 mm, height 4.74 mm; 25 jewels;
21,600 vph; partially skeletonized mainplate;
80-hour power reserve
Functions: hours, minutes, sweep seconds
Case: stainless steel with black PVD, ø 42 mm, height
10.63 mm; sapphire crystal; transparent case back;
water-resistant to 10 atm
Band: textile, folding clasp
Remarks: skeletonized dial
Price: $1,210

Baroncelli Lady Twenty Five

Reference number: M0390071109600
Movement: automatic, Mido Caliber 48.111 (based
on ETA Caliber C26.111); ø 17.2 mm, height 4.92 mm;
24 jewels; 28,800 vph; finely decorated movement;
48-hour power reserve
Functions: hours, minutes, sweep seconds; date
Case: stainless steel, ø 25 mm, height 9.1 mm; sapphire
crystal; transparent case back; water-resistant to 5 atm
Band: stainless steel, folding clasp
Remarks: dial with 12 diamonds
Price: $970

MILUS

Milus is one of those brands that has had quite a journey in recent times. It was founded by Paul William Junod in Biel/Bienne and remained in family hands until the year 2002. A new era began then with the founding of Milus International SA under Jan Edöcs and with investments from the giant Peace Mark Group from Hong Kong.

Within a few years, the brand had made a new name for itself with a triple retrograde seconds module, which was developed together with the specialists at Agenhor in Geneva. And that made all the difference to the Milus image. In the 1970s, the brand had a reputation for jewelry. With Edöcs, it had become a genuine and respected watchmaker, one producing top-drawer horological complications that could compete quite boldly on a market. The TriRetrograde function is a Milus trademark and could be found in a host of models all named after constellations (Tirion, Merea, Zetios).

After the Peace Mark Group collapsed in 2008, Milus quickly found another investor in the Chow Tai Fook Group owned by Dr. Cheng Yu-tung. In 2011, Cyril Dubois took over at the head of the company. Quietly, but surely, the brand expanded on several fronts with the TriRetrogrades in the lead. Unfortunately, it had no staying power, and a family named Tissot bought up the brand in 2017 and started working on streamlining the portfolio. The strategy was simple: have three attractive collections on the affordable end of the market. Thus we find a solid, functional diver, the Archimèdes, with an inner bezel that can be turned using a separate crown and a helium valve. The simple LAB 01 features a modern fiberglass dial. And the third, the Snow Star, is all that's left from the old collections. It dates originally from the 1940s and was rebuilt and modernized. One can imagine that the TriRetrograde mechanism will soon show up.

Milus International SA
Rue de Reuchenette 19
CH-2502 Biel/Bienne
Switzerland

Tel.:
+41-32-344-3939

E-mail:
info@milus.com

Website:
www.milus.com

Founded:
1919

Distribution:
Contact company in Switzerland

Most important collections/price range:
Milus Snow Star / from approx. $1,915; Archimèdes by Milus / from approx. $2,175; Milus LAB 01 / from approx. $1,122

Snow Star

Reference number: MIH.02.002.BG
Movement: automatic, ETA 2892-A2; ø 25.6 mm, 3.60 mm; 21 jewels; 28,800 vph; 42-hour power reserve
Functions: hours, minutes, sweep seconds; date
Case: stainless steel, ø 39 mm, height 9.45 mm; sapphire crystal; water-resistant to 10 atm
Band: stainless steel, with safe release system
Remarks: replica of a watch that pilots had as a barter when flying over the Pacific during WW2
Price: $2,142
Variations: with calfskin band

Archimèdes by Milus

Reference number: MIH.01.002.YS
Movement: automatic, ETA 2892-A2; ø 25.6 mm, height 3.60 mm; 21 jewels; 28,800 vph; 42-hour power reserve
Functions: hours, minutes, sweep seconds; date
Case: stainless steel, ø 41 mm, height 11.9 mm; sapphire glass; bidirectional bezel; screw-in crown, helium valve; water-resistant to 30 atm
Band: rubber, pin buckle
Price: $2,288
Variation: with Milanese mesh bracelet

LAB 01

Reference number: MIL.01.003
Movement: automatic, Sellita SW200; ø 26 mm, height 4.6 mm; 26 jewels; 28,800 vph; 38-hour power reserve
Functions: hours, minutes, sweep seconds
Case: stainless steel, ø 40 mm, height 9.5 mm; sapphire glass; water-resistant to 3 atm
Band: Milanese mesh, folding clasp
Remarks: fiberglass dial
Price: $1,122

Minase
Company representation
H-Development Sarl
Ch. du Long-Champ 99
CH-2504 Biel-Bienne
Switzerland

Tel.:
+41-32-521-06-13

E-mail:
info@h-development.ch

Website:
www.minasewatches.ch
www.h-development.ch

Founded:
2005

U. S. Distribution:
Contact the representation in Switzerland

Annual production:
approx. 500 pieces

Most important collections/price range:
Five Windows, Seven Windows, Horizon, Divido,
Uruga; / $3,800 to $5,000; special editions

MINASE

Successful companies frequently like to build a monument to their achievements. It might be a real structure, like the Chrysler Building in New York, or something more ephemeral, like an arts endowment. In 2005, Kyowa, a toolmaking enterprise founded in Japan in 1963, paid homage to its own skills in working on watch components by launching a watch brand. Its logo, appearing at 12 o'clock on some models, was inspired from a step drill.

Minase Watches was named after a small village some 250 miles north of Tokyo that was absorbed in that same year 2005 into the neighboring city of Yuzawa. Until recently, it produced no more than three hundred watches a year for the Japanese market, but lately it has begun widening its horizons internationally.

The company's timepieces are all made according to *monozukuri* philosophy, which essentially means excellent manufacturing practices. One technique used is *sallaz*, or block polishing, which gives a particularly sparkling polish. The stainless-steel bracelets have been inspired by complex Japanese wooden puzzles.

The brand has three basic collections, each of which expresses the company's dedication to traditional hand-finishing. The Five Windows features multiple sapphire crystals integrated into the cases to reveal each watch's complex case-in-case structure, the intricate dial, and the mechanism inside. The oversized date aperture creates visual space on the dial. A subcollection with two extra openings, the Seven Windows, occasionally becomes a canvas for limited editions decorated by select Japanese artists. Lacquerware specialist Junichi Hakose, for example, used the *maki-e urushi* technique—sap from the urushi tree, with gold sprinklings—to create a riveting pattern on one of the dials.

The Horizon line is more sportive, with an elegantly curved sapphire crystal covering an arched dial on a tonneau case. The Divido is far more classical, with a round dial in a slightly angular case. In 2023, the brand added the Uruga, an equally elegant, but gentler, subline, whose dial features a flowing relief resembling water in the breeze, like the surface of the Minase River.

Divido Urushi Rubber

Reference number: VM14-M01KA4
Movement: automatic, KT7002 (base ETA 2892); ø 25.6 mm, height 3.6 mm; 28,800 vph; 21 jewels; 50-hour power reserve
Functions: hours, minutes, sweep seconds
Case: stainless steel, ø 40.6 mm, height 11 mm; sapphire crystal, transparent case back; water-resistant to 5 atm
Band: rubber, folding clasp
Remarks: dial features shibo urushi technique, a mix of urushi laquer and egg white
Price: $7,150

Uruga 42 mm Leather

Reference number: 15-CDBNGY-SSD
Movement: automatic, KT7002 (base ETA 2892); ø 25.6 mm, height 3.6 mm; 28,800 vph; hand-finished surfaces with perlage, mainplate and bridges in black; blued screws; 21 jewels; 50-hour power reserve
Functions: hours, minutes, sweep seconds; date.
Case: stainless steel, ø 42 mm, height 10.2 mm; sapphire crystal; water-resistant to 5 atm
Band: leather, folding clasp
Remarks: flowing relief design of the dial represents the Minase River
Price: $4,400
Variations: comes with steel bracelet ($5,150); in 31-millimieter case

Windows Hakose Steel

Reference number: 15-CBKMA2-SSD
Movement: automatic, KT7002 (base ETA 2892); ø 25.6 mm, height 3.6 mm; 28,800 vph; 21 jewels; 50-hour power reserve
Functions: hours, minutes, sweep seconds
Case: stainless steel, ø 38 x 47 mm, height 13 mm; domed box sapphire crystal (non-reflective coating) on top, see-through sapphire case back and 5 sapphire crystals at 12, 6 and 9 o'clock, and 2 at 3 o'clock; water-resistant to 3 atm
Band: calfskin, folding clasp
Price: $16,100

MING

Horologer Ming Sdn Bhd
B-3A-3, Sunway Palazzio
1 Jalan Sri Hartamas 3
50480 Kuala Lumpur
Malaysia

E-mail:
hello@ming.watch

Website:
www.ming.watch

Founded:
August 2017

Number of employees:
6

Annual production:
3000+ pieces

Distribution:
online, direct to customer

Most important collections/price range:
20 series, 29 series, 37 series; special projects /
$2,000-$60,000

It takes a certain courage to launch a new watch brand in a crowded market that is subject to emotional swings. Ming, however, is no ordinary brand. It is a cooperative enterprise made up of six watchmaking enthusiasts from around the world. Leading the team is Ming Thein, a well-known photographer, designer, corporate strategist, and watch fan. He hails from Malaysia. Added up, the Ming team computes to a total of eighty solid years' experience collecting watches of all sorts, from vintage pieces to avant-garde works of kinetic art, from robust ground-level timepieces to custom-made products in the six-figure range.

Each of their purchases always gave them a genuine feeling of value and happiness. The mission of the six brand founders was therefore to reconnect with that feeling of emotional excitement that comes from discovering an authentic diamond in the rough. Their strategy was to create a series of watches that are conscientiously finished and stand out thanks to some subtle details in the finishing and the design. These are not flashy pieces, but rather subtle seducers by dint of the details, like the carefully worked lugs or the modified ETA 7001 caliber, turning a fairly square assembly into a delicate and colorful ballet of gearwheels and bridges.

The 2023 crop illustrates the now well-shaped DNA of this young brand well. A world timer without a bezel to confine the eye's gaze. The minimalist dial of the LW.01, with its two ghostly pointers are the visual representation of an ultra-light case made of a special magnesium alloy. And, finally, the Sand watch, which carries the mind to a desert or a beautiful beach, where air and earth join in a harmonious pas de deux.

The watches are all made in cooperation with partners that are compatible with the brand's aesthetic goals and price points. Lately, they have turned to the excellent Schwarz-Etienne movements. All Ming watches are assembled, adjusted, and tested in Switzerland. The final quality control is then done in Kuala Lumpur by Ming Thein in person.

29.01 Worldtimer

Reference number: 29.01
Movement: hand-wound, Schwarz-Etienne Caliber ASE 222 for Ming; ø 30 mm, height 5.70 mm; 31 jewels; 21,600 vph; DLC-coated bridges; diamond chamfering; gold rotor; 70-hour power reserve
Functions: hours, minutes; world time with 24 reference locations
Case: titanium, ø 40 mm, height 11.9 mm; "flying blade" interlocking lugs; sapphire crystal, transparent case back; water-resistant to 5 atm,
Band: Alcantara, buckle with micro-adjustment
Remarks: bezel-less construction, sapphire hands with HyCeram ceramic Super-LumiNova, two-part sapphire dial with luminous city rings over rotating metallic 24h disc and day-night gradient with Super-LumiNova
Price: $22,000; limited to 100 pieces

LW.01 Ultra-Light Manual

Reference number: LW.01-M
Movement: manuall wound, modified ETA 2000-1, ø 19.4 mm, height 3.60 mm; 20 jewels; 28,800 vph; 40-hour power reserve
Functions: hours, minutes, pulsating seconds
Case: magnesium alloy with vanadium (AZ31), anthracite/black treated, ø 38 mm, height 6.5 mm; Gorilla Glass top crystal; water-resistant to 2.5 atm
Band: Alcantara, AZ31 magnesium alloy buckle
Remarks: ultra-light construction made of specifically selected and treated materials, weight of watch head only 8.8 grams.
Price: $22,000; limited to 200 pieces

37.08 Sand

Reference number: 37.08
Movement: hand-wound, Sellita for Ming Cal. 210. M1; ø 25.6 mm, height 3.35 mm; 19 jewels; 28,800 vph; anthracite skeletonized bridges with contrast rhodium circular brushing; 40-hour power reserve
Functions: hours, minutes
Case: stainless steel, ø 38 mm, height 10.9 mm; water-resistant to 10 atm
Band: leather, buckle with micro-adjustment
Remarks: complex structured dial resembling sand dunes
Price: $5,500; limited to 500 pieces

Mk II Corporation
303 W. Lancaster Avenue, #283
Wayne, PA 19087
USA

E-mail:
info@mkiiwatches.com

Websites:
www.mkiiwatches.com
https://tornek-rayville.us/

Founded:
2002

Number of employees:
3

Annual production:
1,200 watches

Distribution:
Direct to consumer sales

Most important collections/price range:
Ready-to-Wear Collection / $500 to $995;
Benchcrafted Collection / $1,000 to $2,000

MK II

If vintage and unserviceable watches had their say, they would probably be naturally attracted to Mk II for the name alone, which is a military designation for the second generation of equipment. The company, which was founded by watch enthusiast and maker Bill Yao in 2002, not only puts retired designs back into service, but also modernizes and customizes them. Before the screwed-down crown, diving watches were not nearly as reliably sealed, for example. And some beautiful old pieces were made with plated brass cases or featured Bakelite components, which are either easily damaged or have aged poorly. The company substitutes not only proven modern materials, but also modern manufacturing methods and techniques to ensure a better outcome.

These are material issues that the team at Mk II handles with great care. They will not, metaphorically speaking, airbrush a Model-T. As genuine watch lovers themselves, they make sure that the final design is in the spirit of the watch itself, which still leaves a great deal of leeway for many iterations, given a sufficient number of parts. In the company's output, vintage style and modern functionality are key. The watches are assembled by hand at the company's workshop in Pennsylvania—and subjected to a rigorous regimen of testing. The components are individually inspected, the cases tested at least three times for water resistance, and at the end the whole watch is regulated in six positions. The ready-to-wear collection is made in Japan and finished in the USA. These watches are robust, timeless, and, for the collector of lesser means, affordable.

Looking to the future, Mk II aspires to carry its clean vintage style into the development of what it hopes will be future classics in their own right.

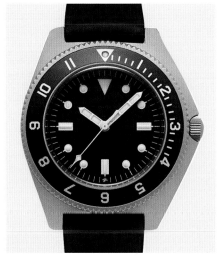

Paradive
Reference number: CD04.2-1011AmB
Movement: automatic (hack setting), TMI Caliber NE15; ø 27.40 mm, height 5.32 mm; 24 jewels; 21,600 vph; 50-hour power reserve; rotor decorated with côtes de Genève
Functions: hours, minutes, sweep seconds
Case: stainless steel, ø 41.2 mm, height 15.50 mm; 120-click unidirectional bezel; high domed sapphire crystal; screw-down case back; screw-in crown; water-resistant to 20 atm
Band: nylon, pin buckle
Price: $895
Variations: with time-elapse bezel, 12-hour acrylic inlay, rubber strap

Stingray
Reference Number: CD02.2-K-1002AmK
Movement: automatic (hack setting), TMI Caliber NE15 (made in Japan); ø 27.40 mm, height 5.32 mm; 24 jewels; 21,600 vph; 50-hour power reserve; rotor decorated with côtes de Genève
Functions: hours, minutes, sweep seconds, date
Case: stainless steel; ø 40.00 mm, height 14.72 mm; 120-click unidirectional bezel; high domed sapphire crystal with antireflective coating; screw-down case back; screw-in crown; water-resistant to 20 atm
Band: nylon, pin buckle
Price: $895
Variations: rubber strap, luminous acrylic inlay

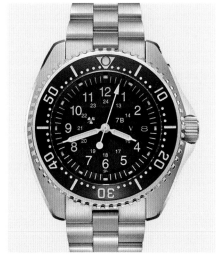

Type 7B "Blakjak"
Reference Number: CG07-1001F
Movement: automatic (hack setting), TMI Caliber NH36 (made in Japan); ø 27.40 mm, height 5.32 mm; 24 jewels; 21,600 vph; 41-hour power reserve
Functions: hours, minutes, sweep seconds, day/date
Case: stainless steel; ø 42.50 mm, height 13.20 mm; unidirectional bezel with 0-120 scale; sapphire crystal; screw-down case back; screw-in crown; water-resistant to 20 atm
Band: steel bracelet
Price: $895
Variations: rubber strap, 12-hour bezel inlay

MONTBLANC

It was with great skill and cleverness that Nicolas Rieussec (1781–1866) used the invention of a special chronograph—the "Time Writer," a device that released droplets of ink onto a rotating sheet of paper—to make a name for himself. Montblanc, once famous only for its exclusive writing implements, borrowed that name on its way to becoming a distinguished watch brand. Within a few years, it had created an impressive range of chronographs driven by in-house calibers: from simple automatic stopwatches to flagship pieces with two independent spring barrels for time and "time-writing."

The Richemont Group, owner of Montblanc, has placed great trust in its "daughter" company, having put the little *manufacture* Minerva, which it purchased at the beginning of 2007, at the disposal of Montblanc. Minerva, which was founded in Villeret in 1858, was already building keyless pocket watches in the 1880s, and by the early twentieth century was producing monopusher chronographs with a reputation for precision. Today, the Minerva Institute serves as a kind of think tank for the future, a place where young watchmakers can absorb the old traditions and skills, as well as the wealth of experience and mind-set of the masters.

Montblanc is maintaining the over 160-year Minerva tradition with four leading collections. The 1858 and the Heritage clearly draw inspiration from the company's past codes, with quotations from the 1920s and 1930s, like those salmon-colored dials. The Star Legacy and the TimeWalker lines allow Montblanc to explore some more complex complications packaged in more modern forms.

Montblanc Montre SA
10, chemin des Tourelles
CH-2400 Le Locle
Switzerland

Tel.:
+41-32-933-8888

E-mail:
service@montblanc.com

Website:
www.montblanc.com

Founded:
1997 (1906 in Hamburg)

Number of employees:
worldwide approx. 3,000

U.S. distributor:
Montblanc North America
645 Fifth Avenue, 7th Floor
New York, NY 10022
800-995-4810
www.montblanc.com

Most important collections:
Heritage Chronométrie, Heritage Spirit, Meisterstück, Minerva, Nicolas Rieussec, 4810, TimeWalker, Collection Villeret, 1858 Collection, Iced Sea

1858 Geosphere Chronograph "Zero Oxygen"

Reference number: 130811
Movement: automatic, Caliber MB 29.27; ø 29,98 mm, height 9.11 mm; 33 jewels; 28,800 vph; 46-hour power reserve
Functions: hours, minutes; additional synchronously counter-rotating world time indicators for northern and southern hemispheres; chronograph; date
Case: titanium, ø 44 mm, height 17.1 mm; bidirectional bezel in stainless steel with ceramic insert and points of the compass; sapphire crystal; water-resistant to 10 atm
Band: textile, triple folding clasp
Remarks: case filled with nitrogen
Price: $9,800; limited to 290 pieces as homage to the 14 peaks of the Himalaya over 8,000 meters

1858 Geosphere "Zero Oxygen"

Reference number: 130982
Movement: automatic, Caliber MB 29.25 (based on Sellita SW300-1 with Montblanc-Modul); ø 25.6 mm; 26 jewels; 28,800 vph; 42-hour power reserve
Functions: hours, minutes; additional synchronously counter-rotating world time indicators for northern and southern hemispheres; date
Case: titanium, ø 42 mm, height 12.8 mm; bidirectional bezel with ceramic insert and points of the compass; sapphire crystal; water-resistant to 10 atm
Band: titanium, double folding clasp
Remarks: nitrogen-filled case; homage to the 14 peaks of the Himalaya over 8,000 meters
Price: $7,600

1858 Automatic Chronograph "Zero Oxygen"

Reference number: 130983
Movement: automatic, Caliber MB 29.13 (based on Sellita SW510); ø 30 mm, height 7.9 mm; 27 jewels; 28,800 vph; 48-hour power reserve
Functions: hours, minutes, subsidiary seconds; chronograph
Case: stainless steel, ø 42 mm, height 12.8 mm; bidirectional bezel with ceramic insert and points of the compass; sapphire crystal; water-resistant to 10 atm
Band: stainless steel, double folding clasp
Remarks: nitrogen-filled case; homage to the 14 peaks of the Himalaya over 8,000 meters
Price: $5,200

1858 Automatic Date "Zero Oxygen"

Reference number: 130984
Movement: automatic, Caliber MB 29.17 (based on Sellita SW200-1); ø 25.6 mm, height 4.6 mm; 26 jewels; 28,800 vph; 38-hour power reserve
Functions: hours, minutes, sweep seconds; date
Case: stainless steel, ø 41 mm, height 11.3 mm; bidirectional bezel with ceramic insert and points of the compass; sapphire crystal; water-resistant to 10 atm
Band: stainless steel, double folding clasp
Remarks: case filled with nitrogen; homage to the 14 peaks of the Himalaya over 8,000 meters
Price: $3,210

1858 Iced Sea Automatic Date

Reference number: 129371
Movement: automatic, Caliber MB 24.17 (based on Sellita SW200); ø 25.6 mm, height 4.6 mm; 26 jewels; 28,800 vph; 38-hour power reserve
Functions: hours, minutes, sweep seconds; date
Case: stainless steel, ø 41 mm, height 12.9 mm; unidirectional bezel with ceramic insert, with 0 60 scale; sapphire crystal; water-resistant to 30 atm
Band: stainless steel, double folding clasp
Price: $3,415
Variations: with rubber strap ($3,210)

1858 Iced Sea Automatic Date

Reference number: 129372
Movement: automatic, Caliber MB 24.17 (based on Sellita SW200); ø 25.6 mm, height 4.6 mm; 26 jewels; 28,800 vph; 38-hour power reserve
Functions: hours, minutes, sweep seconds; date
Case: stainless steel, ø 41 mm, height 12.9 mm; unidirectional bezel with ceramic insert, with 0-60 scale; sapphire crystal; water-resistant to 30 atm
Band: rubber, double folding clasp
Price: $3,210
Variations: with stainless steel bracelet ($3,415)

1858 Iced Sea Automatic Date Boutique Edition

Reference number: 129373
Movement: automatic, Caliber MB 24.17 (based on Sellita SW200); ø 25.6 mm, height 4.6 mm; 26 jewels; 28,800 vph; 38-hour power reserve
Functions: hours, minutes, sweep seconds; date
Case: stainless steel, ø 41 mm, height 12.9 mm; unidirectional bezel with ceramic insert, with 0-60 scale; sapphire crystal; water-resistant to 30 atm
Band: stainless steel, double folding clasp
Price: $3,415

1858 Iced Sea Automatic Date Boutique Edition

Reference number: 130810
Movement: automatic, Caliber MB 24.17 (based on Sellita SW200); ø 25.6 mm, height 4.6 mm; 26 jewels; 28,800 vph; 38-hour power reserve
Functions: hours, minutes, sweep seconds; date
Case: stainless steel, ø 41 mm, height 12.9 mm; unidirectional bezel with ceramic insert, with 0-60 scale; sapphire crystal; water-resistant to 30 atm
Band: rubber, double folding clasp
Price: $3,415

The Unveiled Secret Minerva Monopusher chronograph

Reference number: 131155
Movement: hand-wound, Caliber MB M16.26; ø 37.5 mm, height 7.05 mm; 26 jewels; 18,000 A/h; inverted movement with chronograph construction on the dial side; column-wheel control of the chronograph functions using a single pusher; screw balance; 50-hour power reserve
Functions: hours, minutes, subsidiary seconds; chronograph
Case: stainless steel, ø 43 mm, height 14.18 mm; bezel in white gold; sapphire crystal; water-resistant to 3 atm
Band: reptile skin, triple folding clasp
Remarks: skeletonized dial; limited to 88 pieces
Price: $38,000

1858 The Unveiled Timekeeper Minerva Limited Edition

Reference number: 130987
Movement: hand-wound, Caliber MB M13.21; ø 29.5 mm, height 6.4 mm; 22 jewels; 18,000 vph; bezel used for chronograph functions; screw balance, hairspring with Phillips end curve; 60-hour power reserve
Functions: hours, minutes, subsidiary seconds; chronograph
Case: stainless steel, ø 42 mm, height 13.85 mm; unidirectional white gold bezel to control chronograph functions; sapphire crystal; water-resistant to 3 atm
Band: reptile skin, triple folding clasp
Remarks: limited to 100 pieces
Price: on request

1858 The Unveiled Timekeeper Minerva Limited Edition

Reference number: 130988
Movement: hand-wound, Caliber MB M13.21; ø 29.5 mm, height 6.4 mm; 22 jewels; 18,000 vph; bezel used for chronograph functions; screw balance, hairspring with Phillips end curve; 60-hour power reserve
Functions: hours, minutes, subsidiary seconds; chronograph
Case: yellow gold ("Lime Gold"), ø 42.5 mm, height 13.85 mm; unidirectional white gold bezel to control chronograph functions; sapphire crystal; water-resistant to 3 atm
Band: reptile skin, pin buckle
Remarks: limited to 28 pieces
Price: $56,000

Star Legacy Blue Exploding Star Automatic Date

Reference number: 130956
Movement: automatic, Caliber MB 24.17 (based on Sellita SW200-1); ø 25.6 mm, height 4.6 mm; 26 jewels; 28,800 vph; 38-hour power reserve
Functions: hours, minutes, sweep seconds; date
Case: stainless steel, ø 43 mm, height 11 mm; sapphire crystal; transparent case back; water-resistant to 5 atm
Band: stainless steel, triple folding clasp
Price: $3,405

Star Legacy Blue Exploding Star Chronograph Day & Date

Reference number: 130973
Movement: automatic, Caliber MB 25.07 (based on Sellita SW500-1); ø 30 mm, height 7.9 mm; 25 jewels; 28,800 vph; 48-hour power reserve
Functions: hours, minutes, subsidiary seconds; chronograph; date and weekday
Case: stainless steel, ø 43 mm, height 14.76 mm; sapphire crystal; transparent case back; water-resistant to 5 atm
Band: reptile skin, triple folding clasp
Price: $5,200

Star Legacy Automatic Date

Reference number: 130958
Movement: automatic, Caliber MB 24.17 (based on Sellita SW200-1); ø 25.6 mm, height 4.6 mm; 26 jewels; 28,800 vph; 38-hour power reserve
Functions: hours, minutes, sweep seconds; date
Case: stainless steel, ø 39 mm, height 10.44 mm; sapphire crystal; transparent case back; water-resistant to 5 atm
Band: reptile skin, pin buckle
Price: $2,380; limited to 1786 pieces

Star Legacy Moonphase

Reference number: 130959
Movement: automatic, Montblanc Caliber MB 24.31 (based on Sellita SW380); ø 25.6 mm, height 4.1 mm; 25 jewels; 28,800 vph; 50-hour power reserve
Functions: hours, minutes, sweep seconds; date, moon phase
Case: stainless steel, ø 42 mm, height 11.38 mm; sapphire crystal; transparent case back; water-resistant to 5 atm
Band: reptile skin, triple folding clasp
Price: $4,600; limited to 1786 pieces

Caliber MB M16.29

Hand-wound; column-wheel control of chronograph functions using a single pusher; single spring barrel, 55-hour power reserve
Functions: hours, minutes, subsidiary seconds; chronograph
Diameter: 38.4 mm
Height: 6.3 mm
Jewels: 22
Balance: screw balance
Frequency: 18,000 vph
Hairspring: with Phillips end curve
Remarks: rhodium-plated mainplate with perlage, bridges with côtes de Genève, gold plated gear wheels

Caliber MB M13.21

Hand-wound; column-wheel control of chronograph functions; single spring barrel, 60-hour power reserve
Functions: hours, minutes, subsidiary seconds; chronograph
Diameter: 29.5 mm
Height: 6.4 mm
Jewels: 22
Balance: screw balance with weights
Frequency: 18,000 vph
Hairspring: with Phillips end curve
Shock protection: Incabloc
Remarks: German silver and rhodium-plated plates and bridges, partially with perlage and hand-beveled

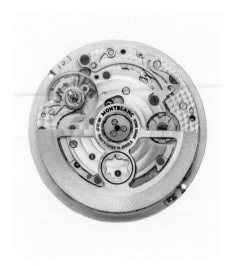

Caliber MB 29.27

Automatic; single spring barrel, 46-hour power reserve
Functions: hours, minutes; second time zone, synchronously counter-rotating world time indicators for northern and southern hemispheres; chronograph; date
Diameter: 29.98 mm
Height: 9.11 mm
Jewels: 33
Frequency: 28,800 vph
Hairspring: flat hairspring
Remarks: rhodium-plated mainplate with perlage

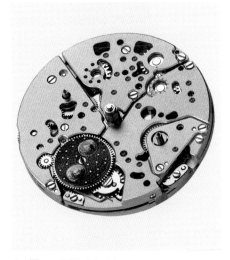

Caliber MB 29.22

Automatic; single spring barrel, 48-hour power reserve
Base caliber: Cartier 1904-PS MC
Functions: hours, minutes; additional 12-hour display (2nd time zone); perpetual calendar with date, weekday, month, moon phase, leap year
Diameter: 28.2 mm
Height: 4.95 mm
Jewels: 77
Frequency: 28,800 vph
Hairspring: flat hairspring
Remarks: 378 parts

Caliber MB M16.31

Hand-wound; monopusher for column-wheel control of chronograph functions, swan-neck fine adjustment; single spring barrel, 50-hour power reserve
Functions: hours, minutes, subsidiary seconds; split-second chronograph
Diameter: 38.4 mm
Height: 8.13 mm
Jewels: 22
Balance: screw balance with Breguet hairspring
Frequency: 18,000 vph
Hairspring: with Phillips end curve
Remarks: rhodium-plated mainplate with perlage, bridges with côtes de Genève, gold plated wheelworks; 262 parts

Caliber MB M29.24

Automatic; one-minute tourbillon with external hairspring; double spring barrel, 48-hour power reserve
Functions: hours, minutes
Diameter: 30.6 mm
Height: 4.5 mm
Jewels: 27
Balance: screw balance with 18 weighted screws
Frequency: 21,600 vph
Hairspring: flat hairspring
Remarks: gold micro-rotor, côtes de Genève on bridges

MÜHLE GLASHÜTTE

Family-run businesses are notoriously successful, especially as each generation must balance tradition with managing the challenges that time brings. Rob. Mühle & Sohn has been doing just this for over 150 years. It started as a manufacturer of precision measuring instruments and managed to survive the ups and downs of German history. Originally, this was for the local watch industry and the German School of Watchmaking. By the early 1920s, the firm was supplying the automobile industry, making speedometers, automobile clocks, tachometers, and other measurement instruments.

As a supplier for the Wehrmacht, it drew Soviet bombers during World War II, and was then nationalized. After the fall of the Iron Curtain, Hans-Jürgen Mühle took the helm, followed, in 2007, by his son, Thilo Mühle.

The wristwatch line was launched as a sideline of sorts in mid-1994 but has now overtaken the nautical instruments for which Mühle was famous. Its collection comprises mechanical wristwatches at entry- and mid-level prices. For these, the company uses Swiss base movements that are equipped with such in-house developments as a patented woodpecker-neck regulation system and the Mühle rotor. The modifications are so extensive that they have led to the calibers having their own names. The traditional line named "R. Mühle & Sohn," introduced in 2014, is equipped with the RMK 1 and RMK 2 calibers. And there are other, somewhat less nautically inspired timepieces, like the Lunova series or the 29ers, which are simply elegant in an unspectacular way. While the watches are by and large in the sportive-elegant segment, the company has shown some boldness in the color of the dials and straps.

Mühle Glashütte GmbH
Nautische Instrumente und Feinmechanik
Altenberger Strasse 35
D-01768 Glashütte
Germany

Tel.:
+49-35053-3203-0

E-mail:
info@muehle-glashuette.de

Website:
www.muehle-glashuette.de

Founded:
first founding 1869; second founding 1993

Number of employees:
47

U.S. distributor:
Mühle Glashütte USA
920 Dr. MLK Jr. Street North
St. Petersburg, FL 33704
727-896-4278
www.muehleglashuetteusa.com

Most important collections/price range:
mechanical wristwatches / approx. $1,399 to $5,400

S.A.R. Mission-Timer Titan

Reference number: M1-51-03-KB
Movement: automatic, Sellita Caliber SW400-1; ø 31 mm, height 4.67 mm; 26 jewels; 28,800 vph; with woodpecker neck regulation, rotor finely processed with special Mühle finish; 41-hour power reserve
Functions: hours, minutes, sweep seconds; date
Case: titanium, ø 43 mm, height 13 mm; bezel in ceramic; sapphire crystal; screw-in crown; water-resistant to 50 atm
Band: rubber, folding clasp, with extension link
Price: $3,299

S.A.R. Rescue-Timer

Reference number: M1-41-03-MB
Movement: automatic, Sellita Caliber SW200-1; ø 25.6 mm, height 4.6 mm; 26 jewels; 28,800 vph; with woodpecker neck regulation, rotor finely processed with special Mühle finish; 41-hour power reserve
Functions: hours, minutes, sweep seconds; date
Case: stainless steel, ø 42 mm, height 13.5 mm; bezel with rubber ring; sapphire crystal; screw-in crown; water-resistant to 100 atm
Band: stainless steel, folding clasp, with extension link
Price: $2,499
Variations: with rubber strap ($2,399); with full lume dial ($2,399)

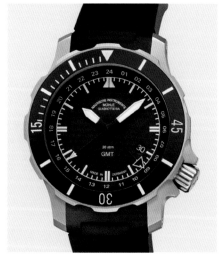

Seebatallion GMT

Reference number: M1-28-62-KB
Movement: automatic, Sellita Caliber SW330-2; ø 25.6 mm, height 4.1 mm; 21 jewels; 28,800 vph; woodpecker neck regulation, rotor finely processed with special Mühle finish; 56-hour power reserve
Functions: hours, minutes, sweep seconds; additional 24-hour display (2nd time zone); date
Case: titanium, ø 45 mm, height 12.7 mm; bidirectional bezel, with 0-60 scale; sapphire crystal; transparent case back; screw-in crown; water-resistant to 30 atm
Band: rubber, folding clasp, with extension link
Price: $3,549

29er Big

Reference number: M1-25-37-CB
Movement: automatic, Sellita Caliber SW200-1;
ø 25.6 mm, height 4.6 mm; 26 jewels; 28,800 vph;
woodpecker neck regulation, rotor finely processed
with special Mühle finish; 41-hour power reserve
Functions: hours, minutes, sweep seconds; date
Case: stainless steel, ø 42.4 mm, height 11.3 mm;
sapphire crystal; transparent case back; screw-in
crown; water-resistant to 10 atm
Band: textile, pin buckle
Price: $1,599
Variations: with stainless steel bracelet ($1,999)

29er Pointer Date

Reference number: M1-25-32-CB
Movement: automatic, Sellita Caliber SW221-1;
ø 25.6 mm, height 5.05 mm; 26 jewels; 28,800 vph;
woodpecker neck regulation, rotor finely processed
with special Mühle finish; 41-hour power reserve
Functions: hours, minutes, sweep seconds; date
Case: stainless steel, ø 42.4 mm, height 12.2 mm;
sapphire crystal; transparent case back;
water-resistant to 10 atm
Band: textile, pin buckle
Price: $1,999
Variations: with stainless steel bracelet ($2,149)

Panova Turquoise

Reference number: M1-40-79-NB-L
Movement: automatic, Sellita Caliber SW200-1;
ø 25.6 mm, height 4.6 mm; 26 jewels; 28,800 vph;
woodpecker neck regulation, rotor finely processed
with special Mühle finish; 41-hour power reserve
Functions: hours, minutes, sweep seconds
Case: stainless steel, ø 40 mm, height 10.4 mm; sapphire
crystal; screw-in crown; water-resistant to 10 atm
Band: calfskin, pin buckle
Price: $1,199
Variations: with textile strap ($1,199)

Lunova Day/Date

Reference number: M1-43-26-LB
Movement: automatic, Sellita Caliber SW220-1;
ø 25.6 mm, height 5.05 mm; 26 jewels; 28,800 vph;
woodpecker neck regulation, rotor finely processed
with special Mühle finish; 41-hour power reserve
Functions: hours, minutes, sweep seconds;
date and weekday
Case: titanium, ø 42.3 mm, height 11 mm; sapphire
crystal; transparent case back; screw-in crown;
water-resistant to 10 atm
Band: reptile skin, pin buckle
Price: $2,299

Teutonia Sport II "Racing Green"

Reference number: M1-29-74-LB
Movement: automatic, Sellita Caliber SW290-1;
ø 25.6 mm, height 5.6 mm; 31 jewels; 28,800 vph;
woodpecker neck regulation, rotor finely processed
with special Mühle finish; 41-hour power reserve
Functions: hours, minutes, subsidiary seconds; date
Case: stainless steel, ø 41.6 mm, height 12.8 mm;
sapphire crystal; transparent case back; screw-in
crown; water-resistant to 10 atm
Band: calfskin, pin buckle
Price: $2,799

Teutonia IV Moon Phase

Reference number: M1-44-05-LB
Movement: automatic, Sellita Caliber SW280-1;
ø 25.6 mm, height 5.4 mm; 26 jewels; 28,800 vph;
woodpecker neck regulation, rotor finely processed
with special Mühle finish; 41-hour power reserve
Functions: hours, minutes, sweep seconds;
date, moon phase
Case: stainless steel, ø 41 mm, height 12.6 mm;
sapphire crystal; transparent case back;
water-resistant to 10 atm
Band: calfskin, double folding clasp
Price: $2,899
Variations: with stainless steel bracelet ($3,049)

NOMOS

Who says Germans have no sense of humor? The best of it is subtle enough to be accessible to the poets and thinkers (*Dichter und Denker*) with command of the language and its many dialects. At its apex, humor must be self-deprecatory and deadpan. This may be the reason for Nomos's global success. Ever since its founding in 1990 by Roland Schwertner and his associate Uwe Ahrendt, the company's marketing measures have harmonized with the product in a subtly playful and humorous manner.

Nomos Glashütte is now the number one producer of mechanical watches in Germany. It manufactures them in the best tradition of the German Werkbund and Bauhaus—research, design, and production work hand in hand. The emphasis on design meant that the brand needed its own calibers, and these are now wisely distributed throughout the thirteen model families with over one hundred variations that grace the company's portfolio. The one that made a loud splash, however, was the DUW 4401 (Deutsche Uhrenwerke Nomos Glashütte), equipped with the "Swing System," an in-house escapement with a spring "made in Germany." Unveiled in 2014, this caliber has gradually become the core regulating instrument for Nomos watches and been integrated into all the brand's movements. Its great advantage is thinness, which lets the company maintain its USP: very elegant, unobtrusively attractive mechanical watches.

Speaking of design, of the over two hundred people who work at Nomos, about twenty or so are members of the Berlin-based company Berlinerblau and the others are spread out across the world, from Glashütte to New York, from Hong Kong and Shanghai to Lake Como in Italy. This aesthetic-philosophical scrim, as it were, has produced such genial watch families as the swimmer's watch Ahoi (as in "ship ahoy!"), with an optional synthetic strap like those that carry locker keys at Germany's public swimming pools. The Autobahn is a panegyric to Germany's favorite playground, the highway. Quirky dial colors are also part of the brand's mission, as are affordable prices (except for a few gold models). The recipe has, so far, earned five stars from the consumers and over 170 prizes for design and quality.

Nomos Glashütte/SA
Roland Schwertner KG
Ferdinand-Adolph-Lange-Platz 2
01768 Glashütte
Germany

Tel.:
+49-35053-404-0

E-mail:
nomos@glashuette.com

Website:
nomos-glashuette.com

Founded:
1990

Number of employees:
over 200

U.S. distributor:
For the U.S. market, please contact:
NOMOS Glashuette USA Inc.
347 W. 36th St.
New York, NY 10018
212-929-2575
contact@nomos-watches.com

Most important collections/price range:
Ahoi / $3,760 to $4,660; Autobahn / $4,800; Club Campus $1,500 to $1,650; Club Sport $3,960; Lambda / $7,500 to $20,000; Ludwig / $1,380 to $10,140; Lux / $19,500 to $21,500; Metro / $2,560 to $10,920; Orion / $1,600 to $4,350; Tangente / $1,440 to $4,980; Tangomat / $2,980 to $4,920; Tetra / $1,660 to $3,860; Zürich / $3,260 to $4,620

Tangente Neomatik 39 Blue Gold

Reference number: 145
Movement: automatic, Nomos Caliber DUW 3001; ø 28.8 mm, height 3.2 mm; 27 jewels; 21,600 vph; three-quarter plate, finely finished movement; 43-hour power reserve
Functions: hours, minutes, subsidiary seconds
Case: stainless steel, ø 38.5 mm, height 6.9 mm; sapphire crystal; water-resistant to 5 atm
Band: horse leather, pin buckle
Price: $3,780

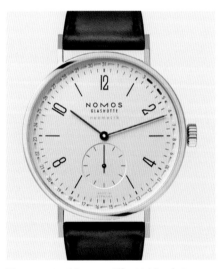

Tangente Neomatik 41 Update

Reference number: 180
Movement: automatic, Nomos Caliber DUW 6101; ø 35.2 mm, height 3.6 mm; 27 jewels; 21,600 vph; three-quarter plate, finely finished movement; 42-hour power reserve
Functions: hours, minutes, subsidiary seconds; date
Case: stainless steel, ø 40.5 mm, height 7.8 mm; sapphire crystal; transparent case back; water-resistant to 5 atm
Band: horse leather, pin buckle
Price: $4,100

Club Sport Neomatik Petrol

Reference number: 745
Movement: automatic, Nomos Caliber DUW 3001; ø 28.8 mm, height 3.2 mm; 27 jewels; 21,600 vph; three-quarter plate, finely finished movement; 43-hour power reserve
Functions: hours, minutes, subsidiary seconds
Case: stainless steel, ø 37 mm, height 8.3 mm; sapphire crystal; water-resistant to 20 atm
Band: stainless steel, folding clasp
Price: $3,150

Tangente 38 Date

Reference number: 130
Movement: hand-wound, Nomos Caliber DUW 4101;
ø 32.1 mm, height 2.8 mm; 23 jewels; 21.600 vph;
three-quarter plate, finely finished movement;
42-hour power reserve
Functions: hours, minutes, subsidiary seconds; date
Case: stainless steel, ø 37.5 mm, height 6.8 mm;
sapphire crystal; transparent case back;
water-resistant to 3 atm
Band: horse leather, pin buckle
Price: $2,780

Tangente Neomatik 41 Update Night Blue

Reference number: 182
Movement: automatic, Nomos Caliber DUW 6101;
ø 35.2 mm, height 3.6 mm; 27 jewels; 21,600 vph;
three-quarter plate, finely finished movement;
42-hour power reserve
Functions: hours, minutes, subsidiary seconds; date
Case: stainless steel, ø 40.5 mm, height 7.8 mm;
sapphire crystal; transparent case back;
water-resistant to 5 atm
Band: horse leather, pin buckle
Price: $4,100

Ludwig Neomatik 41 Date

Reference number: 262
Movement: automatic, Nomos Caliber DUW 6101;
ø 35.2 mm, height 3.6 mm; 27 jewels; 21,600 vph;
three-quarter plate, finely finished movement;
42-hour power reserve
Functions: hours, minutes, subsidiary seconds; date
Case: stainless steel, ø 40.5 mm, height 7.7 mm;
sapphire crystal; transparent case back;
water-resistant to 5 atm
Band: horse leather, pin buckle
Price: $4,000

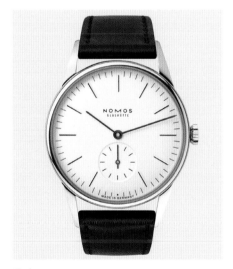

Orion

Reference number: 301
Movement: hand-wound, Nomos Caliber Alpha;
ø 23.3 mm, height 2.6 mm; 17 jewels; 21,600 vph;
43-hour power reserve
Functions: hours, minutes, subsidiary seconds
Case: stainless steel, ø 35 mm, height 7.4 mm;
sapphire crystal; water-resistant to 3 atm
Band: horse leather, pin buckle
Price: $2,020

Metro Neomatik 41 Update

Reference number: 1165
Movement: automatic, Nomos Caliber DUW 6101;
ø 35.2 mm, height 3.6 mm; 27 jewels; 21,600 vph;
three-quarter plate, finely finished movement;
42-hour power reserve
Functions: hours, minutes, subsidiary seconds; date
Case: stainless steel, ø 40.5 mm, height 9.1 mm;
sapphire crystal; transparent case back;
water-resistant to 5 atm
Band: textile, pin buckle
Price: $3,850

Metro Date Gangreserve

Reference number: 1101
Movement: hand-wound, Nomos Caliber DUW 4401;
ø 32.1 mm, height 2.8 mm; 23 jewels; 21,600 vph;
three-quarter plate, finely finished movement;
42-hour power reserve
Functions: hours, minutes, subsidiary seconds;
power-reserve indicator; date
Case: stainless steel, ø 37 mm, height 7.7 mm; sapphire
crystal; transparent case back; water-resistant to 3 atm
Band: horse leather, pin buckle
Price: $3,780

Ahoi Neomatik Atlantic

Reference number: 567
Movement: automatic, Nomos Caliber DUW 3001;
ø 28.8 mm, height 3.2 mm; 27 jewels; 21,600 vph;
three-quarter plate, finely finished movement;
43-hour power reserve
Functions: hours, minutes, subsidiary seconds
Case: stainless steel, ø 36.3 mm, height 9.6 mm;
sapphire crystal; transparent case back;
screw-in crown; water-resistant to 20 atm
Band: textile, pin buckle
Price: $3,400

Tangente Sport Neomatik 42 Date

Reference number: 580
Movement: automatic, Nomos Caliber DUW 6101;
ø 35.2 mm, height 3.6 mm; 27 jewels; 21,600 vph;
three-quarter plate, finely finished movement;
42-hour power reserve
Functions: hours, minutes, subsidiary seconds; date
Case: stainless steel, ø 42 mm, height 10.9 mm;
sapphire crystal; transparent case back;
screw-in crown; water-resistant to 30 atm
Band: stainless steel, folding clasp
Price: $4,980

Zürich Weltzeit

Reference number: 805
Movement: automatic, Nomos Caliber DUW 5201;
ø 31 mm, height 5.7 mm; 26 jewels; 21,600 vph;
42-hour power reserve
Functions: hours, minutes, subsidiary seconds;
world time display (2nd time zone)
Case: stainless steel, ø 39.9 mm, height 10.9 mm;
sapphire crystal; transparent case back;
water-resistant to 3 atm
Band: horse leather, pin buckle
Price: $6,100

Club Sport Neomatik 42 Date Blue

Reference number: 782
Movement: automatic, Nomos Caliber DUW 6101;
ø 35.2 mm, height 3.6 mm; 27 jewels; 21,600 vph;
three-quarter plate, finely finished movement;
42-hour power reserve
Functions: hours, minutes, subsidiary seconds; date
Case: stainless steel, ø 42 mm, height 10.2 mm;
sapphire crystal; transparent case back;
screw-in crown; water-resistant to 30 atm
Band: stainless steel, folding clasp
Price: $3,960

Club Campus 38 Cream Coral

Reference number: 725
Movement: hand-wound, Nomos Caliber Alpha;
ø 23.3 mm, height 2.6 mm; 17 jewels; 21,600 vph;
three-quarter plate, finely finished movement;
43-hour power reserve
Functions: hours, minutes, subsidiary seconds
Case: stainless steel, ø 38.5 mm, height 8.5 mm;
sapphire crystal; water-resistant to 10 atm
Band: suede, pin buckle
Price: $1,650

Club Campus Electric Green

Reference number: 715
Movement: hand-wound, Nomos Caliber Alpha;
ø 23.3 mm, height 2.6 mm; 17 jewels; 21,600 vph;
three-quarter plate, finely finished movement;
43-hour power reserve
Functions: hours, minutes, subsidiary seconds
Case: stainless steel, ø 36 mm, height 8.2 mm;
sapphire crystal; water-resistant to 10 atm
Band: suede, pin buckle
Price: $1,500

Metro Rose Gold 33

Reference number: 1170
Movement: hand-wound, Nomos Caliber Alpha; ø 23.3 mm, height 2.6 mm; 17 jewels; 21,600 vph; three-quarter plate, finely finished movement; 43-hour power reserve
Functions: hours, minutes, subsidiary seconds
Case: rose gold, ø 33 mm, height 7.7 mm; sapphire crystal; transparent case back; water resistant to 3 atm
Band: suede, pin buckle
Price: $8,840

Tetra – Die Unerreichbare

Reference number: 427
Movement: hand-wound, Nomos Caliber Alpha; ø 23.3 mm, height 2.6 mm; 17 jewels; 21,600 vph; three-quarter plate, finely finished movement; 43-hour power reserve
Functions: hours, minutes, subsidiary seconds
Case: stainless steel, 29.5 x 29.5 mm, height 6.3 mm; sapphire crystal; water resistant to 3 atm
Band: vegan suede, pin buckle
Price: $2,080

Tetra – Die Kapriziöse

Reference number: 424
Movement: hand-wound, Nomos Caliber Alpha; ø 23.3 mm, height 2.6 mm; 17 jewels; 21,600 vph; three-quarter plate, finely finished movement; 43-hour power reserve
Functions: hours, minutes, subsidiary seconds
Case: stainless steel, 29.5 x 29.5 mm, height 6.3 mm; sapphire crystal, water-resistant to 3 atm
Band: vegan suede, pin buckle
Price: $2,080

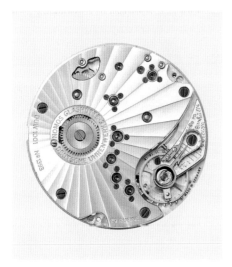

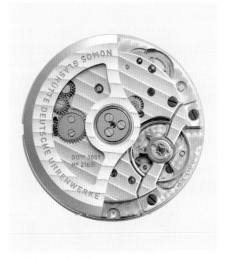

Caliber DUW 1001

Hand-wound; swan-neck fine regulator; double spring barrel, 84-hour power reserve
Functions: hours, minutes, subsidiary seconds; power-reserve indicator
Diameter: 32 mm
Height: 3.6 mm
Jewels: 29, including 5 in screw-mounted gold chatons
Balance: screw balance Frequency: 21,600 vph
Hairspring: Nivarox 1A
Shock protection: Incabloc
Remarks: hand-engraved balance cock, chamfered and polished edges, rhodium-plated movement surfaces, with Glashütte ribbing and perlage decoration

Caliber DUW 6101

Automatic; single spring barrel, 43-hour power reserve
Functions: hours, minutes, subsidiary seconds; date
Diameter: 35.2 mm
Height: 3.6 mm
Jewels: 27
Balance: made in-house
Frequency: 21,600 vph
Hairspring: heat-blued, in-house manufacturing
Shock protection: Incabloc
Remarks: three-quarter plate, rhodium-plated movement surfaces, with Glashütte ribbing and perlage decoration

Caliber DUW 3001

Automatic; single spring barrel, 43-hour power reserve
Functions: hours, minutes, subsidiary seconds
Diameter: 28.8 mm
Height: 3.2 mm
Jewels: 27
Balance: made in-house
Frequency: 21,600 vph
Hairspring: heat-blued, in-house manufacturing
Shock protection: Incabloc
Remarks: three-quarter plate, rhodium-plated movement surfaces, with Glashütte ribbing and perlage decoration

NORQAIN

Norqain was founded in 2018 by CEO Ben Küffer in Nidau near Biel/Bienne, that industrial city at the foot of the Jura Mountains in Switzerland that is home to several watch companies and related enterprises. He invited a number of people as cofounders to form the Board of Directors, notably Ted Schneider, a member of the family that once owned Breitling, and Swiss ice hockey legend Mark Streit, a watch enthusiast and a good ambassador for the new brand. Marc Küffer, Ben's father, was named the Chairman of the Board. He, for his part, had over forty-five years of experience in the manufacturing of Swiss luxury watches and had served on the Board of the Federation of the Swiss Watch Industry for twenty-five years.

The idea was perhaps not terribly original, but in a complicated world with lots of marketing, a clearcut message is often worth a thousand words: affordable quality. The brand's mission statement, as it were, was to be <u>n</u>ew, <u>o</u>pen-minded, <u>r</u>ebellious, <u>q</u>uality time-giving, <u>a</u>dventurous, <u>i</u>ndependent, and <u>n</u>iche-oriented, which spells Norqain. The logo, a kind of N, is also a stylized mountain peak, expressing the sportive feeling.

The company manufactures mechanical watches only, which are assembled by hand in the production facility in Tavannes, a village in the Jura. To ensure high quality, Norqain signed a long-term strategic collaboration with Kenissi in Le Locle, a finicky movement-maker that was founded by Tudor (of Rolex fame) and is twenty percent owned by Chanel. It's an exclusive club, but the fact that Kenissi manager Jean-Paul Girardin is a former Breitling executive surely helped secure the partnership.

The first results of this important alliance were two exclusive manufacture movements. The three-hand caliber NN20/1 and the GMT caliber NN20/2, both with a power reserve of seventy hours and chronometer certification. The three collections—Adventure, Freedom, and Independence—boast quite original, striking design elements. And the conceptual recipe behind the brand seems to have worked because Norqain has become a household name amongst connoisseurs.

Montres Norqain SA
Hauptstrasse 7
CH-2560 Nidau
Switzerland

Tel:
+41-32-505-31-55

E-mail:
info@norqain.com

Founded:
2018

Number of employees:
40

Annual production:
more than 1,000

Distribution:
retailers, own shops

Most important collections/price range:
Adventure, Freedom, Independence / around
$2,000 to $5,000

Adventure Neverest GMT Glacier

Reference number: NN1100SC3CG/G113
Movement: automatic, Norqain Caliber NN20/2 (modified Kenissi); ø 31.8 mm, height 7.52 mm; 28 jewels; 28,800 vph; 70-hour power reserve; COSC-certified chronometer
Functions: hours (crown-adjustable by steps), minutes, sweep seconds; additional 24-hour display (2nd time zone); date
Case: stainless steel, ø 41 mm, height 14.94 mm; bidirectional bezel with ceramic insert, with 0-24 scale; sapphire crystal; transparent case back; screw-in crown; water-resistant to 10 atm
Band: stainless steel, folding clasp, with fine adjustment
Remarks: structured dial with fold inserts to look like glacier crevasses
Price: $4,390

Freedom 60 Chrono

Reference number: N2201S22C/A221
Movement: automatic, Norqain Caliber NN19 (based on Sellita SW510a); ø 30.4 mm, height 7.9 mm; 27 jewels; 28,800 vph; 62-hour power reserve
Functions: hours, minutes, subsidiary seconds; chronograph; date
Case: stainless steel, ø 40 mm, height 14.9 mm; sapphire crystal; transparent case back; screw-in crown; water-resistant to 10 atm
Band: stainless steel, folding clasp
Price: $4,450
Variations: with textile strap made of Nortide recycled plastic ($4,180); with Perlon rubber strap ($4,350)

Independence Wild One Skeleton Turquoise

Reference number: NNQ3000QBQ1AS/B007
Movement: automatic, Norqain Caliber NN08S (based on Sellita SW200-1 S c); ø 25.6 mm, height 4.6 mm; 26 jewels; 28,800 vph; completely skeletonized movement; 38-hour power reserve
Functions: hours, minutes, sweep seconds
Case: carbon fiber (NORTEQ) with a titanium container with rubber shock absorbers, ø 42 mm, height 12.3 mm; sapphire crystal; transparent case back; screw-in crown, with rubber layer; water-resistant to 20 atm
Band: rubber, pin buckle
Price: $5,790

NOVE
Swiss office:
Via ai Boschi 6,
CH-6855 Stabio
Switzerland

Hong Kong office:
NOVE Limited
Unit A, 3/F, Kingsway Industrial Building,
Phase 1, 167-175 Wo Yi Hop Road,
Kwai Chung, N.T., Hong Kong

Email:
mkt@nove.com

Website:
www.nove.com

Founded:
2015 (incorporated 2018)

Number of employees:
About 15 employees

Distribution:
Webshop (see website)

Most important collections/price range:
Atlantean, Gemini, Trident / $280 - $1,880

NOVE

The most popular watch genre is the diver's watch and for good reason. First, these timepieces exude an aura of adventure, danger, and fun, mixed with a bit of lizard-brain survival, all wrapped in one. It's part of their history. After all, have they not served on the wrists of extra-tough special commandos in various countries? The other reason is of course reliability. As genuine tool watches, they must be built with great care and function extremely well, since the users depend on them to know how long they've been underwater and how much time they have left to perform their tasks.

Any brand wanting to release a new diver's watch will face the challenge of innovation and creating a viable USP. Nove, a brand stationed in Hong Kong but with production in Switzerland, came up with the idea of a thin diver's watch, the Trident, which clocks in at 6.2 millimeters thickness in quartz. A second diver, the Atlantean, was conceived with a large dose of Super-LumiNova on the dial, hands, and bezel for good visibility even in deep waters, and an interior bidirectional bezel that can be locked into place with a special hand lever.

To cover its market well, Nove also has rather fresh-looking dress watches, including the clever dual-faced Gemini GMT watch, which reverses using a bespoke lever mechanism, and the Modena chronographs, for the sportive buyer.

Having fresh ideas might be part of the company DNA, because it was founded by Tiffany Meerovitsch in 2015 when she was just 19 years old and about to go to university to study art and later digital marketing. It was a natural passion for her. She grew up steeped in watchmaking while visiting her father's office at a watchmaking company. "He had me working on the assembly line, where I learned how to assemble a watch," she said in an interview. "Seeing all these beautiful designs got me fascinated with the idea of starting my own label with my own designs."

Nove watches are assembled in Switzerland using Swiss parts. They make use of Ronda and Sellita movements mostly.

Modena 500

Reference number: O001-02
Movement: automatic; Sellita SW500a caliber; ø 30 mm; height 7.6 mm; 25 jewels; 28,800 vph; 62-hour power reserve
Functions: hours, minutes, subsidiary seconds; day, date; chronograph with tachymeter scale
Case: stainless steel, ø 44 mm, height 15.7mm; screw-in crowns; sapphire crystal; transparent case back; water-resistant to 20 atm
Band: stainless steel, safety clasp with micro-adjustment
Price: $1,880; limited to 99 pieces

Atlantean

Reference number: I001-02
Movement: automatic, Ronda R150 Caliber; ø 25.6 mm, height 4.4 mm; 25 jewels; 28,800 vph; 40-hour power reserve.
Functions: hours, minutes, sweep seconds; date
Case: stainless steel, 50.5 mm, height 13.95 mm; screw-in crown with guard lock; bidirectional, lever-activated inner bezel; sapphire crystal, transparent case back; water-resistant to 30 atm .
Band: stainless steel, safety clasp with micro-adjustment
Remarks: quick-change strap system; abalone shell dial
Price: $880
Variations: with IP-black case

Trident Automatic

Reference number: G003-02
Movement: automatic, Ronda R150 Caliber; ø 25.6 mm, height 4.4 mm; 25 jewels; 28,800 vph; 40-hour power reserve.
Functions: hours, minutes, sweep seconds; date
Case: stainless steel with IP blue coating; ø 46 mm, height 13.05 mm; screw-in crown; IP Blue; sapphire crystal; transparent case back; water-resistant to 20 atm
Band: stainless steel, folding clasp
Remarks: Haitian mother-of-pearl dial
Price: $830
Variations: IP-black or rose-gold coating; comes in ultra-slim (6 mm) quartz version ($450)

OMEGA

As the largest brand in the SSIH Group, Omega had an important role to play during the quartz crisis that hit the Swiss watch industry in the 1970s. The Société Suisse de l'Industrie Horlogère and the Allgemeine Schweizerische Uhrenindustrie AG (ASUAG) merged to form the founding company of the Swatch Group. It became the flagship brand of the entire group and therefore had a leading position in terms of design, technology, and functionality.

Technology and design are very much responsible for Omega's success. Omega became the first company to try out new materials like titanium and ceramic for the cases, the central tourbillon, or the coaxial escapement designed originally by Englishman George Daniels.

The 15,000-gauss amagnetic movement has now been used in many of the new products. And there is a plethora of new "Master Chronometer" movements, which not only meet the stringent requirements set out by the COSC but also must pass the tests developed by Switzerland's Federal Institute of Metrology (METAS). Swatch Group subsidiary Nivarox-FAR has finally mastered the production of the difficult, oil-free parts of the system designed by George Daniels, although the escapement continues to include lubrication, as the long-term results of "dry" coaxial movements are less than satisfactory. Thus, the most important plus for this escapement design remains a high rate stability after careful regulation.

The most enduring model of the company, the Seamaster, which was born in 1948, was celebrated in 2023. In 1957, Omega introduced the Seamaster 300 automatic watch, specially developed for professional divers. In 1993, the Seamaster Professional Diver pushed the diving watches trend into the modern era, and in 2021, the Ploprof 600 legend was given a facelift. This special model, the Seamaster Planet Ocean Ultra Deep, was developed in 1971 for professional divers (Ploprof stands for "Plongeurs Professionels," professional divers) and is water-resistant to 6,000.

The Seamaster's seventy-fifth anniversary was also celebrated with a series of seawater blue dials ("Summer Blue") for eight models.

Omega SA
Jakob-Stämpfli-Strasse 96
CH-2502 Biel/Bienne
Switzerland

Tel.:
+41-32-343-9211

E-mail:
info@omegawatches.com

Website:
www.omegawatches.com

Founded:
1848

U.S. distributor:
Omega
703 Waterford Way, Suite 920
Miami, FL 33126
800-766-6342
www.omegawatches.com

Most important collections:
Seamaster, Constellation, Speedmaster; as of
$3,200

Speedmaster Super Racing

Reference number: 329.30.44.51.01.003
Movement: automatic, Omega Caliber 9920; ø 32.5 mm, height 8.35 mm; 54 jewels; 28,800 vph; 2 spring barrels, co-axial escapement, silicon balance wheel and hairspring with "Spirate" fine regulation, antimagnetic to 15,000 Gauss; METAS-certified chronometer; 60-hour power reserve
Functions: hours, minutes, subsidiary seconds; chronograph; date
Case: stainless steel, ø 44.25 mm, height 14.9 mm; bezel with ceramic insert; sapphire crystal; transparent case back; water-resistant to 5 atm
Band: stainless steel, double folding clasp
Price: $11,600

De Ville Trésor Power Reserve

Reference number: 435.53.40.22.02.001
Movement: hand-wound, Omega Caliber 8935; ø 29 mm, height 5.5 mm; 30 jewels; 25,200 vph; 2 spring barrels, co-axial escapement, silicon hairspring, antimagnetic to 15,000 Gauss; METAS-certified chronometer; 72-hour power reserve
Functions: hours, minutes, subsidiary seconds; power-reserve indicator
Case: yellow gold, ø 40 mm, height 10.07 mm; sapphire crystal; transparent case back; water-resistant to 3 atm
Band: reptile skin, pin buckle
Price: $20,200

Seamaster Aqua Terra 150M Master Chronometer

Reference number: 220.10.41.21.03.005
Movement: automatic, Omega Caliber 8900; ø 29 mm, height 5.5 mm; 39 jewels; 25,200 vph; double spring barrel, co-axial escapement, silicon balance wheel and hairspring, antimagnetic to 15,000 Gauss; METAS-certified chronometer; 60-hour power reserve
Functions: hours, minutes, sweep seconds; date
Case: Stainless steel, ø 41 mm, height 13.2 mm; sapphire crystal; water-resistant to 15 atm
Band: stainless steel, double folding clasp
Price: $6,600

Seamaster 300

Reference number: 234.92.41.21.10.001
Movement: automatic, Omega Caliber 8912; ø 29 mm,
height 5.5 mm; 38 jewels; 25,200 vph; 2 spring barrels,
co-axial escapement, silicon balance wheel and
hairspring, antimagnetic to 15,000 Gauss;
METAS-certified chronometer; 60-hour power reserve
Functions: hours, minutes, sweep seconds
Case: bronze-gold alloy, ø 41 mm, height 14.4 mm;
unidirectional bezel with ceramic insert, with
0-60 scale; sapphire crystal; transparent case back;
screw-in crown; water-resistant to 30 atm
Band: calfskin, pin buckle
Price: $13,200
Variations: in stainless steel

Seamaster Diver 300M

Reference number: 210.30.42.20.01.001
Movement: automatic, Omega Caliber 8800; ø 26 mm,
height 4.6 mm; 35 jewels; 25,200 vph; co-axial
escapement, silicon balance wheel and hairspring,
antimagnetic to 15,000 Gauss; METAS-certified
chronometer; 55-hour power reserve
Functions: hours, minutes, sweep seconds; date
Case: stainless steel, ø 42 mm, height 13.56 mm;
unidirectional bezel with ceramic insert, with 0-60 scale;
sapphire crystal; transparent case back; screw-in crown,
helium valve; water-resistant to 30 atm
Band: stainless steel, folding clasp
Price: $5,900
Variations: various cases, straps, and dials

Seamaster Diver "Black Black"

Reference number: 210.92.44.20.01.003
Movement: automatic, Omega Caliber 8806; ø 26 mm,
height 4.6 mm; 35 jewels; 25,200 vph; co-axial
escapement, silicon balance wheel and hairspring,
antimagnetic to 15,000 Gauss; METAS-certified
chronometer; 55-hour power reserve
Functions: hours, minutes, sweep seconds
Case: ceramic, ø 43.5 mm, height 14.47 mm;
unidirectional bezel with 0-60 scale; sapphire crystal;
screw-in crown, helium valve; water resistant to 30 atm
Band: rubber, pin buckle
Price: $9,500

Seamaster Diver 300M

Reference number: 210.30.42.20.03.003
Movement: automatic, Omega Caliber 8800; ø 26 mm,
height 4.6 mm; 35 jewels; 25,200 vph; co-axial
escapement, silicon balance wheel and hairspring,
antimagnetic to 15,000 Gauss; METAS-certified
chronometer; 55-hour power reserve
Functions: hours, minutes, sweep seconds; date
Case: stainless steel, ø 42 mm, height 13.56 mm;
unidirectional bezel with ceramic insert, with 0-60 scale;
sapphire crystal; transparent case back; screw-in crown,
helium valve; water-resistant to 30 atm
Band: stainless steel, folding clasp, with extension link
Price: $6,300
Variations: various cases, straps, and dials

Seamaster 300

Reference number: 234.30.41.21.03.002
Movement: automatic, Omega Caliber 8912; ø 29 mm,
height 5.5 mm; 38 jewels; 25,200 vph; 2 spring barrels,
co-axial escapement, silicon balance wheel and
hairspring, antimagnetic to 15,000 Gauss;
METAS-certified chronometer; 60-hour power reserve
Functions: hours, minutes, sweep seconds
Case: stainless steel, ø 41 mm, height 13.85 mm;
unidirectional bezel with ceramic insert, with
0-60 scale; sapphire crystal; transparent case back;
screw-in crown; water-resistant to 30 atm
Band: stainless steel, folding clasp
Price: $7,400

Seamaster Aqua Terra Worldtimer

Reference number: 220.32.43.22.10.001
Movement: automatic, Omega Caliber 8938; ø 29 mm,
height 6.5 mm; 39 jewels; 25,200 vph; co-axial
escapement, silicon balance wheel and hairspring,
antimagnetic to 15,000 Gauss; METAS-certified
chronometer; 60-hour power reserve
Functions: hours, minutes, sweep seconds; world time
display (2nd time zone); date
Case: stainless steel, ø 43 mm, height 14.1 mm; green
anodized bezel; sapphire crystal; transparent case
back; screw-in crown; water-resistant to 15 atm
Band: rubber, folding clasp
Price: $10,700
Variations: various cases and dials

Seamaster Planet Ocean Ultra Deep

Reference number: 215.30.46.21.06.001
Movement: automatic, Omega Caliber 8912; ø 29 mm, height 5.5 mm; 38 jewels; 25,200 vph; 2 spring barrels, co-axial escapement, silicon balance wheel and hairspring, antimagnetic to 15,000 Gauss; METAS-certified chronometer; 60-hour power reserve
Functions: hours, minutes, sweep seconds
Case: stainless steel ("O-Megasteel"), ø 45.5 mm, height 18.12 mm; unidirectional bezel with ceramic insert, with 0-60 scale; sapphire crystal; screw-in crown; water-resistant to 600 atm
Band: stainless steel ("O-Megasteel"), folding clasp
Price: $12,700
Variations: with rubber strap; in titanium with textile strap ($12,300)

Seamaster Planet Ocean Ultra Deep

Reference number: 215.30.46.21.03.002
Movement: automatic, Omega Caliber 8912; ø 29 mm, height 5.5 mm; 38 jewels; 25,200 vph; 2 spring barrels, co-axial escapement, silicon balance wheel and hairspring, antimagnetic to 15,000 Gauss; METAS-certified chronometer; 60-hour power reserve
Functions: hours, minutes, sweep seconds
Case: stainless steel ("O-Megasteel"), ø 45.5 mm, height 18,12 mm; unidirectional bezel with ceramic insert, with 0-60 scale; sapphire crystal; screw-in crown; water-resistant to 600 atm
Band: stainless steel ("O-Megasteel"), folding clasp, with safety lock, with extension link
Price: $13,000

Seamaster "Ploprof"

Reference number: 227.32.55.21.03.001
Movement: automatic, Omega Caliber 8912; ø 29 mm, height 5.5 mm; 38 jewels; 25,200 vph; 2 spring barrels, co-axial escapement, silicon balance wheel and hairspring, antimagnetic to 15,000 Gauss; METAS-certified chronometer; 60-hour power reserve
Functions: hours, minutes, sweep seconds
Case: stainless steel ("O-Megasteel"), 55 x 45 mm, height 15.5 mm; unidirectional bezel with ceramic insert, with 0-60 scale; sapphire crystal; screw-in crown; helium valve; water-resistant to 120 atm
Band: rubber, pin buckle
Price: $14,300
Variations: with stainless steel Milanese mesh bracelet and grey dial ($13,800)

Constellation Master Chronometer

Reference number: 131.33.41.21.04.001
Movement: automatic, Omega Caliber 8900; ø 29 mm, height 5.5 mm; 39 jewels; 25,200 vph; double spring barrel, co-axial escapement, silicon balance wheel and hairspring, antimagnetic to 15,000 Gauss; METAS-certified chronometer; 60-hour power reserve
Functions: hours, minutes, sweep seconds; date
Case: stainless steel, ø 41 mm, height 12.43 mm; sapphire crystal; transparent case back; water-resistant to 5 atm
Band: reptile skin, folding clasp
Price: $7,100
Variations: various dials

Seamaster Aqua Terra Railmaster

Reference number: 220.10.40.20.01.001
Movement: automatic, Omega Caliber 8806; ø 26 mm, height 4.6 mm; 35 jewels; 25,200 vph; co-axial escapement, silicon balance wheel and hairspring, antimagnetic to 15,000 Gauss; METAS-certified chronometer; 55-hour power reserve
Functions: hours, minutes, sweep seconds
Case: stainless steel, ø 40 mm, height 12.65 mm; sapphire crystal; water-resistant to 15 atm
Band: stainless steel, folding clasp
Price: $5,700
Variations: various dials; with calfskin strap; with textile strap

Speedmaster Moonwatch Professional

Reference number: 310.62.42.50.99.001
Movement: hand-wound, Omega Caliber 3861; ø 27 mm, height 6.9 mm; 26 jewels; 21,600 vph; co-axial escapement, silicon balance wheel and hairspring, antimagnetic to 15,000 Gauss; METAS-certified chronometer; 50-hour power reserve
Functions: hours, minutes, subsidiary seconds; chronograph
Case: yellow gold ("Moonshine gold"), ø 42 mm, height 13.2 mm; bezel with ceramic insert; sapphire crystal; transparent case back; water-resistant to 5 atm
Band: rubber, folding clasp
Price: $31,600

YOUR FIRST HAND EXPERIENCE

ROBOT
CZECH MADE WATCHES

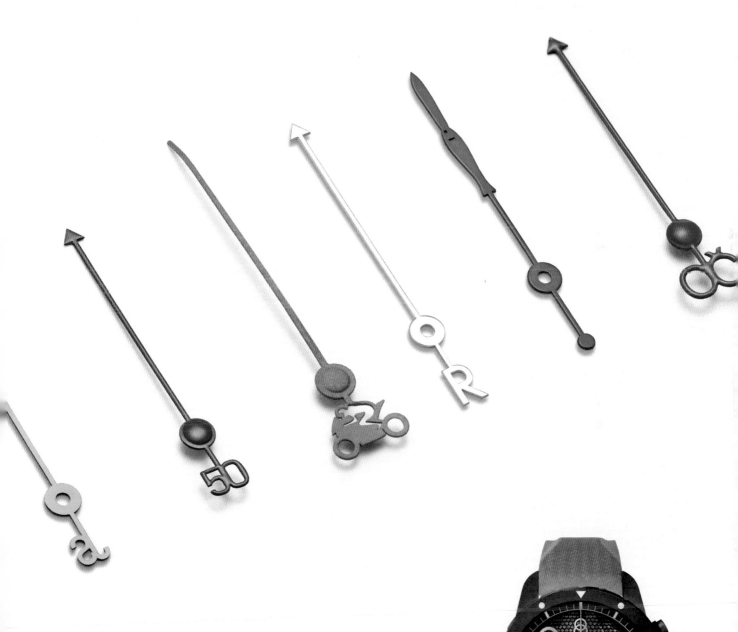

ROBOT watches, handcrafted in our Czech Republic manufactory, offer you the chance to customize your own watch. You don't just buy this watch, we create it together. With pleasure, just for you.

www.robot–watch.com

ROBOT Czech Made Watches: Maiselova 24/2, Prague 1, Czech Republic

Speedmaster Dark Side of the Moon "Apollo 8"

Reference number: 311.92.44.30.01.001
Movement: hand-wound, Omega Caliber 1869;
ø 27 mm, height 6.87 mm; 19 jewels; 21,600 vph;
48-hour power reserve
Functions: hours, minutes, subsidiary seconds;
chronograph
Case: ceramic, ø 44.25 mm, height 13.8 mm; sapphire
crystal; transparent case back; water-resistant to
5 atm
Band: calfskin, pin buckle
Remarks: mainplate and bridges with carefully
replicated moon surface
Price: $10,700

Speedmaster Moonwatch Master Chronometer

Reference number: 310.30.42.50.01.001
Movement: hand-wound, Omega Caliber 3861;
ø 27 mm, height 6.9 mm; 26 jewels; 21,600 vph;
co-axial escapement, silicon balance wheel and
hairspring, antimagnetic to 15,000 Gauss; METAS-
certified chronometer; 50-hour power reserve
Functions: hours, minutes, subsidiary seconds;
chronograph
Case: stainless steel, ø 42 mm, height 14 mm; bezel
with aluminum insert; sapphire crystal; water-resistant
to 5 atm
Band: stainless steel, folding clasp
Price: $7,000
Variations: with textile strap ($6,600)

Speedmaster Moonphase

Reference number: 304.33.44.52.03.001
Movement: automatic, Omega Caliber 9904;
ø 32.5 mm, height 8.35 mm; 54 jewels; 28,800 vph;
2 spring barrels, co-axial escapement, silicon balance
wheel and hairspring, antimagnetic to 15,000 Gauss;
METAS-certified chronometer; 60-hour power reserve
Functions: hours, minutes, subsidiary seconds;
chronograph; date, moon phase
Case: stainless steel, ø 44.25 mm, height 16.85 mm;
bezel with ceramic insert; sapphire crystal;
water-resistant to 10 atm
Band: reptile skin, folding clasp
Price: $11,200
Variations: various cases and dials

De Ville Trésor Small Seconds

Reference number: 435.53.40.21.11.002
Movement: hand-wound, Omega Caliber 8927;
ø 29 mm, height 5.5 mm; 29 jewels; 25,200 vph;
2 spring barrels, co-axial escapement, silicon balance
wheel and hairspring, antimagnetic to 15,000 Gauss;
METAS-certified chronometer; 72-hour power reserve
Functions: hours, minutes, subsidiary seconds
Case: rose gold ("Sedna gold"), ø 40 mm, height
10.7 mm; sapphire crystal; water-resistant to 3 atm
Band: reptile skin, pin buckle
Price: $19,500

Seamaster Diver James Bond Edition

Reference number: 210.90.42.20.01.001
Movement: automatic, Omega Caliber 8806; ø 26 mm,
height 4.6 mm; 35 jewels; 25,200 vph; co-axial
escapement, silicon balance wheel and hairspring,
antimagnetic to 15,000 Gauss; METAS-certified
chronometer; 55-hour power reserve
Functions: hours, minutes, sweep seconds
Case: titanium, ø 42 mm, height 13 mm; unidirectional
bezel with aluminum insert, with 0-60 scale; sapphire
crystal; screw-in crown, helium valve; water-resistant
to 30 atm
Band: titanium-Milanaise, folding clasp
Price: $10,000

Speedmaster '57

Reference number: 332.12.41.51.03.001
Movement: hand-wound, Omega Caliber 9906;
ø 32.5 mm, height 7.6 mm; 44 jewels; 28,800 vph;
co-axial escapement, silicon balance wheel and
hairspring, column-wheel control of chronograph
functions; METAS-certified chronometer;
60-hour power reserve
Functions: hours, minutes, subsidiary seconds;
chronograph; date
Case: stainless steel, ø 40.5 mm, height 13 mm;
sapphire crystal; water-resistant to 10 atm
Band: calfskin, pin buckle
Price: $9,100
Variations: various dials; with stainless steel bracelet

Caliber 8800

Automatic; coaxial escapement; antimagnetic up to 15,000 gauss; METAS-certified chronometer; single spring barrel, 55-hour power reserve
Functions: hours, minutes, sweep seconds; date
Diameter: 26 mm
Height: 4.6 mm
Jewels: 35
Balance: silicon, without regulator
Frequency: 25,200 vph
Hairspring: silicon
Shock protection: Nivachoc
Remarks: blackened screws

Caliber 321B

Hand-wound; Breguet hairspring; column-wheel control of chronograph functions; single spring barrel, 55-hour power reserve
Base caliber: Lémania 2310
Functions: hours, minutes, subsidiary seconds; chronograph
Diameter: 27 mm
Height: 6.87 mm
Jewels: 17
Frequency: 18,000 vph
Remarks: re-edition of historic movement used in first Speedmaster models; red gold plated, finely finished

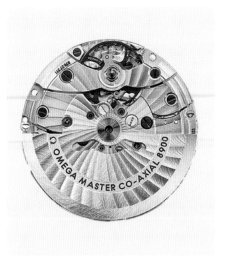

Caliber 8900

Automatic; coaxial escapement; antimagnetic up to 15,000 gauss; METAS-certified chronometer; double spring barrel, 60-hour power reserve
Functions: hours, minutes, sweep seconds; date
Diameter: 29 mm
Height: 5.5 mm
Jewels: 39
Balance: silicon, without regulator
Frequency: 25,200 vph
Hairspring: silicon
Shock protection: Nivachoc
Remarks: mainplate, bridges, and rotor with "arabesque" côtes de Genève, rhodium-plated, spring barrels, blackened balance wheel and screws

Caliber 9900

Automatic; coaxial escapement; column-wheel control of chronograph functions; antimagnetic up to 15,000 gauss; METAS-certified chronometer; double spring barrel, 60-hour power reserve
Functions: hours, minutes, subsidiary seconds; chronograph; date
Diameter: 32.5 mm
Height: 7.6 mm
Jewels: 5.4
Balance: silicon, without regulator
Frequency: 28,800 vph
Hairspring: silicon
Shock protection: Nivachoc
Remarks: mainplate, bridges, and rotor with "arabesque" côtes de Genève

Caliber 8935

Hand-wound; co-axial escapement, antimagnetic to 15,000 gauss; METAS-certified chronometer; 2 spring barrels, 72-hour power reserve
Functions: hours, minutes, subsidiary seconds; power reserve display
Diameter: 29 mm
Height: 5.5 mm
Jewels: 30
Balance: silicon, indexless
Frequency: 25,200 vph
Balance: silicon, indexless
Shock protection: Nivachoc
Remarks: mainplate and bridges with côtes de Genève, "Sednagold" balance bridge; blackened spring barrels, balance wheel and screws

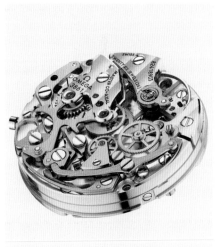

Caliber 3861

Hand-wound; coaxial escapement, antimagnetic protection to 15,000 gauss; METAS-certified chronometer; single spring barrel, 50-hour power reserve
Functions: hours, minutes, subsidiary seconds; chronograph
Diameter: 27 mm
Height: 6.87 mm
Jewels: 26
Frequency: 21,600 vph
Hairspring: silicon
Remarks: gold-plated movement ("Moonshine Gold"); 240 parts

ORIS

Oris, located near Basel, Switzerland, since its founding in 1904, has stuck to its strategic guns for as long as it has existed: affordable quality. The result has been growing international success, now with a portfolio divided up into four "product worlds," each with its own distinct identity: aviation, motor sports, diving, and culture. In utilizing specific materials—a tungsten bezel for the divers, for example—and functions based on these types, Oris makes certain that each will fit perfectly into the world for which it was designed. Yet the heart of every watch houses a small, high-quality "high-mech" movement identifiable by the brand's standard red rotor.

A bold step came in 2014 with the in-house Caliber 110, a plain, but technically efficient, hand-wound movement. It was made together with the engineers from the Technical College of Le Locle and features a massive 6-foot (1.8-meter) mainspring. Almost as regular as clockwork, the brand has produced further calibers, numbered 111, 112 (with GMT function), and 113.

In October 2020, the first wristwatches with the new Caliber 400 were launched. One goal in creating the movement was to eliminate problems even before they occur. Beat Fischli and his team needed five years to meet the established and defined criteria: five-day power reserve, special resistance to magnetic fields, chronometer rate accuracy, and high serviceability with long maintenance intervals of ten years.

The next logical step was the further development to the Caliber 401 and 403, which differ from the Caliber 400 by a subsidiary seconds dial at 6 o'clock and a date hand. The Caliber 400 family debuted in the Aquis series but has already been used in various editions of the Big Crown and Divers Sixty-Five series.

Oris SA
Ribigasse 1
CH-4434 Hölstein
Switzerland

Tel.:
+41-61-956-1111

E-mail:
MyOris@oris.ch

Website:
www.oris.ch

Founded:
1904

Number of employees:
210

U.S. distributor:
Oris Watches USA
50 Washington Street, Suite 302
Norwalk, CT 06854
203-857-4769

Most important collections/price range:
Divers Sixty-Five, Big Crown, Artelier, Aquis, ProPilot / approx. $1,300 to $10,300

Big Crown Calibre 473

Reference number: 01 473 7786 4065
Movement: hand-wound, Oris Caliber 473; ø 30 mm; 27 jewels; 28,800 vph; 120-hour power reserve
Functions: hours, minutes, subsidiary seconds; **power reserve indicator (on movement side); date Case:** stainless steel, ø 38 mm, height 11.8 mm; sapphire crystal; transparent case back; water-resistant to 5 atm
Band: deer skin, pin buckle
Price: $4,400

Oris X Cervo Volante

Reference number: 01 754 7779 4065-Set
Movement: automatic, Oris Caliber 754 (based on Sellita SW200-1); ø 25.6 mm, height 4.6 mm; 26 jewels; 28,800 vph; 38-hour power reserve
Functions: hours, minutes, sweep seconds; date
Case: stainless steel, ø 38 mm, height 12.8 mm; sapphire crystal; transparent case back; water-resistant to 5 atm
Band: deer skin, pin buckle
Price: $2,200
Variations: with green or grey dial

Big Crown ProPilot X Calibre 115

Reference number: 01 115 7759 7153
Movement: hand-wound, Oris Caliber 115; ø 34 mm, height 6 mm; 38 jewels; 21,600 vph; skeletonized movement, centralized, open spring barrel; 240-hour power reserve
Functions: hours, minutes, subsidiary seconds; power-reserve indicator
Case: titanium, ø 44 mm, height 12.5 mm; sapphire crystal; transparent case back; screw-in crown; water-resistant to 10 atm
Band: titanium, folding clasp
Remarks: skeletonized dial
Price: $8,000
Variations: with calfskin strap ($7,600)

ProPilot X Kermit Edition

Reference number: 01 400 7778 7157-Set
Movement: automatic, Oris Caliber 400;
ø 30 mm, height 4.75 mm; 21 jewels; 28,800 vph;
120-hour power reserve
Functions: hours, minutes, sweep seconds; date
Case: titanium, ø 39 mm, height 12 mm;
sapphire crystal; water-resistant to 10 atm
Band: titanium, folding clasp
Remarks: Kermit, the Frog (from the Muppets) appears
in the date window on the first of the month
Price: $4,600

ProPilot Altimeter

Reference number: 01 793 7775 8764-Set
Movement: automatic, Oris Caliber 793 (based on
Sellita SW300-1); ø 25.6 mm, height 3.6 mm; 25 jewels;
28,800 vph; 56-hour power reserve
Functions: hours, minutes, sweep seconds;
barometric altimeter; date
Case: carbon fiber, ø 47 mm; sapphire crystal;
water-resistant to 10 atm
Band: textile, folding clasp
Price: $6,500

Aquis Date Calibre 400

Reference number: 01 400 7763 4157
Movement: automatic, Oris Caliber 400;
ø 30 mm, height 4.75 mm; 21 jewels; 28,800 vph;
120-hour power reserve
Functions: hours, minutes, sweep seconds; date
Case: stainless steel, ø 43.5 mm, height 13.5 mm;
unidirectional bezel with ceramic insert, with
0-60 scale; sapphire crystal; screw-in crown;
water-resistant to 30 atm
Band: stainless steel, folding clasp, with safety lock
and extension link
Price: $3,700

AquisPro 4000m

Reference number: 01 400 7777 7155-Set
Movement: automatic, Oris Caliber 400;
ø 30 mm, height 4.75 mm; 21 jewels; 28,800 vph;
120-hour power reserve
Functions: hours, minutes, sweep seconds; date
Case: stainless steel, ø 49.5 mm, height 23.4 mm;
unidirectional bezel with ceramic insert, with
0-60 scale; sapphire crystal; screw-in crown;
water-resistant to 400 atm
Band: rubber, folding clasp, with safety lock and
extension link
Price: $6,200

Big Crown ProPilot Big Date bronze

Reference number: 01 751 7761 3164-07 3 2003BRLC
Movement: automatic, Oris Caliber 751 (based on
Sellita SW220-1); ø 32.2 mm, height 5.05 mm; 26 jewels;
28,800 vph; 38-hour power reserve
Functions: hours, minutes, sweep seconds; date
Case: bronze, ø 41 mm, height 12 mm; sapphire crystal;
transparent case back; screw-in crown;
water-resistant to 10 atm
Band: textile, folding clasp
Price: $2,300

Divers Sixty-Five Glow

Reference number: 01 733 7707 4053-07 5 20 89
Movement: automatic, Oris Caliber 733 (based on
Sellita SW200-1); ø 25.6 mm, height 4.6 mm; 26 jewels;
28,800 vph; 38-hour power reserve
Functions: hours, minutes, sweep seconds
Case: stainless steel, ø 40 mm, height 13 mm;
unidirectional bezel with 0-60 scale; sapphire crystal;
screw-in crown; water-resistant to 10 atm
Band: calfskin, folding clasp, with extension link
Price: $2,250
Variations: with stainless steel bracelet ($2,420)

PANERAI

Officine Panerai (in English: Panerai Workshops) joined the Richemont Group in 1997. Since then, it has made an unprecedented rise from an insider niche brand to a lifestyle phenomenon. The company, founded in 1860 by Giovanni Panerai, supplied the Italian navy with precision instruments. In the 1930s, the Florentine engineers developed a series of waterproof wristwatches that could be used by commandos under especially extreme and risky conditions. After 1997, under the leadership of Angelo Bonati, the company came out with a collection of oversize wristwatches, both stylistically and technically based on these historical models.

In 2002, Panerai opened a *manufacture* in Neuchâtel, and by 2005 it was already producing its own movements (caliber family P.2000). In 2009, the new "little" Panerai *manufacture* movements (caliber family P.9000) were released. From the start, the idea behind them was to provide a competitive alternative to the base movements available until a couple of years ago. In 2014, a new *manufacture* was inaugurated in Neuchâtel to bring development, manufacturing, assembly, and quality control under one roof.

Parallel to consolidating, the brand has been steadily expanding its portfolio of new calibers. Fairly early on, it came out with an automatic chronograph with a flyback function, the P.9100. This was followed by a string of new calibers, almost one per year, to gradually replace "foreign" movements. Notorious is the P.4000, with an off-center winding rotor. At 3.95 millimeters, it is very thin for Panerai, but then again, it was developed for a new set of models.

The idea of sustainability is continuing to spread among watch manufacturers. Panerai's new eLAB-ID concept watch bears the tagline "Do you want to be part of the solution?" It is made of over ninety-eight percent recycled materials: titanium for the case, sapphire for the glass, silicon for the escapement, PET bottles for the strap, Super-LumiNova for the dial. Only 30 pieces were produced, but Panerai has another solution, too: it uses recycled steel scrap for the case of the new Luminor Marina eSteel.

Officine Panerai
Viale Monza, 259
I-20126 Milan
Italy

Tel.:
+39-02-363-138

Website:
www.panerai.com

Founded:
1860 in Florence, Italy

Number of employees:
Around 1,000 employees

U.S. distributor:
Panerai
645 Fifth Avenue
New York, NY 10022
877-PANERAI
concierge.usa@panerai.com;
www.panerai.com

Most important collections/price range:
Luminor / $5,000 to $25,000; Luminor / $8,000 to $30,000; Radiomir / $8,000 to $133,000; special editions / $10,000 to $125,000; clocks and instruments / $20,000 to $250,000

Submersible QuarantaQuattro

Reference number: PAM01229
Movement: automatic, Panerai Caliber P.900; ø 28 mm, 19 mm, height 4.2 mm; 23 jewels; 28,800 vph; 72-hour power reserve
Functions: hours, minutes, subsidiary seconds; date
Case: stainless steel, ø 44 mm, height 13.35 mm; unidirectionally rotating bezel, with 0-60 scale; sapphire crystal; crown with crown guard and hinged lever; water-resistant to 30 atm
Band: rubber, buckle
Price: $9,500

Submersible QuarantaQuattro Carbotech Blu Abisso

Reference number: PAM01232
Movement: automatic, Panerai Caliber P.900; ø 28.19 mm, height 4.2 mm; 23 jewels; 28,800 vph; 72-hour power reserve
Functions: hours, minutes, subsidiary seconds; date
Case: composite material, ("Carbotech"), ø 44 mm, height 14.25 mm; unidirectionally rotating bezel, with 0-60 scale; sapphire crystal; crown with crown guard and hinged lever; water-resistant to 30 atm
Band: rubber, buckle
Price: $18,600

Submersible QuarantaQuattro

Reference number: PAM01226
Movement: automatic, Panerai Caliber P.900; ø 28.19 mm, height 4.2 mm; 23 jewels; 28,800 vph; 72-hour power reserve
Functions: hours, minutes, subsidiary seconds; date
Case: stainless steel, ø 44 mm, height 13.35 mm; unidirectionally rotating bezel, with 0-60 scale; sapphire crystal; crown with crown guard and hinged lever; water-resistant to 30 atm
Band: rubber, buckle
Price: $9,900

Radiomir Quaranta Goldtech

Reference number: PAM01026
Movement: automatic, Panerai Caliber P.900;
ø 28,19 mm, height 4.2 mm; 23 jewels; 28,800 vph;
72-hour power reserve
Functions: hours, minutes, subsidiary seconds; date
Case: rose gold ("Goldtech"), ø 40 mm, height 10.5 mm;
sapphire crystal; transparent case back; water-resistant
to 5 atm
Band: reptile skin, pin buckle
Price: $18,200

Luminor Due Luna Goldtech

Reference number: PAM01181
Movement: automatic, Panerai Caliber P.900/MP;
ø 28,19 mm, height 5.9 mm; 23 jewels; 28,800 vph;
72-hour power reserve
Functions: hours, minutes, subsidiary seconds;
moon phase
Case: rose gold ("Goldtech"), ø 38 mm; sapphire
crystal; transparent case back; crown with crown
guard and hinged lever; water resistant to 5 atm
Band: reptile skin, pin buckle
Remarks: mother-of-pearl-dial
Price: $21,500

Luminor Chrono

Reference number: PAM01109
Movement: automatic, Panerai Caliber P.9200;
ø 31 mm, height 6.9 mm; 41 jewels; 28,800 vph;
42-hour power reserve
Functions: hours, minutes, subsidiary seconds;
chronograph
Case: stainless steel, ø 44 mm, height 15.65 mm;
sapphire crystal; crown with crown guard and hinged
lever; water-resistant to 10 atm
Band: reptile skin, pin buckle
Remarks: comes with additional rubber strap
Price: $10,000

Radiomir Otto Giorni

Reference number: PAM01348
Movement: hand-wound, Panerai Caliber P.5000;
ø 34.9 mm, height 4.5 mm; 21 jewels; 21,600 vph;
2 spring barrels, 192-hour power reserve
Functions: hours, minutes, subsidiary seconds
Case: recycled steel, ø 45 mm; sapphire crystal;
transparent case back; water-resistant to 10 atm
Band: calfskin, pin buckle
Price: $9,700

Radiomir California

Reference number: PAM01349
Movement: hand-wound, Panerai Caliber P.5000;
ø 34.9 mm, height 4.5 mm; 21 jewels; 21,600 vph;
2 spring barrels, 192-hour power reserve
Functions: hours, minutes
Case: recycled steel, ø 45 mm; sapphire crystal;
water-resistant to 10 atm
Band: calfskin, pin buckle
Remarks: a California dial combines Arabic and
Roman numerals
Price: $12,300

Radiomir Calendario Annuale "Experience"

Reference number: PAM01432
Movement: automatic, Panerai Caliber P.9010/AC;
ø 31 mm, height 7.9 mm; 40 jewels; 28,800 vph; 2 spring
barrels; 72-hour power reserve
Functions: hours, minutes, subsidiary seconds; annual
calendar with date, weekday, month
Case: platinum ("Platinumtech"), ø 45 mm; sapphire
crystal; transparent case back; water-resistant to 10 atm
Band: reptile skin, folding clasp
Remarks: purchase of an "Experience Edition" comes
with an individual guided tour of Rome. The trip can
only be booked at Panerai boutiques.
Price: $88,900

Luminor Quaranta

Reference number: PAM01370
Movement: automatic, Panerai Caliber P.900;
ø 28.19 mm, height 4.2 mm; 23 jewels; 28,800 vph;
72-hour power reserve
Functions: hours, minutes, subsidiary seconds; date
Case: stainless steel, ø 40 mm, height 12.45 mm;
sapphire crystal; crown with crown guard and hinged
lever; water-resistant to 10 atm
Band: reptile skin, pin buckle
Price: $7,800

Luminor Quaranta

Reference number: PAM01372
Movement: automatic, Panerai Caliber P.900;
ø 28,19 mm, height 4.2 mm; 23 jewels; 28,800 vph;
72-hour power reserve
Functions: hours, minutes, subsidiary seconds; date
Case: stainless steel, ø 40 mm, height 12.45 mm;
sapphire crystal; crown with crown guard and hinged
lever; water-resistant to 10 atm
Band: reptile skin, pin buckle
Price: $7,800

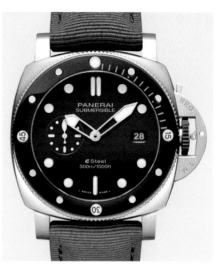

Submersible QuarantaQuattro eSteel Verde Smeraldo

Reference number: PAM01287
Movement: automatic, Panerai Caliber P.900;
ø 28,19 mm, height 4.2 mm; 23 jewels; 28,800 vph;
72-hour power reserve
Functions: hours, minutes, subsidiary seconds; date
Case: recycled steel, ø 44 mm, height 13.35 mm;
unidirectional bezel with ceramic insert, with
0-60 scale; sapphire crystal; crown with crown guard
and hinged lever; water-resistant to 30 atm
Band: recycled textile, pin buckle
Price: $11,600

Submersible QuarantaQuattro eSteel Grigio Roccia

Reference number: PAM01288
Movement: automatic, Panerai Caliber P.900;
ø 28.19 mm, height 4.2 mm; 23 jewels; 28,800 vph;
72-hour power reserve
Functions: hours, minutes, subsidiary seconds; date
Case: recycled steel, ø 44 mm, height 13.35 mm;
unidirectional bezel with ceramic insert, with
0-60 scale; sapphire crystal; crown with crown guard
and hinged lever; water-resistant to 30 atm
Band: recycled textile, pin buckle
Price: $11,600

Luminor Marina eSteel Verde Smeraldo

Reference number: PAM01356
Movement: automatic, Panerai Caliber P.9010; ø 31 mm,
height 6 mm; 31 jewels; 28,800 vph; 2 spring barrels,
72-hour power reserve
Functions: hours, minutes, subsidiary seconds; date
Case: recycled steel, ø 44 mm, height 15.45 mm;
sapphire crystal; crown with crown guard and hinged
lever; water-resistant to 30 atm
Band: recycled textile, folding clasp
Price: $9,400
Variations: with blue or grey strap and dial

Luminor Marina eSteel Blu Profondo

Reference number: PAM01157
Movement: automatic, Panerai Caliber P.9010; ø 31 mm,
height 6 mm; 31 jewels; 28,800 vph; 2 spring barrels,
72-hour power reserve
Functions: hours, minutes, subsidiary seconds; date
Case: recycled steel, ø 44 mm, height 15.45 mm;
sapphire crystal; crown with crown guard and hinged
lever; water-resistant to 30 atm
Band: recycled textile, folding clasp
Price: $9,400
Variations: with green or grey strap and dial

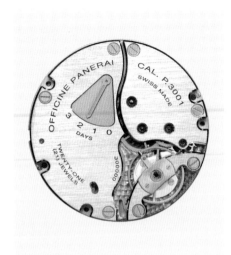

Caliber P.3001

Hand-wound; double, serially arranged spring barrel, 72-hour power reserve
Functions: hours, minutes, subsidiary seconds; power reserve indicator (on the rear)
Diameter: 37.2 mm
Height: 6.3 mm
Jewels: 21
Balance: glucydur
Frequency: 21,600 vph
Remarks: 213 parts

Caliber P.4001

Automatic; micro-rotor; crown-activated stop-seconds mechanism and zero-reset; double spring barrel, 72-hour power reserve
Functions: hours, minutes, subsidiary seconds; additional 24-hour display (2nd time zone), power reserve indicator (on back); date
Diameter: 30 mm
Height: 5.04 mm
Jewels: 31
Balance: glucydur
Frequency: 28,800 vph
Hairspring: flat hairspring
Shock protection: Kif
Remarks: 278 parts

Caliber P.6000

Hand-wound; single spring barrel, 72-hour power reserve
Functions: hours, minutes, subsidiary seconds
Diameter: 34.9 mm
Height: 4.5 mm
Jewels: 19
Balance: glucydur
Frequency: 21,600 vph
Shock protection: Incabloc
Remarks: 110 parts

Caliber P.9010

Automatic; double, serially arranged spring barrel, 72-hour power reserve
Functions: hours, minutes, subsidiary seconds; date
Diameter: 31 mm
Height: 6 mm
Jewels: 31
Balance: Glucydur
Frequency: 28,800 vph
Remarks: 200 parts

Caliber P.2004

Hand-wound; column wheel control of the chronograph-functions, single pusher; 3 serially connected barrel springs, 192-hour power reserve
Functions: hours, minutes, subsidiary seconds; additional 12-hour indication (second time zone), day/night indication, power reserve indication; chronograph
Diameter: 34.9 mm
Height: 8.2 mm
Stones: 29
Balance: glucydur, with variable inertia
Frequency: 28.800 A/h
Remarks: zero position of the second hand when pulling the crown ("Zero Reset" function); 333 parts

Caliber P.4001

Automatic; microrotor; crown-activated stop-seconds mechanism and zero-reset; double spring barrel, 72-hour power reserve
Functions: hours, minutes, subsidiary seconds; additional 24-hour display (2nd time zone), power reserve indicator (on back); date
Diameter: 30 mm
Height: 5.04 mm
Jewels: 31
Balance: glucydur
Frequency: 28,800 vph
Hairspring: flat hairspring
Shock protection: Kif
Remarks: 278 parts

PARMIGIANI

What began as the undertaking of a single man—a gifted watchmaker and reputable restorer of complicated vintage timepieces—in the small town of Fleurier in Switzerland's Val de Travers has now grown into an empire of sorts comprising several factories and more than 400 employees.

Michel Parmigiani is in fact just doing what he has done since 1976, when he began restoring vintage works. An exceptional talent, his output soon attracted the attention of the Sandoz Family Foundation, an organization established by a member of one of Switzerland's most famous families in 1964. The foundation bought 51 percent of Parmigiani Mesure et Art du Temps SA in 1996, turning what was practically a one-man show into a full-fledged and fully financed watch *manufacture*.

After the merger, Swiss suppliers were acquired by the partners, furthering the quest for horological autonomy. Atokalpa SA in Alle (Canton of Jura) manufactures parts such as pinions, wheels, and micro components. Bruno Affolter SA in La Chaux-de-Fonds produces precious metal cases, dials, and other specialty parts. Les Artisans Boitiers (LAB) and Quadrance et Habillage (Q&H) in La Chaux-de-Fonds manufacture cases out of precious metals and dials as well. Elwin SA in Moutier specializes in turned parts. In 2003, the movement development and production department officially separated from the rest as Vaucher Manufacture, now an autonomous entity with a sterling reputation.

Montre Hermès has also held a stake in Vaucher Manufacture, securing the supply of custom watchmaking technology and leather straps for its ambitious model policy.

Parmigiani has enjoyed great independence and was growing strongly for a while, notably in the United States. The old partnership with Bugatti was terminated and more emphasis placed on watches that can be used daily and are not quite what the rest of the industry considers "sportive." Under CEO Guido Terreni, the Tonda PF collection was redesigned, for instance, and given new complications, including a time zone watch with a split-seconds (rattrapante) mechanism for rapidly resetting the second local time.

Parmigiani Fleurier SA
Rue du Temple 11
CH-2114 Fleurier
Switzerland

Tel.:
+41-32-862-6630

E-mail:
info@parmigiani.ch

Website:
www.parmigiani.ch

Founded:
1996

Number of employees:
425

Annual production:
approx. 6,000 watches

U.S. distributor:
Parmigiani Fleurier Distribution Americas LLC
2655 S. Le Jeune Road
Penthouse 1G
Coral Gables, FL 33134
305-260-7770; 305-269-7770
americas@parmigiani.com

Most important collections/price range:
Chronor, Kalpa, Tonda, Toric / approx. $15,000 to
$80,000 for core collections, $300,000+ for *haute
horlogerie* watches; no limit for unique models

Tonda PF Gregorian Calendar

Reference number: PFC907-1020001-100182
Movement: automatic, Parmigiani Caliber PF339;
ø 27.1 mm, height 5.5 mm; 32 jewels; 28,800 vph;
rose gold skeletonized rotor; 50-hour power reserve
Functions: hours, minutes, sweep seconds; annual
calendar with date, weekday, month, moon phase
Case: stainless steel, ø 42 mm, height 11.1 mm; bezel
in platinum; sapphire crystal; transparent case back;
water-resistant to 10 atm
Band: stainless steel, folding clasp
Price: $39,300

Tonda PF Minute Rattrapante

Reference number: PFC904-1020001-100182
Movement: automatic, Parmigiani Caliber PF052;
ø 32 mm, height 4.9 mm; 32 jewels; 21,600 vph;
rose gold micro-rotor, finely finished movement;
48-hour power reserve
Functions: hours, minutes; additional adjustable
minute hand with pusher-activated reset
(split-seconds function)
Case: stainless steel, ø 40 mm, height 10.7 mm;
sapphire crystal; transparent case back; rose gold
pusher; water-resistant to 6 atm
Band: stainless steel, folding clasp
Price: $30,600

Tonda PF Micro-Rotor Platinum

Reference number:
Movement: automatic, Parmigiani Caliber PF703;
ø 30 mm, height 3 mm; 29 jewels; 21,600 vph;
platinum micro-rotor; 48-hour power reserve
Functions: hours, minutes; date
Case: platinum, ø 40 mm, height 7.8 mm; sapphire
crystal; transparent case back; water-resistant to 10 atm
Band: platinum, folding clasp
Price: $92,800

Tonda PF Flying Tourbillon

Reference number: PFH921-2020002-200182
Movement: automatic, Parmigiani Caliber PF517;
ø 32 mm, height 3.4 mm; 29 jewels; 21,600 vph;
flying tourbillon; platinum micro-rotor, finely finished
movement; 48-hour power reserve
Functions: hours, minutes, subsidiary seconds
(on the tourbillon cage)
Case: platinum, ø 42 mm, height 8.6 mm; sapphire
crystal; transparent case back; water-resistant to 10 atm
Band: platinum, white-gold folding clasp
Remarks: limited to 25 pieces
Price: $163,700

Tonda PF Split-Seconds Chronograph

Reference number: PFH916-2010002-200182
Movement: hand-wound, Parmigiani Caliber PF361;
ø 30.6 mm, height 8.45 mm; 35 jewels; 36,000 vph;
skeletonized bridges; 65-hour power reserve;
COSC-certified chronometer
Functions: hours, minutes, subsidiary seconds;
split-seconds chronograph
Case: rose gold, ø 42 mm, height 15 mm; sapphire
crystal; transparent case back; water-resistant to 10 atm
Band: rose gold, folding clasp
Price: $169,100

Tonda PF Xiali Calendar

Reference number: PFK999-2020001-200182
Movement: automatic, Parmigiani Caliber PF008;
ø 32.6 mm, height 6.9 mm; 42 jewels; 28,800 vph;
48-hour power reserve
Functions: hours, minutes, sweep seconds; full
calendar with date, weekday, month, moon phase
(Chinese calendar)
Case: platinum, ø 42 mm, height 11.2 mm; sapphire
crystal; transparent case back; water-resistant to 10 atm
Band: platinum, folding clasp in white gold
Price: $65,300

Tonda PF Micro-Rotor

Reference number: PFC914-1020001-100182
Movement: automatic, Parmigiani Caliber PF703;
ø 30 mm, height 3 mm; 29 jewels; 21,600 vph;
platinum micro-rotor; 48-hour power reserve
Functions: hours, minutes; date
Case: stainless steel, ø 40 mm, height 7.8 mm; sapphire
crystal; transparent case back; water-resistant to 10 atm
Band: stainless steel, folding clasp
Price: $24,000

Tonda PF Micro-Rotor

Reference number: PFC914-2020001-300182
Movement: automatic, Parmigiani Caliber PF703;
ø 30 mm, height 3 mm; 29 jewels; 21,600 vph;
platinum micro-rotor; 48-hour power reserve
Functions: hours, minutes; date
Case: rose gold, ø 40 mm, height 7.8 mm; sapphire
crystal; transparent case back; water-resistant to 10 atm
Band: reptile skin, folding clasp
Price: $40,400
Variations: with rose gold bracelet ($56,800)

Tonda PF Sport Automatic

Reference number: PFC930-1020001-400182
Movement: automatic, Parmigiani Caliber PF770/4100;
ø 25.6 mm, height 3.9 mm; 29 jewels; 28,800 vph;
skeletonized rotor with rose gold oscillating mass;
finely finished movement; 60-hour power reserve
Functions: hours, minutes, sweep seconds; date
Case: stainless steel, ø 41 mm, height 9.8 mm; sapphire
crystal; transparent case back; water-resistant to 10 atm
Band: rubber, folding clasp
Price: $24,000

Tonda PF Automatic 36mm

Reference number: PFC804-2020001-200182
Movement: automatic, Parmigiani Caliber PF777; ø 30 mm, height 3.9 mm; 29 jewels; 28,800 vph; skeletonized rotor in rose gold; 60-hour power reserve
Functions: hours, minutes
Case: rose gold, ø 36 mm, height 8.6 mm; sapphire crystal; transparent case back; water-resistant to 10 atm
Band: rose gold, double folding clasp
Remarks: dial with baguette diamond indices
Price: $54,400

Tonda PF GMT Rattrapante

Reference number: PFC905-1020001-100182
Movement: automatic, Parmigiani Caliber PF051; ø 30 mm, height 4.9 mm; 31 jewels; 21,600 vph; rose gold micro-rotor, finely finished movement; 48-hour power reserve
Functions: hours, minutes; additional 12-hour display (2nd time zone), with pusher reset (split-seconds function)
Case: stainless steel, ø 40 mm, height 10.7 mm; sapphire crystal; transparent case back; rose gold pusher; water-resistant to 6 atm
Band: stainless steel, folding clasp
Price: $29,500

Tonda PF Chronograph

Reference number: PFC915-1020001-100182
Movement: automatic, Parmigiani Caliber PF070; ø 30.6 mm, height 6.95 mm; 42 jewels; 36,000 vph; skeletonized bridges, skeletonized rose gold rotor; 65-hour power reserve; COSC-certified chronometer
Functions: hours, minutes, subsidiary seconds; chronograph; date
Case: stainless steel, ø 42 mm, height 12.4 mm; sapphire crystal; transparent case back; water-resistant to 10 atm
Band: stainless steel, folding clasp
Price: $30,000

Tonda PF Sport Chronograph

Reference number: PFC931-2020001-400182
Movement: automatic, Parmigiani Caliber PF070/6710; ø 30.6 mm, height 6.95 mm; 42 jewels; 36,000 vph; skeletonized rotor with rose gold-oscillating mass, finely finished movement; 65-hour power reserve
Functions: hours, minutes, subsidiary seconds; chronograph; date
Case: rose gold, ø 42 mm, height 12.9 mm; sapphire crystal; transparent case back; water-resistant to 10 atm
Band: rubber, folding clasp
Price: $52,200

Tonda PF Skeleton

Reference number: PFC912-2020001-200182
Movement: automatic, Parmigiani Caliber PF777; ø 30 mm, height 3.9 mm; 29 jewels; 28,800 vph; skeletonized and blackened movement, skeletonized rotor in rose gold; 60-hour power reserve
Functions: hours, minutes
Case: rose gold, ø 40 mm, height 8.4 mm; sapphire crystal; transparent case back; water-resistant to 10 atm
Band: rose gold, folding clasp
Price: $102,600
Variations: in stainless steel ($67,700)

Tonda PF Annual Calendar Rose Gold

Reference number: PFC907-2020001-200182
Movement: automatic, Parmigiani Caliber PF339; ø 27.1 mm, height 5.5 mm; 32 jewels; 28,800 vph; skeletonized rotor in rose gold; 50-hour power reserve
Functions: hours, minutes, sweep seconds; annual calendar with date, weekday, month, moon phase
Case: rose gold, ø 42 mm, height 11.1 mm; sapphire crystal; transparent case back; water-resistant to 10 atm
Band: rose gold, folding clasp
Price: $78,600

Caliber PF051

Automatic; platinum micro-rotor; single spring barrel, 48-hour power reserve
Functions: hours, minutes; additional 12-hour display (second time zone); pusher activated zero-reset (split seconds function)
Diameter: 30 mm
Height: 4.9 mm
Jewels: 31
Frequency: 21,600 vph
Remarks: 207 parts

Caliber PF052

Automatic; rose gold micro-rotor; single spring barrel, 48-hour power reserve
Functions: hours, minutes; additional minute hand with zero reset (split-seconds function)
Diameter: 32 mm
Height: 4.9 mm
Jewels: 32
Frequency: 21,600 vph

Caliber PF703

Automatic; platinum micro-rotor; single spring barrel, 48-hour power reserve
Functions: hours, minutes; date
Diameter: 30 mm
Height: 3 mm
Jewels: 29
Frequency: 21,600 vph
Remarks: 176 parts

Caliber PF517

Automatic; flying tourbillon, platinum micro-rotor; single spring barrel, 48-hour power reserve
Functions: hours, minutes, subsidiary seconds (on the tourbillon cage)
Diameter: 32 mm
Height: 3.4 mm
Jewels: 29
Frequency: 21,600 vph
Remarks: 205 parts

Caliber PF361

Hand-wound; control through two column wheels; skeletonized movement; rose gold mainplate and bridges; single spring barrel, 65-hour power reserve
Functions: hours, minutes, subsidiary seconds; split-seconds chronograph; large date
Diameter: 30.6 mm
Height: 8.45 mm
Jewels: 35
Frequency: 36,000 vph
Remarks: 317 parts

Caliber PF339

Automatic; skeletonized rotor; double spring barrel, 50-hour power reserve; COSC-certified chronometer, Qualité Fleurier
Functions: hours, minutes, sweep seconds; annual calendar with date, weekday, month, moon phase
Diameter: 27.1 mm
Height: 5.5 mm
Jewels: 32
Frequency: 28,800 vph

Patek Philippe SA
Chemin du pont-du-centenaire 141
CH-1228 Plan-les-Ouates
Switzerland

Tel.:
+41-22-884-20-20

Website:
www.patek.com

Founded:
1839

Number of employees:
approx. 2,000 (estimated)

Annual production:
approx. 60,000 watches worldwide per year

U.S. distributor:
Patek Philippe USA
45 Rockefeller Center, Suite 401
New York, NY 10111
212-218-1240

Most important collections
Aquanaut, Calatrava, Ellipse, Gondolo / ladies'
timepieces

...us as the last ...vith two Polish ...Czapek. In 1845, ...her in the mas- ...nding and time- ...ating high-quality ...s. Even among its

...enri and grandson ...mpany through the ...t in line, also Henri,

...ultramodern facilities. ...premises in Geneva, ...single roof with an op- ...ub between La Chaux- de-Fonds anu Lu... ...red, cases are polished, and gem setting is done.

PARMIGIANI

While Patek Philippe's main headquarters rem... the *manufacture* no lon- ger really has a need for that city's famed quality seal: all oi its mechanical watches now feature the "Patek Philippe Seal," the criteria for which far exceed the requirements of the Poinçon de Genève and include specifications for the entire watch, not just the movement. Among the most recent creations to make that grade is the World Time Chro- nograph, a masterful extension of the company's large range of chronographs. To make space, there is no second hand and only a thirty-minute counter. A moving city ring and twenty-four-hour ring have a place on the dial as well, and the whole piece is just over 12 millimeters high.

Chronograph Perpetual Calendar

Reference number: 5270P-014
Movement: hand-wound, Patek Philippe Caliber CH 29-535 PS Q; ø 32 mm, height 7 mm; 33 jewels; 28,800 vph; 55-hour power reserve
Functions: hours, minutes, subsidiary seconds; day/ night indicator; chronograph; perpetual calendar with date, weekday, month, moon phase, leap year
Case: platinum, ø 41 mm, height 12.4 mm; sapphire crystal; transparent case back; water-resistant to 3 atm
Band: reptile skin, folding clasp
Price: $218,820

Chronograph

Reference number: 5172G-010
Movement: hand-wound, Patek Philippe Caliber CH 29-535 PS; ø 29.6 mm, height 5.35 mm; 33 jewels; 28,800 vph; Breguet hairspring, column-wheel control of chronograph functions; 65-hour power reserve
Functions: hours, minutes, subsidiary seconds; chronograph
Case: white gold, ø 41 mm, height 11.45 mm; sapphire crystal; transparent case back; water-resistant to 3 atm
Band: reptile skin, folding clasp
Price: $82,800

World Time Watch

Reference number: 5230P-001
Movement: automatic, Patek Philippe Caliber 240 HU; ø 27.5 mm, height 3.88 mm; 33 jewels; 21,600 vph; silicon Spiromax hairspring, with gold micro-rotor; 48-hour power reserve
Functions: hours, minutes; world time display (2nd time zone)
Case: platinum, ø 38.5 mm, height 10.23 mm; pusher-activated scale ring with reference cities; sapphire crystal; transparent case back; water-resistant to 3 atm
Band: calfskin, folding clasp
Price: $73,330

World Time Watch Flyback Chronograph

Reference number: 5935A-001
Movement: automatic, Patek Philippe Caliber CH 28-520 HU; ø 33 mm, height 7.97 mm; 38 jewels; 28,800 vph; silicon Spiromax hairspring, gold rotor; 50-hour power reserve
Functions: hours, minutes; world time display, day/night indicator (2nd time zone); flyback chronograph
Case: stainless steel, ø 41 mm, height 12.75 mm; pusher-activated scale ring with reference cities; sapphire crystal; transparent case back; water-resistant to 3 atm
Band: calfskin, folding clasp
Remarks: comes with additional calfskin strap in other colors
Price: $63,870

Calatrava Pilot Travel Time chronograph

Reference number: 5924G-010
Movement: automatic, Patek Philippe Caliber 28-520 C FUS; ø 31 mm, height 6.95 mm; 34 jewels; 28,800 vph; silicon Spiromax hairspring, gold rotor; 45-hour power reserve
Functions: hours, minutes; additional 12-hour display (crown-activated second time zone); flyback chronograph; date
Case: white gold, ø 42 mm, height 13.05 mm; sapphire crystal; transparent case back; water-resistant to 3 atm
Band: calfskin, pin buckle
Price: $75,700

Flyback Chronograph Annual Calendar

Reference number: 5905R-010
Movement: automatic, Patek Philippe Caliber CH 28-520 QA 24H; ø 33 mm, height 7.68 mm; 37 jewels; 28,800 vph; Silicon Spiromax hairspring, gold rotor; 45-hour power reserve
Functions: hours, minutes; flyback chronograph; annual calendar with date, weekday, month Case: rose gold, ø 42 mm, height 14.03 mm; sapphire crystal; transparent case back; water-resistant to 3 atm
Band: reptile skin, pin buckle
Price: $75,110

Calatrava

Reference number: 4997/200R-001
Movement: automatic, Patek Philippe Caliber 240; ø 27.5 mm, height 2.53 mm; 27 jewels; 21,600 vph; silicon Spiromax hairspring, off-center gold mini-rotor; 48-hour power reserve
Functions: hours, minutes
Case: rose gold, ø 35 mm, height 7.4 mm; bezel with 76 diamonds; sapphire crystal; transparent case back; water-resistant to 3 atm
Band: calfskin with satin overlay, pin buckle
Price: $38,440

Calatrava

Reference number: 6007G-001
Movement: automatic, Patek Philippe Caliber 26-330 S C; ø 27 mm, height 3.3 mm; 30 jewels; 28,800 vph; silicon Spiromax hairspring, gold rotor; 35-hour power reserve
Functions: hours, minutes, sweep seconds; date
Case: white gold, ø 40 mm, height 9.17 mm; sapphire crystal; transparent case back; water-resistant to 3 atm
Band: calfskin with imprinted carbon fiber motif, pin buckle
Price: $37,850

Calatrava

Reference number: 5226G-001
Movement: automatic, Patek Philippe Caliber 26-330 S C; ø 27 mm, height 3.3 mm; 30 jewels; 28,800 vph; silicon Spiromax hairspring, gold rotor; 35-hour power reserve
Functions: hours, minutes, sweep seconds; date
Case: white gold, ø 40 mm, height 8.53 mm; sapphire crystal; transparent case back; water-resistant to 3 atm
Band: calfskin, pin buckle
Price: $40,220

Nautilus Moon Phase

Reference number: 5712/1R-001
Movement: automatic, Patek Philippe Caliber 240 PS IRM C LU; ø 31 mm, height 3.98 mm; 29 jewels; 21,600 vph; silicon Spiromax hairspring, off-center gold mini-rotor; 38-hour power reserve
Functions: hours, minutes, subsidiary seconds; power-reserve indicator; date, moon phase Case: rose gold, ø 40 mm, height 8.52 mm; sapphire crystal; transparent case back; screw-in crown; water-resistant to 6 atm
Band: rose gold, folding clasp
Price: $82,800

Nautilus Flyback Chronograph Travel Time

Reference number: 5990/1A-011
Movement: automatic, Patek Philippe Caliber CH 28-520 C FUS; ø 31 mm, height 6.95 mm; 34 jewels; 28,800 vph; Silicon Spiromax hairspring, gold rotor; 45-hour power reserve
Functions: hours, minutes, subsidiary seconds; additional 12-hour display (2nd time zone), day/night indicator (crown activated); flyback chronograph; date
Case: stainless steel, ø 40.5 mm, height 12.53 mm; sapphire crystal; transparent case back; screw-in crown; water-resistant to 12 atm
Band: stainless steel, folding clasp
Price: $68,600

Nautilus

Reference number: 5811/1G-001
Movement: automatic, Patek Philippe Caliber 26-330 S C; ø 27 mm, height 3.3 mm; 30 jewels; 28,800 vph; silicon Spiromax hairspring, gold rotor; 35-hour power reserve
Functions: hours, minutes, sweep seconds; date
Case: white gold, ø 41 mm, height 8.2 mm; sapphire crystal; transparent case back; screw-in crown; water-resistant to 12 atm
Band: white gold, folding clasp
Price: $69,790

Aquanaut Luce

Reference number: 5268/200R-010
Movement: automatic, Patek Philippe Caliber 26-330 S C; ø 27 mm, height 3.3 mm; 30 jewels; 28,800 vph; silicon Spiromax hairspring, gold rotor; 35-hour power reserve
Functions: hours, minutes, sweep seconds; date
Case: rose gold, ø 38.8 mm, height 8.5 mm; bezel with 48 diamonds; sapphire crystal; transparent case back; screw-in crown; water-resistant to 12 atm
Band: rubber, folding clasp
Price: $53,820

Aquanaut chronograph

Reference number: 5968R-001
Movement: automatic, Patek Philippe Caliber CH 28-520 C; ø 30 mm, height 6.63 mm; 32 jewels; 28,800 vph; 45-hour power reserve
Functions: hours, minutes, chronograph; date
Case: rose gold, ø 42.2 mm, height 11.9 mm; sapphire crystal; transparent case back; screw-in crown; water-resistant to 12 atm
Band: rubber, folding clasp
Price: $75,700

Aquanaut Luce Annual calendar

Reference number: 5261R-001
Movement: automatic, Patek Philippe Caliber 26-330 S QA LU; ø 30 mm, height 5.32 mm; 34 jewels; 28,800 vph; silicon Spiromax hairspring, gold rotor; 35-hour power reserve
Functions: hours, minutes, sweep seconds; annual calendar with date, weekday, month, moon phase
Case: rose gold, ø 39.9 mm, height 10.9 mm; sapphire crystal; transparent case back; water-resistant to 3 atm
Band: rubber, folding clasp
Price: $61,510

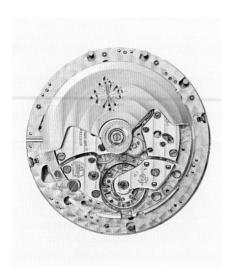

Caliber 324 S Q

Automatic; gold rotor; single spring barrel, 35-hour power reserve
Functions: hours, minutes, sweep seconds; day/night indicator; perpetual calendar with date, weekday, month, moon phase, leap year
Diameter: 32 mm
Height: 4.97 mm
Jewels: 29
Frequency: 28,800 vph

Caliber 31-260 PS QA LU FUS 24H

Automatic; platinum micro-rotor; single spring barrel, 38-hour power reserve
Functions: hours, minutes, subsidiary seconds; additional 12-hour display (2nd time zone), day/night indicator (local and home time); annual calendar with date, weekday, month, moon phase
Diameter: 33 mm
Height: 5.6 mm
Jewels: 47
Balance: Gyromax
Frequency: 28,800 vph
Hairspring: Spiromax silicon spring
Remarks: 409 parts

Caliber CH 29-535 PS

Hand-wound; column-wheel control of chronograph functions, exact jumping 30-minute counter; single spring barrel, 65-hour power reserve
Functions: hours, minutes, subsidiary seconds; split-seconds chronograph
Diameter: 29.6 mm
Height: 7.1 mm
Jewels: 34
Balance: Gyromax, 4-armed, with 4 regulating weights
Frequency: 28,800 vph
Hairspring: Breguet
Shock protection: Incabloc
Remarks: 312 parts

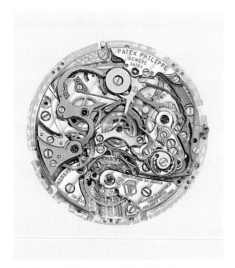

Caliber CHR 29-535 PS Q

Hand-wound; two column wheels to control chronograph functions, flyback mechanism with isolator; single spring barrel, 65-hour power reserve
Functions: hours, minutes, subsidiary seconds; day/night indicator; flyback chronograph; perpetual calendar with date, weekday, month, moon phase, leap year
Diameter: 32 mm
Height: 8.7 mm
Jewels: 34
Balance: Gyromax, 4-armed, with 4 regulating weights
Frequency: 28,800 vph
Hairspring: Breguet
Remarks: 496 parts, including 182 for perpetual calendar and 42 for flyback mechanism with isolator

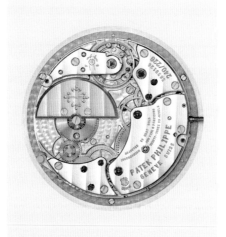

Caliber 240 HU

Automatic; 22-kt gold unidirectional off-center winding micro-rotor on ball-bearings; single spring barrel, 48-hour power reserve
Functions: hours, minutes; world-time display (second time zone)
Diameter: 27.5 mm
Height: 3.88 mm
Jewels: 33
Balance: Gyromax
Frequency: 21,600 vph
Remarks: 239 parts

Caliber CH 28-520 HU

Automatic; single barrel spring, 50-hour power reserve
Functions: hours, minutes, world time indicator (second time zone); flyback chronograph
Diameter: 33 mm
Height: 7.97 mm
Jewels: 38
Balance: Gyromax
Frequency: 28,800 vph
Hairspring: Spiromax silicon spring
Remarks: 343 parts very fine movement finishing

Caliber 26-330 S C

Automatic; gold rotor; single spring barrel, 35-hour power reserve
Functions: hours, minutes, sweep seconds;
date Diameter: 27 mm
Height: 3.3 mm
Jewels: 30
Balance: Gyromax
Frequency: 28,800 vph
Hairspring: Spiromax silicon spring
Remarks: 212 parts

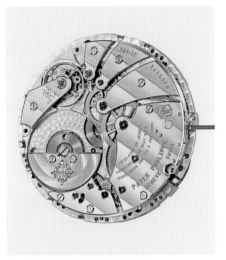

Caliber 31-260 PS FUS 24H

Automatic; platinum micro-rotor; single spring barrel, 48-hour power reserve
Functions: hours, minutes, subsidiary seconds; additional 24-hour display (2nd time zone for local and home time)
Diameter: 31.74 mm
Height: 3.7 mm
Jewels: 44
Balance: Gyromax
Frequency: 28,800 vph
Hairspring: Spiromax silicon spring
Remarks: 240 parts

Caliber CH 28-520 QA 24H

Automatic; gold rotor; single spring barrel, 45-hour power reserve
Functions: hours, minutes; flyback chronograph; annual calendar with date, weekday, month
Diameter: 33 mm
Height: 7.68 mm
Jewels: 37
Frequency: 28,800 vph
Hairspring: Spiromax silicon spring

Caliber CH 28-520 C

Automatic; single spring barrel, 45-hour power reserve
Functions: hours, minutes; chronograph; date
Diameter: 30 mm
Height: 6.63 mm
Jewels: 32
Balance: Gyromax
Frequency: 28,800 vph
Hairspring: Spiromax silicon spring
Remarks: 308 parts

Caliber 240 PS IRM C LU

Automatic; gold micro-rotor; single spring barrel, 38-hour power reserve
Functions: hours, minutes, subsidiary seconds; power-reserve indicator; date, moon phase
Diameter: 31 mm
Height: 3.98 mm
Jewels: 29
Balance: Gyromax, with 8 "masselotte" regulating screws
Frequency: 21,600 vph
Hairspring: Spiromax silicon spring
Shock protection: Kif
Remarks: 265 parts

Caliber 324 S QA LU 24H-303

Automatic; central rotor in 21-karat gold; single spring barrel, 45-hour power reserve
Functions: hours, minutes, sweep seconds; additional 24-hour display (2nd time zone); annual calendar with date, weekday, month, moon phase
Diameter: 32.6 mm
Height: 5.78 mm
Jewels: 34
Balance: Gyromax
Frequency: 28,800 vph
Hairspring: Spiromax silicon spring
Remarks: 347 parts

Paul Gerber
Uhren Konstruktionen
Bockhornstrasse 69
CH-8047 Zürich
Switzerland

Tel.:
+41-44-401-4569

E-mail:
info@gerber-uhren.ch

Website:
www.gerber-uhren.ch

Founded:
1976

Annual production:
up to 50 watches

U.S. distributor:
Intro Swiss—Michel Schmutz
Michel Schmutz
6271 Corinth Rd.
Longmont, CO 80503
303-652-1520
introswiss@gmail.com

Most important collections/price range:
mechanical watches / from approx. $5,175 to
$22,000; tourbillon desk clocks / from approx.
$48,000 to $70,000

PAUL GERBER

In a world that often values hype more than the real thing, people like watchmaker Paul Gerber tend to get overlooked. And it's a shame, because this man, who works out of his basement, where he seems to be puttering around, has encyclopedic knowledge and experience of the industry. He has already developed a vast array of mechanisms and complications, including calendar movements, alarms, and tourbillons, for many brands. Gerber is the one who designed the complicated calendar mechanism for the otherwise minimalist MIH watch conceived by Ludwig Oechslin, curator of the International Museum of Horology (MIH) in La Chaux-de-Fonds and himself a watchmaker. To avoid cluttering a dial for a special customer, he recently devised a battery-run moon phase that fits in the watch strap. His work has twice appeared in *Guinness World Records*.

When his daily work for others lets up, Gerber gets around to building watches bearing his own name with such marvelous features as a retrograde second hand in an elegant thin case and a synchronously, unidirectional rotor system with miniature oscillating weights for his self-winding Retro Twin model. Gerber's works are all limited editions.

After designing a tonneau-shaped hand-wound wristwatch with a three-dimensional moon phase display, Gerber created a simple three-hand watch with an automatic movement conceived and produced completely in-house. It features a 100-hour power reserve and is wound by three synchronically turning gold rotors. Gerber also offers the triple rotor and large date features in a watch with an ETA movement and lightweight titanium case as a classic pilot watch design or in a version with a more modern dial (the Synchron model). The Model 41 has an optional complication that switches the second hand from sweep to dead-beat motion by way of a pusher at 2 o'clock.

Gerber is allegedly retired. But a watchmaker never really retires. Besides continuing to produce outstanding pieces, he occasionally gives three-day workshops for people wanting to get a real feel for the work.

Retrograd

Reference number: 152
Movement: hand-wound, Gerber Caliber 15 (base ETA 7001); ø 28 mm, 2.9 mm; 21 jewels; 21,600 vph
Functions: hours, minutes, subsidiary seconds (retrograde)
Case: yellow gold, ø 36 mm, height 8.5 mm sapphire crystal; transparent case back; water-resistant to 3 atm
Band: reptile skin, buckle
Price: $17,350
Variations: rose gold ($17,350)

Modell 42

Reference number: 420 pilot
Movement: automatic, Gerber Caliber 42 (base ETA 2824); ø 36 mm, height 6.1 mm; 25 jewels; 28,800 vph; automatic winding with 3 synchronously rotating gold rotors
Functions: hours, minutes, sweep seconds; large quick-set date
Case: titanium, ø 42 mm, height 12 mm; sapphire crystal; transparent case back; screw-in crown; water-resistant to 10 atm
Band: calfskin, buckle
Price: $4,900
Variations: synchron ($5,175); pilot's/synchron DaN (day and night) ($6,150); pilot's/synchron DT (Dual Time, $6,100)

Modell 42

Reference number: 420 DaN pilot
Movement: automatic, Gerber Caliber 42 (base ETA 2824); ø 36 mm, height 6.1 mm; 25 jewels; 28,800 vph; automatic winding with 3 synchronously rotating gold rotors
Functions: hours, minutes, sweep seconds; day/night indicator; date
Case: titanium, ø 42 mm, height 12 mm; sapphire crystal; transparent case back; screw-in crown; water-resistant to 10 atm
Band: calfskin, buckle
Price: $6,150
Variations: pilot's/synchron dial ($5,175); as Caliber42 pilot's/synchron Dual Time ($6,100)

PEQUIGNET

The Jura mountains, which saddle Switzerland and France, are not only home to inventive and dogged craftspeople, notably watchmakers, on the Swiss side. In 1973, in Morteau, a small town close to the border, one Emile Pequignet founded a watch and jewelry company producing contemporary pieces that caught the spirit of the age and enjoyed a fair success. In 2004, Pequignet himself retired and sold the brand to one Didier Leibundgut. This whole industry was bursting with energy, creating bigger and crazier watches. Pequignet steered a more conservative course and maintained its classic look. But it did develop its own manufacture movement, investing millions into the Calibre Royal.

The elaborate automatic movement is subject to eight patents. It can drive various functions, like a full calendar with moon phase or a power reserve indicator to tell the wearer how many of the 100 hours the large spring barrel delivers have been used up. Since it does not need any modules, the movement is quite thin and can be configured for other functions quite easily. These functions are available in the Royale Sapphire collection.

The Calibre Royal reinvigorated the company, but it also cost inordinate amounts of money. The decade following was spent under the threat of liquidation. Finally, in December 2021, it was announced that a family fund had purchased the brand and the majority shareholder, Hugues Souparis, was now the new CEO. Morteau (pop. around 6,900) breathed a sigh of relief: maintaining the last independent French watch brand is a matter of honor in the region.

Pequignet still has quite a wide range of collections, but, as a dyed-in-the-wool *manufacture*, focus has been on the calibers inside. In 2021, it released the Calibre Initial, which now drives the Concorde collection.

Montres Péquignet
1, rue du Bief
F-25503 Morteau
France

Tel:
+33 381 67 30 66

E-mail:
contact@pequignet.com

Website:
www.pequignet.com

Founded:
1973

Number of employees:
50

U.S. distributor:
About Time Luxury Group
210 Bellevue Avenue
Newport, RI 02840
401-846-0598

Most important collections / price range:
Men's and women's watches from $1,700 to $12,000

Royale Sapphire Ombres et Lumières
Reference number: 9010833 AGR
Movement: automatic, Calibre Royal EPM01; ø 30 mm, height 5.88 mm; 39 jewels; 21,600 vph; large spring barrel; finely finished with chamfered edges and perlage; 72-hour power reserve
Functions: hours, minutes, subsidiary seconds; power-reserve indicator; large date and weekday, moon phase
Case: stainless steel, ø 42 mm, height 12.3 mm; sapphire crystal; transparent case back; water-resistant to 5 atm
Band: reptile skin, double folding clasp
Remarks: multi-part, translucent sapphire crystal dial
Price: $12,000
Variations: various colors

Concorde Imperial Green
Reference number: 9046493
Movement: automatic, Calibre Initial EPM03; ø 25.6 mm, height 4.2 mm; 21 jewels; 28,800 vph; skeletonized winding rotor; 65-hour power reserve
Functions: hours, minutes, sweep seconds; date
Case: stainless steel, ø 36 mm, height 9.25 mm; sapphire crystal; transparent case back; water-resistant to 10 atm
Band: stainless steel, folding clasp
Price: $4,600
Variations: various colors

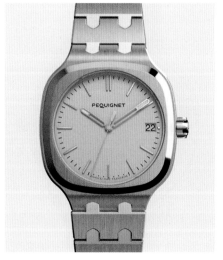

Concorde Pink
Reference number: 9046483
Movement: automatic, Calibre Initial EPM03; ø 25.6 mm, height 4.2 mm; 21 jewels; 28,800 vph; skeletonized winding rotor; 65-hour power reserve
Functions: hours, minutes, sweep seconds; date
Case: stainless steel, ø 36 mm, height 9.25 mm; sapphire crystal; transparent case back; water-resistant to 10 atm
Band: stainless steel, folding clasp
Price: $4,600
Variations: various colors

Perrelet SA
Rue Bubenberg 7
CH-2502 Biel/Bienne
Switzerland

Tel.:
+41-32-346-2626

Fax:
+41-32-346-2627

E-mail:
perrelet@perrelet.com

Website:
www.perrelet.com

Founded:
brand founded in 1777, acquired by Festina Group
in 2004

U.S. distributor:
Perrelet USA
2937 SW 27th Avenue Suite 102
Miami FL 33133
305-588-3628
info@perreletusa.com

Most important collections:
LAB, Turbine, First Class, Diamond Flower,
Weekend

PERRELET

The Perrelet story will sound familiar to anyone who has read about Swiss watchmaking. Abraham-Louis Perrelet (1729–1826) was the son of a middle-class farmer from Le Locle who developed an interest in watchmaking early on in life. He was the first watchmaker in Le Locle to work on cylinder and duplex escapements, and there is a persistent rumor that he was responsible for a repeater that could be heard echoing in the mountains.

Many watchmakers who later became famous were at one time apprenticed to Perrelet, and some historians even suggest that Abraham-Louis Breguet was in this illustrious group. Suffice to say, Perrelet invented a great deal, including the "perpetual" watch from around 1770, a pocket watch that wound itself using the motion of the wearer.

When the brand hit the market in 1995, it came out with a double rotor and a movement, the P-181, which made waves in the industry. The Turbine soon followed, featuring a kind of jet engine fan that decoratively turns over the dial, creating all sorts of effects and giving lots of potential for creative designing. It was all creative and successful enough to attract the attention of Festina Group, which purchased the brand in 2004.

After a few years of silence, during which the company reorganized its distribution network, Perrelet returned to the watch world, having also made improvements to its automatic movements to ensure that their precision was at COSC level. The revised automatic P-411 still drives the LAB, cleverly designed to show the rotor just under a transparent dial. The turbines are back, with that attractive hallmark animation on the dial, driven by the caliber P-331-MH with COSC certificate. The fan-shaped wheel on the upper part of the dial, which rotates at full speed depending on the movements of the wrist, creates fascinating and original visual effects depending on the decoration of the dial below.

LAB Peripheral Dual Time Big Date

Reference number: A1101/5
Movement: automatic, Perrelet Caliber P-421;
ø 34.8 mm, height 6.32 mm; 30 jewels; 28,800 vph;
hubless peripheral rotor; 42-hour power reserve
Functions: hours, minutes, sweep seconds; additional
12-hour display (second time zone, complete set of
hands); day/night indication; large date
Case: stainless steel, ø 42 mm, height 13.5 mm;
sapphire crystal; transparent case back;
water-resistant to 5 atm
Band: calfskin, folding clasp
Remarks: oscillating mass of the hubless rotor visible
on the dial side
Price: $4,980
Variations: with blue, silver, and black dial

Turbine Carbon Midnight Blue

Reference number: A4065/2
Movement: automatic, Perrelet Caliber P-331-
MH (based on Soprod); ø 26.2 mm, height 3.6 mm;
25 jewels; 28,800 vph; 42-hour power reserve;
COSC-certified chronometer
Functions: hours, minutes, sweep seconds
Case: polycarbonate and carbon fiber composite,
ø 44 mm, height 13.82 mm; bezel in stainless steel with
black PVD; sapphire crystal; transparent case back;
water-resistant to 10 atm
Band: calfskin with rubber lining, folding clasp
Remarks: "turbine" animation of anodized aluminum
on the dial (no winding function)
Price: $4,750
Variations: with green dial and strap

Weekend GMT Ice Blue

Reference number: A1304/A
Movement: automatic, Perrelet Caliber P-401 (based
on Soprod); ø 26.2 mm, height 4.25 mm; 25 jewels;
28,800 vph; 42-hour power reserve
Functions: hours, minutes, sweep seconds; additional
24-hour display (2nd time zone); date
Case: stainless steel, ø 39 mm, height 9.5 mm;
sapphire crystal; transparent case back;
water-resistant to 5 atm
Band: calfskin, pin buckle
Price: $1,780
Variations: with blue, black, green or silver dial;
with stainless steel bracelet ($1,880)

PHOENIX WATCH COMPANY

Phoenix Watch Company
333 Washington Street, Suite 634
Boston, MA 02108
USA

Tel:
855-928-2411

Email:
info@phoenixwatchco.com

Website:
www.phoenixwatchco.com

Founded:
2022

Annual production:
250 Watches

Most important collection/price:
Eagle series / $4,680

Getting a brand off the ground always requires founders who know what they are doing. In the case of Phoenix, which saw the light of day in 2022, it was a trio of experts from three key areas of the industry: a collector, a certified master watchmaker, and a member of the watch industry's fourth estate, namely marketing. The first series of the brand is one of the very popular genres: pilot's watches in the form of a chronograph.

The first flight of the Phoenix, as it were, is the Eagle, released in 2023. Essentially, it is a series of three dials, all of which embrace the look and feel of a retro-mod pilot's chronograph, while using a combination of components that take advantage of modern technology and techniques, with respect to historical references.

Design is nothing if the mechanics running a watch are weak, so the company decided to outfit the watches with La Joux Perret's caliber LJP 112. This particular movement is in fact an upgraded design based on the renowned Valjoux 7750 series. Improvements over the original include a power reserve extended to 60 hours, improved winding, stability, and shock resistance thanks to two additional ball bearings in the rotor system, and most critically, the transformation from a heart-cam system to a column-wheel control for the chronograph functions. The transparent case back allows one to see the well-decorated parts.

The unusual choice of an extra-tough authentic style acrylic crystal over the dial is interesting. It was chosen for its superior optical qualities and the fact that the material is functionally shatterproof. Acrylic (hesalite) crystals were de rigueur in the early days of watchmaking and are actually a better choice than sapphire in certain applications.

On the dial side, pilot's watches incorporate various telemeters, tachymeters, turn radius indicators and even circular slide rules—not because they look interesting on the dial, but because they were needed as either primary or backup sources for critical calculations. Today these various scales are rarely used for their ostensible purpose, yet they continue on as inspired designs recalling a more analog age.

Golden Eagle

Movement: automatic, La Joux-Perret Caliber L112); ø 34.40 mm, height 7.90 mm; 26 jewels; 28,800 vph; rotor decorated with côtes de Genève; column-wheel control of chronograph; 60-hour power reserve
Functions: hours, minutes, subsidiary seconds; chronograph
Case: stainless steel; ø 44 mm, height 13.20 mm; extra-thick, shatterproof crystal; transparent case back; water-resistant to 5 atm
Band: calfskin, pin buckle
Price: $4,690; limited to 100 pieces

Strike Eagle

Movement: automatic, La Joux-Perret Caliber L112); ø 34.40 mm, height 7.90 mm; 26 jewels; 28,800 vph; rotor decorated with côtes de Genève; column-wheel control of chronograph; 60-hour power reserve
Functions: hours, minutes, subsidiary seconds; chronograph
Case: stainless steel; ø 44 mm, height 13.20 mm; extra-thick, shatterproof crystal; transparent case back; water-resistant to 5 atm
Band: Milanese Stainless, pin buckle
Price: $4,690; limited to 100 pieces

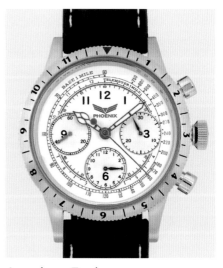

American Eagle

Movement: automatic, La Joux-Perret Caliber L112); ø 34.40 mm, height 7.90 mm; 26 jewels; 28,800 vph; rotor decorated with côtes de Genève; column-wheel control of chronograph; 60-hour power reserve
Functions: hours, minutes, subsidiary seconds; chronograph
Case: stainless steel; ø 44 mm, height 13.20 mm; extra-thick, shatterproof crystal; transparent case back; water-resistant to 5 atm
Band: calfskin, pin buckle
Price: $4,690; limited to 100 pieces

Piaget SA
CH-1228 Plan-les-Ouates
Switzerland

Tel.:
+41-32-867-21-21

E-mail:
info@piaget.com

Website:
www.piaget.com

Founded:
1874

Number of employees:
900

Annual production:
about 15,000 watches

U.S. distributor:
Piaget North America
645 5th Avenue, 6th Floor
New York, NY 10022
212-909-4362
www.piaget.com

Most important collections:
Altiplano, Polo S, Limelight, Possession

PIAGET

Piaget began making watch movements in the secluded Jura village of La Côte-aux-Fées in 1874. For decades, those movements were delivered to other watch brands. The *manufacture* itself, strangely enough, remained in the background. It wasn't until the 1940s that the Piaget family began to offer complete watches under their own name. Even today, Piaget, which long ago moved the business side of things to Geneva, still makes its watch movements at its main facility high in the Jura mountains.

In the late fifties, Piaget began investing in the design and manufacturing of ultrathin movements. This lends these watches the kind of understated elegance that became the company's hallmark. In 1957, Valentin Piaget presented the first ultrathin men's watch, the Altiplano, with the manual caliber 9P, which was 2 millimeters high. Shortly after, it came out with the 12P, an automatic caliber that clocked in at 2.3 millimeters.

The Altiplano has faithfully accompanied the brand for sixty years now. The movement has evolved over time. The recent 900P measures just 3.65 millimeters and is inverted to enable repairs, making the case back the mainplate with the dial set on the upper side.

Piaget is continuing to strive for thinner watches, even in the third millennium. The Altiplano Ultimate Concept, released in 2018, briefly set a world record as the thinnest mechanical watch with manual winding at two millimeters total height. It took four years of research and development.

In 2023, however, it was the Polo collection that experienced expansion, with filigree skeleton versions of the two-hand watch and an ultra-thin perpetual calendar with a movement height of just four millimeters.

Polo Perpetual Calendar Ultrathin

Reference number: G0A48005
Movement: automatic, Piaget Caliber 1255P;
ø 29.9 mm, height 4 mm; 25 jewels; 21,600 vph;
micro-rotor; perlage on mainplate, blued screws, finely
finished with côtes de Genève; 42-hour power reserve
Functions: hours, minutes; perpetual calendar with
date, weekday, month, moon phase, leap year
Case: stainless steel, ø 42.4 mm, height 8.65 mm;
sapphire crystal; transparent case back;
water-resistant to 3 atm
Band: stainless steel, folding clasp
Price: $60,000

Polo Date

Reference number: G0A47010
Movement: automatic, Piaget Caliber 1110P;
ø 25.58 mm, height 4 mm; 25 jewels; 28,800 vph;
perlage on mainplate, blued screws, finely finished
with côtes de Genève; 50-hour power reserve
Functions: hours, minutes, sweep seconds; date
Case: rose gold, ø 42 mm, height 9.4 mm; sapphire
crystal; transparent case back; water-resistant to 10 atm
Band: reptile skin, folding clasp
Price: $30,600

Polo Date

Reference number: G0A48022
Movement: automatic, Piaget Caliber 1110P;
ø 25,58 mm, height 4 mm; 25 jewels; 28,800 vph;
perlage on mainplate, blued screws, finely finished
with côtes de Genève; 50-hour power reserve
Functions: hours, minutes, sweep seconds; date
Case: stainless steel, ø 42 mm, height 9.4 mm;
sapphire crystal; transparent case back;
water-resistant to 10 atm
Band: rubber, folding clasp
Price: $13,300

Polo Skeleton

Reference number: G0A47008
Movement: automatic, Piaget Caliber 1200S1;
ø 29.9 mm, height 2.4 mm; 25 jewels; 21,600 vph;
skeletonized movement, mainplate and bridges with
green PVD; 44-hour power reserve
Functions: hours, minutes
Case: stainless steel, ø 42 mm, height 6.5 mm;
sapphire crystal; transparent case back
Band: stainless steel, folding clasp
Price: $33,100
Variations: with blue PVD

Polo chronograph

Reference number: G0A48024
Movement: automatic, Piaget Caliber 1160P;
ø 25,58 mm, height 5.72 mm; 35 jewels; 28,800 vph;
perlage on mainplate, blued screws, finely finished
with côtes de Genève; 50-hour power reserve
Functions: hours, minutes; chronograph; date
Case: stainless steel, ø 42 mm, height 11.2 mm;
sapphire crystal; transparent case back;
water-resistant to 10 atm
Band: rubber, folding clasp
Price: $19,500

Polo Date

Reference number: G0A47014
Movement: automatic, Piaget Caliber 1110P;
ø 25.58 mm, height 4 mm; 25 jewels; 28,800 vph;
perlage on mainplate, blued screws, finely finished
with côtes de Genève; 50-hour power reserve
Functions: hours, minutes, sweep seconds; date
Case: stainless steel, ø 42 mm, height 9.4 mm;
sapphire crystal; transparent case back;
water-resistant to 10 atm
Band: rubber, folding clasp
Price: $12,400

Altiplano Ultimate Automatic

Reference number: G0A48125
Movement: automatic, Piaget Caliber 910P; ø 41 mm,
height 4.3 (including case and sapphire crystal) mm;
30 jewels; 21,600 vph; inverted movement design as
a single unit with the case, hubless peripheral rotor;
50-hour power reserve
Functions: hours and minutes (off-center)
Case: rose gold, ø 41 mm, height 4,3 mm;
sapphire crystal
Band: reptile skin, pin buckle
Price: $35,300
Variations: in white gold ($35,300)

Possession

Reference number: G0A48080
Movement: quartz, Piaget Caliber 358P
Functions: hours, minutes
Case: stainless steel, ø 29 mm, height 7.5 mm; bezel
set with 46 diamonds; sapphire crystal; water-resistant
to 3 atm
Band: reptile skin, pin buckle
Remarks: mother-of-pearl-dial set with 11 diamonds
Price: $8,150

Polo Date 36mm

Reference number: G0A48026
Movement: automatic, Piaget Caliber 500P1;
ø 20.5 mm, height 3.4 mm; 26 jewels; 21,600 vph;
finely finished movement; 40-hour power reserve
Functions: hours, minutes, sweep seconds; date
Case: stainless steel, ø 36 mm, height 8.8 mm; bezel
in rose gold, with 60 diamonds; sapphire crystal;
transparent case back; rose gold crown;
water-resistant to 5 atm
Band: stainless steel with rose-gold elements,
folding clasp
Remarks: hour indices set with 36 diamonds
Price: $29,400
Variations: various cases, straps, and dials

PILO & CO SA
11 Faubourg-de-Cruseilles
CH-1227 Carouge
Switzerland

Tel.:
+41-22-328-0112

E-mail:
contact@pilo-watches.com

Website:
www.pilo-watches.com

Founded:
2001

Number of employees:
7

U.S. distribution:
Contact main office in Geneva
contact@pilo-watches.com

Most important collections/price range:
Mechanical and quartz watches: Allegra,
Corleone, Doppio Orario, Illusione, Invidia,
Montecristo, Tempo and Exceptional Pieces /
$300 - $5,000

PILO WATCHES

Brimming bank accounts held by mysterious and at times shady characters may not be Geneva's best-kept secret anymore, not in the age of leaks to the media. That is more like the cliché generated by countless spy movies and thrillers and due no doubt to the high concentration of international organizations in the city. Far less known is the fact that Geneva is a veritable hub of all sorts of crafts, notably those associated with watchmaking, and they were at one time concentrated in the district of St. Gervais and referred to as "Les Cabinotiers." Among them are little watch companies that continue to produce excellent timepieces and survive in the shadow of the big brands and groups that have also made the city their home.

One of these independent companies, Pilo & Co., celebrated its twentieth anniversary in 2021 with a get-together in St. Gervais, where it keeps one of two shops. It was founded by Amarildo Pilo, who, while not of Swiss origin, has a very Genevan story. His father was an Albanian diplomat who was called back when the government changed in his native country at the end of the 1980s. His two sons stayed to continue their studies. Amarildo decided on an internship with a watch distributor and ended up traveling a great deal, making numerous contacts, and falling in love with the watch world. One thing led to another, and in 2001 he opened his own brand, Pilo & Co.

Twenty-two years later, his brand is represented throughout Switzerland and has found faithful customers in Europe and in Asia. They manufacture quartz watches but have increasingly been using mechanical movements, which are modified and reworked. The dials, if not in brilliant ceramic colors, are often open-worked or fully skeletonized. The portfolio has now grown to fifteen collections of affordable watches that combine good looks with outstanding workmanship. The Extraneō, released in 2023 and coming in quite a few iterations, is in this style, with a two-level dial; clean, traditional decoration, and a mechanical heart.

Pieces d'Exception

Reference number: P0604HAS
Movement: automatic, Pilo Caliber PW01 Caliber; ø 25.60 mm, height 4.6 mm; 27 jewels; 28,800 vph; 40-hour power reserve
Functions: hours, minutes, sweep seconds; day, date, second time zone; power reserve indicator
Case: stainless steel black PVD, ø 44 mm, height 12.87 mm; sapphire crystal; transparent case back; water-resistant to 5 atm
Band: calfskin, folding clasp
Remarks: silver dial
Price: $5,280

Extraneō

Reference number: P0569HAGR
Movement: automatic, Caliber Soprod P024; ø 25.60 mm, 4.6 mm; 25 jewels; 28,800 vph; 38-hour power reserve
Functions: hours, minutes, sweep seconds
Case: rose gold PVD, ø 40 mm, height 10.7 mm; sapphire crystal; stainless steel case back; water-resistant to 5 atm
Band: rubber & calfskin, folding clasp
Price: $1,660

Tempo

Reference number: P0561HAS
Movement: automatic, modified ETA 2842/2; ø 25.60 mm, height 4.6 mm; 23 jewels; 28,800 vph; openworked ceramic dial; 38-hour power reserve
Functions: hours, minutes, sweep seconds
Case: stainless steel, ø 41 mm, height 9 mm; sapphire crystal; transparent case back; water-resistant to 3 atm
Band: calfskin, folding clasp
Remarks: ceramic dial
Price: $1,690

PORSCHE DESIGN

Porsche Lifestyle Group
Groenerstrasse 5
D-71636 Ludwigsburg
Germany

Tel.:
+49-711-911-0

E-mail:
contact@porsche-design.us

Website:
www.porsche-design.com

Founded:
1972

U.S. distributor:
Porsche Design of America, Inc.
600 Anton Blvd., Suite 1280
Costa Mesa, CA 92626
770-290-7500
timepieces@porsche-design.us
www.porsche-design.com

Most important collections:
Chronograph 1, custom-built timepieces with configurator, 1919 Collection, Chronotimer Flyback

In 1972, Professor Ferdinand Alexander Porsche founded his own design studio with the aim of creating technically inspired products beyond the world of vehicles. From the very beginning, Porsche Design was all about exploring new technical possibilities not only in watches but also in accessories. Just like the first Porsche 911, a key design object in recent history, the iconic Chronograph I was designed by Prof. F. A. Porsche. In 1972, the founder of Porsche Design followed a premise: "My aim was to create a watch to match the car."

The Chronograph I was a timeless sporty precision instrument whose design was derived from the dashboard gauges of the Porsche 911. It was the first time that the design, aesthetics, and functionality of a sports car were reproduced in a watch. The Chronograph I was also the world's first all-black wristwatch.

Porsche Design engineers still inspire themselves from the automobile industry when it comes to materials and functionality. At the heart of the development of the timepieces is the cooperation with Porsche Motorsport, which means that the latest racecar technologies are incorporated into the watches. (Lately, the interior leather has been used for straps, for example).. In keeping with this tradition, Porsche Design dedicated itself to the further development of engines, as it were, and has been relying on exclusive COSC-certified movements since 2017.

In collaboration with the engineers at the Porsche Development Center in Weissach (Germany), the company has produced technical masterpieces and unique calibers that impose Porsche's high quality to the "sports cars on your wrist."

The calibers include Caliber 01.200, with a complex flyback mechanism; Caliber 04.110, with a very clever GMT switching mechanism; and two other calibers, 01.100 and 03.100. Among the newer collections is the Chronograph I, a boldly sportive line with special models, such as the Chronograph 1 - All Black Numbered Edition and Chronograph 1 Utility – Limited Edition. And very much in the spirit of individualization, the company offers a configurator for a chronograph—an opportunity for those Porsche fans who want a genuinely unique piece at an affordable rate.

Chronograph 1 Utility – Limited Edition

Movement: automatic, Porsche Design Caliber WERK 01.240; ø 30 mm, height 7.9 mm; 25 jewels; 28,800 vph; 48-hour power reserve; COSC-certified chronometer
Functions: hours, minutes, sweep seconds, date
Case: titanium carbide with black titanium carbide coating, ø 42.7 mm, height 15.5 mm; sapphire crystal; screw-in crown; water-resistant to 10 atm
Band: calfskin, folding clasp
Price: $13,000; limited to 250 pieces

Chronograph 1 – All Black Numbered Edition

Movement: automatic, Porsche Design Caliber WERK 01.140; ø 30 mm, height 7.9 mm; 25 jewels; 28,800 vph; 48-hour power reserve; COSC-certified chronometer
Functions: hours, minutes, subsidiary seconds; chronograph; date and weekday
Case: titanium with black titanium carbide coating, ø 40.8 mm, height 14.15 mm; sapphire crystal; transparent case back; screw-in crown; water-resistant to 10 atm
Band: titanium with black titanium carbide coating, folding clasp
Price: $9,650; limited to 1,000 pieces per year

Chronograph 1 – 75 Year Porsche Edition

Movement: automatic, Porsche Design Caliber WERK 01.140; ø 30 mm, height 7.9 mm; 25 jewels; 28,800 vph; rotor shaped like the Porsche 911's wheel rim (the famous "Fuchsfelge"); 48-hour power reserve; COSC-certified chronometer
Functions: hours, minutes, subsidiary seconds; chronograph; date and weekday
Case: titanium with black titanium carbide coating, ø 40.8 mm, height 14.15 mm; sapphire crystal; transparent case back; screw-in crown; water-resistant to 10 atm
Band: textile and calfskin, folding clasp
Price: $11,000; limited to 475 pieces

Porsche Design Custom-built Chronograph

Movement: automatic, Porsche Design Caliber WERK 01.100; ø 30 mm, height 7.9 mm; 25 jewels; 28,800 vph; 48-hour power reserve; COSC-certified chronometer
Functions: hours, minutes, subsidiary seconds; chronograph; date
Case: titanium with optional black titanium carbide coating, ø 42 mm, height 15.33 mm; sapphire crystal; transparent case back; screw-in crown; water-resistant to 5 atm
Band: Porsche interior leather or titanium (natural or black titanium carbide coating), titanium double-folding clasp
Remarks: The Porsche Design online watch configurator allows for over 6 million design possibilities to create a unique watch.
Price: Starting at $5,500

Chronotimer Series 1 Flyback

Movement: automatic, Porsche Design Caliber WERK 01.200; ø 30 mm, height 7.9 mm; 25 jewels; 28,800 vph; 48-hour power reserve; COSC-certified chronometer
Functions: hours, minutes; rate control; flyback chronograph; date
Case: titanium with black titanium carbide coating, ø 42 mm, height 14.62 mm; sapphire crystal; transparent case back; screw-in crown; water-resistant to 5 atm
Band: rubber, folding clasp
Price: $6,700

Sport Chrono Subsecond 39 Titanium & Black

Movement: automatic, Porsche Design Caliber WERK 03.200; ø 25.6 mm, height 5.6 mm; 31 jewels; 28,800 vph; 38-hour power reserve; COSC-certified chronometer
Functions: hours, minutes, subsidiary seconds; date
Case: titanium, ø 39 mm, height 12.25 mm; sapphire crystal; screw-in crown; water-resistant to 10 atm
Band: calfskin, folding clasp
Price: $5,350
Variations: Titanium & Blue, Titanium & Brown

Sport Chrono Subsecond 42

Movement: automatic, Porsche Design Caliber WERK 03.200; ø 25.6 mm, height 5.6 mm; 31 jewels; 28,800 vph; 38-hour power reserve; COSC-certified chronometer
Functions: hours, minutes, subsidiary seconds; date
Case: titanium, ø 42 mm, height 12.25 mm; sapphire crystal; screw-in crown; water-resistant to 10 atm
Band: calfskin, folding clasp
Price: $5,350
Variations: Titanium & Black, Titanium & Brown

1919 Globetimer UTC All Titanium Blue

Movement: automatic, Porsche Design Caliber WERK 04.110; ø 28.5 mm, height 6.94 mm; 26 jewels; 28,800 vph; 38-hour power reserve; COSC-certified chronometer
Functions: hours, minutes, subsidiary seconds; date
Case: titanium, ø 42 mm, height 14.90 mm; sapphire crystal; screw-in crown; water-resistant to 10 atm
Band: calfskin, folding clasp
Price: $6,350
Variations: in brown, black, and all black

1919 Chronotimer Flyback

Movement: automatic, Porsche Design Caliber WERK 01.200; ø 30 mm, height 7.90 mm; 25 jewels; 28,800 vph; 48-hour power reserve; COSC-certified chronometer
Functions: UTC function, hours, minutes, sweep seconds; date
Case: titanium, ø 42 mm, height 14.9 mm; sapphire crystal; screw-in crown; water-resistant to 10 atm
Band: calfskin, folding clasp
Price: $6,350
Variations: various dials and straps

RADO

Rado is a relatively young brand, especially for a Swiss one. The company, which grew out of the Schlup clockwork factory, launched its first watches in 1957, but it achieved international fame only five years later, in 1962, when it surprised the world with a revolutionary invention. Rado's oval DiaStar was the first truly scratch-resistant watch ever, sporting a case made of a ceramic and tungsten carbide alloy. In 1985, its parent company, the Swatch Group, decided to put Rado's know-how and extensive experience in developing materials to good use, and from then on, the brand intensified its research activities at its home in Lengnau, Switzerland, and continued to produce only watches with extremely hard cases.

Rado distinguishes between two ceramic variants. The first is high-tech ceramic, which is heated to 1,450 °C and cools to a hard, durable surface. The second is plasma high-tech ceramic, which involves heating the watch case and bracelet links once again, but this time to 20,000 °C until the surface melts into a glass-hard layer.

The continuous research into hard materials has produced generations of collections of watches made of experimental ceramics. In 2011, for example, they produced the ultra-light Ceramos, which went into the D-Star collection. Rado also holds more than thirty patents.

A special material is worth nothing without a strict design code. The reborn diving watch classic, Captain Cook, is one way to present the modern ceramic development from the alchemist's kitchen of Comadur, a sister company within the Swatch Group.

Another is the eye-catching True Square collection, a comfortably wearable timepiece with a 38-millimeter edge length. It is available in black or in metallic shiny plasma ceramic. Further, the True Square and Captain Cook models as well as the brand-new DiaStar Original are now available with exclusive skeleton movements from the Group's sister company ETA.

Rado Uhren AG
Bielstrasse 45
CH-2543 Lengnau
Switzerland

Tel.:
+41-32-655-6111

E-mail:
info@rado.com

Website:
www.rado.com
store.us.rado.com

Founded:
1957

Number of employees:
approx. 470

U.S. distributor:
Rado
The Swatch Group (U.S.), Inc.
703 Waterford Way, Suite 450
Miami, FL 33126
786-725-5393

Most important collections/price range:
Hyperchrome / from approx $1,100; Diamaster / from approx. $1,500; Integral / from approx. $2,000; True Square / from approx. $1,400; Centrix / from approx. $800; Coupole Classic / from approx. $1,000; Tradition / from approx. $2,000

Captain Cook High-Tech Ceramic

Reference number: R32148162
Movement: automatic, ETA Caliber R808; ø 25.6 mm, height 4.74 mm; 25 jewels; 21,600 vph; skeletonized mainplate; 80-hour power reserve
Functions: hours, minutes, sweep seconds
Case: ceramic (plasma treated), ø 43 mm, height 14.6 mm; unidirectional bezel with rose gold PVD and ceramic insert, with 0-60 scale; sapphire crystal; transparent case back; screw-in crown; water-resistant to 30 atm
Band: ceramic (plasma treated), titanium triple folding clasp
Price: $4,400

True Square Skeleton

Reference number: R27124162
Movement: automatic, ETA Caliber R808; ø 25.6 mm, height 4.74 mm; 25 jewels; 21,600 vph; skeletonized mainplate; 80-hour power reserve
Functions: hours, minutes, sweep seconds
Case: ceramic, 38 x 44.2 mm, height 9.7 mm; sapphire crystal; transparent case back; water-resistant to 5 atm
Band: ceramic, titanium triple folding clasp
Remarks: skeletonized dial:
Price: $2,800

DiaStar Original Skeleton

Reference number: R12162153
Movement: automatic, ETA Caliber R808; ø 25.6 mm, height 4.74 mm; 25 jewels; 21,600 vph; skeletonized mainplate; 80-hour power reserve
Functions: hours, minutes, sweep seconds
Case: ceramic, ø 38 mm, height 11.9 mm; sapphire crystal; transparent case back; water-resistant to 10 atm
Band: stainless steel, folding clasp
Remarks: skeletonized dial
Price: $2,050

DiaStar Original

Reference number: R12163118
Movement: automatic, ETA Caliber R764;
ø 25.6 mm, height 4.74 mm; 25 jewels; 21,600 vph;
80-hour power reserve
Functions: hours, minutes, sweep seconds; date
Case: ceramic, ø 38 mm, height 12.3 mm; sapphire
crystal; transparent case back; water-resistant to 10 atm
Band: stainless steel, folding clasp
Remarks: 60th anniversary edition of the DiaStar;
comes with additional textile strap
Price: $2,050

True Square

Reference number: R27078172
Movement: automatic, ETA Caliber R763; ø 25.6 mm,
height 4.74 mm; 25 jewels; 21,600 vph; 80-hour power
reserve
Functions: hours, minutes, sweep seconds; date
Case: ceramic, 38 x 44.2 mm, height 9.7 mm;
sapphire crystal; water-resistant to 5 atm
Band: ceramic, titanium triple folding clasp
Price: $2,150

True Square Skeleton

Reference number: R27125152
Movement: automatic, ETA Caliber R808; ø 25.6 mm,
height 4.74 mm; 25 jewels; 21,600 vph; skeletonized
mainplate; 80-hour power reserve
Functions: hours, minutes, sweep seconds
Case: ceramic (plasma treated), 38 x 44.2 mm, height
9.7 mm; sapphire crystal; transparent case back;
water-resistant to 5 atm
Band: ceramic (plasma treated), titanium triple
folding clasp
Remarks: skeletonized dial
Price: $2,800

True Thinline x Great Gardens of the World

Reference number: R27113152
Movement: automatic, ETA Caliber R766;
ø 25.6 mm, height 4.74 mm; 25 jewels; 21,600 vph;
64-hour power reserve
Functions: hours, minutes
Case: ceramic, ø 40 mm, height 9 mm; sapphire
crystal; water-resistant to 3 atm
Band: ceramic, titanium triple folding clasp
Price: $2,700

Centrix

Reference number: R30018152
Movement: automatic, ETA Caliber R763;
ø 25.6 mm, height 4.74 mm; 25 jewels; 21,600 vph;
80-hour power reserve
Functions: hours, minutes, sweep seconds; date
Case: stainless steel, ø 39.5 mm, height 11.3 mm; bezel
in ceramic; sapphire crystal; transparent case back;
water-resistant to 5 atm
Band: stainless steel with ceramic elements,
triple folding clasp
Price: $2,000

Captain Cook

Reference number: R32136323
Movement: automatic, ETA Caliber R763;
ø 25.6 mm, height 4.74 mm; 25 jewels; 21,600 vph;
80-hour power reserve
Functions: hours, minutes, sweep seconds; date
Case: stainless steel with yellow-gold PVD, ø 42 mm,
height 12.3 mm; unidirectional bezel with ceramic
insert, with 0-60 scale; sapphire crystal; screw-in
crown; water-resistant to 30 atm
Band: stainless steel with yellow-gold PVD,
triple folding clasp
Price: $2,600

RAKETA WATCHES

Raketa Watch Factory LTD
Sankt-Peterburgskiy prospekt, 60
198516 St. Petersburg, Peterhof
Russia

Tel.:
+7-926-304-0591

E-mail:
info@raketa.com

Website:
www.raketa.com

Founded:
1721 /1961

U.S. distributor:
-

Most important collections/price range:
Avant-Garde, Space Launcher, Copernicus,
Baikonur, Russian Code / $ 800 to $3,750

The city of Saint Petersburg, known as Russia's cultural capital, is not that old. Its founding goes back to Czar Peter I, later known as "the Great," who was intent on modernizing his country and decided to have a city built that would face the West and reflect Western values. It was a costly enterprise, especially in lives, since the builders were serfs and the swampy area was rife with disease, but in the end, he got his city. He had a fleet built as well and, in 1721, opened a lapidary known as Petrodvorets (or Peter's Palace), which would later prepare precious stones for the czars.

That factory has had many lives in its three-hundred-year history. Since 1949, after restoration following destruction during World War II, it has been producing watches, first under the name Pobeda (Victory) and Zvezda (Star). On April 12, 1961, Yuri Gagarin orbited Earth once in the Vostok 1 spacecraft, opening the way to human space exploration. The following year saw the launch of the Raketa (rocket) brand at the Petrodvorets factory, which had quite a success with Soviet citizenry.

When David Henderson-Stewart, a young English businessman, visited the factory in 2010, the shine had gone under the onslaught of the free market. A few stalwart employees kept the home fires burning, but everything was run down. Though not from the watch world—an innocence he credits for his spontaneous decision and commitment—he saw the potential. Investors were found, experts brought in, and Raketa was put back into business with several rich collections all made totally in-house and visually unique. Soviet-era or Russian iconography are the main themes. There are military style 24-hour watches from the world of submariners, seamen, soldiers, and cosmonauts, like the Ekranoplan, which pays tribute to a huge hydroplane, or the Russian Code. And there are models honoring some of the artistic movements of the revolutionary era, like the Big Zero Malevich, named after a work by Kazimir Malevich, a founder of the Supremacist movement.

Russian Code 0286

Reference number: W-07-20-10-0286
Movement: automatic, Raketa 2615R (modified to turn counterclockwise); ø 26 mm, height 6.8; 24 jewels; 18,000 vph; rotor with hand-made Neva waves decoration and nanocoating; 40-hour power reserve
Functions: hours, minutes, sweep seconds
Case: stainless steel, ø 40.5 mm, height 16.55 mm; sapphire crystal; transparent case back (mineral glass); water-resistant to 5 atm
Band: leather, buckle
Remarks: replicates the counterclockwise movement of the Earth around the sun.
Price: $1,800; limited to 500 pieces

Ekranoplan 0287

Reference number: W-12-19-30-0287
Movement: automatic, Raketa Caliber 2624; ø 26mm, height 6.8 mm; 24 jewels; 18,000 vph; hand-made Neva waves decoration and nanocoating; 40-hour power reserve
Functions: 24-hour watch, minutes, sweep seconds
Case: stainless steel, ø 41.6 mm, height 14.9 mm; crown with ruby cabochon; sapphire crystal; transparent case back (mineral glass); water-resistant to 20 atm
Band: stainless steel bracelet with extra leather strap, buckle
Remarks: bezel made of metal from the Lun-class Ekranoplan; comes with an extra leather strap.
Price: $2,000; limited to 500 pieces

Big Zero 0283

Reference number: W-11-16-10-0283
Movement: automatic, Raketa 2615; ø 26 mm, height 6.8; 24 jewels; 18,000 vph; laser engraving, Neva waves, red rotor; 40-hour power reserve
Functions: hours, minutes, sweep seconds
Case: stainless steel, ø 40 mm, height 14.05 mm; sapphire crystal; ruby stone inside the crown; transparent case back (mineral glass); water-resistant to 10 atm
Band: leather, buckle
Remarks: "0" instead of "12" on the dial
Price: $1,450
Variations: various strap colors; white dial with black numerals

Reservoir Watch SAS
138, rue du Faubourg Saint-Honoré
F-75008 Paris
France

Tel:
+33 (0)1-42-89-11-79

E-mail:
contact@reservoir-watch.com

Website:
www.reservoir-watch.com

Founded:
2017

Number of employees:
10

U. S. Distributor:
Online sales
Timeless Distribution
contactUSA@reservoir-watch.com
305-588-3628

Most important collections/price range
Cars, Aeronautics, Marine, Music, Comics by
Reservoir / from $3,800

RESERVOIR

One of the most logical inspirations for watches is the humble gauge, and for good reason. It usually has a similar shape to a watch (round), and it serves to depict a certain event or action using a pointing device and numerals. It must also be legible at a glance. In addition, gauges tend to be found precisely where a mechanical process is taking place, and that excites the imagination of any person who appreciates the mesmerizing synergism of gears, cams, rackets, and other parts.

While gauges and meters are used fairly frequently as elements in watchmaking, only a few brands have actually made them the centerpiece of their design strategy. Reservoir, a French brand founded in 2017 by François Moreau, has taken this object mirroring to the nth degree, one could say. Connoisseurs of vintage British cars will easily spot the resemblance of many models to the odometers in the Mini Morris: a big round dial with a fuel gauge at the lower end. Since gauges usually have a single pointer, many Reservoir models have a retrograde minute hand with jumping hours in a separate window below the center. This basic dial serves as a visual pattern for three separate lines, namely air, land, and sea. Car, for example, is composed of three collections: GT Tour, Supercharged, and Longbridge. The latter even includes the oil and ignition lamps, a reminder of the original Smiths odometers used in, among others, the Morris Minor. The other lines are Aeronautic, with gauges from airplanes, and Marine, with, for instance, the Hydrosphere, a real diver's watch with a carefully planned out dial and a helium valve. In 2022, the company created a Music line, inspired from VU meters on hi-fi equipment to create a double retrograde chronograph with a dedicated caliber. Somewhat off-brand is the Comics line with comic strip figures appearing on the dial.

On the subject of movements: Reservoir uses basic ETA and La Joux-Perret movements with special modifications built by Télôs, an exclusive movement and module maker in La Chaux-de-Fonds that specializes in implementing the ideas, no matter how wild, of horological dreamers.

Battlefield D-Day

Reference number: RSV01.BF/230-62
Movement: automatic, Caliber RSV-240 based on La Joux-Perret LP G100; ø 25.6 mm, height 4.45 mm; 24 jewels; 28,800 vph, 56-hour power reserve
Functions: hours (jumping), retrograde minutes; world time with 24 reference locations
Case: stainless steel with gun metal PVD, ø 43 mm, height 12.8 mm; sapphire crystal, transparent case back; water-resistant to 5 atm
Band: leather, folding clasp
Remarks: sand-khaki dial; comes with extra NATO strap with quick release spring bars
Price: $4,400

Sonomaster Chronograph Vintage

Reference number: RSV04.SN/136.BL
Movement: automatic, RSV-Bi120 based on La Joux-Perret LJP-L1CO, ø 30.4 mm, height 7.9 mm; 28 jewels; 28,800 vph; bi-retrograde chronograph movement with column wheel control; 60-hour power reserve
Functions: hours, minutes, retrograde seconds (left side); chronograph with minute and hour totalizers at 12 and 6 o'clock respectively; retrograde date (right side)
Case: stainless steel, ø 43 mm, height 14.5mm; crowns and pushers inspired from level buttons; bezel with tachymeter scale; water-resistant to 5 atm
Band: leather, folding clasp
Remarks: dial design inspired from VU meters of analog recording equipment
Price: $5,750
Variations: in black ($5,750); with steel bracelet ($6,150)

Airfight Chronograph

Reference number: RSV02.AF/136.BL
Movement: automatic, RSV-Bi120 based on La Joux-Perret LJP-L1CO, ø 30.4 mm, height 7.9 mm; 28,800 vph; bi-retrograde chronograph movement with column wheel control; 60-hour power reserve
Functions: hours, minutes, retrograde seconds (left side); chronograph with minute and hour totalizers at 12 and 6 o'clock respectively; retrograde date (right side)
Case: stainless steel with black PVD, ø 43 mm, height 14.5 mm; bezel with tachymeter scale; sapphire crystal; transparent case back; water-resistant to 5 atm
Band: canvas and leather, folding clasp
Remarks: comes with NATO strap; dial inspired from Mustang-51 warbird gauges with green, orange, and red color scheme (for normal/danger/prohibited)
Price: $5,750
Variations: in steel without PVD ($5,750); with steel bracelet ($6,150)

RESSENCE

Belgian Benoit Mintiens had the luck of the newcomer at Baselworld 2010. He showed up at the last minute and found some space to show a strange watch he had conceived, with an almost two-dimensional dial. He returned in 2011 with the Type 1001. It consisted of a large rotating dial carrying a hand that pointed to a minute track on the bezel. Hours, small second, and a day/night indication rotated on dedicated subsidiary dials. All who beheld it were mesmerized. He sold all fifty of his models off the bat.

The mechanics behind the Ressence watches—the name is a compounding of Renaissance of the Essential—are simple: a stripped-down and rebuilt ETA 2824 leaves the minute wheel as the main driver of the other wheels.

In a bid to improve readability, he immersed the dial section in oil, giving the displays a very contemporary two-dimensional look, much like an electronic watch. The movement had to be kept separate from the oil and was connected to the dial using magnets and a set of superconductors and a Faraday cage to protect the movement from magnetism. Baffles compensate for the expanding and contracting of the oil due to temperature shifts. The Type 3 also lost the crown, the only obstacle to making a perfectly smooth watch, in favor of a clever setting and winding mechanism controlled by the case back.

The variations on the theme have been emerging from the Ressence studio at a regular pace. He started experimenting discreetly with the design, produced a diver's watch chic enough to wear for any occasion, and went a bit electronic with a thing called the e-Crown, which allows the wearer to reset the time electronically by discreetly tapping twice on the watch's crystal. Mintiens always preserves the special charm that comes from their rounded, gently curved shape on all sides without a glass holder rim. The curvature of the surface has a radius of 12.5 centimeters, which is approximately the half-diameter of a bowling ball. Lately, the dials have received carefully chosen colorings, or mosaics of luminous substance.

Ressence Watches
Meirbrug 1
2000 Antwerp
Belgium

Tel.:
+32-3-446-0060

E-mail:
hello@ressence.be

Website:
www.ressencewatches.com

Founded:
2010

U.S. distributor:
Totally Worth It (TWI2, Inc.)
76 Division Avenue
Summit, NJ 07901-2309
201-894-4710
724-263-2286
info@totallyworthit.com

Collection prices:
Type 1: $20,600; Type 2: $48,800; Type 3: $42,200;
Type 5: $35,800; Type 8 $15,000

Type 1 DX3

Movement: hand-wound, ROCS 1.3 (modified ETA 2892 caliber); ø 32 mm; 40 jewels; 28,800 vph; case back for winding and time setting; 27 gearwheels; 36-hour power reserve
Functions: hours, minutes, subsidiary seconds (Ressence Orbital Convex System: rotating minute dial with rotating satellites); weekday (off-center, orbiting)
Case: titanium, ø 42.7 mm, height 11 mm; sapphire crystal; splash-resistant to 1 atm
Band: rubber, pin buckle
Remarks: ROCS module propelled by magnetic drive; full-lume dial with cloisonné SuperLumiNova
Price: on request

Type 8S (Sage Green)

Movement: automatic, ROCS 8.1 (Modul, base ETA 2892/2); ø 32 mm; 31 jewels; 28,800 vph; case back for winding and time setting; gear train with 20 gearwheels; 36-hour power reserve
Functions: hours, minutes; Ressence Orbital Convex System (ROCS) rotating minute dial with 1 rotating satellite
Case: titanium, ø 42.9 mm, height 11 mm; sapphire crystal; splash-resistant to 1 atm
Band: leather, buckle
Price: $14,500

Type 3 EE (Eucalyptus)

Movement: automatic, ROCS 3.5 (modified ETA 2824-2 caliber); ø 32 mm; 47 jewels; 28,800 vph; case back for winding and time setting; 44 gearwheels; 36-hour power reserve
Functions: minutes, hours und 180 seconds "runner" (Ressence Orbital Convex System: rotating minute dial with rotating satellites); oil temperature; date and weekday
Case: titanium, ø 44 mm, height 15 mm; sapphire crystal; water-resistant to 1 atm
Band: synthetic, buckle
Remarks: 2 separately sealed case chambers; dial-side chamber filled with oil; display disks propelled by magnetic drive
Price: $43,800
Variations: black dial and black titanium case with black dial

RGM Watch Company
801 W. Main Street
Mount Joy, PA 17552
USA

Tel.:
717-653-9799

E-mail:
sales@rgmwatches.com

Web:
www.rgmwatches.com

Founded:
1992

Number of employees:
12

Annual production:
200–300 watches

Distribution:
RGM deals directly with customers
sales@rgmwatches.com

Most important collection/price range:
Pennsylvania Series (completely made in the U.S.) /
range of different models $2,500 to $125,000

RGM

The traditional values of hard work and persistence are alive and well in Roland Murphy, founder of RGM, one of the U.S.'s most famous and exclusive watch companies. Murphy, born in Maryland, went through the watchmaker's drill, studying at the Bowman Technical School, then in Switzerland, and finally working with Swatch before launching his own business in 1992 in Pennsylvania, which could be considered a kind of "watch valley."

The secret to his success, however, has always been to stay in touch with fundamental American values and icons. His first watch, the Signature, resurrected vintage pocket watch movements developed by Hamilton. The Railroad series today is run on restored Hamilton movements. His second big project was the Caliber 801, the first "high-grade mechanical movement made in series in America since Hamilton stopped production of the 992 B in 1969," Murphy shares with a grin. This was followed by an all-American-made watch, the Pennsylvania Tourbillon.

And so, model by model, Murphy continues to expand his "Made in U.S.A." portfolio. "You cannot compare us to the big brands," says Murphy. "We are small and specialized, the needs are different. We work directly with the customer." This may account for the brand's diversity. There are retro-themed watches, sports-themed watches (honoring baseball or chess), a diver's water-resistant to 70 atm, and the series 400 chronograph with a pulsometer and extra-large subdials for visibility.

Of late, Murphy has turned to the many crafts associated with watchmaking, notably engine-turned guilloché. He has also produced a series of dials with cloisonné enamel motifs or hand-painted images on mother of pearl. In 2023, for example, the Model 25 came out with a stone marquetry dial depicting a tiger.

Model 151-OP "Orange Pilot

Movement: automatic, RGM-Selitta Caliber 300-1; ø 25.6 mm, height 3.6 mm; 25 jewels; 28,800 vph; rhodium finish with perlage and côtes de Genève; up to 56-hour power reserve
Functions: hours, minutes, sweep seconds; date
Case: stainless steel, ø 38.50 mm, height 9.9 mm; sapphire crystal; transparent case back; water-resistant to 5 atm
Band: leather, pin buckle
Price: $3,250
Variations: titanium case ($4,250) optional brushed steel case

Model 25 "Tiger in Stone"

Reference number: Model 25
Movement: automatic, modified ETA Calibre 2892-A2 with solid gold in-house rotor; ø 25.6 mm; 21 jewels; 28,800 vph; rhodium finish with perlage and côtes de Genève; 42-hour power reserve
Functions: hours, minutes, sweep seconds
Case: stainless steel, ø 40 mm, height 10.4 mm; sapphire crystal; transparent case back; water-resistant to 5 atm
Band: calfskin, buckle
Remarks: stone marquetry tiger
Price: $15,900
Variations: custom dial design encouraged

Model 207-EB

Movement: automatic, RGM-Selitta Caliber 300-1; ø 25.6 mm, height 3.6 mm; 25 jewels; 28,800 vph; rhodium finish with perlage and côtes de Genève; up to 56-hour power reserve
Functions: hours, minutes, sweep seconds; date
Case: brushed or polished stainless steel, ø 35 mm, height 8.8 mm; sapphire crystal; transparent case back; water-resistant to 5 atm
Band: leather, pin buckle
Remarks: dial with barley guilloché and blue galvanic treatment
Price: $5,450
Variations: dial in silver; as Pilot ($2,950)

RICHARD MILLE

Mille never stops delivering the wow to the watch world with what he calls his "race cars for the wrist." He is not an engineer, however, but rather a marketing expert who earned his first paychecks in the watch division of the French defense, automobile, and aerospace concern Matra in the early 1980s. "I have no historical relationship with watchmaking whatsoever," says Mille, "and so I have no obligations either. The mechanics of my watches are geared towards technical feasibility."

His early work was with the wizards at Audemars Piguet Renaud & Papi (APRP) in Le Locle, who would take on the Mille challenge. Audemars Piguet even tested some of those scandalous innovations—materials, technologies, functions—in a Richard Mille watch before daring to use them in its own collections (Tradition d'Excellence).

In 2007, Audemars Piguet finally became a shareholder in Richard Mille, and so the three firms are now closely bound. The assembly of the watches is done in the Franches-Montagnes region in the Jura, where Richard Mille opened the firm Horométrie. These days, the watch business is in the hands of daughter Amanda and son Alexandre, so that the father has more time for his racing cars.

To keep its fans happy, the brand enjoys exploring the lunatic fringe of the technically possible. A collaboration with Airbus Corporate Jets gave rise to a case made of a lightweight titanium-aluminum alloy used in turbines. The superlight and tough material called graphene, developed at the University of Manchester, also found its way to Horometrie and McLaren. Richard Mille timepieces have survived on wrists of elite athletes, like tennis star Rafael Nadal and sprinter Yohan Blake. And if anyone thought Mille was ignoring the race to the thinnest watch being run by several big competitors, they have been proven wrong; in a collaboration with Ferrari, the company has reengineered the whole idea of watchmaking to produce a 1.75-millimeter miracle (it's the thickness of a quarter!) that is even fairly shock-resistant.

Richard Mille
c/o Horométrie SA
11, rue du Jura
CH-2345 Les Breuleux
Switzerland

Tel.:
+41-32-959-4353

E-mail:
info@richardmille.ch

Website:
www.richardmille.com

Founded:
2000

Annual production:
approx. 4,600 watches

U.S. distributor:
Richard Mille Americas
8701 Wilshire Blvd.
Beverly Hills, CA 90211
310-205-5555

Richard Mille watches are priced in Swiss francs.

Automatic RM 07-01 Automatic Starry Night

Reference number: RM 07-01 Starry Night
Movement: automatic, Richard Mille Caliber CRMA2; 22 x 29.9 mm, height 4.92 mm; 25 jewels; 28,800 vph; fully skeletonized titanium mainplate and bridges, balance with 4 regulating screws, skeletonized rotor in pink gold with adjustable inertia and winding performance; 50-hour power reserve
Functions: hours, minutes
Case: carbon fiber, (TPT), 31.4 mm x 45.66 mm, height 11.85 mm; bezel set with diamonds (gold claw setting); sapphire crystal; transparent case back; water-resistant to 5 atm
Band: carbon fiber (TPT); folding clasp
Price: CHF 236,000
Variations: "Starry Night"; "Bright Night"; "Dark Night"

RM 07-01 Automatic Red Gold Snow Set

Reference number: RM 07-01
Movement: automatic, Richard Mille Caliber CRMA2; 22 x 29.9 mm, height 4.92 mm; 25 jewels; 28,800 vph; fully skeletonized titanium mainplate and bridges, balance with 4 regulating screws, skeletonized rotor in pink gold with adjustable inertia and winding performance; 50-hour power reserve
Functions: hours, minutes
Case: red gold, 31.4 x 45.66 mm, height 11.85 mm; bezel set with diamonds (snow-setting); sapphire crystal; transparent case back; water-resistant to 5 atm
Band: carbon fiber (TPT), folding clasp
Remarks: skeletonized dial, with snow-set diamonds
Price: CHF 233,000

RM 037 Automatic White Gold Snow Set

Reference number: RM 037
Movement: automatic, Richard Mille Caliber CRMA1; 22.9 x 28 mm, height 4.82 mm; 25 jewels; 28,800 vph; skeletonized movement; winding rotor with variable geometry; 50-hour power reserve
Functions: hours, minutes; crown-activated function display; large date
Case: white gold, 34.4 x 52.2 mm, height 12.5 mm; bezel set with diamonds (snow-setting); sapphire crystal; transparent case back; pusher as function selection
Band: rubber, pin buckle
Remarks: dial center with snow-set diamonds
Price: CHF 338.000

RM 65-01 Automatic Split-Seconds chronograph

Reference number: RM 65-01 Titanium
Movement: automatic, Caliber RMAC4; 31,78 x 29,98 mm, height 8.69 mm; 51 jewels; 36,000 vph; titanium mainplate and bridges, fully skeletonized; winding rotor with adjustable mass inertia; 60-hour power reserve
Functions: hours, minutes, subsidiary seconds; crown mode display; split-seconds chronograph; date Case: titanium, 44.5 x 50 mm, height 16,1 mm; sapphire crystal; transparent case back; crown with selector function; switchable pusher for rapid winding; water-resistant to 5 atm
Band: rubber, pin buckle
Price: CHF 261,000

RM 74-02 Automatic Tourbillon

Reference number: RM 74-02
Movement: automatic, Richard Mille Caliber CRMT5; 23.7 x 30.7 mm, height 6.2 mm; 23 jewels; 28,800 vph; one-minute tourbillon; red-gold skeletonized mainplate; winding rotor with variable geometry; 55-hour power reserve
Functions: hours, minutes
Case: red gold, 34.4 x 52.63 mm, height 13 mm; carbon-fiber bezel and case back (TPT) with gold insert; sapphire crystal; transparent case back; water-resistant to 5 atm
Band: rubber with leather lining, folding clasp
Price: CHF 502,000

RM 67-01 Automatic Extra Flat

Reference number: RM 67-01 Titanium
Movement: automatic, Richard Mille Caliber CRMA6; 29.1 x 31.25 mm, height 3.6 mm; 25 jewels; 28,800 vph; titanium mainplate and bridges; platinum winding rotor; 50-hour power reserve
Functions: hours, minutes; crown function display; date
Case: titanium, 38.7 x 47.5 mm, height 7.75 mm; sapphire crystal; transparent case back; water-resistant to 3 atm
Band: rubber, folding clasp
Price: CHF 113,000

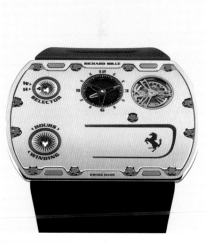

RM 35-03 Automatic Rafael Nadal

Reference number: RM 35-03
Movement: automatic, Richard Mille Caliber RMAL2; 29.45 x 31.25 mm, height 5.92 mm; 38 jewels; 28,800 vph; "butterfly" winding rotor with adjustable geometry; 55-hour power reserve
Functions: hours, minutes, sweep seconds; crown function display, rotor function display
Case: ceramic (TPT-quartz), 43.15 x 49.95 mm, height 13.15 mm; TPT-Quartz bezel and case back; sapphire crystal; transparent case back; pushers with selector function
Band: rubber, pin buckle
Price: CHF 211,000
Variations: with white case and light-blue strap

RM 032 flyback chronograph "Les Voiles de Saint Barth"

Reference number: RM 032
Movement: automatic, Richard Mille Caliber RMAC2; ø 39.15 mm, height 9 mm; 62 jewels; 28,800 vph; unidirectional winding rotor with variable geometry; 50-hour power reserve
Functions: hours, minutes, subsidiary seconds (function control); flyback chronograph; full calendar with large date, month
Case: ceramic (TPT quartz), ø 50 mm, height 17.8 mm; unidirectional bezel of TPT quartz; sapphire crystal; transparent case back; crown and pushers can be locked using central ring on the crown; water-resistant to 30 atm
Band: rubber, folding clasp
Remarks: special limited edition of 120 pieces for the "Voiles de St. Barth" regatta
Price: CHF 220,000

RM UP-01 Ferrari

Reference number: RM UP-01
Movement: hand-wound, Richard Mille Caliber RMUP-01; 41.45 x 28.85 mm, height 1.18 mm; 23 jewels; 28,800 vph; modified lever escapement; titanium mainplate and bridges; 45-hour power reserve
Functions: hours, minutes
Case: titanium, 51 x 39 mm, height 1.75 mm; sapphire crystal (2 crystals 0.2 and 0.4 mm thick)
Band: rubber, buckle
Remarks: winding crown and selector (winding, hand-setting) placed between the back and top plate; currently the world's thinnest mechanical wristwatch
Price: CHF 1,700,000

ROBOT

ROBOT Watch
Bohematic s.r.o.
Maiselova 2
101 00 Prag
Czech Republic

Tel.:
+420-722-977-256

E-mail:
info@bohematic.cz

Website:
www.robot-watch.com

Founded:
2018

Number of employees:
16

Annual production:
approx. 200 watches

Distribution:
direct sales; online shop; please contact the
company directly

Collections and price range:
Various models / $4,000 to $10,000

When brainstorming a name for a new line of watches to be produced by his company, Bohematic, entrepreneur Josef Zajíček decided to tap the Czech Republic's long and rich literary culture and call the line Robot. Few probably know that the word is originally Czech and refers to hard work. As such, it is related to the German word, which in older German actually meant burdensome work, tedium, if you will.

Be that as it may, the name—for the Czech people and those who know the nation's literature—will immediately recall the science fiction play *R.U.R* (it stands for Rossum's Universal Robots) by the famous writer Karel Čapek, written in 1920. In it, Čapek describes androids created by humans to serve them. And that describes what all timepieces do quite well.

The watches are manufactured at Nové Město nad Metují, a center of the Czech precision engineering and watchmaking industry. The tradition of precision manufacturing is not only continued here but constantly developed.

The manufacture was founded in 2018 by Zajíček, the Olgoj Chorchoj design studio, and by a team of experienced watchmakers, designers, and craftsmen. They are all in tune with the rich history of the Czech industrial culture and are intent on implementing their plans for mechanical wristwatches with an independent design and thus to contribute to traditional watchmaking at the highest European level. This translates as watches created by dint of demanding craftsmanship. The designers are inspired by great Czech stories that have left their mark on the world of design, industry, and motor sports. The Aerodynamic, for example, pays tribute to the Czechoslovak Tatra 77—the world's first aerodynamically shaped mass-produced car. The Minor series includes some limited editions that pay tribute to motor sports. But Robot has also thought of elegant dress watches, like the Ada for women, and the Aplos line, which can be worn by anyone. It's worth noting that Zajíček began his enterprise making parts, and as such became familiar with robots and their ability to relieve humans of repetitive and dangerous work. As for the watches' engines, they are usually from Swiss manufacturers, like Eterna and La Joux-Perret.

Graphic Analog

Reference number: 2202ST02
Movement: automatic, La Joux-Perret Caliber G100; ø 25.6 mm, height 4.45 mm; 24 jewels; 28,800 vph; 68-hour power reserve
Functions: hours, minutes, sweep seconds; date
Case: stainless steel with black PVD, ø 42 mm, height 12 mm; sapphire crystal; transparent case back; water-resistant to 5 atm
Band: textile and leather, pin buckle
Remarks: rectangles on dial with luminous mass
Price: $3,320
Variations: various dials

Graphic

Reference number: 1901ST04
Movement: automatic, Eterna Caliber 3909A; ø 30 mm, height 5.6 mm; 29 jewels; 28,800 vph; 65-hour power reserve
Functions: hours, minutes, sweep seconds; date
Case: stainless steel, ø 42 mm, height 12 mm; sapphire crystal; transparent case back; water-resistant to 5 atm
Band: hand-made calfskin, buckle
Remarks: galvanoplasty relief dial, perlage on crown
Price: $3,900
Variations: various dials

IDA

Reference number: 2301ST03
Movement: automatic, La Joux-Perret Caliber G100; ø 25.6 mm, height 4.45 mm; 24 jewels; 28,800 vph; 68-hour power reserve
Functions: hours, minutes, sweep seconds; date
Case: stainless steel, with rose-gold plating, ø 39 mm, height 10.5 mm; sapphire crystal; transparent case back; water-resistant to 5 atm
Band: leather, pin buckle
Price: $3,745
Variations: various cases and dials

Minor Le Mans Blue

Movement: automatic, La Joux-Perret Caliber LJP 8120; ø 30.4 mm, height 7.9 mm; 26 jewels; 28,800 vph; 55-hour power reserve

Functions: hours, minutes, subsidiary seconds; chronograph; date

Case: sand-blasted titanium, ø 44 mm, height 15 mm; bidirectional bezel with 0-12 scale; sapphire crystal; transparent case back; water-resistant to 10 atm

Band: hand-made calfskin, pin buckle

Remarks: perforated blue dial

Price: $5,030; limited to 100 pieces

Minor - Emerson Fittipaldi Limited Edition

Reference number: 2001LE03

Movement: automatic, La Joux-Perret Caliber LJP 8120; ø 30.4 mm, height 7.9 mm; 26 jewels; 28,800 vph; 55-hour power reserve

Functions: hours, minutes, subsidiary seconds; chronograph; date

Case: sand-blasted titanium with black PVD, ø 44 mm, height 15 mm; bidirectional bezel with 0-12 scale; sapphire crystal; transparent case back; water-resistant to 10 atm

Band: hand-made calfskin, pin buckle

Remarks: each dial hand signed by F1 & IndyCar legend Emerson Fittipaldi

Price: $5,880; limited to 100 pieces

Minor Superbike

Movement: automatic, La Joux-Perret Caliber LJP 8120; ø 30.4 mm, height 7.9 mm; 26 jewels; 28,800 vph; 55-hour power reserve

Functions: hours, minutes, subsidiary seconds; chronograph; date

Case: sand-blasted titanium, ø 44 mm, height 15 mm; bidirectional bezel with 0-12 scale; sapphire crystal; transparent case back; water-resistant to 10 atm

Band: hand-made calfskin, pin buckle

Remarks: perforated dial; homage to Jonathan Rea's superbike record on the Most (Czechia) racetrack; comes with keyring with strip of Rea's tire

Price: $5,880; limited to 12 pieces

Aplos

Reference number: 2201ST11

Movement: automatic, La Joux-Perret Caliber G100; ø 25.6 mm, height 4.45 mm; 24 jewels; 28,800 vph; 68-hour power reserve

Functions: hours, minutes, sweep seconds; date

Case: stainless steel with black PVD, ø 42 mm, height 12 mm; sapphire crystal; transparent case back; water-resistant to 5 atm

Band: textile and leather, pin buckle

Price: $2,470

Variations: various dials

Aerodynamic Silver Metallic

Reference number: 2101ST01

Movement: manual, La Joux-Perret Caliber LJP 7513; ø 33 mm, height 4.5 mm; 33 jewels; 28,800 vph; partially skeletonized movement, bridges with sunburst pattern; 192-hour power reserve

Functions: hours, minutes, subsidiary seconds; power-reserve indicator; date

Case: sand-blasted titanium, ø 39 mm, height 12.2 mm; sapphire crystal; transparent case back; water-resistant to 5 atm

Band: hand-made calfskin, pin buckle

Price: $6,300

Variations: various dial colors

Aerodynamic Cobalt Blue

Reference number: 2101ST04

Movement: manual, La Joux-Perret Caliber LJP 7513; ø 33 mm, height 4.5 mm; 33 jewels; 28,800 vph; partially skeletonized movement, bridges with sunburst pattern; 192-hour power reserve

Functions: hours, minutes, subsidiary seconds; power-reserve indicator; date

Case: sand-blasted titanium, ø 39 mm, height 12.2 mm; sapphire crystal; transparent case back; water-resistant to 5 atm

Band: hand-made calfskin, pin buckle

Price: $6,300

Variations: various dial colors

ROLEX

Essentially, the Rolex formula for success has always been "what you see is what you get"—and plenty of it. For over a century now, the company has made wristwatch history without a need for *grandes complications*, perpetual calendars, tourbillons, or exotic materials. And its output in sheer quantity is phenomenal, at not quite a million watches per year. But make no mistake about it: the quality of these timepieces is legendary.

For as long as anyone can remember, this brand has held the top spot in the COSC's statistics, and year after year Rolex delivers just about half of all the official institute's successfully tested mechanical chronometer movements. The brand has also pioneered several fundamental innovations: Rolex founder Hans Wilsdorf invented the hermetically sealed Oyster case in the 1920s, which he later outfitted with a screwed-in crown and an automatic movement wound by rotor. Shock protection, water resistance, the amagnetic Parachrom hairspring, and automatic winding are some of the virtues that make wearing a Rolex timepiece much more comfortable and reliable. As for movements, the automatic caliber 3255 features new materials (nickel-phosphorus), special micromanufacturing technology (LIGA) to make the pallet fork and balance wheel of the Chronergy escapement, and a barrel spring that can store up more energy than ever. Rolex also uses what it calls "Oyster" steel, an alloy of 904L steel, and puts some models on a "Jubilee" bracelet that is five links wide, giving it extra suppleness.

Rolex watches are produced in four different locations in Switzerland. Headquarters in Geneva handles final assembly and quality control and sales. All development, manufacturing, and quality control is done a few miles away in Plan-les-Ouates. Jewel-setting and dial-making are done in the Chêne-Bourg district of Geneva, and movements come from a factory in Biel/Bienne.

Meanwhile the company has built up representation in nearly one hundred countries in the world, with over thirty subsidiaries with customer service centers. The vast network also includes around four thousand watchmakers trained according to Rolex's own standards, who work in the branch offices or at the dealers themselves.

Rolex SA
Rue François-Dussaud 3
CH-1211 Geneva 26
Switzerland

Website:
www.rolex.com

Founded:
1908

Number of employees:
over 2,000 (estimated)

Annual production:
approx. 1,000,000 watches (estimated)

U.S. distributor:
Rolex Watch U.S.A., Inc.
650 Fifth Avenue
New York, NY 10019
212-758-7700
www.rolex.com

Oyster Perpetual GMT-Master II

Reference number: 126720VTNR
Movement: automatic, Rolex Caliber 3285; ø 28.5 mm, height 6.4 mm; 31 jewels; 28,800 vph; Parachrom hairspring, Paraflex shock protection, Chronergy escapement, glucydur balance wheel with Microstella regulating bolts; 70-hour power reserve; COSC-certified chronometer
Functions: hours (crown-activated separate setting), minutes, sweep seconds; additional 24-hour display (2nd time zone); date
Case: stainless steel, ø 40 mm, height 13 mm; bidirectional bezel with ceramic insert, with 0-24 scale; sapphire crystal; screw-in crown; water-resistant to 10 atm
Band: Jubilee stainless steel, folding clasp with safety lock and extension link
Price: $11,250

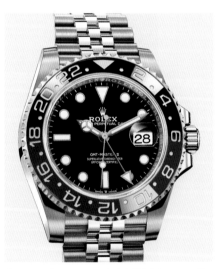

Oyster Perpetual GMT-Master II

Reference number: 126710BLNR
Movement: automatic, Rolex Caliber 3285; ø 28.5 mm, height 6.4 mm; 31 jewels; 28,800 vph; Parachrom hairspring, Paraflex shock protection, Chronergy escapement, glucydur balance wheel with Microstella regulating bolts; 70-hour power reserve; COSC-certified chronometer
Functions: hours (crown-activated separate setting), minutes, sweep seconds; additional 24-hour display (2nd time zone); date
Case: stainless steel, ø 40 mm, height 13 mm; bidirectional bezel with ceramic insert, with 0-24 scale; sapphire crystal; screw-in crown; water-resistant to 10 atm
Band: Jubilee stainless steel, folding clasp with safety lock and extension link
Price: $ 10,700

Oyster Perpetual Deepsea

Reference number: 136660
Movement: automatic, Rolex Caliber 3235; ø 29,1 mm; 31 jewels; 28,800 vph; Parachrom hairspring, Paraflex shock protection, Chronergy escapement, glucydur balance wheel with Microstella regulating bolts; 70-hour power reserve; COSC-certified chronometer
Functions: hours, minutes, sweep seconds; date
Case: stainless steel, ø 44 mm; unidirectional bezel with ceramic insert, with 0-60 scale; sapphire crystal; screw-in crown, helium valve; water-resistant to 390 atm
Band: Oyster stainless steel, folding clasp with safety lock and extension link, with fine adjustment
Price: $14,150

Oyster Perpetual Sea-Dweller

Reference number: 126603
Movement: automatic, Rolex Caliber 3235; ø 29,1 mm; 31 jewels; 28,800 vph; Parachrom hairspring, Paraflex shock protection, Chronergy escapement, glucydur balance wheel with Microstella regulating bolts; 70-hour power reserve; COSC-certified chronometer
Functions: hours, minutes, sweep seconds; date
Case: stainless steel, ø 43 mm, height 13.8 mm; unidirectional bezel in yellow gold with ceramic insert, with 0-60 scale; sapphire crystal; screw-in crown, helium valve; water-resistant to 122 atm
Band: Oyster stainless steel with yellow gold elements, folding clasp with safety link, with fine adjustment
Price: $ 18,000
Variations: in stainless steel ($ 13,250)

Oyster Perpetual Submariner Date

Reference number: 126610LV
Movement: automatic, Rolex Caliber 3230; ø 29,1 mm; 31 jewels; 28,800 vph; Parachrom hairspring, Paraflex shock protection, Chronergy escapement, glucydur balance wheel with Microstella regulating bolts; 70-hour power reserve; COSC-certified chronometer
Functions: hours, minutes, sweep seconds; date
Case: stainless steel, ø 41 mm, height 12.5 mm; unidirectional bezel with ceramic insert, with 0-60 scale; sapphire crystal; screw-in crown; water-resistant to 30 atm
Band: Oyster stainless steel, folding clasp with extension link
Price: $ 10,800
Variations: in white gold ($42,000)

Oyster Perpetual Submariner

Reference number: 124060
Movement: automatic, Rolex Caliber 3230; ø 29,1 mm; 31 jewels; 28,800 vph; Parachrom hairspring, Paraflex shock protection, Chronergy escapement, glucydur balance wheel with Microstella regulating bolts; 70-hour power reserve; COSC-certified chronometer
Functions: hours, minutes, sweep seconds
Case: stainless steel, ø 41 mm, height 12.5 mm; unidirectional bezel with ceramic insert, with 0-60 scale, sapphire crystal; screw-in crown; water-resistant to 30 atm
Band: Oyster stainless steel, folding clasp with extension link
Price: $9,150

Oyster Perpetual Cosmograph Daytona

Reference number: 126506
Movement: automatic, Rolex Caliber 4131; ø 30.5 mm, height 6.5 mm; 44 jewels; 28,800 vph; Parachrom hairspring, Paraflex shock protection, Chronergy escapement; 72-hour power reserve; COSC-certified chronometer
Functions: hours, minutes, subsidiary seconds; chronograph
Case: platinum, ø 40 mm, height 12.8 mm; Cerachrom bezel; sapphire crystal; transparent case back; screw-in crown and pushers; water-resistant to 10 atm
Band: Oyster platinum, folding clasp with safety lock and extension link
Price: $ 77,800,

Oyster Perpetual Cosmograph Daytona

Reference number: 126500LN
Movement: automatic, Rolex Caliber 4131; ø 30.5 mm, height 6.5 mm; 44 jewels; 28,800 vph; Parachrom hairspring, Paraflex shock protection, Chronergy escapement; 72-hour power reserve; COSC-certified chronometer
Functions: hours, minutes, subsidiary seconds; chronograph
Case: stainless steel, ø 40 mm, height 12.8 mm; Cerachrom bezel; sapphire crystal; screw-in crown and pushers; water-resistant to 10 atm
Band: Oyster stainless steel, folding clasp with safety lock and extension link
Price: $ 15,100
Variations: with black dial; in yellow gold ($30,600, with Oysterflex bracelet)

Oyster Perpetual Cosmograph Daytona "Le Mans"

Reference number: 126529LN
Movement: automatic, Rolex Caliber 4132; ø 3.5 mm, height 6.5 mm; 44 jewels; 28,800 vph; Parachrom hairspring, Paraflex shock protection, Chronergy escapement; 72-hour power reserve; COSC-certified chronometer
Functions: hours, minutes, subsidiary seconds; chronograph
Case: white gold, ø 40 mm, height 12.8 mm; Cerachrom bezel; sapphire crystal; screw-in crown and pushers; water-resistant to 10 atm
Band: Oyster white gold, folding clasp with safety lock and extension link
Remarks: special model made for the 100th anniversary of Le Mans racetrack, with 24-hour totalizer
Price: $51,400

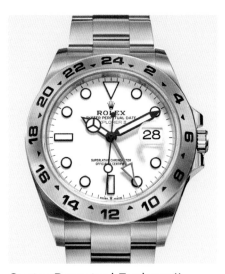

Oyster Perpetual Explorer II

Reference number: 226570
Movement: automatic, Rolex Caliber 3285; ø 28.5 mm;
31 jewels; 28,800 vph; Parachrom hairspring, Paraflex
shock protection, Chronergy escapement, glucydur
balance wheel with Microstella regulating bolts;
70-hour power reserve; COSC-certified chronometer
Functions: hours (incremental setting by the crown),
minutes, sweep seconds; additional 24-hour display
(2nd time zone); date
Case: stainless steel, ø 42 mm; sapphire crystal;
screw-in crown; water-resistant to 10 atm
Band: Oyster stainless steel, folding clasp with
extension link
Price: $9,650
Variations: with black dial

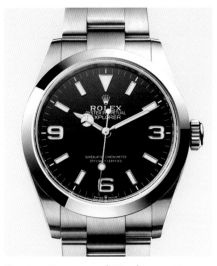

Oyster Perpetual Explorer 40

Reference number: 224270
Movement: automatic, Rolex Caliber 3230; ø 29,1 mm;
31 jewels; 28,800 vph; Parachrom hairspring, Paraflex
shock protection, Chronergy escapement, glucydur
balance wheel with Microstella regulating bolts;
70-hour power reserve; COSC-certified chronometer
Functions: hours, minutes, sweep seconds
Case: stainless steel, ø 40 mm; sapphire crystal;
screw-in crown; water-resistant to 10 atm
Band: Oyster stainless steel, folding clasp with
extension link
Price: $7,700

Oyster Perpetual Air-King

Reference number: 126900
Movement: automatic, Rolex Caliber 3230; ø 28.5 mm,
31 jewels; 28,800 vph; Parachrom hairspring, Paraflex
shock protection, Chronergy escapement, glucydur
balance wheel with Microstella regulating bolts;
70-hour power reserve; COSC-certified chronometer
Functions: hours, minutes, sweep seconds
Case: stainless steel, ø 40 mm, height 11.6 mm; sapphire
crystal; screw-in crown; water-resistant to 10 atm
Band: Oyster stainless steel, folding clasp with safety
lock and extension link
Price: $7,450

Oyster Perpetual Sky-Dweller

Reference number: 336239
Movement: automatic, Rolex Caliber 9002; ø 33 mm,
height 8 mm; 40 jewels; 28,800 vph; Parachrom
hairspring, Paraflex shock protection, glucydur balance
wheel with Microstella regulating bolts; 72-hour power
reserve; COSC-certified chronometer
Functions: hours, minutes, sweep seconds; additional
24-hour display (2nd time zone); annual calendar with
date, month
Case: white gold, ø 42 mm, height 14.1 mm;
bidirectional bezel to control functions; sapphire
crystal; screw-in crown; water-resistant to 10 atm
Band: rubber Oysterflex, folding clasp with fine adjustment
Price: $42,700
Variations: in stainless steel /white gold with
Oysterflex bracelet ($ 15,650); in rose gold

Oyster Perpetual Yacht-Master II

Reference number: 116681
Movement: automatic, Rolex Caliber 4161 (based on
Caliber 4130); ø 31.2 mm, height 8.05 mm; 42 jewels;
28,800 vph; Parachrom hairspring, glucydur balance
wheel with Microstella regulating bolts; 72-hour power
reserve; COSC-certified chronometer
Functions: hours, minutes, subsidiary seconds;
programmable regatta countdown with memory
Case: stainless steel, ø 44 mm, height 13.8 mm;
bidirectional bezel in rose gold with ceramic insert;
sapphire crystal; screw-in crown; water-resistant to 10 atm
Band: Oyster stainless steel with rose-gold elements,
folding clasp with safety lock and extension link
Price: $35,400
Variations: in yellow gold ($43,500); in stainless steel
($18,700)

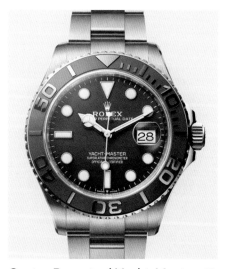

Oyster Perpetual Yacht-Master 42

Reference number: 226627
Movement: automatic, Rolex Caliber 3235; ø 29.1 mm,
height 6 mm; 31 jewels; 28,800 vph; Parachrom
hairspring, Paraflex shock protection, Chronergy
escapement; 48-hour power reserve; COSC-certified
chronometer
Functions: hours, minutes, sweep seconds; date
Case: titanium RLX, ø 42 mm, height 11.9 mm;
bidirectional bezel with ceramic insert, with
0-60 scale; sapphire crystal; screw-in crown;
water-resistant to 10 atm
Band: titanium RLX, folding clasp, with fine adjustment
Price: $14,050

TOURBY

Hagen in Westfalen

we build your watch

Lawless Gradient
Diameter 42mm
Sapphire crystal
Swiss made movement
ETA 2824-2 Automatic
Chronometer
Prices $ 1,800.00

www.tourbywatches.com

urby Watches - Königstr. 78 - 58300 Wetter an der Ruhr (Hagen in Westfalen) - GERMANY - Tel. +49 2335 8463447

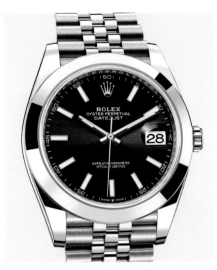

Oyster Perpetual Datejust 41

Reference number: 126300
Movement: automatic, Rolex Caliber 3235; ø 29.1 mm; 31 jewels; 28,800 vph; Parachrom hairspring, Paraflex shock protection, Chronergy escapement, glucydur balance wheel with Microstella regulating bolts; 70-hour power reserve; COSC-certified chronometer
Functions: hours, minutes, sweep seconds; date
Case: stainless steel, ø 41 mm, height 11.6 mm; sapphire crystal; screw-in crown; water-resistant to 10 atm
Band: Jubilee stainless steel, folding clasp with extension link
Price: $8,300

Oyster Perpetual Datejust 41

Reference number: 126333
Movement: automatic, Rolex Caliber 3235; ø 29.1 m; 31 jewels; 28,800 vph; Parachrom hairspring, Paraflex shock protection, Chronergy escapement, glucydur balance wheel with Microstella regulating bolts; 70-hour power reserve; COSC-certified chronometer
Functions: hours, minutes, sweep seconds; date
Case: stainless steel, ø 41 mm, height 11.6 mm; bezel and crown in yellow gold; sapphire crystal; screw-in crown; water-resistant to 10 atm
Band: Jubilee stainless steel with yellow gold elements, folding clasp with extension link
Price: $16,350

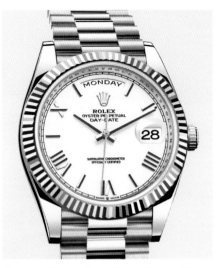

Oyster Perpetual Day-Date 40

Reference number: 228238
Movement: automatic, Rolex Caliber 3255; ø 29.1 mm; height 5.4 mm; 31 jewels; 28,800 vph; Parachrom hairspring, Paraflex shock protection, Chronergy escapement, glucydur balance wheel with Microstella regulating bolts; 70-hour power reserve; COSC-certified chronometer
Functions: hours, minutes, sweep seconds; date and weekday
Case: yellow gold, ø 40 mm, height 11.6 mm; sapphire crystal; screw-in crown; water-resistant to 10 atm
Band: President yellow gold, hidden folding clasp
Price: $38,500
Variations: in white or rose gold ($41,500)

Perpetual 1908

Reference number: 52508
Movement: automatic, Rolex Caliber 7140; ø 28.5 mm, height 4.05 mm; 38 jewels; 28,800 vph; Syloxi hairspring, Paraflex shock protection, Chronergy escapement; 66-hour power reserve; COSC-certified chronometer
Functions: hours, minutes, subsidiary seconds
Case: yellow gold, ø 39 mm, height 9.5 mm; sapphire crystal; transparent case back; water-resistant to 5 atm
Band: reptile skin, double folding clasp
Price: $22,000

Perpetual 1908

Reference number: 52508
Movement: automatic, Rolex Caliber 7140; ø 28.5 mm, height 4.05 mm; 38 jewels; 28,800 vph; Syloxi hairspring, Paraflex shock protection, Chronergy escapement; 66-hour power reserve; COSC-certified chronometer
Functions: hours, minutes, subsidiary seconds
Case: yellow gold, ø 39 mm, height 9.5 mm; sapphire crystal; transparent case back; water-resistant to 5 atm
Band: reptile skin, double folding clasp
Price: $22,000

Perpetual 1908

Reference number: 52509
Movement: automatic, Rolex Caliber 7140; ø 28.5 mm, height 4.05 mm; 38 jewels; 28,800 vph; Syloxi hairspring, Paraflex shock protection, Chronergy escapement; 66-hour power reserve; COSC-certified chronometer
Functions: hours, minutes, subsidiary seconds
Case: white gold, ø 39 mm, height 9.5 mm; sapphire crystal; transparent case back; water-resistant to 5 atm
Band: reptile skin, double folding clasp
Price: $23,300
Variations: with white dial

Caliber 3235

Automatic; optimized Chronergy escapement, nickel-phosphorus pallet lever and escape wheel (LIGA technology); single spring barrel, 70-hour power reserve; COSC-certified chronometer
Functions: hours, minutes, sweep seconds; date
Diameter: 28.5 mm
Height: 6 mm
Jewels: 31
Balance: glucydur with Microstella regulating bolts
Frequency: 28,000 vph
Hairspring: Parachrom Breguet hairspring
Shock protection: Paraflex
Remarks: used in Datejust

Caliber 3255

Automatic; optimized Chronergy escapement, nickel-phosphorus pallet lever and escape wheel (LIGA technology); single spring barrel, 70-hour power reserve; COSC-certified chronometer
Functions: hours, minutes, sweep seconds; date, weekday
Diameter: 29.1 mm
Height: 5.4 mm
Jewels: 31
Balance: glucydur with Microstella regulating bolts
Frequency: 28,800 vph
Hairspring: Parachrom Breguet hairspring
Shock protection: Paraflex
Remarks: used in Day-Date 40

Caliber 4131

Automatic; optimized Chronergy escapement, nickel-phosphorus pallet lever and escape wheel (LIGA technology); single spring barrel, 72-hour power reserve; COSC-certified chronometer
Functions: hours, minutes, subsidiary seconds; chronograph
Diameter: 30.5 mm
Height: 6.5 mm
Jewels: 44
Balance: glucydur with Microstella regulating bolts
Frequency: 28,800 vph
Hairspring: Parachrom Breguet hairspring
Shock protection: Paraflex
Remarks: used in the Daytona model

Caliber 4161

Automatic; single spring barrel, 72-hour power reserve; COSC-certified chronometer
Base caliber: Caliber 4130
Functions: hours, minutes, subsidiary seconds; programmable regatta countdown with memory
Diameter: 31.2 mm
Height: 8.05 mm
Jewels: 42
Balance: glucydur with Microstella regulating bolts
Frequency: 28,800 vph
Hairspring: Parachrom Breguet hairspring
Shock protection: Kif
Remarks: used in Yacht-Master II

Caliber 7140

Automatic; optimized Chronergy escapement, nickel-phosphorus pallet lever and escape wheel (LIGA technology); single spring barrel, 66-hour power reserve; COSC-certified chronometer
Functions: hours, minutes, subsidiary seconds
Diameter: 28.5 mm
Height: 4.05 mm
Jewels: 38
Balance: glucydur with Microstella regulating bolts
Frequency: 28,800 vph Hairspring: Parachrom hairspring
Shock protection: Paraflex
Remarks: used in the Perpetual 1908 model

Caliber 9002

Automatic; optimized Chronergy escapement, nickel-phosphorus pallet lever and escape wheel (LIGA technology); single spring barrel, 72-hour power reserve; COSC-certified chronometer
Functions: hours, minutes, sweep seconds; additional 24-hour display (2nd time zone); annual calendar with date, month
Diameter: 33 mm
Height: 8 mm
Jewels: 40
Balance: glucydur with Microstella regulating bolts
Frequency: 28,800 vph
Hairspring: Parachrom Breguet hairspring
Shock protection: Kif
Remarks: used in the Sky-Dweller models

SCHAUMBURG WATCH

Schaumburg Watch
Kirchplatz 5 and 6
D-31737 Rinteln
Germany

Tel.:
+49-5751-923-351

E-mail:
info@schaumburgwatch.com

Website:
www.schaumburgwatch.com

Founded:
1998

Number of employees:
9

Annual production:
not specified

U.S. distributor:
Schaumburg Watch
About Time Luxury Group
210 Bellevue Avenue
Newport, RI 02840
401-846-0598
nicewatch@aol.com

Most important collections/price range:
mechanical wristwatches / approx. $1,500 to
$13,000

If you are searching for a brand whose brand strategy is anti-brand, then Schaumburg is your brand. Frank Dilbakowski is the owner of this small watchmaking business in Rinteln, Westphalia, which has been producing very unusual yet affordable timepieces since 1998. The name Schaumburg comes from the surrounding region. The firm has gained a reputation for high-performance timepieces for rugged sports and professional use. But expect to be surprised. The portfolio includes such pieces as the chronometer line Aquamatic, with water resistance to 1,000 meters, and the Aquatitan models, secure to 2,000 meters (200 atm). If you are into the worn-down-industrial look, there is the SteamPunk collection, with watches that really look as if they had been buried in someone's garden and have now been unearthed and cleaned up, but not restored. It is an unusual way of surfing the vintage wave.

The patinaed look should not be a deterrent, because Dilbakowski has prioritized robust and traditional watchmaking. The Rinteln workbenches produce the plates and bridges and provide all the finishing as well (perlage, engraving, skeletonizing). Some of the bracelets, cases, and dials are even manufactured in-house, but the base movements come from Switzerland. Besides unadorned one-hand watches like the recent Squarematic Unique, which mixes 1970s-style modernity with a little rusty steampunk, the current portfolio of timepieces includes such outstanding pieces as a whole series of special moon phases that have a mysterious "shadow" crossing over an immobile photo-like reproduction of the moon, which is brightly lit with Super-LumiNova. For those who appreciate a nicely skeletonized watch, Dilbakowski has a whole folder full, including the Craftsman II, and the Old Bridge II, which also reveal hand-engraved bridges and main-plate and daubs of color. Schaumburg is a courageous brand, and one that needs a bit of boldness to invest in. But it does produce genuinely eye-catching pieces.

Unikatorium Old Bridge II

Reference number: Old Bridge II
Movement: hand-wound, Caliber SW 07 (modified Unitas 6498); ø 36.6 mm, height 4.5 mm; 17 jewels; 18,000 vph; extensively hand-skeletonized and finely finished with patinated parts; swan-neck fine adjustment; 46-hour power reserve
Functions: hours, minutes
Case: thermally-patinated stainless steel, ø 42 mm, height 11 mm; sapphire crystal; transparent case back
Band: burlap with leather, buckle
Price: $3,150

Craftsman II

Reference number: 44211
Movement: hand-wound, Caliber SW-07 (modified Unitas 6498); ø 36.6 mm, height 4.5 mm; 17 jewels; 18,000 vph; extensively skeletonized and decorated dial and movement; 46-hour power reserve
Functions: hours (5-minute indices)
Case: stainless steel with ION plating, ø 42 mm, height 10 mm; sapphire crystal; transparent case back, water-resistant to 5 atm
Band: leather, buckle
Remarks: blued wrench-shaped hands
Price: $2,900

MooN Galaxy Planetarium

Reference number: Blood Moon Galaxy
Movement: automatic, Caliber SW-11 (base MAB 88); ø 25.6 mm, height 3.6 mm; 25 jewels; 28,800 vph; astronomically precise moon phase; perlage on movement, côtes de Genève on the rotor; 42-hour power reserve
Functions: hours, minutes; date, moon phase (with Super-LumiNova)
Case: stainless steel, ø 43 mm, height 12.4 mm; sapphire crystal; water-resistant to 5 atm
Band: leather, pin buckle
Remarks: goldstone (an alchemist's secret) dial with photorealistic lunar cycle
Price: $6,000; limited to 25 pieces
Variations: with black PVD ($6,500); various color dials

Schwarz Etienne SA
Route de L'Orée-du-Bois 5
CH-2300 La Chaux-de-Fonds
Switzerland

Tel.:
+41-32-967-9420

E-mail:
info@schwarz-etienne.ch

Website:
www.schwarz-etienne.com

Founded:
1902

Number of employees:
22

Annual production:
300 to 500

Distribution:
Contact company for information.
Retailers in the USA
Esperluxe – Boston MA
Exquisite Timepieces – Naples FL
Goldsmith Complications – Delray FL
Kaufmann de Suisse – Montreal
Manfredi Jewels – Greenwich CT
Oster Jewelers – Denver CO
Rostovsky Watches – Beverly Hills CA

Most important collections:
La Chaux-de-Fonds, Roma, Roswell, Fiji, special
editions

SCHWARZ ETIENNE

When Raffaello Radicchi, who hails from Perugia, Italy, talks about his business, you might think he was talking about a little shop he set up in Neuchâtel. Ask him why he went into watchmaking, he answers, "I was allergic to the metal and could only wear a gold watch." Subtext: He could not afford a gold watch, so he founded a watch company.

Radicchi is a genuine maverick and a lone figure in this somewhat hermetic industry. He arrived in Switzerland at eighteen, a mason. He retrained as a carpenter and started buying and renovating homes, and soon he was earning some serious money. In the early aughts, an acquaintance bought up a watch brand in La Chaux-de-Fonds and suggested that Radicchi buy the building that came with it. The brand, once a big name in the industry and a supplier of movements (to Chanel, among others), had originally been founded by Paul Schwarz and Olga Etienne.

By 2008, Radicchi owned the whole package. He understood that the company needed independence to survive. Having many outstanding suppliers locally to partner with was a good start. But Schwarz Etienne needed movements, so the company set out to make their own, and by 2015 it had three. These calibers now drive a series of watches, including a tourbillon, that are classical in look, yet very modern-technical, thanks to the inverted movement construction that puts the off-center microrotor on the dial. They've recently started appearing in the watches of other brands as well.

For all its traditionalism, the brand still maintains a feeling of youthful creativity with a lot of good and bold humor rarely found in the industry. The Roswell's case, for example, is shaped like a comic-book UFO. And for all its classic layout, the dial of the Roma series can sometimes become asymmetrical, like the 2023 Geometry, which looks like it is being reflected in a hall of mirrors.

Roma Geometry

Reference number: WR023MA08SSVEBCLTD
Movement: automatic, Schwarz Etienne Caliber ASE 200.02 with micro-rotor; ø 30.40 mm, height 5.35 mm; 33 jewels; 21,600 vph; finely finished movement; 86-hour power reserve
Functions: hours, minutes, subsidiary seconds
Case: stainless steel, ø 39 mm, height 11 mm; sapphire crystal; water-resistant to 5 atm
Band: calfskin, triple folding clasp
Remarks: dial with asymmetric sections with clous de Paris and guilloché decoration
Price: $23,490; limited to 50 pieces
Variations: grey and blue dial

Roma Small Seconds

Reference number: WR015MA25SS01AA
Movement: automatic, Schwarz Etienne Caliber ASE 100.00; ø 30.4 mm, height 5.35 mm; 25 jewels; 21,600 vph; finely finished movement; twin spring barrels in parallel; 86-hour power reserve
Functions: hours, minutes, subsidiary seconds
Case: stainless steel, ø 42 mm, height 12.13 mm; sapphire crystal; transparent case back; water-resistant to 5 atm
Band: reptile skin, folding clasp
Remarks: dial with sunburst stamped pattern, outer dial grained, seconds dial in flinqué
Price: $11,800; unique piece
Variations: in red-gold case; different dials (black hour circle, grey hands)

La Chaux-de-Fonds Flying Tourbillon

Reference number: WCF09TSE06RB21AA
Movement: automatic, Schwarz Etienne Caliber TSE 121.00; ø 30.4 mm, height 6.35 mm; 34 jewels; 21,600 vph; finely finished movement; inverted movement with micro-rotor; 1-minute flying tourbillon; 70-hour power reserve
Functions: hours, minutes, seconds on tourbillon cage
Case: red gold, ø 44 mm, height 13.70mm sapphire crystal; transparent case back; water-resistant to 5 atm
Band: reptile skin, pin buckle
Price: $77,640
Variations: stainless steel case

SEIKO

This Japanese watch giant is a part of the Seiko Holding Company, whose story began one hundred and forty years ago, when twenty-two-year-old entrepreneur Kintaro Hattori opened a store in central Tokyo, repairing and selling wristwatches and wall clocks. Today, the company is one of the few watch manufacturers that can carry out all steps of watchmaking in-house, from developing movements to producing parts and assembling all components. Seiko makes every variety of portable timepiece and offers mechanical watches with both manual and automatic winding, quartz watches with battery and solar power or with the brand's own mechanical "Kinetic" power generation, as well as the groundbreaking "Spring Drive" hybrid technology. This intelligent mix of mechanical energy generation and electronic regulation is reserved for Seiko's top models.

Classic Seikos are designed for tradition-conscious buyers. The Astron, however, with its automatic GPS-controlled time setting, was something of a trailblazer. In its second incarnation, the Astron became more compact, and the energy to operate the GPS system inside was supplied by a high-tech solar cell on the dial. As for the new Prospex collection, released for the fiftieth anniversary of the first Seiko diver's watches, it has an unmistakably modern look.

Diving watches from Seiko have been around for over fifty years. They have featured many important innovations, like the first titanium case for a diving watch, or the invention of the "accordion" strap and the single-shell construction of the case with external protection. The 5 Sports series is clearly priced to tap the potential of those without the resources for more costly timepieces. It features a transparent case back, and the crystal is a special hardened glass known as Hardlex.

The Japanese sense of aesthetics is combined with traditional craftsmanship and Seiko's skill in making mechanical watches in the Presage collection. Using a variety of dial materials such as Arita porcelain or enamel, watches are created here that express the passion and high perfection of watchmakers and craftsmen in every detail. This is also evident in the latest "Sharp Edged" series: the traditional shape of the round case is contoured by sharply angled surfaces, which are reflected in the design of the structured dial.

Seiko Holdings
Ginza, Chuo, Tokyo
Japan

Website:
www.seikowatches.com

Founded:
1881

U.S. distributor:
Seiko Corporation of America
1111 MacArthur Boulevard
Mahwah, NJ 07430
201-529-5730
custserv@seikousa.com
www.seikousa.com

Most important collections/price range:
Astron / approx. $1,850 to $3,400; Presage / approx. $425 to $4,500; Prospex / approx. $395 to $6,000

1970 Automatic Diver's "Naomi Uemura"

Reference number: SLA069
Movement: automatic, Seiko Caliber 8L35; ø 28.6 mm; 26 jewels; 28,800 vph; antimagnetic to 4800 A/m; 50-hour power reserve
Functions: hours, minutes, sweep seconds; date
Case: stainless steel, (hard-coated), ø 44 mm, height 13 mm; unidirectional bezel with 0-60 scale; sapphire crystal; screw-in crown; water-resistant to 20 atm
Band: stainless steel (hard-coated), folding clasp with safety lock and extension link
Remarks: modern reinterpretation of the 1970 classic diver's watch from 1970
Price: $2,900; limited to 500 pieces

Automatic GMT Diver's

Reference number: SPB381
Movement: automatic, Seiko Caliber 6R54; ø 27.4 mm, height 4.95 mm; 24 jewels; 21,600 vph; antimagnetic to 4800 A/m; 72-hour power reserve
Functions: hours, minutes, sweep seconds; additional 24-hour display (2nd time zone); date
Case: stainless steel, (hard-coated), ø 42 mm, height 12.9 mm; unidirectional bezel, with 0-60 scale; sapphire crystal; screw-in crown; water-resistant to 20 atm
Band: stainless steel (hard-coated), folding clasp with safety lock and extension link
Price: $1,500

Prospex Solar Chronograph

Reference number: SSC911P1
Movement: quartz, Seiko Caliber V192; power from solar cell in the dial
Functions: hours, minutes, subsidiary seconds; chronograph; date
Case: stainless steel, ø 41.4 mm, height 13 mm; sapphire crystal; water-resistant to 10 atm
Band: stainless steel, folding clasp
Price: $750

Presage Automatic Multifunction Watchmaking 110th Anniversary

Reference number: SPB393
Movement: automatic, Seiko Caliber 6R24; ø 27.4 mm, height 6.15 mm; 31 jewels; 28,800 vph; antimagnetic to 4800 A/m; 45-hour power reserve
Functions: hours, minutes, sweep seconds; power-reserve indicator; date and weekday
Case: stainless steel, (hard-coated), ø 40.2 mm, height 12.0 mm; sapphire crystal; transparent case back, water-resistant to 10 atm
Band: calfskin, folding clasp
Remarks: enamel dial
Price: $1,450; limited to 1,500 pieces

Presage Sharp Edged

Reference number: SPB415J1
Movement: automatic, Seiko Caliber 6R5J; ø 27.4 mm, 24 jewels; 28,800 vph; partially skeletonized mainplate over the escapement; antimagnetic to 4800 A/m; 72-hour power reserve
Functions: hours, minutes, sweep seconds; additional 24-hour display
Case: stainless steel, (hard-coated), ø 40.2 mm, height 13.5 mm; sapphire crystal; transparent case back; water-resistant to 10 atm
Band: stainless steel (hard-coated), folding clasp
Price: $1,200

Presage Style 60's Automatic GMT

Reference number: SSK009
Movement: automatic, Seiko Caliber 4R34; ø 27 mm, height 5.88 mm; 24 jewels; 21,600 vph; antimagnetic to 4800 A/m; 41-hour power reserve
Functions: hours, minutes, sweep seconds; additional 24-hour display (2nd time zone); date
Case: stainless steel, ø 40.8 mm, height 13 mm; Plexiglas; transparent case back; water-resistant to 5 atm
Band: stainless steel, folding clasp
Price: $625

King Seiko

Reference number: SPB369J1
Movement: automatic, Seiko Caliber 6R55; ø 27.4 mm, height 4.95 mm; 24 jewels; 21,600 vph; antimagnetic to 4800 A/m; 72-hour power reserve
Functions: hours, minutes, sweep seconds; date
Case: stainless steel, ø 39 mm, height 11.9 mm; sapphire crystal; water-resistant to 10 atm
Band: stainless steel, double folding clasp
Price: $1,800

Astron GPS Solar

Reference number: SSJ013J1
Movement: quartz, Seiko Caliber 3X62; power delivered by solar cell on the dial
Functions: hours, minutes, sweep seconds; power-reserve indicator, airplane mode; perpetual calendar with date
Case: titanium (hard-coated), ø 41.2 mm, height 12 mm; sapphire crystal; water-resistant to 10 atm
Band: titanium (hard-coated), folding clasp
Price: $2,000

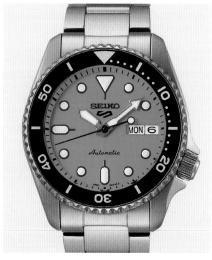

Seiko 5 Sports

Reference number: SRPK33K1
Movement: automatic, Seiko Caliber 4R36; ø 27.4 mm, height 5.32 mm; 24 jewels; 21,600 vph; antimagnetic to 4800 A/m; 40-hour power reserve
Functions: hours, minutes, sweep seconds; date and weekday
Case: stainless steel, ø 38 mm, height 12 mm; unidirectional bezel with 0-60 scale; Hardlex crystal (heat-hardened glass); transparent case back; screw-in crown; water-resistant to 10 atm
Band: stainless steel, folding clasp with safety lock
Price: $325
Variations: various dial colors

SHANGHAI WATCH

One of China's most popular brands of watches bears the name of the country's most cosmopolitan-chic city, Shanghai, and is also one of the oldest in the country. The history of Shanghai watch goes back to 1955.

When Mao Zedong took over China in December 1949, the country had basically been at war with itself and Japan for over 22 years. Much had changed since the end of the Qing Dynasty in 1911, except for the envisioned necessities of the population, the so-called "Three Great Things": a sewing machine, a bicycle, and a watch. The latter was especially important to run a country efficiently, be that in the military, transportation, or industrial sectors. In 1955, in a bid to end foreign dependence on watches and create a domestic industry, the government launched a competition amongst Chinese cities to start a native watch industry. Teams of watchmakers gathered about and went to work. Tianjin (now Sea-Gull) actually came first, but Shanghai took a little more time and retro-engineered a Swiss movement using Japanese and Soviet parts. Their watch, the A581, went on to become an icon: simple, functional, and quite elegant.

The Shanghai watch factory, a stylized image of which is used for the logo, is still manufacturing to this day. The original design of its first watch has been upgraded to suit more modern tastes, but the original, functional look is still dominant. Today, they use Swiss or Chinese calibers and have even come out with an in-house movement.

With the A581, Shanghai Watch is looking at the recent history and culture of the city and at its international past, signaled by the typical old Shanghai "begonia" window embossed on the case back. Chinese culture is also represented in the company's portfolio. The Danqing in the Artisan collection features a special form of embroidery on the dial, which portrays a section of the painting "A thousand li of rivers and mountains," a masterpiece by Wang Ximeng (1096-1119). It depicts a natural scene in perfect harmony. In the same vein, but with a far more modern look, is the Taichi Tourbillon in the Metropolitan collection, which an S-shaped tourbillon bridge suggesting the yin-yang symbol and Shanghai's meandering Huangpu River.

Shanghai Watches Company Ltd
201, Yulin Rd.
Yangpu DIstrict,
Shanghai, China

Tel.:
+86-400-821-6812

E-mail:
bd.shby@shwatch.cn

Website:
https://www.shwatch.cn/

Date founded:
1955

U.S. distributor/retail structure:
Contact the company for information.

Most important collections/price range
(in USD):
Originate, Metropolitan, Artistic / $500 to $5,500

Originate "Sky Silver"

Movement: automatic, (Sea-Gull Caliber ST2130 base), ø 25.6 mm, height 4.6 mm; 28 jewels; 21,600 vph; 42-hour power reserve
Functions: hours, minutes, sweep seconds
Case: stainless steel, ø 39 mm, height 10.95 mm; sapphire crystal; case back featuring typical vintage Shanghai begonia window design and calligraphed company name; water-resistant to 5 atm
Band: calfskin, pin buckle
Remarks: the A581 was the first mass-produced watch manufactured by Shanghai watch
Price: $450
Variations: "Sunset Gold" and "Obsidian Black"

Danqing · A Thousand Li of Rivers and Mountains

Reference number: 22AT-Q-SW30-EMRS
Movement: automatic, Sellita SW300 Caliber; ø 25.6 mm, height 3.6 mm; 25 jewels; 28,800 vph; stop-second mechanism; 50-hour power reserve
Functions: hours, minutes, sweep seconds
Case: stainless steel, ø 41 mm, height 9.44 mm; sapphire crystal; transparent, screw-down case back; screw-down crown; water-resistant to 3 atm
Band: reptile skin, folding clasp
Price: $3,680
Variations: with rose-gold PVD

Tai-Chi Tourbillon

Reference number: 23MT-T-Z07-BKST
Movement: automatic, Shanghai Watch Caliber Z07; ø 31.50 mm, height 7.20 mm; 23 jewels; 21,600 vph; 1-minute tourbillon; 52-hour power reserve
Functions: hours, minutes, seconds on tourbillon cage
Case: stainless steel, ø 42 mm, height 13.50 mm; sapphire crystal; transparent case back; water-resistant to 3 atm
Band: reptile skin, folding clasp
Price: $5,950
Variations: comes with white dial

Sinn Spezialuhren GmbH
Wilhelm-Fay-Strasse 21
D-65936 Frankfurt/Main
Germany

Tel.:
+49-69-9784-14-200

E-mail:
info@sinn.de

Website:
www.sinn.de

Founded:
1961

Number of employees:
approx. 135 (at the Frankfurt location)

Annual production:
approx. 14,000 watches

U.S. distributor:
WatchBuys
888-333-4895
www.watchbuys.com

Most important collections/price range:
Financial District, U-Models, Diapal / from approx.
$1,500 to $17,000

SINN

Pilot and flight instructor Helmut Sinn began manufacturing watches in Frankfurt am Main because he thought the pilot's watches on the market were too expensive. The resulting combination of top quality, functionality, and a good price-performance ratio turned out to be an excellent sales argument. There is hardly another source that offers watch lovers such a sophisticated and reasonable collection of sporty watches, many conceived to survive in extreme conditions by conforming to German DIN industrial norms.

The company remains in Frankfurt (in the Sossenheim district) where its headquarters and manufacturing space are in a two-story building that is the pride of the brand. In 1994, Lothar Schmidt took over leadership, and his product developers began looking for inspiration in other industries and the sciences. They did so out of a practical technical impulse without any plan for launching a trend. Research and development are consistently aimed at improving the functionality of the watches. This includes application of special Sinn technology such as moisture-proofing cases by pumping in an inert gas like argon. Other Sinn innovations include the Diapal (a lubricant-free lever escapement), the Hydro (an oil-filled diver's watch), and tegiment processing (for hardened steel and titanium surfaces). The latest innovation is a patent-pending alloy of bronze with a sixth of gold mixed in, goldbronze 125.

Having noticed a lack of norms for aviator watches, Schmidt negotiated a partnership with the Aachen Technical University to create the *Technischer Standard Fliegeruhren* (TESTAF, or Technical Standard for Pilot's Watches), which is housed at the Eurocopter headquarters.

Sinn also joined forces with two German watch companies, the Sächsische Uhrentechnologie Glashütte (SUG) and the Uhren-Werke-Dresden (UWD). The latter produced the outstanding UWD 33.1 caliber with Sinn as chaperone.

All these moves brought the company enough wherewithal to open new headquarters in the Sossenheim district of Frankfurt. The building offers nearly 25,000 square feet of space, most of which is devoted to assembly and manufacturing. At the heart of the two-story construction is a grandiose atrium with a skylight offering lots of natural light. The roof was also turned into an open-air terrace.

T50 Goldbronze

Reference number: 1052.061
Movement: automatic, Sellita Caliber SW300-1; ø 25.6 mm, height 3.6 mm; 25 jewels; 28,800 vph; 42-hour power reserve
Functions: hours, minutes, sweep seconds; date
Case: bead-blasted goldbronze 125 alloy, ø 41 mm, height 12.3 mm; unidirectional bezel, with 0-60 scale; sapphire crystal; screw-in crown; water-resistant to 50 atm
Band: textile, pin buckle
Remarks: dehumidifying technology (protective gas)
Price: $5,760; limited to 300 pieces

T50 GBDR

Reference number: 1052.020
Movement: automatic, Sellita Caliber SW300-1; ø 25.6 mm, height 3.6 mm; 25 jewels; 28,800 vph; 42-hour power reserve
Functions: hours, minutes, sweep seconds; date
Case: titanium, (bead-blasted) with special gold-bronze alloy, ø 41 mm, height 12.3 mm; unidirectional goldbronze 125 bezel, with 0-60 scale; sapphire crystal; screw-in crown; water-resistant to 50 atm
Band: titanium, folding clasp, with extension link
Remarks: dehumidifying technology (protective gas)
Price: $4,670

T50

Reference number: 1052.010
Movement: automatic, Sellita Caliber SW300-1; ø 25.6 mm, height 3.6 mm; 25 jewels; 28,800 vph; 42-hour power reserve
Functions: hours, minutes, sweep seconds; date
Case: titanium, (bead-blasted), ø 41 mm, height 12.3 mm; unidirectional bezel with 0-60 scale; sapphire crystal; screw-in crown; water-resistant to 50 atm
Band: textile, pin buckle
Remarks: dehumidifying technology (protective gas)
Price: $3,840

EZM 13.1

Reference number: 613.011
Movement: automatic, Sinn Caliber SZ02 (based on Concepto C99001); ø 30.4 mm, height 7.9 mm; 28 jewels; 28,800 vph; antimagnetic, finely finished movement; 46-hour power reserve
Functions: hours, minutes, subsidiary seconds; chronograph; date
Case: stainless steel, ø 41 mm, height 15 mm; sapphire crystal; screw-in crown; water-resistant to 50 atm
Band: stainless steel, folding clasp with extension link
Remarks: dehumidifying technology (protective gas)
Price: $3,640
Variations: with silicone strap ($3,440); with calfskin strap ($3,440)

103 Ti Ar

Reference number: 103.071
Movement: automatic, Concepto Caliber C99001; ø 30.4 mm, height 7.9 mm; 28 jewels; 28,800 vph; antimagnetic according to the German industrial norm (DIN), finely finished movement; 46-hour power reserve
Functions: hours, minutes, subsidiary seconds; chronograph; date and weekday
Case: titanium, ø 41 mm, height 17 mm; bidirectional bezel, with 0-60 scale; sapphire crystal; screw-in crown; water-resistant to 20 atm
Band: textile, pin buckle
Remarks: dehumidifying technology (protective gas)
Price: $3,180
Variations: with Diapal escapement ($4,170)

717

Reference number: 717.010
Movement: automatic, Sinn Caliber SZ01 (based on Concepto C99001); ø 30.4 mm, height 8.5 mm; 28 jewels; 28,800 vph; sweep stop-seconds and minute hands; 46-hour power reserve
Functions: hours, minutes, subsidiary seconds; chronograph; date
Case: tegimented stainless steel, with black hard coating, ø 45 mm, height 15.3 mm; sapphire crystal; screw-in crown; water-resistant to 20 atm
Band: calfskin, pin buckle
Remarks: dehumidifying technology (protective gas)
Price: $5,560

900 Diapal

Reference number: 900.013
Movement: automatic, La Joux-Perret Caliber 8000; ø 30.4 mm, height 7.9 mm; 28 jewels; 28,800 vph; oil-free escapement (Diapal); shock-protected and antimagnetic according to the German industrial norm (DIN); finely finished movement; 55-hour power reserve
Functions: hours, minutes, subsidiary seconds; additional 24-hour display (2nd time zone); chronograph; date
Case: stainless steel, ø 44 mm, height 15.5 mm; crown-activated inner rotating scale ring, with 0-60 scale; sapphire crystal; screw-in crown; water-resistant to 20 atm
Band: calfskin, pin buckle
Remarks: dehumidifying technology (protective gas), antimagnetic to 80,000 A/m
Price: $4,290
Variations: as 900 Flieger without Diapal technology ($3,990)

910 SRS

Reference number: 910.020
Movement: automatic, modified ETA Caliber 7750; ø 30 mm, height 8.4 mm; 25 jewels; 28,800 vph; column-wheel control of the chronograph functions; antimagnetic according to the German industrial norm (DIN); finely finished dial; 46-hour power reserve
Functions: hours, minutes, subsidiary seconds; flyback chronograph; date
Case: stainless steel, ø 41.5 mm, height 15.5 mm; sapphire crystal; transparent case back; water-resistant to 10 atm
Band: horse leather, pin buckle
Price: $4,460

3006 Hunter Chronograph

Reference number: 3006.010
Movement: automatic, Concepto Caliber C99002; ø 30.4 mm, height 7.9 mm; 25 jewels; 28,800 vph; antimagnetic according to the German industrial norm (DIN); 46-hour power reserve
Functions: hours, minutes, subsidiary seconds; additional 24-hour display; chronograph date, weekday, month, moon phase
Case: tegimented stainless steel, ø 44 mm, height 15.5 mm; sapphire crystal; transparent case back; screw-in crown; water-resistant to 20 atm
Band: calfskin, pin buckle
Remarks: dehumidifying technology (protective gas)
Price: $5,440

1739 Ag B

Reference number: 1739.021
Movement: automatic, Sellita Caliber SW300-1;
ø 25.6 mm, height 3.6 mm; 25 jewels; 28,800 vph;
42-hour power reserve
Functions: hours, minutes
Case: polished argentium silver, ø 39 mm, height
9.1 mm; sapphire crystal; transparent case back;
screw-in crown; water-resistant to 10 atm
Band: calfskin, pin buckle
Price: $2,820
Variations: without silver alloy, with silver plated dial
($2,350), without silver alloy, with black dial ($2,350)

104 St Sa I A

Reference number: 104.014
Movement: automatic, Sellita Caliber SW220-1;
ø 25.6 mm, height 4.6 mm; 26 jewels; 28,800 vph;
finely finished movement; 38-hour power reserve
Functions: hours, minutes, sweep seconds;
date and weekday
Case: stainless steel, ø 41 mm, height 11.9 mm;
bidirectional bezel, with 0-60 scale; sapphire crystal;
transparent case back; screw-in crown;
water-resistant to 20 atm
Band: calfskin, pin buckle
Price: $1,640
Variations: with stainless steel bracelet ($1,990)

105 St Sa UTC

Reference number: 105.020
Movement: automatic, Sellita Caliber SW330-1;
ø 25.6 mm, height 4.1 mm; 25 jewels; 28,800 vph;
50-hour power reserve
Functions: hours, minutes, sweep seconds;
additional 24-hour display (2nd time zone); date
Case: stainless steel, ø 41 mm, height 11.9 mm;
hidirectional bezel, with 0-24 scale; sapphire crystal;
transparent case back; screw-in crown;
water-resistant to 20 atm
Band: stainless steel, folding clasp, with safety lock
Price: $2,240
Variations: with white dial

105 St Sa W

Reference number: 105.011
Movement: automatic, Sellita Caliber SW220-1;
ø 25.6 mm, height 5.05 mm; 26 jewels; 28,800 vph;
38-hour power reserve
Functions: hours, minutes, sweep seconds;
date and weekday
Case: stainless steel, ø 41 mm, height 11.9 mm;
bidirectional bezel, with 0-12 scale; sapphire crystal;
transparent case back; screw-in crown;
water-resistant to 20 atm
Band: silicone, pin buckle
Price: $1,730
Variations: with black dial

556 A RS

Reference number: 556.0141
Movement: automatic, Sellita Caliber SW200-1;
ø 25.6 mm, height 4.6 mm; 26 jewels; 28,800 vph;
antimagnetic according to the German industrial norm
(DIN); 38-hour power reserve
Functions: hours, minutes, sweep seconds; date
Case: stainless steel, ø 38.5 mm, height 11 mm;
sapphire crystal; transparent case back; screw-in
crown; water-resistant to 20 atm
Band: stainless steel, folding clasp, with safety lock
Price: $1,690
Variations: with Index-dial ($1,770); with mother-of-
pearl-dial ($1,790)

556 I Mother-of-Pearl S

Reference number: 556.0105
Movement: automatic, Sellita Caliber SW200-1;
ø 25.6 mm, height 4.6 mm; 26 jewels; 28,800 vph;
antimagnetic according to the German industrial norm
(DIN); 38-hour power reserve
Functions: hours, minutes, sweep seconds
Case: stainless steel, ø 38.5 mm, height 11 mm;
sapphire crystal; transparent case back;
screw-in crown; water-resistant to 20 atm
Band: stainless steel, folding clasp, with safety lock
Remarks: mother-of-pearl dial
Price: $1,770
Variations: various colors

6060 B Frankfurt World Time

Reference number: 6060.013
Movement: automatic, Sellita Caliber SW330-1;
ø 25.6 mm, height 4.1 mm; 25 jewels; 28,800 vph;
finely finished dial; 50-hour power reserve
Functions: hours, minutes, sweep seconds; additional
24-hour display (2nd time zone); date
Case: stainless steel, ø 38.5 mm, height 12 mm; crown-
activated inner rotating scale ring, with 0-12 scale;
sapphire crystal; transparent case back; screw-in
crown; water-resistant to 10 atm
Band: stainless steel, double folding clasp
Remarks: comes with additional calfskin strap
Price: $3,140
Variations: with black dial

U2 S

Reference number: 1020.020
Movement: automatic, Sellita Caliber SW330-1;
ø 25.6 mm, height 4.6 mm; 25 jewels; 28,800 vph;
38-hour power reserve
Functions: hours, minutes, sweep seconds; additional
24-hour display (2nd time zone); date
Case: stainless steel (submarine steel), tegimented,
with black hard coating, ø 44 mm, height 15.5 mm;
unidirectional bezel with 0-60 scale; sapphire crystal;
screw-in crown; water-resistant to 200 atm
Band: silicone, folding clasp
Remarks: certified according to European diving norms
Price: $3,730
Variations: without hard coating ($3,440); with
black-coated bezel ($3,540)

U50

Reference number: 1050.010
Movement: automatic, Sellita Caliber SW300-1;
ø 25.6 mm, height 3.6 mm; 25 jewels; 28,800 vph;
42-hour power reserve
Functions: hours, minutes, sweep seconds; date
Case: submarine steel, ø 41 mm, height 11.5 mm;
unidirectional bezel with 0-60 scale; sapphire crystal;
screw-in crown; water-resistant to 50 atm
Band: silicone, folding clasp
Remarks: certified according to European diving norms
Price: $2,710
Variations: with black hard coating ($3,270)

6012

Reference number: 6012.010
Movement: automatic, Sinn Caliber SZ06 (based
on ETA 7751); ø 30.4 mm, height 7.9 mm; 25 jewels;
28,800 vph; antimagnetic according to the German
industrial norm (DIN); 42-hour power reserve
Functions: hours, minutes, subsidiary seconds;
chronograph; full calendar with date, weekday, month,
moon phase
Case: stainless steel, ø 41.5 mm, height 14.5 mm;
sapphire crystal; transparent case back;
water-resistant to 10 atm
Band: calfskin, pin buckle
Remarks: comes with additional stainless-steel bracelet
Price: $5,740

434 St GG B

Reference number: 434.032
Movement: quartz, ETA Caliber E64.101, thermos-
compensated; antimagnetic according to the German
industrial norm (DIN)
Functions: hours, minutes, sweep seconds
Case: stainless steel, ø 34 mm, height 8 mm; bezel in
yellow gold; sapphire crystal; water-resistant to 10 atm
Band: stainless steel, double folding clasp
Remarks: Q-technology to shield electromagnetic
impulses from the quartz movement
Price: $2,060
Variations: with black dial; with stainless-steel bezel
($970)

EZM 12

Reference number: 112.010
Movement: automatic, ETA Caliber 2836-2; ø 25.6 mm,
height 5.05 mm; 25 jewels; 28,800 vph; antimagnetic
to 80,000 A/m according to German Industrial Norm
(DIN); 38-hour power reserve
Functions: hours, minutes, sweep seconds;
date and weekday
Case: tegimented stainless steel, ø 44 mm, height
14 mm; bidirectional bezel with 60-minute division
(counting down); crown-controlled inner bezel with
0-60 scale (upward counting); sapphire crystal,
water-resistant to 20 atm
Band: silicone, folding clasp
Remarks: developed for medevac services; with pulse
scale; dehumidifying technology (protective gas)
Price: $4,120

Speake-Marin
Avenue de Miremont 33C
1206 Geneva
Switzerland

Tel.:
+41-21-695-26-55

E-mail:
info@speake-marin.com

Website:
www.speake-marin.com

Founded:
2002

Number of employees:
9

Annual production:
400 watches

U.S. Distribution
Watches of Switzerland
844-4USAWOS
jkloiber@battalionpr.com

Most important collections:
One & Two, Art Series, Vintage, Haute Horlogerie

SPEAKE-MARIN

So many brands these days bear the name of great watchmakers from the distant past. Speake-Marin is an exception because founder Peter Speake-Marin is very much alive but is no longer connected with his company, other than through his name and style.

This dyed-in-the-wool independent from Essex, England, learned the trade at Hackney College and the famous WOSTEP. In 1996, he moved to Le Locle, Switzerland, to work with Renaud et Papi, at which point he set about making his own pieces. A dual-train tourbillon (the Foundation Watch) opened the door to the prestigious AHCI.

Speake-Marin's watches have a strong connection to the industry's traditions. The topping tool logo suggested the expert handicraft that goes into making a watch, rather than hyper-modern CNC machines. He has also had his skilled fingers in a number of iconic timepieces, like the HM1 of MB&F, the Chapter One for Maîtres du Temps, and the Harry Winston Excenter Tourbillon.

The baton was passed to Christelle Rosnoblet in 2012—and then with more finality in 2017 when Peter Speake-Marin decided to step out completely. She had the delicate task of keeping the old fans happy while letting the brand take on a more distinct identity. The "old bottles," one might say are elements like the small seconds dial at 1:30, which also gives space to a retrograde date on the new One & Two tourbillon collection. There is, too, the conical crown and the famous Piccadilly case, now remodeled. By the same token, the innovations are hardly subtle. The Ripples dials, with their deep, lacquered engravings, show what happens when a strong wind begins blowing on traditional côtes de Genève. And there are the bold colors, like minty greens or eye-smacking pink—perhaps for the Barbie fans? All this on a backdrop of robust watchmaking assisted by the Cercle des Horlogers platform and industry stars like Eric Giroud.

Worthy of note, too, is the brand's commitment to charity work, this year to help an organization working to save the koalas in Australia.

Art Series Koala

Reference number: 414217420
Movement: automatic, SMA-03 Caliber; ø 32 mm, height 4.2 mm; 31 jewels; 21,600 vph; micro-rotor; 52-hour power reserve
Functions: hours, minutes, subsidiary seconds
Case: stainless steel, ø 42 mm, height 10.5 mm; sapphire crystal; transparent case back; water-resistant to 5 atm
Band: recycled nylon with corn-based leather lining, pin buckle
Remarks: gradient green lacquer dial with hand micro-painted koala; watch supports the Queensland Koala Crusaders
Price: $33,400; limited to 6 pieces
Variations: 38-mm case (limited to 3 pieces)

Ripples Metallic Green

Reference number: 604015460
Movement: automatic, SMA-03 Caliber; ø 32 mm, height 4.2 mm; 31 jewels; 21,600 vph; micro-rotor; 52-hour power reserve
Functions: hours, minutes, subsidiary seconds
Case: stainless steel, ø 42 mm, height 10.5 mm; sapphire crystal; transparent case back; water-resistant to 5 atm
Band: stainless steel, buckle
Remarks: engraved wave pattern with green PVD and lacker finish
Price: $26,400; limited to 60 pieces
Variations: 38-mm case; dials in various colors

One & Two Openworked Dual Time Pink

Reference number: 414209290
Movement: automatic, SMA02 Caliber; ø 34 mm, height 6.6 mm; 36 jewels; 28,000 vph; integrated micro-rotor; open-worked dial, 52-hour power reserve
Functions: hours, minutes, subsidiary seconds; 24-hour time zone with day/night indication; retrograde date
Case: titanium with black DLC, ø 42 mm, height 12.35 mm; sapphire crystal; transparent case back; water-resistant to 3 bars
Band: rubber, pin buckle with black DLC
Price: $40,135; limited to 28 pieces
Variations: in various color themes; in 38-mm case ($38,410, limited to 10 pieces)

STOWA

When a watch brand organizes a museum for itself, it is usually with good reason. The firm Stowa may not be the biggest fish in the horological pond, but it has been around for more than eighty years, and its products are well worth taking a look at as expressions of German watchmaking culture. Stowa began in Pforzheim, then moved to the little industrial town of Rheinfelden, and now operates in Engelsbrand, a "suburb" of Pforzheim.

Stowa is one of the few German brands to have operated without interruption since the start of the twentieth century, albeit with a new owner as of 1990. Besides all the political upheavals, it survived the quartz crisis of the 1970s, during which Europe was flooded with cheap watches from Asia and many traditional German watchmakers were put out of business. Founder Walter Storz managed to keep Stowa going, but even a quality fanatic has to pay a price during times of trouble; with huge input from his son, Werner, Storz restructured the company so that it was able to begin encasing reasonably priced quartz movements rather than being strictly an assembler of mechanical ones.

Another watchmaker, Jörg Schauer, took over the brand in 1996. Spurred on by the success of his own brand, he focused on mechanics from the very beginning. Collaboration with designer Hartmut Esslinger, the founder of Frog Design, resulted in a modern design language that is expressed above all in the Flieger collection. After twenty-five years, Schauer sold the Stowa watch brand to the Tempus Arte Group, which includes Lang & Heyne Dresden and the affiliated Uhren Werke Dresden (UWD) and Leinfelder Uhren in Munich. The group also holds a stake in customization specialist Blaken.

Stowa GmbH & Co. KG
Gewerbepark 16
D-75331 Engelsbrand
Germany

Tel.:
+49-7082-942630

E-mail:
info@stowa.com

Website:
www.stowa.com

Founded:
1927

Number of employees:
20

Annual production:
around 4,500 watches

Distribution:
Direct sales; please contact company in Germany; orders taken by phone Monday through Friday 9 a.m. to 5 p.m. European time.

Note: Prices are according to daily euro exchange rate.

Flieger Verus 40

Reference number: FliegerVerus40
Movement: automatic, Sellita Caliber SW200-1; ø 25.6 mm, height 4.6 mm; 26 jewels; 28,800 vph; 38-hour power reserve
Functions: hours, minutes, sweep seconds; date
Case: stainless steel, ø 40 mm, height 10.2 mm; sapphire crystal; transparent case back; water-resistant to 5 atm
Band: calfskin, pin buckle
Price: $1,000
Variations: with date function; with "top" version of the movement ($1,150); with manual winding (€ $1,170)

Flieger Klassik 40

Reference number: FliegerKlassik40
Movement: automatic, Sellita Caliber SW200-1; ø 25.6 mm, height 4.6 mm; 26 jewels; 28,800 vph; 38-hour power reserve
Functions: hours, minutes, sweep seconds
Case: stainless steel, ø 40 mm, height 10.2 mm; sapphire crystal; transparent case back; water-resistant to 5 atm
Band: calfskin, pin buckle
Price: $1,330
Variations: with manual winding ($1,350)

Flieger Bronze Vintage Baumuster "B" 40

Reference number: FliegerbronzeVintageBauB40
Movement: automatic, Sellita Caliber SW200-1; ø 25.6 mm, height 4.6 mm; 26 jewels; 28,800 vph; 38-hour power reserve
Functions: hours, minutes, sweep seconds
Case: bronze, ø 40 mm, height 10.20 mm; sapphire crystal; transparent case back; water-resistant to 5 atm
Band: calfskin, pin buckle
Price: $1,540
Variations: with dates function; with manual winding ($1,560)

Marine Classic 40 Navis Limited

Reference number: Marine40NavisLimited
Movement: automatic, Sellita Caliber SW200-1;
ø 25.6 mm, height 4.6 mm; 26 jewels; 28,800 vph;
38-hour power reserve
Functions: hours, minutes, sweep seconds
Case: stainless steel, ø 40 mm, height 10.30 mm;
sapphire crystal; transparent case back;
water-resistant to 5 atm
Band: calfskin, pin buckle
Price: $1,330
Variations: with blue-black calfskin strap ($1,370)

Marine Original Bronze Vintage

Reference number: MarineOriginalbronzeVintage
Movement: hand-wound, ETA Caliber 6498-1;
ø 37.2 mm, height 4.5 mm; 17 jewels; 18.000 A/h; screw
balance, swan-neck fine regulator, côtes de Genève,
blued screws; 46-hour power reserve
Functions: hours, minutes, subsidiary seconds
Case: bronze, ø 41 mm, height 12 mm; sapphire crystal;
transparent case back; water-resistant to 5 atm
Band: calfskin, pin buckle
Price: $1,900
Variations: with Arabic numerals

Antea Classic 390

Reference number: AnteaKlassik390
Movement: automatic, Sellita Caliber SW200-1;
ø 25.6 mm, height 4.6 mm; 26 jewels; 28,800 vph;
38-hour power reserve
Functions: hours, minutes, sweep seconds; date
Case: stainless steel, ø 39 mm, height 9.2 mm;
sapphire crystal; transparent case back;
water-resistant to 5 atm
Band: calfskin, pin buckle
Price: $1,330
Variations: with manual winding ($1,350)

Verus GMT Chronograph

Reference number: VerusGMTchronograph
Movement: automatic, ETA Caliber 7754; ø 30 mm,
height 7.9 mm; 25 jewels; 28,800 vph; 54-hour power
reserve
Functions: hours, minutes; additional 24-hour display
(2nd time zone); chronograph
Case: stainless steel, ø 41 mm, height 14.7 mm;
sapphire crystal; transparent case back;
water-resistant to 5 atm
Band: calfskin, folding clasp
Price: $2,850

Partitio Classic Black

Reference number: PartitioKlassikschwarz
Movement: automatic, Sellita Caliber SW200-1;
ø 25.6 mm, height 4.6 mm; 26 jewels; 28,800 vph;
38-hour power reserve
Functions: hours, minutes, sweep seconds
Case: stainless steel, ø 37 mm, height 10.8 mm;
sapphire crystal; water-resistant to 5 atm
Band: calfskin, pin buckle
Price: $950
Variations: with manual winding ($1,100)

Prodiver Vintage 95 Limited

Reference number: Prodiver95VintageLimited
Movement: automatic, Sellita Caliber SW200-1;
ø 25.6 mm, height 4.6 mm; 26 jewels; 28,800 vph;
38-hour power reserve
Functions: hours, minutes, sweep seconds
Case: stainless steel, ø 42 mm, height 15.6 mm;
unidirectional bezel with ceramic insert, with
0-60 scale; sapphire crystal; screw-in crown;
water-resistant to 100 atm
Band: rubber, folding clasp, with safety lock
Price: $1,900

TAG HEUER

Measuring speed accurately in ever greater detail was always the goal of TAG Heuer, a company founded in 1860 in St. Imier, Switzerland, by Edouard Heuer. With this in mind, the brand strove for a number of technical milestones, including the first automatic chronograph caliber with a microrotor, created in 1969 with Hamilton-Büren, Breitling, and Dubois Dépraz. That was before Techniques d'Avant Garde (TAG), a high-tech firm, bought the company.

In 1999, TAG Heuer became part of LVMH Group and in addition to producing its own watches also later served as an extended workbench for companion brands Zenith and Hublot.

TAG Heuer has continued to break world speed records for mechanical escapements. For example, the Caliber 360 combined a standard movement with a 360,000-vph (50-Hz) chronograph mechanism able to measure hundredths of a second. And then there is the Mikrotourbillons, which features a separate chronograph escapement driven at a breakneck 360,000 vph.

TAG Heuer, now under CEO Frédéric Arnault, son of LVMH owner Bernard Arnault, is evolving along several lines. One is to re-release Heuer classics in more modern garb. The Heuer 02 manufacture caliber, for example, is a redeveloped chronograph movement, produced in a purpose-built, ultra-modern factory in Chevenez. In addition to cooperations with the sports car manufacturer Porsche and the unchanged strong commitment to Formula 1 (with Red Bull Racing), the company relaunched a streamlined Aquaracer, a watch with a distinctive dodecagonal rotating bezel.

The company has also continued exploring contemporary technology, with a line of connected watches. By the same token, it has not abandoned its pursuit analog pursuits, like an electromagnetic, hairspring-less pendulum watches, or new materials, like graphene.

It's the Carrera, though, that is really the brand emblem, so it appears a lot on the menu. In 2022, for example, the Carrera Plasma became the most expensive watch in the collection, thanks to a dial covered in lab-grown diamonds. To celebrate the model's sixtieth anniversary in 2023, the designers came up with the Carrera 60th Anniversary based on a watch that had been released in 1968, five years following the first model.

The "Glassbox" Carreras released in the summer of 2023 are more modern. The dial extends up to the sides of the watch, where one finds a minute track, and higher up is a tachymeter scale. The sapphire crystal is in fact like a dome, hence the name "Glassbox."

TAG Heuer
Branch of LVMH SA
6a, rue L.-J.-Chevrolet
CH-2300 La Chaux-de-Fonds
Switzerland

Tel.:
+41-32-919-8164

E-mail:
info@tagheuer.com

Website:
www.tagheuer.com

Founded:
1860

Number of employees:
Around 2,000 internationally

Annual production:
Est. 400,000

U.S. distributor:
TAG Heuer/LVMH Watch & Jewelry USA
966 South Springfield Avenue
Springfield, NJ 07081
973-467-1890

Most important collections/price range:
TAG Heuer Carrera, Monaco, Aquaracer, Formula 1, Connected, Autovia, / from approx. $1,450 to $24,000

Monza Flyback Chronometer

Reference number: CR5090.FN6001
Movement: automatic, TAG Heuer Caliber Heuer 02; ø 31 mm, height 6.9 mm; 33 jewels; 28,800 vph; 80-hour power reserve; COSC-certified chronometer
Functions: hours, minutes, subsidiary seconds; flyback chronograph; date
Case: carbon fiber, ø 42 mm; sapphire crystal; transparent case back; screw-in crown; water-resistant to 10 atm
Band: textile, folding clasp
Price: $13,850

Connected Calibre E4 42 mm

Reference number: SBR8081.BT6299
Movement: quartz, Qualcomm Snapdragon 4100+Smartwatch processor with Google's Wear-OS; 330mAh lithium-ion battery
Functions: hours, minutes, seconds (digital); world time display, pulse sensors, compass, speed; near-field communication (NFC), microphone; various micro-apps available; date
Case: titanium with black DLC, ø 42 mm; bezel with ceramic insert; sapphire crystal; water-resistant to 5 atm
Band: silicone, folding clasp
Price: $2,350

Connected Calibre E4 Sport Edition 45 mm

Reference number: SBR8A80.EB0259
Movement: quartz, Qualcomm Snapdragon WearTMSmartwatch processor with Google's Wear-OS; 430mAh lithium-ion battery
Functions: hours, minutes, seconds (digital); world time display, pulse sensors, compass, speed; near-field communication (NFC), microphone; various micro-apps available; date
Case: titanium with black DLC, ø 45 mm; bezel with ceramic insert; sapphire crystal; water-resistant to 5 atm
Band: silicone, pin buckle
Price: $2,600

Carrera Chronograph x Porsche Orange Racing

Reference number: CBN2A1M.FC6526
Movement: automatic, TAG Heuer Caliber Heuer 02; ø 31 mm, height 6.9 mm; 33 jewels; 28,800 vph; 80-hour power reserve; COSC-certified chronometer
Functions: hours, minutes, subsidiary seconds; flyback chronograph; date
Case: stainless steel with black DLC, ø 44 mm, height 15.27 mm; sapphire crystal; transparent case back; screw-in crown; water-resistant to 10 atm
Band: calfskin, folding clasp
Price: $7,050

Carrera Chronograph 60th Anniversary Edition

Reference number: CBK221H.FC8317
Movement: automatic, TAG Heuer Caliber Heuer 02; ø 31 mm, height 6.9 mm; 33 jewels; 28,800 vph; 80-hour power reserve; COSC-certified chronometer
Functions: hours, minutes, subsidiary seconds; flyback chronograph
Case: stainless steel, ø 39 mm, height 13.9 mm; sapphire crystal; transparent case back; screw-in crown; water-resistant to 10 atm
Band: calfskin, folding clasp
Price: $7,400

Carrera Chronograph

Reference number: CBN201D.FC6543
Movement: automatic, TAG Heuer Caliber Heuer 02; ø 31 mm, height 6.9 mm; 33 jewels; 28,800 vph; 80-hour power reserve; COSC-certified chronometer
Functions: hours, minutes, subsidiary seconds; flyback chronograph; date
Case: stainless steel, ø 42 mm, height 14.48 mm; sapphire crystal; transparent case back; screw-in crown; water-resistant to 10 atm
Band: calfskin, folding clasp
Price: $5,750

Carrera Date

Reference number: WBN2312.BA0001
Movement: automatic, TAG Heuer Calibre 7 (based on ETA 2893-2); ø 25.6 mm, height 4.1 mm; 21 jewels; 28,800 vph; 38-hour power reserve
Functions: hours, minutes, sweep seconds; date
Case: stainless steel, ø 36 mm, height 10 mm; sapphire crystal; transparent case back; water-resistant to 10 atm
Band: stainless steel, folding clasp
Price: $3,200
Variations: various colors

Carrera Chronograph Glassbox

Reference number: CBS2212.FC6535
Movement: automatic, TAG Heuer Caliber TH20-00; ø 31 mm, height 6.9 mm; 33 jewels; 28,800 vph; 80-hour power reserve
Functions: hours, minutes, subsidiary seconds; chronograph; date
Case: stainless steel, ø 39 mm, height 13.9 mm; sapphire crystal; transparent case back; water-resistant to 10 atm
Band: calfskin, folding clasp
Price: $6,450

Carrera Chronograph Glassbox

Reference number: CBS2210.FC6534
Movement: automatic, TAG Heuer Caliber TH20-00; ø 31 mm, height 6.9 mm; 33 jewels; 28,800 vph; 80-hour power reserve
Functions: hours, minutes, subsidiary seconds; chronograph; date
Case: stainless steel, ø 39 mm, height 13.9 mm; sapphire crystal; transparent case back; water-resistant to 10 atm
Band: calfskin, folding clasp
Price: $6,450

Carrera Chronograph Tourbillon

Reference number: CBS5010.FC6543
Movement: automatic, TAG Heuer Caliber TH20-09; ø 31 mm, height 6.9 mm; 33 jewels; 28,800 vph; one-minute tourbillon; COSC-certified chronometer
Functions: hours, minutes; chronograph
Case: stainless steel, ø 39 mm, height 13.9 mm; sapphire crystal; transparent case back; water-resistant to 10 atm
Band: calfskin, folding clasp
Price: $24,050

Carrera Plasma Tourbillon Nanograph

Reference number: XCBN5A90.FC8315
Movement: automatic, TAG Heuer Caliber Heuer 02T; ø 31 mm, height 6.9 mm; 33 jewels; 28,800 vph; one-minute tourbillon; COSC-certified chronometer
Functions: hours, minutes; chronograph
Case: aluminum (anodized black) with 48 lab-grown diamonds, ø 44 mm; sapphire crystal; transparent case back; water-resistant to 10 atm
Band: aluminum (black anodized) with diamonds, double folding clasp
Price: $376,000

Aquaracer Professional 200 Solargraph

Reference number: WBP1180.BF0000
Movement: quartz, TAG Heuer Caliber TH50-00
Functions: hours, minutes, sweep seconds; date
Case: titanium, ø 40 mm, height 11 mm; unidirectional bezel with 0-60 scale; sapphire crystal; screw-in crown; water-resistant to 20 atm
Band: titanium, folding clasp
Remarks: power supplied by solar cell integrated in the dial
Price: $3,050

Aquaracer Calibre 5 Professional 200

Reference number: WBP2150.FT6210
Movement: automatic, TAG Heuer Caliber 5 (based on ETA 2824-2); ø 26 mm, height 4.6 mm; 25 jewels; 28,800 vph
Functions: hours, minutes, sweep seconds; date
Case: stainless steel, ø 40 mm, height 11 mm; unidirectional bezel and crown in yellow gold, with 0-60 scale; sapphire crystal; screw-in crown; water-resistant to 20 atm
Band: rubber, folding clasp
Price: $5,050
Variations: various cases, straps, and dials

Aquaracer Professional 200

Reference number: WBP2450.FT6215
Movement: automatic, TAG Heuer Caliber 9 (based on ETA 2000-1); ø 20.6 mm, height 3.6 mm; 18 jewels; 28,800 vph; 40-hour power reserve
Functions: hours, minutes, sweep seconds; date
Case: stainless steel, ø 30 mm; unidirectional bezel and crown in yellow gold, with 0-60 scale; sapphire crystal; screw-in crown, in yellow gold; water-resistant to 20 atm
Band: rubber, folding clasp
Remarks: dial with 11 diamonds
Price: $4,700
Variations: various cases, straps, and dials

Aquaracer Professional 200

Reference number: WBP5152.FT6210
Movement: automatic, TAG Heuer Caliber TH31-00; 30 jewels; 28,800 vph; skeletonized rotor; 80-hour power reserve; COSC-certified chronometer
Functions: hours, minutes, sweep seconds; date
Case: yellow gold, ø 40 mm, height 11 mm; unidirectional bezel with 0-60 scale; sapphire crystal; transparent case back; screw-in crown; water-resistant to 20 atm
Band: rubber, folding clasp
Price: $18,450
Variations: in rose gold ($18,450)

Temption GmbH
Raistinger Str. 46
D-71083 Herrenberg
Germany

Tel.:
+49-7032-977-954

E-mail:
ftemption@aol.com

Website:
www.temption.info

Founded:
1997

Number of employees:
4

Annual production:
700 watches

U.S. distributor:
Debby Gordon
3306 Arrow Creek Dr.
Granbury, TX 76049
debby@temptionusa.com
Toll-free number: 1-888-400-4293

Most important collections/price range:
automatics (three-hand), GMT, chronographs, and
chronographs with complications / approx. $1,900
to $4,200

TEMPTION

Temption has been operating under the leadership of Klaus Ulbrich since 1997. Ulbrich is an engineer with special training in the construction of watches and movements, and right from the start, he intended to develop timekeepers that were modern in their aesthetics but not subject to the whims of zeitgeist. Retro watches would have no place in his collections. The design behind all Temption models is inspired by two contrasting stylistic movements: the modernist design codes of the Irish architect Eileen Gray (1878–1976) and the fascinating Japanese concept of *wabi sabi*, the aesthetics of passing time and its impact on the world we create.

Ulbrich sketches all the watches himself. The components are purchased from various sources, though some are made in-house. Assembly is done in the company facility in Herrenberg, a town just to the east of the Black Forest. The primary functions are always easy to read, even in low light. The company logo is discreetly included on the dial.

Ulbrich works according to a model he calls the "information pyramid." Hours and minutes are at the tip, with all other functions subordinated. To maintain this hierarchy and the calm aesthetics, the date windows are in the same hue as the dials, and the subdials are not framed in any way. The most unimportant information for reading time comes at the end of the "pyramid"; it is the logo, which appears as a shiny image on the dial and can only be identified in lateral light.

The Temption chronographs are perfect expressions of this vision of simplicity even with a naturally complex dial. With the CGK205, Ulbrich took the concept out of the case. Whether it be the leather strap or the stainless-steel bracelet, the watch's attachment is seamlessly integrated into the case, without any visible split. Of late, though, some models have also been given touches of color, notably red coral cabochons in the crown and pushers.

Classic Blau

Reference number: CLB316LSST
Movement: automatic, ETA 7750; ø 30 mm, height 7.9 mm; 25 jewels; 28,800 vph; skeletonized rotor, decorated movement; 42-hour power reserve
Functions: hours, minutes, subsidiary seconds; chronograph; date and weekday
Case: stainless steel with rose-gold PVD, ø 43 mm, height 14.7 mm; sapphire crystal; transparent case back; screw-in crown and pushers, with onyx cabochons; water-resistant to 10 atm
Band: calfskin, pin buckle
Price: $2,480

Chronograph CGK204 White

Reference number: 204V2316BSST
Movement: automatic, Temption Caliber T18.1 (based on ETA 7751); ø 30 mm, height 7.8 mm; 25 jewels; 28,800 vph; finely finished movement; 42-hour power reserve
Functions: hours, minutes, subsidiary seconds; additional 24-hour display (2nd time zone); chronograph; full calendar with date, weekday, month, moon phase
Case: stainless steel, ø 43 mm, height 14 mm; sapphire crystal; transparent case back; screw-in crown and pushers, with coral cabochons; water-resistant to 10 atm
Band: calfskin, folding clasp
Price: $2,700
Variations: with rubber strap

Chronograph CGK205-Blau V2

Reference number: 205V2316BSST
Movement: automatic, Temption Caliber T18.1 (based on ETA 7751); ø 30 mm, height 7.8 mm; 25 jewels; 28,800 vph; finely finished movement; 42-hour power reserve
Functions: hours, minutes, subsidiary seconds; additional 24-hour display; chronograph; full calendar with date, weekday, month, moon phase
Case: stainless steel, ø 43 mm, height 14 mm; sapphire crystal; transparent case back; screw-in crown and pushers, with colored cabochons; water-resistant to 10 atm
Band: calfskin, folding clasp
Remarks: comes with additional stainless steel link bracelet
Price: $3,000

TISSOT

There is Swiss-made, and then there is the Swiss Watch, as a kind of unobtrusive yet clearly-defined icon one you will see on many a Swiss wrist. That's a Tissot. The company was founded in 1853 in the town of Le Locle in the Jura mountains. In the century that followed, it gained international recognition for its Savonnette pocket watch. And even when the wristwatch became popular in the early twentieth century, time and again Tissot managed to attract attention to its products. To this day, the Banana Watch of 1916 and its first watches in the art deco style (1919) remain design icons of that epoch. The watchmaker has always been at the top of its technical game as well: the first amagnetic watch (1930), the first mechanical plastic watch (Astrolon, 1971), and its touch-screen T-Touch (1999) all bear witness to Tissot's remarkable capacity for finding unusual and modern solutions.

Today, Tissot belongs to the Swatch Group and, with its wide selection of quartz and inexpensive mechanical watches, serves as the group's entry-level brand. Within this price segment, Tissot offers something special for the buyer who values traditional watchmaking but is not of limitless financial means. The brand has been cultivating a sportive image of late, expanding into everything from basketball to superbike racing, from ice hockey to fencing—and water sports, of course. Partnerships with several NBA teams have been signed, notably with the Houston Rockets, Chicago Bulls, and Washington Wizards in October 2018. The chronograph Couturier line is outfitted with the new ETA chronograph caliber C01.211. This caliber features a number of plastic parts: another step in simplifying, and lowering the cost of, mechanical movements.

Increasingly, in addition, a number of Tissot models are being equipped with the automatic caliber Powermatic 80, which boasts a silicon hairspring, has outstanding isochronous oscillation, and is impervious to magnetic fields and changes in temperature. And for the buyer, it means only a slight increase in price.

Tissot SA
Chemin des Tourelles, 17
CH-2400 Le Locle
Switzerland

Tel.:
+41-32-933-3111

E-mail:
info@tissot.ch

Website:
www.tissotwatches.com

Founded:
1853

U.S. distributor:
Tissot
The Swatch Group (U.S.), Inc.
703 Waterford Way, Suite 450
Miami, FL 33126
www.us.tissotshop.com

Most important collections/price range:
Ballade / from $925; T-Touch / from $850; NBA Collection / from $375; Chemin des Tourelles / from $795; Seastar from $495; Swissmatic from $395

PRX Powermatic 80

Reference number: T137.407.11.351.00
Movement: automatic, ETA Caliber Powermatic 80 (based on ETA 2824-2); ø 25.6 mm, height 4.74 mm; 23 jewels; 21,600 vph; 80-hour power reserve
Functions: hours, minutes, sweep seconds; date
Case: stainless steel, ø 40 mm, height 10.93 mm; sapphire crystal; transparent case back; water-resistant to 10 atm
Band: stainless steel, folding clasp
Price: $725
Variations: various cases, straps, and dials

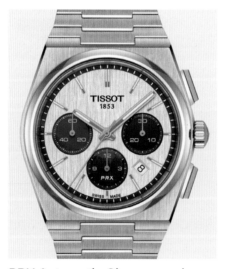

PRX Automatic Chronograph

Reference number: T137.427.11.011.01
Movement: automatic, ETA Caliber A05.H31; ø 30 mm, height 7.9 mm; 27 jewels; 28,800 vph; 60-hour power reserve
Functions: hours, minutes, subsidiary seconds; chronograph; date
Case: stainless steel, ø 42 mm, height 14.5 mm; sapphire crystal; transparent case back; water-resistant to 10 atm
Band: stainless steel, double folding clasp
Price: $1,895
Variations: various dial colors

PRX Powermatic 80

Reference number: T137.407.17.041.00
Movement: automatic, ETA Caliber Powermatic 80 (based on ETA 2824-2); ø 25.6 mm, height 4.74 mm; 23 jewels; 21,600 vph; 80-hour power reserve
Functions: hours, minutes, sweep seconds; date
Case: stainless steel, ø 40 mm, height 10.93 mm; sapphire crystal; transparent case back; water-resistant to 10 atm
Band: rubber, pin buckle
Price: $675

Chemin de Tourelles Powermatic 80

Reference number: T139.807.11.061.00
Movement: automatic, ETA Caliber Powermatic 80 (based on ETA 2824-2); ø 25.6 mm, height 4.74 mm; 23 jewels; 21,600 vph; 80-hour power reserve
Functions: hours, minutes, sweep seconds; date
Case: stainless steel, ø 39 mm, height 11.2 mm; sapphire crystal; transparent case back; water-resistant to 5 atm
Band: stainless steel, double folding clasp
Price: $825

Chemin de Tourelles Powermatic 80

Reference number: T139.807.16.041.00
Movement: automatic, ETA Caliber Powermatic 80 (based on ETA 2824-2); ø 25.6 mm, height 4.74 mm; 23 jewels; 21,600 vph; 80-hour power reserve
Functions: hours, minutes, sweep seconds; date
Case: stainless steel, ø 39 mm, height 11.2 mm; sapphire crystal; transparent case back; water-resistant to 5 atm
Band: calfskin, double folding clasp
Price: $750

Chemin de Tourelles Powermatic 80

Reference number: T139.407.16.261.00
Movement: automatic, ETA Caliber Powermatic 80 (based on ETA 2824-2); ø 25.6 mm, height 4.74 mm; 23 jewels; 21,600 vph; 80-hour power reserve
Functions: hours, minutes, sweep seconds; date
Case: stainless steel, ø 42 mm, height 11.3 mm; sapphire crystal; transparent case back; water-resistant to 5 atm
Band: calfskin, double folding clasp
Price: $750

Seastar 1000 Powermatic 80 Silicium

Reference number: T120.407.17.041.01
Movement: automatic, ETA Caliber Powermatic 80 Si (based on ETA 2824-2); ø 25.6 mm, height 4.74 mm; 23 jewels; 21,600 vph; silicon hairspring; 80-hour power reserve
Functions: hours, minutes, sweep seconds; date
Case: stainless steel, ø 43 mm, height 12.7 mm; unidirectional bezel with ceramic insert, with 0-60 scale; sapphire crystal; transparent case back; screw-in crown; water-resistant to 30 atm
Band: textile, double folding clasp
Price: $875

Seastar 2000 Professional Powermatic 80

Reference number: T120.607.17.441.00
Movement: automatic, ETA Caliber Powermatic 80 (based on ETA 2824-2); ø 25.6 mm, height 4.74 mm; 23 jewels; 21,600 vph; 80-hour power reserve
Functions: hours, minutes, sweep seconds; date
Case: stainless steel, ø 46 mm, height 16.25 mm; unidirectional bezel with ceramic insert, with 0-60 scale; sapphire crystal; transparent case back; screw-in crown, helium valve; water-resistant to 60 atm
Band: rubber, pin buckle
Price: $1,075

Gentleman Powermatic 80 Open Heart

Reference number: T127.407.11.081.00
Movement: automatic, ETA Caliber Powermatic 80 (based on ETA 2824-2); ø 25.6 mm, height 4.74 mm; 25 jewels; 21,600 vph; mainplate partially skeletonized over the escapement; 80-hour power reserve
Functions: hours, minutes, sweep seconds
Case: stainless steel, ø 40 mm, height 11.5 mm; sapphire crystal; transparent case back; water-resistant to 10 atm
Band: stainless steel, double folding clasp
Remarks: dial with opening over the escapement
Price: $895

TOURBY WATCHES

In an industry and a world that tries hard to attract attention at times by fairly spectacular means, Tourby Watches is slowly but surely gathering a following and fan club by keeping it simple and elegant. The company, which is headquartered in the town of Wetter in Westphalia, Germany, manufactures mechanical wristwatches whose design is inspired by classic models. This little brand notably has already quite a following in the U.S. A pilot's watch was made especially for the dangerous deployments of the Strike Fighters Weapons School Pacific, a U.S. Navy training school for fighter pilots.

The story began when Erdal Yildiz inherited a pocket watch from his grandfather. The Unitas movement inside was in need of serious revision. So, he looked around for a proper watchmaker, and was soon enamored with the craft itself. The world of mechanical watches became a genuine passion during his studies. He then contacted a number of suppliers in Germany and Switzerland, and in 2007 founded his own brand. The name Tourby has nothing to do with tourbillons, which his company does not manufacture. Rather, it is his nickname; furthermore, it is short and memorable, and the domain name was still available!

All raw materials are purchased from top-notch suppliers in Germany and Switzerland. Some of the parts are ready to use on delivery; others need to be reworked in the company's own workshops in the cities of Bochum and Hagen. The cases are finished by hand, for example, as are the movements—all Swiss ETA calibers—which are extensively decorated, and the dials, in part at least. The leather straps are stitched by hand. Final assembly, quality control, and after-sales service are all done by the company. Erdal Yildiz ensures that they are adjusted to chronometer precision (top grade).

Tourby Watches produces series, but also does made-to-order pieces. The customer can choose his or her case, dial, hands, strap, and even the movement with its decoration. Another option is skeletonization. It's a good way to get hold of a unique piece.

Tourby Watches
Königstrasse 78
D-58300 Wetter an der Ruhr
Hagen in Westfalen
Germany

Tel:
+49-176-8311-83-82

E-mail:
info@tourbywatches.com

Website:
www.tourbywatches.com

Founded:
2007

Number of employees:
5

Annual production:
500

Distribution:
Direct sales

Most important collections/price range:
Lawless Diver / from $1,400; Art Deco Classic / from $1,800; Ottoman / from $1,575; Planetarium / $9,000; special set

Enamel 40
Reference number: 2010.1
Movement: hand-wound, ETA Caliber 6498-2; ø 37 mm, 17 jewels, 21,600 vph, circular côtes de Genève, double sunburst decoration on wheels, blued screws, skeletonized, blued swan-neck fine adjustment, 60-hour power reserve
Functions: hours, minutes, subsidiary seconds
Case: stainless steel, ø 40.5 mm, height 10.6 mm, arched sapphire crystal, transparent case back, water-resistant to 5 atm
Band: reptile skin, buckle
Remarks: sterling silver dial
Price: $3,000
Variations: various sizes (40, 43 and 45 mm)

Marine Arabic 43 Rose
Reference number: 2002.1
Movement: hand-wound, ETA Caliber 6498-2; ø 37 mm, 17 jewels, 21,600 vph, côtes de Genève, sunburst brushing on wheels, blued screws, 60-hour power reserve
Functions: hours, minutes, subsidiary seconds
Case: stainless steel, ø 43 mm, height 10.4 mm, arched sapphire crystal, transparent case back, water-resistant to 5 atm
Band: reptile skin, buckle
Remarks: sterling silver dial
Price: $3,200
Variations: stainless steel

Art Deco Automatic Salmon Dial 37
Reference number: 2400
Movement: self-winding, ETA Caliber 2824-2; ø 25.6 mm, 25 jewels, 28,800 vph, top grade, skeletonized, 40-hour power reserve
Functions: hours, minutes, sweep seconds
Case: stainless steel, ø 37 mm, height 11 mm, sapphire crystal, transparent case back, water-resistant to 10 atm
Band: reptile skin, buckle
Price: $2,200
Variations: stainless steel

Art Deco Chrono Salmon Dial 43

Reference number: 2500
Movement: self-winding, ETA Caliber 7753; ø 30 mm, 27 jewels, 28,800 vph, top grade, 44-hour power reserve
Functions: hours, minutes, subsidiary seconds; chronograph, date
Case: rose gold-plated stainless steel, ø 40 mm, height 14 mm, sapphire crystal, transparent case back, water-resistant to 5 atm
Band: reptile skin, buckle
Price: $4,700
Variations: stainless steel

Old Military Vintage 45

Reference number: 1404
Movement: hand-wound, ETA Caliber 6498-2; ø 37 mm, height 4.5 mm; 17 jewels, 21,600 vph; skeletonized movement with circular côtes de Genève, double sunburst wheels, blued screws, blued swan-neck fine adjustment, 60-hour power reserve
Functions: hours, minutes, subsidiary seconds
Case: stainless steel, ø 45 mm, height 13.35 mm, arched sapphire crystal, transparent case back, water-resistant to 5 atm
Band: leather, buckle
Price: $2,750
Variations: blue or enamel dial; comes in different case diameters (40, 43 or 45 mm)

Lawless Skeleton 37

Reference number: 6302
Movement: self-winding, ETA Caliber 2824-2; ø 25.6 mm, 25 jewels, 28,800 vph, top grade, skeletonized movement and dial, 40-hour power reserve
Functions: hours, minutes, center seconds
Case: stainless steel, ø 37 mm, height 11 mm, sapphire crystal, transparent case back, water-resistant to 20 atm
Band: rubber strap
Price: $2,500

Lawless Blue 37

Reference number: 6301
Movement: self-winding, ETA Caliber 2824-2; 25.6 mm, 25 jewels, 28,800 vph, top grade, skeletonized movement, 40-hour power reserve
Functions: hours, minutes, center seconds
Case: stainless steel, ø 37 mm, height 11 mm, sapphire crystal, transparent case back, water-resistant to 20 atm
Band: rubber strap
Price: $2,500
Variations: black dial

Lawless Blue 40

Reference number: 6220.2
Movement: self-winding, ETA Caliber 2824-2; ø 25.6 mm, height 4.6 mm; 25 jewels, 28,800 vph, skeletonized movement; top grade; 40-hour power reserve
Functions: hours, minutes, center seconds
Case: stainless steel, ø 40 mm, height 11.8 mm; sapphire crystal, transparent case back; water-resistant to 20 atm
Band: stainless steel, pin buckle
Price: $1,750
Variations: black dial

Lawless GMT 40

Reference number: 6230
Movement: self-winding, ETA Caliber 2893-2; ø 25.6 mm, 21 jewels, 28,800 vph, adjusted in 5 positions, top grade, skeletonized, 42-hour power reserve
Functions: hours, minutes, center seconds, additional 24-hour display (2nd time zone)
Case: stainless steel, ø 40 mm, height 11.8 mm, sapphire crystal, rotating bezel, water-resistant to 20 atm
Band: steel bracelet, pin buckle
Price: $2,000
Variations: black dial

TOWSON WATCH COMPANY

Towson Watch Co.
502 Dogwood Lane
Towson, MD 21286
USA

Tel.:
410-823-1823

Fax:
410-823-8581

E-Mail:
towsonwatchco@aol.com

Website:
www.twcwatches.com

Founded:
2000

Number of employees:
4

Annual production:
200 watches

U.S. Distribution:
Retail

Most important collections/price range:
Skipjack GMT / approx. $2,950; Mission / approx. $2,500; Potomac / approx. $2,000; Choptank / approx. $4,500; Martin / approx. $3,950 ; custom design / $10,000 to $35,000

Spencer Shattuck was thirteen when he wrote an eighth grade thesis on watchmaking. His key source was a week of hanging out with George Thomas and Hartwig Balke, two passionate and highly experienced watchmakers. While close to retirement, the two men founded Towson Watch Company.

Advancing ages increases the number of stories one can tell. Thomas's first tourbillon pocket watches are displayed at the National Watch and Clock Museum in Columbia, Pennsylvania. In 1999, Balke made his first wrist chronograph, the STS-99 Mission, for a NASA astronaut and mission specialist. The two also restored one of the world's oldest watches, one belonging to Philip Melanchthon, friend and fellow traveler of Martin Luther. In 2009, Thomas was invited to open up a pocket watch belonging to President Lincoln, and revealed a secret message engraved by a servicing watchmaker and Union supporter working in Maryland: "Jonathan Dillon April 13 - 1861 Fort Sumpter was attacked by the rebels on the above date. J Dillon."

Towson watches pay tribute to local sites, like the Choptank or Potomac rivers. The timepieces are imaginative, with a retro feel—not to mention affordable. The collection includes a number of chronographs and watches with moon phases. And the brand has also ventured into tonneau cases and one oddity, the Pride II, which pays tribute to Baltimore's own schooner. The case is shaped like the company logo and the crown is a miniature winch.

Their local commitment was also shared by entrepreneur and former University of Maryland football captain Kevin Plank, founder of the sports apparel company Under Armour, who purchased a twenty-five percent stake in Towson. In 2020, he sold it to a friend, the above-mentioned Spencer Shattuck, who aims to refresh the brand, without shedding any of its charm, and to make it better known to a broader public.

Cadet

Reference number: CR250
Movement: automatic Caliber ETA 2824-2 or Selitta SW200-1-2; ø 25.60 mm (Sellita 26 mm); height 4.60 mm; 25 jewels; 28,800 vph; finely finished with black-enameled côtes de Genève on rotor, perlage on mainplate, blued screws; 46-hour power reserve
Functions: hours (with inside military time track), minutes, sweep seconds; date
Case: satin-finished stainless steel; ø 41 mm; height 10.5 mm; sapphire crystal; screwed transparent back with sapphire crystal; water-resistant to 5 atm
Band: calf leather, folding clasp.
Price: $1,325; limited to 250 pieces
Variations: as Recruit

Recruit

Reference number: CR250
Movement: automatic Caliber ETA 2824-2 or Selitta SW200-1-2; ø 25.60 mm (Sellita 26 mm); height 4.60 mm; 25 jewels; 28,800 vph; finely finished with black-enameled côtes de Genève on rotor, perlage on mainplate, blued screws; 46-hour power reserve
Functions: hours (with inside military time track), minutes, sweep seconds; date
Case: satin-finished stainless steel; ø 41 mm; height 10.5 mm; sapphire crystal; screwed transparent back with sapphire crystal; water-resistant to 5 atm
Band: calf leather, folding clasp.
Price: $1,325; limited to 250 pieces
Variations: as Cadet

Half-Skelly

Reference number: HS100
Movement: hand-wound, Unitas Caliber 6498; ø 36.6 mm; height 4.5 mm; 17 jewels; 18,000 vph; partially skeletonized movement, black-coated mainplate; 46-hour power reserve
Functions: hours, minutes, subsidiary seconds
Case: stainless steel; ø 42 mm; height 10.8 mm; domed sapphire crystal; screwed transparent case back; water-resistant to 5 atm
Band: calf leather, buckle
Remarks: silver dial rings; dial and components guilloché by Jochen Benzinger
Price: $12,995
Variations: white dial; with stainless steel mesh bracelet

Mission Moon II

Reference number: MM250
Movement: automatic ETA Caliber 7751; ø 30 mm, height 7.6 mm; 25 jewels; 28,800 vph; fine finishing with côtes de Genève; 54-hour power reserve
Functions: hours, minutes, subsidiary seconds; chronograph with tachymeter scale; weekday, month, date; moon phase; 24-hour display
Case: stainless steel, 42 mm, height 13 mm, sapphire crystal, screwed down back with engraving, water resistant to 5 atm
Band: calf leather, orange stitching, folding clasp.
Price: $3,125; limited to 100 pieces

Skipjack 2.0

Reference number: SKJ100-B2
Movement: Automatic Caliber ETA 2893-2; ø 25.6 mm, height 4.1mm; 21 jewels; 28,800 vph; fine finish with côtes de Genève.
Functions: hours, minutes, sweep seconds; date; 24-hour adjustable hand
Case: stainless steel with cannelage, ø 41.5 mm; sapphire crystal; screwed transparent back with sapphire crystal; water-resistant to 5 atm
Band: calf leather, folding clasp.
Price: $2,269; limited to 100 pieces
Variations: black dial

North.er

Reference number: NP250
Movement: automatic, ETA Caliber 2893-2; ø 25.6 mm, height 4.1 mm; 24 jewels; 28,800 vph; 48-hour power reserve
Functions: hours, minutes, sweep seconds; date; 2nd time zone hand
Case: stainless steel, 42 mm, height 13.5 mm; sapphire crystal, transparent case back, water-resistant to 5 atm
Band: calfskin, folding clasp
Price: $2,425

Benzinger Choptank

Reference number: E250-C2
Movement: automatic, ETA Caliber 7751 Valjoux; ø 30 mm; height 7.9 mm; 25 jewels; 28,800 vph; finely decorated, blued hands; 46-hour power reserve
Functions: hours, minutes, subsidiary seconds; weekday, month, sweep date; moon phase; 24-hour display; chronograph
Case: stainless steel; 40 mm x 44 mm; height 13.4 mm; sapphire crystal at front; transparent screwed-down case back; water resistant to 5 atm
Band: reptile skin with folding clasp
Remarks: guilloché dial by Jochen Benzinger
Price: $6,500; limited to 250 pieces

Classic Chronograph

Movement: automatic, Caliber 7750 Valjoux; ø 30 mm, height 7.9 mm; 21 jewels; 28,800 vph; fine finish with côtes de Genève
Functions: hours, minutes, subsidiary seconds; chronograph; date
Case: stainless steel, ø 41 mm, height 14 mm; sapphire crystal; transparent screwed-down back; water-resistant to 5 atm
Band: reptile skin, folding clasp
Remarks: solid silver hand-guillochéed dial
Price: $6,900

Martin M-130

Reference number: CC100
Movement: automatic, ETA Caliber 7750 Valjoux, ø 30 mm; height 7.9 mm; 25 jewels; 28,800 vph; fine finishing with côtes de Genève; 48-hour power reserve
Functions: hours, minutes, subsidiary second, chronograph, date
Case: stainless steel, ø 42 mm, height 13.5 mm, sapphire crystal, screwed-down case back, water resistant to 5 atm
Band: leather, folding clasp
Remarks: case back with engraving of famous China Clipper flying boat from the 1930s built by the Glenn B. Miller company
Price: $3,745
Variations: mesh stainless steel bracelet ($4,250)

TRILOBE

Gautier Massonneau, son of an architect and an interior designer, has a natural attraction to shapes. Still in his 20s, and just cutting his teeth in the world of infrastructure financing, he decided to buy himself a watch but couldn't find any that met his aesthetic expectations.

And so he stumbled upon a timeless and transcultural form, the trefoil, an arrangement of "leaves" with powerful symbolic value. Indeed, the number 3, or the triangle, suggests completion. Do we not live in a world of three dimensions? And there is the past, the present, and the future; the religious trinities; and each story, that always has a beginning, middle, and an end.

The beating heart is the off-center seconds disc, an open-worked six-leaved trefoil. The other leaves, a minute ring and an hour ring, radiate outwards across the dial, like water on a still pond, or the light of the sun. A poetic image is reflected in the name as well: Les Matinaux (the morning people), a collection of poems by René Char.

To realize the module for his first watch, Massonneau turned to Jean-François Mojon and his engine-making company Chronode in Le Locle, Switzerland. One major challenge was to get the rings to turn without rubbing each other. Together they created the X-Centric Caliber, which is based on an ETA movement. For clients seeking a customized watch, there is a "Secret" version, which has a constellation of Super-LumiNova stars on a dark blue sky on the dial, a constellation representing a precise time given by the owner or the receiver of such a watch.

The second Trilobe collection also plays with turning subdials and rings. The Nuit Fantastique is inspired by the story of a nobleman's crazy night in Vienna, a story by Austrian author Stefan Zweig, famous for his obsessive characters. And in 2022, Massoneau presented Une Folle Journée (a crazy day), also a literary reference, amongst others to the *Marriage of Figaro*. In 2023, the "crazy day" reappeared with 150 diamonds on the hour, minute, and seconds rails set using a unique, invisible technique.

Trilobe Watches SAS
18 rue Volney,
75002, Paris
France

Tel.:
+33-1-4233-5296

E-mail:
cercles@trilobewatches.com

Website:
www.trilobe.com

Founded:
2019

Number of employees:
8

Annual production:
approx. 700 pieces

U.S. distributor:
Totally Worth It (TWI2, Inc.)
76 Division Avenue
Summit, NJ 07901-2309
201-894-4710
724-263-2286
info@totallyworthit.com

Most important collections/price range:
Les Matinaux, La Nuit Fantastique, Une Folle Journée / $8,800 to $22,200

Les Matinaux, Sunray Silver, Rose Gold

Reference number: LM07AS
Movement: automatic, X-Centric Caliber; ø 35.2 mm, height 5.78 mm; 33 jewels; 28,800 vph; 48-hour power reserve
Functions: hours, minutes, small seconds
Case: rose gold, ø 40.5 mm, height 8.8 mm; sapphire crystal; transparent case back; water-resistant to 5 atm
Band: calfskin or reptile skin, pin buckle
Remarks: three off-center concentric and rotating rings for hour, minute, and seconds
Price: $24,900
Variations: comes with different color dials: red, anthracite, green, blue, and more; in 38.5-mm case; stainless steel case ($10,600)

Une Folle Journée Diamant

Reference number: UFJ01BA
Movement: automatic, X-Centric Caliber; ø 35.2 mm, height 6.49 mm; 33 jewels; 28,800 vph; dial of three off-center concentric circles; 48-hour power reserve
Functions: hours, minutes, small seconds
Case: platinum, ø 40.5 mm, height 10.2 mm (17.8 mm incl. the domed sapphire crystal); transparent case back; water-resistant to 5 atm
Band: reptile skin, pin buckle
Remarks: time displayed 10 mm above the dial on rotating rings set with 150 diamonds using a special setting technique
Price: on request
Variations: rose-gold case or titanium case

Nuit Fantastique Brume

Reference number: NF05GB
Movement: automatic, X-Centric Caliber; ø 35.2 mm, height 5.78 mm; 33 jewels; 28,800 vph; 48-hour power reserve
Functions: hours, minutes, small seconds
Case: titanium, ø 40.5 mm, height 9.2 mm; sapphire crystal; transparent case back; water-resistant to 5 atm
Band: reptile skin, pin buckle
Remarks: circular taupe grain d'orge (barley-grain) guilloché on dial, clous de Paris on seconds disk.
Price: $12,900
Variations: rose-gold case ($27,000); also, in 38.5-mm case

Montres Tudor SA
Rue François-Dussaud 3-5-7
1211 Geneva 26
Switzerland

Tel.:
+41-22-302-2200

Website:
www.tudorwatch.com

Founded:
1946

U.S. distributor:
Tudor Watch U.S.A., LLC
665 Fifth Avenue
New York, NY 10022
212-897-9900
www.tudorwatch.com

Most important collections/price range:
Black Bay / $2,475 to $6,800; Heritage / $2,675 to
$6,175; Pelagos / $4,450; 1926 / $1,725 to $3,475

TUDOR

Rolex founder Hans Wilsdorf started Tudor in 1946 as a second brand to offer the legendary reliability of his watches at a more affordable price. Tudor still benefits from the same industrial platform as Rolex, especially in cases and bracelets, assembly, and quality assurance, not to mention distribution and after sales. However, the movements themselves are usually delivered by ETA and "Tudorized" according to the company's own aesthetics and technical criteria.

After coming out of the shadows in 2007, the company had an easy time registering with consumers with the Heritage Black Bay, especially considering the trend towards 1970s nostalgia. The first edition of the model with a wine-red bezel was followed by numerous variants with and without a rotating bezel, and with a GMT function. The latter was the second new development by the Rolex sister brand after the three-hand manufacture calibers. In the summer of 2021, Tudor finally presented a brand new surprise: the Black Bay Ceramic is the first model to feature a ceramic case and a completely magnetic field-resistant movement. As a result, the Black Bay Ceramic even passes the stringent Swiss METAS magnetism test, making Tudor the second brand (after Omega) with a Master Chronometer certificate.

As for movements, the MT-5621 made its debut in the simple North Flag and as the MT-5612 in the Pelagos models. The M5601/5602 calibers, with three hands and a date, were followed by an attractive automatic chronograph using Breitling's B01 Caliber. The Tudor calibers are produced by the movement manufacturer Kenissi, a joint venture with Breitling, among others. The movement of the automatic chronograph, which is basically a Breitling caliber B01, is also "shared" with this brand.

After launching various Black Bay models made of unusual case materials, Tudor invested in the development of the Pelagos special FXD model for professional use with integrated strap bars. Two special editions for the sailing partner in the America's Cup, the Alinghi Red Bull Racing team, use this system, and they also boast bezels inlaid with carbon fiber. Price-conscious Tudor fans will be delighted with the Ranger, which was presented in 2022, a basic three-hander but done with great attention to detail.

Black Bay Master Chronometer

Reference number: 7941A1A0RU
Movement: automatic, Tudor Caliber MT5602-1U;
ø 31.8 mm, height 6.5 mm; 25 jewels; 28,800 vph; silicon hairspring, amagnetic geartrain components; blackened movement; Master Chronometer certification (METAS); 70-hour power reserve; COSC-certified chronometer
Functions: hours, minutes, sweep seconds
Case: stainless steel, ø 41 mm, height 13.6 mm; unidirectional bezel with aluminum number disk, with 0-60 scale; sapphire crystal; screw-in crown; water-resistant to 20 atm
Band: stainless steel with five-link row, folding clasp with fine adjustment
Price: $4,550
Variations: with three-link row ($4,425)

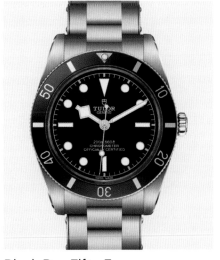

Black Bay Fifty-Four

Reference number: 79000N
Movement: automatic, Tudor Caliber MT5400;
ø 26 mm, height 4.99 mm; 27 jewels; 28,800 vph; silicon hairspring; 70-hour power reserve; COSC-certified chronometer
Functions: hours, minutes, sweep seconds
Case: stainless steel, ø 37 mm; unidirectional bezel with aluminum number disk, with 0-60 scale; sapphire crystal; screw-in crown; water-resistant to 20 atm
Band: stainless steel, folding clasp with fine adjustment
Remarks: inspired by the first Tudor diver's watch, reference number 7922
Price: $3,900
Variations: with textile or leather strap ($3,750)

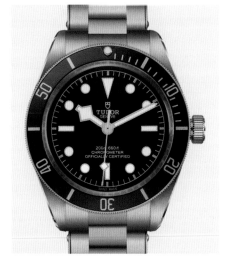

Black Bay Fifty-Eight

Reference number: 79030N
Movement: automatic, Tudor Caliber MT5402; ø 26 mm, height 4.99 mm; 27 jewels; 28,800 vph; silicon hairspring; 70-hour power reserve; COSC-certified chronometer
Functions: hours, minutes, sweep seconds
Case: stainless steel, ø 39 mm, height 11.9 mm; unidirectional bezel with aluminum insert, with 0-60 scale; sapphire crystal; screw-in crown; water-resistant to 20 atm
Band: stainless steel, buckle with safety lock
Price: $3,800
Variations: with textile or leather strap ($3,675)

Black Bay GMT

Reference number: 79830RB
Movement: automatic, Tudor Caliber MT5652;
ø 31.8 mm, height 7.52 mm; 28 jewels; 28,800 vph;
silicon hairspring; 70-hour power reserve;
COSC-certified chronometer
Functions: hours (incremental setting by the crown),
minutes, sweep seconds; additional 24-hour display
(2nd time zone); date
Case: stainless steel, ø 41 mm; bidirectional bezel with
bicolor aluminum numeral disk, with 0-24 scale; sapphire
crystal; screw-in crown; water-resistant to 20 atm
Band: stainless steel, folding clasp, with safety lock
Remarks: return of the PanAm colors
Price: $4,375
Variations: with calfskin or textile strap ($4,050)

Black Bay Bronze

Reference number: 79250BA
Movement: automatic, Tudor Caliber MT5601;
ø 33.8 mm, height 6.5 mm; 25 jewels; 28,800 vph;
silicon hairspring; 70-hour power reserve;
COSC-certified chronometer
Functions: hours, minutes, sweep seconds
Case: bronze, ø 43 mm, height 14.5 mm; unidirectional
bezel with aluminum insert, with 0-60 scale; sapphire
crystal; screw-in crown; water-resistant to 20 atm
Band: textile, pin buckle
Price: $4,475
Variations: with leather strap ($4,475)

Black Bay 41

Reference number: 79680
Movement: automatic, Tudor Caliber MT5601;
ø 33.8 mm, height 6.5 mm; 25 jewels; 28,800 vph;
silicon hairspring; 70-hour power reserve;
COSC-certified chronometer
Functions: hours, minutes, sweep seconds
Case: stainless steel, ø 41 mm, height 11.2 mm; sapphire
crystal; screw-in crown; water-resistant to 10 atm
Band: stainless steel in five rows, folding clasp, with
fine adjustment
Price: $4,125
Variations: with blue dial; also, in 31-, 36- or 39-mm case

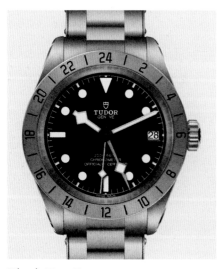

Black Bay Pro

Reference number: 79470
Movement: automatic, Tudor Caliber MT5652;
ø 31.8 mm, height 7.52 mm; 28 jewels; 28,800 vph;
silicon hairspring; 70-hour power reserve;
COSC-certified chronometer
Functions: hours (incremental setting by the crown),
minutes, sweep seconds; additional 24-hour display
(2nd time zone); date
Case: stainless steel, ø 39 mm, height 14.6 mm;
with 0-24 scale; sapphire crystal; screw-in crown;
water-resistant to 20 atm
Band: stainless steel, folding clasp, with safety lock
Price: $4,225
Variations: with calfskin/rubber or textile strap
($3,900)

Black Bay Chrono

Reference number: 79360N
Movement: automatic, Tudor Caliber MT5813;
ø 30.4 mm, height 7.23 mm; 41 jewels; 28,800 vph;
silicon hairspring, balance wheel with variable inertia;
70-hour power reserve; COSC-certified chronometer
Functions: hours, minutes, subsidiary seconds;
chronograph; date
Case: stainless steel, ø 41 mm, height 14.6 mm; aluminum
bezel with aluminum numerals; sapphire crystal; screw-in
crown and pushers; water-resistant to 20 atm
Band: stainless steel, folding clasp, with safety lock
Remarks: comes with additional textile strap
Price: $5,550
Variations: only with leather or textile strap ($5,225);
with black dial

Ranger

Reference number: 79950
Movement: automatic, Tudor Caliber MT5402;
ø 26 mm, height 4.99 mm; 27 jewels; 28,800 vph;
silicon hairspring; 70-hour power reserve;
COSC-certified chronometer
Functions: hours, minutes, sweep seconds **Case:**
stainless steel, ø 39 mm, height 12 mm; sapphire
crystal; screw-in crown; water-resistant to 10 atm
Band: rubber/leather, folding clasp with safety lock
Price: $2,875
Variations: with textile strap ($2,875); with stainless
steel link bracelet ($3,200)

Pelagos LHD

Reference number: 25610TNL
Movement: automatic, Tudor Caliber MT5612LHD; ø 31.8 mm, height 6.5 mm; 25 jewels; 28,800 vph; silicon hairspring; 70-hour power reserve; COSC-certified chronometer
Functions: hours, minutes, sweep seconds; date
Case: titanium, ø 42 mm, height 11.8 mm; unidirectional stainless-steel bezel with ceramic numeral disk, with 0-60 scale; sapphire crystal; screw-in crown, helium valve; water-resistant to 50 atm
Band: titanium, folding clasp, with safety lock, with extension link, with fine adjustment
Remarks: comes with additional rubber strap
Price: $5,025

Pelagos FXD Alinghi Red Bull Racing Edition

Reference number: 25707KN
Movement: automatic, Tudor Caliber MT5602, ø 33.8 mm, height 6.5 mm; 25 jewels; 28,800 vph; silicon hairspring; 70-hour power reserve; COSC-certified chronometer
Functions: hours, minutes, sweep seconds
Case: titanium, ø 42 mm; height 11.8 mm; bidirectional bezel with ceramic numeral disc, with 0-60 scale (countdown); sapphire crystal; screw-in crown; water-resistant to 20 atm
Band: looped-textured fabric, velcro fastener
Remarks: fixed lug screws (tear-protected); special edition commemorating the 2023 collaboration with the Alinghi Red Bull Racing Team
Price: $3,675

Pelagos FXD Chronograph Alinghi Red Bull Racing Edition

Reference number: 25807KN
Movement: automatic, Tudor Caliber MT5813; ø 30.4 mm, height 7.23 mm; 41 jewels; 28,800 vph; silicon hairspring; 70-hour power reserve; COSC-certified chronometer
Functions: hours, minutes, subsidiary seconds; chronograph; date
Case: titanium, ø 43 mm; height 12.75 mm; bidirectional bezel with carbon numeral disc and 0-60 scale (countdown); sapphire crystal; screw-in crown; water-resistant to 20 atm
Band: textile looped-textured fabric, velcro fastener
Remarks: fixed lug screws (tear-protected); special edition commemorating the 2023 collaboration with the Alinghi Red Bull Racing Team
Price: $5,075

Caliber MT5602-U

Automatic; single spring barrel, 70-hour power reserve; antimagnetic gearwheel components; "Master Chronometer" (METAS) and COSC-certification
Functions: hours, minutes, sweep seconds
Diameter: 31.8 mm
Height: 6.5 mm
Jewels: 25
Balance: glucydur with weighted screws
Frequency: 28,800 vph
Hairspring: silicon
Related caliber: MT5601/5612 (insertable diameter 33.8/31.8 mm) without antimagnetic parts

Caliber MT5402

Automatic; single spring barrel, 70-hour power reserve; COSC-certified chronometer
Functions: hours, minutes, sweep seconds
Diameter: 26 mm
Height: 4.99 mm
Jewels: 27
Balance: glucydur with weighted screws
Frequency: 28,800 vph
Hairspring: silicon

Caliber MT5813

Automatic; single spring barrel, 70-hour power reserve; COSC-certified chronometer
Functions: hours, minutes, subsidiary seconds; chronograph; date
Diameter: 30.4 mm
Height: 7.23 mm
Jewels: 41
Balance: glucydur with weighted screws
Frequency: 28,800 vph
Hairspring: silicon

TUTIMA

The name Glashütte is synonymous with watches in Germany. The area, also known for precision engineering, already had quite a watchmaking industry going when World War I closed off markets, followed by the hyperinflation of the early twenties. To rebuild the local economy, a conglomerate was created to produce finished watches, under the leadership of jurist Dr. Ernst Kurtz, consisting of the movement manufacturer UROFA Glashütte AG and UFAG. The top watches were given the name Tutima, derived from the Latin *tutus*, meaning whole, sound. Among the brand's most famous timepieces was a pilot's watch that set standards in terms of aesthetics and functionality.

A few days before World War II ended, Kurtz left Glashütte and founded Uhrenfabrik Kurtz in southern Germany. A young businessman and former employee of Kurtz by the name of Dieter Delecate is credited with keeping the manufacturing facilities and the name Tutima going even as the company sailed through troubled waters. In founding Tutima Uhrenfabrik GmbH in Ganderkesee, this young, resolute entrepreneur prepared the company's strategy for the coming decades.

Delecate has had the joy of seeing Tutima return to its old home and vertically integrated operations, meaning it is once again a genuine *manufacture*. In 2013, Tutima proudly announced a genuine made-in-Glashütte movement (at least 50 percent must be produced in the town), Caliber 617. Tutima Glashütte has started reviving the great watchmaking crafts that have made the region world famous. Among these horological treats is the Hommage minute repeater and the three-hand Patria, which comes in a noble steel or gold case with a blue dial. For a genuine vintage feeling, the brand introduced the Tempostopp, a flyback chronograph run on the Caliber 659, a replica of the legendary Urofa Caliber 59 from the 1940s with a few necessary improvements in the details. More contemporary is the Saxon One line with a range of classic complications. And then there are the military-inspired models for everyday usage based on military watches, like the M2 Coastline, of lightweight titanium but with soft edges that will not ruin a silk shirt cuff.

Tutima Uhrenfabrik GmbH Ndl. Glashütte
Altenberger Strasse 6
D-01768 Glashütte
Germany

Tel.:
+49-35053-320-20

E-mail:
info@tutima.com

Website:
www.tutima.com

Founded:
1927

Number of employees:
approx. 60

U.S. distributor:
Tutima USA, Inc.
P.O. Box 983
Torrance, CA 90508
1-TUTIMA-1927
info@tutimausa.com
www.tutima.com

Most important collections/price range:
Patria, Saxon One, M2, Grand Flieger, Hommage /
approx. $1,650 to $29,500

M2

Reference number: 6450-03
Movement: automatic, Tutima Caliber 521 (based on ETA 7750); ø 30 mm, height 7.9 mm; 25 jewels; 28,800 vph; sweep minute counter, rotor with gold seal; 48-hour power reserve
Functions: hours, minutes, subsidiary seconds; additional 24-hour display; chronograph; date
Case: titanium, ø 46 mm, height 15.5 mm; sapphire crystal; screw-in crown; water-resistant to 30 atm
Band: titanium, folding clasp
Remarks: soft iron core for protection from magnetism
Price: $5,300
Variations: with Kevlar strap ($4,900)

M2 Seven Seas S Black Limited Edition

Reference number: 6156-13
Movement: automatic, Tutima Caliber 330 (based on ETA 2836-2); ø 25.6 mm, height 5.05 mm; 25 jewels; 28,800 vph; rotor with gold seal; 38-hour power reserve
Functions: hours, minutes, sweep seconds; date
Case: stainless steel with black PVD, ø 40 mm, height 12.5 mm; unidirectional bezel, with 0-60 scale; sapphire crystal; screw-in crown; water-resistant to 50 atm
Band: rubber with calfskin overlay, folding clasp
Remarks: limited to 250 pieces
Price: $2,100

M2 Seven Seas

Reference number: 6151-07
Movement: automatic, Tutima Caliber 330 (based on ETA 2836-2); ø 25.6 mm, height 5.05 mm; 25 jewels; 28,800 vph; rotor with gold seal; 38-hour power reserve
Functions: hours, minutes, sweep seconds; date and weekday
Case: titanium, ø 44 mm, height 13 mm; unidirectional bezel with 0-60 scale; sapphire crystal; screw-in crown; water-resistant to 50 atm
Band: rubber with textile overlay, folding clasp
Price: $1,980
Variations: various dials with fitting straps

Grand Flieger Classic Chronograph

Reference number: 6408-02
Movement: automatic, Tutima Caliber 310 (based on ETA 7750); ø 30 mm, height 7.9 mm; 25 jewels; 28,800 vph; rotor with gold seal; 48-hour power reserve
Functions: hours, minutes, subsidiary seconds; chronograph; date
Case: stainless steel, ø 41 mm, height 16 mm; bidirectional bezel, with reference markings; sapphire crystal; transparent case back; screw-in crown; water-resistant to 20 atm
Band: stainless steel, folding clasp
Price: $4,300

Grand Flieger Airport Chronograph

Reference number: 6407-01
Movement: automatic, Tutima Caliber 310 (based on ETA 7750); ø 30 mm, height 7.9 mm; 25 jewels; 28,800 vph; rotor with gold seal; 48-hour power reserve
Functions: hours, minutes, subsidiary seconds; chronograph; date and weekday
Case: stainless steel, ø 41 mm, height 16 mm; bidirectional bezel with ceramic insert, with 0-60 scale; sapphire crystal; transparent case back; screw-in crown; water-resistant to 20 atm
Band: calfskin with textile overlay, folding clasp
Price: $3,900

Flieger

Reference number: 6105-29
Movement: automatic, Tutima Caliber 330 (based on ETA 2836-2); ø 25.6 mm, height 5.05 mm; 25 jewels; 28,800 vph; rotor with gold seal; 38-hour power reserve
Functions: hours, minutes, sweep seconds; date
Case: stainless steel, ø 41 mm, height 13 mm; sapphire crystal; transparent case back; screw-in crown; water-resistant to 10 atm
Band: calfskin, folding clasp
Price: $1,650
Variations: various colors

Saxon One Chronograph

Reference number: 6420-06
Movement: automatic, Tutima Caliber 521 (based on ETA 7750); ø 30 mm, height 7.9 mm; 25 jewels; 28,800 vph; sweep minute counter; rotor with gold seal 48-hour power reserve
Functions: hours, minutes, subsidiary seconds; additional 24-hour display; chronograph; date Case: stainless steel, ø 43 mm, height 15.7 mm; bidirectional bezel, with reference markings; sapphire crystal; transparent case back; screw-in crown; water-resistant to 20 atm
Band: reptile skin, folding clasp
Price: $6,100

Tempostopp

Reference number: 6650-01
Movement: hand-wound, Tutima Caliber 659; ø 33.7 mm, height 6.6 mm; 28 jewels; 21,600 vph; screw balance with gold weight screws and Breguet hairspring; winding wheels with click; hand-engraved balance cock, gold-plated and finely finished movement; 65-hour power reserve
Functions: hours, minutes, subsidiary seconds; flyback chronograph
Case: rose gold, ø 43 mm, height 12.95 mm; sapphire crystal; transparent case back
Band: reptile skin, buckle
Remarks: optimized replica of legendary UROFA Caliber 59 from 1940s
Price: $42,500

Patria GMT

Reference number: 6611-02
Movement: hand-wound, Tutima Caliber 619; ø 31 mm, height 4.78 mm; 20 jewels; 21,600 vph; screw balance with weighted screws and Breguet hairspring; Glashütte three-quarter plate; winding wheels with click; gold-plated and finely finished movement; 65-hour power reserve
Functions: hours, minutes, subsidiary seconds; additional 12-hour display (2nd time zone, adjustable to the minute)
Case: stainless steel, ø 43 mm, height 11.2 mm; sapphire crystal; transparent case back; water-resistant to 5 atm
Band: reptile skin, pin buckle
Price: $9,900

ULYSSE NARDIN

Ulysse Nardin celebrated 175 years in 2021, though a few of those years were dormant. It was Rolf Schnyder who revived the venerable brand after the quartz crisis. At one time it had a reputation for marine chronometers and precision watches. Schnyder had the luck to meet the multitalented Dr. Ludwig Oechslin, who developed a host of innovations for Ulysse Nardin, from intelligent calendar movements to escapement systems. He was the first to use silicon and synthetic diamonds. In fact, just about every Ulysse Nardin has become famous for some spectacular technical innovation, be it the Moonstruck with its stunning moon phase accuracy or the outlandish Freak series that more or less does away with the dial.

After Schnyder's death in 2011, the brand developed a strategy of partnerships and acquisitions, notably of the enameler Donzé Cadrans SA, which gave rise to the Marine Chronometer Manufacture, powered by the Caliber UN-118.

In 2014, the French luxury group Kering, owner of Sowind (Girard-Perregaux), purchased Ulysse Nardin. The two companies were neighbors in La Chaux-de-Fonds, Switzerland, and this has created synergies. Ulysse Nardin continued developing clever solutions such as a new blade-driven anchor escapement and the regatta countdown watch with a second hand that runs counterclockwise first before running clockwise like a conventional chronograph once the race has started.

A joint venture with Sigatec in Sion and its sister company, Mimotec, which specialize in lithogalvanics (LIGA) and processing silicon, allowed Ulysse Nardin to continue developing its advanced technologies. Specialties such as the dual Ulysse escapement in the "Freak" model or the Ulysse anchor escapement in the tourbillon caliber 178 with the flying bearing of the anchor made of silicon would not have been feasible without the new manufacturing possibilities and materials.

Kering Group's sell-off of Ulysse Nardin and Girard-Perregaux in a management buyout under the guidance of Patrick Pruniaux, CEO of both brands, is bringing the two watch brands even closer together. As both companies are based in La Chaux-de-Fonds, the exploitation of production synergies, for example, is obvious. For the moment, the two brands have kept on producing unconventional watches.

Ulysse Nardin SA
3, rue du Jardin
CH-2400 Le Locle
Switzerland

Tel.:
+41-32-930-7400

Website:
www.ulysse-nardin.com

Founded:
1846

U.S. distributor:
Ulysse Nardin Inc.
7900 Glades Rd., Suite 200
Boca Raton, FL 33434
646-500-8664
usa@ulysse-nardin.com

Most important collections:
Freak Collection, Blast Collection, Marine Collection and Diver Collection; Dual Time (also ladies' watches); complications and *métiers d'art* (alarm clocks, perpetual calendar, tourbillons, minute repeaters, jacquemarts, astronomical watches, enamel, micropainting)

Marine Torpilleur

Reference number: 1182-310/42
Movement: automatic, Caliber UN-118; ø 31.6 mm, height 6.45 mm; 50 jewels; 28,800 vph; "DIAMonSIL" escapement, silicon hairspring; 60-hour power reserve; COSC-certified chronometer
Functions: hours, minutes, subsidiary seconds; power-reserve indicator; date
Case: rose gold, ø 42 mm, height 13 mm; sapphire crystal; transparent case back; screw-in crown; water-resistant to 5 atm
Band: reptile skin, folding clasp
Price: $20,400
Variations: with white dial and rubber strap ($22,500)

Marine Torpilleur Moonphase

Reference number: 1192-310-0A/1A
Movement: automatic, Caliber UN-119; ø 31.6 mm, height 6.2 mm; 45 jewels; 28,800 vph; "DIAMonSIL" escapement, silicon hairspring; 60-hour power reserve; COSC-certified chronometer
Functions: hours, minutes, subsidiary seconds; power-reserve indicator; moon phase
Case: rose gold, ø 42 mm, height 13 mm; sapphire crystal; transparent case back; screw-in crown; water-resistant to 5 atm
Band: reptile skin, folding clasp
Price: $19,000

Marine Torpilleur Dual Time

Reference number: 3343-320-3A/1A
Movement: automatic, Caliber UN-24; ø 25.6 mm, height 5.35 mm; 23 jewels; 28,800 vph
Functions: hours, minutes, subsidiary seconds; additional 24-hour display (2nd time zone); large date
Case: stainless steel, ø 42 mm, height 13 mm; ceramic bezel ceramic; sapphire crystal; transparent case back; water-resistant to 5 atm
Band: reptile skin, folding clasp
Price: $12,000

Diver 42 mm

Reference number: 8163-175-7M/92
Movement: automatic, Caliber UN-816 (based on
Sellita SW300); ø 25.6 mm, height 3.6 mm; 25 jewels;
28,800 vph; 42-hour power reserve
Functions: hours, minutes, sweep seconds; date
Case: stainless steel, ø 42 mm, height 10.75 mm;
unidirectional bezel with rubber overlay, with
0-60 scale; sapphire crystal; screw-in crown;
water-resistant to 30 atm
Band: stainless steel, folding clasp
Price: $7,700
Variations: with textile strap ($7,000)

Diver Net Azur

Reference number: 1183-170-2B/3A
Movement: automatic, Caliber UN-118; ø 31.6 mm,
height 6.45 mm; 50 jewels; 28,800 vph;
"DIAMonSIL" escapement, silicon hairspring; 60-hour
power reserve; COSC-certified chronometer
Functions: hours, minutes, subsidiary seconds;
power-reserve indicator; date
Case: stainless steel, ø 44 mm, height
13.1 mm; unidirectional bezel with rubber insert, with
0-60 scale, ceramic glass; transparent case back;
screw-in crown; water-resistant to 30 atm
Band: recycled plastic, pin buckle
Remarks: ceramic glass
Price: $12,600

Diver Chronograph

Reference number: 1503-170-3/93
Movement: automatic, Caliber UN-150; ø 31 mm, height
6.75 mm; 25 jewels; 28,800 vph; silicon escapement;
48-hour power reserve
Functions: hours, minutes, subsidiary seconds;
chronograph; date
Case: titanium, ø 44 mm, height 16.1 mm; unidirectional
bezel with 0-60 scale; sapphire crystal; transparent
case back; screw-in crown; water-resistant to 30 atm
Band: rubber, pin buckle
Price: $13,100
Variations: with textile strap ($13,100); with stainless
steel bracelet ($13,800); in rose gold ($44,500)

Diver X Skeleton

Reference number: 3723-170-1A/3A
Movement: automatic, Caliber UN-372; ø 37 mm,
height 5.86 mm; 23 jewels; 21,600 vph; skeletonized
movement design; double spring barrel; silicon
escapement and hairspring; 96-hour power reserve
Functions: hours, minutes, sweep seconds
Case: titanium, ø 44 mm, height 16 mm; unidirectional
bezel with 0-60 scale; sapphire crystal; transparent
case back; water-resistant to 20 atm
Band: rubber, pin buckle
Price: $26,400
Variations: with azure blue case

Blast Skeleton X

Reference number: 3713-260-3/03
Movement: hand-wound, Caliber UN-371; ø 37 mm,
height 5.86 mm; 23 jewels; 18,000 vph; skeletonized
movement design; double spring barrel; silicon
escapement and hairspring; 96-hour power reserve
Functions: hours, minutes
Case: titanium, ø 42 mm, height 10.85 mm; bezel with
blue PVD; sapphire crystal; transparent case back;
water-resistant to 5 atm
Band: rubber, pin buckle
Price: $22,200
Variations: with reptile skin strap; in carbon fiber;
in titanium

Blast Tourbillon

Reference number: 1723-400-3A/03
Movement: automatic, Caliber UN-172; ø 36.4 mm,
height 6.1 mm; 25 jewels; 18,000 vph; flying tourbillon;
platinum micro-rotor; silicon escapement; skeletonized
movement; 72-hour power reserve
Functions: hours, minutes
Case: titanium, ø 45 mm, height 11 mm; bezel in
ceramic; sapphire crystal; transparent case back;
water-resistant to 5 atm
Band: rubber, folding clasp
Price: $53,800
Variations: with reptile skin strap; in black or white
ceramic-titanium

Blast Tourbillon

Reference number: 1725-400-3A/03
Movement: automatic, Caliber UN-172; ø 36.4 mm, height 6.1 mm; 25 jewels; 18,000 vph; flying tourbillon; platinum micro-rotor; silicon escapement; skeletonized movement; 72-hour power reserve
Functions: hours, minutes
Case: rose gold, ø 45 mm, height 11 mm; bezel in ceramic; sapphire crystal; transparent case back; water-resistant to 5 atm
Band: rubber, folding clasp
Price: $67,000

Blast Hourstriker

Reference number: 6215-400-3A/02
Movement: automatic, Caliber UN-621; ø 35.5 mm, height 10.8 mm; 46 jewels; 28,800 vph; flying 1-minute tourbillon, silicon escapement; platinum micro-rotor (manual winding for the chime), 60-hour power reserve
Functions: hours, minutes "au-passage" hour and half-hour striking on request
Case: rose gold, barrel section of DLC-coated titanium, ø 45 mm; sapphire crystal; transparent case back; water-resistant to 3 atm
Band: rubber, folding clasp
Price: on request
Variations: with reptile skin band

Blast Moonstruck

Reference number: 1063-400-2A/3B
Movement: automatic, Caliber UN-106; 28,800 vph; silicon escapement; microrotor; 50-hour power reserve
Functions: hours, minutes; power-reserve indicator, world time display (2nd time zone), tide display, position indicator for sun and moon; date, moon phase and age
Case: titanium with black DLC, ø 45 mm, height 15.8 mm; sapphire crystal; transparent case back; water-resistant to 3 atm
Band: rubber with reptile skin overlay, folding clasp
Price: $86,500

Freak X

Reference number: 2305-270/02
Movement: automatic, Caliber UN-230; ø 34.5 mm, height 10.1 mm; 21 jewels; 28,800 vph; baguette movement on a rotating carousel, silicon balance, movement components are used as hands, crown-controlled conventional winding and hands-setting; 72-hour power reserve
Functions: hours, minutes
Case: rose gold and titanium with black DLC, ø 43 mm, height 13.5 mm; sapphire crystal; transparent case back
Band: calfskin, folding clasp
Price: $36,900
Variations: with reptile skin strap; with black DLC; in titanium

Freak ONE

Reference number: 2405-500-2A/3D
Movement: automatic, Caliber UN-240; ø 34.5 mm, height 10.1 mm; 21 jewels; 21,600 vph; baguette movement on a rotating carousel; "DIAMonSIL" pallet lever and escape wheel, silicon balance wheel and hairspring; 72-hour power reserve
Functions: hours, minutes
Case: titanium with black DLC, ø 44 mm, height 12 mm; bezel in rose gold; sapphire crystal; transparent case back
Band: rubber, folding clasp
Price: $68,600

Freak S

Reference number: 2513-500LE-2A-BLACK-5N/1A
Movement: automatic, Caliber UN-251; ø 34.5 mm, height 10.1 mm; 21 jewels; 28,800 vph; baguette movement on a peripheral and flying carousel, double silicon escapement and hairspring, movement components are used as hands, crown-controlled conventional winding and hands-setting; 72-hour power reserve
Functions: hours, minutes
Case: titanium with black DLC, ø 45 mm, height 13.8 mm; bezel in rose gold; sapphire crystal; transparent case back; water-resistant to 5 atm
Band: calfskin, folding clasp
Price: $137,200

Urwerk SA
Bourg du Four 5e
CH-1204 Geneva
Switzerland

Tel:
+41-22-900-2027

E-mail:
info@urwerk.com

Website:
www.urwerk.com

Founded:
1995

Annual production:
150 watches

U.S. distributor:
Ildico Inc.
8701 Wilshire Blvd.
Beverly Hills, CA 90211
310-205-5555

URWERK

Many watchmakers make unique pieces, but Felix Baumgartner and designer Martin Frei are in and of themselves unique. Their products are immediately recognizable, their ultra-technical style—never losing sight of the visual codes they laid down when they founded their company in 1997—has always been the source of eye-popping mechanisms. It's all in the name, a play on the words *Uhrwerk*, for movement, and *Urwerk*, meaning a sort of primal mechanism. Their specialty is inventing surprising time indicators featuring digital numerals that rotate like satellites and display the time in a relatively linear depiction on a small "dial" at the front of the flattened case, which could almost—but not quite—be described as oval. Their inspiration goes back to the so-called night clock of the eighteenth-century Campanus brothers, but the realization is purely *2001: A Space Odyssey*.

Urwerk's debut was with the Harry Winston Opus 5. Later, they created the Black Cobra, which displays time using cylinders and other clever ways to recoup energy for driving rather heavy components. The Torpedo is another example of high-tech watchmaking, again based on the satellite system of revolving and turning hands. With each return to the drawing board, Baumgartner and Frei find new ways to explore what has now become an unmistakable form, using high-tech materials, like aluminum titanium nitride (AlTiN), or a gold-silver alloy known as electrum, or finding new functions for the owner to play with.

Urwerk is continually pushing the envelope, even by its own standards. The latest implemented idea is the continuation of the minute hand trajectory along a 20-minute scale representing the 555 kilometers (345 miles) you would travel if standing that long on the equator. A scale opposite tracks your 20-minute journey around the sun as 35,740 kilometers (22,216 miles). This odd display complication has been built into the 100V series of watches, like the Stardust, with a generous sprinkling of diamonds, and this year's Time and Culture series, which is dedicated to the ancient Sumerian city of Ur. The 100V watches are driven by the updated 12.01 movement, now numbered 12.02.

UR-100V Time and Culture II

Movement: automatic, Caliber UR 12.02; 28,800 vph; 40 jewels; with air-brake control; aluminum carousel; carousel and baseplates in ARCAP alloy; finely finished movement with circular graining and shot-blasting; 48-hour power reserve
Functions: satellite hours (on beryllium-bronze Geneva crosses), minutes; track of sun's rotational distance in 20 minutes at the ancient Sumerian city of Ur
Case: titanium with violet DLC, 41 mm x 49.7 mm, height 14 mm; sapphire crystal; transparent case back; water-resistant to 3 atm
Band: rubber, pin buckle
Remarks: watch dedicated to Sumerian culture and the city of Ur; symbols of sun god Utu on the ARCAP cover, moon goddess Nanna on the case between the lugs
Price: $82,000; limited to 30 pieces

UR-230 "Eagle"

Movement: automatic (manual option), Caliber UR-7.30; 50 jewels; on/off winding status, regulation by airbrake; 28,800 vph; wandering aluminum satellites with titanium Geneva Cross control and planetary transmission, finely finished; 48-hour power reserve
Functions: hours (on satellite), minutes (retrograde)
Case: titanium and carbon with black DLC, 53.55 mm x 44.81 mm, height 15.8 mm; sapphire crystal; transparent case back; water-resistant to 3 atm
Band: carbon and rubber, pin buckle with black DLC, buckle
Remarks: protective cover with beak-shaped edge for easy lifting and special mechanism to slow shutting and clicking into place
Price: $205,000; limited to 35 pieces

UR-100V Stardust

Movement: automatic, Caliber UR 12.02; 28,800 vph; 40 jewels; with air-brake control; aluminum carousel; carousel and baseplates in ARCAP alloy; finely finished movement with circular graining and shot-blasting; 48-hour power reserve
Functions: satellite hours (on beryllium bronze Geneva crosses), minutes; rotational distance at the equator in 20 minutes and orbital distance in 20 minutes
Case: titanium with violet DLC, 49.7 mm x 41 mm, height 14 mm; crown set with 24 brilliant cut diamonds; sapphire crystal; transparent case back; water-resistant to 3 atm
Band: fabric, pin buckle set with 22 diamonds
Remarks: case set with 400 snow-set diamonds
Price: $105,000; limited to 10 pieces per year

VACHERON CONSTANTIN

The origins of this oldest continuously operating watch *manufacture* can be traced back to 1755 when Jean-Marc Vacheron opened his workshop in Geneva. His highly complex watches were particularly appreciated by clients in Paris. The development of such an important outlet for horological works there had a lot to do with the emergence of a wealthy class around the powerful French court. The Revolution put an end to all the financial excesses of that market, however, and the Vacheron company suffered as well, until the arrival of marketing wizard François Constantin in 1819.

Fast-forward to the late twentieth century: the brand with the Maltese cross logo had evolved into a tradition-conscious keeper of *haute horlogerie* under the aegis, starting in the mid-1990s, of the Vendôme Luxury Group (today's Richemont SA).

Vacheron Constantin is one of the last luxury brands to have abandoned the traditional way of dividing up labor. Today, most of its basic movements are made in-house at the production facilities and headquarters in Plan-les-Ouates and the workshops in Le Brassus in Switzerland's Jura region.

Products range from the world's most complicated watch, like the 57260, and the finely crafted Les Cabinotiers and Traditionnelle collections. For daily use, there are the elegant Overseas models, and the entry-level collection, the Fiftysix, with a basic movement and no Geneva Seal. In 2019, the brand's competence in movements produced a genuine novelty: a perpetual calendar driven by the "Twin Beat" escapement. It runs at 36,000 vph on the wearer's arm, and can be switched to 8,640 vph when stored, giving it a 65-day power reserve.

And when not looking ahead, Vacheron Constantin is looking back to its great feats of the past, which have their own family, Les Collectionneurs. Among the favorites is a revisited American 1921 model, now made from 100-year-old spare parts and components and manufactured with 100-year-old tools. This watchmaking icon with its boldly oblique dial differs from the current models in the 1921 collection in that the dial and crown are tilted to the left.

Vacheron Constantin
Chemin du Tourbillon
CH-1228 Plan-les-Ouates
Switzerland

Tel.:
+41-22-930-2005

E-mail:
info@vacheron-constantin.com

Website:
www.vacheron-constantin.com

Founded:
1755

Number of employees:
approx. 800

U.S. distributor:
Vacheron Constantin
645 Fifth Avenue
New York, NY 10022
877-701-1755

Most important collections:
Patrimony, Traditionnelle, Métiers d'Art, Overseas, Fiftysix, Historiques and Égérie, Harmony, Patrimony, Traditionnelle, Historiques, Métiers d'Art, Malte, Overseas, Egérie, FiftySix, Quai de l'Île, unique pieces. As well as unique and bespoke timepieces from its Les Cabinotiers department.

Traditionnelle Tourbillon

Reference number: 6000T/000P-H025
Movement: automatic, Vacheron Constantin Caliber 2160/1; ø 30.4 mm, height 5.65 mm; 30 jewels; 18,000 vph; one-minute tourbillon; peripheral gold oscillating mass; 80-hour power reserve; Geneva Seal
Functions: hours, minutes, subsidiary seconds (on the tourbillon cage)
Case: platinum, ø 41 mm, height 10.4 mm; sapphire crystal; transparent case back; water-resistant to 3 atm
Band: reptile skin, folding clasp
Price: on request

Traditionnelle Tourbillon Retrograde Date Openface

Reference number: 6010T/000R-B638
Movement: automatic, Vacheron Constantin Caliber 2162 R31; ø 31 mm, height 6.25 mm; 30 jewels; 18,000 vph; one-minute tourbillon; peripheral gold-oscillating mass; 72-hour power reserve; Geneva Seal
Functions: hours, minutes, subsidiary seconds (on the tourbillon cage); date (retrograde)
Case: rose gold, ø 41 mm, height 11.07 mm; sapphire crystal; transparent case back; water-resistant to 3 atm
Band: reptile skin, folding clasp
Price: on request

Overseas Tourbillon Skeleton

Reference number: 6000V/110T-B935
Movement: automatic, Vacheron Constantin Caliber 2160 SQ; ø 31 mm, height 5.65 mm; 30 jewels; 18,000 vph; one-minute tourbillon; hubless, peripheral winding rotor; 80-hour power reserve; Geneva Seal
Functions: hours, minutes, subsidiary seconds (on the tourbillon cage)
Case: titanium, ø 42.5 mm, height 10.39 mm; sapphire crystal; transparent case back; water-resistant to 5 atm
Band: titanium, folding clasp
Remarks: sapphire crystal dial
Price: $164,000

Fiftysix Automatic

Reference number: 4600E/000A-B442
Movement: automatic, Vacheron Constantin Caliber 1326; ø 25.6 mm, height 4.3 mm; 25 jewels; 28,800 vph; 48-hour power reserve
Functions: hours, minutes, sweep seconds; date
Case: stainless steel, ø 40 mm, height 9.6 mm; sapphire crystal; transparent case back; water-resistant to 3 atm
Band: reptile skin, folding clasp
Price: $12,700
Variations: in rose gold

Fiftysix Complete Calendar

Reference number: 4000E/000R-B438
Movement: automatic, Vacheron Constantin Caliber 2460QCL/1; ø 29 mm, height 5.4 mm; 27 jewels; 28,800 vph; 40-hour power reserve; Geneva Seal
Functions: hours, minutes, sweep seconds; full calendar with date, weekday, month, moon phase
Case: rose gold, ø 40 mm, height 11.6 mm; sapphire crystal; transparent case back; water-resistant to 3 atm
Band: reptile skin, pin buckle
Price: $44,500
Variations: in stainless steel

Historiques American 1921

Reference number: 82035/000R-9359
Movement: hand-wound, Vacheron Constantin Caliber 4400AS; ø 28.6 mm, height 2.8 mm; 21 jewels; 28,800 vph; 65-hour power reserve; Geneva Seal
Functions: hours, minutes, subsidiary seconds
Case: rose gold, 40 x 40 mm, height 8.06 mm; sapphire crystal; transparent case back; water-resistant to 3 atm
Band: reptile skin, pin buckle
Remarks: modeled after a vintage piece from 1921
Price: 40,400

Historiques 222

Reference number: 4200H/222J-B935
Movement: automatic, Vacheron Constantin Caliber 2455/2; ø 26.2 mm, height 3.6 mm; 27 jewels; 28,800 vph; 40-hour power reserve; Geneva Seal
Functions: hours, minutes; date
Case: yellow gold, ø 37 mm, height 7.95 mm; sapphire crystal; transparent case back; water-resistant to 5 atm
Band: yellow gold, triple folding clasp
Remarks: carefully modernized reedition for the 45th anniversary of the "222"
Price: $70,000

Overseas Chronograph

Reference number: 5500V/110R-B952
Movement: automatic, Vacheron Constantin Caliber 5200; ø 30.6 mm, height 6.6 mm; 54 jewels; 28,800 vph; column-wheel control of the chronograph functions; gold rotor; 52-hour power reserve; Geneva Seal
Functions: hours, minutes, subsidiary seconds; chronograph; date
Case: rose gold, ø 42.5 mm, height 13.7 mm; sapphire crystal; transparent case back; screw-in crown and pushers; water-resistant to 15 atm
Band: rose gold, folding clasp
Price: $79,500
Variations: with reptile skin strap

Overseas Chronograph

Reference number: 5500V/110A-B686
Movement: automatic, Vacheron Constantin Caliber 5200; ø 30.6 mm, height 6.6 mm; 54 jewels; 28,800 vph; column-wheel control of the chronograph functions; gold rotor; 52-hour power reserve; Geneva Seal
Functions: hours, minutes, subsidiary seconds; chronograph; date
Case: stainless steel, ø 42.5 mm, height 13.7 mm; sapphire crystal; transparent case back; screw-in crown and pushers; water-resistant to 15 atm
Band: stainless steel, folding clasp
Price: $35,600
Variations: with reptile skin strap

Overseas Moon Phase Retrograde Date

Reference number: 4000V/210A-B911
Movement: automatic, Vacheron Constantin Caliber 2460 R31L/2; ø 27.2 mm, height 5.4 mm; 27 jewels; 28,800 vph; gold rotor; 40-hour power reserve; Geneva Seal
Functions: hours, minutes; date (retrograde), moon phase
Case: stainless steel, ø 41 mm, height 10.48 mm; sapphire crystal; transparent case back; water-resistant to 5 atm
Band: stainless steel, folding clasp
Price: $43,800

Patrimony Retrograde Day-Date

Reference number: 4000U/000P-H003
Movement: automatic, Vacheron Constantin Caliber 2460 R31R7/3; ø 27.2 mm, height 5.4 mm; 27 jewels; 28,800 vph; 40-hour power reserve; Geneva Seal
Functions: hours, minutes; date and weekday (retrograde)
Case: platinum, ø 42.5 mm, height 9.7 mm; sapphire crystal; water-resistant to 3 atm
Band: reptile skin, folding clasp
Price: $62,000

Traditionnelle Complete Calendar

Reference number: 4010T/000R-B344
Movement: automatic, Vacheron Constantin Caliber 2460 QCL/1; ø 25.6 mm, height 5.4 mm; 27 jewels; 28,800 vph; 40-hour power reserve; Geneva Seal
Functions: hours, minutes, sweep seconds; full calendar with date, weekday, month, moon phase
Case: pink gold, ø 41 mm, height 10.72 mm; sapphire crystal; transparent case back; water-resistant to 3 atm
Band: reptile skin, pin buckle
Price: $45,300

Patrimony Self-Winding

Reference number: 85180/000J-9231
Movement: automatic, Vacheron Constantin Caliber 2450 Q6/3; ø 25.6 mm, height 3.6 mm; 27 jewels; 28,800 vph; 40-hour power reserve; Geneva Seal
Functions: hours, minutes, sweep seconds; date
Case: yellow gold, ø 40 mm, height 8.55 mm; sapphire crystal; water-resistant to 3 atm
Band: reptile skin, pin buckle
Price: $31,800

Patrimony Retrograde Day-Date

Reference number: 4000U/000R-B516
Movement: automatic, Vacheron Constantin Caliber 2460 R31R7/3; ø 25.6 mm, height 5.4 mm; 27 jewels; 28,800 vph; 40-hour power reserve; Geneva Seal
Functions: hours, minutes; date and weekday (retrograde)
Case: rose gold, ø 42.5 mm, height 9.7 mm; sapphire crystal; water-resistant to 3 atm
Band: reptile skin, folding clasp
Price: $49,400

Patrimony Perpetual Calendar Ultra-Thin

Reference number: 43175/000R-B519
Movement: automatic, Vacheron Constantin Caliber 1120 QP/1; ø 28 mm, height 4.05 mm; 36 jewels; 19,800 vph; skeletonized rotor with Gold-oscillating mass; 40-hour power reserve; Geneva Seal
Functions: hours, minutes; perpetual calendar with date, weekday, month, moon phase, leap year
Case: rose gold, ø 41 mm, height 8.96 mm; sapphire crystal; transparent case back; water-resistant to 3 atm
Band: reptile skin, folding clasp
Price: $88,000

Overseas Self-Winding

Reference number: 4600V/200R-B979
Movement: automatic, Vacheron Constantin Caliber 1088/1; ø 20.5 mm, height 3.83 mm; 26 jewels; 28,800 vph; gold rotor; 40-hour power reserve
Functions: hours, minutes, sweep seconds; date
Case: rose gold, ø 34.5 mm, height 9.33 mm; sapphire crystal; transparent case back; water-resistant to 15 atm
Band: rose gold, folding clasp
Price: $49,400
Variations: with calfskin strap

Overseas Self-Winding

Reference number: 4605V/200A-B971
Movement: automatic, Vacheron Constantin Caliber 1088/1; ø 20.5 mm, height 3.83 mm; 26 jewels; 28,800 vph; gold rotor; 40-hour power reserve
Functions: hours, minutes, sweep seconds; date
Case: stainless steel, ø 34.5 mm, height 9.33 mm; bezel with 84 diamonds; sapphire crystal; transparent case back; water-resistant to 15 atm
Band: stainless steel, folding clasp
Remarks: comes with additional calfskin strap
Price: $30,500

Égérie Moon Phase

Reference number: 8005F/000R-B958
Movement: automatic, Vacheron Constantin Caliber 1088 L; ø 30 mm, height 5.03 mm; 26 jewels; 28,800 vph; 40-hour power reserve; Geneva Seal
Functions: hours, minutes, sweep seconds; moon phase
Case: rose gold, ø 37 mm, height 9.32 mm; bezel with 58 diamonds; sapphire crystal; transparent case back; crown with moonstone cabochon; water-resistant to 3 atm
Band: reptile skin, pin buckle
Remarks: dial with 36 diamonds; comes with two extra reptile skin straps
Price: $49,400
Variations: with light-colored dial; in stainless steel

Patrimony Self-Winding

Reference number: 4110U/000G-B906
Movement: automatic, Vacheron Constantin Caliber 2450 Q6/3; ø 26.2 mm, height 3.6 mm; 27 jewels; 28,800 vph; 40-hour power reserve; Geneva Seal
Functions: hours, minutes, sweep seconds; date
Case: white gold, ø 36.5 mm, height 8.45 mm; sapphire crystal; transparent case back; water-resistant to 3 atm
Band: reptile skin, pin buckle
Price: $28,900

Traditionnelle Perpetual Calendar Ultra-Thin

Reference number: 4305T/000G-B948
Movement: automatic, Vacheron Constantin Caliber 1120 QP; ø 29.6 mm, height 4.05 mm; 36 jewels; 19,800 vph; 40-hour power reserve; Geneva Seal
Functions: hours, minutes; perpetual calendar with date, weekday, month, moon phase, leap year
Case: white gold, ø 36.5 mm, height 8.43 mm; bezel and lugs set with 76 diamonds; sapphire crystal; transparent case back; crown with diamond; water-resistant to 3 atm
Band: reptile skin, pin buckle set with 17 diamonds besetzt
Price: on request

Traditionnelle moon phase

Reference number: 83570/000G-9916
Movement: hand-wound, Vacheron Constantin Caliber 1410AS; ø 26 mm, height 4.2 mm; 22 jewels; 28,800 vph; 40-hour power reserve; Geneva Seal
Functions: hours, minutes, subsidiary seconds; power-reserve indicator; moon phase
Case: white gold, ø 36 mm, height 9.1 mm; bezel and lugs set with 81 diamonds; sapphire crystal; transparent case back; crown with diamond; water-resistant to 3 atm
Band: reptile skin, pin buckle
Remarks: mother-of-pearl-dial
Price: $45,000
Variations: in rose gold

Caliber 2460 R31R7/3

Automatic; single spring barrel, 40-hour power reserve; Geneva Seal
Functions: hours, minutes; date and weekday (retrograde)
Diameter: 25.6 mm
Height: 5.4 mm
Jewels: 27
Balance: glucydur
Frequency: 28,800 vph
Remarks: skeletonized gold rotor; 276 parts

Caliber 2460 QCL/1

Automatic; stop-seconds mechanism; single spring barrel, 40-hour power reserve; Geneva Seal
Functions: hours, minutes, sweep seconds; full calendar with date, weekday, month
Diameter: 29 mm
Height: 5.4 mm
Jewels: 27
Balance: glucydur
Frequency: 28,800 vph
Remarks: gold rotor; 308 parts

Caliber 2460 R31L/2

Automatic; single spring barrel, 40-hour power reserve; Geneva Seal
Functions: hours, minutes; date (retrograde), moon phase
Diameter: 27.2 mm
Height: 5.4 mm
Jewels: 27
Balance: glucydur
Frequency: 28,800 vph
Remarks: gold rotor; 275 parts

Caliber 2162 R31

Automatic; peripheral hubless winding rotor; one-minute tourbillon; double spring barrel, 72-hour power reserve; Geneva Seal
Functions: hours, minutes, subsidiary seconds (on the tourbillon cage); date (retrograde)
Diameter: 31 mm
Jewels: 30
Balance: glucydur
Frequency: 18,000 vph
Remarks: gold oscillating mass; 242 parts

Caliber 2455/2

Automatic; gold rotor; single spring barrel, 40-hour power reserve; Geneva Seal
Functions: hours, minutes; date
Diameter: 26.2 mm
Height: 3.6 mm
Jewels: 27
Balance: glucydur
Frequency: 28,800 vph
Remarks: 194 parts

Caliber 1120 QP

Automatic; extra-thin construction; winding rotor with supporting ring; single spring barrel, 40-hour power reserve; Geneva Seal
Functions: hours, minutes; perpetual calendar with date, weekday, month, moon phase, leap year
Diameter: 29.6 mm
Height: 4.05 mm
Jewels: 36
Balance: glucydur
Frequency: 19,800 vph
Remarks: skeletonized rotor with Gold-oscillating mass; 276 parts

Caliber 1088 L

Automatic; swan-neck fine regulator; single spring barrel, 40-hour power reserve; Geneva Seal

Functions: hours, minutes, sweep seconds
Diameter: 30 mm
Height: 5.03 mm
Jewels: 26
Balance: glucydur
Frequency: 28,800 vph
Hairspring: flat hairspring
Remarks: skeletonized gold rotor; 172 parts

Caliber 4400 AS

Hand-wound; single spring barrel, 65-hour power reserve; Geneva Seal

Functions: hours, minutes, subsidiary seconds
Diameter: 28.6 mm
Height: 2.8 mm
Jewels: 21
Balance: glucydur
Frequency: 28,800 vph
Remarks: plate with perlage, chamfered edges, bridges with côtes de Genève; 127 parts

Caliber 1326

Automatic; double spring barrel, 48-hour power reserve

Functions: hours, minutes, sweep seconds; date
Diameter: 25.6 mm
Height: 4.3 mm
Jewels: 25
Balance: glucydur Frequency: 28,800 vph
Hairspring: flat hairspring
Remarks: skeletonized gold rotor; finely finished with côtes de Genève; 142 parts

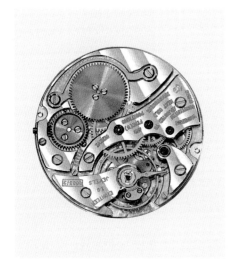

Caliber 1003

Hand-wound; single spring barrel, 31-hour power reserve; Geneva Seal

Functions: hours, minutes
Diameter: 21.1 mm
Height: 1.64 mm
Jewels: 18
Balance: glucydur
Frequency: 18,000 vph
Remarks: currently the thinnest industrially-produced mechanical caliber being produced

Caliber 3300

Hand-wound; column-wheel control of chronograph functions, horizontal clutch; single spring barrel, 65-hour power reserve; Geneva Seal

Functions: hours, minutes, subsidiary seconds; power reserve indicator; chronograph with crown pusher
Diameter: 32.8 mm
Height: 6.7 mm
Jewels: 35
Balance: glucydur
Frequency: 21,600 vph
Remarks: 252 parts

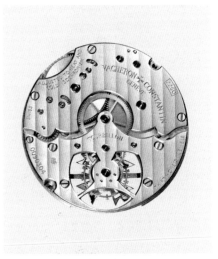

Caliber 2260

Hand-wound; one-minute tourbillon; quadruple spring barrel, 336-hour power reserve; Geneva Seal

Functions: hours, minutes, subsidiary seconds (on the tourbillon cage); power reserve indicator
Diameter: 29.1 mm
Height: 6.8 mm
Jewels: 31
Balance: glucydur
Frequency: 18,000 vph
Remarks: 231 parts

VAN CLEEF & ARPELS

In 1999, while shopping around for more companies to add to its roster of high-end jewelers, Richemont Group decided to purchase Van Cleef & Arpels. The venerable jewelry brand had a lot of name recognition, thanks in part to a host of internationally known customers, like Jacqueline Kennedy Onassis, whose two marriages each involved a Van Cleef & Arpels ring. It also had a reputation for the high quality of its workmanship. It was Van Cleef & Arpels that came up with the mystery setting using a special rail and cut totally hidden from the casual eye.

Van Cleef & Arpels was a family business that came to be when a young stone cutter, Alfred van Cleef, married Estelle Arpels in 1896, and ten years later opened a business on Place Vendôme in Paris with Estelle's brother Charles. More of Estelle's brothers joined the firm, which was soon booming and serving, quite literally, royalty.

Watches were always a part of the portfolio. But after joining Richemont, Van Cleef now had the support of a very complete industrial portfolio that would allow it to make stunning movements that could bring dials to life. Most models today run on the Valfleurier Q020 movement exclusively developed for the company. But it was a collaboration with Jean-Marc Wiederrecht and Agenhor on the Pont des Amoureux with its stunning retrograde complication that became a standard for the brand. The animation idea has been replicated in many of the other Poetic Complications, like the Ballerine Enchantée, whose tutu, on demand, suddenly becomes butterfly wings pointing to the hours and minutes. In 2022, the company came out with another stunner, the Heures Florales, which replicates the concept garden of Swedish botanist and taxonomist Carl Linnaeus, where time could be read according to which flowers are open. And Van Cleef has also looked to the sky for inspiration, with, for instance, a planetarium for the wrist, a collaboration with the eminent watchmaker, Christiaan van der Klaauw.

Van Cleef & Arpels
2, rue du Quatre-Septembre
F-75002 Paris
France

Tel.:
+33-1-70-70-36-56

Website:
www.vancleefarpels.com

Founded:
1906

U.S. distributor:
1-877-VAN-CLEEF

Most important collections:
Charms; Pierre Arpels; Poetic Complications

Lady Arpels Planétarium

Reference number: VCAROAR500
Movement: automatic, Valfleurier Q020; ø 36 mm, height 12.6 mm; with exclusive module (by Christiaan van der Klaauw); 34 jewels; 40-hour power reserve
Functions: retrograde hours and minutes
Case: white gold, ø 38 mm, height 11.8 mm; white gold bezel with round diamonds; sculpted bridge; diamond on crown
Band: reptile skin, white gold buckle
Remarks: planetarium with aventurine dial, pink gold sun and white gold shooting star, pink mother-of-pearl Mercury, green enamel Venus, turquoise Earth, diamond Moon; planets rotate at actual speed
Price: $245,000
Variation: on diamond bracelet ($330,000)

Lady Arpels Heures Florales

Reference number: VCARPBJL00
Movement: automatic, Valfleurier Q020, with special module to open the flowers; ø 36 mm, height 12.6 mm; 93 jewels; 28,8000 vph; 36-hour power reserve
Functions: count open flowers for the hour, minutes in side window
Case: white gold, ø 38 mm, height 14.64 mm; round diamond on crown; water resistant up to 3 atm
Band: reptile skin, pin buckle
Remarks: floral arrangement on the dial inspired by Linnaeus' flower clock; mother-of-pearl marquetry, miniature painting, sapphires and diamonds, and three colors of gold; 424 diamonds in all
Price: $240,000

Lady Arpels Day and Night Watch

Reference number: VCARN25800
Movement: automatic, Caliber 800P (with special 24-hour module by Valfleurier); ø 26.80, height 4 mm; 25 jewels; 21,600 vph; 60-hour power reserve
Functions: hours, minutes; day/night indication
Case: white gold, ø 38.1 mm, height 5.8 mm; set with round diamonds; white-gold bezel; transparent case back; water-resistant to 3 atm
Band: reptile skin, buckle
Remarks: yellow-gold sun with 55 yellow sapphires, white-gold moon with diamonds on aventurine backdrop; mother-of-pearl cap
Price: $110,100

Vortic Watch Co.
324 Jefferson St
Fort Collins, CO 80524
USA

Tel.:
855-285-7884

E-mail:
info@vorticwatches.com

Website:
www.vorticwatches.com

Founded:
2013

Number of employees:
8

Most important collections/price range:
American Artisan Series, Railroad Edition,
Military Edition, "Convert Your Watch" service /
$2,495 to $9,495

VORTIC WATCH COMPANY

The U.S. watch industry produced some very fine timepieces back in the nineteenth century, like Ball, Elgin, Hamilton, and Waltham. So where did the millions of pocket watches go?

Enter R. T. Custer from Pennsylvania. He got wind of companies collecting just the cases of old pocket watches for their gold and silver, and throwing out the movements, dials, hands, and anything deemed worthless to the non-watch fan. So, he took some classes in industrial design, learned all about 3D printing, graduated, and moved out to Colorado. With crowdfunded seed money, and a few friends, he started printing simple cases.

This process, known as upcycling, did not please one brand, Hamilton, whose name appears on some of the dials. It decided to use the staggering cash-power of its parent group, Swatch, to stomp out the upstart in Colorado. After five years of litigation, a judge at the Southern District of New York finally ended the absurd battle in Custer's favor, stating clearly that buyers were not about to be confused by the use of the old Hamilton parts in an upcycled watch. Vortic promptly did a victory lap with a Lancaster 065, with a Hamilton dial and caliber from 1930.

Vortic continues to explore the opportunities of modern technology to redo old movements. Crystals are now made of Corning's specially reinforced Gorilla Glass, for example. Watch fans can send in an old pocket watch for reconditioning and wrist conversion with personal configuration. But even in their modern casings, these watches recall some of the grand old days of American history and business. The difference is subtle at times, but a glance at the Boston (with a Waltham engine) or the Springfield (with an Illinois movement), might be enough to see that while both are in "practical" style, the one is just a touch more elegant and might have belonged to the rider rather than the conductor. Finally, the Military Editions (with Hamiltons inside) are on black DLC. For those who put their money where their wrist is, buying one means a 500-dollar donation to veterans.

American Artisan Series "The Boston 463"

Movement: hand-wound, antique American Waltham Watch Company movement (built in 1924, serial number: 24431537), 12 size (ø 39 mm); 17 jewels; Art Deco decoration, blued steel moon hands; 36-hour power reserve
Functions: hours, minutes, subsidiary seconds
Case: titanium, ø 46 mm, height 12 mm; Gorilla Glass crystal; gold-plated crown; transparent stainless-steel case back, water-resistant to 1 atm
Band: rye leather, buckle
Price: up to $3,195

American Artisan Series "Chicago 009"

Movement: hand-wound, Elgin National Watch Company movement (built 1898, serial number 7323776); 16 size (44 mm); 17 jewels; golden Louis XIV hands; côtes de Genève; 36-hour power reserve
Functions: hours, minutes, subsidiary seconds
Case: titanium, ø 49 mm, height 13.5 mm; Gorilla Glass crystal; nickel plated crown; transparent case back; water-resistant to 1 atm
Band: leather, buckle
Price: up to $3,995

Military Edition "Third Edition"

Movement: hand-wound, Hamilton movement (lot built from 1938 to 1950); ø 39 mm; 22 jewels; original antique hands with hacking sweep seconds in the original movement; 36-hour power reserve
Functions: hours, minutes, subsidiary seconds (hacking)
Case: titanium with black PVD, ø 49 mm; German glass (front); transparent case back with Gorilla glass; water-resistant to 5 atm
Band: military canvas with leather overlay, buckle
Remarks: also comes with bomber jacket leather with stitching
Price: $6,995; limited to 50 pieces

VOSTOK-EUROPE

Vostok-Europe is a young brand with old roots. What started as a joint venture between the original Vostok company—a wholly separate entity—deep in the heart of Russia and a start-up in the newly minted European Union member nation of Lithuania has grown into something altogether different over the years. Originally, every Vostok model had a proprietary Russian engine, a 32-jewel automatic built in Russia. Over the years, demand and the need for alternative complications expanded the portfolio of movements to include Swiss and Japanese ones. While the heritage Russian watch industry is still evident in the inspirations and designs of Vostok-Europe, the watches built today have become favorites of extreme athletes the world over.

"Real people doing real things," is the mantra that Igor Zubovskij, managing director of the company, often repeats. "We don't use models to market our watches. Only real people test our watches in many different conditions."

That community of "real people" includes cross-country drivers in the Dakar Rally, one of the most famous aerobatic pilots in the world, a team of spelunkers who literally went to the bottom of the world in the Krubera Cave, and world free-diving champions. In 2020 the brand became the official watch of the SSN-571 Alumni Association and a part of the history of the world's first nuclear submarine.

In 2023, the brand celebrated its 20th birthday with a special model, and the 700th anniversary of the town of Vilnius, Lithuania, which, legend has it, was founded by the Iron Wolf, who came to Grand Duke Gediminas in a dream, which was interpreted as meaning he should found a town at the spot where he was hunting.

Much of the Vostok-Europe line is of professional dive quality. Some models use tritium tube technology for illumination, which offers about twenty-five years of constant lighting. The vertical tubes are placed in a kind of candleholder-shaped part for full 360-degree illumination.

Koliz Vostok Co. Ltd.
Naugarduko 41
LT-03227 Vilnius
Lithuania
Tel.:
+370-5-2106342

E-mail:
info@vostok-europe.com

Website:
www.vostok-europe.com

Founded:
2003

Number of employees:
24

Annual production:
30,000 watches

U.S. distributor:
Vostok-Europe
Détente Watch Group
244 Upton Road, Suite 4
Colchester, CT 06415
877-486-7865
www.detentewatches.com

Most important collections/price range:
Anchar / from $759; Lunokhod / from $899;
Mriya / from $649

20th Anniversary Special Edition
Reference number: YN84-640E726
Movement: automatic, Seiko Epson YN84; ø 29.36 mm; 22 jewels; 21,600 vph; 40-hour power reserve
Functions: hours, minutes, sweep seconds; power reserve indication, 24-hour display
Case: stainless steel, ø 48 mm, height 17.5 mm; unidirectional bezel with 60-minute divisions, hardened anti-reflective K1 mineral glass; screw-in crown; water-resistant to 20 atm
Band: stainless steel with black PVD, folding clasp
Remarks: "Trigalight" constant tritium illumination; comes with additional silicone strap, changing tool, and dry box; certified meteorite dial.
Price: $2,699; limited to 200 numbered pieces

Engine
Reference number: NH72-571C647
Movement: automatic, Seiko SII NH72; ø 27.40 mm; height 5.32 mm; 24 jewels; 21,600 vph; skeletonized movement; 41-hour power reserve
Case: stainless steel black PVD, ø 47 mm, height 17.5 mm; unidirectional bezel with 0-60 scale, hardened antireflective K1 mineral glass; screw-in crown; water-resistant to 20 atm
Band: leather, buckle
Remarks: First skeletonized watch from Vostok-Europe. "Trigalight" constant tritium illumination in stand-up candle holders for 360° illumination; comes with additional silicon strap, changing tool, and dry box
Price: $1,029; limited to 3,000 numbered pieces

Energia II
Reference number: NH35-575C649
Movement: automatic, Seiko SII NH35; ø 27.40 mm; height 5.32; 24 jewels; 21,600 vph; 41-hour power reserve
Functions: hours, minutes, sweep seconds; date
Case: stainless steel, ø 49 mm, height 17.5 mm; unidirectional bezel with 0-60 scale, hardened antireflective K1 mineral glass; water-resistant to 30 atm, helium release valve
Band: calfskin, buckle
Remarks: comes with additional silicon strap, screwdriver, and dry box; "Trigalight" constant tritium illumination
Price: $899

Energia II

Reference number: NH34-575C719
Movement: automatic, Seiko SII NH34; ø 27.40 mm; height 5.32; 24 jewels; 21,600 vph; 41-hour power reserve
Functions: hours, minutes, sweep seconds; GMT secondary time zone, 24-hour display
Case: stainless steel, ø 49 mm, height 17.5 mm; unidirectional bezel with 0-60 scale, hardened antireflective K1 mineral glass; helium release valve; water-resistant to 30 atm
Band: calfskin, buckle
Remarks: with additional silicone strap, screwdriver, and dry box; "Trigalight" constant tritium illumination
Price: $899

Geležinis Vilkas (Iron Wolf)

Reference number: NH72-592A706
Movement: automatic, Seiko SII NH72; ø 27.40 mm; height 5.32; 24 jewels; 21,600 vph; 41-hour power reserve
Case: stainless steel black PVD, ø 47 mm, height 17.5 mm; unidirectional bezel with 0-60 scale, hardened antireflective K1 mineral glass; screw-in crown; water-resistant to 20 atm
Band: leather, buckle
Remarks: inspired the Iron Wolf legend and the founding of Vilnius, Lithuania, in 1323. The wolf on the underside of the crystal is luminous.
Price: $1029; limited to 3,000 numbered pieces

Atomic Age Fermi Collection

Reference number: NH34-640A701
Movement: automatic, Seiko SII NH34; ø 27.40 mm; height 5.32; 24 jewels; 21,600 vph; 41-hour power reserve
Functions: hours, minutes, sweep seconds; GMT secondary time zone, 24-hour display
Case: stainless steel, ø 48 mm, height 16 mm; unidirectional bezel with 0-60 scale, hardened antireflective K1 mineral glass; screw-in crown; helium release valve; water-resistant to 30 atm;
Band: leather and silicon
Remarks: "Trigalight" tritium illumination in holders for 360° illumination; comes with additional silicone strap, changing tool, and dry box
Price: $1,210; limited to 3,000 numbered pieces

N1 Rocket

Reference number: NH34-225A713
Movement: automatic, Seiko SII NH34; ø 27.40 mm; height 5.32; 24 jewels; 21,600 vph; 41-hour power reserve
Functions: hours, minutes, sweep seconds; GMT secondary time zone, 24-hour display
Case: stainless steel, ø 46 mm, height 16 mm; unidirectional bezel with 0-60 scale, hardened antireflective K1 mineral glass; screw-in crown; water-resistant to 20 atm;
Band: leather and silicon
Remarks: fully luminous dial
Price: $749; limited to 3,000 numbered pieces

SSN 571 Automatic Submarine Watch

Reference number: NH35-5710609
Movement: automatic, Seiko SII NH35; ø 27.40 mm; height 5.32; 24 jewels; 21,600 vph; 41-hour power reserve
Functions: hours, minutes, sweep seconds; power reserve indicator; 24-hour indication
Case: stainless steel, ø 45.7 mm, height 15.6 mm; unidirectional bezel with 0-60 scale, K1 hardened antireflective mineral glass; helium release valve; water-resistant to 30 atm
Band: leather, buckle
Remarks: produced in agreement with "Association of Veterans of US Submarine Service" comes with additional silicon strap, screwdriver, and dry box; "Trigalight" constant tritium illumination
Price: $1,079; limited to 3,000 numbered pieces

Limousine

Reference number: NH38-560D681
Movement: automatic, Seiko Instruments NH38; ø 27.4 mm, height 5.77 mm; 22 jewels; 21,600 vph; 40-hour power reserve
Functions: hours, minutes, sweep seconds; open heart
Case: blue PVD plated, ø 43 mm, height 14 mm; hardened antireflective K1 mineral crystal; water-resistant to 5 atm
Band: calfskin, pin buckle
Price: $649

VULCAIN

For ever so long, watchmakers or companies producing watches kept their names off the face of their products. So, it was not until 1894 that one Maurice Ditisheim put a name to the very fine pocket watches he had been producing in La Chaux-de-Fonds since 1858, the year he opened his little atelier. Among the timepieces in his portfolio were chronographs, a perpetual calendar, and a minute repeater.

Ditisheim understood that the world was bigger than Switzerland and he extended his networks abroad. His son Ernest-Albert took over in the 1890s and continued not only producing excellent watches, but also promoting what was now a brand. He cleverly chose the name Vulcain, or Vulcan, the "patron saint," if you will, of all metal workers. The company became known as Vulcain & Volta in 1911, Vulcain & Studio in the 1950s, and finally, simply and lastly, Vulcain.

The Ditisheims saw the potential of the wristwatch early on and soon began making various models with in-house calibers. The company's major turning point came at the 1947 World's Fair, where it presented its Cricket wristwatch. The aptly named timepiece has an alarm built in that made a loud chirping sound thanks to a double soundboard. The fact that President Truman loved the watch started a tradition: every American president since, except George W. Bush, received a Cricket, even Donald Trump.

After years of ups and downs and changing hands, Vulcain seems to have found its feet again as a partner with Anonimo and under the able management of Carla Duarte. The collections have been extended beyond the fabled Cricket to include the equally fabled Nautical and Skindiver diving watches. Modern production logistics and digital distribution channels have enabled more competitive pricing. Finally, while the vintage flavor is still present, these watches have a clearly modern look.

Manufacture des montres Vulcain S.A.
Chemin des Tourelles 4
CH-2400 Le Locle
Switzerland

Tel:
+41-32-930-5370

E-Mail:
info@vulcain.ch

Website:
ww.vulcain.ch

Founded:
1858

Number of employees:
7

Annual production:
5000 watches

U.S. Distribution
Contact the company headquaerters

Most important collections/price range:
Cricket, Chronograph 1970s, Monopusher, Nautical, Salute, Skindiver Nautique / $1,500 to $6,000

Cricket Tradition 39 mm
Reference number: C6A0008
Movement: hand-wound, Vulcain Caliber V-10; ø 28 mm, height 6.3 mm; 25 jewels; 18,000 vph; 2 spring barrels; alarm lasts about 20 seconds; 52-hour power reserve
Functions: hours, minutes, sweep seconds; alarm
Case: stainless steel, ø 39 mm, height 12.8 mm; sapphire crystal; water-resistant to 5 atm
Band: reptile skin, pin buckle
Price: $4,500
Variations: with calfskin strap; various dials

Cricket Nautical
Reference number: C6A0153
Movement: hand-wound, Vulcain Caliber V-10; ø 28 mm, height 6.3 mm; 25 jewels; 18,000 vph; 2 spring barrels; alarm lasts about 20 seconds; 52-hour power reserve
Functions: hours, minutes, sweep seconds; alarm
Case: stainless steel, ø 42 mm, height 13.6 mm; crown-activated inner rotating scale ring with 0-12 scale at the center of the dial; Plexiglas; screw-in crown; water-resistant to 30 atm
Band: rubber with carbon fiber texture, pin buckle
Price: $4,640
Variations: various bands and dials

Nautic Skindiver
Reference number: C6A0180
Movement: automatic, ETA Caliber 2824-2; ø 25.6 mm, height 4.6 mm; 25 jewels; 28,800 vph; 42-hour power reserve
Functions: hours, minutes, sweep seconds
Case: stainless steel, ø 38 mm, height 12.2 mm; unidirectional bezel with ceramic insert, with 0-60 scale; sapphire crystal; screw-in crown; water-resistant to 20 atm
Band: calfskin, pin buckle
Price: $1,640
Variations: various bands and dials

Gerhard D. Wempe KG
Steinstrasse 23
D-20095 Hamburg
Germany

Tel.:
+49-40-334-480

E-mail:
info@wempe.de

Website:
www.wempe.com

Founded:
1878

Number of employees:
845 worldwide; 72 at Wempe Glashütte I/SA

Annual production:
4,000 watches

U.S. distributor:
Wempe
700 Fifth Avenue
New York, NY 10019
212-397-9000
www.wempe.com

Most important collections/price range:
Wempe Zeitmeister / approx. $1,000 to $4,700;
Wempe Chronometerwerke / approx. $6,000 to
$56,500; Wempe Iron Walker / $1,950 to $4,250

WEMPE GLASHÜTTE I/SA

Ever since 2005, the global jewelry chain Gerhard D. Wempe KG has been putting out watches under its own name again. It was probably inevitable: Gerhard D. Wempe, who founded the company in the late nineteenth century in Oldenburg, was himself a watchmaker. And in the 1930s, the company also owned the Hamburg chronometer works that made watches for seafarers and pilots.

Today, while Wempe remains formally in Hamburg, its manufacturing is done in Glashütte. The move to the fully renovated and expanded Urania observatory in the hills above town was engineered by Eva-Kim Wempe, great-granddaughter of the founder. There, the company does all its after-sales service and tests watches using the strict German Industrial Norm (DIN 8319), with official blessings from the Saxon and Thuringian offices for measurement and calibration, and according to international norms paid out by the German Calibration Service. Among other criteria, a chronometer must be tested in the assembled state, which differs from the Swiss COSC certification method.

The move to Glashütte coincided with a push to verticalize by creating a line of in-house movements reserved for the Chronometerwerke models, like the very retro Chronometerwerke Power Reserve or the . Automatic Moonphase. The calibers, bearing the initials CW, are made in partnership with companies like Nomos in Glashütte or the Swiss workshop MHVJ.

The second Wempe line is called Zeitmeister, or Master of Time. This collection uses more standard, but reworked, ETA or Sellita calibers. It meets all the requirements of the high art of watchmaking and, thanks to its accessible pricing, is attractive for budding collectors. All models are in the middle price range, which the luxury watch industry has long shunned. In 2020, Wempe joined a large community of brands with sportive-elegant timepieces. The Iron Walker series is supposed to be inspired by the workers who built the great skyscrapers of New York in the 1920s. The line is characterized by the elegant bracelet that integrates almost seamlessly into the case. The skyscrapers are hinted at in the shape of the hands.

Chronometerwerke Automatic Moonphase

Reference number: WG 100001
Movement: automatic, Wempe Caliber CW5;
ø 32.8 mm, height 6 mm; 35 jewels; 28,800 vph;
screw balance with variable inertia; 2 spring barrels,
three-quarter plate, hand-engraved balance cock,
6 gold chatons, tungsten micro-rotor, finely finished
with Glashütte ribbing; 90-hour power reserve;
DIN-certified chronometer
Functions: hours, minutes, sweep seconds; date,
moon phase
Case: stainless steel, ø 41 mm, height 11 mm; sapphire
crystal; transparent case back; water-resistant to 3 atm
Band: reptile skin, pin buckle
Price: $7,100
Variations: with brown reptile skin strap ($7,100)

Iron Walker Automatic 40

Reference number: WI 100015
Movement: automatic, Sellita Caliber SW300-1;
ø 25.6 mm, height 3.6 mm; 21 jewels; 28,800 vph; ISO
3159-certified chronometer; 56-hour power reserve
Functions: hours, minutes, sweep seconds; date
Case: stainless steel, ø 40 mm, height 9.75 mm;
sapphire crystal; water-resistant to 10 atm
Band: stainless steel, folding clasp with safety lock
Price: $3,300
Variations: various dial colors

Iron Walker Automatic Chronograph 46

Reference number: WI 690011
Movement: automatic, Sellita Caliber SW500-1;
ø 30 mm, height 7.9 mm; 25 jewels; 28,800 vph; ISO
3159 certified chronometer; 48-hour power reserve
Functions: hours, minutes, subsidiary seconds;
chronograph; date
Case: carbon fiber, ø 46 mm; bezel, crown and pusher
with rubber layer; sapphire crystal; water-resistant to
10 atm
Band: rubber with textile overlay, folding clasp
Price: $8,025

Zeitmeister Classic Chronograph 45

Reference number: WM 550005
Movement: automatic, ETA Caliber A07.211; ø 36.6 mm, height 7.9 mm; 25 jewels; 28,800 vph; modified fine regulator; ISO 3159-certified chronometer; 46-hour power reserve
Functions: hours, minutes, subsidiary seconds; chronograph; date
Case: stainless steel, ø 45 mm, height 15 mm; sapphire crystal; water-resistant to 5 atm
Band: reptile skin, folding clasp
Price: $3,045
Variations: various colors

Iron Walker Automatic Women

Reference number: WI 100018
Movement: automatic, Sellita Caliber SW300-1; ø 25.6 mm, height 3.6 mm; 21 jewels; 28,800 vph; ISO 3159-certified chronometer; 56-hour power reserve
Functions: hours, minutes, sweep seconds; date
Case: stainless steel, ø 36 mm, height 9.75 mm; set bezel with 60 precious stones; sapphire crystal; water-resistant to 10 atm
Band: stainless steel, folding clasp, with safety lock
Price: $6,925

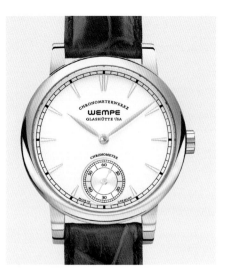

Chronometerwerke Subsidiary Seconds

Reference number: WG 070001
Movement: hand-wound, Wempe Caliber CW 3.1; ø 32.8 mm, height 6.1 mm; 40 jewels; 28,800 vph; three-quarter plate, 3 screw-mounted gold chatons, swan-neck fine regulator, hand-engraved balance cock; ISO 3159-certified chronometer; 42-hour power reserve
Functions: hours, minutes, subsidiary seconds
Case: yellow gold, ø 41 mm, height 12.5 mm; sapphire crystal; transparent case back; water-resistant to 3 atm
Band: reptile skin, pin buckle
Price: $10,190

Chronometerwerke Automatic

Reference number: WG 090001
Movement: automatic, Wempe Caliber CW4; ø 32.8 mm, height 6 mm; 35 jewels; 28,800 vph; 2 spring barrels, three-quarter plate, hand-engraved balance cock, 6 gold chatons, tungsten micro-rotor, finely finished with Glashütte ribbing; 92-hour power reserve; ISO 3159-certified chronometer
Functions: hours, minutes, sweep seconds; date
Case: yellow gold, ø 41 mm, height 11.7 mm; sapphire crystal; transparent case back; water-resistant to 3 atm
Band: reptile skin, pin buckle
Price: $14,950
Variations: in stainless steel ($6,900)

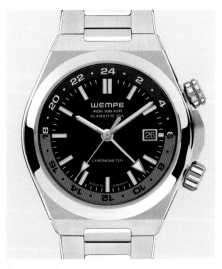

Iron Walker Automatic GMT

Reference number: WI 250002
Movement: automatic, Sellita Caliber SW330; ø 25.6 mm, height 4.1 mm; 21 jewels; 28,800 vph; ISO 3159-certified chronometer; 56-hour power reserve
Functions: hours, minutes, sweep seconds; additional 24-hour display (2nd time zone); date
Case: stainless steel, ø 42 mm, height 11.7 mm; crown-activated inner rotating scale ring with 0-24 scale; sapphire crystal; screw-in crown; water-resistant to 10 atm
Band: stainless steel, folding clasp, with safety lock
Price: $4,440
Variations: with black-white bezel

Iron Walker Automatic Chronograph

Reference number: WI 300002
Movement: automatic, ETA Caliber 7753; ø 30 mm, height 7.9 mm; 27 jewels; 28,800 vph; ISO 3159-certified chronometer; 48-hour power reserve
Functions: hours, minutes, subsidiary seconds; chronograph; date
Case: stainless steel, ø 42 mm, height 13.95 mm; sapphire crystal; screw-in crown; water-resistant to 10 atm
Band: stainless steel, folding clasp, with safety lock
Price: $5,075
Variations: with black dial

YEMA Watches
1 rue Fontaine de l'Epine
F-25500 Morteau
France

Tel.:
+33 381 67 67 67

Email:
privilege@yema.com

Website:
www.yema.com

Founded:
1948

Number of employees:
60

Distribution:
online

Most important collections:
Superman, Navygraf, Meangraf, Rallygraf

YEMA

How difficult it is to live in the shadow of a great and geographically close competitor is illustrated by the little town of Morteau, population just under 7,000, in Burgundy, France. But in the world of watchmaking, it has quite a reputation. It lies in *Pays Horloger* (watch country), in a gentle valley traversed by the meandering Doubs River (hence the name, which means dead, or stagnant, water). Watchmaking came to the region and replaced agriculture as a source of income in the mid-1750s. Today, the town's school has an excellent reputation as an institution that supplies extremely talented workers to the entire industry, notably in Switzerland: Le Locle and La Chaux-de-Fonds, global hubs of Swiss watchmaking, are just a few miles away. Not surprisingly, it has two watch brands, one of which is Yema.

Quietly and steadily, Yema has been producing sports watches for divers, motor sports enthusiasts, pilots, and seafarers since 1948. Among its most important achievements was the first watch able to go 200 meters (660 feet) underwater. The Master Elements of the late 1970s let the user calculate speed, flying time, and the amount of fuel left in flight. And the Spationaute was the first French watch to reach space on the wrist of Jean-Loup Chrétien.

In 2009, the company was bought by a local group, Montres Ambre SA, which chose a flight forward strategy. Leveraging the long experience of the employees, it began manufacturing its own calibers, the Yema 2000 and Yema 3000 (GMT) as well as the Morteau 20. While the first two automatic movements are essentially based on the Swiss standard movements from ETA and Sellita in terms of architecture, dimensions, and rate performance, the Morteau 20 caliber is a modern, extra-thin automatic movement (3.7 millimeters high) with a bidirectional tungsten micro-rotor and 70-hour power reserve. The watches are then assembled and regulated in the Morteau workshops using many individual parts manufactured in-house, though some parts are outsourced to French companies. Also done in Morteau are design, prototyping, and assembly.

Superman 500

Reference number: YSUP22A39-AMS
Movement: automatic, Caliber YEMA2000;
ø 25.6 mm, height 4.6 mm; 29 jewels; 28,800 vph;
42-hour power reserve
Functions: hours, minutes, sweep seconds
Case: stainless steel, ø 39 mm, height 13.4 mm;
unidirectional bezel with 0-60 scale; sapphire crystal;
screw-in crown; water-resistant to 50 atm
Band: stainless steel, folding clasp, with safety lock
and extension link
Price: $1,249
Variations: with 41-millimeter case

Navygraf GMT

Reference number: YNAV23MN-AMS
Movement: automatic, Caliber YEMA3000;
ø 25.6 mm, height 4.6 mm; 29 jewels; 28,800 vph;
42-hour power reserve
Functions: hours, minutes, sweep seconds; additional
24-hour display (2nd time zone)
Case: stainless steel, ø 38.5 mm, height 12 mm;
bidirectional bezel, with 0-24 scale; sapphire crystal;
screw-in crown; water-resistant to 30 atm
Band: stainless steel, folding clasp, with safety lock
and extension link
Price: $1,349

Wristmaster Traveler Micro-Rotor

Movement: automatic, Caliber Manufacture Morteau
CMM20; ø 25.6 mm, height 3.7 mm; 33 jewels;
28,800 vph; tungsten micro-rotor; 70-hour power
reserve
Functions: hours, minutes, sweep seconds
Case: stainless steel, ø 39 mm, height 10 mm;
screw bezel; sapphire crystal; screw-in crown;
water-resistant to 10 atm
Band: stainless steel, folding clasp
Price: $3,600; limited to 1948 pieces of the
manufacture's own calibers

YVAN MONNET

After two decades working with Patek Philippe and Vacheron Constantin, Valais-born Yvan Monnet faced a bit of a dilemma: either continue finding work in the beehives of large companies with security but little autonomy, or set sail on his own. He decided to tap into his extensive experience with what is known as *habillage*, all the jobs related to the complex art of finishing in watchmaking and conceive his own brand.

"For it to be relevant," says Monnet, "it had to be something that was never done before." He wanted a watch that would be essentially unisex, that would reflect his own positive personality traits: sports-loving, entertaining, sociable, communicative. "I wanted a watch I could take to work, to a concert, to a cocktail, and then go take a swim in the lake without having to leave a precious object in my shoes on the beach."

He began by simply brainstorming on paper. The design that stuck was a pentagonal bezel, not very attractive on paper, but after lots of tweaking and fine-tuning, he obtained what he had originally intended in his mind's eye. It is not an easy shape to fit onto a round dial and the barrel. He avoided gilding the lily with lots of decoration, opting for a great degree of coherence between the hands, the colors, and the numerals. The screw-in crown at 2:30 is also pentagonal and allows the watch to dive two-hundred meters. The colors are stark without being overbearing: black, blue, a pine green, and light chocolate. They come in a larger size, the Five, and a smaller size, the Mina. They are driven by a Selitta caliber.

In a bid to spread his pentagonal gospel to a larger market, Monnet then come up with the Tzoumy. This side brand is slightly thinner and runs on a robust Landeron caliber. It, too, comes in a variety of colors that are carefully chosen to stand out without being flamboyant. Yvan Monnet products hide complex design behind a look of simplicity.

Yvan Monnet
Place Simon-Goulart, 2 38
CVH-1201 Genève
Switzerland

Tel:
+41-32-967-97-97

E-mail:
yvan@yvm2.ch

Website:
www.ymonnet.ch

Founded:
2016; Tzoumy in 2021

Number of employees:
5

Number of watches:
100 (Five), Tzoumy (750)

Distributor:
For all questions and orders, contact the company directly

Most important collections/price range:
Five, Mina, Tzoumy; $2,350 – $5,800

Five Black
Reference number: 1001V2
Movement: automatic, Selitta SW400-1; ø 31 mm, height 7.9 mm; 26 jewels; 28,800 vph; custom rotor with black PVD; 38-hour power reserve
Functions: hours, minutes, sweep seconds
Case: stainless steel, ø 43 x 42.1 mm, height 10.80 mm; sapphire crystal; screw-in crown; water-resistant to 20 atm
Band: calfskin, folding clasp
Remarks: comes with additional "waterproof" strap on rubber padding with buckle
Price: $5,780
Variations: comes in different dial colors

Tzoumy Denim
Reference number: TZ01
Movement: automatic, Landeron 24 Caliber; ø 25.6 mm, height 4.6 mm; 25 jewels; 28,800 vph; Tzoumy special rotor, 36-hour power reserve
Functions: hours, minutes, sweep seconds
Case: stainless steel, ø 40.1 x 39.55 mm, height 9.5 mm; sapphire crystal; water-resistant to 5 atm
Band: calfskin, buckle
Remarks: sunburst finishing on the dial
Price: $2,350
Variations: comes in different dial colors

Mina Cacao
Reference number: 2103
Movement: hand-wound, modified Sellita Caliber SW210-1; ø 25.6 mm, height 3.35 mm; 19 jewels; 28,800 vph; 42-hour power reserve
Functions: hours, minutes, sweep seconds
Case: stainless steel, ø 40.1 x 39.55 mm, height 9.5 mm; sapphire crystal; water-resistant to 5 atm
Band: calfskin, buckle
Remarks: comes with additional satin strap and buckle
Price: $3,100
Variations: white or blue lacquered dial; comes in automatic version with Selitta SW300-1 movement ($3,350)

Zenith SA
34, rue des Billodes
CH-2400 Le Locle
Switzerland

Tel.:
+41-32-930-6262

Website:
www.zenith-watches.com

Founded:
1865

Number of employees:
over 330 employees worldwide

U.S. distributor:
Zenith Watches
966 South Springfield Avenue
Springfield, NJ 07081
866-675-2079
contact.zenith@lvmhwatchjewelry.com

Most important collections/price range:
Academy / from $80,900; Elite / from $4,700;
Chronomaster / from $6,700; Pilot / from $5,700;
Defy / from $5,900

ZENITH

Zenith, still housed in a tall, light-bathed industrial building in Le Locle, Switzerland, was founded in 1865 by Georges Favre-Jacot as a small watch reassembly workshop. It has produced all kinds of watches in its long history, but its claim to fame is the El Primero caliber, the first wristwatch chronograph movement boasting automatic winding and a frequency of 36,000 vph, allowing for measurements of a tenth of a second. It was 1969, and only a few manufacturers had risked such a high oscillation frequency—and none of them with such complexity as the integrated chronograph mechanism and bilaterally winding rotor of the El Primero.

LVMH Group bought the brand in 1999, boosting its technical possibilities. Zenith was dusted off and modernized. The historic complex in Le Locle, which was put on UNESCO's World Heritage list in 2009, was thoroughly renovated. Over eighty different crafts are now practiced here, from watchmaking to design, from art to prototyping. Synergies with the Group companions Hublot and TAG Heuer produced the Defy 21, a complex chronograph movement based on the 36,000-vph El Primero. It features two separate gear trains and escapements for time and chronograph functions, respectively. The chronograph movement beats at 360,000 vph, allowing the hundredths of a second to be displayed. The other technical feat is the Zero G that keeps the escapement system in the horizontal position.

Re-releasing older models has led the company to promote a circular economy, whereby older models can be perfectly restored and remain in circulation. The original El Primero was also modernized and is now the Primero 3600 caliber, boasting a little more power reserve than the original.

In addition to the chronographs, the sporty and elegant three-hand watches, and a series of intricate skeletons in the Defy line, Zenith also decided to give the Pilot family a major facelift. The name itself harks back to the days when the company equipped the pioneers of aviation with all kinds of instruments. Now, the Pilot has been given a new place in the collection, as a distinctive and modern sports watch with and without a large date, and with a look that hints at the original Zeniths.

Chronomaster Sport

Reference number: 03.3100.3600/69.M3100
Movement: automatic, Zenith Caliber 3600 "El Primero"; ø 30 mm, height 6.6 mm; 35 jewels; 36,000 vph; 60-hour power reserve
Functions: hours, minutes, subsidiary seconds; chronograph; date
Case: stainless steel, ø 41 mm, height 13.6 mm; ceramic bezel; sapphire crystal; transparent case back; water-resistant to 10 atm
Band: stainless steel, double folding clasp
Price: $11,000
Variations: with rubber strap ($10,500)

Chronomaster Sport

Reference number: 51.3100.3600/69.M3100
Movement: automatic, Zenith Caliber 3600 "El Primero"; ø 30 mm, height 6.6 mm; 35 jewels; 36,000 vph; 60-hour power reserve
Functions: hours, minutes, subsidiary seconds; chronograph; date
Case: stainless steel, ø 41 mm, height 13.6 mm; rose-gold bezel; sapphire crystal; transparent case back; rose-gold crown and pushers; water-resistant to 10 atm
Band: stainless steel with rose-gold elements, double folding clasp
Price: $17,000

Chronomaster Sport

Reference number: 18.3101.3600/21.M3100
Movement: automatic, Zenith Caliber 3600 "El Primero"; ø 30 mm, height 6.6 mm; 35 jewels; 36,000 vph; 60-hour power reserve
Functions: hours, minutes, subsidiary seconds; chronograph; date
Case: rose gold, ø 41 mm, height 13.6 mm; sapphire crystal; transparent case back; water-resistant to 10 atm
Band: rose gold, double folding clasp
Price: $38,200

Chronomaster Sport

Reference number: 03.3100.3600/69.C823
Movement: automatic, Zenith Caliber
3600 "El Primero"; ø 30 mm, height 6.6 mm; 35 jewels;
36,000 vph; 60-hour power reserve
Functions: hours, minutes, subsidiary seconds;
chronograph; date
Case: stainless steel, ø 41 mm, height 13.6 mm;
ceramic bezel; sapphire crystal; transparent case
back; water-resistant to 10 atm
Band: rubber with textile overlay, double folding clasp
Price: $10,500
Variations: with black dial and strap

Chronomaster Open

Reference number: 18.3300.3604/69.C823
Movement: automatic, Zenith Caliber 3604; ø 30 mm,
height 6.6 mm; 35 jewels; 36,000 vph; dial and
movement partially skeletonized over the regulating
section; 60-hour power reserve
Functions: hours, minutes, subsidiary seconds;
chronograph
Case: stainless steel, ø 39.5 mm, height 12.6 mm;
sapphire crystal; transparent case back;
water-resistant to 10 atm
Band: stainless steel, folding clasp
Price: $10,000

Chronomaster Open

Reference number: 03.3300.3604/21.M3300
Movement: automatic, Zenith Caliber 3604; ø 30 mm,
height 6.6 mm; 35 jewels; 36,000 vph; dial and
movement partially skeletonized over the regulating
section; 60-hour power reserve
Functions: hours, minutes, subsidiary seconds;
chronograph
Case: stainless steel, ø 39.5 mm, height 12.6 mm;
sapphire crystal; transparent case back;
water-resistant to 10 atm
Band: stainless steel, folding clasp
Price: $10,000

Chronomaster Original

Reference number: 03.3200.3600/22.C908
Movement: automatic, Zenith Caliber
3600 "El Primero"; ø 30 mm, height 6.6 mm; 35 jewels;
36,000 vph; 60-hour power reserve
Functions: hours, minutes, subsidiary seconds;
chronograph; date
Case: stainless steel, ø 38 mm, height 12.6 mm;
sapphire crystal; transparent case back;
water-resistant to 5 atm
Band: calfskin, triple folding clasp
Price: $9,500

Chronomaster Original

Reference number: 03.3200.3600/69.M3200
Movement: automatic, Zenith Caliber
3600 "El Primero"; ø 30 mm, height 6.6 mm; 35 jewels;
36,000 vph; 60-hour power reserve
Functions: hours, minutes, subsidiary seconds;
chronograph; date
Case: stainless steel, ø 38 mm, height 12.6 mm;
sapphire crystal; transparent case back;
water-resistant to 5 atm
Band: stainless steel, folding clasp
Price: $10,000

Defy Revival Shadow

Reference number: 97.A3642.670/21.M3642
Movement: automatic, Zenith Caliber 670 "Elite";
ø 25.6 mm, height 3.88 mm; 27 jewels; 28,800 vph;
48-hour power reserve
Functions: hours, minutes, sweep seconds; date
Case: titanium (microblasted), ø 37 mm, height 13.60;
sapphire crystal; water-resistant to 30 atm
Band: titanium (microblasted), double folding clasp
Remarks: A modern reinterpretation of the first DEFY
wristwatch model from 1969
Price: $7,400

Defy Skyline

Reference number: 03.9300.3620/51.I001
Movement: automatic, Zenith Caliber 3620 "El Primero"; ø 30 mm; 26 jewels; 36,000 vph; 60-hour power reserve
Functions: hours, minutes, subsidiary seconds (10-second rotation); date
Case: stainless steel, ø 41 mm, height 11.6 mm; sapphire crystal; transparent case back; screw-in crown; water-resistant to 10 atm
Band: stainless steel, folding clasp
Price: $9,000

Defy Skyline Ceramic

Reference number: 49.9300.3620/21.I001
Movement: automatic, Zenith Caliber 3620 "El Primero"; ø 30 mm; 26 jewels; 36,000 vph; 60-hour power reserve
Functions: hours, minutes, subsidiary seconds (10-second rotation); date
Case: ceramic, ø 41 mm, height 11.6 mm; sapphire crystal; transparent case back; screw-in crown; water-resistant to 10 atm
Band: ceramic, folding clasp
Price: $15,000

Defy Skyline Skeleton

Reference number: 03.9300.3620/79.I001
Movement: automatic, Zenith Caliber 3620 "El Primero"; ø 30 mm; 26 jewels; 36,000 vph; skeletonized movement; 60-hour power reserve
Functions: hours, minutes, subsidiary seconds (10-second rotation)
Case: stainless steel, ø 41 mm, height 11.6 mm; sapphire crystal; transparent case back; screw-in crown; water-resistant to 10 atm
Band: rubber, folding clasp
Remarks: skeletonized dial; comes with additional stainless steel bracelet
Price: $10,800

Defy Skyline Skeleton Ceramic

Reference number: 49.9300.3620/78.I001
Movement: automatic, Zenith Caliber 3620 "El Primero"; ø 30 mm; 26 jewels; 36,000 vph; skeletonized movement; 60-hour power reserve
Functions: hours, minutes, subsidiary seconds (10-second rotation)
Case: ceramic, ø 41 mm, height 11.6 mm; sapphire crystal; transparent case back; screw-in crown; water-resistant to 10 atm
Band: ceramic, folding clasp Remarks: skeletonized dial:
Price: $17,000

Defy Extreme

Reference number: 95.9100.9004/01.I001
Movement: automatic, Zenith Caliber 9004 "El Primero"; ø 32 mm, height 7.9 mm; 53 jewels; 36,000 vph; separate chronograph construction with separate escapement (360,000 vph) and power management; Timelab-certified chronometer; 50-hour power reserve
Functions: hours, minutes, subsidiary seconds; power-reserve indicator (for chrono functions); chronograph (indicates 100th of a second)
Case: stainless steel, ø 45 mm, height 15.4 mm; sapphire crystal; transparent case back; water-resistant to 20 atm
Band: stainless steel, double folding clasp
Price: $18,000

Defy Skyline 36mm

Reference number: 03.9400.670/61.I001
Movement: automatic, Zenith Caliber 670 "Elite"; ø 25.6 mm, height 3.88 mm; 27 jewels; 28,800 vph; 48-hour power reserve
Functions: hours, minutes, sweep seconds; date
Case: stainless steel, ø 36 mm; sapphire crystal; transparent case back; screw-in crown; water-resistant to 10 atm
Band: stainless steel, folding clasp
Price: $8,500
Variations: with blue or pink dial; with diamond bezel (€ 12.900,–)

Defy Extreme Carbon

Reference number: 10.9100.9004/22.I200
Movement: automatic, Zenith Caliber
9004 "El Primero"; ø 32 mm, height 7.9 mm; 53 jewels;
36,000 vph; separate chronograph construction
with separate escapement (360,000 vph) and power
management; Timelab-certified chronometer;
50-hour power reserve
Functions: hours, minutes, subsidiary seconds;
power-reserve indicator (for chrono functions);
chronograph (indicates 100th of a second)
Case: carbon fiber, ø 45 mm, height 15.4 mm; sapphire
crystal; transparent case back; water-resistant to 20 atm
Band: textile, double folding clasp
Price: $25,100

Defy Extreme Double Tourbillon

Reference number: 12.9100.9020/78.I200
Movement: automatic, Zenith Caliber
9020 "El Primero"; ø 35.8 mm, height 7.9 mm; 59 jewels;
36,000 vph; based on caliber with double tourbillon;
separate chronograph construction with separate
escapement (360,000 vph) and power management;
Timelab-certified chronometer; 50-hour power reserve
Functions: hours, minutes, subsidiary seconds;
power-reserve indicator (for chrono functions);
chronograph (indicates 100th of a second)
Case: carbon fiber, ø 45 mm, height 15.4 mm; rose-gold
bezel and case flanks; sapphire crystal; transparent
case back; water-resistant to 20 atm
Band: rubber, double folding clasp
Price: $79,700

Pilot Automatic

Reference number: 03.4000.3620/21.I001
Movement: automatic, Zenith Caliber 3620
"El Primero"; ø 30 mm; 26 jewels; 36,000 vph;
60-hour power reserve
Functions: hours, minutes, sweep seconds; date
Case: stainless steel, ø 40 mm; sapphire crystal;
transparent case back; screw-in crown;
water-resistant to 10 atm
Band: rubber with textile overlay, triple folding clasp
Remarks: comes with additional calfskin strap
Price: $8,100

Pilot Automatic

Reference number: 49.4000.3620/21.I001
Movement: automatic, Zenith Caliber 3620
"El Primero"; ø 30 mm; 26 jewels; 36,000 vph;
60-hour power reserve
Functions: hours, minutes, sweep seconds; date
Case: ceramic, ø 40 mm; sapphire crystal; transparent
case back; screw-in crown; water-resistant to 10 atm
Band: rubber with textile overlay, triple folding clasp
Remarks: comes with additional textile strap
Price: $9,600

Pilot Big Date Flyback

Reference number: 03.4000.3652/21.I001
Movement: automatic, Zenith Caliber 3652
"El Primero"; ø 30 mm; 26 jewels; 36,000 vph;
60-hour power reserve
Functions: hours, minutes, subsidiary seconds;
flyback chronograph; large date
Case: stainless steel, ø 42.5 mm; sapphire crystal;
transparent case back; screw-in crown;
water-resistant to 10 atm
Band: rubber with textile overlay, triple folding clasp
Remarks: comes with additional calfskin strap
Price: $11,500

Pilot Big Date Flyback

Reference number: 49.4000.3652/21.I001
Movement: automatic, Zenith Caliber 3652
"El Primero"; ø 30 mm; 26 jewels; 36,000 vph;
60-hour power reserve
Functions: hours, minutes, subsidiary seconds;
flyback chronograph; large date
Case: ceramic, ø 42.5 mm; sapphire crystal;
transparent case back; screw-in crown;
water-resistant to 10 atm
Band: rubber with textile overlay, triple folding clasp
Remarks: comes with additional textile strap
Price: $13,500

Caliber 400 El Primero

Automatic; column-wheel control of the chronograph functions; single spring barrel, 50-hour power reserve
Functions: hours, minutes, subsidiary seconds; chronograph; date
Diameter: 30 mm
Height: 6.5 mm
Jewels: 31
Balance: glucydur
Frequency: 36,000 vph
Hairspring: flat hairspring
Shock protection: Kif
Remarks: 278 parts

Caliber 9020 El Primero

Automatic; independent chronograph construction with separate escapement (360,000 vph) and power management; two tourbillons with carbon nanotube matrix hairspring; Timelab-certified chronometer; single spring barrel, 50-hour power reserve
Functions: hours, minutes; power reserve indicator (for chronograph functions); chronograph with 100th/second indicator
Diameter: 35.8 mm
Height: 7.9 mm
Jewels: 60
Balance: glucydur Frequency: 36,000 vph
Shock protection: Kif
Remarks: blue-coated movement parts; 311 parts

Caliber 9004 El Primero

Automatic; independent chronograph mechanism with separate escapement (360,000 vph) and power management; COSC-certified chronometer; 2 hairsprings of nanotube carbon matrix, impervious to magnetic fields and temperature fluctuations; single spring barrel, 50-hour power reserve; Timelab-certified chronometer
Functions: hours, minutes, subsidiary seconds; power reserve indicator (for chronograph functions); chronograph displays 1/100th of a second
Diameter: 32.8 mm
Height: 7.9 mm
Jewels: 53
Balance: glucydur
Frequency: 36,000 vph
Shock protection: Kif
Remarks: 293 parts

Caliber 670 Elite

Automatic; skeletonized movement; single spring barrel, 50-hour power reserve
Functions: hours, minutes, sweep seconds; date
Diameter: 25.6 mm
Height: 3.88 mm
Jewels: 27
Balance: glucydur
Frequency: 28,800 vph
Hairspring: flat hairspring
Shock protection: Kif
Remarks: 187 parts

Caliber 3600 El Primero

Automatic; silicon anchor and escape wheel; column-wheel control of the chronograph functions; single spring barrel, 60-hour power reserve; COSC-certified chronometer
Functions: hours, minutes, subsidiary seconds; chronograph; date
Diameter: 30 mm
Height: 6.6 mm
Jewels: 35
Balance: glucydur
Frequency: 36,000 vph
Hairspring: flat hairspring
Shock protection: Kif

Caliber 3620 El Primero

Automatic; silicon anchor and escape wheel; single spring barrel, 60-hour power reserve; COSC-certified chronometer
Functions: hours, minutes, subsidiary seconds; date
Diameter: 30 mm
Jewels: 26
Balance: glucydur
Frequency: 36,000 vph
Hairspring: flat hairspring
Shock protection: Kif

ZEROO TIME CO.

Japan has a few very globally famous brands, like Casio, Citizen, and Seiko. But in their shadow, one finds a number of small brands doing excellent work as well: Zeroo Time, for example, was launched in 2017 by a watch designer named Syuu Kiryou, who prefers to go by the name SYUU, all caps. His experience in the watch industry had left him feeling that watches needed strong design but had to be affordable as well, even if they had serious complications, like tourbillons.

The T8 Orion Full Skeleton Tourbillon, for instance, is fully skeletonized, including an elongated sapphire crystal in the case middle to offer a lateral view into the watch. On the T6 Quaser, the tourbillon appears in the middle surrounded by a ring, giving it a somewhat extraterrestrial look. The transparent case back reveals a pinwheel côtes de Genève on the mainplate. And any resemblance between the M2 Subaru and, say a Richard Mille, is not coincidental. As a note, the term "subaru" refers to six stars of the constellation we call the Pleiades.

Special design involves cost, and Zeroo Time intended to make products that would draw attention and were mechanically reliable but would not ruin the buyer. The way to achieve the delicate cost-quality balance was, first, to crowdfund, and avoid many of the extraneous expenses from distribution and retailing. The second strategy was to source low-cost parts, for instance Sea-Gull movements from China, which are taken apart and rigorously worked over by a team of watchmakers in Japan, where the watches are assembled. The company also uses Swiss STP calibers, notably in their M3 Lyra series.

Almost seven years in, Zeroo is making a name for itself. It is present in fifteen countries, including the USA. "We want every watch lover to have one of our watches" says SYUU. "We are planning to develop our own movements in the future and create products that are a cross between Swiss and Japanese made."

Zeroo Time Co.
2-1-3 Naganuma-cho 104
Hachioji-shi
Tokyo 192-09078
Japan

Tel.:
+81-50-3656-4608

Email:
hshiba@zerootime.com

Website:
https://zerootime.com/en-global

Founded:
2017

Number of employees:
10

Annual production:
approx 1,000 pieces

U.S. distributor:
King Jewelers Tennessee
4121 Hillsboro Pike
Nashville, TN 37215
info@kingjewelers.com
www.KingJewelers.com
615-724-5464

Most important collections/price range:
Zeroo T (Tourbillon) series / $3,000 to $5,000

M2 The Subaru Skeleton Mechanical Automatic

Reference number: ZM002BBK
Movement: automatic, Caliber ZM02 (modified STP6-21); ø 25.6 mm, height 4.6 mm; 26 jewels; 28,800 vph; skeletonized movement; 40-hour power reserve
Functions: hours, minutes, sweep seconds
Case: stainless steel with black DLC, 39 mm x 50 mm x 10.5 mm, height 13 mm; sapphire crystal; transparent case back; water-resistant to 3 atm
Band: fluorine rubber, folding buckle
Price: $2,500
Variations: with various color straps and cases

T6 The Quasar

Reference number: ZT006BBK
Movement: hand-wound, Caliber T6; ø 33 mm, height 6.4 mm; 26 jewels; 28,800 vph; with central tourbillon; finely decorated mainplate; 40-hour power reserve
Functions: hours, minutes, sweep seconds
Case: stainless steel with black PVD, ø 43 mm, height 10.5 mm; sapphire crystal; transparent case back; water-resistant to 5 atm
Band: leather, folding buckle
Price: $4,000
Variations: with blue rubber strap; with various color cases

T8 The Orion Full Skeleton Tourbillon

Reference number: ZT008SWLB
Movement: hand-wound, Caliber ZT05 Tourbillon; ø 33.5 mm, height 6.5 mm; 20 jewels; 28,800 vph; 1-minute tourbillon; fully skeletonized movement; dual barrel spring; 60-hour power reserve
Functions: hours, minutes, seconds on tourbillon
Case: stainless steel, ø 43 mm, height 11 mm; sapphire crystal; water-resistant to 3 atm
Band: fluorine rubber, folding buckle
Price: $5,000; limited to 1,000 pieces for each color
Variations: with black or white strap

Zero West LTD
41 Bridgefoot Path
Emsworth
Hampshire
United Kingdom
PO10 7EB

Tel.:
+44 (0)1243-376-676

E-mail:
time@zerowest.co.uk

Website:
www.zerowest.watch

Founded:
2015

Number of employees:
5

U.S. distribution:
Contact the manufacturer directly

Most important collections:
Aviation (Spitfire S1/S2/S3, Hurricane H1);
Marine (Longitude L2); Motorsport (LS-2 Land
Speed Bullhead, Flying Scotsman)

ZERO WEST

Time, place and indeed, history are the reference points for Zero West, a company founded in 2015 by Andrew Brabyn and Graham Collins, a leading graphic designer and an aerospace engineer, respectively. The company name itself refers to the coordinates of the Greenwich Royal Observatory. Their first watch was a statement: The Longitude L1 paid homage to an icon of British even world horology, John Harrison's remarkable H4 maritime clock that managed to keep accurate time on a ship in 1761 contributed to the establishment of the Greenwich prime meridian by George Airy in 1851.

Meanwhile, the company has defined three core collections for their brand: automotive, aviation and marine. Their latest aviation model, for example, celebrates an absolute icon: the Lancaster DB-1. The design recalls the plane's altimeter dial and inside, one finds a smelted disc from the bodywork of ED825, which was along for the famous "Dambusters" (Operation Chastise) raid in 1943, during which the RAF ricocheted special bombs on dams in the Ruhr region to try and cripple Nazi Germany's industrial production.

The automotive portfolio covers machines on wheels, like the TT-58R, featuring a machined disc cut from the drive shaft of the 1958 race winning Aston Martin DBR1 driven by Stirling Moss. A rare watch at only fifty-eight builds. Anyone with a good train set has at least heard of the famous Flying Scotsman, a locomotive that was the first to reach 100 mph, on November 30, 1930. A section of its boiler tube is the guest of honor in the FS-1 reference.

The watches are designed and assembled at the company's workshop and headquarters on the South Coast of England. It is where the two founders do their historical research and brainstorm each new watch dial. It is also where Graham Collins makes the straps for the collections. Low volume ensures high quality. The geographical location on the dials and case back relates to the watch's theme. Each watch is powered by tried-and-true Swiss calibers, like the ETA 2824 and Valjoux 7750 for the chronographs.

Lancaster

Reference number: DB-1
Movement: automatic, ETA 2824; ø 44 mm, height 14.1mm; 26 jewels; 28,800 vph, 41-hour power reserve
Functions: hours, minutes
Case: stainless steel with 8 polished vertically cut ball-nose flutes, ø 44 mm, height 14.1 mm; sapphire crystal, transparent case back; screw-in crown; transparent case back with view of metal disc from a Lancaster ED825 with serial number; water-resistant to 10 atm
Band: fluoroelastomer rubber strap, pin buckle
Remarks: dial inspired from an altimeter gauge from a Lancaster cockpit and paying tribute to Operation Chastise and the Lancaster plane ED825, 1 of 19 on that mission
Price: $4,490; limited to 200 pieces

Flying Scotsman

Reference Number: FS-1
Movement: automatic, Sellita SW200-1 (top premium grade); ø 41 mm, height 13.1 mm; 28,800 vph, 26 jewels; 41-hour power reserve
Functions: hours, minutes
Case: black PVD stainless steel, ø 41mm, height 13.1mm; screw-in crown; sapphire crystal; transparent case back with view of disc from the original Flying Scotsman boiler tube with serial number; water-resistant to 10 atm
Band: fluoroelastomer rubber strap, pin buckle
Remarks: dial inspired from a locomotive gauge; latitude and longitude of Doncaster works where the Flying Scotsman was built, and date of completion printed at 6 o'clock; luminous minute track
Price: $4,490; limited to 100 pieces

Hurricane - Battle of Britain (1940)

Reference Number: H2 P3708
Movement: Sellita SW200-1 (top premium grade); ø 41 mm, height 13.5 mm; 28,800 vph, 26 jewels; 41-hour power reserve
Functions: hours, minutes
Case: stainless steel, matt silver bead blasted with eight vertically cut ball-nose flutes, black PVD, ø 41 mm, height 13.5 mm; screw-in crown; sapphire crystal; transparent case back with view of a disc from a WW2 Hurricane Merlin engine with serial number ; water-resistant to 10 atm
Band: fluroelastomer rubber strap, pin buckle
Remarks: dial inspired from a slip turn indicator from Hurricane P3708; date and longitude positions where the plane was recovered
Price: $4,600; limited to 50 pieces

CONCEPTO

The Concepto Watch Factory, founded in 2006 in La Chaux-de-Fonds, is the successor to the family-run company Jaquet SA, which changed its name to La Joux-Perret a little while ago and then moved to a different location on the other side of the hub of watch-making. In 2008, Valérien Jaquet, son of the company founder Pierre Jaquet, began systematically building up a modern movement and watch component factory on an empty floor of the building.

Today, the Concepto Watch Factory employs eighty people in various departments, such as Development/Prototyping, Decoparts (partial manufacturing using lathes, machining, or wire erosion), Artisia (production of movements and complications in large series), as well as Optimo (escapements). In addition to the standard family of calibers, the C2000 (based on the Valjoux) and the vintage chronograph movement C7000 (the evolution of the Venus Caliber), the company's product portfolio includes various tourbillon movements (Caliber C8000) and several modules for adding onto ETA movements (Caliber C1000). A brand-new caliber series, the C3000, features a retrograde calendar and seconds, a power reserve indicator, and a chronograph. The C4000 chronograph caliber with automatic winding is currently in pre-series testing.

One of Concepto's greatest assets is its flexibility. Most of the company's movements are not sold off the shelf, as it were, but rather designed according to the specific requirements of watchmaking companies with regard to form or technical DNA. Some of these cooperations become long-term relationships. Complicated movements are assembled entirely and tested by the company's watchmakers, while others are sold as kits for assembly by the watchmakers. Annual production is somewhere between 30,000 and 40,000 units, with additional hundreds of thousands of components made for contract manufacturing.

Caliber 1053

Automatic; inverted construction with dial-side escapement; bidirectional off-center winding rotor; single spring barrel; 42-hour power reserve
Functions: hours, minutes, subsidiary seconds (all off-center)
Diameter: 33 mm
Height: 3.75 mm
Jewels: 31
Balance: glucydur
Frequency: 28,800 vph
Balance spring: flat hairspring
Remarks: black finishing on movement

Caliber 2904 (dial side)

Inverted construction with dial-side escapement; single spring barrel; 48-hour power reserve
Functions: hours, minutes, subsidiary seconds
Diameter: 30.4 mm
Height: 4.6 mm
Jewels: 31
Balance: screw balance
Frequency: 28,800 vph
Balance spring: flat hairspring

Caliber 3041 Skeleton (dial side)

Hand-wound; skeletonized symmetrical construction; single spring barrel; 48-hour power reserve
Functions: hours, minutes
Diameter: 32.6 mm
Height: 5.5 mm
Jewels: 21
Balance: screw balance
Frequency: 28,800 vph
Balance spring: flat hairspring
Remarks: extensive personalization options for finishing and accessories

Caliber 2000-RAC

Automatic; column wheel control of chronograph functions; stop-second system; single spring barrel; 48-hour power reserve
Functions: hours, minutes, subsidiary seconds; chronograph
Diameter: 30.4 mm; **Height:** 8.4 mm
Jewels: 26; **Balance:** screw balance
Frequency: 28,800 vph
Balance spring: flat hairspring
Shock protection: Incabloc
Remarks: related calibers: 2000 (without control wheel); with two or three totalizers ("tricompax") with or without date; various additional displays (moon phase, retrograde date hand, additional 24-hour sweep hand, power reserve indicator)

Caliber 8500

Hand-wound; 1-minute tourbillon; column wheel control of chronograph functions; single spring barrel; 50-hour power reserve
Functions: hours, minutes, subsidiary seconds; split-seconds chronograph
Diameter: 31.3 mm
Height: 7.2 mm
Jewels: 31
Balance: screw balance
Frequency: 21,600 vph
Balance spring: flat hairspring
Remarks: very fine movement finishing

Caliber 8950-A

Automatic; 1-minute tourbillon; single spring barrel; 60-hour power reserve
Functions: hours, minutes
Diameter: 30.4 mm
Height: 6.7 mm
Jewels: 27
Balance: glucydur
Frequency: 28,800 vph
Balance spring: flat hairspring
Remarks: related caliber: 8950-M (manual winding); extensive personalization options for the finishing, accessories, and functions

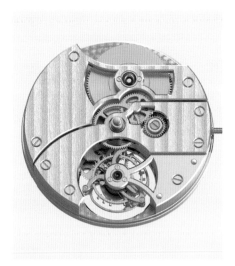

Caliber 8000 (dial side)

Hand-wound; 1-minute tourbillon; single spring barrel; 72-hour power reserve
Functions: hours, minutes
Diameter: 32.6 mm
Height: 5.7 mm
Jewels: 19
Balance: screw balance
Frequency: 21,600 vph
Balance spring: flat hairspring
Remarks: extensive personalization options for the finishing, accessories, and functions

Caliber 8152

Automatic; 1-minute tourbillon; bridges and plate made of sapphire crystal; off-center, bidirectional rotor; single spring barrel; 72-hour power reserve
Functions: hours, minutes
Diameter: 32.6 mm
Height: 8.5 mm
Jewels: 25
Balance: screw balance
Frequency: 21,600 vph
Balance spring: flat hairspring
Remarks: extensive personalization options for the finishing, accessories, and functions

Caliber 8600 (dial side)

Hand-wound; 1-minute tourbillon; double spring barrel; 72-hour power reserve
Functions: hours, minutes; minute repeater with carillon (3 gongs)
Diameter: 34.6 mm
Height: 6.45 mm
Jewels: 36
Balance: screw balance
Frequency: 21,600 vph
Hairspring: flat hairspring
Remarks: many customization options for finishing, equipment and functions

ETA

This Swatch Group movement manufacturer produces more than five million movements a year. And after the withdrawal of Richemont's Jaeger-LeCoultre as well as Swatch Group sisters Nouvelle Lémania and Frédéric Piguet from the business of selling movements on the free market, most watch brands can hardly help but beat down the door of this full-service manufacturer.

ETA offers a broad spectrum of automatic movements in various dimensions with different functions, chronograph mechanisms in varying configurations, pocket watch classics (Calibers 6497 and 98), and hand-wound calibers of days gone by (Calibers 1727 and 7001). This company truly offers everything that a manufacturer's heart could desire—not to mention the sheer variety of quartz technology from inexpensive three-hand mechanisms to highly complicated multifunctional movements and futuristic ETAquartz featuring autonomous energy creation using a rotor and generator.

The almost stereotypical accusation of ETA being "mass goods" is not justified, however, for it is a real art to manufacture filigreed micromechanical technology in consistently high quality. This is certainly one of the reasons why there have been very few movement factories in Europe that can compete with ETA, or that would want to. Since the success of Swatch—a pure ETA product—millions of Swiss francs have been invested in new development and manufacturing technologies. ETA today owns more than twenty production locales in Switzerland, France, Germany, Malaysia, and Thailand.

In 2002, ETA's management announced it would discontinue providing half-completed component kits for reassembly and/or embellishment to specialized workshops, and from 2010 only offer completely assembled and finished movements for sale. The Swiss Competition Commission, however, studied the issue, and a new deal was struck in 2013, phasing out sales to customers over a period of six years. ETA is already somewhat of a competitor of independent reassemblers such as Soprod, Sellita, La Joux-Perret, Dubois Dépraz, and others thanks to its diversification of available calibers, which has led the rest to counter by creating their own base movements.

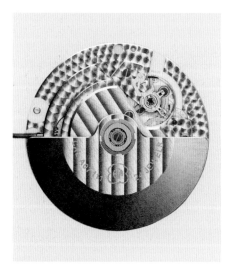

Caliber A07.111

Automatic; ETACHRON regulating system with fine-timing device, rotor on ball bearings, stop-second system; single spring barrel; 48-hour power reserve
Functions: hours, minutes, sweep seconds
Diameter: 37.2
Height: 7.9 mm
Jewels: 24
Frequency: 28,800 vph
Balance spring: flat hairspring
Shock protection: Incabloc
Remarks: related calibers: A07.161 (with power reserve display)

Caliber A07.171 (dial side)

Automatic; ETACHRON regulating system with fine-timing device, rotor on ball bearings, stop-second system; single spring barrel; 48-hour power reserve
Functions: hours, minutes, sweep seconds; 2nd time zone, additional 24-hour display (2nd time zone); quick-set date window
Diameter: 37.2 mm
Height: 7.9 mm
Jewels: 24
Frequency: 28,800 vph
Balance spring: flat hairspring
Shock protection: Incabloc

Caliber A07.211 (dial side)

Automatic; ETACHRON regulating system with fine-timing device, rotor on ball bearings, stop-second system; single spring barrel; 48-hour power reserve
Functions: hours, minutes, subsidiary seconds; chronograph; quick-set date window
Diameter: 37.2 mm
Height: 7.9 mm
Jewels: 25
Frequency: 28,800 vph
Balance spring: flat hairspring
Shock protection: Incabloc

Caliber 2000-1

Automatic; ball bearing–mounted rotor; stop-seconds, ETACHRON regulating system; single spring barrel; 40-hour power reserve

Functions: hours, minutes, sweep seconds; quick-set date window
Diameter: 20 mm
Height: 3.6 mm
Jewels: 20
Balance: glucydur
Frequency: 28,800 vph
Balance spring: flat hairspring
Shock protection: Incabloc

Caliber 2671

Automatic; ball bearing–mounted rotor; stop-seconds, ETACHRON regulating system; single spring barrel; 38-hour power reserve

Functions: hours, minutes, sweep seconds; date window
Diameter: 17.5 mm
Height: 4.8 mm
Jewels: 25
Balance: glucydur
Frequency: 28,800 vph
Balance spring: flat hairspring
Shock protection: Incabloc
Remarks: related calibers: 2678 (additional weekday window, height 5.35 mm)

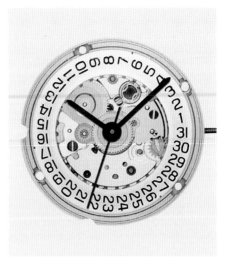

Caliber 2681 (dial side)

Automatic; ball bearing–mounted rotor; stop-seconds, ETACHRON regulating system; single spring barrel; 38-hour power reserve

Functions: hours, minutes, sweep seconds; quick-set date window
Diameter: 20 mm
Height: 4.8 mm
Jewels: 25
Balance: glucydur
Frequency: 28,000 vph
Balance spring: flat hairspring
Shock protection: Incabloc

Caliber 2801-2

Hand-wound; ETACHRON regulating system; 42-hour power reserve

Functions: hours, minutes, sweep seconds
Diameter: 26 mm
Height: 3.35 mm
Jewels: 17
Frequency: 28,800 vph
Related caliber: 2804-2 (with date window and quick set)

Caliber 2824-2

Automatic; ball bearing–mounted rotor; stop-seconds, ETACHRON regulating system; 38-hour power reserve

Functions: hours, minutes, sweep seconds; quick-set date window at 3 o'clock
Diameter: 26 mm
Height: 4.6 mm
Jewels: 25
Frequency: 28,800 vph
Related calibers: 2836-2 (additional day window at 3 o'clock, height 5.05 mm); 2826-2 (with large date, height 6.2 mm)

Caliber 2834-2 (dial side)

Automatic; ball bearing–mounted rotor; stop-seconds, ETACHRON regulating system; single spring barrel; 38-hour power reserve

Functions: hours, minutes, sweep seconds; quick-set date window, quick-set weekday
Diameter: 29.4 mm
Height: 5.05 mm
Jewels: 25
Balance: glucydur
Frequency: 28,800 vph
Balance spring: flat hairspring
Shock protection: Incabloc

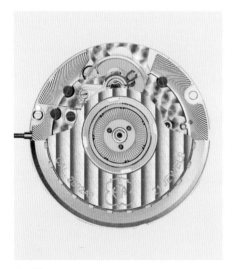

Caliber 2892-A2

Automatic; ball bearing–mounted rotor; stop-seconds, ETACHRON regulating system; single spring barrel; 42-hour power reserve
Functions: hours, minutes, sweep seconds; quick-set date window
Diameter: 26.2 mm
Height: 3.6 mm
Jewels: 21
Balance: glucydur
Frequency: 28,800 vph
Balance spring: flat hairspring
Shock protection: Incabloc

Caliber 2893-1 (dial side)

Automatic; ball bearing rotor; stop-seconds, ETACHRON regulating system; 42-hour power reserve
Functions: hours, minutes, sweep seconds; quick-set date window at 3 o'clock; world time display via central disk
Diameter: 25.6 mm
Height: 4.1 mm
Jewels: 21
Frequency: 28,800 vph
Related calibers: 2893-2 (24-hour hand; 2nd time zone instead of world time disk); 2893-3 (only world time disk without date window)

Caliber 2894-2

Automatic; ball bearing–mounted rotor; stop-seconds, ETACHRON regulating system; single spring barrel; 42-hour power reserve
Functions: hours, minutes, subsidiary seconds; chronograph; quick-set date window
Diameter: 28.6 mm
Height: 6.1 mm
Jewels: 37
Balance: glucydur
Frequency: 28,800 vph
Balance spring: flat hairspring
Shock protection: Incabloc
Related caliber: 2094 (diameter 23.9 mm, height 5.5 mm, 33 jewels)

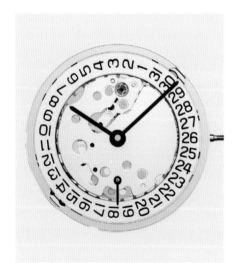

Caliber 2895-2 (dial side)

Automatic; ball bearing–mounted rotor; stop-seconds, ETACHRON regulating system; single spring barrel; 42-hour power reserve
Functions: hours, minutes, subsidiary seconds, at 6 o'clock; quick-set date window
Diameter: 26.2 mm
Height: 4.35 mm
Jewels: 27
Balance: glucydur
Frequency: 28,800 vph
Balance spring: flat hairspring
Shock protection: Incabloc

Caliber 2896 (dial side)

Automatic; ball bearing rotor; stop-seconds, ETACHRON regulating system; 42-hour power reserve
Functions: hours, minutes, sweep seconds; power reserve display at 3 o'clock
Diameter: 25.6 mm
Height: 4.85 mm
Jewels: 21
Frequency: 28,800 vph

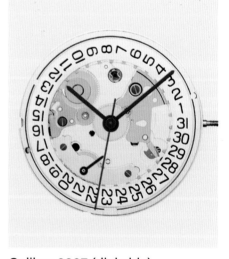

Caliber 2897 (dial side)

Automatic; ball bearing rotor; stop-seconds, ETACHRON regulating system; single spring barrel; 42-hour power reserve
Functions: hours, minutes, sweep seconds; power reserve indicator; quick-set date window
Diameter: 26.2 mm
Height: 4.85 mm
Jewels: 21
Balance: glucydur
Frequency: 28,800 vph
Balance spring: flat hairspring
Shock protection: Incabloc

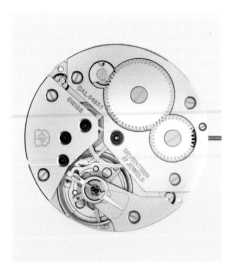

Caliber 6497-1

Hand-wound; ETACHRON regulating system; single spring barrel; 46-hour power reserve
Functions: hours, minutes, subsidiary seconds
Diameter: 37.2 mm
Height: 4.5 mm
Jewels: 17
Frequency: 18,000 vph
Balance spring: flat hairspring
Remarks: pocket watch movement (Unitas model) in Lépine version with subsidiary seconds extending from the winding stem); as Caliber 6497-2 with 21,600 vph and 53-hour power reserve

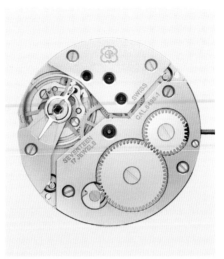

Caliber 6498-1

Hand-wound; ETACHRON regulating system; single spring barrel; 46-hour power reserve
Functions: hours, minutes, subsidiary seconds
Diameter: 37.2 mm
Height: 4.5 mm
Jewels: 17
Frequency: 18,000 vph
Balance spring: flat hairspring
Remarks: pocket watch movement (Unitas model) in savonette version (subsidiary seconds at right angle to the winding stem); as Caliber 6498-2 with 21,600 vph and 53-hour power reserve

Caliber 7001

Hand-wound; ultrathin construction; single spring barrel; 42-hour power reserve
Functions: hours, minutes, subsidiary seconds
Diameter: 23.7 mm
Height: 2.5 mm
Jewels: 17
Frequency: 21,600 vph
Balance spring: flat hairspring

Caliber 7750 (dial side)

Automatic; stop-second system; single spring barrel; 42-hour power reserve
Functions: hours, minutes, subsidiary seconds; chronograph; quick-set date and weekday window
Diameter: 30.4 mm
Height: 7.9 mm
Jewels: 25
Balance: glucydur
Frequency: 28,800 vph
Balance spring: flat hairspring
Shock protection: Incabloc

Caliber 7751 (dial side)

Automatic; stop-second system; single spring barrel; 42-hour power reserve
Functions: hours, minutes, subsidiary seconds; additional 24-hour display; chronograph; full calendar with date, weekday, month, moon phase
Diameter: 30.4 mm
Height: 7.9 mm
Jewels: 25
Balance: glucydur
Frequency: 28,800 vph
Balance spring: flat hairspring
Shock protection: Incabloc
Remarks: related caliber: 7754 with sweep 24-hour hand (2nd time zone)

Caliber 7753

Automatic; stop-second system; single spring barrel; 42-hour power reserve
Functions: hours, minutes, subsidiary seconds; chronograph; quick-set date window with pusher
Diameter: 30.4
Height: 7.9 mm
Jewels: 25
Balance: glucydur
Frequency: 28,800 vph
Balance spring: flat hairspring
Shock protection: Incabloc
Remarks: variation of the Valjoux chronograph caliber with symmetrical "tricompax" layout of the totalizers

MANUFACTURE LA JOUX-PERRET

The re-industrialization of the caliber segment in Switzerland, brought about by some very confusing signals from Swatch Group and the Swiss government's Competition Commission, has created a number of opportunities for caliber builders who had until recently been operating in the shadow of ETA. Among them is Manufacture La Joux-Perret (MLJP), known primarily for its bespoke complication calibers for prestigious brands. It has now decided to enter the ready-to-wear caliber market in 2021 with the revised G100 three-hand automatic movement and the L100 automatic chronograph.

Due to their dimensions and specifications, both movements are suitable as replacements for the widely used 2824 and 7750 ("Valjoux") models, which will no longer be available to the watch industry in sufficient quantities after the expiry of the general supply obligation on the part of Swatch Group subsidiary ETA. The two MLJP calibers compete with Sellita's own high-volume movements SW200 and SW500, but they offer a greater amount of power reserve (68 and 60 hours, respectively) and partly better equipment (column-wheel control). Also in the standard portfolio of this caliber specialist is a classic-a hand-wound movement with the caliber number D100, whose architecture is strongly reminiscent of the pocket watch "Unitas" caliber. Its diameter, however, is only 23.3 millimeters.

MLJP has been part of the Citizen Group (Japan) since 2012. The company's headquarters and production facilities are located in La Chaux-de-Fonds, in the heart of watch country.

G100

Automatic; rotor on ball bearing, second stop; single spring barrel, 68-hour power reserve
Functions: hours, minutes, sweep seconds; date aperture
Diameter: 26 mm
Height: 4.45 mm
Jewels: 24
Balance: glucydur
Frequency: 28,800 vph
Hairspring: flat hairspring
Shock protection: Kif
Remarks: functionality and parts compatibility with ETA 2824-2; various display options, many customization options

L100

Automatic; column wheel control of chronograph functions; second stop; single spring barrel, 60-hour power reserve
Functions: hours, minutes, subsidiary seconds; chronograph; date and weekday aperture with rapid correction
Diameter: 30.4 mm
Height: 7.9 mm
Jewels: 26
Balance: Glucydur
Frequency: 28,800 vph
Hairspring: flat hairspring
Shock protection: Incabloc
Remarks: functionality and parts compatibility with ETA 7750; various display options, many customization options

D100

Hand-wound; single spring barrel, 50-hour power reserve
Functions: hours, minutes, subsidiary seconds
Diameter: 23.3 mm
Height: 2.5 mm
Jewels: 18
Frequency: 21,600 vph
Hairspring: flat hairspring
Shock protection: Incabloc
Remarks: many customization options

RONDA

Ronda is a Swiss company with a long tradition. It was founded by William Mosset, born in 1909 in the village of Hölstein, a man whose gift for micro-engineering declared itself early on when he invented a way to drill thirty-two holes in a metal plate in one operation and with great accuracy. The company was founded in 1946 in Lausen, a little town in the hinterlands of German-speaking Switzerland near Basel, where the first factory was built.

In the meantime the company has turned into a group with five subsidiaries: There are two production sites in Ticino, one in the Jura mountains, one operation in Thailand, and sales offices in Hong Kong. Overall, Ronda employs around 1,800 people in Switzerland and Asia.

The shareholders of the family enterprise, which is now in its second generation, value the company's absolute independence. This is undoubtedly a key advantage for the customer, since Ronda can continue defining its own strategy and can react decisively to customer needs.

That is why the company, which had already made a name for itself with quartz movements, decided to add a portfolio of automatic mechanical movements. The first product batches arrived on the market in early 2017; in the medium term, the mechanical Ronda Caliber R150 is to be produced in batches of six figures per year.

Caliber R150

Automatic; ball bearing–mounted rotor; stop-seconds, index for fine adjustment; single spring barrel; 40-hour power reserve
Functions: hours, minutes, sweep seconds; quick-set date
Diameter: 25.6 mm
Height: 4.4 mm
Jewels: 25
Frequency: 28,800 vph
Balance spring: flat hairspring
Shock protection: Incabloc

Caliber 5040.B

Quartz; 54-month power reserve; single spring barrel
Functions: hours, minutes, subsidiary seconds; chronograph, with add and split function; large date
Diameter: 28.6 mm
Height: 4.4 mm
Jewels: 13

Caliber 7004.P

Quartz; 48-month power reserve; single spring barrel
Functions: hours, minutes, subsidiary seconds; large date and weekday (retrograde)
Diameter: 34.6 mm
Height: 5.6 mm
Jewels: 6

SELLITA

Sellita, founded in 1950 by Pierre Grandjean in La Chaux-de-Fonds, is one of the biggest reassemblers and embellishers in the mechanical watch industry. On average, Sellita embellishes and finishes about one million automatic and hand-wound movements annually—a figure that represents about 25 percent of Switzerland's mechanical movement production, according to Miguel García, Sellita's president.

Reassembly can be defined as the assembly and regulation of components to make a functioning movement. This is the type of work that ETA loved to give to outside companies back in the day in order to concentrate on manufacturing complete quartz movements and individual components for them.

Reassembly workshops like Sellita refine and embellish components purchased from ETA according to their customers' wishes and can even successfully fulfill smaller orders made by the company's estimated 350 clients.

When ETA announced that it would only sell ébauches to companies outside the Swatch Group until the end of 2010, García, who has owned Sellita since 2003, reacted by shifting production to the development and manufacturing of new in-house products.

He planned and implemented a new line of movements based on the dimensions of the most popular ETA calibers, whose patents had expired. The company now has a line of hand-wound or automatic movements with little complications, like a date, weekday, GMT, or a second time zone, as well as chronographs with different display constellations. The new design types are all based on mature models. A whole new line of automatic movements was launched, the Caliber SW1000, which has no ETA parts at all. The way to identify these movements will simply be the four digits. The price range will be similar to that of other products offered by the company.

Caliber SW100-1

Automatic; ball-bearing mounted rotor, stop second mechanism; single spring barrel, 38-hour power reserve
Functions: hours, minutes, sweep seconds; date , with rapid correction
Diameter: 17.2 mm
Height: 4.8 mm
Jewels: 25
Balance: nickel or Glucydur Frequency: 28,800 vph
Hairspring: Nivaflex
Shock protection: Novodiac or Incabloc

Caliber SW200-1

Automatic; ball-bearing mounted rotor, stop-second mechanism; single spring barrel, 38-hour power reserve
Functions: hours, minutes, sweep seconds; date, with rapid correction
Diameter: 25.6 mm
Height: 4.6 mm
Jewels: 26
Balance: nickel or glucydur
Frequency: 28,800 vph
Hairspring: Nivaflex
Shock protection: Novodiac or Incabloc
Related calibers: SW260-1 and SW261-1 (with subsidiary seconds at 6 o'clock); SW290-1 (with subsidiary seconds at 9 o'clock)

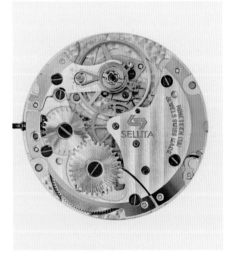

Caliber SW215-1

Hand-wound; stop-second mechanism; single spring barrel, 42-hour power reserve
Functions: hours, minutes, sweep seconds; date
Diameter: 25.6 mm
Height: 3.35 mm
Jewels: 19
Balance: nickel
Frequency: 28,800 vph
Hairspring: Nivaflex
Shock protection: Novodiac or Incabloc
Related caliber: SW210-1 (without date); SW216-1 (with small second and date)

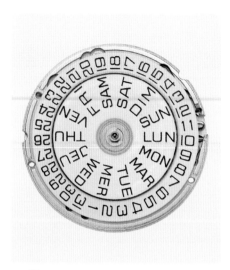

Caliber SW220-1 M

Hand-wound; stop-second mechanism; single spring barrel, 42-hour power reserve

Functions: hours, minutes, sweep seconds; date and weekday with rapid correction
Diameter: 25.6 mm
Height: 3.8 mm
Jewels: 19
Balance: nickel or Glucydur
Frequency: 28,800 vph
Hairspring: flat hairspring, Nivaflex
Shock protection: Novodiac or Incabloc
Related calibers: SW221-1 M (with date hand); SW240-1 M with larger mainplate (ø 29 mm)

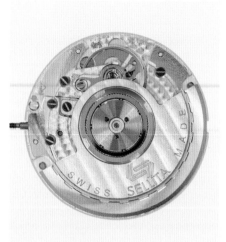

Caliber SW300-1

Automatic; ball bearing–mounted rotor; stop-second system; single spring barrel; 42-hour power reserve

Functions: hours, minutes, sweep seconds; quick-set date
Diameter: 25.6 mm
Height: 3.6 mm
Jewels: 25
Balance: glucydur
Frequency: 28,800 vph
Balance spring: flat hairspring, Nivaflex
Shock protection: Incabloc
Remarks: related caliber: SW360-1 (with subsidiary seconds, height 4.35 mm, 31 jewels); SW330-2 (with additional 24-hour hand for 2nd time zone)

Caliber SW400-1

Automatic; ball-bearing mounted rotor, stop-second mechanism; single spring barrel, 38-hour power reserve

Functions: hours, minutes, sweep seconds; date with rapid correction
Diameter: 31 mm
Height: 4.67 mm
Jewels: 26
Balance: nickel or glucydur
Frequency: 28,800 vph
Hairspring: Nivaflex
Shock protection: Novodiac or Incabloc
Related Caliber: SW461-1 (with subsidiary second)

Caliber SW500-1

Automatic; ball-bearing mounted rotor, stop-second; single spring barrel, 48-hour power reserve

Functions: hours, minutes, subsidiary seconds; chronograph; date and weekday with rapid correction
Diameter: 30 mm
Height: 7.9 mm
Jewels: 25
Frequency: 28,800 vph
Shock protection: Incabloc
Related calibers: SW500 M (hand-wound version, height 7 mm, 21 jewels); SW500 BV (bicompax without subsidiary seconds); SW510 (tricompax with symmetrical totalizers); SW510 BH (bicompax without hour totalizer); SW500/510 MP (monopusher); SW500/510 MPC (crown pusher)

Caliber SW600

Automatic; ball-bearing mounted rotor, stop-second; single spring barrel, 48-hour power reserve

Functions: hours, minutes, sweep seconds; date and weekday with rapid correction
Diameter: 30 mm
Height: 7.9 mm
Jewels: 24
Balance: nickel or glucydur
Frequency: 28,800 vph
Hairspring: Nivaflex
Shock protection: Incabloc
Related caliber: SW690 (with subsidiary seconds)

Caliber SW1000-1

Automatic; ball-bearing mounted rotor, stop second mechanism; single spring barrel, 38-hour power reserve

Functions: hours, minutes, sweep seconds; date with rapid correction
Diameter: 20 mm
Height: 3.9 mm
Jewels: 18
Balance: nickel or glucydur
Frequency: 28,800 vph
Hairspring: Nivaflex
Shock protection: Incabloc

SOPROD

The name Soprod stands for "Société de Production Horlogère" and refers to a company with a fairly long tradition of movement-building, though, admittedly, mostly in quartz. It was originally founded in 1966, though its later reputation rested on its laurels as an external assembly company for ETA movements. Soprod continued enlarging its portfolio, adding customized decorations and finishings as a service and then building modules that could be used to enhance base movements. Around the turn of the millennium, the company finally began to seriously develop its own calibers. This development was accelerated by ETA's announcement that in the foreseeable future, they would no longer supply movement parts kits to external assemblers but would supply end-customers directly.

In the meantime, Soprod had slipped under the wing of the Swiss Festina Group and supplemented the existing capacities in the field of inexpensive quartz movements. But their mechanical division was growing steadily with two caliber lines (M and C) with over fifteen iterations. In 2011, at Baselworld, they presented their Alternance 10, or A10, which had the look and feel of the very popular ETA 2892. As a base movement, it could serve in many cases, and Soprod already had a wide range of modules on tap to supplement it, like large dates, GMT, power reserves, and moon phases.

Soprod continued expanding its production capacities and today, besides a range of calibers, it manufactures its own escapement parts such as anchors, escape wheels, balance wheels, and hairsprings at its founding site in Les Reussilles in the Jura. It is completely self-sufficient.

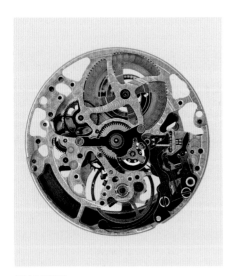

M100SQ

Automatic; skeletonized plate and bridges; bidirectional winding rotor, stop-second mechanism; single spring barrel, 42-hour power reserve
Functions: hours, minutes, sweep seconds; date with rapid correction
Diameter: 25.6 mm
Height: 3.6 mm
Jewels: 25
Frequency: 28,800 vph
Shock protection: Incabloc
Related calibers: M100 (standard version without skeletonization); M100 Balancier Visible (with openworked plate under the escapement parts)

M100

Automatic; bidirectional winding rotor, stop-second mechanism; single spring barrel, 42-hour power reserve
Functions: hours, minutes, sweep seconds; date with rapid correction
Diameter: 25.6 mm
Height: 3.6 mm
Jewels: 25
Frequency: 28,800 vph
Shock protection: Incabloc
Remarks: various regulation options (COSC, among others); various finishings (Optimal, Excellence, Manufacture)

Newton

Automatic; in-house escapement and hairspring; unidirectional winding rotor, stop-second mechanism; single spring barrel, 44-hour power reserve
Functions: hours, minutes, sweep seconds; date, with rapid correction
Diameter: 25.6 mm
Height: 4.6 mm
Jewels: 23
Frequency: 28,800 vph
Shock protection: Incabloc
Remarks: with/without côtes de Genève

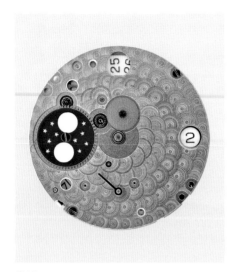

C105

Automatic; bidirectional winding rotor, stop-second mechanism; single spring barrel, 42-hour power reserve
Functions: hours, minutes, subsidiary seconds; date with rapid correction, moon phase Diameter: 25.6 mm
Height: 5.1 mm
Jewels: 33
Frequency: 28,800 vph
Shock protection: Incabloc

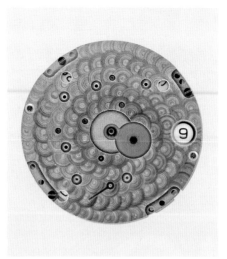

C110

Automatic; bidirectional winding rotor, stop-second mechanism; single spring barrel, 42-hour power reserve
Functions: hours, minutes, subsidiary seconds; date with rapid correction
Diameter: 25.6 mm
Height: 5.1 mm
Jewels: 29
Frequency: 28,800 vph
Shock protection: Incabloc

C115

Automatic; bidirectional winding rotor, stop-second mechanism; single spring barrel, 42-hour power reserve
Functions: hours, minutes, sweep seconds; additional 24-hour display (second time zone), power reserve display; date with rapid correction
Diameter: 25.6 mm
Height: 5.1 mm
Jewels: 33
Frequency: 28,800 vph
Shock protection: Incabloc

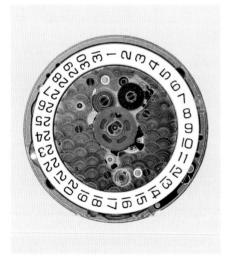

C125

Automatic; bidirectional winding rotor, stop-second mechanism; single spring barrel, 42-hour power reserve
Functions: hours, minutes, sweep seconds; additional 12-hour display (second time zone),
day/night indication (with hour and minute at 6 o'clock); large date with rapid correction
Diameter: 25.6 mm
Height: 5.1 mm
Jewels: 25
Frequency: 28,800 vph
Shock protection: Incabloc

C120

Automatic; bidirectional winding rotor, stop-second mechanism; single spring barrel, 42-hour power reserve
Functions: hours, minutes, sweep seconds; additional 24-hour display (sweep second time zone); date, with rapid correction
Diameter: 25.6 mm
Height: 4.1 mm
Jewels: 25
Frequency: 28,800 vph
Shock protection: Incabloc

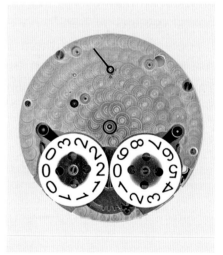

C130

Automatic; bidirectional winding rotor, stop-second mechanism; single spring barrel, 42-hour power reserve
Functions: hours, minutes, sweep seconds; power reserve display; large date with rapid correction
Diameter: 25.6 mm
Height: 5.1 mm
Jewels: 27
Frequency: 28,800 vph
Shock protection: Incabloc
Related calibers: C135 (with additional sweep 24-hour hand and date aperture); C140 (power reserve display und date aperture)

LIVING
WATCHES

You can scroll through thousands of images online, or gaze longingly at the high-resolution images in books like this one, but nothing beats getting a hands-on experience with timepieces and trying them on. That's where the trade fairs and watch festivals come in. The following is just a sampling.

SWITZERLAND

Let us begin in Switzerland, where the decline and fall of Baselworld, the biggest and most dominant show for years, put an end to a behind-the-scenes rivalry in Switzerland between Geneva and Basel. Today, **Watches & Wonders**, which grew out of the SIHH, is held at the Palexpo Convention Center, on the edge of Geneva's airport. In 2024, it will host fifty-five brands between April 9 and 13, spearheaded, of course, by the big names of the sponsoring Richemont Group, which a few years ago had the bright idea to broaden the fair by invit-ing independents and other brands, like MB&F, Louis Moinet, Hermès, Trilobe, and others.

As in the old days, many brands take the opportunity to exhibit in the luxury hotels along the lake so that serious collectors and fans can have first dibs on the novelties, along with journalists, bloggers, and other media. There are several venues near these places that are well worth visiting, like the L'iceBergues (Place des Bergues 3) and the Espace FERT (Rue Barton 7, next to the Fairmont Hotel) **Website: watchesandwonders.com**

If you are looking for a more casual atmosphere, you can travel a few minutes by bus or Uber/taxi to the HEAD (tram stop Guye), where the **Time to Watches** (April 10 to 14) brings together many smaller brands, like Milus, Elka, Azimuth, or Yema in the big hall of the HEAD (University of Art and Design). Wolf 1834, which makes winders and other watch paraphernalia is also present every year.
Website: timetowatches. com

Watch fans traveling to Switzerland in June who really want know what's inside their watches might also want to spend a day or two at the Palexpo Convention Center from June 11 to 14, 2024, roaming around the many booths of the **EPHJ** show. Few actual watch brands exhibit there, but you will find hundreds of companies that make up the great value chain of the industry, from movement makers, to prototype specialists using the latest 3D printing technology, polishers, box makers, and so forth. There are round tables and conferences, and even a prize, which went to MPS Watch in 2023 for a special way to mount a rotor on an automatic. It's esoteric, but it is one of the fairs I do not miss because it adds a lot to one's knowledge and understanding of the watch and its industry.
Website: ephj.ch

Festivals are not only for music and art. Yes, the watch community also gets together to celebrate their art and craft, and visitors are heartily invited for opportunities not only to get a feel of timepieces, but also to meet the watchmakers in a more informal setting and sometimes to try out their hand at assembling a watch. From September 20 to 22, 2024,

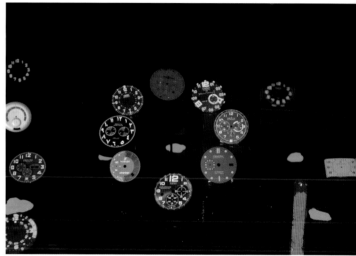

the town of **Yverdon-les-bains**, Switzerland, located between Zurich and Geneva at the southwestern tip of Lake Neuchâtel, will host its annual **Festival Suisse de l'Horlogerie** at the Y-Parc technology center, with demos of *métiers d'art*, in addition to showcasing watches and creations around watches. Yverdon also has a refreshing lake, a restorative modern spa, and hotels and B&Bs that are more affordable than those in, for example, Geneva. And if you need to visit one of Switzerland's cities, remember, the country is small, and everything is accessible by train.
Website: festival-suisse-horlogerie.ch

IRELAND

Imagine going to a small concert in a quaint setting, listening to music, eating some good victuals, and chatting with, say, a few major stars of the music scene (I'll let you imagine which ones). In the watch world, that would be the equivalent of the **International Festival of Time** in Waterford, Ireland. The city lies about two and a half hours south of Dublin by train. The festival's second edition in 2023 drew in some genuine demigods of the industry, like local hero John McGonigle, Andreas Strehler, Paul Gerber, Kari Voutilainen, Simon Brette (who went on to win a prize at the GPHG), and Stefan Kudoke. The festival is held in chambers at the Medieval Museum and the Irish Museum of Time. Interestingly, Waterford was the planned settlement destination of a group of Swiss watchmakers in the late 1780s seeking to escape irksome constraints at home, but most (though not all) decided to cancel. The city does host a Watch Museum. The next

edition of the Waterford Time Festival will not be until May 25, 2025, unfortunately, but you may wish to put it on your calendar. Pack your flannel shirt, jeans, an umbrella, and your funny bone for the Irish jokes.
Website: waterfordtreasures.com

THE AMERICAS

The USA is one of the world's biggest markets, so there is no shortage of trade shows, whereby many are actually billed as jewelry-focused events, like the MJSA Expo in New York, so you have to check each one to see what they are offering. A major fair is the **Couture Show** (May 30 to June 2, 2024), held annually in Las Vegas, which gives some added glitz to the glamour. "Attendees at Couture Watch can expect an intimate and sophisticated atmosphere, fostering networking opportunities and collaborations within the high-end watchmaking community," says the marketing, and those who have attended can concur.
Website: thecoutureshow. com

South of the border, in Mexico City, the **SIAR** (Salón Internacional Alta Relojería México) has been attracting watchmakers, collectors, aficionados, and media people (mostly local) in October since 2007. It is the most important watch fair in Latin America, where high-end and low-end (mostly Asian, according to my source) watches dominate the market. The independent brands are well represented, you will find the Swiss group SIWP there regularly. The SIAR goes beyond being a marketplace; it is a full-fledged celebration of watchmaking with about 46 brands and nearly 4,000

visitors at the last edition, and the usual master classes and conferences.
Website: salonaltarelojeria. com

ASIA

If traveling to Asia in the fall, you may want to begin in Hong Kong with the **Hong Kong Watch and Clock Fair (HKWCF)**, which took off again in 2023 with over 700 exhibitors after the Covid-19 hiatus. The event is very well organized by the Hong Kong Trade Development Council (HKTDC) and takes place in several spacious, pleasantly air-conditioned halls of the modern Hong Kong Convention and Exhibition Centre that overlooks Victoria Harbor.

The HKTDC, along with the Hong Kong Watch Manufacturers Association and The Federation of Hong Kong Watch Trades and Industries, attract a very wide range of industry actors, including many watchmakers from China and Japan, of course, and Europe, giving it—as one Swiss exhibitor noted—a very professional feel and an important overview of the industry in China. It says a lot that Jean-Daniel Pasche, outgoing president of the Federation of the Swiss Watch Industry (FH), showed up for the 2023 edition.

Note that it is one of the world's major fairs and, like Baselworld of old, it is geared towards the whole industry, as it is not sponsored by any big brands. Besides myriad watch and clock makers, the fair attracts, amongst others, makers of tools and machinery, watch hands, cases, movements (Miyota, Peacock, Sea-Gull, for example), sapphire crystal parts, straps, packaging, and, last but not least, a range of services, like OEM and ODM, which is a

Chinese specialty. So, anyone with an idea for a watch in mind will have a lot to choose from. Conferences, after-watch parties, and fashion shows are part of the show. The convention center is centrally located, with many hotels and eating places of all categories nearby. The 2024 edition will be held from September 3 to 7, 2024.

Website: hktdc.com/event/ hkwatchfair

The **Singapore Watch Fair** follows the Hong Kong fair by a few weeks. It's a far more intimate affair and well stocked with independent brands and watchmakers, like Ludovic Ballouard, Antoine Preziuso, Petermann Bédat, Itay Noy, and Krayon. The event is consumer-oriented, but the fair does attract trade professionals who enjoy the congenial and dignified atmosphere that encourages conversations, lively exchanges, and buying of watches.

Website: singaporewatch-fair.com

DUBAI

No list of important trade fairs would be complete without mention of the great **Dubai Watch Week**, which is among the top get-togethers for any watch enthusiast. It is, however, a biennial event, so the next edition in Dubai will not occur until the fall of 2025 (exact dates to be announced), but it is well worth noting in your calendar. The figures for 2023 speak for themselves: 59,000 visitors; 900 conferences and panels, including tête-à-têtes with leaders in all aspects of watchmaking; 63 brands presenting their wares; and, what is most important, 53 new launches, including H. Moser & Cie's Streamliner Small Seconds, a new Czapek & Cie with simple onyx dial, and so on.

Website: dubaiwatchweek. com

FAIRS IN SHORT

USA
iWOW (international World of Watches)
Held in early December
Very popular watch fair held at the American Dream Mall, Newark, New Jersey
Website: intlworldofwatches

GERMANY
Inhorgenta, Munich, Germany
Annual trade show in February for jewelry, gemstones, and watches
Website: inhorgenta.com

ITALY
Vicenzaoro's special VO'Clock Privé
September 6-8 in Vicenza, Italy
(about 2 hours by car or train east of Milan)
The Vicenzaoro's January edition is mostly jewelry, with a large selection of watches
Website: vicenzaoro.com

MONACO
Top Marques
June 5-9 in Monaco
Super cars, super boats, and high-end watches
Website: topmarquesmonaco.com

SWITZERLAND
Geneva Watch Days
August 27 to September 1
In the lakeside hotels, brands' own showrooms, or other venues
Website: gva-watch-days. com

FRANCE
We Love Watches
October 2024, Paris (10th arrondissement)
About fifty brands in an old three-story building
Website: welovewatches.fr

ABU DHABI
The Jewellery and Watch Show (JWS)
November 2024
Website: jws.ae

QATAR
Doha Jewellery and Watches Exhibition
February 2024
Website: decc.qa (convention center's site, search for the show)

WATCH YOUR WATCH

Mechanical watches are not only by and large more expensive and complex than quartzes, they are also a little high-maintenance, as it were. The mechanism within does need servicing occasionally—perhaps a touch of oil and an adjustment. Worse yet, the complexity of all those wheels and pinions engaged in reproducing the galaxy means that a user will occasionally do something perfectly harmless like wind his or her watch up only to find everything grinding to a halt. Here are some tips for dealing with these mechanical beauties for new watch owners and reminders for the old hands.

1. DATE CHANGES

Do not change the date manually (via the crown or pusher) on any mechanical watch—whether manual wind or automatic—when the time indicated on the dial reads between 10 and 2 o'clock. Although some better watches are protected against this horological quirk, most mechanical watches with a date indicator are engaged in the process of automatically changing the date between the hours of 10 p.m. and 2 a.m. Intervening with a forced manual change while the automatic date shift is engaged can damage the movement. Of course, you can make the adjustment between 10 a.m. and 2 p.m. in most cases—but this is just not a good habit to get into. When in doubt, roll the time past 12 o'clock and look for an automatic date change before you set the time and date. The Ulysse Nardin brand is notable, among a very few others, for in-house mechanical movements immune to this effect.

Bovet's barrier to pressing the wrong pusher.

2. CHRONOGRAPH USE

On a simple chronograph, start and stop are almost always the same button. Normally located above the crown, the start/stop actuator can be pressed at will to initiate and end the interval timing. The reset button, normally below the crown, is only used for resetting the chronograph to zero, but only when the chronograph is stopped—never while engaged. Only a "flyback" chronograph allows safe resetting to zero while running. With the chronograph engaged, you simply hit the reset button and all the chronograph indicators (seconds, minutes, and hours) snap back to zero and the chronograph begins to accumulate the interval time once again. In the early days of air travel this was a valuable complication as pilots would reset their chronographs when taking on a new heading—without having to fumble about with a three-step procedure with gloved hands.

Nota bene: Don't actuate or reset your chronograph while your watch is submerged—even if you have one of those that are built for such usage, like Omega, IWC, and a few other brands. Feel free to hit the buttons before submersion and jump in and swim while they run; just don't push anything while in the water.

3. CHANGING TIME BACKWARD

Don't adjust the time on your watch in a counterclockwise direction—especially if the watch has calendar functions. A few watches can tolerate the abuse, but it's better to avoid the possibility of damage altogether. Change the dates as needed (remembering the 10 and 2 rule above).

4. SHOCKS

Almost all modern watches are equipped with some level of shock protection. Best practices for the Swiss brands allow for a three-foot fall onto a hard wood surface. But if your watch is running poorly—or even worse has stopped entirely after an impact—do not shake, wind, or bang it again to get it running; take it to an expert for service as you may do even more damage. Sports like tennis, squash, or golf can have a deleterious effect on your watch, including flattening the pivots, overbanking, or even bending or breaking a pivot.

5. OVERWINDING

Most modern watches are fitted with a mechanism that allows the mainspring to slide inside the barrel—or stops it completely once the spring is fully wound—for protection against overwinding. The best advice here is just don't force it. Over the years, a winding crown may start to get "stickier" and more difficult to turn even when unwound. That's a sure sign it is due for service.

6. JACUZZI TEMPERATURE

Don't jump into the Jacuzzi—or even a steaming hot shower—with your watch on. Better-built watches with a deeper water-resistance rating typically have no problem with this scenario. However, take a 3 or 5 atm water-resistant watch into the Jacuzzi, and there's a chance the different rates of expansion and contraction of the metals and sapphire or mineral crystals may allow moisture into the case.

Panerai makes sure you think before touching the crown.

Do it yourself at your own risk.

7. SCREW THAT CROWN DOWN (AND THOSE PUSHERS)!

Always check and double-check to ensure a watch fitted with a screwed-down crown is closed tightly. Screwed-down pushers for a chronograph—or any other functions—deserve the same attention. This one oversight has cost quite a few owners their watches. If a screwed-down crown is not secured, water will likely get into the case and start oxidizing the metal. In time, the problem can destroy the watch.

8. MAGNETISM

If your watch is acting up, running faster or slower, it may have become magnetized. This can happen if you leave your timepiece near a computer, cell phone, or some other electronic device. Many service centers have a so-called degausser to take care of the problem. A number of brands also make watches with a soft iron core to deflect magnetic fields, though this might not work with the stronger ones.

9. TRIBOLOGY

Keeping a mechanical timepiece hidden away in a box for extended lengths of time is not the best way to care for it. Even if you don't wear a watch every day, it is a good idea to run your watch at regular intervals to keep its lubricating oils and greases viscous. Think about a can of house paint: Keep it stirred and it stays liquid almost indefinitely; leave it still for too long and a skin develops. On a smaller level the same thing can happen to the lubricants inside a mechanical watch.

10. SERVICE

Most mechanical watches call for a three- to five-year service cycle for cleaning, oiling, and maintenance. Some mechanical watches can run twice that long and have functioned within acceptable parameters, but if you're not going to have your watch serviced at regular intervals, you do run the risk of having timing issues. Always have your watch serviced by a qualified watchmaker (see box), not at the kiosk in the local mall. The best you can expect there is a quick battery change.

Gary Girdvainis is the founder of Isochron Media LLC, publishers of WristWatch *and* AboutTime *magazines.*

WATCH REPAIR SERVICE CENTERS

RGM
www.rgmwatches.com/repair

Stoll & Co.
www.americaswatchmaker.com

Swiss Watchmakers & Company
www.swisswatchland.com

Universal Watch Repair
www.universalwatch.net

Watch Repairs USA
www.watchrepairsusa.com

GLOSSARY

ANNUAL CALENDAR

The automatic allowances for the different lengths of each month of a year in the calendar module of a watch. This type of watch usually shows the month and date, and sometimes the day of the week (like this one by Patek Philippe) and the phases of the moon.

ANTIMAGNETIC

Magnetic fields found in common everyday places affect mechanical movements, hence the use of anti- or non-magnetic components in the movement. Some companies encase movements in antimagnetic cores such as Sinn's Model 756, the Duograph, shown here.

ANTIREFLECTION

A film created by steaming the crystal to eliminate light reflection and improve legibility. Antireflection functions best when applied to both sides of the crystal, but because it scratches, some manufacturers prefer to have it only on the interior of the crystal. It is mainly used on synthetic sapphire crystals. Dubey & Schaldenbrand applies antireflection on both sides for all of the company's wristwatches, such as this Aquadyn model.

AUTOMATIC WINDING

A rotating weight set into motion by moving the wrist winds the spring barrel via the gear train of a mechanical watch movement. Automatic winding was invented during the pocket watch era in 1770, but the breakthrough automatic winding movement via rotor began with the ball bearing Eterna-Matic in the late 1940s. Today we speak of unidirectional winding and bidirectionally winding rotors, depending on the type of gear train used. Shown is IWC's automatic Caliber 50611.

BALANCE

The beating heart of a mechanical watch movement is the balance. Fed by the energy of the mainspring, a tirelessly oscillating little wheel, just a few millimeters in diameter and possessing a spiral-shaped balance spring, sets the rhythm for the escape wheel and pallets with its vibration frequency. Today the balance is usually made of one piece of antimagnetic glucydur, an alloy that expands very little when exposed to heat.

BAR OR COCK

A metal plate fastened to the base plate at one point, leaving room for a gear wheel or pinion. The balance is usually attached to a bar called the balance cock. Glashütte tradition dictates that the balance cock be decoratively engraved by hand like this one by Glashütte Original.

BEVELING

To uniformly file down the sharp edges of a plate, bridge, or bar and give it a high polish. The process is also called *anglage*. Edges are usually beveled at a 45° angle. As the picture shows, this is painstaking work that needs the skilled hands and eyes of an experienced watchmaker or *angleur*.

BRIDGE

A metal plate fastened to the base plate at two points leaving room for a gear wheel or pinion. This vintage Favre-Leuba movement illustrates the point with three individual bridges.

CARBON FIBER

A very light, tough composite material, carbon fiber is composed of filaments comprised of several thousand seven-micron carbon fibers held together by resin. The arrangement of the filaments determines the quality of a component, making each unique. Carbon fiber is currently being used for dials, cases, and even movement components.

CALIBER

A term, similar to type or model, that refers to different watch movements. Pictured here is Heuer's Caliber 11, the legendary automatic chronograph caliber from 1969. This movement was a coproduction jointly researched and developed for four years by Heuer-Leonidas, Breitling, and Hamilton-Büren. Each company gave the movement a different name after serial production began.

CHAMPLEVÉ

A dial decoration technique, whereby the metal is engraved, filled with enamel, and baked, as in this cockatoo on a Cartier Tortue, enhanced with mother-of-pearl slivers.

CERAMIC

An inorganic, nonmetallic material formed by the action of heat and practically unscratchable. Pioneered by Rado, ceramic is a high-tech material generally made from aluminum and zirconia oxide. Today, it is used generally for cases and bezels and now comes in many colors.

CHRONOGRAPH

From the Greek *chronos* (time) and *graphein* (to write). Originally a chronograph literally wrote, inscribing the time elapsed on a piece of paper with the help of a pencil attached to a type of hand. Today this term is used for watches that show not only the time of day, but also certain time intervals via independent hands that may be started or stopped at will. Stopwatches differ from chronographs because they do not show the time of day. This exploded illustration shows the complexity of a Breitling chronograph.

CHRONOMETER

Literally, "measurer of time." As the term is used today, a chronometer denotes an especially accurate watch (one with a deviation of no more than 5 seconds a day for mechanical movements). Chronometers are usually supplied with an official certificate from an independent testing office such as the COSC. The largest producer of chronometers in 2008 was Rolex, with 769,850 officially certified movements. Chopard came in sixth with more than 22,000 certified L.U.C mechanisms, like the 4.96 in the Pro One model shown here.

COLUMN WHEEL

The component used to control chronograph functions within a true chronograph movement. The presence of a column wheel indicates that the chronograph is fully integrated into the movement. In the modern era, modules are generally used that are attached to a base caliber movement. This particular column wheel is made of blued steel.

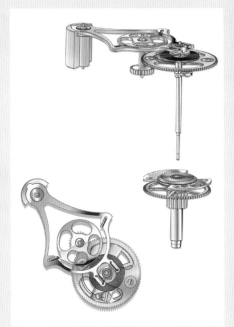

CONSTANT FORCE MECHANISM

Sometimes called a constant force escapement, it isn't really: in most cases this mechanism is "simply" an initial tension spring. It is also known in English by part of its French name, the *remontoir*, which actually means "winding mechanism." This mechanism regulates and portions the energy that is passed on through the escapement, making the rate as even and precise as possible. Shown here is the constant force escapement from A. Lange & Söhne's Lange 31—a mechanism that gets as close to its name as possible.

COSC

The Contrôle Officiel Suisse de Chronométrage, the official Swiss testing office for chronometers. The COSC is the world's largest issuer of so-called chronometer certificates, which are only otherwise given out individually by certain observatories (such as the one in Neuchâtel, Switzerland). For a fee, the COSC tests the rate of movements that have been adjusted by watchmakers. These are usually mechanical movements, but the office also tests some high-precision quartz movements. Those that meet the specifications for being a chronometer are awarded an official certificate as shown here.

CÔTES DE GENÈVE

Also called *vagues de Genève* and Geneva stripes. This is a traditional Swiss surface decoration comprising an even pattern of parallel stripes, applied to flat movement components with a quickly rotating plastic or wooden peg. Glashütte watchmakers have devised their own version of *côtes de Genève* that is applied at a slightly different angle, called Glashütte ribbing.

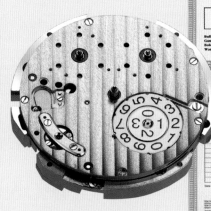

CROWN

The crown is used to wind and set a watch. A few simple turns of the crown will get an automatic movement started, while a manually wound watch is completely wound by the crown. The crown is also used for the setting of various functions, almost always including at least the hours, minutes, seconds, and date. A screwed-down crown like the one on the TAG Heuer Aquagraph pictured here can be tightened to prevent water entering the case or any mishaps while performing extreme sports such as diving.

EQUATION OF TIME

The mean time that we use to keep track of the passing of the day (24 hours evenly divided into minutes and seconds) is not equal to true solar time. The equation of time is a complication devised to show the difference between the mean time shown on one's wristwatch and the time the sun dictates. The Équation Marchante by Blancpain very distinctly indicates this difference via the golden sun-tipped hand that also rotates around the dial in a manner known to watch connoisseurs as *marchant*. Other wristwatch models, such as the Boreas by Martin Braun, display the difference on an extra scale on the dial.

ESCAPEMENT

The combination of the balance, balance spring, pallets, and escape wheel, a subgroup which divides the impulses coming from the spring barrel into small, accurately portioned doses. It guarantees that the gear train runs smoothly and efficiently. The pictured escapement is one newly invented by Parmigiani, containing pallet stones of varying colors, though they are generally red synthetic rubies. Here one of them is a colorless sapphire, or corundum, the same geological material that ruby is made of.

FLINQUÉ

A dial decoration in which a guilloché design is given a coat of enamel, softening the pattern and creating special effects, as shown here on a unique Bovet.

FLYBACK CHRONOGRAPH

A chronograph with a special dial train switch that makes the immediate reuse of the chronograph movement possible after resetting the hands. It was developed for special timekeeping duties such as those found in aviation, which require the measurement of time intervals in quick succession. A flyback may also be called a *retour en vol*. An elegant example of this type of chronograph is Corum's Classical Flyback Large Date shown here.

GEAR TRAIN

A mechanical watch's gear train transmits energy from the mainspring to the escapement. The gear train comprises the minute wheel, the third wheel, the fourth wheel, and the escape wheel.

GLUCYDUR

Glucydur is a functional alloy of copper, beryllium, and iron that has been used to make balances in watches since the 1930s. Its hardness and stability allow watchmakers to use balances that were poised at the factory and no longer required adjustment screws.

GUILLOCHÉ

A surface decoration usually applied to the dial and the rotor using a grooving tool with a sharp tip, such as a rose engine, to cut an even pattern onto a level surface. The exact adjustment of the tool for each new path is controlled by a device similar to a pantograph, and the movement of the tool can be controlled either manually or mechanically. Real *guillochis* (the correct term used by a master of guilloché) are very intricate and expensive to produce, which is why most dials decorated in this fashion are produced by stamping machines. Breguet is one of the very few companies to use real guilloché on every one of its dials.

INDEX

A regulating mechanism found on the balance cock and used by the watchmaker to adjust the movement's rate. The index changes the effective length of the balance spring, thus making it move more quickly or slowly. This is the standard index found on an ETA Valjoux 7750.

JEWEL

To minimize friction, the hardened steel tips of a movement's rotating gear wheels (called pinions) are lodged in synthetic rubies (fashioned as polished stones with a hole) and lubricated with a very thin layer of special oil. These synthetic rubies are produced in exactly the same way as sapphire crystal using the same material. During the pocket watch era, real rubies with hand-drilled holes were still used, but because of the high costs involved, they were only used in movements with especially quickly rotating gears. The jewel shown here on a bridge from A. Lange & Söhne's Double Split is additionally embedded in a gold chaton secured with three blued screws.

LIGA

The word LIGA is actually a German acronym that stands for lithography (*Lithografie*), electroplating (*Galvanisierung*), and plastic molding (*Abformung*). It is a lithographic process exposed by UV or X-ray light that literally "grows" perfect micro components made of nickel, nickel-phosphorus, or 23.5-karat gold in a plating bath. The components need no finishing or trimming after manufacture.

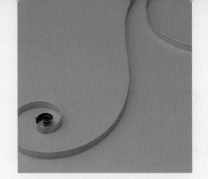

LUMINOUS SUBSTANCE

Tritium paint is a slightly radioactive substance that replaced radium as a luminous coating for hands, numerals, and hour markers on watch dials. Watches bearing tritium must be marked as such, with the letter *T* on the dial near 6 o'clock. It has now for the most part been replaced by nonradioactive materials such as Superluminova. Traser technology (as seen on these Ball timepieces) uses tritium gas enclosed in tiny silicate glass tubes coated on the inside with a phosphorescing substance. The luminescence is constant and will hold around twenty-five years.

MAINSPRING

The mainspring, located in the spring barrel, stores energy when tensioned and passes it on to the escapement via the gear train as the tension relaxes. Today, mainsprings are generally made of Nivaflex, an alloy invented by Swiss engineer Max Straumann at the beginning of the 1950s. This alloy basically comprises iron, nickel, chrome, cobalt, and beryllium.

MINUTE REPEATER

A striking mechanism with hammers and gongs for acoustically signaling the hours, quarter hours, and minutes elapsed since noon or midnight. The wearer pushes a slide, which winds the spring. Normally a repeater uses two different gongs to signal hours (low tone), quarter hours (high and low tones in succession), and minutes (high tone). Some watches have three gongs, called a carillon. The Chronoswiss Répétition à Quarts is a prominent repeating introduction of recent years.

PERPETUAL CALENDAR

The calendar module for this type of timepiece automatically makes allowances for the different lengths of each month as well as leap years until the next secular year, which will occur in 2100. A perpetual calendar usually shows the date, month, and four-year cycle, and may show the day of the week and moon phase as well, as does this one introduced by George J von Burg at Baselworld 2005. Perpetual calendars need much skill to complete.

PERLAGE

Surface decoration comprising an even pattern of partially overlapping dots, applied with a quickly rotating plastic or wooden peg, as shown here on the plates of Frédérique Constant's *manufacture* Caliber FC 910-1.

PLATE

A metal platform having several tiers for the gear train. The base plate of a movement usually incorporates the dial and carries the bearings for the primary pinions of the "first floor" of a gear train. The gear wheels are made complete by tightly fitting screwed-in bridges and bars on the back side of the plate. A specialty of the so-called Glashütte school, as opposed to the Swiss school, is the reverse completion of a movement not via different bridges and bars, but rather with a three-quarter plate. Glashütte Original's Caliber 65 (shown) displays a beautifully decorated three-quarter plate.

POWER RESERVE DISPLAY

A mechanical watch contains only a certain amount of power reserve. A fully wound modern automatic watch usually possesses between 36 and 42 hours of energy before it needs to be wound again. The power reserve display keeps the wearer informed about how much energy his or her watch still has in reserve, a function that is especially practical on manually wound watches with several days of possible reserve. The Nomos Tangente Power Reserve pictured here represents an especially creative way to illustrate the state of the mainspring's tension. On some German watches the power reserve is also displayed with the words "auf" and "ab."

PULSOMETER

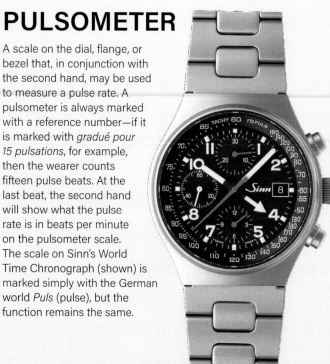

A scale on the dial, flange, or bezel that, in conjunction with the second hand, may be used to measure a pulse rate. A pulsometer is always marked with a reference number—if it is marked with *gradué pour 15 pulsations*, for example, then the wearer counts fifteen pulse beats. At the last beat, the second hand will show what the pulse rate is in beats per minute on the pulsometer scale. The scale on Sinn's World Time Chronograph (shown) is marked simply with the German world *Puls* (pulse), but the function remains the same.

QUALITÉ FLEURIER

This certification of quality was established by Chopard, Parmigiani Fleurier, Vaucher, and Bovet Fleurier in 2004. Watches bearing the seal must fulfill five criteria, including COSC certification, passing several tests for robustness and precision, top-notch finishing, and being 100 percent Swiss-made (except for the raw materials). The seal appears here on the dial of the Parmigiani Fleurier Tonda 39.

RETROGRADE DISPLAY

A retrograde display shows the time linearly instead of circularly. The hand continues along an arc until it reaches the end of its scale, at which precise moment it jumps back to the beginning instantaneously. This Nienaber model not only shows the minutes in retrograde form, it is also a regulator display.

ROTOR

The rotor is the component that keeps an automatic watch wound. The kinetic motion of this part, which contains a heavy metal weight around its outer edge, winds the mainspring. It can either wind unilaterally or bilaterally (to one or both sides) depending on the caliber. The rotor from this Temption timepiece belongs to an ETA Valjoux 7750.

SAPPHIRE CRYSTAL

Synthetic sapphire crystal is known to gemologists as aluminum oxide (Al_2O_3) or corundum. It can be colorless (corundum), red (ruby), blue (sapphire), or green (emerald). It is virtually scratchproof; only a diamond is harder. The innovative Royal Blue Tourbillon by Ulysse Nardin pictured here features not only sapphire crystals on the front and back of the watch, but also actual plates made of both colorless and blue corundum within the movement.

SCREW BALANCE

Before the invention of the perfectly weighted balance using a smooth ring, balances were fitted with weighted screws to get the exact impetus desired. Today a screw balance is a subtle sign of quality in a movement due to its costly construction and assembly utilizing minuscule weighted screws.

SEAL OF GENEVA

Since 1886 the official seal of this canton has been awarded to Genevan watch *manufactures* who must follow a defined set of high-quality criteria that include the following: polished jewel bed drillings, jewels with olive drillings, polished winding wheels, quality balances and balance springs, steel levers and springs with beveling of 45 degrees and *côtes de Genève* decoration, and polished stems and pinions. The list was updated in 2012 to include the entire watch and newer components. Testing is done on the finished piece. The Seal consists of two, one on the movement, one on the case. The pictured seal was awarded to Vacheron Constantin, a traditional Genevan *manufacture*.

SILICIUM/SILICON

Silicon is an element relatively new to mechanical watches. It is currently being used in the manufacture of precision escapements. Ulysse Nardin's Freak has lubrication-free silicon wheels, and Breguet has successfully used flat silicon balance springs.

SKELETONIZATION

The technique of cutting a movement's components down to their weight-bearing basic substance. This is generally done by hand in painstaking hours of microscopic work with a small handheld saw, though machines can skeletonize parts to a certain degree, such as the version of the Valjoux 7750 that was created for Chronoswiss's Opus and Pathos models. This tourbillon created by Christophe Schaffo is additionally—and masterfully—hand-engraved.

SONNERIE

A variety of minute repeater that—like a tower clock—sounds the time not at the will of the wearer, but rather automatically *(en passant)* every hour *(petite sonnerie)* or quarter hour *(grande sonnerie)*. Gérald Genta designed the most complicated sonnerie back in the early nineties. Shown is a recent model from the front and back.

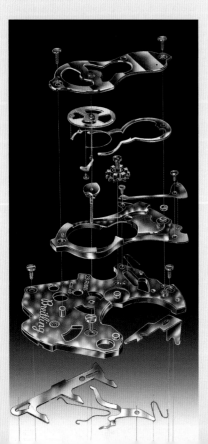

SPLIT-SECONDS CHRONOGRAPH

Also known in the watch industry by its French name, the *rattrapante* (exploded view at left). A watch with two second hands, one of which can be blocked with a special dial train lever to indicate an intermediate time while the other continues to run. When released, the split-seconds hand jumps ahead to the position of the other second hand. The PTC by Porsche Design illustrates this nicely.

SPRING BARREL

The spring barrel contains the mainspring. It turns freely on an arbor, pulled along by the toothed wheel generally doubling as its lid. This wheel interacts with the first pinion of the movement's gear train. Some movements contain two or more spring barrels for added power reserve.

SWAN-NECK FINE ADJUSTMENT

A regulating instrument used by the watchmaker to adjust the movement's rate in place of an index. The swan neck is especially prevalent in fine Swiss and Glashütte watchmaking (here, Lang & Heyne's Moritz model). Mühle Glashütte has varied the theme with its woodpecker's neck.

TACHYMETER

A scale on the dial, flange, or bezel of a chronograph that, in conjunction with the second hand, gives the speed of a moving object. A tachymeter takes a value determined in less than a minute and converts it into miles or kilometers per hour. For example, a wearer could measure the time it takes a car to pass between two mile markers on the highway. When the car passes the marker, the second hand will be pointing to the car's speed in miles per hour on the tachymetric scale.

TOURBILLON

A technical device invented by Abraham-Louis Breguet in 1801 to compensate for the influence of gravity on the balance of a pocket watch. The entire escapement is mounted on an epicyclic train in a "cage" and rotated completely on its axis over regular periods of time. This superb horological highlight is seen as a sign of technological know-how in the modern era. Harry Winston's Histoire de Tourbillon 4 is a spectacular example.

VIBRATION FREQUENCY (VPH)

The spring causes the balance to oscillate at a certain frequency measured in hertz (Hz) or vibrations per hour (vph). Most of today's wristwatches tick at 28,800 vph (4 Hz) or 21,600 vph (3 Hz). Less usual is 18,000 vph (2.5 Hz). Zenith's El Primero was the first serial movement to beat at 36,000 vph (5 Hz), and the Breguet Type XXII runs at 72,000 vph.

WATER RESISTANCE

Water resistance is an important feature of any timepiece and is usually measured in increments of one atmosphere (atm or bar, equal to 10 meters of water pressure) or meters and is often noted on the dial or case back. Watches resistant to 100 meters are best for swimming and snorkeling. Timepieces resistant to 200 meters are good for scuba diving. To deep-sea dive there are various professional timepieces available for use in depths of 200 meters or more. The Hydromax by Bell & Ross (shown) is water-resistant to a record 11,000 meters.

Copyright © 2024 HEEL Verlag GmbH, Königswinter, Germany

English-language translation copyright © 2024 Abbeville Press,
655 Third Avenue, New York, NY 10017

Editor-in-chief: Peter Braun
Editor: Marton Radkai
Production manager: Louise Kurtz
Copy Editors: Cynthia K. Barton, Stephanie Sarkany, Katherine Macedon
Composition: Erin Morris, Evergreen Design Studio
Project Management: Kourtnay King, Layman Poupard Publishing

For more information about advertising, please contact:
Gary Girdvainis
25 Gay Bower Road, Monroe, CT 06468
203-952-3522, garygeorgeg@gmail.com

ISBN 978-0-7892-1479-9

Twenty-fifth edition
10 9 8 7 6 5 4 3 2 1

Library of Congress Cataloging-in-Publication Data available upon request

For bulk and premium sales and for text adoption procedures, write to Customer Service Manager,
Abbeville Press, 655 Third Avenue, New York, NY 10017, or call 1-800-Artbook.

Visit Abbeville Press online at www.abbeville.com.

ISBN 978-0-7892-1479-9   U.S. $39.95

EAN

9 780789 214799   53995